Fundamentals of Computer Security

Springer
Berlin
Heidelberg
New York
Hong Kong
London
Milan
Paris
Tokyo

Josef Pieprzyk
Thomas Hardjono
Jennifer Seberry

Fundamentals of Computer Security

With 98 Figures

Springer

Prof. Dr. Josef Pieprzyk
Macquarie University
Department of Computing
Sydney, NSW 2109
Australia

josef@ics.mq.edu.au

Dr. Thomas Hardjono
VeriSign INC.
401 Edgewater Place, Suite 280
Wakefield, MA 01880
USA

thardjono@verisign.com

Prof. Dr. Jennifer Seberry
University of Wollongong
School of Information Technology
and Computer Science
Wollongong, NSW 2522
Australia

jennifer_seberry@uow.edu.au

Cataloging-in-Publication Data applied for

Bibliographic information published by Die Deutsche Bibliothek
Die Deutsche Bibliothek lists this publication in the Deutsche Nationalbibliografie;
detailed bibliographic data is available in the Internet at http://dnb.ddb.de

ISBN 3-540-43101-2 Springer-Verlag Berlin Heidelberg New York

Springer-Verlag Berlin Heidelberg New York,
a member of BertelsmannSpringer Science+Business Media GmbH

http://www.springer.de

© Springer-Verlag Berlin Heidelberg 2003
Printed in Germany

Cover Design: *KünkelLopkaWerbeagentur*
Typesetting: Camera ready by authors
Printed on acid-free paper   SPIN: 10859891   45/3142/X0 - 5 4 3 2 1 0

Preface

The primary goal of this book is to present the basic concepts in computer and network security. The starting point for the book was the lecture notes that were used for teaching the undergraduate course on computer security at the University of Wollongong (Australia). Later more topics were added to the book. These topics were mainly taught to postgraduate students as an advanced cryptography course. Some chapters, especially those towards the end of the book, were included to help students in their seminar presentations. The book was recently used as the textbook for a new course, Cryptography and Information Security, offered for third-year students in the Computing Department at Macquarie University (Australia).

The book contains 18 chapters. It starts with an introductory chapter (Chap. 1) that gives a brief summary of the history of cryptography. As the book is meant to be self-contained, the necessary background knowledge is given in the theory chapter (Chap. 2). It starts with elements of number theory, goes through algebraic structures, the complexity of computing, and elements of information theory.

The chapter on private-key cryptosystems (Chap. 3) covers classical ciphers, the DES family of ciphers, and a selected subset of modern cryptosystems submitted for the AES call. An introduction to differential and linear cryptanalysis closes the chapter. The next chapter (Chap. 4) sets the background for public-key cryptography. It describes the concept of a public key and discusses its implementations. The RSA cryptosystem deserves special attention for at least two reasons. The first one is that its security nicely relates to the difficulty of factoring. The other one is the widespread use of RSA for communication security. Probabilistic encryption and modern public-key cryptosystems close the chapter.

In Chap. 5, pseudorandomness is studied and the concept of polynomial indistinguishability is introduced. Next, pseudorandom generators of bits, functions, and permutations are described. Hashing is studied in Chap. 6. The birthday paradox is presented and its application for breaking hash functions explored. The main part of the chapter is devoted to the MD family of hash functions (MD5, SHA-1, RIPEMD-160, and HAVAL). Keyed hashing closes the chapter.

Chapter 7 deals with signature schemes and starts with one-time signature schemes. The basic signature schemes examined in this chapter are the RSA and ElGamal signatures. In addition, the chapter discusses blind, undeniable, and fail-stop signatures. Authentication, although related to digital signatures, has developed its own theory and vocabulary, which are presented in Chap. 8.

Secret sharing is one of the main cryptographic tools that enables groups to perform cryptographic operations. The basic theory of secret sharing is given in Chap. 9 and the application of secret sharing in cryptography is presented in Chap. 10.

The key establishment protocols discussed in Chap. 11 can be split into two broad categories: key-agreement and key-distribution protocols. These two categories normally relate to the case when two parties wish to generate a fresh and secret key. Multiparty versions of key establishment protocols are of growing interest and are also presented in the chapter. A short exposition of the BAN logic concludes the chapter.

Zero-knowledge proof systems are interactive systems in which two parties – the prover and verifier – interact. The prover claims that a statement is true and the verifier wants to be convinced that it is true. The parties interact, and at the end of the interaction the verifier is either convinced that the statement is true or, alternatively, the verifier discovers that the statement is not true. This topic is studied in Chap. 12.

Identification is discussed in Chap. 13. The discussion starts with a review of biometric techniques applied to user identification. Next, passwords and challenge-response identification are examined. The main part of the chapter is, however, devoted to identification based on zero-knowledge proofs.

The chapter on intrusion detection (Chap. 14) first discusses two generic approaches: anomaly and misuse detection. The former approach makes decisions about a suspected intrusion using the profile of the behavior of the user. The latter approach uses a single profile that characterizes misuse of the computing resources. Selected implementations of host and network intrusion detection systems are also examined.

Chapter 15 is an introduction to the technical aspects of e-commerce and it covers electronic elections and electronic money. Chapter 16 looks at database security with an emphasis on security filters, cryptographic methods, and database views. A review of security features applied in Oracle8 concludes the chapter.

Chapter 17 explores access control. Three models are considered: mandatory, discretionary, and role-based access control. Some selected implementations are described as well. Chapter 18 deals with the IPSec protocol and computer viruses.

The contents of the book can be roughly divided into two parts:

1. Cryptography (Chaps. 3 to 13)
2. Computer and Network Security (Chaps. 14 to 18)

The chapters can be arranged into the following hierarchy:

Introduction		Background Theory	
Cryptography			
Private-key Cryptosystems	Public-key Cryptosystems	Secret Sharing	Authentication
Pseudorandomness	Hashing	Zero-knowledge Proof Systems	
Digital Signatures			
Group-Oriented Cryptography	Key Establishment Protocols	Identification	
Computer and Network Security				
Intrusion Detection	Electronic Elections and Digital Money	Database Protection and Security	Access Control	Network Security

The cryptography part includes four basic chapters: private-key cryptosystems, public-key cryptosystems, secret sharing, and authentication. They can be studied independently as they overlap very little (see the third row of the above table). Chapters on pseudorandomness, hashing, and zero-knowledge proof systems (the fourth row of the table) build on knowledge of the material given in the basic chapters. For instance, zero-knowledge proof systems require a good grasp of public-key cryptosystems. The hashing chapter is less dependent on basic chapters but, certainly, hashing uses both private- and public-key cryptography. Digital signature concepts are tightly coupled with private- and public-key cryptography, and with hashing. The bottom chapters of the cryptography part include chapters on complex topics and the reader is encouraged to be sure that the concepts in the chapters in the two preceding rows are first understood. In particular, to follow material in the chapter on

- group-oriented cryptography, working through the chapters on public-key cryptosystems, secret sharing, hashing, and digital signatures is recommended;
- key establishment protocols, the reader is required to know public-key cryptography, including the theory behind digital signatures;
- identification, it is advisable to know digital signatures and zero-knowledge proof systems.

The book can be used as a text for undergraduate and postgraduate courses. The list below gives examples of possible courses that can be supported by the book:

- Introduction to Cryptography: Background Theory, Private-Key Cryptosystems, Public-Key Cryptosystems, Hashing, and Digital Signatures.
- Electronic Commerce: Background Theory, Public-Key Cryptosystems, Hashing, Digital Signatures, Electronic Elections, and Digital Money.
- Advanced Cryptography: Authentication, Secret Sharing, Group-Oriented Cryptography, Key Establishment Protocols, Zero-Knowledge Proof Systems, and Identification.
- Computer and Network Security: Intrusion Detection, Database Protection and Security, Access Control, and Network Security.

The contributions to the book are shown in the following table:

Coauthor Name	Chapters
Josef Pieprzyk	All chapters
Thomas Hardjono	14 and 16
Jennifer Seberry	3 and 18

Acknowledgements The authors are grateful to the persons who provided comments and constructive criticism. We are especially thankful to

Marc Fischlin, Ron Rivest, and Abhi Shelat

for their critical reviews, suggestions, and improvements. We also indebted to many colleagues who devoted their time and effort to give us their feedback. The list includes:

Colin Boyd	Nicolas Courtois
Ivo Desmedt	Dieter Gollmann
Hossein Ghodosi	Jeffrey Horton
Andrew Klapper	Keith Martin
Anish Mathuria	Krystian Matusiewicz
Igor Shparlinski	Michał Sramka
Janusz Stokłosa	Huaxiong Wang
Xianmo Zhang	

We apologize to those colleagues whose names have inadvertently been dropped from the list.

The project would never have happened without the strong support and encouragement from Alfred Hofmann and his team at Springer-Verlag, including Ingeborg Mayer, Frank Holzwarth and Ronan Nugent. Thank you. We also thank Kate Krastev and Deanne van der Myle for their help in getting the book into its final form.

Readers who spot any omissions or errors are requested to contact the authors with details.

November 2002   Josef Pieprzyk, Thomas Hardjono, and Jennifer Seberry

Table of Contents

1 Introduction

1.1 Preamble

In 1988, the *New Encyclopædia Britannica* defined *cryptology* as:

> The science concerned with communications in secure and usually secret form. It encompasses both cryptography and cryptanalysis. The former involves the study and application of the principles and techniques by which information is rendered unintelligible to all but the intended receiver, while the latter is the science and art of solving cryptosystems to recover such information.

Today this definition needs to be extended as modern cryptology focuses its attention on the design and evaluation of a wide range of methods and techniques for information protection. Information protection covers not only secrecy (a traditional protection against eavesdropping) but also authentication, integrity, verifiability, nonrepudiation and other more specific security goals. The part of cryptology that deals with the design of algorithms, protocols, and systems which are used to protect information against specific threats is called *cryptography*.

To incorporate information protection into a system, protocol, or service, the designer needs to know:

- a detailed specification of the environment in which the system (protocol or service) is going to work, including a collection of security goals,
- a list of threats together with the description of places in the system where adverse tampering with the information flow can occur,
- the level of protection required or amount of power (in term of accessible computing resources) that is expected from an attacker (or adversary), and
- the projected life span of the system.

Cryptography provides our designer with tools to implement the information protection requested or, in other words, to achieve the security goals expected. The collection of basic tools includes encryption algorithms, authentication codes, one-way functions, hashing functions, secret sharing schemes, signature schemes, pseudorandom bit generators, zero-knowledge proof systems, etc. From these elementary tools, it is possible to create more complex tools and services, such as threshold encryption algorithms, authentication protocols, key establishment protocols, and a variety of application-oriented protocols, including electronic payment systems, electronic election, and electronic commerce protocols. Each tool is characterized by its security specification which usually indicates the recommended configuration and its strength against specific threats, such as eavesdropping and illegal modification of information. The designer can use all the tools provided by cryptography to combine them into a single solution. Finally, the designer has to verify the quality of the solution, including a careful analysis of the overall security achieved.

The second part of cryptology is *cryptanalysis*. Cryptanalysis uses mathematical methods to prove that the design (an implementation of information protection) does not achieve a security goal or that it cannot withstand an attack from the list of threats given in the security specification of the design. This may be possible if the claimed security parameters are grossly overestimated or, more often, if the interrelations among different threats are not well understood.

An attentive reader could argue that cryptography includes cryptanalysis as the designer always applies some sort of analysis of the information protection achieved. To clarify this point, note that the aim of cryptography is the design of new (hopefully) secure algorithms, protocols, systems, schemes, and services, while cryptanalysis concentrates on finding new *attacks*. Attacks (which are a part of cryptanalysis) are translated into the so-called *design criteria* or *design properties* (which are a part of cryptography). The design criteria obtained from an attack allow us to design a system that is immune against the attack.

Cryptography tries to prove that the obtained designs are secure, using all available knowledge about possible attacks. Cryptanalysis carefully examines possible and realistic threats to find new attacks and to prove that the designs are not secure (are breakable). In general, it is impossible to prove that information protection designs are unbreakable, while the opposite is possible – it is enough to show an attack.

1.2 Terminology

Cryptography has developed an extensive vocabulary. More complex terms will be introduced gradually throughout the book. However, a collection of basic terms is presented below.

There is a list of basic security requirements. This list includes: secrecy (or confidentiality), authenticity, integrity, and nonrepudiation. *Secrecy* ensures that information flow between the sender and the receiver is unintelligible to outsiders. It protects information against threats based on eavesdropping. *Authenticity* allows the receiver of messages to determine the true identity of the sender. It guards messages against impersonation, substitution, or spoofing. *Integrity* enables the receiver to verify whether the message has been tampered with by outsiders while in transit via an insecure channel. It ensures that any modification of the stream of messages will be detected. Any modification that results from changing the order of transmitted messages, deleting some parts of messages, or replaying old messages will be detected. *Nonrepudiation* prevents the sender of a message from claiming that they have not sent the message.

Encryption was the first cryptographic operation used to ensure secrecy or confidentiality of information transmitted across an insecure communication channel. The encryption operation takes a piece of information (also called the message, message block, or plaintext) and translates it into a cryptogram (ciphertext or codeword) using a secret cryptographic key. *Decryption* is the reverse operation to encryption. The receiver who holds the correct secret key can recover the message (plaintext) from the cryptogram (ciphertext).

The step-by-step description of encryption (or decryption) is called the *encryption algorithm* (or *decryption algorithm*). If there is no need to distinguish encryption from decryption, we are going to call them collectively *ciphers, cryptoalgorithms*, or *cryptosystems*.

Private-key or symmetric cryptosystems use the same secret key for encryption and decryption. More precisely, the encryption and decryption keys do not need to be identical – the knowledge of one of them suffices to find the other (both keys must be kept secret).

Public-key or asymmetric cryptosystems use different keys for encryption and decryption. The knowledge of one key does not compromise the other.

Hashing is a cryptographic operation that generates a relatively short *digest* for a message of arbitrary length. Hashing algorithms are required to be *collision-resistant*, i.e. it is "difficult" to find two different messages with the same digest.

One-way functions are functions for which it is easy to compute their values from their arguments but it is difficult to reverse them, i.e. to find their arguments knowing their values.

The *electronic signature* is a public and relatively short string of characters (or bits) that can be used to verify the authorship of an electronic document (a message of arbitrary length) by anybody.

Secret sharing is the method of distribution of a secret amongst participants so that every large enough subset of participants is able to recover collectively the secret by pooling their *shares*. The class of all such subsets is called the *access structure*. The secret sharing is set up by the so-called *dealer* who, for the given secret, generates all shares and delivers them to all participants. The recalculation of the secret is done by the so-called *combiner* to whom all collaborating participants entrust their shares. Any participant or any collection of participants outside the access structure is not able to find out the secret.

Cryptanalysis has its own terminology as well. In general, cryptographic designs can be either unconditionally or conditionally secure. An *unconditionally secure* design is immune against any attacker with an *unlimited* computational power. For a *conditionally secure* design, its security depends on the difficulty of reversing the underlying cryptographic problem. At best, the design can be only as strong as the underlying cryptographic problem.

An *attack* is an efficient algorithm that, for a given cryptographic design, enables some protected elements of the design to be computed "substantially" quicker than specified by the designer. Some other attacks may not contradict the security specification and may concentrate on finding overlooked and realistic threats for which the design fails. Any encryption algorithm that uses secret keys can be subject to an *exhaustive search attack*. The attacker finds the secret key by trying all possible keys.

Encryption algorithms can be analyzed using the following typical attacks:

- *Ciphertext-only attack* – the cryptanalyst knows the encrypted messages (cryptograms) only. The task is to either find the cryptographic key applied or decrypt one or more cryptograms.

- *Known-plaintext attack* – the adversary has access to a collection of pairs (message and the corresponding cryptogram) and wants to determine the key or decrypt some new cryptograms not included in the collection.
- *Chosen-plaintext attack* – this is the known-plaintext attack for which the cryptanalyst can choose messages and read the corresponding cryptograms.
- *Chosen-ciphertext attack* – the enemy can select her own cryptograms and observe the corresponding messages for them. The aim of the enemy is to find out the secret key. In private-key encryption, the attacker may encrypt new messages into valid cryptograms. In public-key encryption, she may create valid cryptograms from the sample of observed valid cryptograms (*lunchtime attack*).

Authentication algorithms allow senders to incorporate their identity to transmitted messages so each receiver can verify the owner (or sender) of the message. Authentication algorithms can be evaluated using their resistance against the following attacks:

- *Impersonation attack* – the cryptanalyst knows the authentication algorithm and wants to construct a valid cryptogram for a false message, or determine the key (the encoding rule).
- *Substitution attack* – the enemy cryptanalyst intercepts a cryptogram and replaces it with another cryptogram (for a false message).
- *Spoofing attack* – the adversary knows a collection of different cryptograms (codewords) and plans to either work out the key (encoding rule) applied or compute a valid cryptogram for a chosen false message.

Attacks on cryptographic hashing are efficient algorithms that allow a *collision*, i.e. two different messages with the same digest, to be found. All hashing algorithms are susceptible to the so-called *birthday attack*. A weaker form of attack on hashing produces *pseudocollisions*, i.e. collisions with specific restrictions imposed, usually on the initial vectors.

Secret sharing is analyzed by measuring the difficulty of retrieving the secret by either an outsider or an unauthorized group of participants. More sophisticated attacks could be launched by a cheating participant who sends a false share to the combiner. After the reconstruction of the invalid secret (which is communicated to all collaborating participants), the cheater tries to compute the valid one.

1.3 Historical Perspective

The beginnings of cryptography can be traced back to ancient times. Almost all ancient civilisations developed some kind of cryptography. The only exception was ancient China. This could be attributed to the Chinese complex ideogram alphabet – writing down the message made it private, as few could read. In ancient Egypt secret writing was used in inscriptions on sarcophaguses to increase the mystery of the place. Ancient India used its allusive languages to create a sort of impromptu cryptography. Kahn [264] gives an exciting insight into secret communications from ancient to modern times.

Steganography, or secret writing, was probably the first widely used method for secure communication in a hostile environment. The secret text was hidden on a piece of paper by using a variety of techniques. These techniques included the application of invisible ink, masking of the secret text inside an inconspicuous text, and so forth. This method of secure communication was rather weak if the document found its way to an attacker who was an expert in steganography. Cryptography in its early years very much resembled secret writing – the well-known Caesar cipher is an excellent example of concealment by ignorance. This cipher was used to encrypt military orders which were later delivered by trusted messengers. This time the ciphertext was not hidden but characters were transformed using a very simple substitution. It was reasonable to assume that the cipher was "strong" enough as most of the potential attackers were illiterate and it was hoped that the others thought that the document was written in an unknown foreign language.

It was quickly realized that the assumption about an ignorant attacker was not realistic. Most early European ciphers were designed to withstand attacks from educated opponents who knew the encryption process but did not know the secret cryptographic key. Additionally, it was necessary that encryption and decryption processes could be done quickly, usually by hand or with the aid of mechanical devices such as the cipher disk invented by Leon Battista Alberti[1].

At the beginning of the nineteenth century the first mechanical-electrical machines were introduced for "fast" encryption. This was the first breakthrough

---

[1] Leon Battista Alberti (1404–1472) was born in Genoa, Italy. He was a humanist, architect and principal founder of Renaissance art theory. Alberti is also called the Father of Western Cryptology because of his contributions to the field [264].

in cryptography. Cryptographic operations (in this case encryption and decryption) could be done automatically with minimal operator involvement.

Cipher machines could handle relatively large volumes of data. The German ENIGMA and Japanese PURPLE are examples of cipher machines. They were used to protect military and diplomatic information.

The basic three-wheel ENIGMA was broken by Marian Rejewski, Jerzy Różycki, and Henryk Zygalski, a team of three Polish mathematicians. Their attack exploited weaknesses in the operating procedure used by the sender to communicate the settings of the machine rotors to the receiver [16, 96]. The British team of Alan Turing at Bletchley Park perfected the attack and broke the strengthened versions of ENIGMA. Churchhouse in [97] describes the cryptanalysis of the four-wheel ENIGMA. These remarkable feats were possible due to careful analysis of the cryptographic algorithms, the predictable selection of the cipher machine parameters (poor operational procedures), and significant improvements in computational power. Cryptanalysis was first supported by application of the so-called crypto bombs, copies of the original cipher machines used to test some of the possible initial settings. Later cryptanalysts applied the early computers to speed up computations.

The advent of computers gave both the designers and cryptanalysts new powerful tools for fast computations. New cryptographic algorithms were designed and new attacks were developed to break them. The new impetus in cryptology was not given by new designing tools but rather by new emerging applications of computers and new requirements for the protection of information. Distributed computation and sharing information in computer networks were among those new applications that demonstrated, sometimes very dramatically, the necessity of providing tools for reliable and secure information delivery. Recent progress in Internet applications illustrates the fact that new services can be put on the Net only after a careful analysis of their security features. Secrecy is no longer the most important security issue. In the network environment, the authenticity of messages and the correct identification of users have become the two most important requirements.

The scope of cryptology has increased dramatically. It is now seen as the field that provides the theory and a practical guide for the design and analysis of cryptographic tools, which can then be used to build up complex secure protocols and services. The secrecy part of the field, traditionally concentrated around the design of new encryption algorithms, was enriched by the addition of authentication, cryptographic hashing, digital signatures, secret sharing schemes, and zero-knowledge protocols.

1.4 Modern Cryptography

In 1949 Claude Shannon [467] laid the theoretical foundations of modern private-key cryptography in his seminal work by using information theory to analyze ciphers. He defined the *unicity distance* in order to characterize the strength of a cipher against an opponent with unlimited computational power. He also considered the so-called *product ciphers*. Product ciphers use small substitution boxes connected to larger permutation boxes. Substitution boxes (also called *S-boxes*) are controlled by a relatively short cryptographic key. They provide confusion (because of the unknown secret key). Permutation boxes (*P-boxes*) have no key – their structure is fixed and they provide diffusion. Product ciphers are also termed *substitution-permutation* or *S-P networks*. As the decryption process applies the inverses of S-boxes and P-boxes in the reverse order, decryption in general cannot be implemented using the encryption routine. This is expensive in terms of both hardware and software.

In the early 1970s, Feistel [168] used the S-P network concept to design the Lucifer encryption algorithm. It encrypts 128-bit messages into 128-bit cryptograms using a 128-bit cryptographic key. The designer of the Lucifer algorithm was able to modify the S-P network in such a way that both the encryption and decryption algorithms could be implemented by a single program or a piece of hardware. Encryption (or decryption) is done in 16 iterations (also called rounds). Each round acts on a 128-bit input (L_i, R_i) and generates a 128-bit output (L_{i+1}, R_{i+1}) using a 64-bit partial key k_i. A single round can be described as

$$R_{i+1} = L_i \oplus f(k_i, R_i)$$
$$L_{i+1} = R_i \tag{1.1}$$

where L_i and R_i are 64-bit long sequences, $f(k_i, R_i)$ is a cryptographic function (also called the round function) which represents a simple S-P network. In the literature, the transformation defined by (1.1) is referred to as the Feistel permutation. Note that a round in the Lucifer algorithm is always a permutation regardless of the form of the function $f()$. Also the inverse of a round can use the original round routine with the swapped input halves. The strength of the Lucifer algorithm directly relates to the strength of the cryptographic function $f()$. Another interesting observation is that the design of a Lucifer-type cryptosystem is equivalent to the design of its $f()$ function, which operates on shorter sequences.

The *Data Encryption Standard* (DES) was developed from Lucifer [383] and very soon became a standard for encryption in banking and other non-military applications. It uses the same Feistel structure with shorter 64-bit message/cryptogram blocks and a shorter 64-bit key. As a matter of fact, the key contains 56 independent and 8 parity-check bits. Due to its wide utilization, DES has been extensively investigated and analyzed. The differential cryptanalysis invented by Biham and Shamir [33] was first applied to the DES. Also the linear cryptanalysis by Matsui [320, 321] was tested on the DES.

The analysis of the DES gave a valuable insight into the design properties of cryptographic algorithms. Successors of the DES, whose structures were based on Feistel permutation, include the Fast Encryption Algorithm (FEAL) [347], the International Data Encryption Algorithm (IDEA) [294], and some algorithms submitted as candidates for the Advanced Encryption Standard (AES) and the New European Schemes for Signatures, Integrity, and Encryption (NESSIE) project.

On October 2, 2000 the US National Institute of Standards and Technology announced the winner of their AES competition, the Rijndael algorithm from a team in Belgium. Unlike the DES algorithm that uses the Feistel permutation, Rijndael is based on the general S-P network and needs two separate algorithms, one for encryption and the other for decryption.

Cryptographic hashing has become an important component of cryptographic primitives, especially in the context of efficient generation of digital signatures. MD4 [429] and its extended version MD5 [430] are examples of the design that combines Feistel structure with C language bitwise operations for fast hashing. Although both MD4 and MD5 have been shown to have security weaknesses, their design principles seem to be sound and can be used to develop more secure hashing algorithms.

Both private-key encryption and hashing algorithms can be designed using one-way functions. These constructions are conditionally secure as the security of the algorithms depends upon the difficulty of reversing the underlying one-way functions. In 1976 Diffie and Hellman in their visionary paper [152] introduced a class of trapdoor one-way functions that are easy to invert with the help of some extra information. They showed that such functions can be used to design public-key cryptosystems. Soon after, in 1978, two practical implementations of public-key cryptosystems were published. Rivest, Shamir, and Adleman [428] based their algorithm (the RSA system) on factorization and discrete logarithms. Merkle and Hellman [339] used the knapsack function. Unfortunately, the Merkle-Hellman cryptosystem was broken six years later.

Conventional cryptographic algorithms have a limited lifetime – an algorithm "dies" if an exhaustive attack[2] becomes possible due to progress in computing technology. Conditionally secure cryptographic algorithms are insensitive to the increment of computational power of the attacker. It is enough to select larger security parameters for the algorithm and be sure that the algorithm is still secure.

The design and analysis of conditionally secure cryptographic algorithms is related to easy and difficult problems defined in Complexity Theory. A cryptographic algorithm can be applied in two ways: legally by an authorized user, or illegally by an adversary. Naturally, the authorized use of the cryptographic algorithm should be as efficient as possible, while the illegal handling ought to be difficult. This brings us to the notion of provable security, where breaking a cryptographic algorithm is equivalent to finding an efficient algorithm for solving an intractable problem (such as a factoring, discrete logarithm, or knapsack problem, or any other problem believed to be intractable).

---

[2] In the case of encryption algorithms, this means that the secret key space can be exhaustively searched. In the case of hashing algorithms, this means that the birthday attack becomes viable.

2 Background Theory

This chapter covers the main concepts and notions from Number Theory, Information Theory, and Complexity Theory that are frequently used in cryptology. Those readers with a strong mathematical background may wish to browse through this chapter or skip it completely.

2.1 Elements of Number Theory

Denote the set of *natural numbers* as $\mathcal{N} = \{1, 2, \ldots\}$, the set of *integers* as $\mathcal{Z} = \{\ldots, -1, 0, +1, \ldots\}$, the set of *rational numbers* as $\mathcal{Q}$, the set of *irrational numbers* as $\mathcal{I}$, and the set of *real numbers* as $\mathcal{R}$.

2.1.1 Divisibility and the Euclid Algorithm

Let a be a nonzero integer. We can create the set $\{\ldots, -3a, -2a, 0, a, 2a, 3a, \ldots\}$ of all integers that are *multiples* of a. Any integer b from the set $\{\ldots, -3a, -2a, 0, a, 2a, 3a, \ldots\}$ is *divisible* by a or a divides b without a remainder. This fact can be expressed in short as $a \mid b$. All integers which are divisible by other integers with no remainder are called *composites*. Divisibility has the following properties [366]:

1. If $n \mid a$ and $n \mid b$, then n divides both $(a+b)$ and $(a-b)$ (the set of multiples of n is closed under addition).
2. If $a \mid b$ and $b \mid c$, then a divides c (transitivity).
3. For any nonzero $b \in \mathcal{Z}$, if $n \mid a$, then n divides ab.
4. For any nonzero $b \in \mathcal{Z}$, $\mid a \mid \leq \mid b \mid$ if $a \mid b$.
5. If $a \mid b$ and $b \mid a$, then $\mid a \mid = \mid b \mid$ (antisymmetry).

Integers different from ± 1, which are divisible by themselves and 1 only are called *prime numbers* or simply *primes*. The set of all primes is denoted by $\mathcal{P}$.

The fundamental theorem of arithmetic states that any natural number can be uniquely factored into the product of primes, i.e., any $n \in \mathcal{N}$ can be written as

$$n = \prod_{p \in \mathcal{P}} p^{e_p}, \tag{2.1}$$

where e_p is the exponent of the prime p $(p \neq 1)$. The representation of n on the right-hand side of (2.1) is called its *factorization* and the primes p its *factors*.

Let a and b be two natural numbers. The *least common multiple (lcm)* of a and b is the smallest integer which is divisible by both a and b. How can we find $lcm(a,b)$? Clearly, both a and b have their unique factorizations, so $a = \prod_i p_i^{a_i}$ and $b = \prod_i p_i^{b_i}$. Thus, if the factorizations of a and b are given, then their least common multiple can be computed as

$$lcm(a,b) = \prod_i p_i^{\max(a_i,b_i)}, \tag{2.2}$$

where $\max(a_i, b_i)$ selects the maximum exponent for the given factor and i indexes all factors of the integer. Consider $a = 882$ and $b = 3465$. Their factorizations are: $a = 2 \cdot 3^2 \cdot 7^2$ and $b = 3^3 \cdot 5 \cdot 7 \cdot 11$. Thus $lcm(a,b) = 2 \cdot 3^3 \cdot 5 \cdot 7^2 \cdot 11 = 145530$.

The *greatest common divisor (gcd)* is another integer that expresses a relation between two natural numbers a and b. The greatest common divisor of a and b is the largest integer which divides with no remainder both a and b. Therefore

$$gcd(a,b) = \prod_i p_i^{\min(a_i,b_i)} \tag{2.3}$$

where $a = \prod_i p_i^{a_i}$ and $b = \prod_i p_i^{b_i}$ and i indexes all factors of the integer. The function $\min(a_i, b_i)$ produces the smallest exponent for the given factor. For our two integers $a = 882$ and $b = 3465$, their greatest common divisor is $gcd(a,b) = 3^2 \cdot 7 = 63$. Both *lcm* and *gcd* work with an arbitrary number of arguments and can be defined recursively as follows:

$$lcm(a,b,c) = lcm(lcm(a,b),c) \text{ and } gcd(a,b,c) = gcd(gcd(a,b),c). \tag{2.4}$$

Some of the properties of *lcm* and *gcd* are:

1. If there is an integer $d \in \mathcal{Z}$ such that $d \mid n_i$ for all $n_i \in \mathcal{N}$ $(i = 1, \ldots, k)$, then $d \mid gcd(n_1, \ldots, n_k)$.
2. If $n_1 \mid m, \ldots, n_k \mid m$ $(m \in \mathcal{Z})$, then $lcm(n_1, \ldots, n_k) \mid m$.
3. If $d = gcd(n_1, \ldots, n_k)$ and $b_i = \frac{n_i}{d}$, then $gcd(b_1, \ldots, b_k) = 1$.
4. $lcm(a,b) \cdot gcd(a,b) = a \cdot b$.

Two integers a and b are said to be *coprime* or relatively prime if their $gcd(a,b) = 1$. For example, $a = 15$ and $b = 77$ are coprime as their $gcd(15, 77) = 1$. Their $lcm(15, 77) = 15 \cdot 77$.

How can we compute the greatest common divisor? Clearly, the *gcd* can be computed from factorizations of the integers. However, no one knows of an efficient factoring algorithm for large numbers. An excellent alternative not based on factoring is the well-known *Euclid algorithm* which is very efficient, even for very large numbers.

Euclid algorithm – finds the greatest common divisor of two numbers $a, b \in \mathcal{N}$.

E1. Initialize $r_0 = a$ and $r_1 = b$.
E2. Compute the following sequence of equations:

$$r_0 = q_1 r_1 + r_2,$$
$$r_1 = q_2 r_2 + r_3,$$
$$\vdots \tag{2.5}$$
$$r_{n-3} = q_{n-2} r_{n-2} + r_{n-1},$$
$$r_{n-2} = q_{n-1} r_{n-1} + r_n,$$

until there is a step for which $r_n = 0$ while $r_{n-1} \neq 0$.
E3. The greatest common divisor is equal to r_{n-1}.

Theorem 1. *Let the sequence r_k be defined as in (2.5), then $r_{n-1} = gcd(a, b)$ when n is the first index for which $r_n = 0$.*

Proof. Using induction, we will show that both $r_{n-1} \mid gcd(a, b)$ and $gcd(a, b) \mid r_{n-1}$, which implies that $gcd(a, b) = r_{n-1}$.

Note that $r_{n-1} \mid r_{n-2}$ as $r_{n-2} = q_{n-1} r_{n-1}$. Further, $r_{n-1} \mid r_{n-3}$ as $r_{n-3} = q_{n-2} q_{n-1} r_{n-1} + r_{n-1}$, and so forth. Finally, $r_{n-1} \mid a$ and $r_{n-1} \mid b$. This implies that $r_{n-1} \mid gcd(a, b)$. By definition, $gcd(a, b)$ divides both a and b and we conclude that $gcd(a, b) \mid r_{n-1}$. □

For example, assume we have two integers $a = 882$ and $b = 3465$. The Euclid algorithm will give the following equations:

$$3465 = 3 \cdot 882 + 819$$

$$882 = 1 \cdot 819 + 63$$
$$819 = 13 \cdot 63 + 0$$

The remainder in the last equation is zero so the algorithm terminates and $gcd(882, 3465) = 63$.

The Euclid algorithm can be implemented as a computer program. A C language implementation of the algorithm is given below.

C implementation of Euclid algorithm

```
/* gcd finds the greatest common divisor for a and b */
long gcd(long a, long b)
{
    long r0,r1,r2;

    if(a==0 || b==0) return(0);
                        /* if one is zero output zero */
    r0=a;
    r1=b;               /* initialisation */
    r2=r0 % r1;
    while(r2) {
            r0=r1;
            r1=r2;
            r2=r0 % r1;
    }
    if(r1>0)
            return(r1);
    else
            return(-r1);
}
```

Observe that we do not need to compute q_i in the Euclid algorithm as we are looking for the last nonzero remainder.

The number of iterations n in the Euclid algorithm is proportional to $\log_2 a$ where a is the larger integer from the pair. To justify this, it is enough to observe that the divisor in each iteration is bigger than or equal to 2. If the divisor were always 2, then the number of iterations would be exactly equal to $\log_2 a$. In other words, every iteration reduces the length of the remainder by at least one bit. How many steps are consumed by a single iteration? Let our two integers be a and b ($a > b$). To produce two integers q and r such that $a = q \cdot b + r$, we will need at most $\log_2 a$ subtractions. This can be seen if we represent a and b in binary and carry out the division. A single subtraction takes at most $\log_2 a$-bit operations. Altogether the Euclid algorithm needs $O(\log_2^3 a)$ steps. This upper bound can be refined to $O(\log_2^2 a)$ after a more detailed analysis.

2.1.2 Primes and the Sieve of Eratosthenes

The fact that any integer can be uniquely represented by its prime factors emphasizes the importance of primes. Primes are "building blocks" for the construction of all other integers. In cryptography most primes that are used are relatively large (typically more than 100 decimal digits). One could ask whether it is possible to generate large primes and to decide whether an integer is prime. Another question could relate to the distribution of primes or how often they occur. The answer to the first question was given by Euclid who showed that there are infinitely many primes. His proof is one of the gems of Number Theory [455].

Theorem 2. *There are infinitely many primes.*

Proof. (By contradiction) Assume that the number of primes is finite. Then there is the largest prime p_{max}. Consider the number N that is the product of all primes plus "1", i.e.,

$$N = p_1 \cdot \ldots \cdot p_{max} + 1.$$

The number N is bigger than p_{max} so it cannot be prime. Therefore N has to be composite. But this is impossible as any of the known primes $p_1, \ldots, p_{max}$ divides N leaving the remainder 1. Thus, there is a prime N larger then p_{max}. This is a contradiction, which leads us to the conclusion that there are infinitely many primes. □

Eratosthenes gave a method which generates all primes smaller than a given number N. His method is referred to as the *sieve of Eratosthenes*.

Sieve of Eratosthenes – determines all primes smaller than N.

S1. Create an initial set of all numbers $\mathcal{N}_N = \{2, 3, 4, \ldots, N - 1\}$ smaller than N.

S2. For all integers $n < \sqrt{N}$ (that are still in the set $\mathcal{N}_N$), remove all multiples of n from the set $\mathcal{N}_N$ (leaving n itself in the set).

S3. The final reduced set $\mathcal{N}_N$ contains all primes smaller than N.

Let the upper limit N be 20. The set $\mathcal{N}_{20} = \{2, 3, \ldots, 19\}$. We need to remove all multiples of 2, 3 and 4 ($n < \sqrt{20}$). After removing all multiples of 2, the set is

$$\{2, 3, 5, 7, 9, 11, 13, 15, 17, 19\}.$$

After removing all multiples of 3, the set reduces to

$$\{2, 3, 5, 7, 11, 13, 17, 19\}.$$

The number 4 is not in the set so our sieving is completed. The set contains all primes smaller than 20.

Denote by $\pi(x)$ a function that gives the number of all primes contained in the interval $\langle 1, x \rangle$. Alternatively, $\pi(x)$ is named the *prime-counting function*. Gauss claimed that $\pi(x) \approx \frac{x}{\ln x}$. A better approximation of $\pi(x) \approx \frac{x}{\ln x - 1.08366}$ was given by Legendre. Hadamard and de la Vallée-Poussin proved the *prime number theorem* which says that

$$\lim_{x \to \infty} \frac{\pi(x) \ln(x)}{x} = 1. \tag{2.6}$$

For more details, readers are referred to [366, 455].

A Mersenne number is an integer of the form $M_p = 2^p - 1$ where p is a prime. If a Mersenne number is itself prime then it is called a *Mersenne prime*. The number $M_3 = 2^3 - 1 = 7$ is a Mersenne prime. Two consecutive primes separated by a single even number are called *twin primes*. The numbers 5 and 7 are twin primes.

2.1.3 Congruences

Modular arithmetic is often introduced in school as *clock arithmetic*. Fourteen hours after 3 p.m. is 5 a.m. the next morning. Simply,

$$14 + 3 \equiv 5 \quad (\text{mod } 12) \text{ or } 14 + 3 = 1 \cdot 12 + 5.$$

The formula $a \equiv b \bmod N$ is a *congruence* and can be read as "a is congruent to b modulo N." It holds for integers a, b and $N \neq 0$ if and only if

$$a = b + kN \text{ for some integer } k$$

or $N \mid (a - b)$.

If $a \equiv b \bmod N$, b is called a *residue* of a modulo N. In our example, $17 \equiv 5 \bmod 12$, or 5 is a residue of 17 modulo 12. A set $\{r_1, r_2, \ldots, r_n\}$ is called a complete set of residues modulo N if for every integer a exactly one r_i in the set satisfies $a \equiv r_i \bmod N$. For any modulus N, $\{0, 1, \ldots, N-1\}$ forms a complete set of residues modulo N. For $N = 12$ the set of complete residues is $\{0, 1, \ldots, 11\}$. We usually prefer to use integers from $\{0, \ldots, N-1\}$ but sometimes integers in the set $\{-\frac{1}{2}(N-1), \ldots, \frac{1}{2}(N-1)\}$ may be more useful (N is odd). Note that

$$\ldots - 12 \pmod 7 \equiv -5 \pmod 7 \equiv 2 \pmod 7 \equiv 9 \pmod 7 \equiv \ldots$$

Congruences have the following properties:

1. If $a \equiv A \bmod N$ and $b \equiv B \bmod N$, then $a + b \equiv A + B \bmod N$ and $a \cdot b \equiv A \cdot B \bmod N$.
2. $a \equiv b \bmod N$ if and only if $N \mid (a - b)$.
3. If $ab \equiv ac \bmod N$ and $gcd(a, N) = 1$, then $b \equiv c \bmod N$.

For example, the rule of "casting out nines" relies on adding all the digits of a number. If you add to 9, then ultimately the original number is divisible by 9. For instance, in order to determine whether 46909818 is divisible by 9 we sum the digits $4 + 6 + 9 + 9 + 8 + 1 + 8 = 45$ and repeat this by summing $4 + 5 = 9$, which indicates that the number is divisible by 9. The method relies on the fact that:

$$10 \equiv 1 \pmod 9$$
$$10^2 \equiv 10 \pmod 9 \cdot 10 \pmod 9 \equiv 1 \pmod 9$$
$$10^3 \equiv 10^2 \pmod 9 \cdot 10 \pmod 9 \equiv 1 \pmod 9$$
$$\vdots$$

Any integer a is represented by the sequence of its successive decimal digits $a = (a_m \ldots a_2 a_1 a_0)_{10}$ and $a = a_m \cdot 10^m + \ldots + a_2 \cdot 10^2 + a_1 \cdot 10 + a_0$. So the integer,

$$a \equiv (a_m \ldots a_2 a_1 a_0)_{10} \pmod 9$$
$$\equiv a_m \cdot 10^m + \cdots + a_2 \cdot 10^2 + a_1 \cdot 10 + a_0 \pmod 9$$
$$\equiv a_m + \cdots + a_2 + a_1 + a_0 \pmod 9.$$

The casting out nines rule illustrates the fact that the calculation of powers of an integer in congruences can be done very efficiently.

Algorithm for fast exponentiation – computes a^e mod N.

1. Find the binary representation of the exponent e. Let it be $e = e_k \cdot 2^k + \ldots + e_1 \cdot 2 + e_0$ where e_i are bits ($e_i \in \{0, 1\}$) for all i and $e_k = 1$.
2. Initiate an accumulator $accum$ (which will be used to store partial results) to 1.
3. For $i = 0, \ldots, k$, multiply modulo N the contents of $accum$ by a^{e_i} and save a^2 in a.
4. The result is stored in $accum$.

Observe that all the computations can be done "on the fly." For every i, it is enough to square the power of a and modify the accumulator only if $e_i = 1$. The modulus N can be represented as a string of $\ell = \lfloor \log_2 N \rfloor + 1$ bits. Exponentiation can be done using at most $\log_2 e$ modular multiplications.

An example of the algorithm implementation in C is given below.

C implementation of fast exponentiation

```
/* fastexp returns a to the power of e modulo N */
long fastexp(long a, long e, long N)
{
        long accum=1;

        while(e) {
                while(!(e%2)) {
                        e/=2;
                        a=((a % N)*(a % N)) % N;
                }
                e--;
                accum=((accum % N)*(a % N)) % N;
        }
        return(accum);
}
```

Suppose we wish to find 7^5 mod 9. We first note that 5 is $e = 1 \cdot 2^2 + 0 \cdot 2 + 1$ or $e = (101)_2$ in binary. We start from the least significant (the rightmost) bit e_0 of the exponent. As $e_0 = 1$ so $a = 7$ and $accum = 7$. Since the second rightmost digit is zero, we square a but do not multiply it onto $accum$:

$$a = 7^2 = 49 \equiv 4 \pmod{9}, \text{ and } accum = 7.$$

Now, the leftmost digit of e is 1, so we square a and multiply it onto *accum* to get the result

$$a = 7^4 \equiv 4^2 = 16 \equiv 7 \pmod 9, \text{ and } accum = 7^2 = 4.$$

Note that if the fast exponential is used for very long integers (i.e., longer than the length of the long integer type in your C compiler), then special care must be taken to prevent overflow. Software packages such as MATHEMATICA and MAPLE provide multiprecision arithmetic that handles arbitrarily long integers.

The inverse problem to that of finding powers of numbers in modular arithmetic is that of finding the *discrete logarithm* $\log_a b \pmod N$. It means that we are looking for an integer e such that

$$a^e \equiv b \pmod N.$$

Unlike exponentiation, finding discrete logarithms is generally not an easy problem.

Consider an example in which we show how discrete logarithms may be solved by applying exponentiation. Find two exponents e, f such that the two following congruences are satisfied: $3^e \equiv 4 \bmod 13$ and $2^f \equiv 3 \bmod 13$. Let us compute $3^1 \equiv 3$, $3^2 \equiv 9$, $3^3 \equiv 1$, $3^4 \equiv 3, \ldots \bmod 13$ which clearly has no solution. On the other hand, for the congruence $2^f \equiv 3 \bmod 13$, we have the following sequence:

$$2^1 \equiv 2, \quad 2^2 \equiv 4, \quad 2^3 \equiv 8, \quad 2^4 \equiv 3,$$
$$2^5 \equiv 6, \quad 2^6 \equiv 12, \quad 2^7 \equiv 11, \quad 2^8 \equiv 9,$$
$$2^9 \equiv 5, \quad 2^{10} \equiv 10, \quad 2^{11} \equiv 7, \quad 2^{12} \equiv 1 \pmod{13}.$$

So $f = 4$.

2.1.4 Computing Inverses in Congruences

Unlike ordinary integers, sometimes residues do have multiplicative inverses. So given $a \in \{0, \ldots, N-1\}$ there may be a unique $x \in \{0, \ldots, N-1\}$ such that,

$$ax \equiv 1 \pmod N.$$

For example, $3 \cdot 7 \equiv 1 \bmod 10$.

Consider the following lemma.

Lemma 1. *If $gcd(a, N) = 1$ then,*

$$a \cdot i \neq a \cdot j \pmod{N}$$

for all numbers $0 \leq i < j < N$ $(i \neq j)$.

Proof. We proceed by contradiction. Assume $a \cdot i \equiv a \cdot j \bmod N$. This means that $N \mid a(i - j)$. This implies that $i - j \equiv 0 \bmod N$ as $gcd(a, N) = 1$. Since $i, j < N$, we conclude that $i = j$ which is a contradiction. $\square$

Corollary 1. *If $gcd(a, N) = 1$, then the collection of numbers $a \cdot i \bmod N$ for $i = 0, 1, \ldots, N - 1$ is a permutation of the numbers from 0 to $N - 1$.*

For example, if $a = 3$ and $N = 7$ then the congruence $3 \cdot i$ (mod 7) yields the following sequence of numbers $\{0, 3, 6, 2, 5, 1, 4\}$ for all successive $i = 0, 1, \ldots, 6$. The sequence is just a permutation of the set $\{0, 1, 2, 3, 4, 5, 6\}$. This is not true when $gcd(a, N) \neq 1$. For example, if $a = 2$ and $N = 6$ then for $i = 0, 1, \ldots, 5$ the congruence $2 \cdot i \bmod 6$ generates all multiples of 2 smaller than 6.

Theorem 3. *If $gcd(a, N) = 1$, then the inverse element a^{-1}, $0 < a^{-1} < N$, exists, and*

$$a \cdot a^{-1} \equiv 1 \pmod{N}.$$

Proof. From Corollary 1 we know that $a \cdot i \bmod N$ is a permutation of $0, 1, \ldots, N - 1$. Thus there must be an integer i such that $a \cdot i \equiv 1 \bmod N$. $\square$

A *reduced set of residues* is a subset of the complete set of residues that are relatively prime to N. For example, the complete set of residues modulo 10 is $\{0, 1, 2, 3, 4, 5, 6, 7, 8, 9\}$, but of these only 1, 3, 7, 9 do not have a factor in common with 10. So the reduced set of residues modulo 10 is $\{1, 3, 7, 9\}$. The elements that have been excluded to form the reduced set are the multiples of 2 and the multiples of 5. It is easy to see that for the modulus $N = p \cdot q$ $(p, q$ are different primes), the number of elements in the reduced set of residues is $(p - 1)(q - 1)$.

The complete set of residues modulo 11 is $\{0, 1, 2, 3, \ldots, 10\}$. Of these, only one element, 0, is removed to form the reduced set of residues, which has 10 elements. In general, for a prime modulus, the reduced set of residues contains $(N - 1)$ elements.

Table 2.1. Euler's totient function

Modulus		Reduced set	$\varphi(N)$
$N = p$	(p prime)	$\{1, 2, \ldots, p-1\}$	$p-1$
$N = p^2$	(p prime)	$\{1, 2, \ldots, p-1, p+1, \ldots,$	$p(p-1)$
		$2p-1, 2p+1, \ldots, p^2-1\}$	
	$\vdots$	$\vdots$	$\vdots$
$N = p^r$	(p prime)	$\{1, 2, \ldots, p^r-1\}$	$(p^r-1) - (p^{r-1}-1)$
		$-$ multiples of $p < p^r$	$= p^{r-1}(p-1)$
$N = pq$	(p, q prime, $p \neq q$)	$\{1, 2, \ldots, pq-1\}$	$(pq-1) - (q-1) - (p-1)$
		$-$ multiples of p	$= (p-1)(q-1)$
		$-$ multiples of q	
	$\vdots$	$\vdots$	$\vdots$
$N = \prod_{i=1}^{t} p_i^{e_i}$;	(p_i prime)		$\prod_{i=1}^{t} p_i^{e_i-1}(p_i-1)$

The reduced set of residues modulo $27 = 3^3$ is:

$$\{1, 2, 4, 5, 7, 8, 10, 11, 13, 14, 16, 17, 19, 20, 22, 23, 25, 26\},$$

which has 18 elements. The number 18 is obtained from the observation that the reduced set of residues modulo 3 has 2 elements, 1 and 2, and all the elements are either $3i + 1$ or $3i + 2$ for $i = 0, 1, \ldots, 8$. In general, for a prime power N^r, the reduced set of residues has $(N-1) \cdot N^{r-1}$ elements.

The *Euler totient function* $\varphi(N)$ is the number of elements in the reduced set of residues. This is tabulated in Table 2.1.

Theorem 4. (*Euler's Theorem*) *Let* $\gcd(a, N) = 1$, *then*

$$a^{\varphi(N)} \pmod{N} = 1. \tag{2.7}$$

Proof. Let $R = \{r_1, \ldots, r_{\varphi(N)}\}$ be a reduced set of residues modulo N. Then $\{ar_1, ar_2, \ldots, ar_{\varphi(N)}\}$ is a permutation of R for any $a = 1, 2, \ldots, N-1$. Thus,

$$\prod_{i=1}^{\varphi(N)} r_i = \prod_{i=1}^{\varphi(N)} ar_i \equiv a^{\varphi(N)} \cdot \prod_{i=1}^{\varphi(N)} r_i \pmod{N}.$$

Hence $a^{\varphi(N)} \equiv 1 \pmod{N}$. □

Euler's Theorem is also called the generalization of Fermat's theorem.

Theorem 5. (*Fermat's Little Theorem*) *Let p be a prime and suppose the* $gcd(a, p) = 1$ *then*

$$a^{p-1} \equiv 1 \pmod{p}. \tag{2.8}$$

To understand the security of many public-key algorithms, we need to study how efficiently we can find inverses in modular arithmetic. Algorithms for finding inverses $a^{-1} \bmod N$ include:

− Search through $1, \ldots, N-1$ until an a^{-1} is found such that $a \cdot a^{-1} \bmod N = 1$. This algorithm is not feasible when N is large.
− Compute

$$a^{-1} \equiv a^{\varphi(N)-1} \pmod{N}$$

if $\varphi(N)$ is known.
− Use the Euclid algorithm if $\varphi(N)$ is not known; see (2.5).

Consider the third algorithm from the above list. Recall (2.5), which describes the Euclid algorithm. We are going to show how to adjust it to find inverses. It starts with the following substitutions: $r_0 = N$ and $r_1 = a$, where N is the modulus and a is the number for which the inverse is sought. The first step is $r_0 = q_1 r_1 + r_2$. The equation can be rewritten as

$$r_2 = r_0 - q_1 r_1.$$

As $r_0 = N$ so $r_2 \equiv -q_1 r_1 \bmod N$. We store the coefficient against r_1 in $x_1 = -q_1$ so $r_2 = x_1 r_1$. The second step $r_1 = q_2 r_2 + r_3$ can be presented as

$$r_3 = r_1 - q_2 r_2 = r_1 - q_2 x_1 r_1 = (1 - q_2 x_1) r_1 = x_2 r_1,$$

where $x_2 = (1 - q_2 x_1)$. The third step proceeds as

$$r_4 = r_2 - q_3 r_3 = x_1 r_1 - q_3 x_2 r_1 = x_3 r_1,$$

and $x_3 = (x_1 - q_3 x_2)$. In general, the ith step is

$$r_{i+1} = r_{i-1} - q_i r_i = x_i r_1,$$

where $x_i = (x_{i-2} - q_i x_{i-1})$. The computations end when there is a step $n - 1$ for which $r_n = 0$ and $r_{n-1} = 1$. The equation for the previous step is

$$r_{n-1} = r_{n-3} - q_{n-2}r_{n-2} = x_{n-2}r_1 = 1.$$

The value of x_{n-2} is the inverse of $a = r_1$.

To illustrate the algorithm, consider the following example in which we find the inverse of 5 modulo 23.

$$3 = 23 - 4 \cdot 5 \equiv -4 \cdot 5 \pmod{23},$$
$$2 = 5 - 1 \cdot 3 = 5 - 1(-4 \cdot 5) = 5 \cdot 5,$$
$$1 = 3 - 1 \cdot 2 = (-4 \cdot 5) - 1(5 \cdot 5) = -9 \cdot 5.$$

So $1 \equiv -9 \cdot 5 \pmod{23}$ and $-9 \equiv 14 \pmod{23}$ is the inverse.

C implementation of the Euclid algorithm for finding inverses

```
/* inverse returns an element x such that */
/* a*x=1 mod N */
long inverse(long N, long a)
{
    long r0,r1,r2,q1,q2,x0,x1,x2;

    r0=N; r1=a;
    x0=1; /* initialization */
    q1=r0/r1; r2=r0 % r1;
    x1=-q1;
    while(r2){
        r0=r1; r1=r2;
        q1=r0/r1; r2=r0 % r1;
        x2=x0-q1*x1;
        x0=x1; x1=x2;
    }
    if(r1!=1){
        printf("NO INVERSE \n");
        exit(1);
    }
    if(x0>0) return(x0);
    return(N+x0);
}
```

Algorithms for finding inverses can be used to solve congruences

$$ax \equiv b \pmod{N}. \tag{2.9}$$

To find an integer x which satisfies (2.9), first compute the inverse of a, i.e.,

$$ay \equiv 1 \pmod{N},$$

and $x \equiv yb \pmod{N}$. For instance, to solve $5x \equiv 9 \pmod{23}$, we first solve $5y \equiv 1 \pmod{23}$ getting $y = 14$ and thus $x = 14 \cdot 9 \equiv 11 \pmod{23}$.

Theorem 6. *If $d = gcd(a, N)$ and $d \mid b$, then the congruence $ax \equiv b \pmod{N}$ has d solutions*

$$x_{i+1} \equiv \left(\frac{b}{d} \cdot x_0 + i \cdot \frac{N}{d} \right) \pmod{N}, \tag{2.10}$$

for $i = 0, 1, \ldots, d - 1$, and x_0 is the solution to

$$\frac{a}{d} x \equiv 1 \pmod{\frac{N}{d}},$$

otherwise it has no solution.

Proof. If $ax \equiv b \bmod N$ has a solution in $[1, N - 1]$, then $N \mid (ax - b)$. The fact that $d \mid N$ and $d \mid a$ implies that $d \mid b$. Hence the congruence

$$\frac{a}{d} x \equiv 1 \pmod{\frac{N}{d}}$$

has a unique solution x_0 in $[1, \frac{N}{d} - 1]$. Thus $x_1 \equiv \frac{b}{d} x_0 \bmod \frac{N}{d}$ is a solution of

$$\frac{a}{d} x \equiv \frac{b}{d} \pmod{\frac{N}{d}},$$

therefore $\frac{a}{d} x_1 - \frac{b}{d} = k \cdot \frac{N}{d}$ for some k. Multiplication by d gives

$$ax_1 - b = kN,$$

so x_1 is a solution of $ax \equiv b \bmod N$. But any $x \in \{1, \ldots, N - 1\}$ such that $x \equiv x_1 \bmod \frac{N}{d}$ is also a solution. So all solutions are:

$$x_{i+1} = \frac{b}{d} x_0 + i \frac{N}{d} \text{ for } i = 1, \ldots, d - 1.$$

□

Suppose we wish to solve $9x \equiv 6 \bmod 12$. We denote $d = gcd(9,12) = 3$ and 3 divides 6 so there are three solutions. We first solve:

$$3x_1 = 2 \quad (\bmod \; 4)$$

by finding the solution to:

$$3x_0 = 1 \quad (\bmod \; 4).$$

Now $x_0 = 3$ and so $x_1 = 3 \cdot 2 = 6 \equiv 2 \bmod 4$. Thus the three solutions are:

$$x_{i+1} = 2 + i \cdot 4, \quad i = 0, 1, \text{ and } 2.$$

That is, $x = 2$, 6 and 10.

Diophantine equations are equations with solutions in the set of integers or natural numbers. Congruences have an intimate relation with Diophantine equations. The congruence $a \cdot x \equiv b \bmod N$ has its Diophantine counterpart

$$a \cdot x = k \cdot N + b.$$

To solve it, it is enough to show pairs (x, k) which satisfy the equation for the given (a, b).

2.1.5 Legendre and Jacobi Symbols

Consider the following quadratic congruence

$$x^2 \equiv a \quad (\bmod \; p) \tag{2.11}$$

where p is a prime integer. Note that squaring takes two values x and $-x$ and produces the same result x^2. Therefore the quadratic congruence (2.11) may have one, two or no solutions. More precisely, the quadratic congruence may have

1. one solution if $a \equiv 0 \quad (\bmod \; p)$,
2. two solutions if a is a *quadratic residue modulo* p,
3. no solution if a is a *quadratic nonresidue modulo* p.

The Legendre symbol is defined as follows:

$$\left(\frac{a}{p} \right) = \begin{cases} 0 & \text{if } a = 0, \\ 1 & \text{if } a \text{ is a quadratic residue modulo } p, \\ -1 & \text{if } a \text{ is a quadratic nonresidue modulo } p. \end{cases} \tag{2.12}$$

Below we list some properties of the Legendre symbol.

– The value of the Legendre symbol can be computed from the congruence

$$\left(\frac{a}{p}\right) \equiv a^{\frac{1}{2}(p-1)} \pmod{p}.$$

It is easy to check that the congruence holds for $a = 0$ (or $p \mid a$). Note that for $a \neq 0$ Fermat's Little Theorem says that $a^{(p-1)} \equiv 1 \pmod{p}$ so $a^{(p-1)/2} \pmod{p}$ is ± 1. Now we show that a is a quadratic residue modulo p if and only if $a^{(p-1)/2} = 1$. ($\Rightarrow$) Clearly if a is a quadratic residue, then there is a number x such that $x^2 = a$. According to Fermat's Little Theorem, we have $a^{(p-1)/2} = x^{(p-1)} = 1$. ($\Leftarrow$) Assume that there is a number a for which $a^{(p-1)/2} = 1$. This means that $a^{(p-1)/4} = \pm 1$ or in other words there is a number $x = a^{1/2}$ such that $x^{(p-1)/2} = \pm 1$. The case when the Legendre symbol is equal to -1 follows as there are three possible values it can take.

– The Legendre symbol is multiplicative or $\left(\frac{ab}{p}\right) = \left(\frac{a}{p}\right)\left(\frac{b}{p}\right)$. To see that this holds, consider the following sequence of congruences:

$$\left(\frac{ab}{p}\right) = (ab)^{(p-1)/2} = a^{(p-1)/2}b^{(p-1)/2} = \left(\frac{a}{p}\right)\left(\frac{b}{p}\right).$$

– If $a \equiv b \pmod{p}$, then $\left(\frac{a}{p}\right) = \left(\frac{b}{p}\right)$.
– The sets of nonresidues and residues modulo p are of the same cardinality.

The Jacobi symbol is a generalization of the Legendre symbol for the case when the quadratic congruence is considered for an arbitrary modulus N (N need not be a prime). The Jacobi symbol for a given quadratic congruence $x^2 = a$ (mod N), where $N = p_1 \cdots p_r$, is defined as

$$\left(\frac{a}{N}\right) = \prod_{i=1}^{r}\left(\frac{a}{p_i}\right),$$

where N is a composite integer, p_i are factors of N, and $\left(\frac{a}{p_i}\right)$ are Legendre symbols.

Jacobi symbols are easy to compute using exponentiation when the factors of N are known. If factors of N are not known, then Jacobi symbols can still be computed efficiently using the Euclid algorithm with $O(\log_2^2 N)$ steps (for details see [102]).

2.1.6 Chinese Remainder Theorem

Solving congruences for moduli which are composite is equivalent to the solution of systems of congruences. If the congruence is $ax \equiv b \bmod p \cdot q$, then we solve two congruences $ax \equiv b \bmod p$, $ax \equiv b \bmod q$ and combine the results. The Chinese Remainder Theorem (CRT) shows how we can solve a single congruence modulo N by solving the system of congruences for factors of N.

Theorem 7. *Let $p_1, \ldots, p_r$ be pairwise coprime and $f(x)$ an arbitrary congruence. Further let $N = p_1 \cdot \ldots \cdot p_r$. Then,*

$$f(x) \pmod{N} \equiv 0 \text{ iff } f(x) \pmod{p_i} \equiv 0$$

for $i = 1, \ldots, r$.

Proof. The p_i are pairwise coprime so

$$f(x) = kN = k \cdot p_1 \cdot \ldots \cdot p_r \Rightarrow p_i \mid f(x)$$

for any i. □

Theorem 8. (*Chinese Remainder Theorem*) *Let $p_1, \ldots, p_r$ be pairwise coprime, where $N = p_1 \cdot \ldots \cdot p_r$. Then the system of congruences*

$$x \equiv x_i \pmod{p_i}, \quad i = 1, \ldots, r$$

has a common solution x in $\{0, \ldots, N-1\}$.

Proof. For each i, $gcd(p_i, \frac{N}{p_i}) = 1$. Therefore there exists a y_i such that:

$$\frac{N}{p_i} \cdot y_i \equiv 1 \pmod{p_i}$$

and

$$\frac{N}{p_i} \cdot y_i \equiv 0 \pmod{p_j}$$

for all $j \neq i$ and $p_j \mid \frac{N}{p_i}$. Let $x \equiv \sum_{i=1}^{r} \frac{N}{p_i} \cdot x_i y_i \bmod N$. Then x is a solution of $x_i = x \bmod p_i$ because, $x = \frac{N}{p_i} \cdot x_i y_i \equiv x_i \bmod p_i$. □

For example, suppose we wish to solve two congruences $x \equiv 1 \bmod 5$ and $x \equiv 10 \bmod 11$ to find a solution modulo 55. First find the inverse of 11 modulo 5

$$\frac{55}{5} y_1 \equiv 1 \pmod{5} \text{ or } 11 y_1 \equiv 1 \pmod{5} \Rightarrow y_1 = 1.$$

Next, find the inverse of 5 modulo 11

$$\frac{55}{11} y_2 \equiv 1 \pmod{11} \text{ or } 5 y_2 \equiv 1 \pmod{11} \Rightarrow y_2 = 9.$$

Thus $x = \frac{55}{5} \cdot x_1 y_1 + \frac{55}{11} \cdot x_2 y_2 \equiv 11 \cdot 1 \cdot 1 + 5 \cdot 10 \cdot 9 \equiv 21 \bmod 55$.

CRT algorithm – generates the solution for $x \bmod N$ from $x_i \bmod p_i$, where $N = p_1 \cdot \ldots \cdot p_r$, $i = 1, \ldots, r$.

1. Precomputation: For all $i = 1, \ldots, r$, find all inverses y_i of $\frac{N}{p_i}$ modulo p_i and store them as the vector $(y_1, \ldots, y_r)$.
2. Composition: For the given vector of residues $x_1, \ldots, x_r$, create the solution $x \equiv \sum_{i=1}^{r} \frac{N}{p_i} \cdot x_i y_i \bmod N$.

The CRT asserts the equivalence of the representation of integers in modular arithmetic, i.e. $x \bmod N$ is equivalent to the vector representation $(x_1, \ldots, x_r)$. From a cryptographic point of view, both the recovery procedure of x from its vector $(x_1, \ldots, x_r)$ and the reverse operation (i.e., finding the vector from the integer x) are very efficient only if the factors of N are known (see Knuth [282]).

2.2 Algebraic Structures in Computing

Cryptography exploits a variety of algebraic structures. Most computations are done in finite groups, rings, and fields. In this section, we introduce basic algebraic concepts and explore the properties of basic algebraic structures.

2.2.1 Sets and Operations

Computing always involves passive entities (numbers) and active entities (operations). Algebra provides a well-developed theory that deals with such objects. An algebraic structure is defined as the collection of a set with one or more operations which can be performed on elements of the set. Let $\mathcal{S}$ be a set of elements and $\diamond$ be an operation. The operation $\diamond$ acts on a pair of elements $a, b \in \mathcal{S}$ and assigns an element $c = a \diamond b \in \mathcal{S}$. Note that, in general, the order of elements is important, as $a \diamond b \neq b \diamond a$.

A *group* $G = \langle \mathcal{S}, \diamond \rangle$ is an algebraic structure that satisfies the following conditions:

G1. For any two elements $a, b \in \mathcal{S}$, $c = a \diamond b \in \mathcal{S}$. This property is called closure.
G2. For any three elements $a, b, c \in \mathcal{S}$, the group operation is associative, i.e.,

$$(a \diamond b) \diamond c = a \diamond (b \diamond c).$$

G3. There is a *neutral (identity) element* $e \in \mathcal{S}$ such that

$$\forall_{a \in \mathcal{S}} \ a \diamond e = e \diamond a = a.$$

G4. Each element $a \in \mathcal{S}$ has its inverse, i.e.,

$$\forall_{a \in \mathcal{S}} \ \exists_{a^{-1} \in \mathcal{S}} \ a \diamond a^{-1} = a^{-1} \diamond a = e.$$

An *Abelian group* is a group whose group operation is commutative:

G5. For any two $a, b \in \mathcal{S}$,

$$a \diamond b = b \diamond a.$$

The following structures are examples of groups.

- The set of integers with addition as the group operation $\langle \mathcal{Z}, + \rangle$ is a group. The identity element is zero and the inverse element of $a \in \mathcal{Z}$ is $-a \in \mathcal{Z}$. The group is Abelian as $\forall_{a,b \in \mathcal{Z}} \ a + b = b + a$. The group is infinite.
- The set of nonzero rationals $\mathcal{R}$ under multiplication creates an Abelian group $\langle \mathcal{R} \setminus \{0\}, \cdot \rangle$. The identity element is 1 and the inverse of a is $\frac{1}{a}$. The group is infinite.
- The set $\mathcal{Z}_N = \{0, 1, \ldots, N-1\}$ with addition modulo N is an Abelian group $\mathcal{Z}_N = \langle \mathcal{Z}_N, + \rangle$. The identity element is 0. The inverse of a is $(N-a)$. The group is finite.
- The group $\mathcal{Z}_2 = \langle \mathcal{Z}_2, + \rangle$ has a special practical significance. It has two elements only. The group addition is equivalent to the binary Exclusive-Or operation $\oplus$.
- The set $\mathcal{Z}_N^* = \{1, 2, \ldots, N-1\}$ with multiplication, i.e., $\mathcal{Z}_N^* = \langle \mathcal{Z}_N^*, \cdot \rangle$ is an Abelian group if N is prime. The identity element is 1. The inverse element of a is a^{-1} such that $a \cdot a^{-1} \equiv 1 \pmod{N}$. The group is finite.

The *order* of a finite group is the number of elements in the group. A group $G_1 = \langle \mathcal{S}_1, \diamond \rangle$ is a *subgroup* of the group $G = \langle \mathcal{S}, \diamond \rangle$ if $\mathcal{S}_1 \subset \mathcal{S}$.

Theorem 9. (*Lagrange theorem*) *The order of a subgroup H of a finite group G divides the order of G.*

Proof. The idea of the proof is to show that there is an equivalence relation that partitions the elements of G into disjoint subsets (cosets). The relation is defined as $a \sim b$ if and only if $a^{-1} \diamond b \in H$. We now verify that the relation is reflexive, symmetric, and transitive. The relation is clearly reflexive as $a \sim a$ means that $a^{-1} \diamond a = e \in H$. The relation is symmetric as $a \sim b$ implies $b \sim a$.

This is true as the following sequence of implications holds: $a \sim b$ is equivalent to $a^{-1} \diamond b \in H$. This implies that $(a^{-1} \diamond b)^{-1} \in H$ and $b^{-1} \diamond a \in H$, which is equivalent to $b \sim a$. The relation is also transitive (we need to check that $a \sim b$ and $b \sim c$ implies $a \sim c$). This means that $a^{-1} \diamond b \in H$ and $b^{-1} \diamond c \in H$. So $(a^{-1} \diamond b) \diamond (b^{-1} \diamond c) = a^{-1} \diamond c \in H$, which is equivalent to $a \sim c$.

As $\sim$ is an equivalence relation, it partitions elements of G into disjoint cosets each having the number of elements equal to the order of H. Since each element of G is in some coset, the order of H divides the order of G. □

A *cyclic group* is a group whose elements are generated by a single element g (also called *the generator of the group*).

Consider the multiplicative group Z_7^*. Note that the identity element $1 \in Z_7^*$ generates the *trivial group* $\langle \{1\}, \cdot \rangle$. The element $6 \equiv -1 \pmod 7$ generates a bigger subgroup, namely $\langle \{1, 6\}, \cdot \rangle$. The element 2 generates the following subgroup: $2^1 = 2$, $2^2 = 2 \cdot 2 = 4$, $2^3 = 2 \cdot 2 \cdot 2 = 8 \equiv 1 \pmod 7$ of Z_7^*. Obviously we can rewrite $2^3 \equiv 2^0 \pmod 7$. The subgroup generated by 2 is $\langle \{1, 2, 4\}, \cdot \rangle$. The element 3 yields the following:

$$3^1 = 3,$$
$$3^2 = 3 \cdot 3 \equiv 2 \pmod 7,$$
$$3^3 = 3 \cdot 3 \cdot 3 \equiv 6 \pmod 7,$$
$$3^4 = 3 \cdot 3 \cdot 3 \cdot 3 \equiv 4 \pmod 7,$$
$$3^5 = 3 \cdot 3 \cdot 3 \cdot 3 \cdot 3 \equiv 5 \pmod 7,$$
$$3^6 = 3 \cdot 3 \cdot 3 \cdot 3 \cdot 3 \cdot 3 \equiv 1 \pmod 7.$$

The element 3 generates the whole group Z_7^*. Powers of 4 are: $4^1 = 4$, $4^2 \equiv 2 \pmod 7$, and $4^3 \equiv 1 \pmod 7$. The subgroup $\langle \{1, 2, 4\}, \cdot \rangle$ is generated by 4. Finally, the element 5 produces $5^1 = 5$, $5^2 \equiv 4 \pmod 7$, $5^3 \equiv 6 \pmod 7$, $5^4 \equiv 2 \pmod 7$, $5^5 \equiv 3 \pmod 7$, and $5^6 \equiv 1 \pmod 7$, i.e., the whole group Z_7^*. The number of elements in each subgroup is directly related to the factorization of $\varphi(N) = 6$. Altogether, the trivial and nontrivial factors are: 1, 2, 3, and 6. If we deal with larger N, and the factorization of $\varphi(N)$ has n nontrivial factors, then the probability that a randomly selected element from Z_N^* generates the whole group is $\approx \frac{1}{n+1}$.

The *mapping* $f : \mathcal{X} \to \mathcal{Y}$ is a generalization of a function, i.e., for every element of the set $\mathcal{X}$ it assigns an element from the set $\mathcal{Y}$. Let $\langle G, \diamond \rangle$ and $\langle H, \circ \rangle$

be two groups, then the mapping $f : G \rightarrow H$ is a group *homomorphism* if

$$\forall_{a,b \in G} \ f(a \diamond b) = f(a) \circ f(b). \tag{2.13}$$

If some additional conditions are imposed on the homomorphism, it is called an:

- *Epimorphism* – the image of the homomorphism covers the whole set H or $f(G) = H$.
- *Monomorphism* – there exists an inverse mapping $f^{-1} : H \rightarrow G$ such that
  $$\forall_{a \in G} \ f^{-1}(f(a)) = a.$$
- *Isomorphism* – monomorphism with $f(G) = H$.

A *ring* is an algebraic structure with the set $\mathcal{S}$ and two operations, addition, $+$, and multiplication, $\cdot$; i.e., $R = \langle \mathcal{S}, +, \cdot \rangle$ such that

R1. For each pair $a, b \in \mathcal{S}$, $a + b$ and $a \cdot b$ belong to $\mathcal{S}$.

R2. $\langle \mathcal{S}, + \rangle$ is an additive Abelian group.

R3. The multiplication operation is associative, i.e., for any $a, b, c \in \mathcal{S}$

$$(a \cdot b) \cdot c = a \cdot (b \cdot c).$$

R4. The multiplication operation is distributive with respect to addition, i.e., for any three elements $a, b, c \in \mathcal{S}$,

$$a(b + c) = ab + ac \ \text{ and } \ (a + b)c = ac + bc.$$

Let p, q be two odd primes and the modulus $N = pq$. The set $Z_N = \{0, 1, \ldots, N - 1\}$ with addition and multiplication modulo N is a ring. It is easy to check that $\langle Z_N, + \rangle$ is an Abelian group. Multiplication is associative and is also distributive with respect to addition. The ring Z_N describes the algebraic structure of the well-known Rivest-Shamir-Adleman public-key cryptosystem. Using the CRT, any element $a \in Z_N$ can be equivalently represented as a vector

$$a \equiv (a_1, a_2) \text{ with } a_1 \equiv a \bmod p \text{ and } a_2 \equiv a \bmod q.$$

Note that all elements $a \in Z_N$ whose vector components are different from zero $a_1 \neq 0$ and $a_2 \neq 0$ have additive and multiplicative inverses. Under multiplication, the set of these elements forms a finite group Z_N^* of order $\varphi(N)$. The group is cyclic and any element generates a subgroup of an order which divides $\varphi(N)$. Elements with one component equal to zero do not have multiplicative inverses. The collection of all elements $(0 \bmod p, a_2 \bmod q)$ includes the set of all multiples of p, i.e., $\{ip \mid i = 0, 1, \ldots, q-1\}$. The other set of multiples is $\{iq \mid i = 0, 1, \ldots, p-1\}$. These two sets have special properties: they are closed under addition and any product of their elements with an arbitrary element of Z_N falls back into the sets. The sets are called ideals.

More formally, an *ideal* in a ring R is a nonempty subset I ($I \subset R$) such that

I1. For any pair of elements $a, b \in I$, $(a+b) \in I$ – ideal is closed under addition.
I2. For any $a \in I$ and any $b \in R$, both ab and ba belong to I.

The ring Z_N ($N = pq$, p and q primes) contains two ideals: $I_1 = \{ip \mid i = 0, 1, \ldots, q-1\}$ and $I_2 = \{iq \mid i = 0, 1, \ldots, p-1\}$.

As not all elements of rings have multiplicative inverses, computations that involve division may not be possible unless special care is exercised. To make sure that all nonzero elements have their multiplicative inverses, computations should be done in rings with division. Commutative rings with division are called fields.

A *field* $F = \langle S, +, \cdot \rangle$ is a set S with two operations, addition and multiplication, with the following properties:

F1. $\langle S, +, \cdot \rangle$ is a commutative ring – it satisfies all the conditions for rings, and also multiplication is commutative, i.e., for all $a, b \in S$, $ab = ba$.
F2. There is an identity element 1 with respect to multiplication, i.e., for all $a \in S$, there is $e = 1 \in S$ such that $a \cdot 1 = 1 \cdot a = a$.
F3. Any nonzero element $a \in S$ has its unique inverse and $a \cdot a^{-1} = a^{-1} \cdot a = 1$.

$Z_N = \langle \{0, 1, \ldots, N-1\}, +, \cdot \rangle$ is a field if N is prime. Some other important fields can be constructed using polynomials.

2.2.2 Polynomial Arithmetic

Let F be a field. Consider a function $f : F \rightarrow F$ of the form

$$f(x) = a_0 + a_1 x + \ldots + a_n x^n, \tag{2.14}$$

where $a_i \in F$ for $i = 0, 1, \ldots, n$. Any function which can be written in the form of (2.14) is called a *polynomial*. Any polynomial $f(x) \neq 0$ has its degree – the highest power of x. For the polynomial (2.14) its *degree* is equal to n or, in other words, $\deg f(x) = n$. Two polynomials $p(x) = a_0 + a_1 x + \ldots + a_n x^n$ and $q(x) = b_0 + b_1 x + \ldots + b_m x^m$ can be added and subtracted

$$p(x) \pm q(x) = (a_0 \pm b_0) + (a_1 \pm b_1)x + \ldots$$
$$+ (a_m \pm b_m)x^m + a_{m+1}x^{m+1} + \ldots + a_n x^n, \tag{2.15}$$

where $n > m$. Their product is also a polynomial and

$$p(x)q(x) = a_0 b_0 + (a_0 b_1 + a_1 b_0)x + \ldots + a_n b_m x^{n+m}$$
$$= \sum_{i=0}^{n} \sum_{j=0}^{m} a_i b_j x^{i+j}. \tag{2.16}$$

It is easy to verify that the collection of all polynomials over the field F with polynomial addition (2.15) and multiplication (2.16) create a commutative ring $F[x]$.

Theorem 10. (*Division Algorithm*) *Let* $a(x) = a_0 + a_1 x + \ldots + a_n x^n$ *and* $b(x) = b_0 + b_1 x + \ldots + b_m x^m$ *be two polynomials from* $F[x]$ *(n > m). Then we can find two polynomials* $q(x)$ *and* $r(x)$ *such that*

$$a(x) = q(x) \cdot b(x) + r(x), \tag{2.17}$$

where $q(x)$ *is a quotient and* $r(x)$ *is a remainder whose degree is smaller than* m.

Proof. We apply induction on the degrees n and m.

1. $n < m$, then clearly $a(x) = 0 \cdot b(x) + a(x)$.
2. $n \geq m$, then

$$a(x) = \tilde{a}(x) + \frac{a_n}{b_m} x^{n-m} b(x). \tag{2.18}$$

The degree of $\tilde{a}(x)$ is smaller than n and equal to k. Assume that (2.17) is true for any $k > m$. From this assumption we can draw the conclusion that

$$\tilde{a}(x) = q_1(x)b(x) + r_1(x).$$

By putting the above expression for $\tilde{a}(x)$ into (2.18), we obtain the final result (2.17).

$\square$

This algorithm is an extension of the division algorithm for integers. The algorithm works for polynomials if the coefficients have multiplicative inverses – the coefficient $a_n b_m^{-1}$ in (2.18) has to exist. That is why polynomial coefficients have to be from a field.

Consider the ring $Z_7[x]$. The division of $a(x) = 2x^4 + x^2 + 5x + 3$ by $b(x) = 4x^2 + 3$ proceeds as follows:

$$
\begin{array}{l}
2x^4 + x^2 +5x +3 \ / \ 4x^2 + 3 = 4x^2 + 6 \\
\underline{-2x^4 -5x^2} \\
3x^2 +5x +3 \\
\underline{-3x^2 -4} \\
5x +6
\end{array}
$$

So, finally, $2x^4 + x^2 + 5x + 3 = (4x^2 + 3)(4x^2 + 6) + (5x + 6)$.

A polynomial $a(x)$ is *irreducible* over a field F if for all polynomials $b(x) \in F[x]$ with $\deg b(x) < \deg a(x)$, the following holds:

$$a(x) = q(x)b(x) + r(x),$$

where $\deg r(x) < \deg b(x)$ and $r(x) \neq 0$. All *reducible polynomials* have two or more nontrivial factor polynomials, or simply factors. Any irreducible polynomial $p(x) = p_0 + p_1 x + \ldots p_n x^n \in F[x]$ can be represented as $p(x) = a \cdot p'(x)$ where $a \in F$. We can normalize $p(x)$ so its leading coefficient $p_n = 1$. This can be done by dividing the polynomial by the leading coefficient. Such a polynomial is called *monic*. In polynomial arithmetic, there is also the unique factorization theorem which is equivalent to the fundamental theorem of arithmetic. It says that every polynomial over a field F can be uniquely represented as a product of a constant (an element of the field F) and monic irreducible polynomials. Thus notions such as the greatest common divisor and the least common multiple can be extended for polynomials. The Euclid algorithm can be easily modified to generate the *gcd* of two polynomials.

Euclid algorithm – finds the greatest common divisor of two polynomials $a(x), b(x) \in F[x]$.

E1. Initialize $r_0(x) = a(x)$ and $r_1(x) = b(x)$.

E2. Compute the following sequence of equations:

$$
\begin{aligned}
r_0(x) &= q_1(x)r_1(x) + r_2(x), \\
r_1(x) &= q_2(x)r_2(x) + r_3(x), \\
&\ \vdots \\
r_{k-3}(x) &= q_{k-2}(x)r_{k-2}(x) + r_{k-1}(x), \\
r_{k-2}(x) &= q_{k-1}(x)r_{k-1}(x) + r_k(x),
\end{aligned}
\tag{2.19}
$$

until there is a step for which $r_k(x) = 0$ while $r_{k-1}(x) \neq 0$ ($\deg r_i(x) >$ $\deg r_{i+1}(x)$ for all $i = 2, \ldots, k$).

E3. The greatest common divisor is equal to $r_{k-1}(x)$.

Let $p(x) = p_0 + p_1 x + \ldots p_n x^n \in F[x]$ be a polynomial. Then two polynomials $a(x), b(x) \in F[x]$ are congruent modulo $p(x)$, or

$$a(x) \equiv b(x) \pmod{p(x)},$$

if $p(x) \mid (a(x) - b(x))$. For instance, consider $Z_5[x]$, $3x^3 + 2x + 4 \equiv 4x + 4 \bmod x^2 + 1$ as $3x^3 + 2x + 4 - (4x + 4) = 3x^3 + 3x = 3x(x^2 + 1)$. Most properties discussed for congruences modulo N hold for congruences modulo $p(x)$, including the Chinese Remainder Theorem.

Assume that $p(x) \in F[x]$ is an irreducible polynomial over field F with $\deg p(x) = n$. A *set of residues* modulo $p(x)$ is a set $F[x]/p(x)$ of all polynomials whose degree is smaller than the degree of $p(x)$. The set of residues also includes all elements of the field F. It is easy to check that the set of residues (modulo irreducible polynomial $p(x)$) with polynomial addition and multiplication modulo $p(x)$ is a field. The only point that needs some elaboration is the existence of multiplicative inverses. Let $a(x), b(x) \in F[x]/p(x)$. Assume that $a(x)$ and $p(x)$ are given, and that we would like to find $b(x) = a^{-1}(x)$ such that

$$a(x) \cdot b(x) \equiv 1 \pmod{p(x)}.$$

We apply the Euclid algorithm (2.19) for $r_0(x) = p(x)$ and $r_1(x) = a(x)$. At each step we express $r_i(x)$ as a multiple of $a(x)$ modulo $p(x)$. Therefore $r_0(x) = 0$, $r_1(x) = a(x)$, $r_2(x) = -q_1(x)a(x) = m_1(x)a(x)$, $r_3(x) = (1 + q_1 q_2)a(x) = m_2(x)a(x)$, and so on. This leads us to a version of the Euclid algorithm that computes the inverse elements.

Euclid algorithm – finds the inverse of $a(x)$ modulo $p(x)$ ($p(x) \in F[x]$ is irreducible).

E1. Initialize $r_0(x) = p(x)$ and $r_1(x) = a(x)$.

E2. Compute the following sequence of equations:

$$r_0(x) = q_1(x)r_1(x) + r_2(x),$$
$$\Rightarrow r_2(x) \equiv -q_1(x)a(x) = m_1(x)a(x) \pmod{p(x)},$$
$$r_1(x) = q_2(x)r_2(x) + r_3(x),$$
$$\Rightarrow r_3(x) = r_1(x) - q_2(x)r_2(x) = m_2(x)a(x),$$

$$\vdots \qquad\qquad\qquad\qquad (2.20)$$

$$r_{k-3}(x) = q_{k-2}(x)r_{k-2}(x) + r_{k-1}(x),$$
$$\Rightarrow r_{k-1}(x) = r_{k-3}(x) - q_{k-2}(x)r_{k-2}(x) = m_{k-4}(x)a(x),$$
$$r_{k-2}(x) = q_{k-1}(x)r_{k-1}(x) + r_k(x),$$

until there is a step for which $r_k(x) = 0$ while $r_{k-1}(x) = c \in F$ ($\deg r_i(x) > \deg r_{i+1}(x)$ for $i = 2, \ldots, k$).

E3. The inverse is equal to $c^{-1}(m_{k-4}(x) - q_{k-2}(x)m_{k-3}(x))$.

The field defined over the set of residues $F[x]/p(x)$ with the addition and multiplication modulo $p(x)$, where $p(x)$ is irreducible, is called a *Galois field*. If the field F is Z_N (N is prime) then the corresponding Galois field over $Z_N[x]/p(x)$ is denoted $GF(N^n)$ ($n = \deg p(x)$). Note that $GF(N)$ is the field of coefficients with addition and multiplication modulo N.

2.2.3 Computing in Galois Fields

Many cryptographic designs extensively use binary Galois fields $GF(2^n)$. Consider an example that shows how computations can be done in $GF(2^3)$ with an irreducible polynomial $p(x) = x^3 + x + 1 \in Z_2[x]$ (in binary Galois fields all polynomials are monic).

The Galois field $GF(2^3)$ has the following elements: $0, 1, x, x+1, x^2, x^2+1, x^2+x$, and x^2+x+1. Zero is equivalent to any multiple of $p(x) = x^3 + x + 1$. This fact is equivalent to $x^3 = x + 1$. This equation can be used to reduce any polynomial of degree higher than or equal to 3 to a polynomial of degree at most 2. For instance, $(x^2 + 1)^2$ is equal to $x^4 + 1$, and using the fact that $x^3 = x + 1$ we have

$$x^4 + 1 = x \cdot x^3 + 1 = x \cdot (x+1) + 1 = x^2 + x + 1.$$

To do computations in the field, it suffices to build up two tables, one for addition and the other for multiplication (Table 2.2).

All nonzero elements of $GF(2^n)$ under multiplication modulo $p(x)$ ($p(x)$ is an irreducible polynomial of degree n) constitute a cyclic group with $2^n - 1$ elements. The Euler totient function can also be extended for polynomials and $\varphi(p(x)) = 2^n - 1$. There is a polynomial version of Fermat's theorem which states that

Table 2.2. The addition and multiplication tables for $GF(2^3)$

+	0	1	010	011	100	101	110	111
0	0	1	010	011	100	101	110	111
1	1	0	011	010	101	100	111	110
$x = 010$	010	011	0	1	110	111	100	101
$x + 1 = 011$	011	010	1	0	111	110	101	100
$x^2 = 100$	100	101	110	111	0	1	010	011
$x^2 + 1 = 101$	101	100	111	110	1	0	011	010
$x^2 + x = 110$	110	111	100	101	010	011	0	1
$x^2 + x + 1 = 111$	111	110	101	100	011	010	1	0

×	1	010	011	100	101	110	111
1	1	010	011	100	101	110	111
$x = 010$	010	100	110	011	1	111	110
$x + 1 = 011$	011	110	101	111	100	1	010
$x^2 = 100$	100	011	111	110	010	101	1
$x^2 + 1 = 101$	101	1	100	010	111	011	110
$x^2 + x = 110$	110	111	1	101	011	010	100
$x^2 + x + 1 = 111$	111	101	010	1	110	100	011

$$\forall_{a \in GF(2^n); a \neq 0} \quad a^{\varphi(p(x))} \equiv 1 \pmod{p(x)}.$$

Thus exponentiation can be used to find multiplicative inverses in $GF(2^n)$ as

$$\forall_{a \in GF(2^n); a \neq 0} \quad a^{-1} \equiv a^{\varphi(p(x))-1} \equiv a^{2^n - 2} \pmod{p(x)}.$$

Any nonzero element of $GF(2^n)$ generates a cyclic group whose order j divides $(2^n - 1)$, or in other words $j \mid (2^n - 1)$. If, for some reason, one would like all nonzero elements (different from 1) to generate the whole cyclic group, then it is enough to select a field for which $2^n - 1$ is a Mersenne prime.

$GF(2^3)$ has its totient function $\varphi(x^3 + x + 1) = 7$ and 7 is a Mersenne prime. Therefore there should be no surprise to learn that any nonzero element (different from 1) in $GF(2^3)$ generates the whole set of nonzero elements of the field. Let $(x + 1)$ be a tested element. We have the following sequence of powers: $(x + 1)^2 = x^2 + 1$, $(x + 1)^3 = x^2$, $(x + 1)^4 = x^2 + x + 1$, $(x + 1)^5 = x$, $(x + 1)^6 = x^2 + x$, and $(x + 1)^7 = 1$.

Computations in $GF(2^n)$ are often desirable for the following reasons:

1. Algorithms for computation in $GF(2^n)$ are usually more efficient than their counterparts in $GF(N)$. There is also the other side of the coin: crypto-

graphic designs based on integer arithmetic in $GF(N)$ are usually more secure than their equivalents based on polynomial arithmetic in $GF(2^n)$ when both fields have similar sizes.

2. Polynomial arithmetic in $GF(2^n)$ is more efficient as nothing is carried and there is no need to divide by the modulus in order to perform addition or subtraction. For example the C language offers the bit-by-bit Exclusive-Or (XOR) operation which provides a very fast implementation of addition in $GF(2^n)$.

3. The cost of the hardware depends on the choice of modulus. For instance, we can use a trinomial $p(x) = x^k + x + 1$ as the modulus to speed up multiplication as the string involved in the operation contains mostly zeros.

2.3 Complexity of Computing

Evaluating the security of cryptographic designs is in general a difficult business. It is not unusual to find out that the security evaluation has been upheld by a statement "as the design is based on the well-known intractable problem, a successful attack will be equivalent to finding an algorithm that solves all instances of the problem in polynomial time." Cryptanalysis is a part of cryptology whose ultimate goal is to demonstrate the existence of a polynomial-time algorithm that enables the computation of some of the secret elements of the design. In this section we present the basic results of Complexity Theory and discuss their applicability in cryptography and cryptanalysis.

2.3.1 Asymptotic Behavior of Functions

Assume that there are two algorithms that can be applied to solve a numerical task. To select a better algorithm we need to know how the efficiency of algorithms can be measured. One of the measurements is the so-called *time complexity function*. It describes how many steps (time intervals) must be performed before the algorithm generates the result for an instance of length n. Time complexity functions are usually compared using their asymptotic behavior.

Let $f(n)$ and $g(n)$ be two functions whose rates of growth are to be compared. The following notations are commonly used.

– "Little o" notation – the function $f(n)$ is *"little oh"* of $g(n)$ when the quotient of $f(n)$ by $g(n)$ converges to zero, or

$$f(n) = o(g(n)) \text{ if } \lim_{n \to \infty} \frac{f(n)}{g(n)} = 0. \tag{2.21}$$

For instance, $3n^3 = o(7n^4)$ and $2 = o(n)$.

− "Big O" notation – the function $f(n)$ is "*big oh*" of $g(n)$, or

$$f(n) = O(g(n)), \tag{2.22}$$

if there is a constant $C \in \mathcal{R}$ such that $\lim_{n \to \infty} |\frac{f(n)}{g(n)}| < C$. The function $3n^7 + n^3 = O(n^7)$.

− Ω notation – the function $f(n) = \Omega(g(n))$ iff $g(n) = O(f(n))$. For instance, $3x^4 = \Omega(x^4)$ but also $x^5 = \Omega(x^4)$, $x^6 = \Omega(x^4)$, and $x^7 = \Omega(x^4)$.

− Θ notation – the function $f(n)$ is *theta of* $g(n)$ if there is a pair of positive nonzero constants c_1, c_2 such that

$$c_1 g(n) < f(n) < c_2 g(n)$$

for all big enough n. For example, $3x^8 + x^5 + 1 = \Theta(x^8)$.

− $\sim$ notation – the function $f(n)$ is *asymptotically equal to* or $f(n) \sim g(n)$ if

$$\lim_{n \to \infty} \frac{f(n)}{g(n)} = 1.$$

For instance, $4x^2 + 3 \sim 4x^2 + 3x + 3$.

Consider the problem of multiplying of two $n \cdot n$ matrices. As the resulting product matrix contains n^2 elements and each element involves n multiplication, we can say we can multiply two matrices in time $O(n^3)$. Strassen showed that it is possible to multiply matrices quicker in time $O(n^{2.81})$. On the other hand, we cannot multiply matrices quicker than n^2, as $2n^2$ entries of matrices have to be read from the input. So multiplication of two matrices can be performed in time $\Omega(n^2)$. Or, in other words, any algorithm for matrix multiplications has to take at least n^2 steps. More details about the asymptotic notations together with an extensive discussion can be found in the book by Brassard and Bratley [60].

2.3.2 Hierarchy of Functions

Consider two algorithms. The first runs in time given by the polynomial $f_1(n) = n^a$ where n is an input length, and a is a fixed positive integer. The second has its time complexity function $f_2(n) = 2^n$. Consider the following question. Is there any integer $N \in \mathcal{N}$ such that

$$\forall_{n \geq N} \exists_{a \in \mathcal{N}} \ n^a \leq 2^n \ ?$$

In order to answer the question, take the equality $n^a = 2^n$. As $n \in \mathcal{N}$, the equality can be rewritten as

$$a = \frac{n}{\log_2 n}.$$

The function $\frac{n}{\log_2 n}$ grows to infinity as $n \to \infty$. So there is an integer N such that for all $n > N$, $n^a < 2^n$.

So even for large exponents a, the rate of growth of polynomials is negligible compared to the rate of exponential functions. For instance, assume we have two algorithms. The first runs in polynomial time $f_1(n) = n^{1000}$, the second in exponential time $f_2(n) = 2^{0.001n}$. Of course, the second algorithm is much more efficient than the first for small n. But, for $n > 2^{25}$, the situation changes and the polynomial-time algorithm is more efficient as it requires $\sim 2^{25000}$ steps while the exponential one needs $\sim 2^{32000}$ steps. This example is unrealistic but illustrates what we mean by the asymptotic behavior of functions.

In general, we can introduce a hierarchy of functions depending on their rates of growth [529].

1. *Logarithmic functions* – slow-growing functions. A typical representative of the class is $f(n) = \log_2 n$.
2. *Polynomial functions* – functions of the form $f(n) = n^a$ where a is a constant $(a \in \mathcal{N})$.
3. *Subexponential functions* – functions from the following set:

$$\{f(n) \mid f(n) = \Omega(n^a) \text{ for all } a \in \mathcal{N} \text{ and}$$
$$f(n) = o((1 + \varepsilon)^n) \text{ for all } \varepsilon \in \mathcal{R}; \varepsilon > 0\}.$$

A function $f(n) = 2^{p(\log(n))}$ is a typical example of a member of this class, where $p(x)$ is a polynomial.

4. *Exponential functions* – a function $f(n)$ is exponential if there is a constant $a \in \mathcal{N}$ such that $f(n) = \Omega(a^n)$ and there is another constant $b \in \mathcal{N}$ such that $f(n) = O(b^n)$. The function $f(n) = 2^n$ is a typical representative of this class.

5. *Super-exponential functions* – all functions whose rates of growth are higher than for previous classes, i.e., $f(n)$ is super-exponential if every exponential function $g(n) = o(f(n))$. Examples of such functions include $n!$ and 2^{n^2}.

2.3.3 Problems and Algorithms

A *problem* is a general question with associated parameters and variables whose values are not specified. The definition of a problem consists of two parts. The first one gives a general setting of the problem with a precise description of the problem parameters. The second part determines the requested answer or solution.

Consider the problem of finding the greatest common divisor. The problem can be defined as follows.

Name: GCD problem.
Instance: Two natural numbers $a, b \in \mathcal{N}$.
Question: What is the greatest common divisor of a and b?

Clearly, any problem consists of the collection of *instances* for whom all values are fixed. An instance of the GCD problem is: what is $gcd(24, 16)$?

An *algorithm* is a step-by-step procedure which for an instance produces the correct answer. An algorithm is said to solve a problem if it produces the correct answers for all instances of the problem (Fig. 2.1).

Obviously, there are some instances of a problem for which the answer is generated quicker than for the others. For example, it is much easier to compute

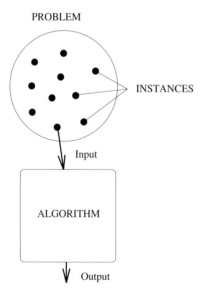

Fig. 2.1. Relation among a problem, its instances, and an algorithm

$gcd(2,4)$ than $gcd(1245, 35820)$. The commonly accepted characterization of the instance complexity is the number of symbols necessary to represent it uniquely using an acceptable encoding scheme.

The *time complexity function* (TCF) of an algorithm expresses how many steps (time intervals) are necessary to produce the solution for a given instance of the size n. The TCF of an algorithm depends upon

– the scheme used to encode instances, and
– the model of computer.

Assume that the TCF of an algorithm belongs to either polynomial, subexponential, or exponential class of functions from the Sect. 2.3.2 hierarchy. Observe that the TCF will stay in its class even for a wide range of possible encoding schemes. Any encoding scheme which differs polynomially from the best encoding scheme is acceptable as it leaves the TCF in the same class.

There are many computer models. But all realistic models are polynomially equivalent to the *deterministic Turing machine* (DTM) [191]. Moreover, Church's hypothesis says that any realistic notion of an algorithm is equivalent to a DTM.

The class of all problems can be divided into two broad subclasses:

– *undecidable* or provably intractable problems,
– *decidable* problems.

A problem belongs to the class of undecidable problems if there is *no algorithm* that solves it. The existence of such problems was proved by Alan Turing in 1936. Being more specific, Turing showed that the *Halting problem* is undecidable. Briefly, the Halting problem can be described as follows: Given an arbitrary DTM and an input, determine whether the machine will eventually halt. Another example of an undecidable problem is Hilbert's Tenth Problem.

Name: Hilbert's Tenth Problem.
Instance: A polynomial equation with integer coefficients in an arbitrary number of unknowns.
Question: Are there integers that are solutions of the equation?

2.3.4 Classes P and NP

A problem is considered to be solved if we can provide an answer to the question. The amount of information required can range from a simple question about

PROBLEM

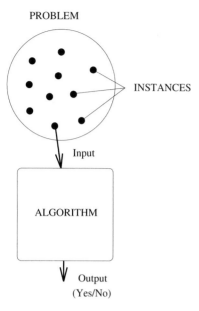

INSTANCES

Input

ALGORITHM

Output
(Yes/No)

Fig. 2.2. Decision problem

the existence of a solution to the question in which we require the enumeration of all possible solutions. In general, the more information that is required, the more computation effort is expected. A class of *decision problems* includes all problems for which the answer sought is either "yes" or "no" (Fig. 2.2).

Name: Knapsack problem.
Instance: A finite set $U = \{u_i \mid i = 1, \ldots, n\}$, a size $s(u_i)$ of any element of $u_i \in U$, and an integer B.
Question: Is there a subset $U' \subseteq U$ such that $\sum_{u_i \in U'} s(u_i) = B$?

The Knapsack problem given above requires a binary yes/no answer.

A class of decision problems which are solvable in polynomial time using a DTM is called the class **P**. Note that we are not particularly concerned about the efficiency of algorithms as long as they run in polynomial time. For instance, the matrix multiplication problem can be rephrased as a decision problem.

Name: Matrix multiplication problem.
Instance: Given three $n \cdot n$ matrices A, A_1, A_2.
Question: Does $A = A_1 \cdot A_2$?

As noted in Sect. 2.3.1, there are at least two polynomial-time algorithms for finding the product matrix of two matrices. This problem, however, requires a binary answer (yes/no) only. The "no" answer may be generated quicker if, for instance, matrices A_1 and A_2 are not of the correct dimensions. The "yes" answer typically will require generating the product $A_1 \cdot A_2$ and next comparing the product with A.

As we have indicated the classification of problems mainly depends on the computer model used. A *nondeterministic Turing machine* (NDTM) is much more powerful than a deterministic Turing machine. The NDTM works in two stages: guessing and checking. Informally, the guessing stage is where the computing power of the NDTM is "concentrated." In this stage, a correct solution (witness) is guessed. The solution (witness) is verified against the parameters of the instance and the final yes/no answer is produced. A decision problem is *solvable* by the NDTM if the NDTM produces the "yes" answer whenever there is a solution. There is a fine point which needs to be clarified. The solvability of a problem by the NDTM requires the correct "yes" answer for all "yes" instances of the problem. On the other hand, the NDTM can either produce the correct "no" answer or run forever for "no" instances of the problem.

A class of decision problems which are solvable in polynomial time by the nondeterministic Turing machine is called the class **NP**. **NP** can be thought of as a class of decision problems whose solutions (if they exist) can be verified in polynomial time.

The class **P** contains all problems that are easy to solve. Clearly, any problem from **P** belongs to **NP**. An embarrassing fact in the theory of computational complexity is that we do not know whether **P** is really different from **NP**. In 1971 Cook made a major contribution to the theory of computational complexity. He showed that there is a decision problem which is the hardest in the class **NP**. The problem used by Cook was the Satisfiability problem.

Name: Satisfiability problem (SAT).
Instance: A set U of variables and a collection C of clauses over U.
Question: Is there a satisfying truth assignment for C?

2.3.5 NP Completeness

The main tool used in proving the existence of equivalence subclasses in **NP** is the so-called *polynomial reduction*. Assume we have two decision problems

$Q_1, Q_2 \in \mathbf{NP}$ with their corresponding sets of instances I_1 and I_2. Let I_1^+ and I_2^+ be subsets of all "yes" instances of I_1 and I_2, respectively. We say that Q_1 is *polynomially reducible* to Q_2 if there is a function $f : I_1 \rightarrow I_2$ which

1. is computable in polynomial time by a DTM,
2. for all instances $x \in I_1^+$ if and only if $f(x) \in I_2^+$.

This fact can be written shortly as

$Q_1 \leq_{\text{poly}} Q_2$.

If we know an algorithm A_2 that solves Q_2 and we are able to polynomially reduce Q_1 to Q_2, then we can create an algorithm A_1 to solve Q_1. A_1 is a concatenation of the function f and A_2, i.e., $A_1(x) = A_2(f(x))$ where f is the function that establishes the polynomial reducibility between Q_1 and Q_2. If $Q_2 \in \mathbf{P}$, then $Q_1 \in \mathbf{P}$. Although being polynomial, the complexity of $A_1(x)$ can be significantly larger. If Q_1 has a higher than polynomial-time complexity, i.e., $Q_1 \notin \mathbf{P}$, then of course $Q_2 \notin \mathbf{P}$ either.

Cook's theorem can be rephrased as follows: *Any* **NP** *problem Q is polynomially reducible to the satisfiability problem*, or

$Q \leq_{\text{poly}} \text{SAT}$.

The proof of the theorem starts from the observation that for each problem in **NP**, there is a NDTM program which solves it (in polynomial time). Next, it is shown that any NDTM program can be polynomially reduced to an instance of the SAT problem. The construction of the function which forces the polynomial reducibility is quite complex. The reader who wishes to learn more about the proof is referred to [191].

The SAT problem is **NP**-complete or **NPC**, as any other problem from **NP** is polynomially reducible to it, i.e.,

$\forall_{Q \in \mathbf{NP}}\ Q \leq_{\text{poly}} \text{SAT}$.

The class **NPC** is nonempty as SAT belongs to it. Are there any other problems in it? The answer is positive and we know many other **NPC** problems. Core problems which share the same computational complexity with SAT are: 3-satisfiability (3-SAT), 3-dimensional matching (3DM), vertex cover (VC), partition, Hamiltonian circuit (HC), etc. To prove that a given problem $Q \in \mathbf{NP}$ is in **NPC** is enough to show that the satisfiability problem or any other **NPC** problem is polynomially reducible to Q, i.e., $\text{SAT} \leq_{\text{poly}} Q$.

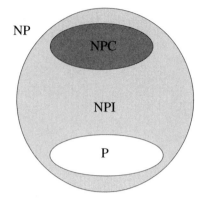

Fig. 2.3. NP world

If we assume that **P** $\neq$ **NP** then we can identify three subclasses: **P**, **NPC**, and **NPI** = **NP** \ (**NPC** $\cup$ **P**) (Fig. 2.3).

2.3.6 Complementary Problems in NP

Let us define the class of complementary problems as:

$$\textbf{co-NP} = \{\hat{Q} \; ; \; Q \in \textbf{NP}\}$$

where $\hat{Q}$ means the complementary problem to Q. A complementary problem $\hat{Q}$ can be easily generated from Q as follows:

Name: Complementary problem $\hat{Q}$.
Instance: The same as for Q.
Question: The complementary answer required.

Consider the following two problems.

Name: Factorization problem (FACT).
Instance: Positive integer N.
Question: Are there integers p and q such that $N = p \cdot q$ $(p, q \geq 2)$?

and

Name: Primality problem (PRIM).
Instance: Positive integer N.
Question: Is N prime?

It is easy to notice that the FACT problem is a complementary problem to the PRIM problem. In our case, $\overline{\text{PRIM}}$ = FACT. So, having the PRIM problem,

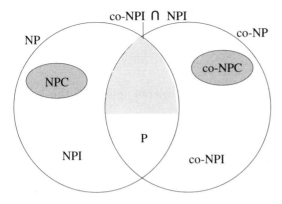

Fig. 2.4. Classes **NP** and **co-NP**

we can create the FACT problem by putting *not (Is N prime?)* in the Question part. Of course, "not (Is N prime?)" is equivalent to "Is N Composite?" and it is the same as "Are there integers p, q such that: $N = p \cdot q$?". Consider an instance x of both PRIM and FACT. The answer is "yes" for $x \in$ PRIM if and only if the answer is "no" for the same instance x considered as a member of FACT.

In general, however, such an observation cannot be made for all problems in **NP** and numerous examples lead us to the assumption that:

$$\text{co-NP} \neq \text{NP}.$$

In other words, the answer "yes" for an instance $x \in Q$ does not guarantee that the answer is "no" for the same instance x in $\hat{Q}$. If we consider the class $\mathbf{P} \subset \mathbf{NP}$ then it is easy to prove that **co-P** = **P**, i.e., the class **P** is closed under complementation.

The next question concerns the interrelation between the class **NPC** and the class **co-NPC**. The answer is given in the following theorem.

Theorem 11. *If there exists an* **NP**-*complete problem* Q *such that* $\hat{Q} \in$ **NP**, *then* **NP** = **co-NP**.

The proof can be found in Garey and Johnson [191] (p. 156). Our discussion is summarized in Fig. 2.4 (assuming that $\mathbf{P} \neq \mathbf{NP}$ and $\mathbf{NP} \neq \mathbf{co\text{-}NP}$). Going back to the pair of FACT and PRIM problems, Theorem 11 suggests that they must not belong to **NPC**. On the other hand there is a common consensus that the FACT problem does not belong to **P** as all existing factorization algorithms run in a time longer than or equal to

$$e^{\sqrt{\ln(n)\ln\ln(n)}}.$$

Thus we can assume that both PRIM and FACT problems belong to the intersection **NPI ∩ co-NPI**.

2.3.7 NP-Hard and #P-Complete Problems

The theory of **NP**-completeness relates to decision problems only. Most problems used in cryptography are search problems so statements which are true for the **NP** class are not necessarily correct if we deal with search problems. A *search problem* Q consists of a set of instances denoted by I. For each instance $x \in I$, we have a set $S_Q(x)$ of all solutions for x. An algorithm is said to *solve the problem* Q if it gives a solution from the set $S_Q(x)$ for an instance x whenever $S_Q(x)$ is not empty. Otherwise, the algorithm returns a "no" answer. The knapsack problem can be rewritten as a search problem.

Name: Knapsack search problem.
Instance: A finite set $U = \{u_i \mid i = 1, \ldots, n\}$, a size $s(u_i)$ of any element of $u_i \in U$, and an integer B.
Question: What is a subset $U' \subseteq U$ such that $\sum_{u_i \in U'} s(u_i) = B$?

Informally, a search problem Q_s is **NP**-hard if there is a decision problem $Q_d \in$ **NPC** which is polynomially reducible to it, i.e., $Q_d \leq_{\text{poly}} Q_s$. **NP**-hard problems are believed to be at least as hard as **NPC** problems. If there existed a polynomial-time algorithm for an **NP**-hard problem, then all **NPC** problems would collapse into the class **P**.

Another class of problems which is closely related to search problems is the class of enumeration problems. The *enumeration problem* based on the search problem Q (with the set $S_Q(x)$ of all solutions for an instance x) asks about the cardinality of $S_Q(x)$. The knapsack enumeration problem can be defined as follows.

Name: Knapsack enumeration problem.
Instance: A finite set $U = \{u_i \mid i = 1, \ldots, n\}$, a size $s(u_i)$ of any element of $u_i \in U$, and an integer B.
Question: How many subsets $U' \subseteq U$ satisfy the equation $\sum_{u_i \in U'} s(u_i) = B$?

The class of **#P**-complete problems comprises the hardest problems of enumer-ation equivalents of **NPC**. If a **#P**-complete problem was solvable in polyno-mial time, then **P=NP**.

2.3.8 Problems Used in Cryptography

There are many problems that have been used in cryptography. We have already discussed the PRIM and FACT problems. There is another problem that shares the same computational complexity as PRIM and FACT problems. This is the discrete logarithm problem or DL problem.

Name: DL problem.
Instance: Integers (g, s) that belong to $GF(p)$ determined by a prime p.
Question: Is there a positive integer h ($h = 1, \ldots, p$) such that $h = \log_g s$ (mod p)?

The DL problem or, more precisely, its search-problem variant is extensively used in conditionally secure cryptographic designs. There is a general-purpose algorithm that solves instances of DL in subexponential time. Let us briefly describe a version of the algorithm that is applicable for $GF(2^n)$.

Assume that $g \in GF(2^n)$ is a primitive element of $GF(2^n)$. We would like to compute h such that $s = g^h$. The index-calculus algorithm starts from the preprocessing stage, which can be done once for the given primitive element g of $GF(2^n)$. In the preprocessing stage, a "big enough" set D of discrete logarithms of g is computed. The elements of D are usually irreducible polynomials of degree m where m is appropriately selected.

Once the set D is created, we can proceed with the main stage of computa-tions in which we select repeatedly at random an integer $a = 1, \ldots, 2^n - 1$ and compute

$$\hat{s} = s \cdot g^a.$$

Then the polynomial $\hat{s}$ is factorized into irreducible polynomials. If all factors are in D then

$$\hat{s} = \prod_{p \in D} p^{b_p(\hat{s})}.$$

As polynomials $p \in D$ are discrete logarithms of g, we know the exponents of g for any given $p \in D$. Therefore

$$h = \log_g s = \sum_{p \in D} b_p(\hat{s}) - a \pmod{2^n - 1}.$$

The algorithm needs to be run for many random a. It will terminate once all factors of $\hat{s}$ are in D. Probabilistic arguments can be used to prove that on average the algorithm takes the following number of steps

$$e^{((1+o(1)) \frac{n}{m} \log \frac{m}{n})}.$$

The Diffie-Hellman problem relates to the DL problem and is one of the most frequently used in cryptography. It was first applied by Diffie and Hellman for their key-agreement protocol. Below we define the decision DH problem for which the answer to the question is binary yes/no. Note that Diffie and Hellman used a search version of the DH problem.

Name: DH decision problem.
Instance: Integers $g^k \pmod{p}$, $g^s \pmod{p}$, and $g^r \pmod{p}$, where p is
    prime, g generates Z_p^*, and k, s, r are integers.
Question: Is the integer $r = ks \pmod{p-1}$ or equivalently does the following
    congruence hold

$$(g^k)^s = (g^s)^k \equiv g^r \pmod{p}?$$

The search version of the DH problem can be easily derived by putting two integers $g^k \pmod{p}$ and $g^s \pmod{p}$ into the instance part and asking for g^{sk} in the question part. It is easy to notice that the DH problem is not harder than the related DL problem.

The knapsack problem is also used in cryptography. The problem was applied in cryptography to build one of the first public-key cryptosystems. Unfortunately, this application did not lead to a secure design despite the fact that the knapsack problem belongs to the **NPC** class! The statement that the knapsack problem belongs to **NPC** does not mean that all its instances are of the same complexity. It is possible to define an easy knapsack problem whose instances can be solved using a linear-time algorithm.

Name: Easy knapsack problem.
Instance: The n-dimension vector space V over $GF(2)$ with the basis $v_1 =$
    $(1, 0, \ldots, 0)$, $\ldots$, $v_n = (0, \ldots, 0, 1) \in V$, the vector of sizes $S = (s(v_1), \ldots,$
    $s(v_n))$ such that $s_{i+1} > \sum_{j=0}^{i} s_j$, and an integer B.
Question: Is there a binary vector $v' \in V$ such that $v' \cdot S = B$?

In general, any **NPC** problem consists of easy instances which are solvable in polynomial time and difficult ones for which there is no polynomial-time algorithm unless **P** = **NP**. When an intractable problem is used in a cryptographic design to thwart some possible attacks, it is essential to make sure that almost all instances applied are difficult ones.

2.3.9 Probabilistic Computations

As mentioned before, the efficiency of algorithms depends on the encoding scheme used to represent instances and the model of computation. As there is no substantial room for improvement if you use a reasonable encoding scheme, the only way to increase the efficiency of algorithms is to apply a different model of computations.

Probabilistic methods in computations are mostly used to simulate large systems which work in a probabilistic environment. By its nature probabilistic computations do not guarantee "error-free" computations. Sometimes when the error rate can be made as small as required, probabilistic computations may be an attractive alternative.

The reader should be warned that there is no consensus about the definitions of the probabilistic algorithms discussed below. Our definitions are in line with those accepted by Brassard and Bratley [60] and Gill [201].

A *Monte Carlo* algorithm is a probabilistic algorithm which solves a decision problem. A yes-biased Monte Carlo algorithm never makes mistakes if it deals with "yes" instances. If the algorithm handles a "no" instance, it may make a mistake with the probability ε. A no-biased algorithm correctly solves "no" instances making mistakes for "yes" instances with probability ε.

A *Las Vegas* algorithm is a probabilistic algorithm which for any instance of the problem may either give the correct answer with the probability $1 - \varepsilon$ or fail with probability ε. If the algorithm fails, it returns "no answer."

The primality testing (the PRIM problem) calculated using a DTM requires subexponential time. It can be run faster, as a matter of fact, in polynomial time if we are ready to accept a small chance of mistakes in computations. The probabilistic algorithm for solving PRIM returns either "prime" or "composite." If the tested integer is prime, the algorithm never makes mistakes. If, however, the tested integer is composite, it returns "prime" with some probability $\varepsilon <$ 1. The algorithm can be repeated n times for n independent inputs. If the algorithm consistently has answered "prime," we can assume that the integer is prime. The probability of a mistake (i.e., the integer is in fact composite) is ε^n.

2.3.10 Quantum Computing

A new paradigm in computation which has an explosive potential to revolutionize the theory and practice of computation is *quantum computing*. Unlike classical computers, the quantum ones are based on the rules of quantum mechanics. The idea of quantum computing emerged in early 1980 when Richard Feynman [180] asked about the suitability of using classical computers to simulate physics. He also gave an abstract model of a quantum simulator. In 1985 David Deutsch [150] gave a model of a universal quantum computer. The power of the quantum computer comes from the phenomenon of *quantum parallelism*. Roughly speaking, a classical bit can be either 0 or 1 while a quantum bit is a superposition of both 0 and 1. Thus a register of n quantum bits can be seen as a collection of 2^n potential states existing at the same time. A confirmation of the extraordinary power of quantum computers came when Peter Shor showed that the factoring and discrete logarithm problems are computable in polynomial time! This development has a dramatic impact on the RSA cryptosystem as the security of RSA depends upon the intractibility of factoring.

The crucial issue related to the quantum computer is its implementation. We can build some components, such as negation gates and 2-bit quantum gates. The full general-purpose quantum computer is still far away. We may expect that some specialized quantum computers will be easier to implement. These include a factoring engine. Readers who would like to find out more about the topic are referred to [59, 243, 533].

2.4 Elements of Information Theory

It would be difficult to discuss any matter concerning cryptography without referring to the fundamental precepts of *information theory*. Claude Shannon, who is seen as the father of this discipline, published in 1948 the seminal work [466], in which he formulated principles of reliable communication via a noisy channel. One year later Shannon extended his information theoretic approach to secrecy systems [467] and provided the greater portion of the theoretical foundation for modern cryptography. The principal tools of secure communications across a channel are *codes* and *ciphers*. A code is a fixed predetermined "dictionary," where for every valid message there is an equivalent encoded message called a *codeword*. Coding theory addresses itself to the "noisy channel" problem, where by selecting a particular code, if a message M is distorted to M' during transmission, this error can be detected and hopefully corrected to the original message. On the other hand, ciphers are a general method of transforming messages into a format whose meaning is not apparent.

2.4.1 Entropy

An information source is one of the basic components of any communication and secrecy system. It generates messages which are later transmitted over a communication channel. In most cases, a probabilistic model of the information source seems to be adequate. So the source is represented by a random variable S with the collection of source states (also called messages) $\mathcal{S} = \{s_1, s_2, \ldots, s_k\}$ and associated probabilities $P(S = s_i) = p(s_i)$ for each state $i = 1, \ldots, k$. The *entropy* of a discrete message source is defined as:

$$H(S) = \sum_{i=1}^{k} p(s_i) \log_2 \frac{1}{p(s_i)}. \tag{2.23}$$

Each $\log_2(p(s_i)^{-1})$ term represents the number of bits needed to encode the message optimally. When all the messages are equally likely, i.e., $p(s_1) = p(s_2) = \ldots = p(s_k) = \frac{1}{k}$, then $H(S)$ is $\log_2 k$. If $k = 2^n$, then n bits are needed to encode each message. The value of $H(S)$ ranges between its maximum value $\log_2 k$ and its minimum of zero when there is a single message with the probability 1. Note that when there is only one message, there is no choice of messages. The entropy of a source $H(S)$ also measures its *uncertainty*, in that it indicates the number of bits of information that must be acquired to recover the message. The uncertainty of a message cannot exceed $\log_2 k$ bits, where k is the possible number of messages.[1]

---

[1] If a message is known to contain a marital status, either married or single, then the uncertainty is only *one* bit, since there are only two possibilities for the first character, and once this is determined the message can be recovered. If the message was a student number, then the uncertainty is greater than one bit but will not exceed $\log_2 k$ bits.

Consider a random variable that takes on two values s_1 and s_2 with probabilities

$$p(s_1) = \varepsilon \quad \text{and} \quad p(s_2) = 1 - \varepsilon.$$

What is the maximum entropy of the random variable, and how does the entropy behave as a function of ε? First of all, we apply the definition of entropy to obtain

$$H(S) = \sum_{i=1}^{2} p(s_i) \log_2 \frac{1}{p(s_i)} = -\varepsilon \log_2 \varepsilon - (1 - \varepsilon) \log_2(1 - \varepsilon).$$

As $H(S)$ is a function of ε, we find its derivative:

$$\frac{dH(S)}{d\varepsilon} = -\log_2 \varepsilon + \log_2(1 - \varepsilon).$$

Clearly,

$$\frac{dH(S)}{d\varepsilon} = 0 \quad \text{for } \varepsilon = \frac{1}{2}.$$

As the second derivative

$$\frac{d^2 H(S)}{d\varepsilon^2} = -\frac{1}{\ln 2}\left(\frac{1}{\varepsilon} + \frac{1}{1 - \varepsilon}\right)$$

is negative for $\varepsilon = \frac{1}{2}$, $H(S)$ can have its maximum at $\varepsilon = \frac{1}{2}$ unless it has its maximum at $\varepsilon = 0$ or $\varepsilon = 1$. We calculate the values of $H(S)$ at points

$$H(S) \mid_{\varepsilon=0} = \lim_{\varepsilon \to 0} \left(\varepsilon \log_2 \frac{1}{\varepsilon} + (1 - \varepsilon) \log_2 \frac{1}{1 - \varepsilon} \right)$$

and

$$H(S) \mid_{\varepsilon=1} = \lim_{\varepsilon \to 1} \left(\varepsilon \log_2 \frac{1}{\varepsilon} + (1 - \varepsilon) \log_2 \frac{1}{1 - \varepsilon} \right).$$

Now, as $\lim_{\varepsilon \to 0}(\varepsilon \log_2 \varepsilon) = 0$, $H(S) \mid_{\varepsilon=0} = H(S) \mid_{\varepsilon=1} = 0$. In other words the maximum entropy of the random variable with just two values is attained for the uniform distribution $p(s_1) = p(s_2) = \frac{1}{2}$, and then $H(S) = \log_2 2 = 1$ (Fig. 2.5).

Let S and X be two random variables defined over the sets $S = \{s_1, \ldots, s_k\}$ and $X = \{x_1, \ldots, x_n\}$, respectively. Assume that for every value of $x_j \in X$, we know conditional probabilities $p(s_i \mid x_j) = P(S = s_i \mid X = x_j)$. Now we can define the entropy in S conditional on x_j as follows: $H(S \mid x_j) = -\sum_{i=1}^{k} p(s_i \mid x_j) \log_2 p(s_i \mid x_j)$. The conditional entropy

$$H(S \mid X) = \sum_{j=1}^{n} H(S \mid x_j) P(X = x_j)$$

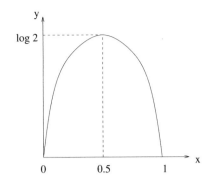

Fig. 2.5. The entropy function $y = H(x)$

is also called *equivocation* and characterizes the uncertainty about S knowing X. The following properties hold for the entropy:

1. $H(S \mid X) \leq H(S)$ – any side information X never increases the entropy of S.
2. $H(S, X) = H(S) + H(X \mid S) = H(X) + H(S \mid X)$ – the joint entropy of the pair (S, X) is the sum of uncertainty in X and the uncertainty in S provided X is known.
3. If S and X are independent random variables then $H(S, X) = H(S) + H(X)$.
4. If $(X_1, \ldots, X_n)$ is a collection of random variables, then $H(X_1, \ldots, X_n) = H(X_1) + H(X_2 \mid X_1) + \ldots + H(X_n \mid X_1, \ldots, X_{n-1})$.

The properties can be easily proven and the proofs are left to the reader as an exercise.

2.4.2 Huffman Codes

Assume we have a discrete source that is represented by the random variable S. Clearly, $H(S)$ specifies the average number of bits necessary to represent messages from the set $S = \{s_1, \ldots, s_k\}$. Can we encode messages in such a way that their average length is as short as possible and hopefully equal to $H(S)$? The Huffman algorithm gives the answer to this question.

Huffman code – produces an optimal binary representation of messages of the source defined by $S = \{s_1, \ldots, s_k\}$ with their probabilities $p(s_1), \ldots, p(s_k)$ (recursive algorithm).

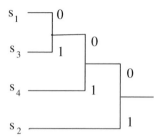

Fig. 2.6. An example of Huffman code

H1. Recursive step: Assume that there are j messages ($j \le k$). Order the messages according to their occurrence probabilities. The ordered collection of messages is $x_1, \ldots, x_j$ ($j \le k$) and $p(x_1) \le p(x_2) \le \ldots \le p(x_j)$. Suppose further that the encodings of the original messages $s_1, \ldots, s_k$ have their partial codes $b_1, \ldots, b_k$. At the beginning, all b_is are empty. Choose the two first messages and merge them creating a new message $x_{1,2}$ with its occurrence probability $p(x_{1,2}) = p(x_1) + p(x_2)$. If s_i has been merged into x_1, assign the prefix 0 to the encoding, i.e., b_i becomes $0\|b_i$. If s_i has been merged into x_2, assign the prefix 1 to the encoding, i.e., b_i becomes $1\|b_i$. Otherwise the encodings are unchanged. Note that $\|$ stands for the concatenation. Repeat the algorithm for the collection of $x_{1,2}, x_3, \ldots, x_j$ messages.

H2. Stopping step: There are two messages x_1 and x_2 only. Create the final codes by putting 0 at the front of all encodings of messages which have been merged into x_1 and 1 otherwise.

Consider a source $\mathcal{S} = \{s_1, s_2, s_3, s_4\}$ with corresponding probabilities $\frac{1}{8}, \frac{1}{2}, \frac{1}{8}, \frac{1}{4}$. The messages (s_1, s_3, s_4, s_2) are ordered and their probabilities are $\frac{1}{8}, \frac{1}{8}, \frac{1}{4}, \frac{1}{2}$. The partial encodings are $b_1 = 0$ and $b_3 = 1$, and s_1 and s_3 are merged into x_1, and x_1 occurs with the probability $\frac{1}{4}$. The messages (x_1, s_4, s_2) are already in the requested order so x_2 is a merge of x_1 and s_4. The partial encodings are $b_1 = 00$, $b_3 = 01$, and $b_4 = 1$. Finally x_2 is merged with s_2 and the codes are: $b_1 = 000$, $b_3 = 001$, $b_4 = 01$, and $b_2 = 1$. It is easy to check that $H(S) = \frac{14}{8} = 1.75$ and the average length of the Huffman code is $L = 3 \cdot \frac{1}{8} + 3 \cdot \frac{1}{8} + 2 \cdot \frac{1}{4} + \frac{1}{2} = 1.75$. The code is illustrated in Fig. 2.6

2.4.3 Redundancy of the Language

Any natural language can be treated as a message source with a complex structure. Entropy is a convenient tool that can be used to specify probabilistic behavior of the language. Let $S^{(k)}$ be a random variable defined over the set $\underbrace{S \cdot S \cdot \ldots \cdot S}_{k}$ with the corresponding probability distribution for sequences of length k where $\mid S \mid = N$ indicates the number of letters in the alphabet. The *rate of language* $S^{(k)}$ for messages of length k is defined as

$$r_k = \frac{H(S^{(k)})}{k},$$

which denotes the average number of bits of information in each character. For English, when k is large, r_k has been estimated to lie between 1.0 and 1.5 bits/letter. The *absolute rate* of a language is the maximum number of bits of information that could be encoded in each character assuming that all combinations of characters are equally likely. If there are $\mid S \mid = N$ letters in the alphabet, then the absolute rate is given by $R = \log_2 N$, which is the maximum entropy of the individual characters. For a 26-character alphabet this is 4.7 bits/letter. The actual rate of English is much less as it is highly *redundant*, like all natural languages. Redundancy stems from the underlying structure of a language. In particular, certain letters and combinations of letters occur frequently, while others have a negligible likelihood of occurring (e.g., in English the letters *e*, *t*, and *a* occur very frequently, as do the pairs, or digrams, *th* and *en*, while *z* and *x* occur less frequently).[2]

The *redundancy* of a language with rate r is defined as $D = R - r$. When $r = 1$ and $R = 4.7$ then the ratio $\frac{D}{R}$ shows that English is about 79% redundant.

Consider a language that consists of the 26 letters of the set $S = \{A, B, C, D, E, F, G, H, I, J, K, L, M, N, O, P, Q, R, S, T, U, V, W, X, Y, Z\} = \{s_1, s_2, \ldots, s_{26}\}$. Suppose the language is characterized by the following sequence of probabilities:

---

[2] In coding theory, *redundancy* refers to that portion of a codeword that is used to transmit *check symbols*, so as to allow error detection and possible correction. This portion of the codeword contains no information.

$$P(s_1) = \tfrac{1}{2}, \quad P(s_2) = \tfrac{1}{4},$$

$$P(s_i) = \tfrac{1}{64} \quad \text{for} \qquad i = 3, 4, 5, 6, 7, 8, 9, 10,$$

$$P(s_i) = \tfrac{1}{128} \quad \text{for} \qquad i = 11, \ldots, 26.$$

The entropy of our single-letter language is:

$$r_1 = H(S)$$

$$= \Sigma_{i=1}^{26} P(s_i) \log_2 \tfrac{1}{P(s_i)}$$

$$= \tfrac{1}{2} \log_2 2 + \tfrac{1}{4} \log_2 4 + 8(\tfrac{1}{64} \log_2 64) + 16(\tfrac{1}{128} \log_2 128)$$

$$= 2.625.$$

Now the language has $N = 26$ letters, so

$$R = \log_2 26 = 4.7.$$

In other words, the redundancy of the language calculated for single-letter probabilities is

$$D_1 = R - r_1 = 4.7 - 2.625 = 2.075.$$

This example only applies to a language structure that is described by the probability distribution of single letters only. This description should be treated as the very first approximation of a language's statistical structure. As a matter of fact, a natural language's structure is far more complex and the second approximation of a language's structure gives a better picture of its statistical properties.

Let our language be defined as in the previous example and let its conditional probability distribution be given as follows:

$$P(s'_{i+1} \mid s_i) = P(s'_{i+2} \mid s_i) = \tfrac{1}{2} \quad \text{for } i = 1, \ldots, 24,$$

$$P(s'_{26} \mid s_{25}) = P(s'_1 \mid s_{25}) = \tfrac{1}{2},$$

$$P(s'_1 \mid s_{26}) = P(s'_2 \mid s_{26}) = \tfrac{1}{2},$$

where $P(s'_{i+1} \mid s_i)$ means the conditional probability that the second letter is s_{i+1} provided that the first letter is s_i.

Now, we calculate the probability distribution of two-letter sequences:

$$P(s_1, s_2') \; = P(s_2' \mid s_1)P(s_1) \qquad = \tfrac{1}{4},$$

$$P(s_1, s_3') \; = P(s_3' \mid s_1)P(s_1) \qquad = \tfrac{1}{4},$$

$$P(s_2, s_3') \; = P(s_3' \mid s_2)P(s_2) \qquad = \tfrac{1}{8},$$

$$P(s_2, s_4') \; = P(s_4', \mid s_2)P(s_2) \qquad = \tfrac{1}{8},$$

$$P(s_i, s_{i+1}') = P(s_{i+1}' \mid s_i)P(s_i) \qquad = \tfrac{1}{128} \text{ for } i{=}3, \ldots, 10,$$

$$P(s_i, s_{i+2}') = P(s_{i+2}' \mid s_i)P(s_i) \qquad = \tfrac{1}{128} \text{ for } i{=}3, \ldots, 10,$$

$$P(s_i, s_{i+1}') = P(s_{i+1}' \mid s_i)P(s_i) \qquad = \tfrac{1}{256} \text{ for } i{=}11, \ldots, 24,$$

$$P(s_i, s_{i+2}') = P(s_{i+2}' \mid s_i)P(s_i) \qquad = \tfrac{1}{256} \text{ for } i{=}11, \ldots, 24,$$

$$P(s_{25}, s_{26}') = P(s_{25}, s_1') = P(s_{26}, s_1') = P(s_{26}, s_2') = \tfrac{1}{256}.$$

All other probabilities are equal to zero and, in this case, the entropy of two-letter language sequences is equal to:

$$H(S^{(2)}) = \sum_{i,j=1}^{26} P(s_i, s_j') \log_2 \tfrac{1}{P(s_i, s_j')}$$

$$= 2(\tfrac{1}{4} \log_2 4) + 2(\tfrac{1}{8} \log_2 8) + 16(\tfrac{1}{128} \log_2 128) + 32(\tfrac{1}{256} \log_2 256)$$

$$= 3.625.$$

Consider, for the moment, the entropy $H(S)$ from the previous example and compare it to $H(S^{(2)})$. We can immediately state that $H(S^{(2)}) - H(S) = 1$. This equation means that, having the first letter, we can obtain the second one using one bit only. This results from the fact that there are two equally probable candidates. For example, if the first letter is $s_3 = C$, then the second letter may be either $s_4' = D$ or $s_5' = E$.

Returning to our example, we calculate the rate of the language for messages of length 2, namely,

$$r_2 = \frac{1}{2}H(S^{(2)}) = 1.8125.$$

As the absolute rate of our language is fixed and depends on the number of letters only, the redundancy D_2 is:

$$D_2 = R - r_2 = 2.9.$$

We can now state that the language considered is 60% redundant.

We note that the more redundant a language is, the stronger the statistical relations between the letters in a sequence. On the other hand, if a language has no redundancy, then occurrences of subsequent letters are statistically independent.

Once we have dealt with a natural language, we can easily calculate the entropy of a single letter $r_1 = H(S)$. Also the entropy $r_2 = H(S^{(2)})/2$ of two-letter words can be found relatively easily. Unfortunately, the amount of calculation for $r_n = H(S^{(n)})/n$ grows exponentially as a function of n. So, the real redundancy of a language, which can be expressed as

$$r_\infty = \lim_{n \to \infty} \frac{H(S^{(n)})}{n},$$

is estimated using several earlier-evaluated entropies.

2.4.4 Key Equivocation and Unicity Distance

Consider the encryption system in Fig. 2.7. The cryptosystem consists of three basic components: the message source, the key generator, and the encryption block. The message source is characterized by the random variable M and describes statistical properties of the language generated by the source. The set of all characters in the language alphabet is $\mathcal{M}$. The key generator selects keys randomly with uniform probability from the whole set $\mathcal{K}$. Once chosen, the key stays fixed for some time. The encryption block uses a publicly known algorithm to encrypt messages into cryptograms under the control of the secret key. The set of possible cryptograms is denoted by $\mathcal{C}$.

The sender applies the cryptosystem (or cipher) for n consecutive messages and produces n corresponding cryptograms (ciphertexts). An enemy cryptan-

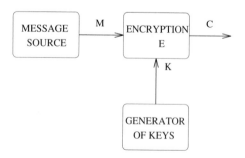

Fig. 2.7. Graphical presentation of the interrelations between messages and cryptograms in a binary cryptosystem

alyst who does not know the secret key but can read cryptograms, may try to

- recover messages from cryptograms, or
- recover the secret key.

The attacker is also assumed to know the statistical properties of the message source, and thus can calculate the message and key equivocation to find out the collection of most probable messages and keys. As the attacker knows n cryptograms, he/she can compute the *message equivocation* as follows:

$$H(M^{(n)} \mid C^{(n)}) = \sum_{c \in \mathcal{C}^n} p(c) \sum_{m \in \mathcal{M}^n} p(m \mid c), \log_2 \left(\frac{1}{p(m \mid c)} \right), \tag{2.24}$$

where $\mathcal{C}^n = \underbrace{\mathcal{C} \cdots \cdots \mathcal{C}}_{n}$, $\mathcal{M}^n = \underbrace{\mathcal{M} \cdots \cdots \mathcal{M}}_{n}$, and $p(m \mid c)$ is the conditional probability of the sequence m provided c has been observed. Similarly, the enemy can compute the *key equivocation* according to

$$H(K \mid C^{(n)}) = \sum_{c \in \mathcal{C}^n} p(c) \sum_{k \in \mathcal{K}} p(k \mid c), \log_2 \left(\frac{1}{p(k \mid c)} \right), \tag{2.25}$$

where $p(k \mid c)$ is the probability of k given c.

The *unicity distance* of the cryptosystem (or cipher) is the parameter n for which

$$H(K \mid C^{(n)}) \approx 0. \tag{2.26}$$

In other words, the unicity distance is the amount of ciphertext needed to uniquely determine the key applied. Intuitively, as the number of observations increases, the key equivocation stays the same or decreases.

The unicity distance can be used to define two classes of cryptosystems (ciphers):

- *Unbreakable*, whose unicity distance is infinite and $\lim_{n \to \infty} H(K \mid C^{(n)}) = H(K)$.
- *Breakable*, whose unicity distance is finite.

The class of unbreakable cryptosystems is also called *ideal ciphers*. Ideal ciphers are immune against any attacker who knows the statistical properties of the language (message source) and has access to cryptograms (communication channel) even if the attacker has unlimited computational power! Cryptographic designs that are secure against an enemy with unlimited computational power are called unconditionally secure.

2.4.5 Equivocation of a Simple Cryptographic System

Consider the cryptographic system (Fig. 2.7) that encrypts binary messages using binary keys according to the following formula:

$$c = m \oplus k,$$

where $c \in C$, $m \in M$, $k \in K$ are a cryptogram (ciphertext), a message, and a key, respectively ($C = M = K = \{0,1\}$ and $\oplus$ stands for addition modulo 2). The message source is known to generate elementary messages (bits) with probabilities,

$$P(M = 0) = v \quad \text{and } P(M = 1) = 1 - v,$$

while $0 \leq v \leq 1$. For each transmission session, a cryptographic key K is selected from equally probable binary elements, namely,

$$P(K = 0) = P(K = 1) = \frac{1}{2}.$$

Our task is to calculate the cipher equivocation and estimate the unicity distance.

Assume that our cryptosystem has generated n binary cryptograms so that the probability $P(A)$, where A is the event that *the ordered cryptogram sequence consists of i zeros and $n - i$ ones*, is equal to:

$$P(A) = P(A, (K = 0 \text{ or } K = 1))$$

$$= P(A, K = 0) + P(A, K = 1)$$

$$= P(A \mid K = 0)P(K = 0) + P(A \mid K = 1)P(K = 1).$$

The conditional probability $P(A \mid K = 0)$ is equal to the probability that the ordered message sequence consists of i zeros and $n - i$ ones. On the other hand, $P(A \mid K = 1)$ equals the probability that the ordered message sequence contains $n - i$ zeros and i ones. Therefore,

$$P(A \mid K = 0) = v^i(1 - v)^{n-i} \text{ and } P(A \mid K = 1) = (1 - v)^i v^{n-i}.$$

As the result, we have:

$$P(A) = \frac{1}{2}\left(v^i(1 - v)^{n-i} + (1 - v)^i v^{n-i}\right).$$

Assume that $C_{i,n}$ is the event that *the unordered cryptogram sequence contains i zeros and $n - i$ ones*; then

$$P(C_{i,n}) = \frac{1}{2} \binom{n}{i} \left(v^i (1-v)^{n-i} + (1-v)^i v^{n-i} \right).$$

Of course, the conditional key probability is equal to:

$$P(K = 0 \mid C_{i,n}) = \frac{P(C_{i,n} \mid K = 0)P(K = 0)}{P(C_{i,n})}.$$

The probability $P(C_{i,n} \mid K = 0)$ is equal to the probability that the unordered message sequence obtains i zeros and $n - i$ ones. Substituting values, we get the following expression:

$$P(K = 0 \mid C_{i,n}) = \frac{1}{1+a} \quad \text{while } a = \frac{v^{n-i}(1-v)^i}{v^i(1-v)^{n-i}}.$$

Considering the second conditional probability of the key, we obtain:

$$P(K = 1 \mid C_{i,n}) = \frac{a}{1+a}.$$

Clearly, the conditional entropy $H(K \mid C_{i,n})$ of the key can be calculated according to the following formula:

$$H(K \mid C_{i,n}) = \sum_{k \in \mathcal{K}} P(k \mid C_{i,n}) \log_2 \frac{1}{P(k \mid C_{i,n})}$$

$$= P(K = 0 \mid C_{i,n}) \log_2 \frac{1}{P(K = 0 \mid C_{i,n})}$$

$$+ P(K = 1 \mid C_{i,n}) \log_2 \frac{1}{P(K = 1 \mid C_{i,n})}$$

$$= \log_2(1 + a) - \frac{a}{1+a} \log_2 a.$$

So, the equivocation of the cipher (or the average conditional entropy of the cryptographic key) can be presented as:

$$H(K \mid C_n) = \sum_{i=0}^{n} P(C_{i,n}) H(K \mid C_{i,n}).$$

Substituting values, we obtain:

$$H(K \mid C_n) = \frac{1}{2} \sum_{i=0}^{n} \binom{n}{i} v^i (1-v)^{n-i}(1+a) \left(\log_2(1+a) - \frac{a}{1+a} \log_2 a \right).$$

Figure 2.8 shows the equivocation $EQ(n) = H(K \mid C_n)$ for five different parameters of v, namely $v = 0.5, 0.4, 0.3, 0.2,$ and 0.1.

First consider the case when $v = 0.5$. The equivocation is constant and equals 1. This means that the uncertainty in the key is fixed no matter how

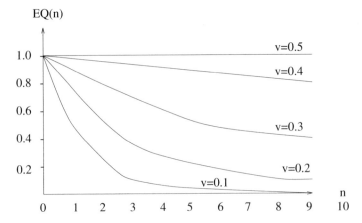

Fig. 2.8. Diagram of $EQ(n)$ for different values of v

Table 2.3. The equivocation for $v = 0.1$ with various numbers of observations

Number of observations n	$EQ(n) \mid_{v=0.1}$
1	0.47
2	0.26
3	0.14
4	0.078
5	0.043
6	0.025
7	0.014
8	0.0081
9	0.0046
10	0.0027

much of the cryptogram sequence is known. In other words, the key applied can be determined by selecting from two equally probable elements from all observations of cryptograms.

The second case is for $v = 0.1$. More exact values of $EQ(n)$ for $n = 1, \ldots, 10$ are given in Table 2.3.

Our equivocation is the entropy of two value random variables. Now consider such a variable which is characterized by two probabilities $P(a) = \varepsilon$, $P(b) = 1 - \varepsilon$. Its entropy H_ε is presented in Table 2.4. From the two tables, we can state the equivocation $EQ(n)$ for $v = 0.1$ and $n = 4$ is less than H_ε, i.e.,

$$EQ(4) = 0.078 < H_\varepsilon = 0.081.$$

Table 2.4. Some probabilities and entropies

Value of probability ε	entropy H_ε
0.5	1
0.4	0.91
0.3	0.88
0.2	0.72
0.1	0.47
0.05	0.29
0.01	0.081

Therefore, in this case, the unicity distance equals 4. In other words, after observing four elementary cryptograms, we are able to discover the key applied with the probability 0.99. Moreover, if we accept the threshold probability 0.9 instead of 0.99, then the unicity distance equals 1, as

$$EQ(1) = 0.47 \leq H_\varepsilon = 0.47.$$

As you can see in the above example, the calculation of equivocation becomes more and more complicated as the number of elementary messages and keys grows. Sometimes, we can calculate (or estimate) the unicity distance of a cipher, but, unfortunately, we may not be able to use this knowledge to break the cipher.

In the above example the unicity distance stays the same only when the language (message source) has no redundancy (the case $v = 0.5$). But we must not draw a conclusion that this is an ideal cipher as the infinite unicity distance results from the lack of redundancy of the language rather than the strength of the cryptosystem. The ideal cipher should keep the unicity distance infinite for all message sources no matter how redundant they are. It is possible to improve the cipher considered in the example and make it ideal. How? It is enough to generate the cryptographic key independently and uniformly for every single message. The resulting cipher is the well-known *Vernam one-time pad*. Gilbert Vernam invented the cipher in 1917 for encryption of telegraphic messages. Although the one-time pad provides the perfect secrecy, the price to pay for it is the length of the cryptographic key – it has to be as long as the message (or cryptogram) itself.

2.5 Problems and Exercises

1. Show that the following properties of lcm and gcd hold:
   a) If there is an integer $d \in \mathcal{Z}$ such that $d \mid n_i$ for all $n_i \in \mathcal{N}$ ($i = 1, \ldots, k$), then $d \mid gcd(n_1, \ldots, n_k)$.
   b) If $n_1 \mid m, \ldots, n_k \mid m$ ($m \in \mathcal{Z}$), then $lcm(n_1, \ldots, n_k) \mid m$.
   c) If $d \mid gcd(n_1, \ldots, n_k)$ and $b_i = \frac{n_i}{d}$, then $gcd(b_1, \ldots, b_k) = 1$.
   d) $lcm(a, b) \cdot gcd(a, b) = a \cdot b$.

2. Apply the Euclid algorithm to find the following:
   - $gcd(111, 141)$
   - $gcd(208, 264)$
   - $gcd(57998, 162432)$
   - $gcd(785437, 543889)$

3. Write a C program that accepts two arguments *lower_bound* and *upper_bound* and generates all twin primes between two bounds.

4. Write a C program that produces all Mersenne primes smaller than an integer given as an argument to the program.

5. Use the sieve of Eratosthenes to determine all primes smaller than 10000. Write a C program to execute the computations.

6. Justify that the Euler totient function is equal to:
   - $N(N - 1)$ for the modulus N^2 (N is prime), and
   - $(p - 1)(q - 1)$ for the modulus pq (p and q are primes).

7. To compute inverses modulo N, it is possible to use at least the three following methods: exhaustive search through all elements, exponentiation if $\varphi(N)$ is known, or the Euclid algorithm. Analyze the efficiency of these methods.

8. Use the exponentiation to find inverses a^{-1} of
   - $a = 87543$ for the modulus $N = 111613 = 239 \cdot 467$,
   - $a = 8751$ for the modulus $N = 12347$.

9. Apply the Euclid algorithm to find inverses a^{-1} of the following integers:
   - $a = 2317$ modulo 3457,
   - $a = 111222$ modulo 132683.

10. Write a C language implementation of the CRT algorithm. It should accept an arbitrary number of primes as the command line arguments (primes $p_1, \ldots, p_r$) and convert any vector $(a_1, \ldots, a_r)$ given from the standard input into the corresponding integer a (where $a_i = a \bmod p_i$).

11. Let $p_1 = 11$, $p_2 = 13$ and $p_3 = 17$. Find the integer representation of the following vectors:
    - $a = (5 \bmod 11, 7 \bmod 13, 3 \bmod 17)$,
    - $a = (2 \bmod 11, 11 \bmod 13, 2 \bmod 17)$.

12. Implement a polynomial version of the Euclid algorithm for finding gcd. The program can be written in C or another language. Assume that the coefficients are from the field $GF(N)$ where N is prime.

13. Modify your program for the gcd of two polynomials so it computes the inverse of a polynomial $a(x)$ modulo $p(x)$.

14. Consider polynomials $Z_2[x]$ over the binary field. Write a program (in C or another language) which generates all irreducible polynomials of a given degree. The degree should be an input argument passed to the program.

15. Create the multiplication and addition tables for
    - $GF(2^2)$ generated by an irreducible polynomial $p(x) = x^2 + x + 1$,
    - $GF(2^3)$ generated by an irreducible polynomial $p(x) = x^3 + x^2 + 1$.

16. Take a function $g(n) = 12n^6 + 34n^5 + 23$. Give examples of the function $f(n)$ such that
    - $f(n) = o(g(n))$,
    - $f(n) = O(g(n))$,
    - $f(n) = \Theta(g(n))$,
    - $f(n) = \Omega(g(n))$.

17. Define conditional entropy and show that
    - $H(S \mid X) \le H(S)$,
    - $H(S, X) = H(S) + H(X \mid S)$,
    - $H(S, X) = H(S) + H(X)$ if S and X are independent random variables.

18. Design a Huffman code for a message source $S = \{s_1, s_2, s_3, s_4, s_5\}$ with the probabilities $p(s_1) = 1/2$, $p(s_2) = 3/16$, $p(s_3) = 1/8$, $p(s_4) = 1/8$, and $p(s_5) = 1/16$. Calculate the average length of the code and compare it to the entropy of the source.

19. Design an algorithm for measuring the statistical properties of the English language. Your algorithm should count the occurrences of single characters and output the complete statistics for all single letters. Implement the algorithm in C or any other high-level programming language. Test your program for different texts and discuss the results. Compute the redundancy D_1 of English for single letters. Modify your program so it will output statistics of two-letter strings. Compute the redundancy D_2 of English for two-letter sequences.

20. Show that the one-time pad cipher is ideal.

3 Private-Key Cryptosystems

Section 3.1 presents some classical ciphers for which both plaintext and cipher-text are characters or strings of characters. Section 3.2 covers the theory of modern cryptosystems and describes two early ciphers: Lucifer and DES. Section 3.3 presents five private-key block ciphers: FEAL, IDEA, RC6, Rijndael, and Serpent, of which the last three took part in the recent AES competition. The Rijndael algorithm won this and is currently proposed as the encryption standard. Section 3.4 and 3.5 introduce differential and linear cryptanalysis, respectively. Finally, Sect. 3.6 studies the principles of secure S-box design.

3.1 Classical Ciphers

The private-key ciphers enable two parties, the sender and receiver, to talk in secrecy via an insecure channel (Fig. 3.1).

Before any communication of messages takes place, both parties must exchange the secret key $k \in \mathcal{K}$ via a secure channel. The secure channel can be

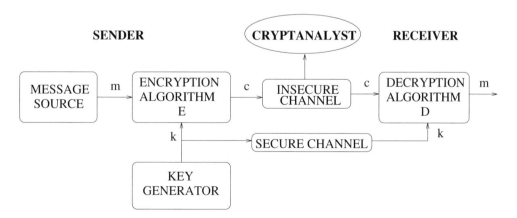

Fig. 3.1. Diagram of a private-key cryptosystem

implemented using a messenger or registered mail. If the distribution of the key is done, the sender can select message $m \in \mathcal{M}$, apply the encryption algorithm $E : \mathcal{M} \times \mathcal{K} \to \mathcal{C}$, and put the corresponding cryptogram $c = E_k(m)$ into the insecure channel, where $\mathcal{M}, \mathcal{C}, \mathcal{K}$ are sets of messages, cryptograms, and keys, respectively. The receiver recreates the message from the cryptogram using the decryption algorithm $D : \mathcal{C} \times \mathcal{K} \to \mathcal{M}$, i.e., $m = D_k(c)$. Clearly, the cryptosystem works correctly if $D_k(E_k(m)) = m$ for all keys $k \in \mathcal{K}$. Note that if the parties communicate using a particular language, the sender always chooses letters according to the probability distribution which characterizes the language.

We must assume that an enemy cryptanalyst knows the statistical properties of the message source (language) and reads all cryptograms that are being sent via the insecure channel. This adversary may want to either recreate messages or determine the secret key from cryptograms. This is the so-called *ciphertext-only attack*.

Early encryption algorithms were *monoalphabetic ciphers* where the encryption and decryption were done independently for each character. Consequently, messages and letters are used interchangeably.

3.1.1 Caesar Ciphers

Julius Caesar used a cipher which moved each letter of the alphabet to the letter three to the left in the predetermined order of the letters of the alphabet, so:

Messages	A B C D E F G H I J K L M
Cryptograms	D E F G H I J K L M N O P
Messages	N O P Q R S T U V W X Y Z
Cryptograms	Q R S T U V W X Y Z A B C

The last three substitutions are $X \to A$, $Y \to B$, and $Z \to C$. It is much more convenient to convert letters of the alphabet into integers. The most natural conversion is to assign to each letter an integer which indicates the position of the letter in the alphabet:

Letters	A	B	C	D	E	F	G	H	I	J	K	L	M
Integers	0	1	2	3	4	5	6	7	8	9	10	11	12
Letters	N	O	P	Q	R	S	T	U	V	W	X	Y	Z
Integers	13	14	15	16	17	18	19	20	21	22	23	24	25

If we use this conversion, then encryption in the above cipher can be defined as

$$c = E_k(m) = m + 3 \pmod{26}.$$

The decryption is

$$m = D_k(c) = c - 3 \pmod{26}.$$

Notice that the cipher does not have any key! The integer 3 which determines the rotation is fixed (and perhaps known to the cryptanalyst). If we replace the integer by the key, we get the *Caesar cipher*.

The cryptanalysis of the cipher is easy – there are 26 possible keys only. In Fig. 3.2 we have a histogram of the percentage frequency of English characters in text. In Fig. 3.3 this has been shifted using the Caesar cipher with $k = 3$. So if a ciphertext is given, it is easy to get the frequency of characters in the ciphertext and compare it with the frequency of the language. So, having the ciphertext

$$L\ FDPH\ L\ VDZ\ L\ FRQTXHUHG$$

it is easy to find out that $k = 3$ and the plaintext is:

$$I\ CAME\ I\ SAW\ I\ CONQUERED$$

Caesar cipher

Message Space: $\mathcal{M} = \{0, 1, \ldots, 25\}$ – letters converted to their positions in the alphabet.

Cryptogram Space: $\mathcal{C} = \{0, 1, \ldots, 25\}$.

Fig. 3.2. English character frequencies

Key Space: $\mathcal{K} = \{0, 1, \ldots, 25\}$, $|\mathcal{K}| = 26$, and $H(K) \approx 4.7$.

Encryption: $c = E_k(m) = m + k \pmod{26}$.

Decryption: $m = D_k(c) = c - k \pmod{26}$.

Unicity Distance: $N \approx \frac{H(K)}{D} \approx 1.5$ letters (assuming $D = 3.2$).

Cryptanalysis: Uses letter frequency distributions. If encipherment is achieved by a simple letter shift then a frequency count of the letter distributions in the ciphertext will yield the same pattern as the original host language of the plaintext but shifted.

3.1.2 Affine Ciphers

This is a generalization of the Caesar cipher obtained by numbering the letters of the alphabet and then multiplying the number of the letter to be enciphered by k_1, where $gcd(k_1, 26) = 1$, and adding a constant k_2. The answer is then reduced modulo 26. Figure 3.4 shows what happens to the histogram of Fig. 3.2 when the affine cipher $c = E_k(m) = k_1 m + k_2 \pmod{26}$ is applied with $k_1 = 5$ and $k_2 = 7$.

Decryption $m = D_k(c) = (c - k_2)k_1^{-1} \pmod{26}$ recovers the message m from the cryptogram c. It works only if k_1 has its inverse k_1^{-1} or, equivalently, $gcd(k_1, 26) = 1$.

Suppose we have to decipher:

WZDUY ZZYQB OTHTX ZDNZD KWQHI BYQBP WZDUY ZXZDSS

We note that:

Fig. 3.3. Encryption character frequencies with $c = m + 3 \pmod{26}$

Fig. 3.4. Encryption character frequencies with $c = 5m + 7$

$$Z \qquad \text{occurs 8 times,}$$
$$D \qquad \text{occurs 5 times,}$$
$$Y \qquad \text{occurs 4 times,}$$
$$\text{W, Q, B occur 3 times each.}$$

Assuming the language is English, we note that the most frequently occurring letters in English text are, in order:

$$E, T, R, I, N, O, A$$

This leads us to try $Z \to E$ and $D \to T$ or $Y \to T$. That is, we try to simultaneously solve,

$$\boxed{\begin{aligned} 25 &\equiv 4k_1 + k_2 \quad (\text{mod } 26) \\ 3 &\equiv 19k_1 + k_2 \quad (\text{mod } 26) \end{aligned}} \quad \text{or} \quad \boxed{\begin{aligned} 25 &\equiv 4k_1 + k_2 \quad (\text{mod } 26) \\ 24 &\equiv 19k_1 + k_2 \quad (\text{mod } 26) \end{aligned}}$$

which have as a solution $k_1 = 2$, $k_2 = 17$ in the first case (we reject it as k_1^{-1} does not exist), and $k_1 = 19$, $k_2 = 1$ in the second. If we try to decipher the letters WZDUY (the integers 22, 25, 3, 20, and 24) using $(c - k_2) \cdot k_1^{-1}$, which, in this case, is $(c - 1) \cdot 19^{-1}$ or $(c - 1) \cdot 11$, we will get the following plaintext

$$23, 4, 22, 1, 7 \quad \text{or} \quad XEWBH$$

which is not a part of any recognizable English expression or word. In fact, we could try all combinations $Z \to E$ with other letters and find that, in fact, Z does not map to E.

After much trial and error, we would find that $Z \to O$ (we would expect the most common letter to be a vowel). Now let us try $Z \to O$ and $D \to T$ or $Y \to$ T. That is, we simultaneously try to solve

$$\boxed{\begin{array}{l} 25 \equiv 14k_1 + k_2 \quad (\text{mod } 26) \\ 3 \;\equiv 19k_1 + k_2 \quad (\text{mod } 26) \end{array}} \quad \text{or} \quad \boxed{\begin{array}{l} 25 \equiv 14k_1 + k_2 \quad (\text{mod } 26) \\ 24 \equiv 19k_1 + k_2 \quad (\text{mod } 26) \end{array}}$$

which have solutions $k_1 = 6$ and $k_2 = 19$ or $k_1 = 5$ and $k_2 = 7$.

Now if we use the second of these to decode

$$WZDUYZ \qquad \text{(the integers 22, 25, 3, 20, 24, and 25)}$$

using $(c - k_2) \cdot k_1^{-1} = (c - 7) \cdot 21$, we get 3, 14, 20, 13, 19, and 14 or $DOUNTO$ which is recognizable as the words $DO\ UNTO$. We leave the reader to decipher the remainder of the message.

Affine cipher

Message Space: $\mathcal{M} = \{0, 1, \dots, 25\}$ – letters converted to their positions in the alphabet.

Cryptogram Space: $\mathcal{C} = \{0, 1, \dots, 25\}$.

Key Space: $\mathcal{K} = \{k = (k_1, k_2) \mid k_1, k_2 \in \{0, 1, \dots, 25\}, gcd(k_1, 26) = 1\}$, $\mid \mathcal{K} \mid = 312$, $H(K) \approx 8.3$.

Encryption: $c = E_k(m) = k_1 m + k_2 \pmod{26}$.

Decryption: $m = D_k(c) = (c - k_2)k_1^{-1} \pmod{26}$.

Unicity Distance: $N \approx \frac{H(K)}{D} \approx 2.6$ letters $(D = 3.2)$.

Cryptanalysis: Uses letter frequency distributions. The letter frequencies are still preserved but permuted according to the secret key $k = (k_1, k_2)$.

3.1.3 Monoalphabetic Substitution Ciphers

It is a common practice to use a secret word or words, not repeating letters, and write them in a rectangle to use as a mnemonic to translate plaintext into ciphertext. Suppose the secret words were $STAR\ WARS$. We note that $STAR\ WARS$ has the letters A, R, and S repeated so we use only the letters S, T, A, R, and W. We write these first and then fill out the rectangle with the unused letters of the alphabet:

$$\begin{array}{ccccc} S & T & A & R & W \\ B & C & D & E & F \\ G & H & I & J & K \\ L & M & N & O & P \\ Q & U & V & X & Y \\ Z & & & & \end{array}$$

Columns are then read off to give us the following plaintext to ciphertext transformation:

0	1	2	3	4	5	6	7	8	9	10	11	12	13	14	15	16	17	18	19	20	21	22	23	24	25
A	B	C	D	E	F	G	H	I	J	K	L	M	N	O	P	Q	R	S	T	U	V	W	X	Y	Z
S	B	G	L	Q	Z	T	C	H	M	U	A	D	I	N	V	R	E	J	O	X	W	F	K	P	Y

Thus,

$$I\ KNOW\ ONLY\ THAT\ I\ KNOW\ NOTHING$$

becomes:

$$H\ UINF\ NIAP\ OCSO\ H\ UINF\ INOCHIT$$

The above cipher is a substitution cipher. The nice property of it is that the secret permutation can be readily reconstructed from a relatively short and easy-to-memorize word or sentence. A general instance of a substitution cipher can be obtained if the secret word consists of a random permutation of 26 letters. Unfortunately, such a secret is difficult to learn by heart. Mathematically, the secret key is the permutation $\pi : \mathcal{Z}_{26} \rightarrow \mathcal{Z}_{26}$, where $\mathcal{Z}_{26} = \{0, 1, \ldots, 25\}$. A message $m \in \mathcal{Z}_{26}$ is encrypted into $c = \pi(m)$. The decryption is $m = \pi^{-1}(c)$ where π^{-1} is the inverse permutation of π.

Cryptanalysis uses frequency analysis on the letters of the alphabet. Short amounts of ciphertext can readily be attacked by computer search but even reasonable amounts of ciphertext are easy to decipher by hand. For example, to decipher

$$BRYH\ DRL\ R\ ITEEIA\ IRBS\ TEF\ CIAAXA\ NFR\ NDTEA\ RF\ FGKN$$
$$RGL\ AOAYJNDAYA\ EDRE\ BRYH\ NAGE\ EDA\ IRBS\ NRF\ FMYA$$
$$EK\ ZK\ TE\ CKIIKNAL\ DAY\ EK\ FXDKKI\ KGA\ LRH\ NDTXD\ NRF$$
$$RZRTGFE\ EDA\ YMIAF$$

we do a frequency analysis and note the following distribution of letters:

A	B	C	D	E	F	G	H	I	J	K	L	M	N	O	P	Q	R	S	T	U	V	W	X	Y	Z
17	4	2	10	13	10	5	3	9	1	9	4	2	9	1			15	2	6				3	6	2

So the most frequent letters are:

$$A,\ R,\ E,\ D\ or\ F,\ I\ or\ K\ or\ N.$$

There is a one-letter word so R is I or A. The two most common three-letter words in English are THE and AND. So we guess EDA is one of these. Since the most common letters in English are

$$E, T, R, I, N, \ldots,$$

we will guess EDA is THE and that R is A so our message becomes:

BaYH HaL a ITttle IaBS TtF CIeeXe NaF NhDte aF FGKN aGL eOeYJNheYe that BaYH NeGT the IaBS NaF FMYe tK ZK Tt CKI-IKNeL heY tK FXhKKI KGe LaH NhTXh NaF aZaTGFt the YMIeF

Which resolves to:

mary had a little lamb its fleece was white as snow and everywhere that mary went the lamb was sure to go it followed her to school one day which was against the rules

---

Monoalphabetic substitution cipher

Message Space: $\mathcal{M} = \{0, 1, \ldots, 25\} = \mathcal{Z}_{26}$.
Cryptogram Space: $\mathcal{C} = \{0, 1, \ldots, 25\} = \mathcal{Z}_{26}$.
Key Space: $\mathcal{K} = \{\pi \mid \pi : \mathcal{Z}_{26} \to \mathcal{Z}_{26}\}$, $\mid \mathcal{K} \mid = 26!$, and $H(K) = \log_2 26! \approx 88.3$.
   To evaluate $\log_2 26!$, Sterling's approximation can be used and $\log_2 26! \approx 26 \log_2 \frac{26}{e}$.
Encryption: $c = E_k(m) = \pi(m)$.
Decryption: $m = D_k(c) = \pi^{-1}(c)$.
Unicity Distance: $N \approx \frac{H(K)}{D} \approx 27.6$ letters (assuming $D = 3.2$).
Cryptanalysis: Uses letter frequency distributions. The letter frequencies are still preserved but permuted according to the permutation π.

3.1.4 Transposition Ciphers

The other principal technique for use on alphabets is transposition of characters. Thus,

$$\text{plaintext} \to \text{rearrange characters} \to \text{ciphertext}.$$

Write the plaintext *CRYPTANALYST* as a 3×4 matrix:

$$1\ 2\ 3\ 4$$
$$C\ R\ Y\ P$$
$$T\ A\ N\ A$$
$$L\ Y\ S\ T$$

and read off the columns in the order 2, 4, 1, 3 to get,

$$RAYPATCTLYNS$$

This technique can also be used for n-dimensional arrays. Transposition ciphers often use a *fixed period d*. Let $\mathcal{Z}_d$ be the integers from 0 to $d-1$, and $\pi : \mathcal{Z}_d \to \mathcal{Z}_d$ be a permutation. Then the *key* is the pair $k = (d, \pi)$ and blocks of d characters are enciphered at a time. Thus, the sequence of letters

$$m_0 \cdots m_{d-1}\ m_d \cdots m_{2d-1} \cdots$$

is enciphered to

$$m_{\pi(0)} \cdots m_{\pi(d-1)}\ m_{d+\pi(0)} \cdots m_{d+\pi(d-1)} \cdots$$

Suppose $d = 4$ and $\pi = (\pi(0), \pi(1), \pi(2), \pi(3)) = (1, 2, 3, 0)$. Then the following shows a message broken into blocks and enciphered:

Plaintext: *CRYP TOGR APHY*

Ciphertext: *PCRY RTOG YAPH*

Note that the frequency distribution of the characters of the ciphertext is exactly the same as for the plaintext. A knowledge of the most frequent *pairs* and *triples* in a language is used with *anagramming*. The most frequent pairs of letters in English, on a relative scale from 1 to 10, are:

TH 10.00	ED 4.12	OF 3.38
HE 9.50	TE 4.04	IT 3.26
IN 7.17	TI 4.00	AL 3.15
ER 6.65	OR 3.98	AS 3.00
RE 5.92	ST 3.81	HA 3.00
ON 5.70	AR 3.54	NG 2.92
AN 5.63	ND 3.52	CO 2.80
EN 4.76	TO 3.50	SE 2.75
AT 4.72	NT 3.44	ME 2.65
ES 4.24	IS 3.43	DE 2.65

We note some other salient features of English:

1. The vowel-consonant pair is most common – no high-frequency pair has two vowels.
2. Letters that occur in many different pairs are probably vowels.
3. Consonants, except for N and T, occur most frequently with vowels.
4. If XY and YX both occur, one letter is likely to be a vowel.

The most frequent three-letter combinations, on a scale of 1 to 10, are:

THE	10.00	FOR	1.65	ERE	1.24
AND	2.81	THA	1.49	CON	1.20
TIO	2.24	TER	1.35	TED	1.09
ATI	1.67	RES	1.26	COM	1.08

Decipher the following ciphertext:

LDWEOHETTHSESTRUHTELOBSEDEFEIVNT

We start by looking at blocks of various lengths by dividing up the text:

LD WE OH ET TH SE ST RU HT EL OB SE DE FE IV NT

Is $d = 2$? The pairs LD and WE, which can only be permuted to DL and EW, tell us no.

LDW EOH ETT HSE STR UHT ELO BSE DEF EIV NT

Is $d = 3$? The triple LDW in any permutation tells us no.

LDWE OHET THSE STRU HTEL OBSE DEFE IVNT

Is $d = 4$? This case is a bit harder because we have to try 16 permutations on the first two groups of four letters but we become convinced that none of these makes sense.

LDWEO HETTH SESTR UHTEL OBSED EFEIV NT

Is $d = 5$? A bit harder because we have to try 5! permutations on the first two groups of five letters but become convinced that none of these makes sense.

LDWEOH ETTHSE STRUHT ELOBSE DEFEIV NT

Is $d = 6$? The second group of six letters suggests

THESET or TTHESE.

That means we try the following permutations for deciphering:

$$(205134), (250134), (405132), (450132)$$
$$(501234), (301245), (510243), (310245)$$

When we try (450132) on the other blocks we recover the following message:

WE HOLD THESE TRUTHS TO BE SELF EVIDENT

Transposition cipher

Message Space: $\mathcal{M} = \underbrace{\mathcal{Z}_{26} \times \ldots \mathcal{Z}_{26}}_{d} = \mathcal{Z}_{26}^{d}$ – collection of sequences with d letters.

Cryptogram Space: $\mathcal{C} = \mathcal{Z}_{26}^{d}$ – d-letter sequences.

Key Space: $\mathcal{K} = \{\pi \mid \pi : \mathcal{Z}_d \rightarrow \mathcal{Z}_d\}$, $\mid \mathcal{K} \mid = d!$ and $H(K) = \log_2 d! \approx d \log_2(d/e)$.

Encryption: A message $m = (m_0, \ldots, m_{d-1})$ is encrypted into cryptogram $c = E_k(m) = (c_0, \ldots, c_{d-1}) = (m_{\pi(0)}, \ldots, m_{\pi(d-1)})$.

Decryption: $m = D_k(c) = (c_{\pi^{-1}(0)}, \ldots, c_{\pi^{-1}(d-1)})$.

Unicity Distance: $N \approx \frac{H(K)}{D}$ (Table 3.1).

Table 3.1. The period and associated unicity distance

d	$N = 0.3d \log_2(d/e)$	N
3	$0.9 \log_2(3/e)$	0.12804
4	$1.2 \log_2(4/e)$	0.66877
5	$1.5 \log_2(5/e)$	1.31885
6	$1.8 \log_2(6/e)$	2.05608
7	$2.1 \log_2(7/e)$	2.86579

Cryptanalysis: Uses letter frequency distributions. First, the period d needs to be guessed. Next single-letter frequencies combined with the most frequent pairs and triples allow us to break the cipher.

3.1.5 Homophonic Substitution Ciphers

Letters which occur frequently may be mapped into more than one letter in the ciphertext to flatten the frequency distribution. The number of cipher letters for a given character is determined by its frequency in the original language.

Suppose the alphabet is mapped into the numbers 0 to 99, then

> map E to 17, 19, 23, 47, and 64
> map A to 8, 20, 25, and 49
> map R to 1, 29, and 65
> map T to 16, 31, and 85

but otherwise the ith letter maps to the integer $3i$. Then the plaintext

MANY A SLIP TWIXT THE CUP AND THE LIP

will become

M	A	N	Y	A	S	L	I	P	T	W	I	X	T	T
08		20						16					31	85

36 08 39 72 20 54 33 24 45 16 66 24 69 31 85

H	E	C	U	P	A	N	D	T	H	E	L	I	P
17			25		16		47						

21 17 06 60 45 25 39 09 16 21 47 33 24 45

If a letter is to be encrypted, a single element is chosen at random from all homophones associated with the letter.

For each message $m \in \mathcal{Z}_{26}$, the cipher assigns the set $\mathcal{H}_m$ of homophones or positive integers. Each set contains at least one element. Usually the cardinality of a set $\mathcal{H}_m$ is proportional to the frequency of the letter m in the language. The cryptogram space $\mathcal{C} = \bigcup_{m \in \mathcal{M}} \mathcal{H}_m \subset \mathcal{Z}_H$ where $\mathcal{Z}_H$ is the smallest possible set that contains all homophones. The parameters and properties of the cipher are summarized below.

Homophonic cipher

Message Space: $\mathcal{M} = \mathcal{Z}_{26}$.
Cryptogram Space: $\mathcal{C} = \bigcup_{m \in \mathcal{M}} \mathcal{H}_m \subseteq \mathcal{Z}_H$.
Key Space: The secret key is the assignment of homophones to all messages so
   $k = (\mathcal{H}_0, \mathcal{H}_1, \ldots, \mathcal{H}_{25})$. If we assume that sizes of $\mathcal{H}_i$ for $i = 0, \ldots, 25$ are
   known (or easy to guess from the statistical analysis of the language), then
   the number of possible keys is equal to the number of possible arrangements
   of H elements into 26 compartments. Each compartment has to contain

$n_i = |\mathcal{H}_i|$ different elements. Thus the number of all keys is $|\mathcal{K}| = \binom{H}{n_0}$

$\binom{H - n_0}{n_1} \cdots \binom{n_{24} + n_{25}}{n_{24}}$ where $H = \sum_{i=0}^{25} n_i$.

Encryption: A message $m \in \mathcal{M}$ is encrypted by random selection of a homophone from $\mathcal{H}_m$, i.e., $c = E_k(m) = h \in_R \mathcal{H}_m$ (where $\in_R$ means that the
element is chosen randomly and uniformly).

Decryption: Knowing a cryptogram $c \in \mathcal{C}$, the decryption relies on finding the
set $\mathcal{H}_m$ to which c belongs – the message is m.

Unicity Distance: If sets of homophones contain single elements only, the cipher
becomes a monoalphabetic substitution cipher with $|\mathcal{K}| = 26!$ and the
unicity distance ≈ 27.6. If each set of homophones has exactly v elements
and $H = 26 \cdot v$, then $|\mathcal{K}| = \frac{(26v)!}{(v!)^{26}}$ and the unicity distance is $N \approx 38.2 \cdot v$
(note that this approximation does not work very well for small $v = 1, 2, 3$).

Cryptanalysis: Uses homophone frequency distributions. If there is enough ciphertext, it is easy to determine the set $\mathcal{C}$. From the language frequency
distribution, guesses about n_i can be made. The final stage would involve
enumeration of possible assignments of homophones to messages.

3.1.6 Polyalphabetic Substitution Ciphers

Whereas homophonic substitution ciphers hide the distribution via the use of
homomorphisms, *polyalphabetic substitution ciphers* hide it by making multiple substitutions. Leon Battista Alberti (see [264]) used two discs which were
rotated according to the key. In effect this gave, for a period d, d different
substitutions. Thus polyalphabetic substitution ciphers apply d different permutations

$$\pi_i : \mathcal{Z}_{26} \to \mathcal{Z}_{26} \text{ for } i = 1, \ldots, d,$$

and the message,

$$m = m_1, m_2, \ldots, m_d, m_{d+1}, m_{d+2}, \ldots m_{2d},$$

becomes

$$E_k(m) = \pi_1(m_1), \pi_2(m_2), \ldots, \pi_d(m_d), \pi_1(m_{d+1}), \ldots, \pi_d(m_{2d}).$$

Note that if $d = 1$, we get back the monoalphabetic substitution cipher. We
now give a few methods for obtaining polyalphabetic ciphers.

Vigenère cipher

Message Space: $\mathcal{M} = \mathbb{Z}_{26}^d$ – d-letter sequences.

Cryptogram Space: $\mathcal{C} = \mathbb{Z}_{26}^d$ – d-letter sequences.

Key Space: $\mathcal{K} = \mathbb{Z}_{26}^d$, $k = (k_1, \ldots, k_d)$, $|\mathcal{K}| = 26^d$, and $H(K) \approx 4.7d$.

Encryption: $c = E_k(m_1, \ldots, m_d) = (c_1, \ldots, c_d)$ and $c_i = \pi_i(m_i) \equiv m_i + k_i$
(mod 26) for $i = 1, \ldots, d$.

Decryption: $m = D_k(c_1, \ldots, c_d) = (m_1, \ldots, m_d)$ and $m_i = \pi_i^{-1}(c_i) \equiv c_i - k_i$
(mod 26) for $i = 1, \ldots, d$.

Unicity Distance: $N \approx \frac{H(K)}{D} \approx 1.47d$ (assuming $D = 3.2$).

Cryptanalysis: If the period d is not known, then it can be determined using
the Kasiski or index of coincidence methods (see Sect. 3.1.7). Once the
period d is known, cryptanalysis reduces to the simultaneous analysis of d
independent Caesar ciphers.

Let us consider how the Vigenère cipher can be used. Encipher the message
INDIVIDUAL CHARACTER with the key *HOST*:

$$
\begin{array}{ll}
m & = INDI \quad VIDU \quad ALCH \; ARAC \; TER \\
k & = HOST \; HOST \quad HOST \; HOST \; HOS \\
E_k(m) & = PBVB \; CWVN \; HZUA \; HFSV \; ASJ
\end{array}
$$

Beauford cipher

Message Space: $\mathcal{M} = \mathbb{Z}_{26}^d$ – d-letter sequences.

Cryptogram Space: $\mathcal{C} = \mathbb{Z}_{26}^d$ – d-letter sequences.

Key Space: $\mathcal{K} = \mathbb{Z}_{26}^d$, $k = (k_1, \ldots, k_d)$, $|\mathcal{K}| = 26^d$, and $H(K) \approx 4.7d$.

Encryption: $c = E_k(m_1, \ldots, m_d) = (c_1, \ldots, c_d)$ and $c_i = \pi_i(m_i) \equiv k_i - m_i$
(mod 26) for $i = 1, \ldots, d$.

Decryption: $m = D_k(c_1, \ldots, c_d) = (m_1, \ldots, m_d)$ and $m_i = \pi_i^{-1}(c_i) \equiv k_i - c_i$
(mod 26) for $i = 1, \ldots, d$.

Unicity Distance: $N \approx \frac{H(K)}{D} \approx 1.47d$ (assuming $D = 3.2$).

Cryptanalysis: If the period d is not known, then it can be determined using
the Kasiski or index of coincidence methods. Once the period d is known,
cryptanalysis reduces to the simultaneous analysis of d independent affine
ciphers with the known multiplier.

Observe that for the Beauford cipher

$$\pi_i(m_i) \equiv (k_i - m_i) \pmod{26} \text{ and } \pi_i^{-1}(c_i) \equiv (k_i - c_i) \pmod{26},$$

so the same algorithm can be used for encryption and decryption as $\pi_i = \pi_i^{-1}$!
In other words, encryption and decryption in the Beauford cipher can be done
using a single algorithm while the Vigenère cipher requires two algorithms: one
for encryption and one for decryption.

3.1.7 Cryptanalysis of Polyalphabetic Substitution Ciphers

To break a polyalphabetic substitution cipher, the cryptanalyst must first determine the period of the cipher. This can be done using two main tools: the
Kasiski method, which is named after its inventor Friedrich Kasiski, and the
index of coincidence.

The Kasiski method uses repetitions in the ciphertext to give clues to the
cryptanalyst about the period. For example, suppose the plaintext *TO BE OR
NOT TO BE* has been enciphered using the key *NOW*, producing the ciphertext
below:

$$\begin{aligned} m &= \textit{TOBEO \ RNOTT \ OBE} \\ k &= \textit{NOWNO \ WNOWN \ OWN} \\ E_k(m) &= \textbf{GCXRC \ NACPG \ CXR} \end{aligned}$$

Since the characters that are repeated, **GCXR**, start nine letters apart we
conclude that the period is probably 3 or 9.

The index of coincidence (*IC*), introduced in the 1920s by Friedman [188,
264], measures the variation in the frequencies of the letters in a ciphertext.
If the period of the cipher is one ($d = 1$), i.e., a simple substitution has been
used, there will be considerable variation in the letter frequencies and the *IC*
will be high. As the period increases, the variation is gradually eliminated (due
to diffusion) and the *IC* is low (Table 3.2).

Assume that there is an alphabet of n letters uniquely identifiable by their
positions from the set $\mathcal{Z}_n = \{0, 1, \ldots, n-1\}$. Each character is assigned its
corresponding frequency expressed by the probability $P(M = m) = p_m$ where
$m \in \mathcal{Z}_n$. Note that $\sum_{i=0}^{n} p_i = 1$. Following Sinkov [479], we shall derive the *IC*
by first defining a *measure of roughness*, *MR*, which gives the variation of the
frequencies of individual characters relative to a uniform distribution. So the
measure of roughness of the language with $\mathcal{Z}_n$ and $\{p_i \mid i = 0, 1, \ldots, n-1\}$ is

Table 3.2. Languages and their indices of coincidence

Language	IC
Arabic	0.075889
Danish	0.070731
Dutch	0.079805
English	0.066895
Finnish	0.073796
French	0.074604
German	0.076667
Greek	0.069165
Hebrew	0.076844
Italian	0.073294
Japanese	0.077236
Malay	0.085286
Norwegian	0.069428
Portuguese	0.074528
Russian	0.056074
Serbo-Croatian	0.064363
Spanish	0.076613
Swedish	0.064489

$$MR = \sum_{i=0}^{n-1} \left(p_i - \frac{1}{n} \right)^2. \tag{3.1}$$

For English letters we have

$$MR = \sum_{i=0}^{25} \left(p_i - \frac{1}{26} \right)^2 \approx \sum_{i=0}^{25} p_i^2 - 0.038.$$

$\sum_{i=0}^{25} p_i^2$ expresses the probability that two characters generated by the language are identical. If we want to compute either MR or $\sum_{i=0}^{25} p_i^2$, we have to estimate these from a limited number of observed cryptograms.

Suppose we have seen a ciphertext with N characters. For every character in the ciphertext, let F_i express how many times it has occurred in the ciphertext. Obviously, $\sum_{i=0}^{25} F_i = N$. Note that F_i can be used to estimate p_i as $p_i \approx F_i/N$. It is possible to create

$$\binom{N}{2} = \frac{N(N-1)}{2}$$

pairs of characters out of N observed in the ciphertext. The number of pairs (i, i) containing just the letter i is:

$$\frac{F_i(F_i - 1)}{2}.$$

The IC is defined as:

$$IC = \sum_{i=0}^{25} \frac{F_i(F_i - 1)}{N(N - 1)}, \tag{3.2}$$

and gives the probability that two letters observed in the ciphertext are, in fact, the same. It is not difficult to see that $IC \approx \sum_{i=0}^{25} p_i^2$. To prove this, it is enough to note that $F_i \approx p_i \cdot N$ and

$$IC \approx \sum_{i=0}^{25} \frac{p_i^2(N - \frac{1}{p_i})}{N - 1}.$$

IC becomes closer and closer to $\sum_{i=0}^{25} p_i^2$ as the number of observed characters in the ciphertext increases. The IC estimate can be used to compute the corresponding measure of roughness:

$$MR \approx IC - 0.038.$$

Index of coincidence (an algorithm)

IC1. Collect N ciphertext characters.
IC2. Find the collection $\mathcal{F} = \{F_i \mid i \in \mathcal{Z}_n\}$ of frequencies for all characters.
Note that $\sum_i F_i = N$.
IC3. Compute

$$IC = \sum_{i=0}^{n} \frac{F_i(F_i - 1)}{N(N - 1)}.$$

For a flat distribution of a 26-character alphabet, all letters have the same frequency, $1/26$, and the sum of the squares is $(1/26)^2 \times 26$. Hence the MR for a flat distribution is $1/26 - 1/26 = 0$. When the MR is 0, corresponding to a flat distribution, we say it has infinite period ($d = \infty$). At the other extreme we have period one ($d = 1$) for simple substitution. English with period one has $MR = 0.028$. Thus we have:

$$0.038 \quad < IC < 0.066 = 0.038 + 0.028.$$
$$\text{(period } \infty) \qquad\qquad\qquad \text{(period 1)}$$

Table 3.3. Periods and associated indices of coincidence for English

d	IC
1	0.0660
2	0.0520
3	0.0473
4	0.0450
5	0.0436
6	0.0427
7	0.0420
8	0.0415
9	0.0411
10	0.0408
11	0.0405
12	0.0403
13	0.0402
14	0.0400
15	0.0399
16	0.0397
17	0.0396
18	0.0396
19	0.0395
20	0.0394

For a cipher of period d, the expected value of IC is given by:

$$\exp(IC) = \frac{N-d}{d(N-1)}(0.066) + \frac{(d-1)N}{d(N-1)}(0.038).$$

Thus, while we can get an estimate of d from the ciphertext, it is not exact but is statistical in nature, and a particular ciphertext might give misleading results. Table 3.2 gives the index of coincidence for some other languages. For English, the relation between IC and d is given in Table 3.3.

The following attack provides a concrete example of this method. Decrypt the following ciphertext which was produced using the Vigenère cipher:

> TSMVM MPPCW CZUGX HPECP REAUE IOBQW PPIMS
> FXIPC TSQPK SZNUL OPACR DDPKT SLVFW ELTKR
> GHIZS FNIDF   ARMUE NOSKR GDIPH WSGVL EDMCM
> SMWKP IYOJS   TLVFA HPBJI RAQIW HLDGA IYOU

Given that the cipher was produced using a Vigenère cipher, we would first like to determine the period that has been used. The Kasiski method allows us to do that, assuming the repetitions are not coincidental. Examining the trigraphs we find two occurrences of IYO and LVF. The IYOs are 25 letters apart and the LVFs are 55 apart. The common factors are 1 and 5.

Let us now examine the *IC*. The frequency count gives us:

$$
\begin{array}{lllll}
a \to 6 & g \to 5 & 1 \to 6 & q \to 3 & v \to 4 \\
b \to 2 & h \to 5 & m \to 8 & r \to 6 & w \to 6 \\
c \to 6 & i \to 10 & n \to 3 & s \to 10 & x \to 2 \\
d \to 6 & j \to 2 & o \to 5 & t \to 5 & y \to 2 \\
e \to 5 & k \to 5 & p \to 13 & u \to 5 & z \to 3 \\
f \to 6 & & & &
\end{array}
$$

Thus the $IC = 0.04066$. From the table of ICs (Table 3.3) it appears more likely that 10 alphabets were used than 5, but we will proceed with an assumption of 5. We split the ciphertext into five sections, getting:

(a) *TMCHRIPFTSODSEGFANGWESITHRHI*
$\qquad\qquad$ from text positions $5i$, $i = 0, 1, \ldots, 27$.

(b) *SPZPFOPXSZPDLLHNRODSDMYLPALY*
$\qquad\qquad$ from text positions $5i + 1$, $i = 0, 1, \ldots, 27$.

(c) *MPUEABIIQNAPVTIIMSIGMWOVBQDO*
$\qquad\qquad$ from text positions $5i + 2$, $i = 0, 1, \ldots, 27$.

(d) *VCGCUQMPPUCKFKZDUKPVCKJFJIGU*
$\qquad\qquad$ from text positions $5i + 3$, $i = 0, 1, \ldots, 27$.

(e) *MWXPEWSCKLRTWRSFERHLMPSAIWA*
$\qquad\qquad$ from text positions $5i + 4$, $i = 0, 1, \ldots, 27$.

In Table 3.4, the frequency distribution for each of these five sections is shown. Each column of Table 3.4 corresponds to the frequency distribution of the section indicated by the text position in the heading. Thus, column 4, headed by $5i + 3$, corresponds to the fourth section which gave text positions $5i + 3$.

It would be best to consider columns 2 and 4 as their *IC* is 0.06614 which corresponds most closely to English. In the second column of Table 3.4 we see L and P occur frequently, suggesting that they might be A and E, respectively. In the fourth column we are more uncertain what initial guess to try for A so we will try the three most frequent values as guesses for A, i.e., U, C, and K.

The second section is:

Table 3.4. Frequency distribution for the five sections of the ciphertext

text	$5i$	$5i+1$	$5i+2$	$5i+3$	$5i+4$
a →	1	1	2	0	2
b →	0	0	2	0	0
c →	1	0	0	4	1
d →	1	3	1	1	0
e →	2	0	1	0	2
f →	2	1	0	2	1
g →	2	0	1	2	0
h →	3	1	0	0	1
i →	3	0	5	1	1
j →	0	0	0	2	0
k →	0	0	0	4	1
l →	0	4	0	0	2
m →	1	1	3	1	2
n →	1	1	1	0	0
o →	1	2	2	0	0
p →	1	5	2	3	2
q →	0	0	2	1	0
r →	2	1	0	0	3
s →	3	3	1	0	3
t →	3	0	1	0	1
u →	0	0	1	4	0
v →	0	0	2	2	0
w →	1	0	1	0	4
x →	0	1	0	0	1
y →	0	2	0	0	0
z →	0	2	0	1	0
IC	0.04233	0.06614	0.05026	0.06614	0.04843

$$SPZPFOPXSZPDLLHNRODSDMYLPALY$$

Since P is the most common letter we are going to use the replacements P → E, Q → F, ..., getting:

$$HEOEUDEMHOESAAWCGDSHSBNAEPAN$$

The fourth section is:

$$VCGCUQMPPUCKFKZDUKPVCKJFJIGU$$

Hence, replacing U → A, V → B, ..., we get:

BIMIAWSVVAIQLQFJAQVBIQPLFOMA

which we quickly decide is unlikely to be English because of the number of Qs. The other choices for A from the frequency distribution are C → A or K → A. Trying these gives, respectively:

TAEASOKNNSAIDIXBSINTAIHDHGES

CGCEGCFFECAFAJDEAFFCADFDCGE

Of these two the first looks the most promising so we look at what we have for our five sections as rows:

```
.  .    .   .    .   .    .    .   .   .   .   .    .   .   .    .   .   .   .   .    .   .   .
H  E   O  E  U  D  E  M  H  O  E  S  A  A  W  C  G  D  S  H  S  B  N  A  E  P  A  N
.  .    .   .    .   .    .    .   .   .   .   .    .   .   .    .   .   .   .   .    .   .   .
T  A   E   A   S   O   K   N  N  S  A  I  D  I  X  B  S  I  N  T  A  I  H  D  H  G  E  S
.  .    .   .    .   .    .    .   .   .   .   .    .   .   .    .   .   .   .   .    .   .   .
```

Neither row is part of a sentence so we look down the first column and decide that since the most common first word in English is THE we will start by leaving the first row as it is and use the replacements M → E, N → F, ..., in the third row, giving:

```
T  M  C  H  R  I  P  F  T  S  O  D  S  E  G  F  A  N  G  W  E  S  I  T  H  R  H  I
H  E  O  E  U  D  E  M  H  O  E  S  A  A  W  C  G  D  S  H  S  B  N  A  E  P  A  N
E  H  M  W  S  T  A  A  I  F  S  H  N  L  A  A  E  K  A  Y  E  O  G  N  T  I  V  G
T  A  E  A  S  O  K  N  N  S  A  I  D  I  X  B  S  I  N  T  A  I  H  D  H  G  E  S
.  .  .  .  .  .  .  .  .  .  .  .  .  .  .  .  .  .  .  .  .  .  .  .  .  .  .  .
```

Hence we decide that the plaintext is:

THE TIME HAS COME THE WALRUS SAID TO SPEAK OF MANY THINGS OF SHOES AND SHIPS AND SEALING WAX OF CAB-BAGES AND KINGS AND WHY THE SEA IS BOILING HOT AND WHETHER PIGS HAVE WINGS

Looking at the character which gave A in each of the five alphabets gives us the key *ALICE*.

3.2 DES Family

This section discusses modern cryptographic algorithms. The discussion starts from the description of Shannon's concept of product ciphers. Later Feistel

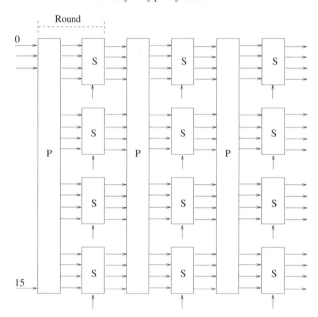

Fig. 3.5. S-P network

transformations are studied. The Lucifer algorithm and the Data Encryption Standard (DES) are presented.

3.2.1 Product Ciphers

Shannon [467] proposed composing different kinds of simple and insecure ciphers to create complex and secure cryptosystems. These complex cryptosystems were called *product ciphers*. Shannon argued that to obtain secure ciphers the designer had to operate on large message and key spaces and use simple transformations to incorporate *confusion* and *diffusion*. The concept is illustrated in Fig. 3.5. The S-boxes are simple substitution ciphers and they provide confusion because of the secret keys used. Permutation boxes (P-boxes) diffuse partial cryptograms across the inputs to the next stage. The P-boxes have no secret key. They have a fixed topology of input-output connections. The product cipher needs to have a number of iterations or rounds. A single round consists of concatenation of a single P-box with the subsequent layer of S-boxes. The more rounds, the better mixing of partial cryptograms. Consequently the probability distribution of the cryptograms becomes flatter. Product ciphers based on

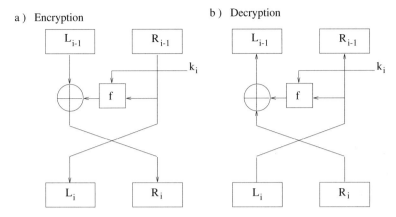

Fig. 3.6. Feistel permutation

substitution and permutation boxes are also known as *substitution-permutation networks* (S-P networks). S-P networks are expected to have [67]:

- *Avalanche* property – a single input bit change should force the complementation of approximately half of the output bits [168].
- *Completeness* property – each output bit should be a complex function of every input bit [265].

In general, to implement product ciphers, it is necessary to have two algorithms: one for encryption and the other for decryption. This can be expensive in terms of both hardware and software. Feistel [168] showed an elegant variant of S-P networks that could be implemented using a single algorithm for both encryption and decryption. A single round of this variant is shown in Fig. 3.6. Note the following interesting properties of the round:

- It is always a permutation regardless of the form of the f function.
- As $L_i = R_{i-1}$, the function f is evaluated on the same input for both encryption and decryption.
- The design of a cipher $E : \mathcal{K} \times \mathcal{M} \to \mathcal{C}$ with $\mathcal{M} = \mathcal{C} = \Sigma^n$ reduces to the design of the function $f : \mathcal{K} \times \Sigma^{\frac{n}{2}} \to \Sigma^{\frac{n}{2}}$ where $\Sigma = \{0,1\}$.

Definition 1. *A* Feistel transformation *is a permutation* $F_{k_i} : \Sigma^n \to \Sigma^n$ *that takes an input* $L_{i-1}, R_{i-1} \in \Sigma^{\frac{n}{2}}$ *and assigns the output* $F_{k_i}(L_{i-1}, R_{i-1}) = (L_i, R_i)$ *according to the following equations:*

$$L_i = R_{i-1} \quad and \quad R_i = L_{i-1} \oplus f(k_i, R_{i-1}), \tag{3.3}$$

where the function f is any function of the form $f : \mathcal{K} \times \Sigma^{\frac{n}{2}} \rightarrow \Sigma^{\frac{n}{2}}$ and $k_i \in \mathcal{K}$ is a cryptographic key (where $\oplus$ stands for a bit-by-bit XOR operation).

A cryptographic system is called a *Feistel-type cryptosystem* if it applies ℓ rounds of a Feistel transformation (Feistel permutation) yielding an encryption function of the form:

$$E_k = F_{k_\ell} \circ F_{k_{\ell-1}} \circ \cdots \circ F_{k_1}. \tag{3.4}$$

The decryption applies the inverse Feistel transformations in the reverse order. The cryptographic key is $k = (k_1, \ldots, k_\ell)$.

An encryption algorithm should allow a user to select an encryption function from a large enough collection of all possible functions through the random selection of a cryptographic key. Note that for a plaintext/ciphertext block of n bits, the collection of all possible permutations contains $2^n!$ elements and is called the symmetric group. If we assume that the size of the key block is also n bits, then the selection of permutations is restricted to 2^n out of $2^n!$ by random selection of the key. To generate a random permutation efficiently, it is enough to iterate Feistel permutations many times. The single iteration is controlled by a shorter partial key which is usually generated from the cryptographic key. Therefore the iteration has to be seen as a collection of permutations, each of which is indexed by the partial key.

Coppersmith and Grossman [109] studied iterations of basic permutations and their suitability to encryption. They defined the *k-functions*. Each *k*-function along with its connection topology produces a single iteration permutation which can be used as a generator of other permutations by composing them. Coppersmith and Grossman proved that these generators produce at least the alternating group using a finite number of their compositions. It means that using composition and with generators of relatively simple structure, it is possible to produce at least half of all the permutations. Even and Goldreich [164] proved that the Feistel permutations can also generate the alternating group. It turns out [407] that even if the function $f(k, R)$ is restricted to one-to-one mappings, the Feistel permutations still generate the alternating group. In other words, having $(2^{n/2})!$ generators, it is possible to produce $\frac{(2^n)!}{2}$ different permutations. Bovey and Williamson reported in [52] that an ordered pair of generators can produce either the alternating group A_{V_n} or the symmetric group S_{V_n} with a probability greater than $1 - \exp(-\log^{1/2} 2^n)$. So if we select the pair at random, there is a high probability that it generates at least A_{V_n}.

3.2.2 Lucifer Algorithm

The first cryptosystem developed using Feistel transformations, was the Lucifer algorithm. It was designed at the IBM Watson Research Laboratory in the early 1970s by a team including Horst Feistel, William Notz, and J. Lynn Smith [168, 169, 486].

Lucifer cryptosystem

Message Space: $\mathcal{M} = \Sigma^{128}$.

Cryptogram Space: $\mathcal{C} = \Sigma^{128}$.

Key Space: $\mathcal{K} = \Sigma^{128}$, $|\mathcal{K}| = 2^{128}$, and $H(K)=128$. A cryptographic key is
   $k = (k_1, \ldots, k_{16})$.

Encryption: $E_k = F_{k_{16}} \circ \cdots \circ F_{k_1}$.

Decryption: $D_k = F_1^{-1} \circ \cdots \circ F_{k_{16}}^{-1}$.

Unicity Distance: $N \approx \frac{H(K)}{D} \approx 40$ letters (assuming $D = 3.2$).

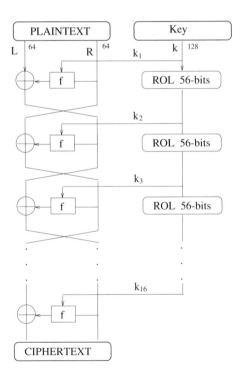

Fig. 3.7. Lucifer algorithm

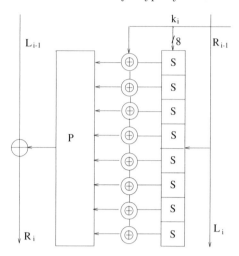

Fig. 3.8. Lucifer function f

The Lucifer operation operates on 128-bit messages and encrypts them into 128-bit cryptograms under a 128-bit key. The general scheme of the Lucifer system is given in Fig. 3.7. The core element is the function f (Fig. 3.8). It translates 64-bit inputs into 64-bit outputs using a 64-bit partial key k_i, $i = 1, \ldots, 16$. A 64-bit input R_{i-1} to the function f goes to eight identical S-boxes. Each S-box is a simple substitution cipher with a single-bit key (0 or 1). The eight bits needed to control S-boxes are extracted from the partial key k_i. The outputs from S-boxes are XORed with the partial key k_i. Finally, bits of the resulting sequence are permuted according to the fixed wire-crossing topology of the block P.

The key schedule of Lucifer is very regular. Partial keys are selected from 64 lower bits of the key. After every extraction of the partial key, the contents of the 128-bit key register are rotated 56 bits to the left.

3.2.3 DES Algorithm

The Data Encryption Standard (DES) [383] or Data Encryption Algorithm (DEA) was developed at IBM in the mid-1970s and was the outgrowth of Lucifer. There is an interesting story behind the design and adoption of DES as a US encryption standard for nonmilitary applications. Readers are referred to Schneier's book [451] for details. It is no surprise to learn that the DES algorithm repeats the Lucifer general structure. The algorithm is summarized in

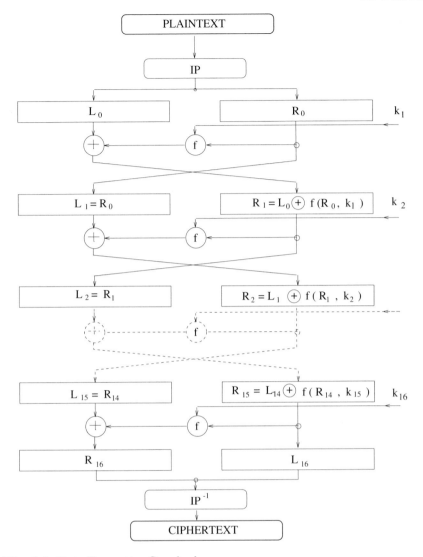

Fig. 3.9. Data Encryption Standard

Fig. 3.9. DES processes 64-bit blocks of data under a 56-bit key using 16 rounds (or iterations).

DES cryptosystem

Message Space: $\mathcal{M} = \Sigma^{64}$.
Cryptogram Space: $\mathcal{C} = \Sigma^{64}$.

Table 3.5. **a** Initial permutation IP and **b** Final permutation IP^{-1}

58 50 42 34 26 18 10 2	40 8 48 16 56 24 64 32
60 52 44 36 28 20 12 4	39 7 47 15 55 23 63 31
62 54 46 38 30 22 14 6	38 6 46 14 54 22 62 30
64 56 48 40 32 24 16 8	37 5 45 13 53 21 61 29
57 49 41 33 25 17 9 1	36 4 44 12 52 20 60 28
59 51 43 35 27 19 11 3	35 3 43 11 51 19 59 27
61 53 45 37 29 21 13 5	34 2 42 10 50 18 58 26
63 55 47 39 31 23 15 7	33 1 41 9 49 17 57 25
(a)	(b)

Key Space: $\mathcal{K} = \Sigma^{56}$, $| \mathcal{K} |= 2^{56}$, and $H(K){=}56$. A cryptographic key is $k = (k_1, \ldots, k_{16})$.

Encryption: $E_k = F_{k_{16}} \circ \cdots \circ F_{k_1}$.

Decryption: $D_k = F_1^{-1} \circ \cdots \circ F_{k_{16}}^{-1}$.

Unicity Distance: $N \approx \frac{H(K)}{D} \approx 17.5$ letters (assuming $D = 3.2$).

There was a disagreement over whether a 56-bit key is sufficiently long. Diffie and Hellman [153] had predicted the DES algorithm would be vulnerable to an exhaustive search attack by a special-purpose machine. Indeed, Michael Wiener [528] at the Crypto '93 rump session gave technical details of a key search chip which could test 5×10^7 keys per second. A search machine which used 5760 chips could search the entire DES key space in 35 hours and cost \$100000.

The algorithm can be used for both encryption and decryption. An input x can be either a plaintext or a ciphertext block. The sequence x is first transposed under an initial permutation (IP). The 64-bit output $IP(x)$ is divided into halves L_0 and R_0. The pair (L_0, R_0) is subject to 16 Feistel transformations, each of which uses the function $f(k_i, L_i)$, $i = 1, \ldots, 16$. Finally, the pair (L_{16}, R_{16}) is transposed under the inverse permutation IP^{-1} to produce the output y. The permutations IP and IP^{-1} are given in Table 3.5. The IP and IP^{-1} tables (as well as the other permutation tables described later) should be read left-to-right, top-to-bottom (e.g., IP transposes a binary string $x = (x_1 x_2 \ldots x_{64})$ into $(x_{58} x_{50} \ldots x_7)$). All tables are fixed.

Note that after the last iteration, the left and right halves are not exchanged; instead the concatenated block $(R_{16} L_{16})$ is input to the final permutation IP^{-1}.

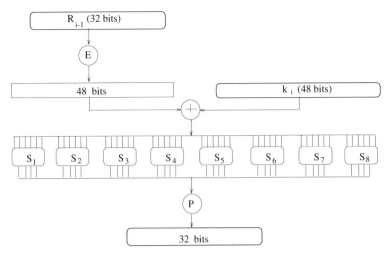

Fig. 3.10. DES function $f(k_i, R_{i-1})$

Table 3.6. Bit-selection function E

32	1	2	3	4	5
4	5	6	7	8	9
8	9	10	11	12	13
12	13	14	15	16	17
16	17	18	19	20	21
20	21	22	23	24	25
24	25	26	27	28	29
28	29	30	31	32	1

This is necessary to ensure that the algorithm can be used both to encipher and decipher.

The Function f and S-boxes. Figure 3.10 shows the components of the function $f(k_i, R_{i-1})$. First R_{i-1} is expanded to a 48-bit string $E(R_{i-1})$ using the bit-selection function E shown in Table 3.6. This table is used in the same way as the permutation tables, except that some bits of R_{i-1} are selected more than once; thus, given $R_{i-1} = r_1 r_2 \ldots r_{32}$, $E(R_{i-1}) = r_{32} r_1 r_2 \ldots r_{32} r_1$. Next, the XOR of $E(R_{i-1})$ and k_i is calculated and the result is broken into eight 6-bit blocks $B_1, \ldots, B_8$, where

$$E(R_{i-1}) \oplus k_i = B_1 B_2 \ldots B_8.$$

Table 3.7. Permutation P

16	7	20	21
29	12	28	17
1	15	23	26
5	18	31	10
2	8	24	14
32	27	3	9
19	13	30	6
22	11	4	25

Each 6-bit block B_j is then used as the input to a selection (substitution) function (*S-box*) S_j, which returns a 4-bit block $S_j(B_j)$. These blocks are concatenated, and the resulting 32-bit block is transposed by the permutation P shown in Table 3.7. Thus, the block returned by $f(k_i, R_{i-1})$ is

$$P(S_1(B_1)\dots S_8(B_8)).$$

Each S-box S_j maps a 6-bit sequence $B_j = b_1 b_2 b_3 b_4 b_5 b_6$ into a 4-bit sequence as defined in Table 3.8. This is done as follows: The integer corresponding to $b_1 b_6$ selects a row in the table, while the integer corresponding to $b_2 b_3 b_4 b_5$ selects a column. The value of $S_j(B_j)$ is then the 4-bit representation of the integer in that row and column. For example, if $B_1 = 011100$, then S_1 returns the value in row 0, column 14; this is 0, which is represented as 0000. If $B_7 = 100101$, then S_7 returns the value in row 3, column 2; this is 13, which is represented as 1101.

Although the DES algorithm was made public, the collection of tests used to select S-boxes and the P-box was not revealed until 1994 [108]. The collection of tests is equivalently referred in the literature as *the design criteria/properties*. A summary of the design properties used during the design of S-boxes and the P-box can be found in [67] and [379]. Some S-box design properties are:

– Each row function in an S-box is a permutation (S-boxes produce sequences with a balanced number of zeros and ones).
– No S-box is a linear or affine function of the input (S-boxes are nonlinear).
– A single-bit change on the input of an S-box changes at least two output bits (S-boxes provide an "avalanche" effect).
– For each S-box S, $S(x)$ and $S(x \oplus 001100)$ must differ in at least two bits.
– $S(x) \neq S(x \oplus 11ef00)$ for any choice of bits e and f.

Table 3.8. DES S-boxes

Row	\multicolumn{16}{c}{Column}																Box
	0	1	2	3	4	5	6	7	8	9	10	11	12	13	14	15	
0	14	4	13	1	2	15	11	8	3	10	6	12	5	9	0	7	
1	0	15	7	4	14	2	13	1	10	6	12	11	9	5	3	8	S_1
2	4	1	14	8	13	6	2	11	15	12	9	7	3	10	5	0	
3	15	12	8	2	4	9	1	7	5	11	3	14	10	0	6	13	
0	15	1	8	14	6	11	3	4	9	7	2	13	12	0	5	10	
1	3	13	4	7	15	2	8	14	12	0	1	10	6	9	11	5	S_2
2	0	14	7	11	10	4	13	1	5	8	12	6	9	3	2	15	
3	13	8	10	1	3	15	4	2	11	6	7	12	0	5	14	9	
0	10	0	9	14	6	3	15	5	1	13	12	7	11	4	2	8	
1	13	7	0	9	3	4	6	10	2	8	5	14	12	11	15	1	S_3
2	13	6	4	9	8	15	3	0	11	1	2	12	5	10	14	7	
3	1	10	13	0	6	9	8	7	4	15	14	3	11	5	2	12	
0	7	13	14	3	0	6	9	10	1	2	8	5	11	12	4	15	
1	13	8	11	5	6	15	0	3	4	7	2	12	1	10	14	9	S_4
2	10	6	9	0	12	11	7	13	15	1	3	14	5	2	8	4	
3	3	15	0	6	10	1	13	8	9	4	5	11	12	7	2	14	
0	2	12	4	1	7	10	11	6	8	5	3	15	13	0	14	9	
1	14	11	2	12	4	7	13	1	5	0	15	10	3	9	8	6	S_5
2	4	2	1	11	10	13	7	8	15	9	12	5	6	3	0	14	
3	11	8	12	7	1	14	2	13	6	15	0	9	10	4	5	3	
0	12	1	10	15	9	2	6	8	0	13	3	4	14	7	5	11	
1	10	15	4	2	7	12	9	5	6	1	13	14	0	11	3	8	S_6
2	9	14	15	5	2	8	12	3	7	0	4	10	1	13	11	6	
3	4	3	2	12	9	5	15	10	11	14	1	7	6	0	8	13	
0	4	11	2	14	15	0	8	13	3	12	9	7	5	10	6	1	
1	13	0	11	7	4	9	1	10	14	3	5	12	2	15	8	6	S_7
2	1	4	11	13	12	3	7	14	10	15	6	8	0	5	9	2	
3	6	11	13	8	1	4	10	7	9	5	0	15	14	2	3	12	
0	13	2	8	4	6	15	11	1	10	9	3	14	5	0	12	7	
1	1	15	13	8	10	3	7	4	12	5	6	11	0	14	9	2	S_8
2	7	11	4	1	9	12	14	2	0	6	10	13	15	3	5	8	
3	2	1	14	7	4	10	8	13	15	12	9	0	3	5	6	11	

– The S-boxes minimize the difference between the number of ones and zeros in any S-box output when any single bit is constant.

S-box design criteria can be defined using the information theory concept of mutual information. This approach was applied by Forre in [187] and Dawson and Tavares in [128]. They argued that the mutual information between inputs and outputs of S-boxes should be as small as possible. The study of the DES S-boxes gave rise to a new field called the S-box theory.

Davies [124] and Davio, Desmedt, Goubert, Hoornaert, and Quisquater [125] analyzed the concatenation of the P-box and bit-selection function E. Assume that the input to an S-box is *abcdef*. The following observations can be made [67]:

– Each S-box input bit comes from the output of a different S-box.
– No input bit to a given S-box comes from the output of the same S-box.
– An output from S_{i-1} goes to one of the *ef* input bits of S_i, and further via E an output from S_{i-2} goes to one of the *ab* input bits.
– An output of S_{i+1} goes to one of the *cd* inputs bits of S_i.
– For each S-box output, two bits go to *ab* or *ef* input bits, the other two go to *cd* input bits.

The above properties allow a quick diffusion of partial cryptograms between two consecutive rounds.

DES Key Scheduling. Each iteration uses a different 48-bit key k_i derived from the initial key k. Figure 3.11 illustrates how this is done. The initial key is input as a 64-bit block, with 8 parity bits in positions 8, 16, ..., 64. The permutation PC1 (permuted choice 1) discards the parity bits and transposes the remaining 56 bits as shown in Table 3.9. The result, PC1(k), is then split into halves C_0 and D_0 used to derive each partial key k_i. Subsequent values of (C_i, D_i) are calculated as follows:

$$C_i = LS_s(C_{i-1}),$$
$$D_i = LS_s(D_{i-1}),$$

where LS_s is a left circular shift by the number of positions shown in Table 3.10. Key k_i is then given by

$$k_i = PC2(C_i D_i),$$

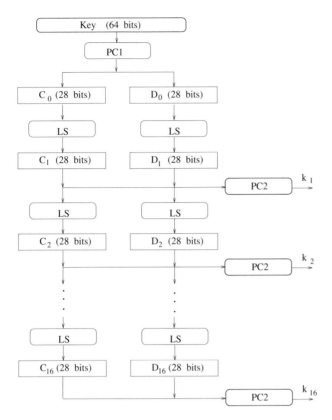

Fig. 3.11. DES key schedule

Table 3.9. Key permutation PC1

57	49	41	33	25	17	9
1	58	50	42	34	26	18
10	2	59	51	43	35	27
19	11	3	60	52	44	36
63	55	47	39	31	23	15
7	62	54	46	38	30	22
14	6	61	53	45	37	29
21	13	5	28	20	12	4

where PC2 is the permutation shown in Table 3.11.

The key schedule works well for most keys. However, if the key is $k = 01010101\ 01010101_x$, then all partial keys are $k_i = 0000000\ 0000000_x$ where the subscript x denotes a hexadecimal number. Note the key k has 8 parity bits

Table 3.10. Key schedule of left shifts LS_s

Iteration s	Iteration s
1	1	9	1
2	1	10	2
3	2	11	2
4	2	12	2
5	2	13	2
6	2	14	2
7	2	15	2
8	2	16	1

Table 3.11. Key permutation PC2

14	17	11	24	1	5
3	28	15	6	21	10
23	19	12	4	26	8
16	7	27	20	13	2
41	52	31	37	47	55
30	40	51	45	33	48
44	49	39	56	34	53
46	42	50	36	29	32

which are stripped off later in the key scheduling. In general, all keys whose partial keys are the same must be avoided. These keys are termed as *weak keys*. DES has 16 weak keys. There is also a class of *semiweak keys*. A key is called semiweak if the key scheduling scheme produces two different partial keys only (instead of 16).

3.2.4 DES Modes of Operation

Encryption and decryption are usually done for larger than 64-bit blocks of data. The method of processing a large number of 64-bit data blocks is called the *mode of operation*. There are several modes of operation, including the following four most common ones:

− *Electronic codebook mode (ECB)* − a data block m of arbitrary length is divided into 64-bit blocks $m_1, m_2, \ldots, m_\ell$. The last block, if it is shorter than 64 bits, needs to be padded to the full length of 64 bits. The DES algorithm

Encryption

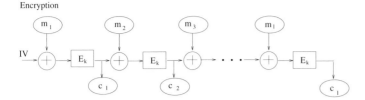

Decryption

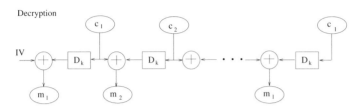

Fig. 3.12. CBC mode

is applied independently to each block using the same cryptographic key k, producing ciphertext

$$c = (c_1, \ldots, c_\ell) = (E_k(m_1), \ldots, E_k(m_\ell)).$$

The decryption in the ECB mode is

$$m = (m_1, \ldots, m_\ell) = (D_k(c_1), \ldots, D_k(c_\ell)).$$

As the blocks are independent, the receiver of ciphertext blocks is not able to determine the correct order of the blocks, or to detect duplicates or missing blocks.

– *Cipher block chaining mode (CBC)* – the initial vector IV needs to be known at both sides but does not need to be secret (Fig. 3.12). For encryption, cryptograms are created for the current message block and the previous cryptogram according to the following equation:

$$c_i = E_k(m_i \oplus c_{i-1}),$$

where $c_1 = E_k(m_1 \oplus IV)$ and $i = 2, \ldots, \ell$. The decryption process unravels the ciphertext

$$m_i = D_k(c_i) \oplus c_{i-1},$$

for $i = 2, \ldots, \ell$ and $m_1 = D_k(c_1) \oplus IV$.

– *Cipher feedback mode (CFB)* – in this mode cryptograms are equal to (Fig. 3.13)

Encryption

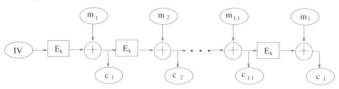

Decryption

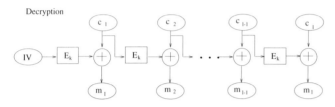

Fig. 3.13. CFB mode

$$c_i = m_i \oplus E_k(c_{i-1}),$$

where $c_1 = m_1 \oplus E_k(IV)$ and $i = 2, \ldots, \ell$. The decryption uses the E_k function as well, therefore

$$m_i = c_i \oplus E_k(c_{i-1}),$$

and the decryption D_k is never used. Note that the sequence $E_k(c_i)$ mimics a random key in the one-time pad system.

– *Output feedback mode (OFB)* – if the pseudorandom string $E_k(c_i)$ ($i = 1, \ldots, \ell$) in CFB is simplified to the string $E_k^i(IV)$, then this mode of operation becomes OFB, where $E_k^i = \underbrace{E_k \circ E_k \circ \ldots \circ E_k}_{i}$.

CBC and CFB modes are useful for message-integrity checking as any interference with the original contents of the transmission will generate, after the decryption, a number of meaningless messages. Assume that we have received a ciphertext sequence $(c_1, \ldots, c_{j-1}, c_j', c_{j+1}, \ldots)$ where the cryptogram c_j was modified (accidently or otherwise) during the transmission. For the both modes, the messages m_j and m_{j+1} cannot be recovered.

3.2.5 Triple DES

As soon as the DES algorithm was published, it was clear that the proposed cipher was intentionally weakened by the use of a relatively short 56-bit cryptographic key [153]. The exhaustive search of the key space is possible, as documented in [528].

To thwart the exhaustive search attack on the key space, the key length must be increased. Consider double DES encryption with two independent keys or $c = E_{k_1}(E_{k_2}(m))$ where k_1, k_2 are 56-bit independent keys. Clearly, the exhaustive search becomes infeasible as the key space contains now 2^{112} candidates. However, assume that the attacker knows a valid pair (m, c) obtained under the double DES. The attacker can produce two sets

$$\mathcal{E} = \{e = E_{k_1}(m) | k_1 \in \mathcal{K}\}$$

and

$$\mathcal{D} = \{d = E_{k_2}^{-1}(c) | k_2 \in \mathcal{K}\},$$

where $\mathcal{K}$ is the set of DES keys with 2^{56} elements, and $E_{k_2}^{-1}$ is the DES decryption for the key k_2. Observe that for the correct pair of keys partial encryption/decryption must be the same or $e = d$. This also means that the pair (m, c) allows the attacker to create 2^{56} possible pairs of keys among which there must be the correct one. This obviously reduces the exhaustive search to 2^{56} candidates which is far smaller than the expected 2^{112}. Needless to say, a second pair of (message, cryptogram) points out with a high probability the correct pair of keys.

This observation leads us to the conclusion that to expand the key space at least triple encryption (triple DES) must be applied. The following list shows possible implementations of the triple DES:

− $E_{k_1}(E_{k_2}(E_{k_3}(m)))$ – implementation with three independent keys, i.e., encryption is used three times (EEE triple DES).
− $E_{k_1}(E_{k_2}^{-1}(E_{k_3}(m)))$ – implementation with three independent keys, the encryption transformation uses the sequences encrypt, decrypt, and encrypt of DES (EDE triple DES).
− $E_{k_1}(E_{k_2}^{-1}(E_{k_1}(m)))$ – the triple encryption-decryption-encryption DES with two independent keys.

The triple DES with two independent keys is recommended in the ANSI X.9.17 and ISO 8732 standards for banking key management. The two-key triple DES is subject to a known-plaintext attack, as described in [393].

3.3 Modern Private-Key Cryptographic Algorithms

This section presents five cryptographic algorithms that are good examples of different approaches to the design of modern ciphers. The five algorithms are: FEAL, IDEA, RC6, Rijndael, and Serpent. The FEAL algorithm belongs to the DES family of ciphers with both S-boxes and key scheduling replaced by functions which can be run very fast. The IDEA algorithm uses a modified Feistel structure with cryptographic operations performed by carefully selected algebraic group operations. The RC6 algorithm again uses the Feistel structure with heavy use of word instructions (rotation, shifting, and bit-by-bit Boolean instructions). The Rijndael algorithm uses a S-P network with operations performed in $GF(2^8)$. The Serpent algorithm is another example of a S-P network with S-boxes derived from those used in DES with extensive use of word shift and rotation.

3.3.1 Fast Encryption Algorithm (FEAL)

FEAL is a Japanese encryption algorithm designed by researchers from NTT, Japan [468]. The main objective was to design an algorithm that would be as secure as DES but much faster. The FEAL algorithm processes 64-bit messages using a 64-bit key (Fig. 3.14). It applies four Feistel permutations (rounds) with the function f shown in Fig. 3.15. The function f uses two S-functions, S_0 and S_1, of the form

$$S_0(x, y) = ((x + y \bmod 256) \ll 2)$$
$$\text{and } S_1(x, y) = ((x + y + 1 \bmod 256) \ll 2)$$

where $(x \ll s)$ stands for rotation of the word x by s positions to the left. The key schedule applies another function f_k which is also based on Sf_0 and Sf_1 (Fig. 3.16).

In the literature the original FEAL is called FEAL-4 because it uses 4 rounds. There are also other versions with more rounds such as FEAL-8 or FEAL-32. The generic name FEAL-N refers to the FEAL with N rounds.

3.3.2 IDEA

IDEA stands for International Data Encryption Algorithm. The algorithm was designed by researchers from the Swiss Federal Institute of Technology in 1990

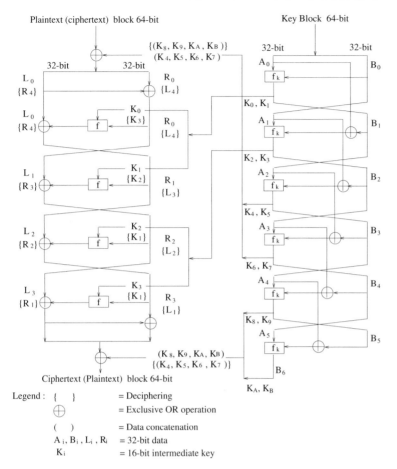

Fig. 3.14. FEAL algorithm

[294, 295]. The algorithm uses a modified Feistel structure with eight rounds and a message block size of 64-bits. Cryptographic keys are 128-bits long. All transformations used in the algorithm are based on the following three operations in $GF(2^{16})$:

- bit-by-bit XOR operation (denoted by $\oplus$),
- addition modulo 2^{16} (denoted by $\boxplus$),
- multiplication modulo $(2^n + 1)$ (denoted by $\odot$).

The algorithm applies an S-box which accepts two 16-bit input words and generates two 16-bit output words under the control of two 16-bit words of the round key. The S-box is called the multiplication-addition (MA) structure and

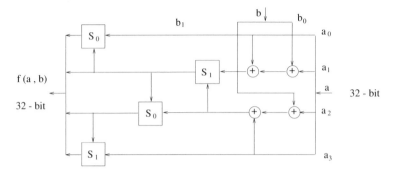

Fig. 3.15. Function f

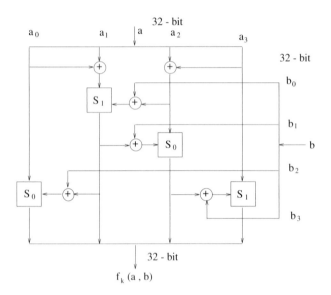

Fig. 3.16. Function f_k

is a permutation for a fixed key. The data flow during encryption is presented in Fig. 3.17. Encryption applies eight rounds followed by the final transformation. Each round takes a 64-bit input block (divided into four 16-bit words) and translates it into four output words using a 6-word round key. The first four words of the round key are mixed with the input words (using $\odot$ and $\boxplus$ operations) while the last two words control the MA structure that produces the output words (note the swap of the internal words of the output).

The key schedule takes the 128-bit primary key K and generates 6-word round keys for eight rounds plus 4 words for the output transformation (al-

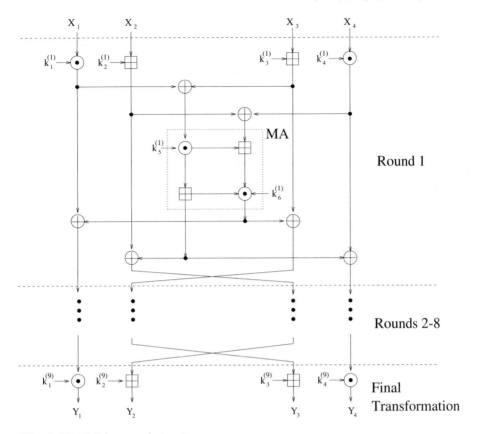

Fig. 3.17. IDEA general structure

together 52 16-bit words). The key generation runs according to the following steps:

- The primary key is divided into eight 16-bit words, so

$$K = (k_1^{(1)}, \ldots, k_6^{(1)}, k_1^{(2)}, k_2^{(2)}).$$

- The primary key is rotated 25 bits left and the result is divided into the next 8 words. This step is repeated until all 52 key words have been generated.

The decryption process uses the same algorithm with rounds performed in reverse order. Note that the S-box is invertible if the same keys are applied (for encryption and decryption). Wherever mixing operations $\odot$ are applied (keys $k_1^{(i)}, k_4^{(i)}$), the decryption uses their multiplicative inverses. On the other hand, if the addition $\boxplus$ is used, the additive inverse has to be used (keys $k_2^{(i)}, k_3^{(i)}$). Also observe that the multiplication $\odot$ is modified in such a way that the key

$k_i^{(j)} = 0$ has its inverse. This is done by assigning $k_i^{(j)} = 2^{16}$ whose inverse is 2^{16} modulo $2^{16} + 1$.

IDEA is a strong encryption algorithm. The only weakness reported so far is related to the existence of *weak keys*, i.e., a key is weak if it belongs to a set of keys in which membership can be efficiently tested [118, 235].

3.3.3 RC6

RC6 was designed by researchers from MIT and RSA Laboratories and submitted as a candidate for the AES competition. A description of the algorithm can be found at *http://www.nist.gov/aes*. RC6 is a strengthened version of the RC5 algorithm that maintains the efficiency of RC5. RC6 is in fact a family of encryption algorithms indexed by three parameters (w, r, b), where w is the size of the word (typically forced by the underlying hardware architecture), r is the number of rounds used (which specifies the tradeoff between efficiency and security), and b is the length of the primary cryptographic key K (in bytes).

The collection of operations used in RC6 includes

- Integer addition modulo 2^w denoted by $\boxplus$.
- Bit-by-bit XOR denoted by $\oplus$.
- Integer multiplication modulo 2^w denoted by $\otimes$. The function $f(a) = a \otimes (2a \boxplus 1)$.
- Rotation denoted by $a \lll b$. It rotates the word a to the left by the least-significant $\log_2 w$ bits of b. Similarly, $a \ggg b$ denotes rotation of the word a to the right by the least-significant $\log_2 w$ bits of b.

RC6 consists of r rounds, and all operations are performed on four words (A, B, C, D) each of w bits (Fig. 3.18). Encryption starts by adding keys $K[0]$ and $K[1]$ to words B and D, respectively. For each round the following operations are performed:

$$t = f(B) \lll \log w,$$
$$u = f(D) \lll \log w,$$
$$A = ((A \oplus t) \lll u) \boxplus K[2i],$$
$$C = ((C \oplus u) \lll t) \boxplus K[2i + 1].$$

The vector (A, B, C, D) is rotated so $(A, B, C, D) = (B, C, D, A)$. After r rounds, the cryptogram is $(A \boxplus K[2r + 2], B, C \boxplus K[2r + 3], D)$.

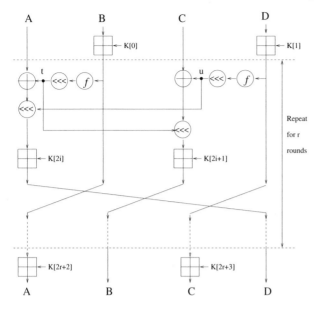

Fig. 3.18. Encryption in RC6

The RC6 key schedule generates $2r + 4$ words (keys $K[0], \ldots, K[2r + 3]$) from the primary key K of b bytes. First, a sufficiently large array L of c words is allocated so it can hold the key K. Next, the key K is stored in L and the unused bits of the last word are filled by zeros. So the first word $L[0]$ contains the first bytes of the key, and the last word $L[c-1]$ contains the tail of the key padded with zeros to the full size of the word. The key schedule uses two *magic constants* P_w and Q_w. P_w is a word derived from the constant e, the base of the natural logarithm, while the word Q_w is obtained from binary expansion of the Golden Ratio constant. For instance, for $w = 32$, the words $P_{32} =$0xB7E15163 and $Q_{32} =$0x9E3779B9. Keys $K[i]$ are first initialized

$$K[0] = P_w \text{ and } K[i] = K[i-1] \boxplus Q_w,$$

for $i = 1, \ldots, 2r + 3$. Next the four variables A, B, i, j are set to zero and the constant $v = 3 \max (c, 2r + 4)$ is computed. Round keys are calculated by repeating the following sequence of operations v times:

$$A = K[i] = (K[i] \boxplus A \boxplus B) \lll 3,$$
$$B = L[j] = (L[j] \boxplus A \boxplus B) \lll (A \boxplus B),$$
$$i = (i+1) \pmod{2r + 4},$$
$$j = (j+1) \pmod c.$$

Decryption follows the footsteps of encryption in reverse and applies the additive inverse of the keys. Each round starts from rotation $(A, B, C, D) = (D, A, B, C)$ and

$$t = f(B) \lll \log w,$$
$$u = f(D) \lll \log w,$$
$$A = ((A \boxplus (-K[2i])) \ggg u) \oplus t,$$
$$C = ((C \boxplus (-K[2i+1])) \ggg t) \oplus u.$$

There is little literature on the cryptographic strength of RC6, but the fact that it went through to the second round of the AES call indicates its quality (for more details go to *http://www.nist.gov/aes*). Some conclusions about its security can be derived from analysis done for RC5. For instance, Knudsen and Meier [281] demonstrated the existence of weak keys with respect to differential cryptanalysis and showed some weaknesses in the structure of the cipher.

3.3.4 Rijndael

The Rijndael cipher was the winner of the AES competition and was designed by researchers from Belgium [119]. Its description is taken from the NIST website *http://www.nist.gov/aes*. The cipher works for three block sizes: 128, 192, and 256 bits. Rijndael applies the Shannon product cipher concept and is not based on the Feistel structure. Cryptographic operations are based on arithmetic in $GF(2^8)$.

Denote N_b and N_k as the number of 32-bit words in the message (cryptogram) and the key, respectively. The cipher uses a sequence of rounds, which varies depending on the length of the message and key:

- If $N_b = N_k = 4$, the number of rounds is $N_r = 10$.
- If both $N_b \leq 6$ and $N_k \leq 6$ but not simultaneously equal to 4, $N_r = 12$.
- Otherwise, $N_r = 14$.

The cipher applies the following transformations:

- ByteSub – an input block with $4N_b$ bytes is subject to a byte-by-byte transformation using the S-box.
- ShiftRow – the bytes of the input are arranged into four rows and every row is rotated a fixed number of positions.
- MixColumn – the bytes of the input are arranged into four rows and every column is transformed using polynomial multiplication over $GF(2^8)$.

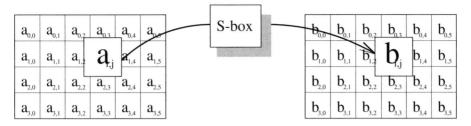

Fig. 3.19. ByteSub transformation

– AddRoundKey – the input block is XOR-ed with the round key.

The ByteSub transformation (Fig. 3.19) takes an input $A = (a_{0,0}, \ldots, a_{0,N_b-1}, \ldots, a_{3,0}, \ldots, a_{3,N_b-1})$ and outputs $B = (b_{0,0}, \ldots, b_{0,N_b-1}, \ldots, b_{3,0}, \ldots, b_{3,N_b-1})$ such that $b_{i,j} = S(a_{i,j})$ for $i = 0, 1, 2, 3$ and $j = 0, \ldots, N_{b-1}$. $S(x)$ is the S-box (permutation) described as follows:

$$
S(x) = \begin{bmatrix}
10001111 \\
11000111 \\
11100011 \\
11110001 \\
11111000 \\
01111100 \\
00111110 \\
00011111
\end{bmatrix} x^{-1} + \begin{bmatrix}
1 \\
1 \\
0 \\
0 \\
0 \\
1 \\
1 \\
0
\end{bmatrix},
$$

where $x^{-1} \in GF(2^8)$ is the multiplicative inverse of x if $x \neq 0$ or zero if $x = 0$ (Fig. 3.20). Note that the affine transformation $L(x) = S(x^{-1})$. The S-box

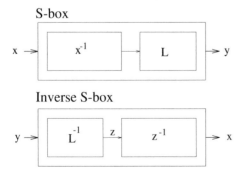

Fig. 3.20. S-box in Rijndael

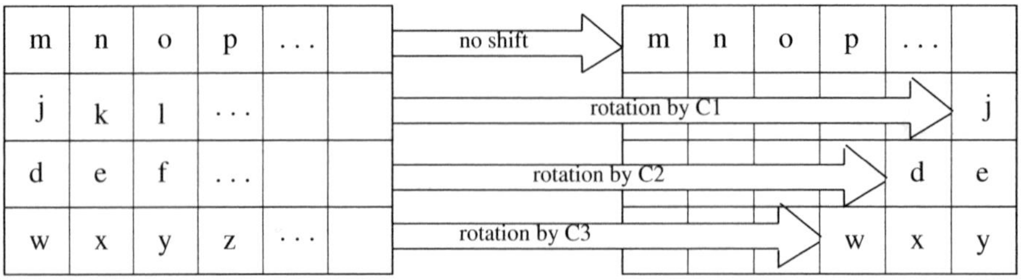

m	n	o	p	...
j	k	l	...	
d	e	f	...	
w	x	y	z	...

no shift → | m | n | o | p | ... |

rotation by C1 → | j |

rotation by C2 → | d | e |

rotation by C3 → | w | x | y |

Fig. 3.21. ShiftRow transformation

outputs an element from $GF(2^8)$. Note that for decryption $S^{-1}(x)$ must be used. In this case, the inverse affine transformation is used followed by finding the multiplicative inverse in $GF(2^8)$.

The ShiftRow transformation (Fig. 3.21) takes the input

$$a_0 = (a_{0,0}, \ldots, a_{0,N_b-1}),$$
$$a_1 = (a_{1,0}, \ldots, a_{1,N_b-1}),$$
$$a_2 = (a_{2,0}, \ldots, a_{2,N_b-1}),$$
$$a_3 = (a_{3,0}, \ldots, a_{3,N_b-1}),$$

and returns $a_0 \ggg C_0, a_1 \ggg C_1, a_2 \ggg C_2, a_3 \ggg C_3$ where $a \ggg C$ is the rotation of the sequence a of bytes to the right by C bytes. The values of C_i are given below:

$$C_0 = 0, \quad C_1 = 1, \quad C_2 = \begin{cases} 2 & \text{if } N_b = 4, 6 \\ 3 & \text{otherwise} \end{cases}, \quad \text{and} \quad C_3 = \begin{cases} 3 & \text{if } N_b = 4, 6 \\ 4 & \text{otherwise} \end{cases}.$$

In decryption mode, ShiftRow rotates the corresponding sequence of bytes the same number of positions but to the left.

The MixColumn transformation (Fig. 3.22) takes the input

$$a_0 = (a_{0,0}, \ldots, a_{0,N_b-1}),$$
$$a_1 = (a_{1,0}, \ldots, a_{1,N_b-1}),$$
$$a_2 = (a_{2,0}, \ldots, a_{2,N_b-1}),$$
$$a_3 = (a_{3,0}, \ldots, a_{3,N_b-1}),$$

creates N_b polynomials $A_j(x) = a_{3,j}x^3 + a_{2,j}x^2 + a_{1,j}x + a_{0,j}$, $j = 0, \ldots, N_b-1$, and multiplies $A_j(x)$ by the polynomial $C(x) = c_3x^3 + c_2x^2 + c_1x + c_0$, where $c_3 = \text{0x03}$, $c_2 = \text{0x01}$, $c_1 = \text{0x01}$, and $c_0 = \text{0x02}$ (all polynomials are over $GF(2^8)$). MixColumn returns $B_j = b_{3,j}x^3 + b_{2,j}x^2 + b_{1,j}x + b_{0,j}$ such that $B_j(x) = A_j(x) \times C(x)$, where

$$b_0 = (b_{0,0}, \ldots, b_{0,N_b-1}),$$
$$b_1 = (b_{1,0}, \ldots, b_{1,N_b-1}),$$
$$b_2 = (b_{2,0}, \ldots, b_{2,N_b-1}),$$
$$b_3 = (b_{3,0}, \ldots, b_{3,N_b-1}).$$

In the decryption mode, `MixColumn` multiplies the respective columns by the inverse $D(x) = C(x)^{-1}$ or $D(x) \times C(x) = 1 \in GF(2^8)$.

The key schedule procedure `KeyExpansion` produces key material $W = (W_0, \ldots, W_{N_b(N_r+1)-1})$ from the primary key $K = (K_0, \ldots, K_{N_k-1})$ where W_i, K_i are 32-bit words. It applies two functions:

– `SubByte`(a, b, c, d) that accepts four bytes and returns $(S(a), S(b), S(c), S(d))$,
– `RotByte`$(a, b, c, d) = (b, c, d, a)$ that rotates bytes.

`KeyExpansion` has two versions: one for $N_k \leq 6$ and the other for $N_k > 6$. The first version (for $N_k \leq 6$) takes two phases:

– Initialization where $W_i = K_i$ for $i = 0, \ldots, N_K - 1$.
– Expansion phase which takes the last computed word and extends it for the next one. The steps are as follows:

$$\text{tmp} = W_{i-1},$$
if $i \pmod{N_k} = 0$, then tmp=`SubByte`(`RotByte`(tmp))$\oplus$ `Rcon`$_{\lfloor i/N_k \rfloor}$,
$$W_i = W_{i-N_k} \oplus \text{tmp},$$

where the constants `Rcon`$_i = (RC_i, 0, 0, 0)$ and $RC_i = RC_{i-1} = x^{i-1}$ where x is an element of $GF(2^8)$.

The second version (for $N_k > 6$) takes two phases:

– Initialization where $W_i = K_i$ for $i = 0, \ldots, N_K - 1$.

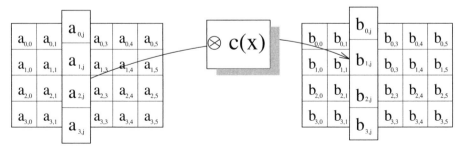

Fig. 3.22. `MixColumn` transformation

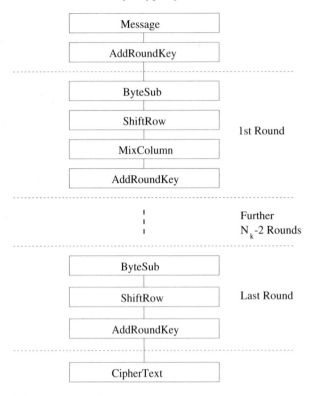

Fig. 3.23. Rijndæl encryption

– Expansion phase which takes the last computed word and extends it for the next one. The steps are as follows:

$\text{tmp} = W_{i-1},$
if $i \pmod{N} = 0$, then $\text{tmp}=\texttt{SubByte}(\texttt{RotByte}(\text{tmp})) \oplus \texttt{Rcon}_{\lfloor i/N_k \rfloor},$
else if $i \pmod{N_k} = 4$ then $\text{tmp}=\texttt{SubByte}(\text{tmp}),$
$W_i = W_{i-N_k} \oplus \text{tmp}.$

The encryption process is illustrated in Fig. 3.23. Clearly, decryption employs inverse transformation in the reverse order.

The Rijndæl algorithm is the new Advanced Encryption Standard and it is going to be scrutinized in a way similar to the DES algorithm before. It remains to be seen whether the balance between security and efficiency is right and whether Rijndæl survives the test of time. The algorithm is immune against linear and differential attacks (Sect. 3.4). The best-known attacks reported in [177] are based on the Square attack. For instance, 6-round Rijndæl is breakable in a time proportional to 2^{44} with 2^{32} chosen plaintexts. An attack on 7-round Rijndael takes 2^{120} steps and $2^{128} - 2^{119}$ chosen plaintexts. An attack on the 256-bit Rijndael with eight rounds requires 2^{204} steps and $2^{128} - 2^{119}$ chosen plaintexts.

The Rijndael algorithm has a nice algebraic structure. The relation between the input and output can be expressed as a system of polynomials over $GF(2^8)$ or a single polynomial over a proper Galois field. It is also interesting to note that the structure can be equivalently represented as a system of quadratic equations over $GF(2)$. The algebraic representation of Rijndael provides a mathematical model in which attacks can be converted into their equivalent problems of solving systems of equations.

3.3.5 Serpent

The Serpent cipher was an AES submission from an international team (UK, Israel, and Norway). A description of the cipher can be found at the AES website *http://www.nist.gov/aes*. A very first version of the algorithm called Serpent-0 was presented at the Fast Software Encryption Workshop in 1998 [32].

Serpent handles 128-bit messages and cryptograms using a cryptographic key which can be either 128-, 192-, or 256-bits long. It implements a Shannon S-P network. The basic cryptographic operations are:

- S-boxes – there are 8 different S-boxes, $S_0, \ldots, S_7$. Each S-box is a permutation mapping 4-bit input into 4-bit output. The ith round applies 32 copies of the same S-box $S_{i \bmod 8}$, $i = 0, \ldots, 7$.
- Linear transformation L – it takes four 32-bit words, X_0, X_1, X_2, X_3, and performs the following operations:

$$X_0 = X_0 \lll 13,$$
$$X_2 = X_2 \lll 3,$$
$$X_1 = X_1 \oplus X_0 \oplus X_2,$$
$$X_3 = X_3 \oplus X_2 \oplus (X_0 \ll 3),$$
$$X_1 = X_1 \lll 1,$$
$$X_3 = X_3 \lll 7,$$
$$X_0 = X_0 \oplus X_1 \oplus X_3,$$
$$X_2 = X_2 \oplus X_3 \oplus (X_1 \ll 7),$$

$$X_0 = X_0 \lll 5,$$
$$X_2 = X_2 \lll 22,$$

and returns X_0, X_1, X_2, X_3, where $X \lll s$ stands for rotation of X by s bits to the left and $X \ll s$ means left shift of X by s bits.

The S-boxes used in Serpent have the following properties:

1. Probabilities of differential characteristics are smaller than $1/4$ and a 1-bit difference never translates into a 1-bit output difference (for definitions of differential characteristics see Sect. 3.4).
2. Probabilities of linear characteristics are within the range $0.5 \pm 1/4$ and the correlations between pairs of input/output bits are expressed by probabilities in the range $0.5 \pm 1/8$ (for definitions of linear characteristics see Sect. 3.5).
3. The nonlinearity of the output bits is a maximum (see Sect. 3.5).

The designers of Serpent intended to convince potential users that the S-boxes used in the algorithm had no hidden trapdoors. The S-boxes can be obtained using a simple procedure that first takes a subset of permutations from the DES S-boxes and next modifies them so the resulting permutations (S-boxes) have "good" differential and linear properties. The procedure uses an array sbox[][] with 32 rows and 16 columns. The rows of the array are initialized by 32 permutations from the DES S-boxes. An array serpent[] with 16 4-bit entries is used to point out the entry of sbox[][] which is chosen for modification. The array serpent[] is initialized to the least-significant four bits of each of 16 ASCII characters in the string sboxesforserpent. The following procedure is used to generate the necessary eight S-boxes:

```
index=0
repeat
  currentsbox=index mod 32
  for i=0 to 15 do
    j=sbox[(currentsbox+1)mod32][serpent[i]]
    swapentries(sbox[currentsbox][i],sbox[currentsbox][j])
  if sbox[currentsbox][] has the desired properties, save it
  index=index+1
until eight S-boxes have been saved
```

Table 3.12. Serpent S-boxes

S_0	3	8	15	1	10	6	5	11	14	13	4	2	7	0	9	12
S_1	15	12	2	7	9	0	5	10	1	11	14	8	6	13	3	4
S_2	8	6	7	9	3	12	10	15	13	1	14	4	0	11	5	2
S_3	0	15	11	8	12	9	6	3	13	1	2	4	10	7	5	14
S_4	1	15	8	3	12	0	11	6	2	5	4	10	9	14	7	13
S_5	15	5	2	11	4	10	9	12	0	3	14	8	13	6	7	1
S_6	7	2	12	5	8	4	6	11	14	9	1	15	13	3	10	0
S_7	1	13	15	0	14	8	2	11	7	4	12	10	9	3	5	6

The modification of S-boxes is based on swapping entries of the row indexed by the `currentsbox` index. S-boxes obtained according to the prescription described above are shown in Table 3.12.

The encryption begins with an initial permutation (IP), runs through 32 rounds and concludes with the final permutation (FP) which is the inverse of IP (Fig. 3.24). The input to the ith round is first XORed with the round key K_i and next put into inputs of 32 copies of the same S-box (one of the eight generated from DES S-boxes), $i = 0, \ldots, 30$. The outputs are transformed by the linear transformation L. The last (32nd) round replaces L by XOR of the key K_{32}.

There are eight S-boxes only so the execution of 32 rounds requires that the same S-box is used in four rounds. The S-box S_i is used in rounds $i, 8 + i, 16 + i, 24 + i$ for $i = 0, \ldots, 7$. The decryption requires that the inverse operations (including inverse S-boxes) have to be used in reverse order.

Key scheduling is used to produce the 33 128-bit subkeys used. As we have already mentioned, the main key is expanded to the 256-bit primary key K. Denote the key K as a sequence of eight 32-bit words $K = (w_{-8}, \ldots, w_{-1})$. The necessary key material is generated word by word according to the following equation:

$$w_i = (w_{i-8} \oplus w_{i-5} \oplus w_{i-1} \oplus \phi \oplus i) \lll 11,$$

where ϕ is part of the decimal extension of the Golden Ratio ($\phi = $0x9e3779b9), $i = 0, \ldots, 131$. The words of round keys are computed using consecutive 4-word pieces $(w_{4i}, w_{4i+1}, w_{4i+2}, w_{4i+3})$ for $i = 1, 2, \ldots, 32$:

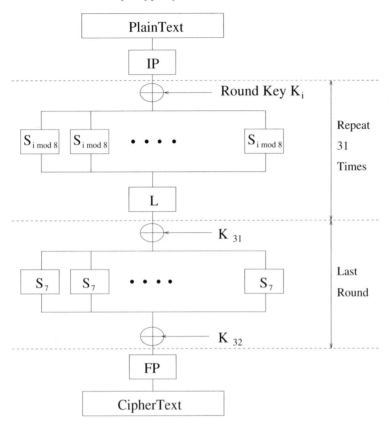

Fig. 3.24. Serpent encryption

$$K_0 = (k_0, k_1, k_2, k_3) = S_3(w_0, w_1, w_2, w_3),$$
$$K_1 = (k_4, k_5, k_6, k_7) = S_2(w_4, w_5, w_6, w_7),$$
$$K_2 = (k_8, k_9, k_{10}, k_{11}) = S_1(w_8, w_9, w_{10}, w_{11}),$$
$$K_3 = (k_{12}, k_{13}, k_{14}, k_{15}) = S_0(w_{12}, w_{13}, w_{14}, w_{15}),$$
$$K_4 = (k_{16}, k_{17}, k_{18}, k_{19}) = S_7(w_{16}, w_{17}, w_{18}, w_{19}),$$
$$\vdots$$
$$K_{31} = (k_{124}, k_{125}, k_{126}, k_{127}) = S_4(w_{124}, w_{125}, w_{126}, w_{127}),$$
$$K_{32} = (k_{128}, k_{129}, k_{130}, k_{131}) = S_3(w_{128}, w_{129}, w_{130}, w_{131}).$$

The Serpent cipher was one of the five finalists chosen in the second round of the AES call. The 32-round Serpent is a strong cipher, and standard attacks based on linear and differential cryptanalysis are not better than the exhaustive attack. Even significantly reduced versions of Serpent preserve their cryptographic strength well. Following the results in [285], 6-round Serpent can be attacked using differential cryptanalysis with 2^{83} chosen plaintexts and 2^{90} trail encryptions. The 256-bit Serpent with nine rounds can be broken after 2^{252} trail encryptions and with 2^{110} chosen plaintexts using the Amplified Boomerang Technique.

3.3.6 Other Ciphers

The LOKI algorithm was designed in Australia. The first version called LOKI'89 was published at the AUSCRYPT'90 conference [69]. The revised version LOKI'91 can be found in the proceedings of the ASIACRYPT'91 conference [68]. Interestingly enough, LOKI applies many copies of a single S-box which is based on cubing in $GF(2^8)$.

The GOST algorithm is a Russian cipher [384] with a Feistel structure. It applies eight S-boxes which are permutations of 4-bit integers. The details of the S-boxes, however, are left unspecified suggesting that the algorithm was designed to encourage users to apply for S-boxes to the central authority. Note that the central authority could choose weak S-boxes on purpose to be able to read encrypted data. This looks like the Russian version of key escrowing.

The 2nd-round finalists of the AES call were RC6, Rijndael, Serpent, MARS, and Twofish. We have described the first three. Now let us briefly discuss the remaining two.

The MARS algorithm is an IBM cipher (see *http://www.nist.gov/aes*). The designers differentiated between internal rounds and external ones (also called "wrapper layers"). The internal rounds are seen as "the core" of the algorithm (provide mostly confusion) while external ones use noncryptographic mixing (diffusion).

The Twofish algorithm was an AES candidate designed by a team of researchers from Counterpane Systems, Hi/fn, Inc., and the University of California, Berkeley. It is a Feistel cipher with 16 uniform rounds. The round function $F : \Sigma^{64} \to \Sigma^{64}$ consists of two copies of the function $g : \Sigma^{32} \to \Sigma^{32}$. The function g is built using four 8-bit S-boxes. Each S-box is a permutation controlled by a cryptographic key. The outputs from the four S-boxes are mixed using maximum-distance separable code. The outputs from the two copies of g are combined using modular addition.

3.4 Differential Cryptanalysis

Private-key cryptographic algorithms can be subject to the following general attacks:

- *Ciphertext-only attack* – the cryptanalysts know the cryptograms only. They know $E_k(m_1)$, $E_k(m_2)$, ..., $E_k(m_\ell)$ and want to find out either the key k or one or more messages m_i for some $i = 1, \ldots, \ell$. This attack takes place if the cryptanalyst is able to eavesdrop the communication channel.
- *Known-plaintext attack* – the adversary has access to a collection of pairs $\{(m_i, E_k(m_i)) \mid i = 1, \ldots, \ell\}$ and wants to determine the key k or to decrypt a cryptogram $E_k(m_{\ell+1})$ not included in the collection. The adversary in this attack can not only eavesdrop the communication channel but also can, in some way, access a part of the plaintext. This happens if, for example, messages have a predictable structure so the attacker knows or can guess that the header of the plaintext starts from "How are you?" or "Dear Sir/Madam" and ends with "Sincerely yours."
- *Chosen-plaintext attack* – this is a known-plaintext attack for which the cryptanalyst may choose messages and read the corresponding cryptograms. This scenario may happen if the encryption equipment is left without supervision for some time, and the attackers can play with it assuming they cannot access the key.
- *Chosen-ciphertext attack* – the enemy can select their own cryptograms and observe the corresponding messages for them. The aim of the enemy is to find out the secret key or encrypt a new message into the valid cryptogram. This attack may happen if the decryption equipment is left unsupervised and the attacker can try different cryptograms (assuming that the equipment is tamper-proof, the attacker cannot access the secret key).

Biham and Shamir invented differential cryptanalysis in 1990 [33, 35]. This is a chosen-plaintext attack which is not only applicable for encryption algorithms but also can be used for other cryptographic algorithms including hashing.

3.4.1 XOR Profiles

The basic tool used in the analysis is a table which shows differences between the input and output of S-boxes. This table is further referred to as the *XOR profile* of an S-box. Assume that we have an S-box that transforms input strings according to the following function

$$f : \Sigma^n \to \Sigma^m.$$

For a given pair of input strings (s_1, s_2), the S-box generates outputs $s_1^* = f(s_1)$ and $s_2^* = f(s_2)$. The pair of input/output tuples $\{(s_1, s_1^*), (s_2, s_2^*)\}$ is characterized by the input and output XOR differences $\delta = s_1 \oplus s_2$ and $\Delta = s_1^* \oplus s_2^*$. Denote

$$\mathcal{S}_\Delta^\delta = \{(s_1, s_2; s_1^*, s_2^*) \mid s_1 \oplus s_2 = \delta, s_1^* \oplus s_2^* = \Delta;$$
$$s_1, s_2 \in \Sigma^n, s_1^*, s_2^* \in \Sigma^m, s_1^* = f(s_1), s_2^* = f(s_2)\},$$

the set consists of elements (4-tuple) whose δ and Δ are fixed. For instance, the set $\mathcal{S}_{2_x}^{3C_x} = \{(3_x, 3F_x; F_x, D_x), (17_x, 2B_x; B_x, 9_x), (2B_x, 17_x; 9_x, B_x), (3F_x, 3_x; D_x, F_x)\}$ is computed for S_1 of DES. It means that there are four elements in the set. Note that there are actually two different elements as only the remaining two are permutations of their inputs and outputs. That is why the cardinality of $\mathcal{S}_\Delta^\delta$ is always an even number. There are also some δ and Δ for which the set $\mathcal{S}_\Delta^\delta$ is empty. Indeed, any set $\mathcal{S}_\Delta^{0_x}$ for $\Delta \neq 0$ is empty. This happens because any 4-tuple for two identical inputs is of the form $(x_i, x_i; y_i, y_i)$ and the corresponding Δ must be zero. The number of 4-tuples in $\mathcal{S}_{0_x}^{0_x}$ is equal to 2^n.

Definition 2. *The XOR profile of an S-box defined by $f : \Sigma^n \to \Sigma^m$ is a table which has 2^n rows and 2^m columns. Each row and column is indexed by δ and Δ, respectively. Each entry (δ, Δ) of the table shows the number of elements in the set $\mathcal{S}_\Delta^\delta$.*

The XOR profile of the DES S_1 is presented in Table 3.13. For the full collection of XOR profiles of other DES S-boxes, the reader is referred to [35]. For the rest of this section we will use S_1 of DES in our examples.

The properties of XOR profiles can be summarized as follows:

− All entries in the table are zeros or positive even integers.

Table 3.13. XOR profile of DES S_1

	Output XOR - Δ															
δ	0_x	1_x	2_x	3_x	4_x	5_x	6_x	7_x	8_x	9_x	A_x	B_x	C_x	D_x	E_x	F_x
0_x	64	0	0	0	0	0	0	0	0	0	0	0	0	0	0	0
1_x	0	0	0	6	0	2	4	4	0	10	12	4	10	6	2	4
2_x	0	0	0	8	0	4	4	4	0	6	8	6	12	6	4	2
3_x	14	4	2	2	10	6	4	2	6	4	4	0	2	2	2	0
4_x	0	0	0	6	0	10	10	6	0	4	6	4	2	8	6	2
5_x	4	8	6	2	2	4	4	2	0	4	4	0	12	2	4	6
6_x	0	4	2	4	8	2	6	2	8	4	4	2	4	2	0	12
7_x	2	4	10	4	0	4	8	4	2	4	8	2	2	2	4	4
8_x	0	0	0	12	0	8	8	4	0	6	2	8	8	2	2	4
9_x	10	2	4	0	2	4	6	0	2	2	8	0	10	0	2	12
A_x	0	8	6	2	2	8	6	0	6	4	6	0	4	0	2	10
B_x	2	4	0	10	2	2	4	0	2	6	2	6	6	4	2	12
C_x	0	0	0	8	0	6	6	0	0	6	6	4	6	6	14	2
D_x	6	6	4	8	4	8	2	6	0	6	4	6	0	2	0	2
E_x	0	4	8	8	6	6	4	0	6	6	4	0	0	4	0	8
F_x	2	0	2	4	4	6	4	2	4	8	2	2	2	6	8	8
10_x	0	0	0	0	0	0	2	14	0	6	6	12	4	6	8	6
11_x	6	8	2	4	6	4	8	6	4	0	6	6	0	4	0	0
12_x	0	8	4	2	6	6	4	6	6	4	2	6	6	0	4	0
13_x	2	4	4	6	2	0	4	6	2	0	6	8	4	6	4	6
14_x	0	8	8	0	10	0	4	2	8	2	2	4	4	8	4	0
15_x	0	4	6	4	2	2	4	10	6	2	0	10	0	4	6	4
16_x	0	8	10	8	0	2	2	6	10	2	0	2	0	6	2	6
17_x	4	4	6	0	10	6	0	2	4	4	4	6	6	6	2	0
18_x	0	6	6	0	8	4	2	2	2	4	6	8	6	6	2	2
19_x	2	6	2	4	0	8	4	6	10	4	0	4	2	8	4	0
$1A_x$	0	6	4	0	4	6	6	6	6	2	2	0	4	4	6	8
$1B_x$	4	4	2	4	10	6	6	4	6	2	2	4	2	2	4	2
$1C_x$	0	10	10	6	6	0	0	12	6	4	0	0	2	4	4	0
$1D_x$	4	2	4	0	8	0	0	2	10	0	2	6	6	6	14	0
$1E_x$	0	2	6	0	14	2	0	0	6	4	10	8	2	2	6	2
$1F_x$	2	4	10	6	2	2	2	8	6	8	0	0	0	4	6	4
20_x	0	0	0	10	0	12	8	2	0	6	4	4	4	2	0	12
21_x	0	4	2	4	4	8	10	0	4	4	10	0	4	0	2	8
22_x	10	4	6	2	2	8	2	2	2	2	6	0	4	0	4	10
23_x	0	4	4	8	0	2	6	0	6	6	2	10	2	4	0	10
24_x	12	0	0	2	2	2	2	0	14	14	2	0	2	6	2	4
25_x	6	4	4	12	4	4	4	10	2	2	2	0	4	2	2	2
26_x	0	0	4	10	10	10	2	4	0	4	6	4	4	4	2	0
27_x	10	4	2	0	2	4	2	0	4	8	0	4	8	8	4	4
28_x	12	2	2	8	2	6	12	0	0	2	6	0	4	0	6	2
29_x	4	2	2	10	0	2	4	0	0	14	10	2	4	6	0	4
$2A_x$	4	2	4	6	0	2	8	2	2	14	2	6	2	6	2	2
$2B_x$	12	2	2	2	4	6	6	2	0	2	6	2	6	0	8	4
$2C_x$	4	2	2	4	0	2	10	4	2	2	4	8	8	4	2	6
$2D_x$	6	2	6	2	8	4	4	4	2	4	6	0	8	2	0	6
$2E_x$	6	6	2	2	0	2	4	6	4	0	6	2	12	2	6	4
$2F_x$	2	2	2	2	2	6	8	8	2	4	4	6	8	2	4	2
30_x	0	4	6	0	12	6	2	2	8	2	4	4	6	2	2	4
31_x	4	8	2	10	2	2	2	2	6	0	0	2	2	4	10	8
32_x	4	2	6	4	4	2	2	4	6	6	4	8	2	2	8	0
33_x	4	4	6	2	10	8	4	2	4	0	2	2	4	6	2	4
34_x	0	8	16	6	2	0	0	12	6	0	0	0	0	8	0	6

Table 3.13. (continued)

								Output XOR - Δ								
δ	0_x	1_x	2_x	3_x	4_x	5_x	6_x	7_x	8_x	9_x	A_x	B_x	C_x	D_x	E_x	F_x
35_x	2	2	4	0	8	0	0	0	14	4	6	8	0	2	14	0
36_x	2	6	2	2	8	0	2	2	4	2	6	8	6	4	10	0
37_x	2	2	12	4	2	4	4	10	4	4	2	6	0	2	2	4
38_x	0	6	2	2	2	0	2	2	4	6	4	4	4	6	10	10
39_x	6	2	2	4	12	6	4	8	4	0	2	4	2	4	4	0
$3A_x$	6	4	6	4	6	8	0	6	2	2	6	2	2	6	4	0
$3B_x$	2	6	4	0	0	2	4	6	4	6	8	6	4	4	6	2
$3C_x$	0	10	4	0	12	0	4	2	6	0	4	12	4	4	2	0
$3D_x$	0	8	6	2	2	6	0	8	4	4	0	4	0	12	4	4
$3E_x$	4	8	2	2	2	4	4	14	4	2	0	2	0	8	4	4
$3F_x$	4	8	4	2	4	0	2	4	4	2	4	8	8	6	2	2

– The row for $\delta = 0$ has only one nonzero entry equal to 2^n (n is the number of input bits of the S-box).
– The sum of entries in each row is equal to 2^n.
– An input difference δ may cause an output difference Δ with probability $p = \frac{\alpha}{2^n}$ where α is the entry of (δ, Δ). In other words, α is the number of input pairs $(s_1, s_1 \oplus \delta)$ such that the corresponding output difference is Δ, where $s_1 \in \Sigma^n$. This is denoted as $\delta \rightarrow \Delta$.
– If an entry (δ, Δ) is zero, then the input difference δ cannot cause the difference Δ on the output.

Suppose both δ and Δ are known. What can be said about actual values of the input? Obviously, the input must occur in some tuples from $\mathcal{S}_\Delta^\delta$. For example, the set $\mathcal{S}_{2_x}^{3C_x}$ computed for S_1 of DES contains four inputs $s \in \{3_x, 3F_x, 17_x, 2B_x\}$. Consider the DES S_1 with a 6-bit partial key k XORed to the input (Fig. 3.25). The XOR profile of S_1 with the key is identical to the XOR profile of the original S-box. This results from the fact that $(s_1 \oplus k) \oplus (s_2 \oplus k) = s_1 \oplus s_2$. The differential attack is based on this observation and exploits the fact that the XOR profile does not depend on the cryptographic key used.

Now assume that the values s_1, s_2 and Δ are known. What can we say about the key? First, observe that both $s_1 \oplus k$ and $s_2 \oplus k$ must occur in $\mathcal{S}_\Delta^\delta$, where $\delta = s_1 \oplus s_2$. So we can extract all input values from the set $\mathcal{S}_\Delta^\delta$. Let the set of the inputs be $\mathcal{X} = \{s_{i_1}, \ldots, s_{i_j}\}$ where $j = |\mathcal{S}_\Delta^\delta|$. Then the key k must belong to the set $\mathcal{K} = \mathcal{X} \oplus s_1 = \mathcal{X} \oplus s_2 = \{s_{i_1} \oplus s_1, \ldots, s_{i_j} \oplus s_1\} = \{s_{i_1} \oplus s_2, \ldots, s_{i_j} \oplus s_2\}$.

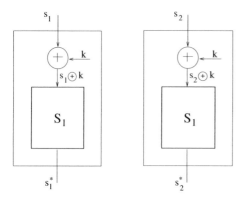

Fig. 3.25. Differential analysis of S_1

Consider an example. Let an input $(s_1, s_2) = (21_x, 38_x)$ have the output difference $\Delta = 1_x$. The set

$$S_{1_x}^{19_x} = \{(2_x, 1B_x; 4_x, 5_x), \ (1B_x, 2_x; 5_x, 4_x),$$
$$(22_x, 3B_x; 1_x, 0_x), \ (2C_x, 35_x; 2_x, 3_x),$$
$$(35_x, 2C_x; 3_x, 2_x), \ (3B_x, 22_x; 0_x, 1_x)\}.$$

The collection of all inputs is $\mathcal{X} = \{2_x, 1B_x, 22_x, 3B_x, 2C_x, 35_x\}$. The applied key must be in the set $\mathcal{K}_1 = \mathcal{X} \oplus s_1 = \mathcal{X} \oplus s_2 = \{23_x, 3A_x, 3_x, 1A_x, D_x, 14_x\}$. If the second observation is done for the input $(s_1, s_2) = (14, 23)$, and $\Delta = 2_x$, the set $S_{2_x}^{37_x}$ has 12 elements and is equal to

$$S_{2_x}^{37_x} = \{(E_x, 39_x; 8_x, A_x), \ (F_x, 38_x; 1_x, 3_x),$$
$$(11_x, 26_x; A_x, 8_x), \ (12_x, 25_x; A_x, 8_x),$$
$$(18_x, 2F_x; 5_x, 7_x), \ (19_x, 2E_x; 9_x, B_x),$$
$$(25_x, 12_x; 8_x, A_x), \ (26_x, 11_x; 8_x, A_x),$$
$$(2E_x, 19_x; B_x, 9_x), \ (2F_x, 18_x; 7_x, 5_x),$$
$$(38_x, F_x; 3_x, 1_x), \ (39_x, E_x; A_x, 8_x)\}.$$

The set of inputs is $\mathcal{X} = \{E_x, 39_x, F_x, 38_x, 11_x, 26_x, 12_x, 25_x, 18_x, 2F_x, 19_x, 2E_x\}$. The key applied must be in the set $\mathcal{K}_2 = \mathcal{X} \oplus s_1 = \mathcal{X} \oplus s_2 = \{1A_x, 2D_x, 2C_x, 1B_x, 32_x, 5_x, 31_x, 6_x, 3B_x, C_x, 3A_x, D_x\}$. The intersection of the sets $\mathcal{K}_1 \cap \mathcal{K}_2 = \{1A_x, D_x, 3A_x\}$. The secret key must be there. Yet another observation should be enough to find out the unique key. Indeed, let $(s_1, s_2) = (14_x, 1C_x)$ and $\Delta = 9_x$, then we have $\mathcal{X} = \{6_x, E_x, 20_x, 28_x, 25_x, 2D_x\}$ and $\mathcal{K}_3 = \mathcal{X} \oplus s_1 = \mathcal{X} \oplus s_2 = \{12_x, 1A_x, 34_x, 3C_x, 31_x, 39_x, \}$. The only key in all sets $\mathcal{K}_1, \mathcal{K}_2, \mathcal{K}_3$ is $1A_x$.

At this stage we know how a single S-box can be analyzed using input observations and the corresponding output differences. The following points summarize our considerations:

- The XOR profile of an S-box with the secret key XORed with the input is identical to the XOR profile of the S-box without the key.
- Every input observation (s_1, s_2) and corresponding output difference Δ allows the cryptanalyst to find a set $\mathcal{K}$ of key candidates, and

$$|\mathcal{K}| = |\mathcal{S}_\Delta^\delta|,$$

  where $\delta = s_1 \oplus s_2$ and $\Delta = f(s_1) \oplus f(s_2)$.
- The analysis of differences for a single S-box allows one to retrieve the key that is XORed to the input of an S-box.

Now we would like to extend our analysis to the DES algorithm. Consider the last round of DES. As DES uses Feistel permutations, inputs to all S-boxes used in the last round can be observed by looking at the second half of the cryptogram. The problem is that we cannot see the corresponding output differences. Fortunately, Biham and Shamir demonstrated that there is a probabilistic argument that allows one to make guesses about Δ. To explain the idea, we need to introduce the so-called *characteristics* of DES rounds.

3.4.2 DES Round Characteristics

An important feature of XOR profiles is that the input difference $\delta = 0$ forces the output difference Δ to be zero as well. Consider a single DES round with two input sequences $(A_1, 0)$ and $(A_2, 0)$. So their input difference is $\Omega_{\text{in}} = (A_1 \oplus A_2, 0) = (\delta_A, 0)$. The inputs to S-boxes are identical so their output differences are zero. Finally, the output difference $\Omega_{\text{out}} = (\delta_A, 0)$, shown in Fig. 3.26.

Consider the XOR profile of S_1. Our goal now is to find a characteristic that feeds a nonzero input difference into S_1 while other input differences of $S_2, \ldots, S_8$ are set to zero. Additionally, the characteristic should work with a high probability. If we have a fixed input difference, then output differences happen with the probability proportional to the corresponding entries in the XOR profile. One of the largest entries is 14 and occurs in many places in the table. The first occurrence is in $(3_x, 0_x)$. It means that the input difference 00 00 11 produces the output difference 00 00. The two nonzero bits on the S_1

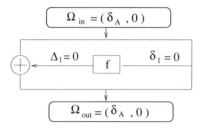

$$\Omega_{in} = (\delta_A, 0)$$

$\Delta_1 = 0$ $\delta_1 = 0$ f

$$\Omega_{out} = (\delta_A, 0)$$

Fig. 3.26. A single-round characteristic of DES

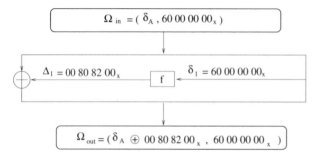

$$\Omega_{in} = (\delta_A, 60\ 00\ 00\ 00\ 00_x)$$

$\Delta_1 = 00\ 80\ 82\ 00_x$ $\delta_1 = 60\ 00\ 00\ 00\ 00_x$ f

$$\Omega_{out} = (\delta_A \oplus 00\ 80\ 82\ 00_x, \ 60\ 00\ 00\ 00\ 00_x)$$

Fig. 3.27. Another single-round characteristic of DES

input have had to pass through the expansion block E so they are duplicated on the input of S_2. The only pair of bits that is not duplicated in other S-boxes is the pair of two middle bits (in the E table marked as bits 2 and 3). So we have to look at rows $00\ 01\ 00 = 4_x$, $00\ 10\ 00 = 8_x$, and $00\ 11\ 00 = C_x$. The only row with an entry 14 is the last one $\delta = C_x$. The pair of differences (C_x, E_x) happens with probability $\frac{14}{64}$. The characteristic is depicted in Fig. 3.27. The binary string $(00\ 80\ 82\ 00_x)$ is obtained by permuting $(E0\ 00\ 00\ 00_x)$ according to the DES permutation block P.

The two single-round characteristics can be concatenated to create the 2-round characteristic shown in Fig. 3.28. Its probability is $\frac{14}{64}$ as the second round happens always (with the probability 1).

This informal discussion can be generalized for an arbitrary Feistel-type cryptosystem. The cryptosystem processes n-bit messages and uses a round function $f_k : \Sigma^{\frac{n}{2}} \rightarrow \Sigma^{\frac{n}{2}}$. The cryptographic key k is XORed to the inputs of S-boxes.

Definition 3. *An m-round characteristic of a Feistel-type cryptosystem is a sequence*

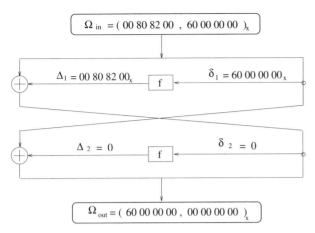

Fig. 3.28. A two-round characteristic of DES

$$(\Omega_{\text{in}}, \delta_1, \Delta_1, \ldots, \delta_m, \Delta_m, \Omega_{\text{out}}) = (\Omega_{\text{in}}, \Omega_\Delta, \Omega_{\text{out}})$$

where Ω_{in} and Ω_{out} are input and output differences. The pairs (δ_i, Δ_i), $i = 1, \ldots, m$, are consecutive input and output differences for the round function f_k.

Characteristics can be concatenated in a similar way as we have done to create 2-round characteristic from two single ones. Let $\Omega^1 = (\Omega_{\text{in}}^1, \Omega_\Delta^1, \Omega_{\text{out}}^1)$ and $\Omega^2 = (\Omega_{\text{in}}^2, \Omega_\Delta^2, \Omega_{\text{out}}^2)$ be two characteristics. They can be concatenated if the swapped halves of Ω_{in}^2 are equal to Ω_{out}^1 and the concatenation $\Omega = (\Omega_{\text{in}}^1, \Omega_\Delta^{1,2}, \Omega_{\text{out}}^2)$, where $\Omega_\Delta^{1,2}$ is the concatenation of the two sequences Ω_Δ^1 and Ω_Δ^2.

Any characteristic has a probability attached to it. Let our m-round characteristic be $(\Omega_{\text{in}}, \delta_1, \Delta_1, \ldots, \delta_m, \Delta_m, \Omega_{\text{out}}$. Then its probability

$$P(\Omega) = \prod_{i=1}^{m} p_{\Delta_i}^{\delta_i},$$

where $p_{\Delta_i}^{\delta_i}$ is the probability that input difference δ_i causes the output difference Δ_i for the function f_k in the ith round.

3.4.3 Cryptanalysis of 4-Round DES

First, recall that to be able to recover keys we have to concentrate on the last round. For a given pair of plaintexts, we need to know values given to the function f_k in the last round. These values are known as they are the right

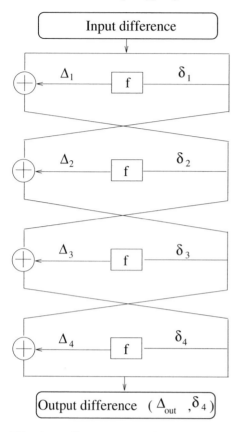

Fig. 3.29. Four-round DES

halves of the cryptograms. The main goal is to find the output differences which occur on S-boxes in the last round.

We use a characteristic given in Fig. 3.26 for $\delta_A = 20\ 00\ 00\ 00_x$, which works always (with probability 1). The general scheme of differences in the 4-round DES is given in Fig. 3.29. We start from an observation that

$$\Delta_4 = \Delta_{\text{out}} \oplus \Delta_2 \oplus \delta_1. \tag{3.5}$$

Δ_{out} is known from the cryptograms (left halves) and δ_1 is given from the input (right halves). Take a closer look at Δ_1 and Δ_2. As $\delta_1 = 0$, $\Delta_1 = 0$ as well. On the other hand, $\delta_2 = 20\ 00\ 00\ 00_x$ so the input difference on S_1 becomes $00\ 10\ 00$ leaving the other S-boxes with zero differences (notice that the two middle bits of S_1 are not duplicated in other S-boxes by the bit-selection block E). This means that all output differences of $S_2, \ldots, S_8$ are forced to zero – we know differences on their outputs. Thus 28-bits of Δ_2 are known. From (3.5), we conclude that 28 bits of Δ_4 are known. Being more specific, we know inputs of seven S-boxes and their output differences in the last round. By the differential analysis given in Sect. 3.4.1, we can find $7 \times 6 = 42$ bits out of the 48-bit key k_4.

To be able to analyze S_1 in the 4th round, we need another characteristic. We can use the same one, but for $\delta_A = 04\ 44\ 44\ 44_x$. As previously, $\delta_1 = \Delta_1 = 0$ but $\delta_2 = 04\ 44\ 44\ 44_x$. As the input difference on S_1 is zero in the second round, the output difference on S_1 is also zero. From (3.5), the 4-bit difference on the output of S_1 in the 4th round can be determined. Note that the permutation block P behind S-boxes is used in all rounds so the corresponding bits always meet. Once this is done, the missing part of the key can be recovered by the differential analysis of S_1.

Having the partial key k_4, we can strip off the last round and analyze the 3-round DES. After finding k_3, we are left with 2-round DES which can be easily analyzed. The analysis assumes that keys are independent in each round so the introduction of long randomly selected keys for each round does not protect the cryptosystem against the differential analysis. This is one of the very strong advantages of this attack. On the other hand, a "weak" key schedule may allow us to deduce the initial key from the partial key used in the last round.

3.4.4 Cryptanalysis of 6-Round DES

Figure 3.30 shows the general scheme of differences in the 6-round DES. As before, in order to find the key k_6 used in the sixth round, we have to determine the output difference Δ_6. The following equation can be easily established:

$$\Delta_6 = \Delta_{\text{out}} \oplus \Delta_4 \oplus \delta_3. \tag{3.6}$$

To derive δ_3, we use the two 3-round characteristics given in Figs. 3.31 and 3.32. The first characteristic uses

$$\delta_3 = 04\ 00\ 00\ 00_x.$$

Δ_{out} is available as it is the difference between the left halves of the cryptograms. To determine Δ_4, consider $\delta_4 = 40\ 08\ 00\ 00_x$. In the fourth round, S-boxes S_2, S_5, S_6, S_7, and S_8 have their input differences set to zero so their output differences are forced to zero. This means that we can find differences in the sixth round for S_2, S_5, S_6, S_7, and S_8. This time the analysis of S-boxes is

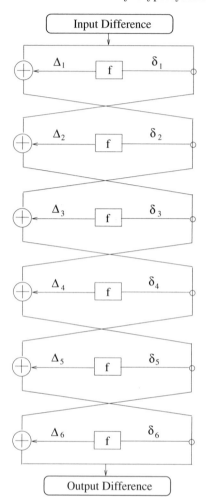

Fig. 3.30. Six-round DES

not deterministic due to the fact that $\delta_4 = 40\ 08\ 00\ 00_x$ occurs with the probability $\frac{1}{16}$. This of course complicates the analysis as we cannot reduce the set of candidate keys after every observation. Indeed, we need to count all the candidate keys. It is expected that the right key will have a higher frequency than the others. Thus, after enough observations we can find 30 bits of k_6.

The second characteristic produces

$$\delta_4 = 00\ 20\ 00\ 08,$$

so input differences in the fourth round are zeroes for S_1, S_2, S_4, S_5, and S_6. Δ_4 has zero output differences for these S-boxes. From (3.6), we can find

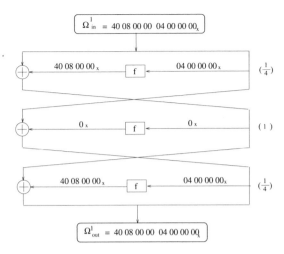

Fig. 3.31. First 3-round characteristic

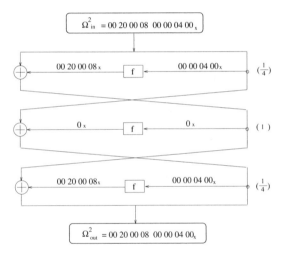

Fig. 3.32. Second 3-round characteristic

Δ_6 for these S-boxes. By counting keys for S_1 and S_4, we can determine the corresponding 12 bits of k_6. So we know 42 out of 48 bits of k_6.

The missing 6 bits of the key (used in S_3) can be determined by using 42 already recovered bits. To do this, we first identify pairs of plaintext/ciphertext which behave according to the characteristic. These pairs are called *right pairs*. The identification can be done by checking if the differences on the outputs of S-boxes in the fourth round are zeroes. As we know 42 bits of k_6, we can

Table 3.14. Cryptanalysis of DES

No. of rounds	Chosen plaintexts	Analysed plaintexts	Complexity of analysis
8	2^{14}	4	2^9
9	2^{24}	2	2^{32}
10	2^{24}	2^{14}	2^{15}
11	2^{31}	2	2^{32}
12	2^{31}	2^{21}	2^{21}
13	2^{39}	2	2^{32}
14	2^{39}	2^{29}	2^{29}
15	2^{47}	2^7	2^{37}
16	2^{47}	2^{36}	2^{37}

generate the corresponding 28 bits of Δ_6' (using the seventh round). Knowing Δ_{out}, we verify whether

$$\Delta_6' \oplus \Delta_{\text{out}} = \Delta_4 \oplus \delta_3.$$

If the equation is not satisfied, we reject the pair as there is an overwhelming probability that this is not the right pair.

For every right pair, we guess the 6-bit part of k_6 XORed to the input of S_3. Now the 48-bit k_6 is used to determine Δ_6'. Next we calculate $\delta_5' = \Delta_{\text{out}} \oplus \Delta_6'$ and verify whether values of differences in S_2, S_3, and S_8 in the fifth round satisfy the equation $\Delta_5 = \delta_4 \oplus \delta_6$. After at most 2^6 tries, we have all bits of k_6. The still missing $56 - 48 = 8$ bits can be reconstructed by an exhaustive search of $2^8 = 256$ possibilities.

3.4.5 Analysis of Other Feistel-Type Cryptosystems

Similar analysis can be conducted for versions of DES with more rounds. Table 3.14 summarizes the results (for more details consult [36]). It is no surprise that the efficiency of the attack drops exponentially with the number of rounds. This is due to the fact that longer characteristics have smaller probabilities associated with them.

Murphy [362] has shown that the FEAL-4 algorithm is vulnerable to the differential analysis with 20 chosen plaintexts only. Biham and Shamir [34] demonstrated that FEAL-N with N smaller than 32 is subject to the differential cryptanalysis whose efficiency is higher than the exhaustive search of the key space.

The main features of the differential analysis are summarized below.

– The differential analysis can be applied to Feistel cryptosystems with t rounds where it is possible to see inputs to the round function and deduce or guess (with high probability) the corresponding output differences.
– Characteristics are useful in guessing the correct output differences of the round function. It is enough to have a $(t-3)$-round characteristic to find output differences in the t-round Feistel cryptosystem.
– As the differential analysis enables us to find keys applied in the last round function, it bypasses the key schedule. It works under the assumption that round keys are statistically independent.
– Once the key in the last round is found, the last round can be stripped off by applying the extra round which is the inverse of the last round. The analysis can now be applied to a system with $t-1$ rounds (peeling-off technique).

To make a Feistel cryptosystem immune to differential analysis, the following points need to be addressed:

– The XOR profile must not have entries with large numbers.
– The best $(t-3)$-round characteristics should work with probabilities smaller than the probability of guessing the right key (t is the number of rounds in the cryptosystem).
– The S-boxes should depend on the secret key in a nonlinear way. This will ensure that the XOR profiles of the S-boxes become more complex. One way of implementing this idea would be an on-the-fly selection of S-boxes depending on the round key.

3.5 Linear Cryptanalysis

At Eurocrypt '93 Matsui presented a new class of general attacks which exploits a low nonlinearity of S-boxes. The attack, referred to as *linear cryptanalysis*, is a known-plaintext attack. Linear cryptanalysis can also work as a ciphertext-only attack. The principles of linear cryptanalysis are explained in [321]. Linear cryptanalysis of DES is described in [320].

3.5.1 Linear Approximation

A Boolean function $h : \Sigma^n \to \Sigma$ in n variables $s_1, \ldots, s_n$ is *linear* if it can be represented as $h(s) = a_1 s_1 \oplus \ldots \oplus a_n s_n$ for some $a_i \in \Sigma = \{0, 1\}$, $i = 1, \ldots, n$. The set of all linear Boolean functions in n variables is denoted by

$$\mathcal{L}_n = \{h : \Sigma^n \to \Sigma \mid h = a_1 s_1 \oplus \ldots \oplus a_n s_n\}.$$

A Boolean function $f : \Sigma^n \to \Sigma$ is called *affine* if either $f(s) = h(s)$ or $f(s) = h(s) \oplus 1$, for some $h(s) \in \mathcal{L}_n$. The set of all affine Boolean functions in n variables is

$$\mathcal{A}_n = \mathcal{L}_n \cup \{h \oplus 1 \mid h \in \mathcal{L}_n\} = \mathcal{L}_n \cup \overline{\mathcal{L}_n},$$

i.e., $\mathcal{A}_n$ consists of all linear functions and their negations. A Boolean function $f : \Sigma^n \to \Sigma$ is uniquely represented by the corresponding truth table. Assume that the argument $\alpha_i \in \Sigma^n$ runs through all its possible values $0, 1, \ldots, 2^n - 1$ so $\alpha_0 = (00 \ldots 0)$, $\alpha_1 = (00 \ldots 1)$, and so forth, until $\alpha_{2^n-1} = (11 \ldots 1)$. The truth table of f is equivalent to the following vector

$$f = (f(\alpha_0), f(\alpha_1), \ldots, f(\alpha_{2^n-1})),$$

where $f(\alpha_i)$ specifies the value of the function for the argument expressed by the vector α_i $(i = 0, \ldots, 2^n - 1)$. The *Hamming distance* $d(f, g)$ between two Boolean functions $f, g : \Sigma^n \to \Sigma$ is the number of 1s in the vector

$$(f(\alpha_0) \oplus g(\alpha_0), f(\alpha_1) \oplus g(\alpha_1), \ldots, f(\alpha_{2^n-1}) \oplus g(\alpha_{2^n-1})),$$

or conversely, the number of disagreements between f and g.

Definition 4. *The nonlinearity $N(f)$ of a Boolean function $f : \Sigma^n \to \Sigma$ is*

$$N(f) = \min_{h \in \mathcal{A}_n} d(h, f),$$

i.e., it is the minimal distance between the function f and its best linear approximation.

The cryptographic strength of a modern encryption algorithm mainly rests on an appropriately chosen cryptographic structure of the cipher round. Those structures can always be seen as a collection of Boolean functions or S-boxes tying input and output bits of the round. More precisely, an $(n \times m)$ S-box $S : \Sigma^n \to \Sigma^m$ is a collection of m functions $f_i : \Sigma^n \to \Sigma$, $i = 1, \ldots, m$, in n Boolean variables $s = (s_1, \ldots, s_n)$ for which

Table 3.15. The truth table of $f(s) = s_1 s_2$ and linear functions from $\mathcal{L}_2$

$s_2 s_1$	f	0	s_1	s_2	$s_1 \oplus s_2$	$f \oplus s_1$	$f \oplus s_2$	$f \oplus s_1 \oplus s_2$
00	0	0	0	0	0	0	0	0
01	0	0	1	0	1	1	0	1
10	0	0	0	1	1	0	1	1
11	1	0	1	1	0	0	0	1

$$S(s) = (f_1(s), \ldots, f_m(s)).$$

The notion of nonlinearity can be extended as in the following definition.

Definition 5. *The nonlinearity of an $(n \times m)$ S-box $S = (f_1, \ldots, f_m)$ is*

$$N(S) = \min_{w=(w_1,\ldots,w_m)\in\Sigma^m; v\in\Sigma} N(w_1 f_1 \oplus \ldots \oplus w_m f_m \oplus v). \tag{3.7}$$

For instance, consider $f : \Sigma^2 \to \Sigma$ where $f(s) = s_1 s_2$. The truth table and all linear functions from $\mathcal{L}_2 = \{0, s_1, s_2, s_1 \oplus s_2\}$ are presented in Table 3.15. So the distances are $d(f, 0) = d(f, s_1) = d(f, s_2) = 1$ and $d(f, s_1 \oplus s_2) = 3$.

Knowing the distance $d(f, h) = d_{f,h}$ where $h \in \mathcal{L}_n$, it is easy to obtain $d(f, h \oplus 1) = 2^n - d_{f,h}$. So to determine the nonlinearity of a function $f : \Sigma^n \to \Sigma$, it is enough to find all distances between the function and the set of linear functions. The distances for the affine functions from the set $\overline{\mathcal{L}_n}$ can be computed from the distances of linear functions.

In the DES algorithm, there are eight S-boxes $S_i : \Sigma^6 \to \Sigma^4$ for $i = 1, \ldots, 8$. Each S-box can be treated as a collection of four Boolean functions. For a given S-box, we can create a table of distances as follows. Rows of the table are indexed by a linear function $\ell \in \mathcal{L}_6$. There are $2^6 = 64$ possible linear functions. The index of the row is a hexadecimal number which represents the linear function. So the index $31_x = 11\ 0001$ corresponds to the linear function $\ell(s) = s_6 \oplus s_5 \oplus s_1$ where $s = (s_6, s_5, s_4, s_3, s_2, s_1)$. The columns of the table are indexed by linear combinations of S-box outputs. So if the S-box function $S = (f_4, f_3, f_2, f_1)$, the linear combination $f = (a_4 f_4 \oplus a_3 f_3 \oplus a_2 f_2 \oplus a_1 f_1)$, where $a_4 a_3 a_2 a_1$ is the column index in the hexadecimal notation. For instance, the index $9_x = 1001$ corresponds to the linear combination of outputs $f_4 \oplus f_1$. There are 15 nonzero columns. The entry (ℓ, f) gives the Hamming distance $d(\ell, f)$. This table is called the *linear profile* of an S-box.

The linear profile of S_5 is given in Table 3.16. All entries are even numbers, which results from the fact that all outputs in all S-boxes have equal numbers

Table 3.16. Linear profile of S_5

	Combinations of Outputs														
	1_x	2_x	3_x	4_x	5_x	6_x	7_x	8_x	9_x	A_x	B_x	C_x	D_x	E_x	F_x
0_x	32	32	32	32	32	32	32	32	32	32	32	32	32	32	32
1_x	32	32	32	32	32	32	32	32	32	32	32	32	32	32	32
2_x	36	30	34	30	34	28	32	36	32	34	30	34	30	32	28
3_x	32	34	26	34	34	28	36	32	32	34	26	34	34	28	36
4_x	34	30	32	32	34	30	32	32	34	34	36	28	30	30	32
5_x	30	30	36	32	22	38	36	32	30	42	32	28	34	30	28
6_x	34	36	38	34	36	30	32	32	34	32	34	38	40	30	32
7_x	34	32	34	30	40	38	32	28	38	32	26	30	32	26	28
8_x	32	34	38	32	32	30	26	30	34	36	20	34	38	28	36
9_x	36	26	34	32	36	38	38	26	34	32	36	30	38	40	36
A_x	28	32	32	34	38	30	30	30	30	34	30	28	36	36	32
B_x	36	36	36	38	34	30	30	30	30	30	34	32	24	28	32
C_x	30	32	34	32	30	28	22	34	28	34	40	34	28	38	36
D_x	38	32	34	32	30	36	22	30	32	30	36	30	40	26	32
E_x	30	30	32	30	36	32	34	30	32	36	34	28	38	30	28
F_x	34	34	24	26	28	32	30	30	28	24	34	24	38	30	32
10_x	34	30	32	32	30	26	24	32	30	30	28	32	34	42	12
11_x	30	34	32	28	30	34	36	28	30	30	32	40	38	30	28
12_x	34	32	34	30	36	34	40	28	26	28	26	34	28	38	32
13_x	26	32	34	30	36	34	32	36	26	36	34	26	36	30	32
14_x	28	36	32	32	32	32	32	36	36	28	28	32	28	36	32
15_x	36	32	28	28	36	24	24	32	32	28	36	40	36	32	36
16_x	32	38	38	34	30	36	32	36	32	38	34	34	34	32	32
17_x	28	38	34	26	34	36	28	28	36	38	30	34	30	32	28
18_x	26	32	30	28	42	36	30	30	32	34	32	30	28	34	36
19_x	34	36	26	32	30	36	30	38	40	38	36	42	32	34	28
$1A_x$	34	34	24	30	36	32	34	30	32	36	34	32	30	30	32
$1B_x$	30	26	36	38	32	32	30	26	24	32	34	36	38	34	32
$1C_x$	32	30	34	36	32	26	34	30	38	28	32	34	30	32	32
$1D_x$	28	34	26	40	32	34	30	22	34	40	40	30	30	32	28
$1E_x$	36	40	32	34	34	34	30	34	30	34	26	28	28	28	32
$1F_x$	28	40	24	34	26	26	30	30	34	30	30	24	32	32	28
20_x	32	32	32	32	32	32	32	32	32	32	32	32	32	32	32
21_x	32	32	32	32	32	32	32	32	32	32	32	32	32	32	32
22_x	28	30	34	30	34	28	40	28	32	26	38	34	30	16	20
23_x	32	34	34	26	34	36	28	32	32	34	34	34	26	28	36
24_x	30	38	36	32	38	30	36	36	26	30	36	32	46	34	32
25_x	26	30	32	32	26	30	32	36	38	30	40	32	34	26	36
26_x	30	28	34	34	32	30	36	28	34	36	34	26	32	34	32
27_x	22	32	30	38	36	38	28	32	38	20	34	34	32	38	28
28_x	36	30	30	32	36	26	34	34	26	36	32	38	30	28	32
29_x	32	30	26	32	32	26	30	30	34	40	32	34	38	32	32
$2A_x$	32	36	40	26	26	26	38	26	30	34	34	40	28	36	28
$2B_x$	40	32	36	38	30	26	38	34	38	30	38	28	32	36	36
$2C_x$	30	28	38	32	38	32	26	34	36	30	36	34	28	26	32
$2D_x$	30	28	30	32	30	24	34	30	32	26	24	30	32	30	36
$2E_x$	38	34	28	38	36	36	30	22	24	32	30	36	30	34	32
$2F_x$	26	38	36	26	36	28	34	30	28	28	38	32	30	34	36
30_x	34	30	32	28	26	30	28	36	34	34	32	32	34	34	36
31_x	30	34	32	32	34	30	32	32	34	34	36	32	30	30	28
32_x	26	32	34	34	24	30	28	32	22	32	30	34	28	30	32
33_x	26	32	42	34	32	30	28	32	38	32	22	34	36	30	32
34_x	32	44	28	36	32	28	40	36	32	36	32	36	36	32	32

Table 3.16. (continued)

	\multicolumn{16}{c}{Combinations of Outputs}
	1_x	2_x	3_x	4_x	5_x	6_x	7_x	8_x	9_x	A_x	B_x	C_x	D_x	E_x	F_x
35_x	24	32	32	40	28	36	32	32	28	28	32	36	36	28	36
36_x	36	30	26	30	30	40	32	36	28	30	30	38	34	28	32
37_x	40	38	38	38	26	32	28	20	32	30	34	30	30	28	36
38_x	30	28	38	32	34	28	34	38	28	38	32	26	28	34	32
39_x	30	40	34	28	38	28	26	30	28	34	36	30	32	34	32
$3A_x$	38	22	32	34	36	32	30	38	28	32	34	36	30	30	28
$3B_x$	34	38	36	42	32	40	34	42	28	28	34	32	30	34	28
$3C_x$	24	26	30	32	28	34	34	26	34	36	32	42	30	36	36
$3D_x$	28	30	30	28	28	34	30	34	22	32	32	30	30	28	32
$3E_x$	36	28	36	30	30	34	30	30	34	34	34	28	36	32	28
$3F_x$	28	28	28	46	38	26	30	34	30	38	30	32	32	28	32

of 0s and 1s (the output functions are balanced). The nonlinearity of a linear combination of outputs can be found by looking for the smallest and the biggest entry in the corresponding column f. Let the two entries be $d_{\min} = d_{f,r1}$ and $d_{\max} = d_{f,r2}$. The nonlinearity of the function f is the smaller integer from $(d_{\min}, 2^6 - d_{\max})$. The best linear approximation of the column function is either the linear function ℓ_{r1} if $d_{\min} < 2^6 - d_{\max}$ or the negation of the linear function ℓ_{r2}, i.e., the affine function $\ell_{r2} \oplus 1$ where ℓ_{r1} and ℓ_{r2} are linear functions that correspond to the rows $r1$ and $r2$, respectively.

The best linear approximation of a function $f : \Sigma^n \to \Sigma$ is the affine function $\ell \in \mathcal{A}_n$ that is closest (in the sense of Hamming distance) to the function f and the distance $d(\ell, f)$ is the nonlinearity of the function. For instance, the function f_{8_x} has the best linear approximation

$$\ell_{f_{8_x}} = s_6 \oplus s_5 \oplus s_3 \oplus s_2 \oplus s_1$$

(the row 37_x) and nonlinearity $N(f_{8_x}) = 20$. The function f_{4_x} is best approximated by

$$\ell_{f_{4_x}} = s_6 \oplus s_5 \oplus s_4 \oplus s_3 \oplus s_2 \oplus s_1 \oplus 1$$

(the row $3F_x$). The nonlinearity of f_{4_x} is $64 - 46 = 18$.

The global characterization of an S-box can be done by the selection of the pair: the smallest $d^g_{\min}$ and biggest entry $d^g_{\max}$. The nonlinearity of the S-box is the minimum of $d^g_{\min}$ and $2^n - d^g_{\max}$. For S_5 the nonlinearity of the S-box is 12 (the entry for the row 10_x and the column F_x) – so f_{F_x} can be approximated by s_5. This is the best available approximation in S_5 and, as a matter of fact, in all S-boxes.

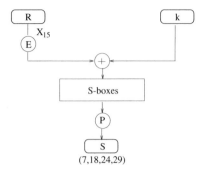

Fig. 3.33. Linear approximation in a single-round of DES

Let a function $f : \Sigma^n \to \Sigma$ and its linear approximation $\ell : \Sigma^n \to \Sigma$ be given. How well does ℓ approximate f? The distance $d(\ell, f)$ gives the number of input values for which the functions differ. So if we randomly select an input, we have the probability

$$\frac{2^n - d(\ell, f)}{2^n}$$

that the outputs of ℓ and f will be the same. The worst case is when the best linear approximation ℓ differs for about half of the possible input values, i.e., $d(\ell, f) \approx 2^{n-1}$. The probability that $\ell(s) \neq f(s)$ or $\ell(s) = f(s)$ is ≈ 0.5 for a random $s \in \Sigma^n$.

3.5.2 Analysis of 3-Round DES

Now we use the linear approximation from the previous section to devise an efficient attack on 3-round DES. The attack uses the best linear approximation of S_5. This approximation is

$$s_1^* \oplus s_2^* \oplus s_3^* \oplus s_4^* = s_5,$$

where s_i^* are outputs and s_5 is an input of S_5. This equation translates to (Fig. 3.33)

$$R_{(15)} \oplus k_{(22)} = S_{(7)} \oplus S_{(18)} \oplus S_{(24)} \oplus S_{(29)} \overset{\text{def}}{=} S_{(7,18,24,29)}$$

in a single-round of DES.

For 3-round DES (Fig. 3.34), we can establish the following equations:

$$R2_{(7,18,24,29)} \oplus L1_{(7,18,24,29)} = k1_{(22)} \oplus R1_{(15)}, \tag{3.8}$$

$$R2_{(7,18,24,29)} \oplus L3_{(7,18,24,29)} = k3_{(22)} \oplus R3_{(15)}. \tag{3.9}$$

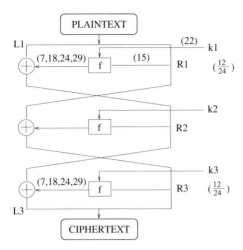

Fig. 3.34. Three-round linear characteristic

If we merge (3.8) and (3.9), we obtain

$$L1_{(7,18,24,29)} \oplus L3_{(7,18,24,29)} \oplus R1_{(15)} \oplus R3_{(15)} = k1_{(22)} \oplus k3_{(22)}. \qquad (3.10)$$

What is the probability that (3.10) is true? Equation (3.10) is true in the two cases: first, if (3.8) and (3.9) are true; or, second, if the equations are simultaneously false. Therefore the probability is $(\frac{52}{64})^2 + (\frac{12}{64})^2 \approx 0.7$.

Note that (3.10) ties bits of plaintext and ciphertext with bits of the secret key. The secret key is fixed so the right-hand side of the equation is constant (either 0 or 1). The left-hand side relates to specific subset of bits of a single plaintext/ciphertext observation and equals the constant with the probability ≈ 0.7. This means that having a large enough collection of observations of plaintext/ciphertext pairs, the frequency distribution of the results is biased and the higher occurrence indicates the correct value of the constant $k1_{(22)} \oplus k3_{(22)}$. The attack could proceed by choosing other good approximations and assemble linear equations for other key bits. If we had enough linearly independent equations, we could find the key.

3.5.3 Linear Characteristics

Take a look at Fig. 3.35, which shows 5-round DES. In the first and fifth round the 15th bit coming out of the round function is approximated using the following equation

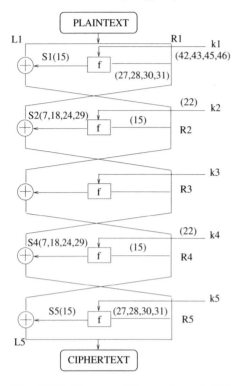

Fig. 3.35. Five-round linear characteristic

$$\overset{\backprime}{S}_{(15)} = k_{(27)} \oplus k_{(28)} \oplus k_{(30)} \oplus k_{(31)} \oplus R_{(27)} \oplus R_{(28)} \oplus R_{(30)} \oplus R_{(31)}$$
$$\overset{\text{def}}{=} k_{(27,28,30,31)} \oplus R_{(27,28,30,31)}. \tag{3.11}$$

This bit comes from S_1 and its nonlinearity is 22. The following two equations are derived for the 1st and 5th round

$$R2_{(15)} = L1_{(15)} \oplus S1_{(15)} = L1_{(15)} \oplus k1_{(27,28,30,31)} \oplus R1_{(27,28,30,31)},$$
$$R4_{(15)} = L5_{(15)} \oplus S5_{(15)} = L5_{(15)} \oplus k5_{(27,28,30,31)} \oplus R5_{(27,28,30,31)}.$$

The 2nd and 4th rounds use the same approximation as in the previously discussed 3-round DES, so we have

$$R3_{(7,18,24,29)} = R1_{(7,18,24,29)} \oplus S2_{(7,18,24,29)} = R1_{(7,18,24,29)} \oplus k2_{(22)} \oplus R2_{(15)},$$
$$R3_{(7,18,24,29)} = R5_{(7,18,24,29)} \oplus S4_{(7,18,24,29)} = R5_{(7,18,24,29)} \oplus k4_{(22)} \oplus R4_{(15)}.$$

After merging these two, we get

$$R1_{(7,18,24,29)} \oplus R5_{(7,18,24,29)} = k2_{(22)} \oplus R2_{(22)} \oplus k4_{(22)} \oplus R4_{(22)}.$$

Now we substitute $R2_{(22)}$ and $R4_{(22)}$ by their linear approximations and we have the final linear characteristic

$$L1_{(15)} \oplus L5_{(15)} \oplus R1_{(7,18,24,27,28,29,30,31)} \oplus R5_{(7,18,24,27,28,29,30,31)} \qquad (3.12)$$

$$= k1_{(27,28,30,31)} \oplus k2_{(22)} \oplus k4_{(22)} \oplus k5_{(27,28,30,31)}. \qquad (3.13)$$

The characteristic uses four linear approximations. Each approximation has the associated probability which expresses the accuracy of the approximation. How can we compute the probability that (3.12) holds? The answer is given in the following theorem.

Theorem 12. (*Matsui* [321]) *Given n independent random variables $X_1, \ldots, X_n$ such that $P(X_i = 0) = p_i$ and $P(X_i = 1) = 1 - p_i$ for $i = 1, \ldots, n$. Then the probability that $X_1 \oplus \ldots \oplus X_n = 0$ is*

$$\frac{1}{2} + 2^{n-1} \prod_{i=1}^{n} (p_i - 0.5). \qquad (3.14)$$

Note that to produce the characteristic from (3.12), we have used four approximations whose probabilities are: $\frac{42}{64}, \frac{52}{64}, \frac{52}{64}, \frac{42}{64}$. The probability that (3.12) holds is ≈ 0.519. It means that after ≈ 2800 pairs of plaintext/ciphertext the right-hand value of $k1_{(27,28,30,31)} \oplus k2_{(22)} \oplus k4_{(22)} \oplus k5_{(27,28,30,31)}$ can be found.

Linear characteristics are linear approximations of some of the key bits by a combination of plaintext/ciphertext bits. The efficiency of a characteristic is measured by the probability that the characteristic is true (or all approximations in the characteristic hold). It can be computed from probabilities of S-box approximations by applying Theorem 12.

Matsui also introduced a nice improvement which speeds up the analysis. The improvement can be used in the first and last round when we can see the inputs to the round functions. Instead of approximation, we try to guess the right bits of a part of the round key (only those bits of the key which influence the characteristic). Assume that the characteristic depends on v bits of the key (in the first or last round). We can evaluate the characteristic for all possible patterns of v bits simultaneously. Due to the probabilistic nature of characteristics, it is expected that the correct value of v bits will cause a noticeable bias in counting, which must be proportional to the probability of the characteristic. This allows us to retrieve v bits of the key.

The analysis of 16-round DES can be done by using two linear characteristics. The second characteristic is obtained from the first one by swapping plaintext bits with ciphertext bits in the equation. The characteristics approximate all rounds except the first and last ones. For the first and last rounds, we guess parts of the round keys. This produces 12 bits of the key plus 1 bit from the characteristic. As the attack uses 2 characteristics, we can determine 26 bits of the key. The remaining 30 bits are found by the exhaustive search. To break DES, it takes 2^{43} steps and the success rate is 85% if 2^{43} pairs (plaintext, ciphertext) are known.

The FEAL cipher was the first algorithm Matsui and Yamagishi [323] attacked using linear cryptanalysis. The attack was much easier to launch due to the structure of the S-boxes. Matsui and Yamagishi [323] noted that the S-boxes have low nonlinearity and, in particular, the least-significant bit is linear. Consequently, they demonstrated that FEAL-4 is breakable with 5 observations and FEAL-8 with 2^{15} observations.

How can cryptographic systems be protected against linear cryptanalysis? The answer seems to be easy: use highly nonlinear S-boxes. For a highly nonlinear S-box, each linear approximation of the S-box function works with low probability. However, it is also possible to increase the immunity of the system against linear analysis by permuting S-boxes [322]. This is due to the fact that, for a carefully chosen order of S-boxes in the round function, concatenation of linear approximations fails to create a good linear characteristic.

3.6 S-box Theory

Shannon's concept of product ciphers uses two basic transformations: confusion and diffusion. All modern cryptographic algorithms use in some way or another a collection of S-boxes that provide confusion and P-boxes which spread out the output bits to different S-boxes of the next round. P-boxes have usually a fixed permutation of input and output bits. The strength of product ciphers mainly comes from the "properly" designed S-boxes. The definition of cryptographically strong S-boxes is to some extent arbitrary. It is well known that weaknesses of S-boxes may be compensated for by the increased number of rounds. This is precisely the case with the FEAL algorithm, which becomes immune against linear cryptanalysis when the number of rounds is bigger than 32. Note that if a cryptographic algorithm is to be both cryptographically strong and fast, then a careful design of all its components is of utmost importance.

Each general cryptographic attack that is better than the exhaustive search explores some weakness in S-boxes. In response, a new S-box criterion is introduced. If the criterion is incorporated into S-boxes, it makes the cryptographic algorithm immune against the attack. For instance, the differential attack brought to our attention the need for good XOR profiles in S-box design.

3.6.1 Boolean Functions

Recall that $\Sigma = \{0, 1\}$. The simplest field which can be defined over Σ is $GF(2) = \langle \Sigma, \oplus, \times \rangle$ with the addition $\oplus$ and multiplication $\times$. $GF(2)$ is called the *binary field*. Clearly, addition is $0 \oplus 0 = 1 \oplus 1 = 0$ and $0 \oplus 1 = 1 \oplus 0 = 1$. Multiplication is defined as $0 \times 0 = 1 \times 0 = 0 \times 1 = 0$ and $1 \times 1 = 1$.

Consider a Boolean function $f : \Sigma^n \to GF(2)$ that assigns a binary element $f(x) \in \Sigma$ to a vector $x = (x_1, \ldots, x_n) \in \Sigma^n$. For simplicity, we will denote elements (vectors) of Σ^n by their decimal representations used as the subscript, so

$$
\begin{aligned}
\alpha_0 \quad &= (00 \ldots 00), \\
\alpha_1 \quad &= (00 \ldots 01), \\
&\vdots \\
\alpha_{2^n - 1} &= (11 \ldots 11).
\end{aligned}
$$

Let $f : \Sigma^n \to GF(2)$ be a Boolean function. The binary sequence

$$(f(\alpha_0), f(\alpha_1), \ldots, f(\alpha_{2^n - 1}))$$

is called the *truth table* of the function f. The sequence with components from $\{1, -1\}$ defined by

$$((-1)^{f(\alpha_0)}, (-1)^{f(\alpha_1)}, \ldots, (-1)^{f(\alpha_{2^n - 1})})$$

is called the *sequence* of the function f. A $2^n \times 2^n$ matrix F with entries $f_{i,j} = (-1)^{f(\alpha_i \oplus \alpha_j)}$ is called the *matrix* of the function f.

Consider an example. Let $f(x) = x_1 x_2 x_3 \oplus x_1 x_3 \oplus x_2 \oplus x_3 \oplus 1$ be a function on Σ^3. It is easy to check that

$$
\begin{aligned}
f(000) &= 1, \ f(001) = 0, \ f(010) = 0, \ f(011) = 1, \\
f(100) &= 1, \ f(101) = 1, \ f(110) = 0, \ f(111) = 1.
\end{aligned}
$$

So the truth table of f is (10011101) and the sequence of f is $(-1, 1, 1, -1, -1, -1, 1, -1)$ or $(-++----+-)$ where $+$ and $-$ stand for $+1$ and -1, respectively. The matrix of f is

$$F = \begin{bmatrix} -++----+- \\ +---+----+ \\ +---++---- \\ -++---+-- \\ ---+---++- \\ ---+++---+ \\ +----+---+ \\ -+----++- \end{bmatrix}.$$

A Boolean function $f : \Sigma^n \to GF(2)$ is said to be *balanced* if its truth table has 2^{n-1} zeros (or ones). For instance, the function $f(x) = x_1 x_2 \oplus x_3$, $x \in \Sigma^3$, is balanced, since the truth table of f is (01010110) and the function takes the value zero the prescribed four times.

A Boolean function $f : \Sigma^n \to GF(2)$ is *affine* if it can be represented in the form

$$f(x_1, \ldots, x_n) = a_0 \oplus a_1 x_1 \oplus \cdots \oplus a_n x_n,$$

where $a_i \in \Sigma$ for $i = 0, \ldots, n$. The set of all affine functions over Σ^n is denoted by $\mathcal{A}_n$. An affine function f is called *linear* if $a_0 = 0$. The sequence of an affine (or linear) function is called an affine (or linear) sequence. The function $f(x_1, x_2, x_3) = x_3 \oplus x_1 \oplus 1$ is affine, and the function $f(x_1, x_2, x_3) = x_3 \oplus x_1$ is linear.

The *Hamming weight* of a binary vector $\alpha \in \Sigma^n$, denoted by $W(\alpha)$, is the number of ones it contains. For example, $W(010011) = 3$. Given two functions $f, g : \Sigma^n \to GF(2)$, the *Hamming distance* between them is defined as

$$d(f, g) = W(f(x) \oplus g(x)),$$

where $W(f(x) \oplus g(x))$ is the weight of the truth table of the function $f(x) \oplus g(x)$. Let $f(x) = x_1 x_2$ and $g(x) = x_1 \oplus x_2$ be two Boolean functions. Then

$$d(f, g) = W(f(x) \oplus g(x)) = W(x_1 x_2 \oplus x_1 \oplus x_2).$$

As the truth table of the function $f \oplus g = x_1 x_2 \oplus x_1 \oplus x_2$ is (0111), the distance $d(f, g) = 3$.

Let $\alpha = (a_1,\ldots,a_n)$ and $\beta = (b_1,\ldots,b_n)$ be two vectors (or sequences), the *scalar product* of α and β, denoted by $\langle \alpha, \beta \rangle$, is defined as the sum of the component-wise multiplications. In particular, when α and β are from Σ^n, $\langle \alpha, \beta \rangle = a_1 b_1 \oplus \cdots \oplus a_n b_n$. If α and β are $(1,-1)$-sequences, the scalar product $\langle \alpha, \beta \rangle = \sum_{i=1}^{n} a_i b_i$, and the addition and multiplication is taken over the reals.

Lemma 2. *If* $\xi = (a_0,\ldots,a_{2^n-1})$ *and* $\eta = (b_0,\ldots,b_{2^n-1})$ *are the sequences of functions* $f_1, f_2 : \Sigma^n \to GF(2)$, *respectively, then*

$$\xi * \eta = (a_0 b_0, a_1 b_1, \ldots, a_{2^n-1} b_{2^n-1})$$

is the sequence of $f_1(x) \oplus f_2(x)$, *where* $x = (x_1, x_2, \ldots, x_n)$.

Let $f_1(x) = x_1 x_2$ $(x \in \Sigma^2)$ that has its sequence

$$\xi = \left((-1)^{f_1(0,0)}, (-1)^{f_1(0,1)}, (-1)^{f_1(1,0)}, (-1)^{f_1(1,1)}\right) = (1 \; 1 \; 1 \; -),$$

where $-$ stands for -1. The function $f_2(x) = x_2$ $(x \in \Sigma^2)$, which has the function sequence

$$\eta = \left((-1)^{f_2(0,0)}, (-1)^{f_2(0,1)}, (-1)^{f_2(1,0)}, (-1)^{f_2(1,1)}\right) = (1 - 1-).$$

Now $f_1(x) \oplus f_2(x) = x_1 x_2 \oplus x_2$ has the sequence $(1 - 1 \; 1)$, which is $\xi * \eta = (1 \; 1 \; 1-) * (1 - 1-) = (1 - 1 \; 1)$.

An $r \times r$ matrix with entries from $\{1, -1\}$ is called a *Hadamard matrix* if

$$HH^T = rI_r,$$

where H^T is the transpose of H and I_r is the $r \times r$ identity matrix. It is well known that Hadamard matrices exist when $n = 1, 2$ or n is a multiple of 4 [518]. A *Sylvester-Hadamard* or *Walsh-Hadamard matrix* is a $2^n \times 2^n$ matrix H_n which is generated according to the following recursive relation:

$$H_0 = 1, \quad H_n = \begin{bmatrix} H_{n-1} & H_{n-1} \\ H_{n-1} & -H_{n-1} \end{bmatrix}, \quad n = 1, 2, \ldots.$$

The way the matrix H_n is constructed from H_{n-1} is written shortly as $H_n = H_1 \otimes H_{n-1}$ where $\otimes$ means the *Kronecker product*. For instance, let

$$A = \begin{bmatrix} a_1 & a_2 \\ a_3 & a_4 \end{bmatrix}, \quad B = \begin{bmatrix} b_1 & b_2 & b_3 \\ b_4 & b_5 & b_6 \\ b_7 & b_8 & b_9 \end{bmatrix},$$

then

$$A \otimes B = \begin{bmatrix} a_1 B & a_2 B \\ a_3 B & a_4 B \end{bmatrix} \quad \text{and} \quad B \otimes A = \begin{bmatrix} b_1 A & b_2 A & b_3 A \\ b_4 A & b_5 A & b_6 A \\ b_7 A & b_8 A & b_9 A \end{bmatrix}.$$

An interesting relation between Walsh-Hadamard matrices and the collection of linear functions is described in the next lemma.

Lemma 3. *The ith row (column) of H_n is the sequence of a linear function $\varphi_i(x) = \langle \alpha_i, x \rangle$, where $x, \alpha_i \in \Sigma^n$ and α_i is the binary representation of the integer i, $i = 0, 1, \ldots, 2^n - 1$.*

Proof. By induction on n. Let $n = 1$. Note that $H_1 = \begin{bmatrix} + & + \\ + & - \end{bmatrix}$ where $+$ and $-$ stand for 1 and -1, respectively. The first row of H_1 is $\ell_0 = (+\ +)$ which is equal to $\langle 0, x \rangle$. The corresponding function is the constant function $f(x) = 0$. The second row of H_1 is $\ell_1 = (+\ -)$ which is the same as the sequence of $\langle 1, x \rangle$ where $x \in \Sigma$. The corresponding function is $f(x) = x$.

Suppose the lemma is true for $n = 1, 2, \ldots, k - 1$. Since $H_k = H_1 \otimes H_{k-1}$, each row of H_n can be written as either (ℓ, ℓ) or $(\ell, -\ell)$ where ℓ is a row in H_{k-1}. From the assumption, ℓ is the sequence of some linear function $\varphi(x)$ where $x = (x_2, \ldots, x_k) \in \Sigma^{k-1}$. Thus (ℓ, ℓ) is the sequence of the function $\phi(y) = \varphi(x)$ where $y = (x_1, \ldots, x_k) \in \Sigma^k$ and $(\ell, -\ell)$ is the sequence of the function $\phi(y) = \varphi(x) \oplus x_1$ where $y = (x_1, \ldots, x_n) \in \Sigma^k$. Thus the lemma is true for k. Since H_k is symmetric, the lemma is also true for columns.   □

The first four Walsh-Hadamard matrices are:

$$H_0 = [1], \quad H_1 = \begin{bmatrix} 1 & 1 \\ 1 & -1 \end{bmatrix},$$

$$H_2 = \begin{bmatrix} 1 & 1 & 1 & 1 \\ 1 & -1 & 1 & -1 \\ 1 & 1 & -1 & -1 \\ 1 & -1 & -1 & 1 \end{bmatrix},$$

$$H_3 = \begin{bmatrix} 1 & 1 & 1 & 1 & 1 & 1 & 1 & 1 \\ 1 & -1 & 1 & -1 & 1 & -1 & 1 & -1 \\ 1 & 1 & -1 & -1 & 1 & 1 & -1 & -1 \\ 1 & -1 & -1 & 1 & 1 & -1 & -1 & 1 \\ 1 & 1 & 1 & 1 & -1 & -1 & -1 & -1 \\ 1 & -1 & 1 & -1 & -1 & 1 & -1 & 1 \\ 1 & 1 & -1 & -1 & -1 & -1 & 1 & 1 \\ 1 & -1 & -1 & 1 & -1 & 1 & 1 & -1 \end{bmatrix}.$$

Let $\delta = (i_1, i_2, \ldots, i_p)$ be a constant vector from Σ^p. Then $D_\delta : \Sigma^p \to \Sigma$ is defined as

$$D_\delta(y_1, y_2, \ldots, y_p) = (y_1 \oplus \bar{i}_1)(y_2 \oplus \bar{i}_2) \cdots (y_p \oplus \bar{i}_p),$$

where $\bar{i}_j$ is the complement of i_j for $j = 1, 2, \ldots, p$. The D-function of δ is useful in obtaining the function representation for the concatenation of binary sequences. Let $f_i : \Sigma^q \to GF(2)$, $i = 0, \ldots, 2^p - 1$, be a collection of 2^p Boolean functions. Also let ξ_i be the sequence of $f_i(x_1, \ldots, x_q)$. Now we create the concatenation ξ of the sequences ξ_i, $i = 0 \ldots, 2^p - 1$, so

$$\xi = (\xi_0, \xi_1, \ldots, \xi_{2^p-1}).$$

Obviously, the function that corresponds to ξ is the Boolean function $f : \Sigma^{p+q} \to GF(2)$ and

$$f(y, x) = \bigoplus_{\delta \in \Sigma^p} D_\delta(y) f_{\alpha_\delta}(x), \tag{3.15}$$

where $y = (y_1, \ldots, y_p)$, $x = (x_1, \ldots, x_q)$, and α_δ is the decimal representation of δ. For example, if ξ_1, ξ_2 are the sequences of functions f_1, f_2 ($f_1, f_2 : \Sigma^n \to GF(2)$) then $\xi = (\xi_1, \xi_2)$ is the sequence of the function $g : \Sigma^{n+1} \to GF(2)$ and

$$g(u, x_1, \ldots, x_n) = (1 \oplus u) f_1(x) \oplus u f_2(x).$$

3.6.2 S-box Design Criteria

The design of cryptographic algorithms is still in its infancy despite an impressive progress. The S-box theory emerged as an attempt to formalize defences that can be incorporated into S-boxes to strengthen the algorithm against cryptographic attacks. Any new attack typically results in a new design criterion that indicates what properties an S-box must have to resist the attack. There is a set of design criteria which are believed to be essential in the design of cryptographic algorithms. If S-boxes do not satisfy one of the criteria, the cryptographic design based on the S-boxes may be cryptographically weak (or easy to attack) or, alternatively, the design may need extra rounds to compensate the weakness (resulting in an inefficient design). The collection of essential S-box design criteria includes

- completeness,
- balance,
- nonlinearity,
- propagation criterion, and
- good XOR profile.

The *completeness* criterion was introduced by Kam and Davida [265]. The criterion is applicable to the whole cryptographic design (or S-P network) rather than a single S-box. Given S-boxes with a fixed structure, it is necessary to design a suitable permutation box (P-box) and compute how many rounds are necessary to build up the cross dependencies so any binary output is a complex function of every binary input. The lack of these dependencies enables an opponent to use the "divide and conquer" strategy to analyze the design.

A Boolean function $f : \Sigma^n \to GF(2)$ is said to be *balanced* if its truth table has 2^{n-1} zeros (or ones). For instance, $f = x_1 x_2 \oplus x_3$, a Boolean function on Σ^3, is balanced since the truth table of f is (01010110) and the function takes the value zero $2^{3-1} = 4$ times. The lack of balance in an S-box means that each time the S-box is used it produces outputs with a bias. So some output strings are more probable than other. Even worse, as any cryptographic design uses many rounds with the same S-box, the bias tends to accumulate making the bias larger when the number of rounds grow. This opens up the design to all sorts of attacks which explore a nonuniform output string probability distribution.

Given a balanced function $f : \Sigma^n \to GF(2)$, what are the possible input transformations such that the resulting function preserves the balance?

Lemma 4. *Let*

$$g(x) = f(xB \oplus \beta),$$

where B is any $n \times n$ nonsingular matrix and $\beta \in \Sigma^n$ is a vector. Then g is balanced if and only if f is balanced.

Proof. Note that if B is nonsingular, then for x running through all input values from the set $\{\alpha_0, \ldots, \alpha_{2^n-1}\}$, $y = xB \oplus \beta$ also takes on the same collection of values. Hence if $f(x)$ is balanced so is $g(x) = f(xB \oplus \beta)$ as the output values of g are permuted values of the function f.   □

Let $g(x) = f(xB \oplus \beta)$ where $\beta = (1,1,1)$ and

$$B = \begin{bmatrix} 1 & 1 & 0 \\ 1 & 0 & 1 \\ 0 & 1 & 0 \end{bmatrix}.$$

Thus $g(x_1, x_2, x_3) = f(x_1 \oplus x_2 \oplus 1, \ x_1 \oplus x_3 \oplus 1, \ x_2 \oplus 1)$. Clearly, g is also balanced since $g(x_0) = 0$ if and only if $f(x_0 B \oplus \beta) = 0$.

Lemma 5. *Let $f : \Sigma^n \to GF(2)$ and $g : \Sigma^m \to GF(2)$ be Boolean functions. Then the function $h : \Sigma^{n+m} \to GF(2)$ defined as $h(x, y) = f(x) \oplus g(y)$ is balanced if f is balanced.*

Proof. Observe that $g(\alpha)$ is constant for given α and the truth table of $f(x)$ is zero (one) half the time. Consequently, the truth table of $f(x) \oplus g(y)$ is zero (one) half the time.   □

The *nonlinearity* of a Boolean function can be defined as the distance between the function and the set of all affine functions [405]. More precisely, the *nonlinearity* of a Boolean function $f : \Sigma^n \to GF(2)$ is

$$N_f = \min_{g \in \mathcal{A}_n} d(f, g),$$

where $\mathcal{A}_n$ is the set of all affine functions over Σ^n. Consider the function $f(x_1, x_2) = x_1 x_2$. What is its nonlinearity? The set $\mathcal{A}_2 = \{0, x_1, x_2, x_1 \oplus x_2, 1, x_1 \oplus 1, x_2 \oplus 1, x_1 \oplus x_2 \oplus 1\}$.

$x_1 x_2$	$f(x) = x_1 x_2$	$\ell_1(x) = x_1$	$\ell_2(x) = x_2$	$\ell_3(x) = x_1 \oplus x_2$
00	0	0	0	0
01	0	0	1	1
10	0	1	0	1
11	1	1	1	0

So that $d(f, \ell_1) = d(f, \ell_2) = 1$, $d(f, \ell_3) = 3$. For the missing affine functions the distances are either 1 or 3, so the nonlinearity of f is 1.

Lemma 6. *Let* $f, g : \Sigma \to GF(2)$ *then*

$$d(f, g) = 2^{n-1} - \frac{1}{2}\langle \xi, \eta \rangle,$$

where ξ, η *are the sequences of* f *and* g, *respectively.*

Proof. Denote $\xi = (a_0, a_1, \ldots, a_{2^n-1})$ and $\eta = (b_0, b_1, \ldots, b_{2^n-1})$. Let $\rho(+)$ denote the number of positions for which two sequences are the same ($a_j = b_j$). The integer $\rho(-)$ gives the number of positions where the two sequences differ or $a_j \neq b_j$. Hence, $\langle \xi, \eta \rangle = \rho(+) - \rho(-) = 2^n - 2\rho(-)$ and $\rho(-) = 2^{n-1} - \frac{1}{2}\langle \xi, \eta \rangle$. Obviously, $\rho(-) = d(f, g)$. □

The next lemma can be easily verified using the definition of nonlinearity.

Lemma 7. *Let* ξ *be the sequence of a function* f *on* Σ^n. *Then the nonlinearity of the function is expressible by*

$$N_f = 2^{n-1} - \frac{1}{2}\max_{i=0,\ldots,2^n-1}\{|\langle \xi, \ell_i \rangle|\},$$

where ℓ_i *is the* i*th row of* H_n.

Lemma 8. *Let* f *be an arbitrary function on* Σ^n. *The nonlinearity of* f *satisfies the following relation*

$$N_f \leq 2^{n-1} - 2^{\frac{1}{2}n-1}.$$

Proof. Let ξ be the sequence of f. Let ℓ_j be the jth row (column) of the Walsh-Hadamard matrix H_n, $j = 0, 1, \ldots, 2^n - 1$. Note that

$$\xi H_n = (\langle \xi, \ell_0 \rangle, \langle \xi, \ell_1 \rangle, \ldots, \langle \xi, \ell_{2^n-1} \rangle).$$

Clearly, $\xi H_n H_n \xi^T = \sum_{j=0}^{2^n-1}\langle \xi, \ell_j \rangle^2$. As $H_n H_n = 2^n I_{2^n}$, $2^n \xi \xi^T = \sum_{j=0}^{2^n-1}\langle \xi, \ell_j \rangle^2$, where I_{2^n} is a $2^n \times 2^n$ identity matrix. The product $\xi \xi^T$ is always equal to 2^n, so

$$\sum_{j=0}^{2^n-1}\langle \xi, \ell_j \rangle^2 = 2^{2n}. \tag{3.16}$$

Equation (3.16) is called *Parseval's equation* [317]. Thus there exists an index j, $0 \leq j \leq 2^n - 1$, such that $\langle \xi, \ell_j \rangle^2 \geq 2^n$, and equivalently either $\langle \xi, \ell_j \rangle \geq 2^{\frac{1}{2}n}$ or $\langle \xi, \ell_j \rangle \leq -2^{\frac{1}{2}n}$.

From Lemma 3, ℓ_j is the sequence of some linear function φ_j. For the case $\langle \xi, \ell_j \rangle \geq 2^{\frac{1}{2}n}$, we can use Lemma 6 and conclude that $d(f, \varphi_j) \leq 2^{n-1} - 2^{\frac{1}{2}n-1}$.

For the case $\langle \xi, \ell_j \rangle \leq -2^{\frac{1}{2}n}$, we have $\langle \xi, -\ell_j \rangle \geq 2^{\frac{1}{2}n}$. Note that $-\ell_j$ is the sequence of the affine function $1 \oplus \varphi_j$. From Lemma 6, $d(f, 1 \oplus \varphi_j) \leq 2^{n-1} - 2^{\frac{1}{2}n-1}$. So finally we have that $N_f \leq 2^{n-1} - 2^{\frac{1}{2}n-1}$. □

The nonlinearity of a Boolean function is invariant under a nonsingular linear transformation.

Lemma 9. *Let f be a Boolean function over Σ^n, B be an $n \times n$ nonsingular matrix, and β a constant vector from Σ^n. Then the function $g(x) = f(xB \oplus \beta)$ has the same nonlinearity as the function f so $N_g = N_f$.*

Proof. From the definition of the nonlinearity, there exists an affine function $\varphi(x) \in \mathcal{A}_n$ such that $d(f, \varphi) = N_f$. Consider the function $\psi(x) = \varphi(xB \oplus \beta)$. Obviously $d(g, \psi) = d(f, \varphi)$ and the function ψ is also an affine function, i.e., $\psi(x) \in \mathcal{A}_n$. From the definition of nonlinearity, we can deduce that $N_g \leq d(g, \psi)$. This proves that $N_g \leq N_f$. Since B is nonsingular, the process can be repeated (for B^{-1}) and thus we derive that $N_f \leq N_g$. □

The notion of nonlinearity can be generalized for a collection of Boolean functions. Let the function $f : \Sigma^n \to \Sigma^m$. The nonlinearity of the function (Nyberg [377]) is

$$N_f = \min_{\alpha \in \Sigma^m, \alpha \neq 0} N_{f\alpha},$$

where $f_\alpha = \langle \alpha, f \rangle = \alpha_1 f_1 \oplus \cdots \oplus \alpha_m f_m$ is a linear combination of component functions $f = (f_1, \ldots, f_m)$ defined by the vector $\alpha = (\alpha_1, \ldots, \alpha_m)$.

The *Strict Avalanche Criterion*, or SAC, was introduced by Webster and Tavares [521]. Informally, an S-box satisfies the SAC if a single bit change on the input results in changes on half of the output bits. Note that if the S-box is used to construct an S-P network, then a single change on the input of the network causes an avalanche of changes. More formally, a function $f : \Sigma^n \to GF(2)$ satisfies the SAC if

$$f(x) \oplus f(x \oplus \alpha)$$

is balanced for all α whose weight is 1, i.e., $W(\alpha) = 1$. In other words, the SAC characterizes the output when there is a single bit change on the input. The *higher-order SAC* is a generalization of the SAC property where the number of input changes is bigger than one. Both the SAC and the higher-order SAC are collectively called propagation criteria [2, 414].

We say that f satisfies the *propagation criterion with respect to the vector* α if $f(x) \oplus f(x \oplus \alpha)$ is a balanced function, where $x, \alpha \in \Sigma^n$ and α is a non-zero vector. A function which holds the propagation criterion with respect to all $\alpha \in \Sigma^n$, whose weights are $1 \leq W(\alpha) \leq k$, is said to satisfy the *propagation criterion of degree k*.

Consider the function $f = x_1 x_2 \oplus x_3$ over Σ^3. Let $\alpha = (1, 1, 0)$. It is easy to check that

$$f(x) \oplus f(x \oplus \alpha) = (x_1 x_2 \oplus x_3) \oplus ((x_1 \oplus 1)(x_2 \oplus 1) \oplus x_3) = x_1 \oplus x_2 \oplus 1$$

is balanced. So f satisfies the propagation criterion with respect to the vector $\alpha = (1, 1, 0)$. Take the following function over Σ^5

$$f(x_1, x_2, x_3, x_4, x_5) = x_1 \oplus x_1 x_5 \oplus x_2 x_4 \oplus x_2 x_5 \oplus x_2 x_4 x_5 \oplus x_3 x_4 x_5.$$

Let the vector $\alpha = (0, 0, 1, 0, 0)$, then the function

$$f(x) \oplus f(x \oplus \alpha) = x_3 x_4 x_5 \oplus (x_3 \oplus 1) x_4 x_5 = x_4 x_5$$

is not balanced. In fact, f does not satisfy the propagation criterion with respect to any vector in the subset

$$\Re = \{(0,0,0,0,0), (0,0,0,0,1), (0,0,0,1,0), (0,0,1,0,0), (0,0,1,1,1)\}.$$

The next theorem shows how a nonsingular linear transformation can be used to obtain a function which satisfies the SAC.

Theorem 13. *Let $f : \Sigma^n \to GF(2)$ be a Boolean function and A be an $n \times n$ nonsingular matrix with entries from $GF(2)$. If $f(x) \oplus f(x \oplus \gamma)$ is balanced for each row γ of A, then the function $\psi(x) = f(xA)$ satisfies the SAC.*

For instance, consider the function $f = x_1 x_2 \oplus x_3$ which does not satisfy SAC, as

$$f(x) \oplus f(x \oplus e_3) = x_1 x_2 \oplus x_3 \oplus x_1 x_2 \oplus (x_3 \oplus 1) = 1$$

is not balanced for the vector $e_3 = (001)$. On the other hand,

$$f(x) \oplus f(x \oplus e_1) = x_2,$$
$$f(x) \oplus f(x \oplus e_2) = x_1, \text{ and}$$
$$f(x) \oplus f(x \oplus \gamma) = x_1 \oplus x_2 \oplus 1$$

are balanced for the vectors $e_1 = (100)$, $e_2 = (010)$, and $\gamma = (111)$, respectively. Consider the matrix built from these vectors:

$$A = \begin{bmatrix} e_1 \\ e_2 \\ \gamma \end{bmatrix} = \begin{bmatrix} 1 & 0 & 0 \\ 0 & 1 & 0 \\ 1 & 1 & 1 \end{bmatrix}.$$

From Theorem 13 we conclude that $g(x) = f(xA)$ satisfies the SAC.

Theorem 13 can be generalized and used to design a collection of functions, each satisfying the SAC.

Theorem 14. *Let $f_1, \ldots, f_m$ be functions over Σ^n and the set of vectors over Σ^n be*

$$\Re = \{\alpha | f_j(x) \oplus f_j(x \oplus \alpha) \text{ is not balanced for } j, \ 1 \le j \le m\}.$$

If $|\Re| < 2^{n-1}$ then there exists a nonsingular $n \times n$ matrix with entries from $GF(2)$ such that each $\psi_j(x) = f_j(xA)$ satisfies the SAC.

Consider the following three functions $f_1 = x_1 \oplus x_3 \oplus x_2 x_3$, $f_2 = x_1 \oplus x_2 \oplus x_1 x_2 \oplus x_2 x_3$, and $f_3 = x_1 x_2 \oplus x_2 x_3 \oplus x_1 x_3$. The function f_1 does not satisfy the propagation criterion with respect to the vector $(1, 0, 0)$ only. The function f_2 satisfies it with respect to $(1, 0, 1)$ only and f_3 with respect to $(1, 1, 1)$ only. Therefore $\Re = \{(1, 0, 0), (1, 0, 1), (1, 1, 1)\}$ and $|\Re| = 3 < 2^{n-1}$, where $n = 3$. From Theorem 14, there exists a nonsingular 3×3 matrix A such that each function $\psi_j(x) = f_j(xA)$ satisfies the SAC. For example, A can be chosen as

$$A = \begin{bmatrix} 0 & 0 & 1 \\ 0 & 1 & 0 \\ 1 & 1 & 0 \end{bmatrix}.$$

A Boolean function may not satisfy the propagation criterion. The ultimate failure happens when the function $f(x) \oplus f(x \oplus \alpha)$ is constant. Being more precise, let f be a function over Σ^n. A vector, α, is called a *linear structure* of f if $f(x) \oplus f(x \oplus \alpha)$ is constant. Every function has at least one linear structure – the zero vector. For instance, consider the function $f = x_1 x_2 \oplus x_3$ over Σ^3. The vector $\beta = (0, 0, 1)$ is a linear structure of f, as

$$f(x) \oplus f(x \oplus \beta) = (x_1 x_2 \oplus x_3) \oplus (x_1 x_2 \oplus x_3 \oplus 1) = 1.$$

Needless to say, nonzero linear structures should be avoided in S-boxes as they force the corresponding differences of functions to be constant.

The XOR profile was introduced in Sect. 3.4.1. The criterion is not very restrictive as the designer of S-boxes needs to take care that the XOR profile does not contain entries with "large" numbers. In addition, the XOR profile must be considered in the context of the best round characteristics. It is possible to trade off the largest entries of the XOR profile with the number of rounds.

In some circumstances, we may require that a collection of Boolean functions be linearly nonequivalent [82]. The collection of functions $\{f_1, \ldots, f_m\}$, $f_i : \Sigma^n \to GF(2)$ is linearly nonequivalent if there is no affine transformation for which $f_i(x) = f_j(Ax + \beta)$ where A is an $n \times n$ nonsingular matrix and $\beta \in \Sigma^n$ ($i \neq j$).

Any Boolean function can be represented in many ways depending on the choice of underlying logical operations. Two canonical forms (disjunctive and conjunctive) lead to expressions that are not unique and then one can try to find the shortest expression (the minimization procedure). On the other hand, the algebraic normal form is unique. The function $f : \Sigma^n \to GF(2)$ is written in the algebraic normal form if

$$f(x) = a_0 \oplus \sum_{1 \leq i \leq n} a_i x_i \oplus \sum_{1 \leq i < j \leq n} a_{ij} x_i x_j \oplus \cdots \oplus a_{12\ldots n} x_1 x_2 \cdots x_n.$$

The requirement to have a short algebraic normal form of a Boolean function becomes essential when the function is too big to be stored as a lookup table. So the function needs to be evaluated "on the fly." Clearly, shorter functions consume less evaluation time.

3.6.3 Bent Functions

In 1976 Rothaus introduced the so-called *bent functions* [435]. Because of their properties, they can be used as building blocks to design Boolean functions with high nonlinearity [1, 289, 391, 541]. Bent functions from $\mathcal{Z}_q^n$ to $\mathcal{Z}_q$ are defined and studied in [290].

A Boolean function f over Σ^n is called bent if

$$2^{-\frac{n}{2}} \sum_{x \in \Sigma^n} (-1)^{f(x) \oplus \langle \beta, x \rangle} = \pm 1$$

for all $\beta \in \Sigma^n$.

The following statements are equivalent.

(i) f is bent.
(ii) $\langle \xi, \ell \rangle = \pm 2^{\frac{1}{2}n}$ for any affine sequence ℓ of length 2^n, where ξ is the sequence of f.

(iii) $2^{-\frac{1}{2}n}H_n\xi^T$ is equal to ± 1.

(iv) $f(x) \oplus f(x \oplus a)$ is balanced for any nonzero vector $a \in \Sigma^n$, where $x = (x_1, x_2, \ldots, x_n)$.

(v) The matrix F of the function f is a Hadamard matrix.

(vi) The nonlinearity N_f satisfies $N_f = 2^{n-1} - 2^{\frac{1}{2}n-1}$.

The proof that the statements are equivalent can be found in [1, 457, 541]. Note that the equivalence of (i), (ii), (iii), and (iv) is easy to prove.

As an exercise, we are going to prove that (ii) $\Leftrightarrow$ (vi).

First, we prove that (ii) $\Rightarrow$ (vi). Assume that (ii) holds, i.e., $\langle \xi, \ell_j \rangle = \pm 2^{\frac{1}{2}n}$ for each linear sequence ℓ_j of length 2^n and the linear function φ_j corresponds to the linear sequence ℓ_j. Note that $\langle \xi, 1+\ell_j \rangle = \mp 2^{\frac{1}{2}n}$ for each linear sequence of length 2^n. Note that $1+\ell_j$ is the sequence of the affine function $1 \oplus \varphi_j$. From Lemma 6, for any linear φ_j, either $d(f, \varphi_j) = 2^{n-1} - 2^{\frac{1}{2}n-1}$ or $d(f, 1 \oplus \varphi_j) = 2^{n-1} - 2^{\frac{1}{2}n-1}$. This proves (vi).

Now we prove that (vi) $\Rightarrow$ (ii). This is done by contradiction. Assume that the statement (ii) is false. From (3.16), we can state that there exists a linear sequence ℓ of length 2^n and its linear function φ such that $|\langle \xi, \ell \rangle| > 2^{\frac{1}{2}n}$. Thus either $\langle \xi, \ell \rangle > 2^{\frac{1}{2}n}$ or $\langle \xi, \ell \rangle < -2^{\frac{1}{2}n}$. In the first case, by Lemma 6, $d(f, \varphi_j) < 2^{n-1} - 2^{\frac{1}{2}n-1}$ so $N_f < 2^{n-1} - 2^{\frac{1}{2}n-1}$. In the second case, we know that $\langle \xi, -\ell \rangle > 2^{\frac{1}{2}n}$. Note that $-\ell$ is the sequence of the affine function $1 \oplus \varphi$. Using the same argument, we have $d(f, 1 \oplus \varphi_j) < 2^{n-1} - 2^{\frac{1}{2}n-1}$ so $N_f < 2^{n-1} - 2^{\frac{1}{2}n-1}$. This gives the requested contradiction that $N_f \neq 2^{n-1} - 2^{\frac{1}{2}n-1}$ which concludes the proof.

Bent functions have some remarkable properties. Let f be a bent function over Σ^n and ξ be a sequence of the function f (the sequence is called bent if it represents a bent function). The basic properties of bent functions are:

1. n must be even – bent functions exist for even values of n.
2. For $n \neq 2$, the degree of $f \leq \frac{1}{2}n$ – the degree of f written in the algebraic normal form.
3. For any affine function φ, $f \oplus \varphi$ is also bent.
4. $f(xA \oplus a)$ is also bent where A is any nonsingular matrix of order n, and a is any vector in Σ^n.
5. f takes the value zero $2^{n-1} \pm 2^{\frac{1}{2}n-1}$ times.
6. $2^{-\frac{1}{2}n}H_n\xi^T$ is also a bent sequence.

We now verify some of the properties for the bent function $f(x) = x_1 x_2$ over Σ^2:

- The truth table of f has to contain $2^1 \pm 2^0$ ones (or zeros). As $f(0,0) = 0$, $f(0,1) = 0$, $f(1,0) = 0$, and $f(1,1) = 1$, the truth table is (0001), so the weight of it is 1.
- The 4×4 Sylvester-Hadamard matrix is

$$
H_2 = \begin{bmatrix} + & + & + & + \\ + & - & + & - \\ + & + & - & - \\ + & - & - & + \end{bmatrix} = \begin{bmatrix} \ell_1 \\ \ell_2 \\ \ell_3 \\ \ell_4 \end{bmatrix}.
$$

The sequence of $f = x_1 x_2$ is $\xi = (+ + + -)$. It is easy to compute that $\langle \xi, \ell_1 \rangle = 2$, $\langle \xi, \ell_2 \rangle = 2$, $\langle \xi, \ell_3 \rangle = 2$, and $\langle \xi, \ell_4 \rangle = -2$. This property is consistent with statement (ii).

- The matrix of f is

$$
F = \begin{bmatrix} + & + & + & - \\ + & + & - & + \\ + & - & + & + \\ - & + & + & + \end{bmatrix},
$$

which is a Hadamard matrix as $FF^T = 4I_4$.

- According to statement (iv), $f(x) \oplus f(x \oplus a)$ has to be balanced for all nonzero $\alpha \in \Sigma^2$. Indeed, $f(x) \oplus f(x \oplus a) = x_1 x_2 \oplus (x_1 \oplus a_1)(x_2 \oplus a_2) = a_1 x_2 \oplus a_2 x_1 \oplus a_1 a_2$ is an affine function, and is thus 0-1 balanced.

Consider another bent function $f = x_1 x_2 \oplus x_3 x_4$ over Σ^n. The truth table of f is

0, 0, 0, 1, 0, 0, 0, 1, 0, 0, 0, 1, 1, 1, 1, 0.

The function f takes on the value zero $2^{4-1} + 2^{\frac{1}{2}4-1} = 8 + 2 = 10$ times. The function is not balanced.

3.6.4 Propagation and Nonlinearity

There is an intrinsic relation between propagation properties and the nonlinearity of Boolean functions. For instance, bent functions satisfy propagation criteria with respect to all nonzero vectors. Now we are going to investigate the relation between propagation and nonlinearity for arbitrary Boolean functions.

Let f be a function over Σ^n and $\xi(\alpha)$ be the sequence of the function $f(x \oplus \alpha)$. Using our notation, it is obvious that $\xi(0) * \xi(\alpha)$ is the sequence of $f(x) \oplus f(x \oplus \alpha)$. The *autocorrelation* of f with a shift α is defined as

$$\Delta(\alpha) = \langle \xi(0), \xi(\alpha) \rangle.$$

Lemma 10. *Let f be a function over Σ^n. Then the Hamming weight of $f(x) \oplus f(x \oplus \alpha)$ is equal to $2^{n-1} - \frac{1}{2}\Delta(\alpha)$.*

Proof. Let e_+ (e_-) denote the number of ones (minus ones) in the sequence of $\xi(0) * \xi(\alpha)$. Thus $e_+ - e_- = \Delta(\alpha)$ and $(2^n - e_-) - e_- = \Delta(\alpha)$, so $e_- = 2^{n-1} - \frac{1}{2}\Delta(\alpha)$. Note that e_- is also the number of ones in the truth table of $f(x) \oplus f(x \oplus \alpha)$. Thus the lemma holds. $\square$

The following corollary is a simple conclusion from Lemma 10.

Corollary 2. $\Delta(\alpha) = 0$ *if and only if $f(x) \oplus f(x \oplus \alpha)$ is balanced, i.e., f satisfies the propagation criterion with respect to α.*

Note that if $|\Delta(\alpha)| = 2^n$ then $f(x) \oplus f(x \oplus \alpha)$ is constant and then α is a linear structure [377]. In practice, for most Boolean functions, the propagation criterion with respect to arbitrary α is not satisfied and also α is not a linear structure. For some cases, $\Delta(\alpha) \neq 0$ and is relatively small so $f(x) \oplus f(x \oplus \alpha)$ is almost balanced, and the function f has "good" propagation properties. To measure the global propagation property of a function f with respect to all vectors in Σ^n, we can use the number

$$\sum_{\alpha \in \Sigma^n} \Delta^2(\alpha).$$

Ideally, we expect the number to be as small as possible. In fact, it is smallest for bent functions and largest for affine functions.

Let F be the matrix of $f : \Sigma^n \to GF(2)$ and ξ be the sequence of f. It is easy to verify that the first row of FF^T is

$$(\Delta(\alpha_0), \Delta(\alpha_1), \cdots, \Delta(\alpha_{2^n - 1})).$$

Now consider the Fourier transform of the function f written in the form $2^{-n}H_n F H_n$. According to the result by McFarland (see Theorem 3.3 in [155]), the matrix F can be represented as

$$F = 2^{-n} H_n \operatorname{diag}(\langle \xi, \ell_0 \rangle, \cdots, \langle \xi, \ell_{2^n - 1} \rangle) H_n, \tag{3.17}$$

where ℓ_i is the ith row of a Sylvester-Hadamard matrix H_n and diag$(a_0, \cdots, a_{2^n-1})$ is a $2^n \times 2^n$ matrix with all zero entries except for the diagonal whose entries are $(a_0, \cdots, a_{2^n-1})$. Using (3.17), the matrix FF^T takes on the form

$$FF^T = 2^{-n} H_n \operatorname{diag}(\langle \xi, \ell_0 \rangle^2, \cdots, \langle \xi, \ell_{2^n-1} \rangle^2) H_n.$$

Note that f and H_n are symmetric so $F = F^T$ and $H_n = H_n^T$. The first row of FF^T is

$$2^{-n}(\langle \xi^*, \ell_0 \rangle, \cdots, \langle \xi^*, \ell_{2^n-1} \rangle) = 2^{-n} \xi^* H_n,$$

where $\xi^* = (\langle \xi, \ell_0 \rangle^2, \cdots, \langle \xi, \ell_{2^n-1} \rangle^2)$. Thus

$$(\Delta(\alpha_0), \Delta(\alpha_1), \cdots, \Delta(\alpha_{2^n-1})) = 2^{-n}(\langle \xi, \ell_0 \rangle^2, \cdots, \langle \xi, \ell_{2^n-1} \rangle^2) H_n.$$

So the following theorem has been proved.

Theorem 15. *Let f be a function over Σ^n. Then*

$$(\Delta(\alpha_0), \Delta(\alpha_1), \cdots, \Delta(\alpha_{2^n-1})) H_n = (\langle \xi, \ell_0 \rangle^2, \cdots, \langle \xi, \ell_{2^n-1} \rangle^2).$$

As $\langle \xi, \ell_i \rangle$ expresses the distance between the function f and the linear function which corresponds to the sequence ℓ_i, Theorem 15 characterizes the relation between the nonlinearity and the propagation. Let us investigate the relation in more detail. First denote $\eta = (\Delta(\alpha_0), \Delta(\alpha_1), \cdots, \Delta(\alpha_{2^n-1}))$. The expression $\langle \xi^*, \xi^* \rangle = \langle \eta H_n, \eta H_n \rangle = \eta H_n H_n^T \eta^T = 2^n \langle \eta, \eta \rangle$. As $\langle \xi^*, \xi^* \rangle = \sum_{j=0}^{2^n-1} \langle \xi, \ell_j \rangle^4$, we have shown that the following corollary is true.

Corollary 3. *Let f be a function over Σ^n. Then*

$$\sum_{\alpha \in \Sigma^n} \Delta^2(\alpha) = 2^{-n} \sum_{j=0}^{2^n-1} \langle \xi, \ell_j \rangle^4.$$

Corollary 3 gives an insight into the relation between propagation properties expressed by $\Delta(\alpha)$ and the nonlinearity characterized by distances of f to the set of linear functions. Clearly, the larger the nonlinearity of f the better the propagation of the function. It is convenient to describe the nonlinearity and propagation of the function f by the parameter

$$\sigma(f) = \sum_{\delta \in \Sigma^n} \Delta^2(\alpha) = 2^{-n} \sum_{j=0}^{2^n-1} \langle \xi, \ell_j \rangle^4. \tag{3.18}$$

The parameter $\sigma(f)$ is called the *global propagation* of the function f. It would be interesting to know how it behaves depending on the function f. The next theorem gives the answer.

Theorem 16. *Let f be a function over Σ^n. Then*

(i) $2^{2n} \leq \sigma(f) \leq 2^{3n}$,
(ii) $\sigma(f) = 2^{2n}$ *if and only if f is a bent function,*
(iii) $\sigma(f) = 2^{3n}$ *if and only if f is an affine function.*

Proof. Statement (i). By the definition, we have

$$\sigma(f) = 2^{-n} \sum_{j=0}^{2^n-1} \langle \xi, \ell_j \rangle^4 \leq 2^{-n} \left(\sum_{j=0}^{2^n-1} \langle \xi, \ell_j \rangle^2 \right)^2.$$

From (3.16), we have

$$\sum_{j=0}^{2^n-1} \langle \xi, \ell_j \rangle^2 = 2^{2n}.$$

Thus $\sigma(f) \leq 2^{-n} 2^{4n} = 2^{3n}$.

Statement (ii). Note that always $\Delta(0) = 2^n$. So $\sigma(f) = \sum_{\alpha \in \Sigma^n} \Delta^2(\alpha) = \Delta^2(0) = 2^{2n}$ happens if and only if $\Delta(\alpha) = 0$ for any $\alpha \neq 0$. This means that f is bent.

Statement (iii). Denote $y_j = \langle \xi, \ell_j \rangle^2$. By Parseval's equation, $\sum_{j=0}^{2^n-1} y_j = 2^n$. The following statements are equivalent: $\sigma(f) = 2^{3n} \Longleftrightarrow 2^{-n} \sum_{j=0}^{2^n-1} y_j^2 = 2^{3n}$ $\Longleftrightarrow \sum_{j=0}^{2^n-1} y_j^2 = 2^{4n} \Longleftrightarrow \sum_{j=0}^{2^n-1} y_j^2 = (\sum_{j=0}^{2^n-1} y_j)^2 \Longleftrightarrow y_i y_j = 0$ if $j \neq i \Longleftrightarrow$ there exists a j_0 such that $y_{j_0} = 2^{2n}$ and $y_j = 0$ if $j \neq j_0 \Longleftrightarrow$ there exists a j_0 such that $\langle \xi, \ell_{j_0} \rangle = \pm 2^n$ and $\langle \xi, \ell_j \rangle = 0$ if $j \neq j_0 \Longleftrightarrow$ there exists a j_0 such that $\xi = \pm \ell_{j_0}$, i.e., f is an affine function. $\qquad \square$

3.6.5 Constructions of Balanced Functions

Bent functions have the largest nonlinearity and good propagation properties but are not balanced. The lack of balance complicates the use of bent functions. Nevertheless, bent functions are still major building blocks for the design of cryptographically strong S-boxes. We study two methods of the construction of balanced functions. The first method concatenates bent functions. The second one applies linear functions. Readers interested in details are referred to [457, 458, 459, 460].

Concatenating Bent Functions. There are two cases. In both cases, we start from a bent function over Σ^{2k}. The bent function is used to construct balanced functions over Σ^{2k+1} (the first case) and Σ^{2k+2} (the second case). Our considerations start from the first case.

Let $f : \Sigma^{2k} \to GF(2)$ be a bent function and g be a function over Σ^{2k+1} defined by

$$g(x_1, x_2, \ldots, x_{2k+1}) = x_1 \oplus f(x_2, \ldots, x_{2k+1}).$$

This construction is embedded in the permutations $g(x) = x^3$ over $GF(2^{2k+1})$ [404]. The function g is balanced, as its truth table is the concatenation of the truth tables of the original function f and its negation, i.e., the function $f \oplus 1$. The function g satisfies the propagation criterion with respect to all nonzero vectors $\alpha \in \Sigma^{2k+1}$ and is different from $(1, 0, \ldots, 0)$. This happens as $g(x) \oplus g(x \oplus \alpha)$ is balanced for all $\alpha \notin \{(0, \ldots, 0), (1, 0, \ldots, 0)\}$ (or $\Delta(\alpha) = 0$). If $\alpha = (1, 0, \ldots, 0) = \alpha_1$, then $g(x) \oplus g(x \oplus \alpha_1) = 1$ for all $x \in \Sigma^{2k+1}$ and $\Delta(\alpha_1) = -2^{2k+1}$. The vector α_1 is a nonzero linear structure of g. The global propagation $\sigma(g)$ can be calculated, and

$$\sigma(g) = \sum_{\alpha \in \Sigma^{2k+1}} \Delta^2(\alpha) = \Delta^2(0) + \Delta^2(\alpha_1) = 2 \cdot 2^{4k+2} = 2^{4k+3}.$$

The lower bound of $\sigma(h)$, where h is a function on Σ^{2k+1}, is 2^{4k+2}. This bound is attained by bent functions only. But bent functions exist in even-dimensional vector spaces only.

Denote $g^*(x) = g(xA)$, where A is a nonsingular $(2k+1) \times (2k+1)$ matrix with entries from $GF(2)$. The function g^* is a balanced function on Σ^{2k+1}. Note that $\sigma(g)$ is invariant under any nondegenerate linear transformation on the variables. Thus $\sigma^*(g^*) = 2^{4k+3}$. Clearly, the nonlinearity and the number of vectors for which the propagation criterion is satisfied are the same for g^* and g. Unfortunately, g has a linear structure although it satisfies the propagation criterion with respect to other nonzero vectors.

Let f be a bent function over Σ^{2k-2} and g be a function over Σ^{2k} defined by

$$g(x_1, x_2, \ldots, x_{2k}) = x_1 \oplus x_2 \oplus f(x_3, \ldots, x_{2k}).$$

For any nonzero vector $\alpha \in \Sigma^{2k}$, consider $g(x) \oplus g(x \oplus \alpha)$. Denote $\alpha_1 = (1, 0, \ldots, 0)$, $\alpha_2 = (0, 1, \ldots, 0)$, and $\alpha_3 = (1, 1, \ldots, 0)$. First, assume that $\alpha \neq \alpha_1, \alpha_2, \alpha_3$. From the definition of the function g, it is easy to conclude that $g(x) \oplus g(x \oplus \alpha)$ is balanced and $\Delta(\alpha) = 0$. On the other hand, suppose that $\alpha = \alpha_j$, $j = 1, 2, 3$. From the definition of g, we have that $g(x) \oplus g(x \oplus \alpha_j) = 1$,

$j = 1, 2$, for all $x \in \Sigma^{2k+1}$. Also $\Delta(\alpha_j) = -2^{2k}$ for $j = 1, 2$. For α_3, $g(x) \oplus g(x \oplus \alpha_3) = 0$ and $\Delta(\alpha_3) = 2^{2k}$. The global propagation $\sigma(g)$ is easy to compute and

$$\sigma(g) = \sum_{\alpha \in \Sigma^{2k}} \Delta^2(\alpha) = \Delta^2(0) + \sum_{j=1}^{3} \Delta^2(\alpha_j) = 4 \cdot 2^{4k} = 2^{4k+2}.$$

The collection of balanced function can be expanded by using a nonsingular linear transformation. Denote

$$g^*(x) = g(xA),$$

where A is any nonsingular $2k \times 2k$ matrix over $GF(2)$. It can be proved that the function g^* is balanced and satisfies the propagation criterion with respect to all but three nonzero vectors. The nonlinearity of g^* satisfies $N_{g^*} \geq 2^{2k-1} - 2^k$. Note that $\sigma(g)$ is invariant under any nondegenerate linear transformation on the variables. Thus $\sigma(g^*) = 2^{4k+2}$. This value compares quite favorably with the lower bound on $\sigma(h)$ which is 2^{4k}. Unfortunately, the function g has three linear structures although it satisfies the propagation criterion with respect to other nonzero vectors.

The constructions presented above modify bent functions so the resulting functions are balanced and maintain high nonlinearity. An alternative approach applies linear functions (always balanced) and combines them in such a way that the resulting function attains high nonlinearity.

Concatenating Linear Functions. Assume we have two collections of Boolean variables $y = (y_1, \ldots, y_p)$ and $x = (x_1, \ldots, x_q)$ $(p < q)$. We can build up a Boolean function over Σ^{p+q} by concatenating 2^p linear functions, each over Σ^q. The collection of nonzero linear functions used in the construction is denoted by $\Re = \{\varphi_0, \ldots, \varphi_{2^p-1}\}$ and $\varphi_i \neq \varphi_j$ for any $i \neq j$, $\varphi_i : \Sigma^q \rightarrow GF(2)$. More precisely, we construct balanced, nonlinear functions by combining the linear functions from $\Re$ as follows:

$$g(z) = g(y, x) = \bigoplus_{\delta=0,\ldots,2^p-1} D_\delta(y)\varphi_\delta(x). \tag{3.19}$$

The properties of the resulting function are summarized below (the proof of the properties can be found in [458]).

PR1. The function g is balanced.
PR2. The nonlinearity of g satisfies $N_g \geq 2^{p+q-1} - 2^{q-1}$.

PR3. The function g satisfies the propagation criterion with respect to any $\gamma = (\beta, \alpha)$ with $\beta \neq 0$ where $\beta \in \Sigma^p$ and $\alpha \in \Sigma^q$.

PR4. The degree of the function g (in the algebraic normal form) can be $p+1$ if $\Re$ is appropriately chosen.

Let ξ_δ be the sequence of φ_δ and η be the sequence of g. Clearly, from the construction, η is the concatenation of 2^p distinct ξ_δ. Note that $H_{p+q} = H_p \otimes H_q$. So each row of H_{p+q}, say L, can be represented as the Kronecker product $L = \ell' \otimes \ell''$, where ℓ' is a row of H_p and ℓ'' is a row of H_q. If $\ell' = (a_0, \ldots, a_{2^p-1})$, then $\ell' \otimes \ell'' = (a_0 \ell'', \ldots, a_{2^p-1} \ell'')$ and the string $a_i \ell''$ is equal to ℓ'' if $a_i = 1$ or $-\ell''$ if $a_i = -1$. Since different rows of H_p are orthogonal, we have

$$\langle \eta, L \rangle = \begin{cases} 2^q \text{ if } f \in \Re, \text{ where } L = \ell' \otimes \ell'', \\ 0 \text{ if } f \notin \Re, \text{ where } L = \ell' \otimes \ell'', \end{cases} \tag{3.20}$$

where f is the linear function corresponding to ℓ''. There are $2^p \cdot 2^p$ different vectors $L = \ell' \otimes \ell''$ which can be constructed from 2^p linear functions from $\Re$. From (3.18) and (3.19), we can obtain that the global propagation of g is

$$\sigma(g) = 2^{-p-q} 2^p \cdot 2^p \cdot 2^{4q} = 2^{p+3q}.$$

The parameter $\sigma(g)$ is invariant under any nondegenerate linear transformation on the variables. Thus $\sigma(g^*) = 2^{p+3q}$ where $g^*(z) = g(Az)$. The lower bound of $\sigma(f)$, where f is a function on V_{p+q}, is 2^{2p+2q}. As we know this bound is reached only by bent functions. The nonlinearity and the number of vectors for which the propagation criterion is satisfied are the same for both g and g^*.

The above construction applies 2^p different nonzero linear functions. There are no other restrictions imposed on the set $\Re$. We can improve the construction when we select the set $\Re$ more carefully. The *rank* of the set of linear functions is the number of all linearly independent elements (functions) in the set. Assume that there is a δ_0 such that the rank of the set

$$\{\varphi_\delta \oplus \varphi_{\delta_0} | \delta = 0, \ldots, 2^p - 1\} \tag{3.21}$$

is equal to q. Next we are going to show that the function g defined by (3.19) has no linear structure. Consider

$$g(z) \oplus g(z \oplus \gamma) = g(y, x) \oplus g(y \oplus \beta, x \oplus \alpha). \tag{3.22}$$

As we know the function (3.22) is balanced for $\beta \neq 0$ (see the property PR3), we can find linear structures only when $\beta = 0$. The expression (3.22) reduces to

$$g(z) \oplus g(z \oplus \gamma) = g(y, x) \oplus g(y, x \oplus \alpha)$$

$$= \bigoplus_{\delta=0,\dots,2^p-1} D_\delta(y)(\varphi_\delta(x) \oplus \varphi(x \oplus \alpha)) = \bigoplus_{\delta=0,\dots,2p-1} D_\delta(y)\varphi_\delta(\alpha). \quad (3.23)$$

Clearly, $\gamma = (0, \alpha)$ is a linear structure if and only if (3.23) is constant or equivalently $\varphi_\delta(\alpha) = c$. This is true when

$$\varphi_\delta(\alpha) \oplus \varphi_{\delta_0}(\alpha) = 0 \quad (3.24)$$

for every $\delta = 0, \dots, 2^p - 1$, where $c \in \Sigma$. Since the rank of $\{\varphi_\delta \oplus \varphi_{\delta_0} | \delta = 0, \dots, 2^p - 1\} = q$, there exists no nonzero α satisfying (3.24) which is equivalent to the set of linear equations. This proves that g has no linear structures.

The condition imposed on the set $\Re$ is easy to satisfy. For example, the following collection of linear functions $h_1(x) = x_1$, $h_2(x) = x_2$, ..., $h_q(x) = x_q$ are linearly independent over Σ^q. Let φ_0 be an arbitrary linear function on Σ^q. Denote $\varphi_j = h_j \oplus \varphi_0$, $j = 1, 2, \dots, q$. Thus $\varphi_1 \oplus \varphi_0$, ..., $\varphi_q \oplus \varphi_0$ are linearly independent. The set $\Re$ has to have 2^p linear functions. It contains the following linear functions: $\varphi_1 = h_1 \oplus \varphi_0$, ..., $\varphi_q = h_q \oplus \varphi_0$, is φ_0 where the $(q+1)$th linear function. The others can be selected arbitrarily from the other nonzero linear functions.

3.6.6 S-box Design

Single Boolean functions are basic elements that can be used to construct complex (and useful from a cryptographic point of view) S-boxes. An $n \times k$ S-box is a mapping from Σ^n to Σ^k and

$$S(x) = (f_1(x), \dots, f_k(x)),$$

where $n \geq k$ and $f_j : \Sigma^n \to GF(2)$.

The collection of cryptographically essential properties for an S-box includes the following:

S1. Any nonzero linear combination of $f_1, \dots, f_k$, i.e., $f = c_1 f_1 \oplus \cdots \oplus c_k f_k$, $(c_1, \dots, c_k) \neq (0, \dots, 0)$, should be balanced.

S2. Any nonzero linear combination of $f_1, \dots, f_k$ should be highly nonlinear.

S3. Any nonzero linear combination of $f_1, \dots, f_k$ should satisfy the SAC.

S4. The S-box $S(x)$ should be *regular*, i.e., each vector in Σ^k should occur 2^{n-k} times while x runs through Σ^n.

S5. $S(x)$ should have a good XOR profile, i.e., $S(x) \oplus S(x \oplus \alpha)$ runs through some 2^{k-1} vectors in Σ^k each 2^{n-k+1} times while x runs through Σ^n but does not take on other 2^{k-1} vectors.

Observe that properties S2 and S4 are equivalent. Other properties may not hold simultaneously but a "reasonable" tradeoff can always be negotiated.

To illustrate the properties, consider a simple example. Let our S-box be the mapping from Σ^3 to Σ^3 such that

$$S(x) = (f_1(x), f_2(x), f_3(x)),$$

where $f_1 = x_1 \oplus x_3 \oplus x_2 x_3$, $f_2 = x_1 \oplus x_2 \oplus x_1 x_2 \oplus x_2 x_3$, and $f_3 = x_1 x_2 \oplus x_2 x_3 \oplus x_1 x_3$. The properties S1–S5 can be verified as follows.

S1. Any nonzero linear combination of f_1, f_2, f_3, say $f = c_1 f_1 \oplus c_2 f_2 \oplus c_3 f_3$, $(c_1, c_2, c_3) \neq (0, 0, 0)$, is balanced.

S2. Any nonzero linear combination f of f_1, f_2, f_3 has nonlinearity 2, i.e., $N_f \geq 2$ (the maximum for balanced functions on Σ^3).

S3. Any nonzero linear combination of f_1, f_2, f_3 satisfies the propagation criterion except for a single vector.

S4. $S(x)$ is regular as it is a permutation.

S5. $S(x)$ has a good XOR profile, i.e., $S(x) \oplus S(x \oplus a)$ runs through some 2^2 vectors in Σ^3 each twice while x runs through Σ^3 once and does not take on other 2^2 vectors. More precisely, let $a = (001)$. Then $S(x) \oplus S(x \oplus a)$ runs through vectors (010), (011), (100), (101) twice while x runs through Σ^3 once. If $a = (111)$, then $S(x) \oplus S(x \oplus a)$ runs through vectors (001), (011), (101), (111) twice while x runs through Σ^3 once.

Permutations defined in $GF(2^n)$ also need to be chosen as some of them exhibit good cryptographic properties. It turns out [404] that exponentiation can produce cryptographically strong S-boxes. Being more specific, the S-boxes $S : \Sigma^n \to \Sigma^n$ defined as $S(x) = x^3$, $x \in GF(2^n)$, where n is odd, are permutations with the following properties [404, 376, 377, 30]:

S1' Any nonzero linear combination of the coordinate functions is balanced. This results from the fact that cubing is a permutation. Any nonzero linear combination f of the coordinate functions has a high nonlinearity and $N_f \geq 2^{n-1} - 2^{\frac{1}{2}(n-1)}$.

S3' Any nonzero linear combination of the coordinate functions satisfies the propagation criterion except for a single nonzero vector.

S5' $S(x)$ has a good XOR profile, i.e., $S(x) \oplus S(x \oplus a)$ runs through a subset of 2^{n-1} vectors in Σ^n twice while x runs through Σ^n once. The remaining 2^{n-1} vectors do not occur.

The design of S-boxes is not free of pitfalls. Special care needs to be exercised when a cryptographically strong S-box is modified by adding or reducing output bits. Consider an S-box $S(x) = (f_1(x), \ldots, f_k(x))$ which is regular and has a good XOR profile where $f_i : \Sigma^n \to GF(2)$ for $i = 1, \ldots, k$. It turns out [461] that $S(x) = (f_1(x), \ldots, f_t(x))$, where $t < k$, is regular but does not have a good XOR profile.

On the other hand, for any regular S-box $S(x) = (f_1(x), \ldots, f_k(x))$ with a good XOR profile, there is a collection of functions $f_{k+1}(x), \ldots, f_s(x)$ such that the extended S-box $S'(x) = (f_1(x), \ldots, f_k(x), f_{k+1}(x), \ldots, f_s(x))$ is a regular mapping from Σ^n to Σ^s but does not have a good XOR profile.

3.7 Problems and Exercises

1. Write C programs for the implementation of the following ciphers:
   - the Caesar cipher,
   - the affine cipher,
   - the monoalphabetic substitution cipher,
   - the transposition cipher,
   - the homophonic substitution cipher,
   - the Vigenère cipher,
   - the Beauford cipher.
   Your programs should include routines for both encryption and decryption.
2. The Caesar cipher is relatively easy to break. Write a C program which is first fed by a sample text to collect statistical properties of the language. Then use the statistics to cryptanalyze a given ciphertext by comparing it with the statistics computed for the ciphertext.
3. Design and implement a C program for cryptanalysis of the affine cipher. Your program must not use the enumeration of all possible keys but should use the frequencies of characters to make "optimal" guesses about the key.
4. Write a computer program which calculates the index of coincidence. Run the program for different texts. Try an English text, a text of a high-level programming language, and a text of random characters generated by a pseudorandom generator. Compare and discuss the results.
5. Let the message space $\mathcal{M} = \mathcal{Z}_{26}^4$ and $m = (m_1, m_2, m_3, m_4)$ where $m_i \in \mathcal{Z}_{26}$ for $i = 1, 2, 3, 4$. Design a product cipher $c = E_k(m)$, where $m, c, k \in \mathcal{Z}_{26}^4$, based on the network of P-boxes and S-boxes. Use the P-box $P : \mathcal{Z}_{26}^4 \to \mathcal{Z}_{26}^4$ where $P(x_1, x_2, x_3, x_4) = (x_1, x_3, x_2, x_4)$, and the S-box $S : \mathcal{Z}_{26}^2 \to \mathcal{Z}_{26}^2$, defined as
   $$S(x, y) = (x + k_1 y \bmod 26, k_2 x + y \bmod 26),$$
   where $k = (k_1, k_2)$ and $gcd(k_i, 26) = 1$ for $i = 1, 2$. Derive the encryption and decryption formulas for a cipher with n iterations. Analyze the cipher and try to break it under the known-plaintext attack. How does the security depend on the number of iterations?

6. Consider the above product cipher with the S-box built using a Feistel permutation defined as

$$S(x, y) = (x, y + k_1 x^{k_2} \bmod 26).$$

Derive encryption and decryption formulas for the cipher with n iterations. Analyze the cipher for the known-plaintext attack and discuss its strength in relation to the number of iterations.

7. Design a DES-type cryptosystem which encrypts 16-bit messages into 16-bit cryptograms and applies functions $f : \Sigma^8 \to \Sigma^8$ of the form:

$$f(k_i, R_{i-1}) = (k_i \oplus R_{i-1})^e,$$

for $e = 7$ in $GF(2^8)$. What would happen if the exponent was $e = 2, 3, 4, 5,$ or 6? Implement the cipher. Assume a reasonable key scheduling.

8. The DES algorithm satisfies the complementation property which can be expressed as $E_k(m) = \overline{E_{\bar{k}}(\bar{m})}$. Give a justification of why the property holds.

9. The key schedule is an essential component of any encryption algorithm. Assume that your key scheduling algorithm is to generate subkeys $k_i \in \Sigma^8$ from the key $k \in \Sigma^{16}$ for $i = 1, \ldots, 16$. Consider the following key schedules:

   - The key k is placed into a 16-bit register. k_1 is the 8-bit sequence of less-significant bits. Next the contents of the register are rotated α positions to the left. The key k_2 is again the 8-bit sequence of less-significant bits. The process continues for the requested number of times.
   - The key k is an argument of a one-way function $f : \Sigma^{512} \to \Sigma^{512}$. Subkeys are generated by applying a one-way function so $k_1 = f(k) \mid_8$ where $f(k) \mid_8$ stands for the 8-bit string of less-significant bits, $k_2 = f(f(k)) \mid_8$ and so forth.

   Assume that you happen to know the last subkey k_{16} (for instance, extracted using the differential cryptanalysis). What you can tell about the other subkeys and the key k for the two key scheduling algorithms?

10. In the ECB mode, encryption is applied independently for each message block m_i for $i = 1, 2, \ldots$. The sequence of cryptograms $c_i = E_k(m_i)$ is subject to many attacks which exploit the lack of links between consecutive cryptograms. Consider the following chaining scheme in which $c_i = E_k(m_i) \oplus c_{i-1}$ for $i = 1, 2, \ldots$. Is this scheme better than the ECB mode? Justify your answer.

11. Assume that encryption applies the CBC mode and during transmission a single cryptogram $c_i = E_k(m_i \oplus c_{i-1})$ has been corrupted due to noise in the communication channel. Which messages cannot be reconstructed at the receiver side? Support your answer with a detailed analysis.

12. Suppose the sender uses the CFB mode to protect the transmitted messages against tampering with the sequence of cryptograms. Let the sender transmit a sequence of cryptograms $c_1, c_2, c_3, c_4, c_5, c_6$. An attacker has changed the order of cryptograms so the receiver gets $c_1, c_2, c_4, c_3, c_5, c_6$. Which messages will be correctly recovered by the receiver?

13. Consider $GF(2^3)$ with addition and multiplication given in Table 2.2. Let an S-box be defined by $s^* = f(s) = s^3$ in $GF(2^3)$ where $s \in GF(2^3)$. Construct an XOR profile of the S-box.

14. An S-box is defined by Table 3.17. The XOR profile of the S-box is given below:

$\delta \setminus \Delta$	0	1	2	3	4	5	6	7
0	8	-	-	-	-	-	-	-
1	-	2	-	2	-	2	-	2
2	-	-	2	2	2	2	-	-
3	-	2	2	-	2	-	-	2
4	-	-	-	-	2	2	2	2
5	-	2	-	2	2	-	2	-
6	-	-	2	2	-	-	2	2
7	-	2	2	-	-	2	2	-

The key is XOR-ed with the input of the S-box. Given two observations $s_1 \oplus k = 3$ and $s_2 \oplus k = 7$ and their corresponding output difference $\Delta = s_1^* \oplus s_2^* = 5$, what can you tell about the key k?

Table 3.17. An example of an S-box

s	s^*
0	0
1	1
2	3
3	4
4	5
5	6
6	7
7	2

15. We are given a DES-type encryption algorithm which encrypts 6-bit messages into 6-bit cryptograms using four rounds. Each round applies the S-box described in Table 3.17. A subkey k_i ($i = 1, 2, 3, 4$) is XORed to the input of the S-box where the subkey k_i is used in the ith iteration. Assume some values of the subkeys and use differential cryptanalysis to break the algorithm.

16. Take the encryption algorithm from the previous exercise. Find the best linear approximation of the S-box outputs and derive the necessary linear characteristics. Apply the linear cryptanalysis to recover the cryptographic key.

17. Write the polynomial of a function over Σ^3 whose truth table is (10101001).

18. Consider a Boolean function $f : \Sigma^3 \to \Sigma$ such that $f(x_1, x_2, x_3) = x_1 x_2 \oplus x_1 x_3 \oplus x_2$. Find out its truth table. Is the function balanced?

19. Let $f(x_1, x_2, x_3, x_4) = x_1 x_2 x_3 \oplus x_3 x_4 \oplus x_2$. Find the truth table, sequence, and matrix of f, $W(f)$, N_f and $\Delta(\alpha)$ for $\alpha = (1111)$.

20. Given two Boolean functions $f(x_1, x_2, x_3) = x_1 x_2 x_3 \oplus x_2$ and $g(x_1, x_2) = x_1 \oplus x_2$. What is the distance $d(f, g)$?

21. Determine all affine functions from the set $\mathcal{A}_3$.

22. Find the nonlinearity of the function $f(x_1, x_2, x_3) = x_1 \oplus x_2 x_3$. The function f can be extended for an arbitrary number of variables. Let $f(x_1, \ldots, x_n) = x_1 \oplus x_2 x_3$ where $n > 3$. What is the nonlinearity of the extended function?

23. Assume that f, g, and h are functions on Σ^n with $W(f) = 0$, $W(g) = 1$, and $W(h) = 2^n$. Find the nonlinearities N_f, N_g, and N_h.

24. Let $f(x_1, x_2, x_3, x_4, x_5) = x_1 x_3 \oplus x_2 x_5 \oplus x_2 x_4 x_5$. Determine the set of vectors $\mathfrak{R}$ for which the function does not satisfy the SAC.

25. Prove that any function of the form $f(x_1, \ldots, x_n) = x_1 x_2 \oplus x_3 x_4 \oplus \cdots \oplus x_{n-1} x_n$ is bent when n is even and bigger than 2.

26. Calculate the nonlinearity of $f(x_1, \ldots, x_n) = x_1 x_2 \oplus x_2 x_3 \oplus \cdots \oplus x_{n_1} x_n \oplus x_n x_1$ where $n \geq 3$ and is odd.

27. Take two functions $f(x_1, x_2, x_3, x_4) = x_1 x_2 \oplus x_2 x_3 \oplus x_3 x_4 \oplus x_4 x_1$ and $g(x_1, x_2, x_3, x_4) = x_1 \oplus x_2 \oplus x_3 \oplus x_4$. Compute their autocorrelation functions $\Delta_f(\alpha)$ and $\Delta_g(\alpha)$. Discuss the results.

28. Let f be a function over Σ^n. Consider the following statements:
    - If $N_f = 0$, then $f = 0$.
    - If $N_f = 2$, then $W(f) = 2$.
    - $d(f, f \oplus g) = 2^{n-1}$ for some linear function g.
    - $N_{f \oplus g} = N_f$ for any linear function g.

4 Public-Key Cryptosystems

In 1976 Diffie and Hellman [152] described the framework for public-key cryptography. It was not until 1978 that three designs for public-key cryptosystems were published. Rivest, Shamir, and Adleman [431] showed how the discrete logarithm and factorization problems could be used to construct a public-key cryptosystem. This is the well-known RSA cryptosystem. Merkle and Hellman [339] used the knapsack problem in their construction. McEliece [329] built a system based on error correcting codes. Later in 1985 ElGamal [163] designed a public-key cryptosystem using the discrete logarithm problem. Koblitz [283] and Miller [346] suggested the use of elliptic curves in the design of public-key cryptosystems. Nowadays, there are quite a few more suggestions as to how to design public-key cryptosystems, but none so popular as the RSA and ElGamal cryptosystems.

In Sect. 4.1, we introduce the notion of public-key cryptography. In the next four sections we discuss the basic implementations of the RSA, MH, McEliece, and ElGamal cryptosystems. Sect. 4.7 presents probabilistic encryption. Sect. 4.8 studies the hierarchical structure of public-key security levels and their impact on public-key design.

4.1 Concept of Public-Key Cryptography

In private-key cryptosystems, both encryption and decryption apply secret keys. Typically, both keys are the same or the knowledge of one of them is enough to determine the other. That is why private-key systems are also called symmetric. Public-key cryptosystems use two different keys. One is public while the other is kept secret. Clearly, it is necessary that computing the secret key from the public key has to be intractable. Public-key cryptosystems are also called asymmetric. As public-key cryptosystems use two keys, it is possible to make public either the encryption or decryption key. If the encryption key is

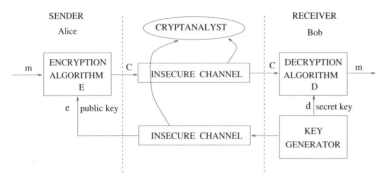

Fig. 4.1. Diagram of a public-key cryptosystem

public, we deal with cryptosystems in which anybody can encrypt a message (plaintext) into a cryptogram (ciphertext) but only the receiver can decrypt the cryptogram. The system can be used for secrecy only. If the decryption key is public, anybody can read cryptograms, but only the holder of the secret encryption key can generate meaningful cryptograms – the system can be used for authenticity only. In this chapter we will concentrate on secrecy systems in which encryption keys are public.

A cryptosystem with a public encryption key is depicted in Fig. 4.1. The sets of messages, cryptograms, and keys are $\mathcal{M}$, $\mathcal{C}$, and $\mathcal{K}$, respectively. The setup of the system is done by the receiver Bob who generates a pair of keys $(e, d) \in \mathcal{K}$. Bob broadcasts the encryption key e and keeps the decryption key d secret. Assume that Alice wants to communicate secretly a message $m \in \mathcal{M}$ to Bob. She uses the known encryption algorithm $E : \mathcal{K} \cdot \mathcal{M} \to \mathcal{C}$ and the public key to compute the cryptogram $c = E_e(m) \in \mathcal{C}$. The cryptogram is sent over the insecure channel to Bob. Bob now applies his secret key d together with the decryption algorithm $D : \mathcal{K} \cdot \mathcal{C} \to \mathcal{M}$ to recover the message $m = D_d(c)$. The cryptosystem has to be efficient and secure. The efficiency requirement can be translated into the following conditions:

1. Calculation of the pair (the public key e, the secret key d) can be done by the receiver in polynomial time.
2. The sender, knowing the public key e and a message m, can determine in polynomial time the corresponding cryptogram,

$$c = E_e(m). \tag{4.1}$$

3. The receiver, knowing the cryptogram c and the secret key d, can compute the original form of m in polynomial time,

$$m = D_d(c) = D_d(E_e(m)). \tag{4.2}$$

The security requirement is equivalent to the following conditions:

1. The task of computing the secret key d from the public key e must be intractable for any instance of the public key.
2. Any attempt to recover the message m from the pair (e, c) must be equivalent to solving an intractable instance of a suitable problem.

Assume that for a parameter $n \in \mathcal{N}$, we have a set of encryption functions

$$E^{(n)} = \{E_e \mid E_e : \Sigma^n \to \Sigma^{\beta(n)}\},$$

where $\beta(n)$ is a polynomial in n. Every element of the set $E^{(n)}$ is indexed by the public key $e \in \mathcal{K}$. So the set $E^{(n)}$ consists of all encryption functions which can be used in the system for the fixed n. The family

$$E = \{E^{(n)} \mid n \in \mathcal{N}\} \tag{4.3}$$

describes the public encryption. The integer n is also called the security parameter as it indicates the size of the message and cryptogram spaces. Now we can define two search problems. The first problem is called the *public encryption* and has the following form:

Name: Public encryption.
Instance: Given a security parameter $n \in \mathcal{N}$, public-key scheme with the family $E = \{E^{(n)} \mid n \in \mathcal{N}\}$ of encryption functions, public key $e \in \mathcal{K}$, and message $m \in \Sigma^n$.
Question: What is the cryptogram $c = E_e(m) \in \Sigma^{\beta(n)}$ where $E_e \in E^{(n)}$?

The second problem is called the *public decryption* and has the form:

Name: Public decryption.
Instance: Given a security parameter $n \in \mathcal{N}$, public-key scheme with the family $E = \{E^{(n)} \mid n \in \mathcal{N}\}$ of encryption functions, public key $e \in \mathcal{K}$, and cryptogram $c \in \Sigma^{\beta(n)}$.
Question: What is the message $m = E_e^{-1}(c) \in \Sigma^n$?

Clearly, the public encryption must belong to the class **P** while the public decryption should belong to **NP**-hard. **NP**-hardness of decryption is necessary but not sufficient for security of public-key cryptosystems. Ideally, for a large enough n, we would hope that all instances of the public decryption are intractable or hard. In practice, we may have to accept that some instances of the public decryption are easy with the caveat that the probability of occurrence of such instances is negligible. The pair of the public encryption and decryption problems uses the family of encryption functions E. The family is an example of a *one-way function*. For a large enough security parameter n and a message m, it is easy to compute $c = E_e(m)$ while computing $m = E_e^{-1}(c)$ is hard.

Public-key cryptography works on the assumption that potential users have access to authentic public keys. By encrypting a message using a public key, the sender creates a ciphertext that can be decrypted by the holder of the corresponding secret key only. Therefore, any mistake while choosing public keys results in unintentional change of the destination in which the cryptogram can be decrypted. The Public Key Infrastructure (PKI) provides a mechanism for users to obtain authentic public keys together with the unique identifier of the owner of the corresponding secret key [132, 447].

4.2 RSA Cryptosystem

The RSA system applies the factorization problems as the underlying intractable problem. In the system, messages, cryptograms, and keys (public and secret) belong to the set $\mathcal{Z}_N$. The integer N is the product of two distinct primes p and q, i.e., $N = p \cdot q$. The set $\mathcal{Z}_N$ along with addition and multiplication modulo N creates a ring. For a given public key e and message m, the encryption function is

$$c = E_e(m) \equiv m^e \pmod{N}. \tag{4.4}$$

The decryption function applies the secret key $d \in \mathcal{Z}_N$ to the cryptogram $c \in \mathcal{Z}_N$ as follows:

$$m = D_d(c) \equiv c^d \pmod{N}. \tag{4.5}$$

Clearly, the encryption and decryption process should allow us to recover the original message m, so

$$m = D_d(E_e(m)).$$

Combining (4.4) and (4.5), we get:

$$(m^e)^d \equiv m \pmod{N}. \tag{4.6}$$

The congruence must be true for all messages. It is known that the congruence (4.6) has a solution if and only if

$$e \cdot d \equiv 1 \pmod{lcm(p-1, q-1)}. \tag{4.7}$$

This follows from a standard application of Fermat's Little Theorem.

The system is set up by the receiver Bob who

– chooses two large enough primes p and q,
– announces the modulus $N = p \cdot q$ while keeping the factors p, q secret,
– selects at random the key $e \in_R \mathcal{Z}_N$ which is coprime to $lcm(p-1, q-1)$ and makes it public,
– computes the secret key d according to congruence (4.7).

The sender, Alice, encrypts a message m using congruence (4.4) and sends the corresponding cryptogram to Bob. Upon receiving the cryptogram, Bob applies congruence (4.5) to recover the message.

RSA cryptosystem

Problems Used: Factorization.

The modulus $N = p \cdot q$ is public, the primes p, q are secret.
Message Space: $\mathcal{M} = \mathcal{Z}_N$.
Cryptogram Space: $\mathcal{C} = \mathcal{Z}_N$.
Public Key: A random integer $e \in \mathcal{Z}_N$, $gcd(e, lcm(p-1, q-1)) = 1$.
Secret Key: An integer $d \in \mathcal{Z}_N$ such that $d \cdot d \equiv 1 \pmod{lcm(p-1)(q-1)}$.
Encryption: $c = E_e(m) \equiv m^e \pmod{N}$.
Decryption: $m = D_d(c) \equiv c^d \pmod{N}$.

Consider a simple example. Assume that Bob intends to create an instance of the RSA cryptosystem. First, Bob selects integers $p = 7$ and $q = 11$. Next, he calculates $lcm(6, 10) = 30$, and randomly selects the public key $e = 13$. Subsequently, he finds the secret key by solving the congruence (4.7), so

$$13 \cdot d \equiv 1 \pmod{30} \Rightarrow d = 7.$$

The above congruence can be solved using the Euclid algorithm (see Sect. 2.1.1). The pair $(N = 77, e = 13)$ is published. If Alice now wants to transmit the message $m = 36$, she calculates the cryptogram

$$c = m^e = 36^{13} \equiv 71 \pmod{77}$$

and forwards it to Bob. Since Bob knows the secret key d, he recreates the message according to the following congruence:

$$m = c^d = 71^7 \equiv 36 \pmod{77}.$$

The above system is an instance with a very low security parameter and is insecure because anybody can guess the factors of the modulus. Given p, q, an adversary can recover d from e using congruence (4.7).

To have a "secure" instance of the RSA system, we have to pick a large modulus N so both an instance of the public decryption problem and an instance of the factorization problem (factorization of N) are intractable. The primes p and q used in the RSA system have to be at least 100 decimal digits long. Thus the modulus N has 200 decimal digits and the best known factoring and discrete logarithm algorithms take $\approx 10^{23}$ steps each. On the other hand, the implementation of public encryption can be done by using the fast exponentiation algorithm from Sect. 2.1.3. As the holder of the secret key knows factors of N, decryption can be sped up by using the fast exponentiation independently for the moduli p and q and merging the results using CRT.

There are many RSA implementations in hardware. Their speed depends on the length of the moduli used. A typical VLSI chip for RSA handles 512-bit-long moduli and processes plaintext/ciphertext at the rate 64 kilobits per second which is roughly 1000 times slower than for DES. More secure hardware implementations use moduli of length 768, 1024, or 2048 bits [300].

4.2.1 Variants of RSA

In some circumstances, senders may have limited computational power. This usually happens when the encryption is being done by a smart card which has limited memory and CPU power. Clearly, we can reduce the number of computations by restricting the value of the public key.

Rabin [421] suggested an RSA variant with the public key $e = 2$. This is the smallest nontrivial exponent. The public encryption is

$$c = m^2 \pmod{N}, \tag{4.8}$$

where N, as before, is the product of two primes p and q. The receiver, who knows the factorization of N, can decrypt c by solving the two following congruences: $\sqrt{c} \equiv m_1 \pmod{p}$ and $\sqrt{c} \equiv m_2 \pmod{q}$. In fact, the first congruence has two possible solutions $\pm m_1$ and so does the second $\pm m_2$. To compose the original message m using the Chinese Remainder Theorem, the receiver needs to guess correctly the signs of m_1 and m_2. Rabin's system has a 4:1 ambiguity in the decrypted message.

Williams [531] showed how to improve Rabin's scheme. He observed that the decryption process can be simplified for all messages m whose Jacobi symbol [1] is $\left(\frac{m}{N}\right) = 1$, where $N = p \cdot q$ and the primes are chosen such that $p \equiv -1 \pmod 4$ and $q \equiv -1 \pmod 4$. In other words, p and q have to be *Blum integers*. If the modulus p is a Blum integer ($p \equiv -1 \pmod 4$), there is no polynomial-time algorithm to calculate square roots of quadratic residues modulo p. The deciphering process is expressed by the following congruence:

$$c^d \equiv \pm m \pmod N, \tag{4.9}$$

where the secret key d is equal to

$$d = \frac{1}{2}\left(\frac{(p-1)(q-1)}{4} + 1\right). \tag{4.10}$$

In Williams's modification, the receiver Bob selects two Blum primes p and q and computes the modulus $N = p \cdot q$ and a small integer S such that $\left(\frac{S}{N}\right) = -1$. Next, he publishes N and S but keeps secret the key d determined by (4.10). For a message m, the sender Alice calculates c_1 ($c_1 \in \{0,1\}$) such that $\left(\frac{m}{N}\right) = (-1)^{c_1}$ and creates the message

$$m' \equiv S^{c_1} \cdot m \pmod N, \quad m' \in \mathcal{Z}_N. \tag{4.11}$$

Finally, the cryptogram is computed for m' according to (4.8), and Alice forwards the triple (c, c_1, c_2), where $c_2 \equiv m' \pmod 2$.

To recover the clear message, Bob computes $m_t \equiv c^d \pmod N$ according to congruence (4.9). The proper sign of m_t is given by c_2 (i.e., $m = m_t$ if $c_2 \equiv m_t \pmod N$, or $m = -m_t$ otherwise). It is easy to verify that the original message m is equal to

$$m \equiv S^{-c_1}(-1)^{c_1} m_t \pmod N, \tag{4.12}$$

as the message m' is even. The enciphering and deciphering processes described above are illustrated in the following example.

---

[1] Recall the Jacobi symbol $\left(\frac{a}{b}\right)$ is defined by $\left(\frac{a}{b}\right) = \left(\frac{a}{b_1}\right) \cdots \left(\frac{a}{b_n}\right)$, where $b = b_1 \cdots b_n$ is the factorization of b and $\left(\frac{a}{b_i}\right) \equiv a^{(b_i-1)/2} \pmod{b_i}$ is the Legendre symbol for $i = 1, \ldots, n$.

Suppose the receiver Bob has selected $p = 7$, $q = 11$ (note $p \equiv -1 \pmod{4}$, and $q \equiv -1 \pmod{4}$). Bob next chooses the small integer $S = 2$ for which the Jacobi symbol is $\left(\frac{S}{N}\right) = \left(\frac{2}{77}\right) = -1$. The values $(N = 77, S = 2)$ are sent to the sender Alice while the key $d = 8$ is kept secret.

If Alice wishes to transmit the message $m = 54$, she first calculates the Jacobi symbol $\left(\frac{M}{N}\right) = \left(\frac{5}{477}\right) = 1$. It implies that the binary number $c_1 = 0$. According to (4.11), the message $m' = m = 54$, and the cryptogram c is equal to:

$$c = m^2 = 54^2 \equiv 67 \pmod{77}.$$

Finally, Alice forwards the triple $(c, c_1, c_2) = (67, 0, 0)$ as the cryptogram.

After obtaining the triple, Bob computes

$$m_t = c^d = 67^8 \equiv 23 \pmod{77}.$$

As $c_2 = 0$, the message m must be even so $m = N - m_t = 54$.

Williams [532] considered the cryptosystem for which the public key is fixed and equal to 3 ($e = 3$). He showed its construction and proved that it is as difficult to break as it is to factor the modulus N. Another modification of the basic RSA system for $e \equiv 3 \pmod{18}$ has been presented by Loxton, Khoo, Bird, and Seberry [306] who recommend that it should be used for those e whose binary representation has many zeros. Their cryptosystem is defined in the ring $Z[\omega]$, where ω is a primitive cube root. They also showed that their system is as difficult to break as factoring N.

4.2.2 Primality Testing

To set up RSA, the receiver has to generate two long primes p and q. In Sect. 2.1.2 the prime-counting function $\pi(x)$ was introduced. It approximates the number of primes in the interval $(0, x]$. If we want to choose a prime at random from the interval $(0, 10^{100}]$, then the probability that the selected integer is a prime is

$$\frac{\pi(10^{100})}{10^{100}} = \frac{1}{100 \ln 10} \approx \frac{1}{230}.$$

This means that, on average, every 230th integer is prime. Hence, there is a good chance that after 230 consecutive tries, there is at least one prime. In order to exploit this, we need an efficient primality test.

From Sect. 2.3.6, we know that both primality and factorization problems belong to **NPI∩co-NPI**. This means that there is no polynomial-time deterministic algorithm for primality testing. There is, however, a class of probabilistic algorithms which can be used if we accept a small probability of error (Sect. 2.3.9).

We start from Fermat's Little Theorem (Sect. 2.1.4) which can be used to design a simple primality test algorithm. The theorem asserts that if the modulus p is prime then the following congruence is true

$$a^{p-1} \equiv 1 \pmod{p}, \tag{4.13}$$

for any nonzero integer $a \in \mathcal{Z}_p$. A Monte Carlo algorithm based upon the congruence will always generate the correct answer if the tested integer is indeed prime no matter what the value of a is. Unfortunately, if p is composite congruence (4.13) may also be satisfied for some integers. These numbers are called *pseudoprimes*. For example, each of the Fermat numbers $F_n = 2^{2^n} + 1$ satisfies congruence (4.13) but not all these are primes. The situation becomes worse when the tested number p is a *Carmichael number*. Carmichael numbers satisfy (4.13) for every a which is coprime to p (i.e., $gcd(a,p) = 1$). In other words, we need a stronger primality test.

Fermat's Little Theorem can still be useful for primality testing. However, to avoid problems with pseudoprimes, it is necessary to modify the testing procedure. Note that we do not need to use the congruence $a^{p-1} \equiv 1 \pmod{p}$. Instead we may apply the congruence

$$a^{\frac{p-1}{2}} \pmod{p}.$$

If p is prime the congruence is equal to either 1 or -1. A fast test which looks into factors of $p - 1$ in order to determine the primality of the modulus p was developed by Miller [345] and Rabin [422]. In the *Miller-Rabin test*, first $p-1$ is represented in the form $2^r \cdot s$ where s is an odd number. As the tested integer p is odd (even integers are not prime), $p-1$ is even, so this representation is always valid. The testing starts by checking if $a^s \equiv \pm 1 \pmod{p}$ for a random nonzero $a \in \mathcal{Z}_p$. If the congruence is true, we conclude that p is prime. Otherwise, we check whether $a^{2^i s} \equiv -1 \pmod{p}$ for $i = 1, \ldots, r - 1$. If there is some i for which the congruence is true, the test returns "p is prime," otherwise it returns "p is composite."

Miller-Rabin primality test – checks whether an integer p is prime.

T1. Find an odd integer s such that $p - 1 = 2^r \cdot s$.

T2. Select at random a nonzero integer $a \in_R \mathbb{Z}_p$.

T3. Compute

$$b = a^s \pmod{p}.$$

If $b = \pm 1$, return "p is prime" and quit.

T4. For $i = 1, \ldots, r - 1$, calculate

$$c \equiv b^{2^i} \pmod{p}.$$

If $c = -1$, return "p is prime" and quit.

T5. Otherwise return "p is composite."

The test always gives the correct answer if the integer p is indeed prime. For composite p, the following theorem characterizes the test.

Theorem 17. (*Rabin* [422]) *If p is composite, then the Miller-Rabin test fails for at least one quarter of integers a where $0 < a \le p - 1$. In other words, the test erroneously returns "p is prime" for at most $\frac{1}{4}$ of all integers a if p is composite.*

So now we have a fast Monte Carlo algorithm for primality testing. It never makes mistakes when p is prime. If p is composite, it returns "p is prime" with probability $\frac{1}{4}$. For instance, in order to bound the probability of error to be smaller than 2^{-50}, it is enough to use the Miller-Rabin test 25 times.

4.2.3 Factorization

The most obvious attack on RSA is to try to factor the public modulus N. Knowing the factors of N, it is easy to recover the secret key. The factorization problem is believed to be intractable so we may not hope for a polynomial-time algorithm. But certainly we need to know how efficient the existing factoring algorithms are.

The sieve of Eratosthenes (Sect. 2.1.2) is a factorization algorithm whose efficiency is $O(\sqrt{N})$ or $O(2^{\frac{n}{2}})$ where $n = \lfloor log_2 N \rfloor$. For moduli $\approx 10^{200}$, the sieve of Eratosthenes would take $O(10^{100})$ steps. It is easy to check that this algorithm starts to be unworkable for moduli larger than 10^{20}.

More efficient algorithms take advantage of the following theorem.

Theorem 18. *Let N be a composite natural number and X, Y be a pair of integers such that $X + Y \neq N$. If $X^2 \equiv Y^2 \pmod{N}$, then $gcd(X + Y, N)$ and $gcd(X - Y, N)$ are nontrivial factors of N.*

The following example shows how Theorem 18 can be used to factor $N = 77$. We start with the two following congruences: $72 \equiv -5 \pmod{77}$ and $45 \equiv -32 \pmod{77}$. Multiplying the separate sides gives:

$$72 \cdot 45 \equiv (-5) \cdot (-32) \pmod{77}.$$

The congruence can be rewritten as

$$2^3 \cdot 3^4 \cdot 5 \equiv (-1)^2 \cdot 5 \cdot 2^5 \pmod{77},$$

which yields upon reduction $9^2 \equiv 2^2 \pmod{77}$. Hence $gcd(9 + 2, 77)$ and $gcd(9 - 2, 77)$ give the primes $p = 11$ and $q = 7$.

Quadratic Sieve (QS). Let us discuss briefly the basic *Quadratic Sieve* algorithm for factoring an integer N. The algorithm proceeds as follows.

Quadratic sieve algorithm – finds factors of integer N.

F1. Initialization: a sequence of quadratic residues $Q(x) = (m + x)^2 - N$ is generated for small values of x where $m = \lfloor \sqrt{N} \rfloor$.

F2. Forming the factor base: the base consists of a small collection of small primes. The set is $FB = \{-1, 2, p_1, \ldots, p_{t-1}\}$.

F3. Sieving: the quadratic residues $Q(x)$ are now factored using the factor base. The sieving stops when t full factorizations of $Q(x)$ have been found.

F4. Forming and solving the matrix: for the collection of fully factored $Q(x)$, a matrix F is constructed. The matrix contains information about the factors. The goal of this stage is to find a linear combination of $Q(x)$'s which gives the quadratic congruence from Theorem 18. The congruence gives a nontrivial factor of N with the probability $\frac{1}{2}$.

Let us illustrate steps of the algorithm using a simple numerical example. Assume that we wish to find factors of $N = 4841$. First we generate a sequence of quadratic residues $Q(x)$. To keep $Q(x)$ as small as possible, we find $m = \lfloor \sqrt{N} \rfloor = 69$ and compute

$$Q(x) = (m + x)^2 - N \tag{4.14}$$

for $x = -8, \ldots, -1, 0, 1, \ldots, 8$. The sequence of Q's is as follows:

$$x = -8 \rightarrow Q(x) = -1120 = (-1) \cdot 2^5 \cdot 5 \cdot 7,$$

$$x = -7 \rightarrow Q(x) = -997 = (-1) \cdot 997,$$

$$x = -6 \rightarrow Q(x) = -872 = (-1) \cdot 2^3 \cdot 109,$$

$$x = -5 \rightarrow Q(x) = -745 = (-1) \cdot 5 \cdot 149,$$

$$x = -4 \rightarrow Q(x) = -616 = (-1) \cdot 2^3 \cdot 7 \cdot 11,$$

$$x = -3 \rightarrow Q(x) = -485 = (-1) \cdot 5 \cdot 97,$$

$$x = -2 \rightarrow Q(x) = -352 = (-1) \cdot 2^5 \cdot 11,$$

$$x = -1 \rightarrow Q(x) = -217 = (-1) \cdot 7 \cdot 31,$$

$$x = 0 \rightarrow Q(x) = -80 = 2^4 \cdot 5,$$

$$x = 1 \rightarrow Q(x) = 59 = 59,$$

$$x = 2 \rightarrow Q(x) = 200 = 2^3 \cdot 5^2,$$

$$x = 3 \rightarrow Q(x) = 343 = 7^3,$$

$$x = 4 \rightarrow Q(x) = 488 = 2^3 \cdot 61,$$

$$x = 5 \rightarrow Q(x) = 635 = 5 \cdot 127,$$

$$x = 6 \rightarrow Q(x) = 784 = 2^4 \cdot 7^2,$$

$$x = 7 \rightarrow Q(x) = 935 = 5 \cdot 11 \cdot 17,$$

$$x = 8 \rightarrow Q(x) = 1088 = 2^6 \cdot 17.$$

A factor base can be a collection of the smallest consecutive primes so $FB = \{-1, 2, 3, 5, 7, 11\}$. Note that $Q(-8)$, $Q(-4)$, $Q(-2)$, $Q(0)$, $Q(2)$, $Q(3)$, and $Q(6)$ have all their factors in the set FB. These are the required full factorizations. There are eight fully factored Q's and the number of elements in the set FB is six so there is a good chance of finding a quadratic congruence $X^2 \equiv Y^2$ (mod N) as required in Theorem 18.

For a fully factored $Q(x)$, we create a binary vector $F(x)$ of length $\ell = |FB|$ whose coordinates indicate the presence or absence of the factor from FB. Thus, for $Q(-8)$, the vector $F(-8) = [1, 1, 0, 1, 1, 0]$ as its factorization contains primes -1, 2, 5, and 7. The collection of all vectors F for fully factored Q's, is:

$$Q(-8) \rightarrow F(-8) = [1, 1, 0, 1, 1, 0],$$

$$Q(-4) \rightarrow F(-4) = [1, 1, 0, 0, 1, 1],$$

$$Q(-2) \rightarrow F(-2) = [1, 1, 0, 0, 0, 1],$$

$$Q(0) \rightarrow F(0) = [0, 1, 0, 1, 0, 0],$$
$$Q(2) \rightarrow F(2) = [0, 1, 0, 1, 0, 0],$$
$$Q(3) \rightarrow F(3) = [0, 0, 0, 0, 1, 0],$$
$$Q(6) \rightarrow F(6) = [0, 1, 0, 0, 1, 0].$$

The vectors $F(x)$ form the rows of our matrix F:

$$F = \begin{bmatrix} F(-8) \\ F(-4) \\ F(-2) \\ F(0) \\ F(2) \\ F(3) \\ F(6) \end{bmatrix} = \begin{bmatrix} 1, 1, 0, 1, 1, 0 \\ 1, 1, 0, 0, 1, 1 \\ 1, 1, 0, 0, 0, 1 \\ 0, 1, 0, 1, 0, 0 \\ 0, 1, 0, 1, 0, 0 \\ 0, 0, 0, 0, 1, 0 \\ 0, 1, 0, 0, 1, 0 \end{bmatrix}. \tag{4.15}$$

Now we look for a collection of rows such that

$$F(i_1) \oplus F(i_2) \oplus \ldots \oplus F(i_r) = 0.$$

This step can be done using standard row-reducing techniques. Observe that $F(-4) \oplus F(-2) \oplus F(3) = 0$. Take the corresponding $Q(-4)$, $Q(-2)$, and $Q(3)$ and write them as:

$$Q(-4) \equiv (69 - 4)^2 \pmod{4841},$$
$$Q(-2) \equiv (69 - 2)^2 \pmod{4841},$$
$$Q(3) \equiv (69 + 3)^2 \pmod{4841}.$$

On the other hand, we can use their factorizations for a second set of relations:

$$Q(-4) \equiv (-1) \cdot 2^3 \cdot 7 \cdot 11 \pmod{4841},$$
$$Q(-2) \equiv (-1) \cdot 2^5 \cdot 11 \pmod{4841},$$
$$Q(3) \equiv 7^3 \pmod{4841}.$$

The requested congruence $X^2 \equiv Y^2 \pmod{N}$ can be constructed as follows:

$$Q(-4)Q(-2)Q(3) \equiv 2^8 \cdot 7^4 \cdot 11^2 \pmod{4841}.$$

Note that the left-hand side is $Q(-4)Q(-2)Q(3) = (69 - 4)^2(69 - 2)^2(69 + 3)^2$ and the right-hand side is $2^8 \cdot 7^4 \cdot 11^2$. Therefore, both sides are powers of two. The left integer is

$$X = (69 - 4)(69 - 2)(69 + 3) \equiv 3736 \pmod{4841},$$

and the right integer is

$$Y = \sqrt{(-1)2^3 \cdot 7 \cdot 11 \cdot (-1)2^5 \cdot 11 \cdot 7^3} = 2^4 \cdot 7^2 \cdot 11 \equiv 3783 \quad (\text{mod } 4841).$$

As $X + Y \neq i \cdot N$, we obtain the factors of N. Indeed, $gcd(3736 - 3783, 4841) = 47$ and $gcd(3736 + 3783, 4841) = 103$. So $N = 47 \cdot 103$.

Concept of Number Field Sieve (NFS). The main idea is to produce two integers X and Y such that $X^2 \equiv Y^2 \bmod N$, where N is an integer to be factored. Unlike the Quadratic Sieve, the Number Field Sieve uses two different algebraic structures:

- *ring* $\mathcal{Z}_N$ – this is the algebraic structure where quadratic equations are sieved to find factors.
- *number field* $\mathcal{K} = \mathcal{R}(\alpha)$ – for some algebraic integer α that is the root of an irreducible monic polynomial $p(x) \in \mathcal{R}[x]$ of degree d or $p(\alpha) = 0$. Assume that an integer m is known such that

$$p(m) = \ell \cdot N \tag{4.16}$$

for some integer ℓ.

In both algebraic structures we look for quadratic equations. Suppose that we find two such equations

$$a + b \cdot m = X^2 \bmod N \text{ in the ring } \mathcal{Z}_N,$$

and

$$a + b \cdot \alpha = \beta^2 \text{ in the field } \mathcal{R}(\alpha),$$

for some integers a, b. Clearly, to use the second equation, we have to transform it into $\mathcal{Z}_N$. For this purpose, we define a homomorphism

$$\psi : \mathcal{Z}_\mathcal{K} \to \mathcal{Z}_N,$$

where $\mathcal{Z}_\mathcal{K}$ denotes all integers in $\mathcal{K}$ and $\psi(\alpha) = m \bmod N$ while $\psi(a) = a \bmod N$ for all $a \in \mathcal{Z}_N$.

This idea is best illustrated by an example. Suppose $N = 161$ is to be factored. Define the number field $\mathcal{K} = \mathcal{R}(\alpha)$ where α is the root of the polynomial $p(x) = x^2 - 2$ or $(p(\alpha) = 0)$. Note that the condition in (4.16) holds, i.e.,

$$p(18) = 2 \cdot 161.$$

for $m = 18$. Now we take element $\beta \in \mathcal{K}$ and compute its squares $\beta^2 = a + b \cdot \alpha$ and check whether the corresponding equation $a + b \cdot m \stackrel{?}{=} Y^2 \bmod N$. If the second equation holds, then we transform the first equation using the homomorphism ψ. Here we need to extend our homomorphism so it works for elements of the form $(a + b \cdot \alpha)$ where $a, b \in \mathcal{Z}_N$. The extended homomorphism is defined as follows:

$$\psi(b \cdot \alpha) = \begin{cases} m \bmod N & \text{if } b = 1; \\ b(b^{-1}a + m) \bmod N & \text{if } b \text{ has its inverse in } \mathcal{Z}_N. \end{cases}$$

Note that, with an overwhelming probability, the element b has its inverse (otherwise a nontrivial factor of N is found). The computations can progress by random selection of quadratic equations as shown below.

Field $\mathcal{K}$	a, b	Ring $\mathcal{Z}_N$
$(\alpha + 1)^2 = 3 + 2\alpha$	$(3, 2)$	$3 + 2 \cdot 18 = 39$
$(\alpha + 2)^2 = 6 + 4\alpha$	$(6, 4)$	$4 + 4 \cdot 18 = 78$
$(2\alpha + 1)^2 = 9 + 4\alpha$	$(9, 4)$	$9 + 4 \cdot 18 = 81 = 9^2$

The last row gives us two quadratic equations, one in $\mathcal{K}$ and the other in $\mathcal{Z}_N$. Now we transform the equation in $\mathcal{K}$ into $\mathcal{Z}_N$ using the homomorphism ψ, i.e.,

$$\psi(9 + 4\alpha) = 9 + 4 \cdot m \text{ and } \psi(2\alpha + 1) = 37.$$

We combine the two equations and get

$$9^2 \equiv 37^2 \bmod N$$

and two nontrivial factors $gcd(37 - 9, 161) = 7$ and $gcd(37 + 9, 161) = 23$.

To factor a large integer, guessing a and b will not lead to an efficient implementation of NFS. Like in QS, NFS uses a factor base to work around this problem. What differs between QS and NFS is the fact that NFS uses two different factor bases, one in $\mathcal{Z}_N$ and the other in $\mathcal{Z}_{\mathcal{K}}$. The factor base in $\mathcal{Z}_N$ can be easily generated and typically includes all primes not exceeding some bound B. Generation of the factor base in $\mathcal{Z}_{\mathcal{K}}$ is more complicated as it involves the selection of the so-called *prime ideals* of $\mathcal{Z}_{\mathcal{K}}$. The description of the NFS algorithm is beyond the scope of the book and the reader is referred to [102] for details.

Factorization is considered to be a part of cryptanalysis since progress in factoring tends to weaken the existing RSA hardware implementations. There are several classes of factorization algorithms:

- Quadratic sieve [126, 127, 411, 470],
- Residue list sieve [111],
- Number field sieve [299],
- Continued fraction [353], and
- Elliptic curve [301].

QS has been extensively used as it is the fastest known algorithm to factor integers shorter than 130 decimal digits. In 1994 Atkins, Graff, Lenstra, and Leyland successfully factored a 129 decimal-digit-long modulus of RSA (known as RSA-129 on the RSA factoring challenge list). The factorization was done using computing resources donated from around the world. As the whole communication was done by electronic mail, the project was called "factoring by e-mail." For details see [10]. This proved that 512-bit moduli of RSA are no longer secure against a powerful attacker who can match the resources used in the factorization.

NFS is the newest algorithm, and the fastest as its asymptotic running time is

$$O\left(e^{(1.92+o(1))(\ln n)^{\frac{1}{3}}(\ln \ln n)^{\frac{2}{3}}}\right),$$

which compares favorably with the asymptotic running time of the QS algorithm

$$O\left(e^{(1+o(1))(\ln n \ln \ln n)^{\frac{1}{2}}}\right).$$

The NFS algorithm outperforms QS if factored integers are longer than 130 decimal digits.

4.2.4 Security of RSA

An instance of RSA can be compromised if the corresponding instances of the factorization problems are easy to compute. Interestingly enough, the security of some versions of RSA are equivalent to the difficulty of factoring the modulus.

Consider the Rabin scheme. Assume that the adversary tries to decrypt a ciphertext c of an unknown plaintext having access to the encryption algorithm that is public (everybody knows the encryption key). The adversary can decrypt c if he/she is able to find the square root of c modulo N. Clearly, finding the square root modulo N is equivalent to factoring N. If we assume that factoring

N is intractable, then the Rabin scheme is immune against a chosen plaintext attack.

Assume that the adversary has access to the decryption algorithm (this is also called the lunchtime attack or midnight attack). So the adversary can choose a ciphertext and the decryption algorithm returns the message m such that $m^2 \equiv c \pmod{N}$. This is a chosen ciphertext attack. The adversary can then use the decryption algorithm to factor N as follows:

1. Select at random a message $m \in \mathbb{Z}_N$.
2. Calculate the cryptogram $c = m^2 \pmod{N}$.
3. Apply the decryption algorithm $m' = D(c, N)$.
4. If $m = \pm m'$, go to Step 1 and select another message. Otherwise, compute $gcd(m - m', N)$ which is either p or q.

Hence, the Rabin scheme is insecure against a chosen ciphertext attack.

Simmons and Norris [478] showed that RSA is breakable if the multiplicative group contains short cycles. Let the opponent know the public elements (N, e) and a cryptogram $c \in \mathbb{Z}_N$. Clearly, the opponent can generate the following sequence:

$$c_i \equiv c_{i-1}^e \pmod{N},$$

where $c_1 = c$ and $i = 2, 3, \ldots$. If there is an element c_j such that $c = c_j$, then the message used to generate c is c_{j-1}.

The iteration attack can be seen as a clumsy way of factoring N [425]. Note that the iteration attack works only if the following two congruences hold at the same time:

$$c^{e^r} \equiv c \pmod{p} \text{ and } c^{e^r} \equiv c \pmod{q}$$

for some r. Clearly, before reaching this point in the sequence of exponentiation, there are many cases where one congruence holds while the other does not. For instance,

$$c^{e^r} \equiv c \pmod{p} \text{ and } c^{e^r} \not\equiv c \pmod{q}.$$

In this case, however, it is possible to factor N as $c^{e^r} - c$ is a multiple of p.

If $\varphi(N)$ is public, then anyone can find d from e or vice versa. Assume that Euler's totient function $\varphi(N)$ has been made public. Take a closer look at $\varphi(N)$, which is

$$\varphi(N) = (p-1)(q-1) = N - p - q + 1 = N - p - \frac{N}{p} + 1.$$

This equation can be rewritten as

$$p^2 + p(\varphi(N) - N - 1) + N = 0.$$

Clearly, the equation has two solutions: the factors p and q. The conclusion is that revealing $\varphi(N)$ allows an adversary to factor N and compute d from e.

Can the modulus N be shared amongst several RSA schemes? This can be an attractive solution when a single user would like to use the same N after the decryption key has been compromised. Or perhaps several cooperating users would like to use the same modulus N to establish their public schemes. To be more precise, assume that two pairs of keys have been compromised and made public. Is it possible to find factors of N or equivalently $\varphi(N)$? Denote the two pairs as (e_1, d_1) and (e_2, d_2). All keys have to be odd numbers. They can be represented as

$$e_1 d_1 - 1 \equiv \alpha_1 2^{r_1} p' q',$$
$$e_2 d_2 - 1 \equiv \alpha_2 2^{r_2} p' q',$$

where $p - 1 = 2p'$, $q - 1 = 2q'$, and α_1, α_2 are two odd numbers. It is easy to compute $gcd(e_1 d_1 - 1, e_2 d_2 - 1) = \gamma 2^{|r_1 - r_2|}$. Note that if $\gamma = 1$, then $\varphi(N)$ can be determined as $p'q'$ is easy to calculate. This happens if α_1 and α_2 are coprime. As pairs of keys are randomly chosen, we may assume that α_1 and α_2 are also two odd random integers. What is the probability that two odd integers smaller than N selected randomly and uniformly are coprime?

To answer the question consider a collection of sets D_d. The set D_d consists of odd integers less than N and divisible by d. Then

$$P(\alpha_1, \alpha_2 \text{ are coprime}) = \sum_{d=1; d \text{ is odd}}^{N} \mu(d) P(\alpha_1, \alpha_2 \in D_d),$$

where $\mu(d)$ is the Möbius function, $\mu(1) = 1$, and

$$\mu(d) = \begin{cases} (-1)^k & \text{if } d = p_1 \cdots p_k, \\ & \text{where } p_i, i = 1, \ldots, k, \text{ are distinct primes,} \\ 0 & \text{otherwise.} \end{cases}$$

Denote $P_d = P(\alpha_1, \alpha_2 \in D_d)$, then $P_d = \lfloor \frac{N}{d} \rfloor^2 N^{-2}$ and $P_d = \frac{1}{d^2} + O\left(\frac{1}{N}\right)$. Note that $\lfloor \frac{N}{d} \rfloor$ stands for the integral part of the fraction. Now, choosing $M = \lfloor N^{\frac{1}{2}} \rfloor$, we have

$$P(\alpha_1, \alpha_2 \text{ are coprime}) = \sum_{d=1; d \text{ is odd}}^{M} \mu(d)\left(\frac{1}{d^2} + O(\frac{1}{N})\right) + O\left(\sum_{d \geq M} \frac{1}{d^2}\right)$$

$$= \sum_{d=1; d \text{ is odd}}^{M} \frac{\mu(d)}{d^2} + O(N^{-\frac{1}{2}}).$$

Let us consider:

$$\sum_{d=1; d \text{ is odd}}^{M} \frac{\mu(d)}{d^2} = \sum_{d=1; d \text{ is odd}}^{\infty} \frac{\mu(d)}{d^2} + O\left(\sum_{d \geq M} \frac{1}{d^2}\right)$$

$$= \prod_{p \geq 3} (1 - \frac{1}{p^2}) + O(N^{-\frac{1}{2}})$$

$$= \frac{4}{3} \prod_{p \geq 2} (1 - \frac{1}{p^2}) + O(N^{-\frac{1}{2}})$$

$$= \frac{4}{3} \frac{6}{\pi^2} + O(N^{-\frac{1}{2}})$$

$$= \frac{8}{\pi^2} + O(N^{-\frac{1}{2}}).$$

Thus, $P(\alpha_1, \alpha_2 \text{ are coprime})$ is approximately $\frac{8}{\pi^2}$.

The RSA system is the most popular cryptosystem which can provide both privacy and authentication. It is widely used to secure communication passing through insecure networks such as the Internet. RSA provides the security of e-mail systems, Web-based applications, and many e-commerce applications. Since its birth in 1977, RSA has been subject to many attacks but none of them was devastating. Boneh [48] defines four categories of attacks that can be launched against RSA: elementary attacks, low private exponent attacks (private exponent must never be low), low public exponents, and implementation attacks.

4.3 Merkle-Hellman Cryptosystem

The knapsack decision problem belongs to the class **NPC** and its search equivalent to the class **NP**-hard. Merkle and Hellman [339] based their public-key cryptosystem on the knapsack problem. The Merkle-Hellman cryptosystem or MH system encrypts an n-bit message $m = (\alpha_1, \ldots, \alpha_n) \in \mathcal{M}$ using a public key $e = (\beta_1, \ldots, \beta_n)$ where $\alpha_i \in \{0, 1\}$ and $\beta_i \in \mathcal{Z}_q$, $i = 1, \ldots, n$ and q is prime. The cryptogram $c \in \mathcal{C}$ is calculated as

$$c = \sum_{i=1}^{n} \alpha_i \beta_i. \tag{4.17}$$

The enciphering is simple and very efficient.

The public key and secret elements are generated by the receiver Bob who sets up the whole system. Bob first selects a sequence of superincreasing integers $w = (w_1, \ldots, w_n)$ where

$$w_i > \sum_{j=1}^{i-1} w_j. \tag{4.18}$$

Note that the initial condition w defines an instance of the easy knapsack problem which is solvable in linear time. Now Bob selects a big enough field $\mathcal{Z}_q$ (q is prime) and a multiplier $r \in \mathcal{Z}_q$. Both the prime q and r can be chosen at random provided that

$$q > \sum_{i=1}^{n} w_i.$$

Next Bob transforms the superincreasing vector w according to the following congruence

$$\beta_i \equiv w_i \cdot r \pmod{q} \tag{4.19}$$

for $i = 1, \ldots, n$. The sequence $(\beta_1, \ldots, \beta_n)$ constitutes the public key of the system. Note that the vector w, multiplier r, and prime q are kept secret by the receiver.

Assume that Bob has received a cryptogram c created according to (4.17). Bob converts the cryptogram as follows:

$$c' \equiv c \cdot r^{-1} \pmod{q}.$$

Using (4.17) and (4.19), we have

$$c' \equiv \sum_{i=1}^{n} \alpha_i \beta_i r^{-1} \equiv \sum_{i=1}^{n} \alpha_i w_i \pmod{q}.$$

The transformed cryptogram c' corresponds to an instance of the easy knapsack problem, so Bob finds bits α_i of the message m.

MH cryptosystem

Problems Used: Knapsack.

The secret easy knapsack is a superincreasing sequence of integers $w = (w_1, \ldots, w_n)$ such that $w_i > \sum_{j=1}^{i-1} w_j$.

Message Space: $\mathcal{M} = \Sigma^n$.

Cryptogram Space: $\mathcal{C} = \mathcal{Z}$.

Public Key: $e = (\beta_1, \ldots, \beta_n)$ where $\beta_i \equiv w_i \cdot r \pmod{q}$.

    Both the modulus q and the multiplier r are secret.

Secret Key: The easy knapsack $w = (w_1, \ldots, w_n)$, q and r.

Encryption: $c = E_e(m) = \sum_{i=1}^{n} \alpha_i \cdot \beta_i$ where $m = (\alpha_1, \ldots, \alpha_n)$.

Decryption: Conversion of the cryptogram c into an instance of the easy knapsack $c' = c \cdot r^{-1} \pmod{q}$.

To illustrate the MH system, assume that 5-bit messages are to be transmitted. Bob initiates the algorithm by choosing the vector

$$w = (w_1, w_2, w_3, w_4, w_5) = (2, 3, 6, 12, 25).$$

Note that:

$$w_2 > w_1,$$
$$w_3 > w_1 + w_2,$$
$$w_4 > w_1 + w_2 + w_3,$$
$$w_5 > w_1 + w_2 + w_3 + w_4.$$

Next he chooses the pair (r, q) at random provided that q is prime and $q > \sum_{i=1}^{5} w_i = 48$. Let $q = 53$ and $r = 46$. It is easy to check that $r^{-1} = 15 \pmod{53}$. Subsequently, the receiver calculates the public key using congruence (4.19), namely:

$$\beta_1 \equiv w_1 r \pmod{q} \equiv 39 \pmod{53},$$
$$\beta_2 \equiv w_2 r \pmod{q} \equiv 32 \pmod{53},$$
$$\beta_3 \equiv w_3 r \pmod{q} \equiv 11 \pmod{53},$$
$$\beta_4 \equiv w_4 r \pmod{q} \equiv 22 \pmod{53},$$
$$\beta_5 \equiv w_5 r \pmod{q} \equiv 37 \pmod{53}.$$

So, the public key $e = (\beta_1, \beta_2, \beta_3, \beta_4, \beta_5) = (39, 32, 11, 22, 37)$ is sent to the sender Alice. Suppose now that Bob has received the cryptogram $c = 119$. To decrypt it, he first transforms it, as follows,

$$c' = c \cdot r^{-1} = 119 \cdot 15 = 36 \pmod{53},$$

and next solves the easy knapsack instance

$$c' = 36 > w_5 = 25 \Rightarrow \alpha_5 = 1,$$
$$c' - w_5 = 11 < w_4 \qquad \Rightarrow \alpha_4 = 0,$$
$$c' - w_5 = 11 > w_3 = 6 \Rightarrow \alpha_3 = 1,$$
$$c' - w_5 - w_3 = 5 > w_2 = 3 \Rightarrow \alpha_2 = 1,$$
$$c' - w_5 - w_3 - w_2 = 2 = w_1 = 2 \Rightarrow \alpha_1 = 1.$$

In other words, the receiver has recreated the message $m = (1, 1, 1, 0, 1)$.

4.3.1 Security of Merkle-Hellman Cryptosystem

The MH system was broken by Shamir [465] who presented a polynomial-time algorithm which calculates easy knapsack from the public key. Shamir used the superincreasing property of easy knapsack integers to derive a system of linear inequalities. The system was later efficiently solved using Lenstra's integer programming algorithm.

There is also a version of the MH system which applies multiple modular multiplications to hide easy knapsacks. This version of the system is called the iterated MH system. Adleman [3] used the L^3 algorithm [298] to analyze a doubly iterated knapsack system. Brickell [63] and Lagarias and Odlyzko [293] showed that any low-density knapsack is solvable in polynomial-time. Finally, Brickell [64] invented a polynomial-time algorithm which for k-iterated MH systems extracts easy knapsack integers from the public key. Readers interested in the details of breaking the Merkle-Hellman system are referred to the review paper by Brickell and Odlyzko [65] and the book by O'Connor and Seberry [378].

4.4 McEliece Cryptosystem

McEliece suggested [329] that error correcting codes are excellent candidates for designing public-key cryptosystems. His work has not received the prominence or detailed study it deserves because error correcting codes are effective by virtue of their redundancy. This leads to data expansion, which has not been considered desirable in cryptography. Other cryptosystems related to the McEliece design include the Niederreiter scheme and the Stern scheme [513].

Assume we have a message space $\mathcal{M} = GF(2^k)$ and a codeword space $\mathcal{C} = GF(2^n)$. For any message $m \in \mathcal{M}$, a code assigns a codeword $c \in \mathcal{C}$ and

$c = L(m)$. A code L is linear if the sum of any two codewords $c_1 + c_2$ is equivalent to the codeword of the sum of their messages $m_1 + m_2$, i.e., $L(m_1 + m_2) = L(m_1) + L(m_2) = c_1 + c_2$. Any linear code can be described as

$$c = m \cdot G,$$

where $m \in GF(2^k)$, $c \in GF(2^n)$, and G is the $(k \cdot n)$ generating matrix.

McEliece based his cryptosystem on the Goppa codes, a superset of the BCH or the Hamming codes, because they are easy to implement in hardware and a fast decoding algorithm exists for the general Goppa codes while no such fast decoding algorithm exists for a general linear code. Goppa codes can be defined by their generating polynomial

$$p(x) = x^t + p_{t-1}x^{t-1} + \cdots + p_1 x + 1$$

of degree t over $GF(2^u)$. For messages of length k, the Goppa code produces codewords of length $n = 2^u$ and the code is capable of correcting any pattern of t or fewer errors.

The receiver Bob chooses a desirable value of n and t and then randomly picks an irreducible polynomial of degree t over $GF(2^u)$. The probability that a randomly selected polynomial of degree t is irreducible is about $1/t$ and Berlekamp [27] describes a fast algorithm for testing the irreducibility of polynomials. Next Bob produces a $k \cdot n$ generator matrix G for the code, which is in canonical form, that is:

$$G = [I_k \ F_{k(n-k)}],$$

where I_k is the identity matrix.

The usual error correction method would now multiply a message vector $m = (\alpha_1, \ldots, \alpha_k)$ onto G to form the codeword c which is transmitted via a noisy channel. The channel usually corrupts the codeword to c' which must then be corrected and then the message recovered. If m were multiplied onto G in the canonical form, c would be:

$$c = (\alpha_1, \ldots, \alpha_k, f_1(m), \ldots, f_{n-k}(m)).$$

If there was no corruption, the message is trivially recovered as the first k bits of c.

Thus McEliece "scrambles" G by selecting a random dense $k \cdot k$ nonsingular matrix S, and a random $n \cdot n$ permutation matrix P. He then computes

$$G' = SGP,$$

which generates a linear code with the same rate and minimum distance as the code generated by G. G' is called the *public generator matrix* and constitutes the public key.

To encrypt a binary message $m \in GF(2^k)$, Alice uses the public key G' and computes the corresponding cryptogram

$$c = m \cdot G' + e,$$

where e is a locally generated random vector of length n and weight t. The vector e is kept secret by Alice. The decryption is done by Bob who calculates

$$c' = c \cdot P^{-1},$$

where P^{-1} is the inverse of the permutation matrix P. The vector c' will then be a codeword of the Goppa code previously chosen. The decoding algorithm is then used to find $m = m'S^{-1}$.

McEliece cryptosystem

Problems Used: General Coding.

A Goppa code characterized by its generating matrix G which specifies an instance.

Message Space: $\mathcal{M} = GF(2^k)$.

Cryptogram Space: $\mathcal{C} = GF(2^n)$.

Public Key: Public key $G' = SGP$.

Secret Key: Matrices S, G, and P.

Encryption: $c = E_K(m) = m \cdot G' + e$,

where e is a secret random binary string of weight t generated by Alice.

Decryption: Bob computes $c' = c \cdot P^{-1}$, decodes c', and obtains m'.

Finally, Bob translates m' into m applying $m = m'S^{-1}$.

4.4.1 Security of McEliece Cryptosystem

We need to determine the security of the system. If an opponent knows G' and intercepts c, can he/she recover m? There are two possible attacks:

1. To try to recover G from G' and therefore be able to use the decoding algorithm;
2. To attempt to recover m from c without knowing G.

The first attack is equivalent to the decomposition of G' into three matrices S, G, and P. Note that from the adversary point of view, the decomposition is not unique. The number of invertible matrices S is $\approx 0.29 \cdot 2^{k^2}$. There are $\approx 2^{ut}/t$ different Goppa codes (matrices G) and $n!$ different permutation matrices P. We do not know a decomposition algorithm that is better than the exhaustive search of all Goppa codes.

The second attack seems more promising but the basic problem to be solved is that of decoding a more or less arbitrary (n, k) linear code in the presence of up to t errors. Berlekamp, McEliece, and van Tilborg [26] have proved that the general coding problem for linear codes is **NP**-complete, so one can certainly expect that, if the code parameters are large enough, this attack will also be infeasible.

If $n = 1024 = 2^{10}$ and $t = 50$ there are about 10^{149} possible Goppa polynomials and a vast number of choices for S and P. The dimension of the code will be about 524. Hence, a brute-force approach to decoding based on comparing C to each codeword has a work factor of about $2^{524} = 10^{158}$, and a brute-force approach based on coset leaders has a work factor of about $2^{500} = 10^{151}$.

4.5 ElGamal Cryptosystem

In 1985 ElGamal [163] published a public-key cryptosystem which uses the discrete logarithm problem. Bob, the designer of the system, chooses a large enough prime p and selects an element g that generates the cyclic group $\mathcal{Z}_p^*$. The element g can be found quickly by choosing at random g many times until $g^{(p-1)/2} = -1$ which guarantees that g is primitive (assuming that $g \neq -1$). The probability that a single random element generates $\mathcal{Z}_p^*$ is quite high and equals $\varphi(p-1)/(p-1)$, where $\varphi(p-1)$ is the Euler totient function. Later Bob picks up an integer $k < p - 1$. Bob computes $g^k \pmod{p}$ and publishes the modulus p, primitive element g, and integer g^k. The exponent k is kept secret.

To encrypt a message $m \in GF(p)$, Alice selects first her secret element s at random from $\mathcal{Z}_{p-1}$ and prepares a cryptogram which consists of two parts $c = (c_1, c_2)$, where

$$c_1 \equiv m \cdot (g^k)^s \pmod{p},$$
$$c_2 \equiv g^s \pmod{p}.$$

The pair is dispatched to Bob. On receiving the cryptogram, Bob computes $c_2^k \equiv g^{sk}$ (mod p). Next he finds the inverse g^{-ks}, and computes the message

$$m \equiv c_1 \cdot g^{-ks} \pmod{p}.$$

The steps in ElGamal systems are summarized below.

ElGamal cryptosystem

Problems Used: Discrete logarithm.

Bob selects the modulus p, primitive element g, and the exponent k. The modulus p and element g are public.

Message Space: $\mathcal{M} = GF(p)$.

Cryptogram Space: $\mathcal{C} = GF(p) \cdot GF(p)$.

Public Key: Public key g^k (mod p).

Secret Key: $k \in \mathcal{Z}_{p-1}$.

Encryption: Alice selects at random an exponent $s \in \mathcal{Z}_{p-1}$. The exponent s is secret. The cryptogram is $c = (c_1, c_2)$ where $c_1 \equiv m \cdot (g^k)^s$ (mod p) and $c_2 \equiv g^s$ (mod p).

Decryption: Bob computes $(g^k)^s = c_2^k \equiv g^{sk}$ (mod p), its inverse g^{-sk}, and the message $m \equiv c_1 \cdot g^{-sk}$ (mod p).

4.5.1 Security of ElGamal Cryptosystem

The security of the system is related to the difficulty of solving instances of the DH problem. To have a secure instance of the ElGamal system, the modulus needs to be larger than 200 decimal digits or 660 bits. The modulus p must be selected in such a way that $p-1$ has at least one large factor, preferably $p-1 = 2q$ where q is a prime. For $p = 2^n$, using Mersenne numbers is recommended (as $p-1$ is prime). Readers interested in algorithms for solving discrete logarithm problems are directed to Odlyzko's paper [380].

4.6 Elliptic Cryptosystems

Both the RSA and ElGamal cryptosystems extensively use the cyclic groups which exist in the underlying algebraic structure. Elliptic curves can also be used to define cyclic groups which are suitable for cryptographic applications. There is a common belief that a cryptosystem based on elliptic curves provides the same security as a system based on multiplicative groups $\mathcal{Z}_p$ with the advantage that the cryptographic keys used by elliptic curve systems are shorter. These systems are relatively new and they have not been subject to the same scrutiny as older systems. This could be perceived as the main weakness. The idea of applying elliptic curves in cryptography was first suggested by Koblitz [283] and Miller [346]. Readers who want to study the subject in more detail are directed to the books by Menezes [335] and Koblitz [284].

4.6.1 Elliptic Curves

Elliptic curves are interesting geometric objects that exhibit remarkable algebraic properties. To present their application in cryptography, we need to introduce necessary definitions and notation and briefly discuss their algebraic properties.

Assume we have two fields $\mathcal{F}$ and $\mathcal{K}$. $\mathcal{K}$ is an *extension field* of $\mathcal{F}$ if $\mathcal{F}$ is contained in $\mathcal{K}$. The extension field $\mathcal{K}$ is always a vector space over $\mathcal{F}$. If the dimension of the vector space is finite then we deal with a *finite extension*. The field $\mathcal{K}$ and its vector structure is determined by a unique monic irreducible polynomial $f(x) \in \mathcal{F}[x]$ such that $f(\alpha) = 0$ for an element $\alpha \in \mathcal{K}$ ($\alpha \notin \mathcal{F}$). The polynomial $f(x)$ is called a *minimal polynomial* of α.

If the degree of $f(x)$ is d, the extension field $\mathcal{F}(\alpha)$, i.e., the smallest field containing $\mathcal{F}$ and the element α, is a vector space with the base

$$1, \alpha, \alpha^2, \ldots, \ldots \alpha^{d-1}.$$

Consider the field $\mathcal{Q}$ of all rational numbers. Take an element $\alpha = \sqrt{2}$. Then the minimal polynomial is

$$f(x) = x^2 - 2 \in \mathcal{Q}[x].$$

It is easy to check that $f(\alpha) = 0$. The extension field $\mathcal{Q}(\sqrt{2})$ is a vector space with the base $(1, \alpha)$. For example, the product of two elements $(a + b\alpha)$ and $(c + d\alpha)$ from $\mathcal{Q}(\sqrt{2})$ is equal to

$$(a + b\alpha)(c + d\alpha) = ac + ad\alpha + bc\alpha + bd\alpha^2$$
$$= (ac + 2bd) + (ad + bc)\alpha$$

because $f(\alpha) = 0$ implies that $\alpha^2 = 2$.

We say that $\mathcal{F}$ is *algebraically closed* if every polynomial with coefficients from $\mathcal{F}$ factors into polynomials of degree one. The *algebraic closure* $\bar{\mathcal{F}}$ is the smallest algebraically closed extension of $\mathcal{F}$.

A field $\mathcal{F}$ has the *characteristic* (denoted as $char(\mathcal{F})$):

– zero if repeated addition of the multiplicative identity never produces zero;
– nonzero and equal to p if adding the multiplicative identity p times produces zero.

A *discriminant* Δ of a monic polynomial $f(x)$ of degree d with roots $(\alpha_1, \ldots, \alpha_d)$ is

$$\Delta = \prod_{i \neq j} (\alpha_i - \alpha_j).$$

A curve defined over a field $\mathcal{F}$ is a collection of points $(x, y) \in \mathcal{F}^2$ satisfying a generalized Weierstrass equation of the form

$$y^2 + a_1 xy + a_3 y = x^3 + a_2 x^2 + a_4 x + a_6, \tag{4.20}$$

where the coefficients $a_i \in \mathcal{F}$ for $i = 1, \ldots, 6$. Equation (4.20) defines an elliptic curve if the equation is *smooth*, i.e., the two partial derivatives of $f(x, y) = y^2 + a_1 xy + a_3 y - x^3 - a_2 x^2 - a_4 x - a_6$ do not vanish simultaneously, or

$$\frac{\partial f}{\partial x} \neq 0 \text{ or } \frac{\partial f}{\partial y} \neq 0$$

in any point of the curve.

The general form given by (4.20) can be simplified if we know the characteristic of the field $\mathcal{F}$. If $char(\mathcal{F}) \neq 2$, then we can apply the substitution

$$(x, y) \rightarrow \left(x, y - \frac{a_1}{2}x - \frac{a_3}{2} \right),$$

which produces an isomorphic curve

$$y^2 = x^3 + a_2' x^2 + a_4' x + a_6'. \tag{4.21}$$

If $char(\mathcal{F}) \neq \{2, 3\}$, then the elliptic curve (4.21) can further be subject to the following substitution:

$$(x, y) \rightarrow \left(\frac{2x - 3a_2'}{36}, \frac{y}{216} \right).$$

The transformation reduces the curve to one of the form

$$y^2 = x^3 + ax + b,$$

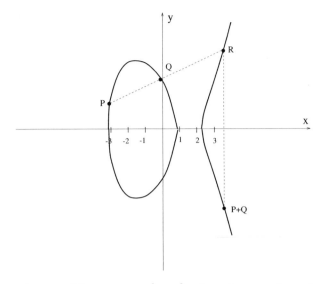

Fig. 4.2. Elliptic curve $y^2 = x^3 - 8x + 6$ over real numbers

which is smooth if the polynomial $x^3 + ax + b$ has no multiple roots or, equivalently, if the discriminant $\Delta = -(4a^3 + 27b^2) \neq 0$.

If $char(\mathcal{F}) = 2$, we have two cases: $a_1 = 0$ or $a_1 \neq 0$ in (4.20).

1. *Supersingular elliptic curve* $(a_1 = 0)$ – the transformation

   $$(x, y) \rightarrow (x + a_2, y)$$

   produces the curve of the form

   $$y^2 + a_3' y = x^3 + a_4' x + a_6'.$$

2. *Nonsupersingular elliptic curve* $(a_1 \neq 0)$ – the substitution

   $$(x, y) \rightarrow \left(a_1^2 x + \frac{a_3}{a_1}, a_1^3 y + \frac{a_1^2 a_4 + a_3^2}{a_1^3} \right)$$

   gives the curve

   $$y^2 + xy = x^3 + a_2' x^2 + a_6'.$$

4.6.2 Addition of Points

Elliptic curves can be graphically illustrated as shown in Fig. 4.2. It is possible to define addition of points on elliptic curves. Moreover, the set of points on the curve together with addition defines an Abelian group. This point is crucial for our discussion and we are going to prove that the points on an elliptic curve form an Abelian group. We start from definitions of the group structure.

- The group identity element $\mathcal{O}$ is the point at infinity, and for each point P

$$\mathcal{O} + P = P + \mathcal{O}.$$

- The inverse of the point $P = (x, y)$ is the point

$$-P = (x, -y).$$

- Two points P and Q with different x coordinates (see Fig. 4.2) are added as follows:
  1. Construct a line which intersects both P and Q. The line meets the curve at the third point R.
  2. The inverse of the point R is the requested element $P + Q$ or $P + Q = -R$.
- The point P can be added to itself. The line, which in the previous case intersected the two points, is now replaced by the tangent line to the curve at the point P.

The above definition gives an explicit formula for addition. To derive this formula, assume that two points P and Q are given, and

$$P = (x_1, y_1) \text{ and } Q = (x_2, y_2).$$

We would like to find a point $P + Q = (x_3, y_3)$. Note that the line intersecting P and Q has the form

$$\ell(x) = \ell_1 x + \ell_2,$$

where $\ell_1 = \frac{y_2 - y_1}{x_2 - x_1}$ and $\ell_2 = y_1 - \ell_1 x_1$. The line $\ell(x)$ intersects the elliptic curve at points (x, y), each of which satisfies

$$f(x) = (\ell_1 x + \ell_2)^2 - x^3 - ax - b = 0. \tag{4.22}$$

The polynomial $f(x)$ is of degree 3 and has three different roots for $x \in \{x_1, x_2, x_3\}$ or, equivalently,

$$f(x) = (x - x_1)(x - x_2)(x - x_3) = 0. \tag{4.23}$$

Comparison of (4.22) and (4.23) leads us to the conclusion that

$$x_1 + x_2 + x_3 = \ell_1^2 \text{ or } x_3 = \ell_1^2 - x_1 - x_2.$$

The case for $P = Q = (x_1, y_1)$ is similar, with the difference that $\ell_1 = \frac{dy}{dx} = \frac{3x_1^2 + a}{2y_1}$ at point P. The expressions for the addition of two points are therefore

$$x_3 \equiv \lambda^2 - x_1 - x_2,$$
$$y_3 \equiv \lambda(x_1 - x_3) - y_1,$$

(4.24)

where

$$\lambda = \begin{cases} \dfrac{y_1 - y_2}{x_1 - x_2} & \text{if } P \neq Q \\[2ex] \dfrac{3x_1^2 + a}{2y_1} & \text{if } P = Q \end{cases}.$$

From now on, we denote an Abelian group generated by the points on the curve

$$y^2 \equiv x^3 + ax + b \pmod{p}$$

by $\mathcal{E}_p(a, b)$ where the field $\mathcal{F} = \mathcal{Z}_p$.

For example, consider an elliptic curve $\mathcal{E}_7(1, 6)$ with points satisfying the congruence $y^2 \equiv x^3 + x + 6 \pmod{7}$. The collection of all points is

$$\mathcal{E}_7(1, 6) = \{(1, 1), (1, 6), (2, 3), (2, 4), (3, 1), (3, 6), (4, 2), (4, 5), (6, 2), (6, 5), \mathcal{O}\}.$$

Because the order of the group is 11, the group is isomorphic to $\mathcal{Z}_{11}^*$ and any point different from $\mathcal{O}$ generates the group. For instance,

$$2 \cdot (2, 3) = (4, 2),$$
$$3 \cdot (2, 3) = (3, 1),$$
$$4 \cdot (2, 3) = (6, 5),$$
$$5 \cdot (2, 3) = (1, 1),$$
$$6 \cdot (2, 3) = (1, 6),$$
$$7 \cdot (2, 3) = (6, 2),$$
$$8 \cdot (2, 3) = (3, 6),$$
$$9 \cdot (2, 3) = (4, 5),$$
$$10 \cdot (2, 3) = (2, 4),$$
$$11 \cdot (2, 3) = \mathcal{O}.$$

4.6.3 Elliptic Curve Variant of RSA

Koyama, Maurer, Okamoto, and Vanstone [286] presented an implementation of RSA using elliptic curves. Demytko [134] showed a variant which is less restrictive as to the types of elliptic curves used in the cryptosystem.

We will describe the first system by Koyama, Maurer, Okamoto, and Vanstone. Let the number of points in $\mathcal{E}_p(a, b)$ or the order of the group be $\#\mathcal{E}_p(a, b)$. If we know $\mathcal{E}_p(a, b)$, then we can use the elliptic curve for encryption in a way very similar to that of the basic RSA system. To encrypt a message we add the message e times. To decrypt the ciphertext, we need to add the ciphertext d times so we get back to the original message. It is easy to see that to do that it is enough to choose e and d so their product is a multiple of $\#\mathcal{E}_p(a, b)$.

In general, we know that

$$\#\mathcal{E}_p(a, b) = p + 1 + t,$$

where $|t| \leq 2\sqrt{p}$. Schoof [453] invented an algorithm that computes the order of an elliptic curve in $O((\log p)^8)$ steps. The algorithm becomes impractical for large p. However, the order of the elliptic curves is known explicitly in the two cases:

(1) If the modulus p is an odd prime $p \equiv 2 \pmod 3$ and the parameter $a = 0$. The group $\mathcal{E}_p(0, b)$ is cyclic with the order $p + 1$ $(0 < b < p)$.
(2) If the modulus p is a prime satisfying $p \equiv 3 \pmod 4$ and $b = 0$. The group $\mathcal{E}_p(a, 0)$ is cyclic with the order $p + 1$ if a is a quadratic residue modulo p $(0 < a < p)$.

The RSA variant based on elliptic curves is described below. It is based on the elliptic curve $\mathcal{E}_N(0, b)$ with $N = p \cdot q$ and $p \equiv q \equiv 2 \pmod 3$. Note that $\#\mathcal{E}_N(0, b) = lcm(p + 1, q + 1)$.

Elliptic curve RSA cryptosystem

Problems Used: Factorization and discrete logarithm.

The modulus $N = p \cdot q$ is public, the primes p, q are secret. The elliptic curve used is $\mathcal{E}_N(0, b)$ (or $\mathcal{E}_N(a, 0)$).

Message Space: $\mathcal{M} = \mathcal{E}_N(0, b)$.

Cryptogram Space: $\mathcal{C} = \mathcal{E}_N(0, b)$.

Public Key: $e \in_R \{1, \ldots, \#\mathcal{E}_N(0, b)\}$ and $gcd(e, \#\mathcal{E}_N(0, b)) = 1$.

Secret Key: $d \in \{1, \ldots, \#\mathcal{E}_N(0, b)\}$ such that $e \cdot d \equiv 1 \pmod{\#\mathcal{E}_N(0, b)}$.

Encryption: Let $m = (m_x, m_y)$ be a point on the elliptic curve $E_N(0, b)$.

$c = E_e(m) = e \cdot m$ over $E_N(0, b)$.

Decryption: $m = D_d(c) = d \cdot c$ over $E_N(0, b)$.

The security of elliptic curve RSA systems is related to the difficulty of factorization of the modulus N. Kurosawa, Okada, and Tsujii report that elliptic curve RSA is not secure with low exponents [292].

Let us illustrate the system for small parameters. The receiver Bob selects two primes $p = 239$ and $q = 401$. Note that the primes are congruent to 2 modulo 3. In other words, Bob has decided to use the group $\mathcal{E}_N(0, b)$. Next he computes $N = p \cdot q = 95839$, $\#\mathcal{E}_N(0, b) = lcm(p+1, q+1) = 16080$ and selects at random a public key e. Let it be $e = 5891$ $(gcd(N, e) = 1)$. A secret key $d = 12971$ satisfies the congruence $e \cdot d \equiv 1 \bmod 16080$. Bob announces the modulus N and the public key e.

Alice takes her message $m = (m_x, m_y) = (66321, 24115)$, which is a point on the elliptic curve $\mathcal{E}_N(0, b)$. Alice may even compute b as for all points (x, y) on the curve $y^2 \equiv x^3 + b \bmod N$ $(b \equiv y^2 - x^3 \bmod N)$. Addition in $\mathcal{E}_N(0, b)$ does not depend on b. The sender computes the cryptogram $c = e \cdot m \bmod N$ which for the assumed values is the point $c = (79227, 19622)$. Bob can easily decrypt the cryptogram by multiplying it by the secret key so $m = d \cdot c = 12971(79227, 19622) = (66321, 24115)$.

Multiplication of points on elliptic curves may be conveniently implemented using any system for algebraic computations, such as MAPLE, MATHEMAT-ICA, or MAGMA, that supports multiprecision arithmetic. An example of a MAPLE program for addition and multiplication over an elliptic curve in given below.

```
# To load it into MAPLE, type:
# read'<namefile>';
# where <namefile> is a file with the code in the same directory
# MAPLE software is run.
#-------------------------------------------------------------------------
# Program adds two points on the elliptic curve y^2 = x^3 + b modulo N.
# Point in infinity is represented by (0,0) and the inverse of
# any point (x,y) is (x,-y)
#-------------------------------------------------------------------------
ad := proc(x1,y1,x2,y2, N)
local lambda, x3, y3, result;

if x1=x2 then
if modp(y1+y2, N)=0 then RETURN( 0, 0 ); fi;
fi;
```

```
if x1=0 then
if y1=0 then RETURN( x2, y2 ); fi;
fi;
if x2=0 then
if y2=0 then
result[1] := x1; result[2] := y1;
RETURN( x1, y1 );
fi;
fi;
if x1 <> x2 then
lambda := modp((y1-y2)/(x1-x2), N);
else
lambda := modp((3*(x1^2))/(2*y1), N);
fi;
x3 := modp(lambda^2-x1-x2,N);
y3 := modp(lambda*(x1-x3)-y1, N);
RETURN( x3, y3 );
end;
#-----------------------------------------------------------------------
# mult function multiplies a point (x,y) by k modulo N on the
# curve (the function calls ad function).
#-----------------------------------------------------------------------
mult := proc( k, x, y, N)
local a,i,j,alpha,beta,base,s,accum ;
a := array ( 1 .. 1000 , sparse );
base := array( 1 .. 1000, 1..2, sparse);

if k=0 then RETURN( 0,0 ); fi;
if k=1 then RETURN( x,y ); fi;
i := k; j := 1;
while i > 0 do
alpha := irem(i,2,'q');
beta  := iquo(i,2,'r');
i := beta; a[j] := alpha; j := j+1;
od;
base[1,1] := x; base[1,2] := y;
accum[1] := 0; accum[2] := 0;
if a[1]=1 then
accum[1] := x; accum[2] := y;
fi;
for i from 2 to j-1 do
s := ad( base[i-1,1],base[i-1,2],base[i-1,1],base[i-1,2],N);
```

```
base[i,1] := s[1]; base[i,2] := s[2];
if a[i]=1 then
    accum := ad( base[i,1],base[i,2],accum[1],accum[2],N);
fi;
od;
RETURN( accum );
end;
```

The function `mult()` can be used directly for encryption and decryption. Note that the function performs an operation that is equivalent to the RSA exponentiation. It works relatively fast for moduli whose size is several hundreds of bits, making computations quite realistic.

4.6.4 Elliptic Curve Variant of ElGamal

The system described below was invented by Menezes and Vanstone [338].

Elliptic curve ElGamal cryptosystem

Problems Used: Discrete logarithm.

Bob selects a large prime $p > 3$ (the modulus), an elliptic curve $\mathcal{E}_p$ (the corresponding discrete logarithm problem has to be intractable), and a point $P \in \mathcal{E}_p$. The elliptic curve $\mathcal{E}_p$, the modulus, and the point P are public.

Message Space: $\mathcal{M} = \mathcal{Z}_p \cdot \mathcal{Z}_p$.

Cryptogram Space: $\mathcal{C} = \mathcal{E}_p \cdot \mathcal{Z}_p \cdot \mathcal{Z}_p$.

Public Key: a point $d \cdot P \in \mathcal{E}_p$.

Secret Key: an integer $d \in \mathcal{Z}$ (d smaller than the order of the cyclic group).

Encryption: Alice selects at random a multiplier $s \in \mathcal{Z}_p$, calculates the point $R = s \cdot P \in \mathcal{E}_p$, and finds a point $Q = s \cdot d \cdot P = (\alpha_x, \alpha_y) \in \mathcal{E}_p$. For the message $m = (m_x, m_y)$, she computes the cryptogram $c = E_e(m) = (R, c_x, c_y)$ where $c_x = \alpha_x m_x \pmod{p}$ and $c_y = \alpha_y m_y \pmod{p}$. The multiplier s is kept secret by Alice.

Decryption: Bob uses the point R to recover the point Q as $Q = dR = dsP = (\alpha_x, \alpha_y) \in \mathcal{E}_p$. Next $m = D_d(c) = (c_x \alpha_x^{-1} \pmod{p}, c_y \alpha_y^{-1} \pmod{p})$.

For example, consider an ElGamal system on an elliptic curve $\mathcal{E}_p(0, b)$ for $p = 71$ ($71 \equiv 2 \bmod 3$). Bob publishes p and a point on the curve $P = (25, 33)$ and the public key $dP = (33, 39)$ for his secret key $d = 43$. To encrypt a message $m = (m_x, m_y) = (22, 44)$, Alice first selects her secret s at random. Assume that the secret $s = 29$. Then she finds two points $R = sP = (33, 32)$ and $Q = s(dP) = (25, 38)$. The message m is encrypted using coordinates of the point Q so $c_x \equiv m_x \cdot 25 \equiv 53 \bmod 71$ and $c_y \equiv m_y \cdot 38 \equiv 39 \bmod 71$. The cryptogram $c = (R, 53, 39)$ is communicated to Bob.

Bob reconstructs the point Q using his secret integer d as $Q = dR = (25, 38)$, and computes $25^{-1} \equiv 54 \bmod 71$ and $38^{-1} \equiv 43 \bmod 71$. Clearly $m_x \equiv 53 \cdot 54 \equiv 22 \bmod 71$ and $m_y \equiv 39 \cdot 43 \equiv 44 \bmod 71$.

Menezes, Okamoto, and Vanstone [336] demonstrated that the discrete logarithm problem on a supersingular elliptic curve can be reduced to the (classical) logarithm problem in a finite field. This result shows that care must be exercised in the selection of elliptic curves so the corresponding logarithm problems are harder than the (classical) logarithm problem.

4.7 Probabilistic Encryption

The concept of probabilistic encryption was introduced and studied by Goldwasser and Micali in [209]. Their goal was to design an encryption that is semantically secure. *Semantic security* requires that a polynomially bounded attacker is not able to tell apart a ciphertext of one message from a ciphertext of another. In other words, cryptograms provide no information about encryption. This requirement must hold even if encryption is used for binary messages only.

A probabilistic public key cryptosystem applies to the set of messages $\mathcal{M} = \{0, 1\}$, the set of keys $\mathcal{K}$, the set of cryptograms $\mathcal{C}$, and the set $\mathcal{R} = \mathcal{R}_0 \cup \mathcal{R}_1$. The encryption proceeds using the encryption function $c = E_e(m, r)$ where $r \in_R \mathcal{R}_m$ and $m \in \{0, 1\}$. During the decryption process, the message $m = 0$ if $D_d(c) \in \mathcal{R}_0$ or $m = 1$, otherwise. The encryption function induces a pair of two ensembles: $\mathcal{C}_0 = E_e(\mathcal{R}_0)$ and $\mathcal{C}_1 = E_e(\mathcal{R}_1)$. The proof of security of a probabilistic public key cryptosystem can be reduced to the assertion that the two ensembles $\mathcal{C}_0$ and $\mathcal{C}_1$ are polynomially indistinguishable (or polynomially secure). It turns out that semantic security and polynomial indistinguishability are equivalent and they are the cornerstone of the theory of conditionally secure cryptosystems.

4.7.1 GM Probabilistic Encryption

The Goldwasser-Micali (GM) probabilistic encryption assumes that the quadratic residuosity problem is intractable. The idea is to generate cryptograms which are either quadratic or nonquadratic residues modulo a composite $N = p \cdot q$ with their Jacobi symbol equal to 1. Thus, the system applies two indistinguishable sets: $\mathcal{Z}_N^{Q+}$ and $\mathcal{Z}_N^{Q-}$. The set $\mathcal{Z}_N^{Q+}$ consists of all elements from $\mathcal{Z}_N$ that are quadratic residues modulo N. The set $\mathcal{Z}_N^{Q-}$ contains nonquadratic residues of the form

$$\mathcal{Z}_N^{Q-} = \{x \in \mathcal{Z}_N : \left(\frac{x}{p}\right) = \left(\frac{x}{q}\right) = -1\}.$$

Note that their Jacobi symbol $\left(\frac{x}{N}\right) = \left(\frac{x}{p}\right)\left(\frac{x}{q}\right) = 1$. Other nonquadratic residues are not used in the encryption.

Assume that whenever the message is 0, the GM system generates a random element from $\mathcal{Z}_N^{Q+}$, otherwise it produces a random number from $\mathcal{Z}_N^{Q-}$. The sender can produce the quadratic residues by random selection of element $r \in \mathcal{Z}_N$ and then squaring it. To enable the sender to produce random nonquadratic residue from $\mathcal{Z}_N^{Q-}$, there must be a public integer $u\mathcal{Z}_N^{Q-}$ which is used for this purpose.

GM probabilistic encryption

Problems Used: The quadratic residuosity problem. Given a composite integer
  N with two factors p and q. The modulus N is public but the factors are
  secret. An element $u \in \mathcal{Z}_N^{Q-}$ is public.
Message Space: $\mathcal{M} = \{0, 1\}$.
Cryptogram Space: $\mathcal{C} = \mathcal{Z}_N$.
Encryption: For a message $m \in \mathcal{M}$, select $r \in \mathcal{Z}_N$ and compute $c = E_e(m, r) = u^m r^2 \bmod N$.
Decryption: $m = D_d(c) = \begin{cases} 0 & \text{if } c \in \mathcal{Z}_N^{Q+} \\ 1 & \text{if } c \in \mathcal{Z}_N^{Q-} \end{cases}$.

Clearly, all cryptograms c have their Jacobi symbol equal to 1. To distinguish which one carries the 0 bit, the receiver has to know the factorization of N and calculate $\left(\frac{c}{p}\right) = c^{(p-1)/2}$. If this is equal to 1, $u^m = 1$ so $m = 0$.

4.7.2 BG Probabilistic Encryption

Blum and Goldwasser [45] generalized the GM public key encryption. They used the BBS pseudorandom generator to design a probabilistic public key encryption for short binary messages (not necessarily single bits). Their system is further referred to as the BG probabilistic encryption.

BG probabilistic encryption

Problems Used: The quadratic residuosity problem. Given a composite integer
N with two factors p and q such that $p \equiv q \equiv 3 \bmod 4$. The modulus N is
public. The factors p and q are secret.

Message Space: $\mathcal{M} = \Sigma^t$.

Cryptogram Space: $\mathcal{C} = \mathbb{Z}_N$.

Encryption: 1. For a given seed x_0, generate $(x_1, \ldots, x_t)$ using the BBS generator (Sect. 5.3.2).

 2. For a given message $m = (m_1 \ldots m_t) \in \mathcal{M}$ compute $c_i \equiv x_i + m_i \bmod 2$, $i = 1, \ldots, t$.

 3. Calculate $c_{t+1} = x_0^{2^{t+1}} \bmod N$.

 4. Send the cryptogram $c = (c_1, \ldots, c_{t+1})$.

Decryption: 1. Recover the seed x_0 from c_{t+1}.

 2. For the seed x_0, generate $(x_1, \ldots, x_t)$ using the BBS generator.

 3. Recreate the message string $m_i \equiv c_i + x_i \bmod 2$ for $i = 1, \ldots, t$.

The method to retrieve x_0 from c_{t+1} needs some clarification. Assume that
$\alpha \in \mathbb{Z}_N^{Q+}$, then α has two square roots, namely $\pm\sqrt{\alpha} = \pm\alpha^{\frac{p+1}{4}}$. Indeed,

$$\left(\alpha^{\frac{p+1}{4}}\right)^2 = \alpha^{\frac{p+1}{2}} = \alpha^{\frac{p-1}{2}}\alpha$$

as $\alpha \in \mathbb{Z}_N^{Q+}$ so $\left(\frac{\alpha}{p}\right) = \alpha^{(p-1)/2} = 1$ and $\left(\alpha^{\frac{p+1}{4}}\right)^2 = \alpha$. So the squaring has its
inverse $2^{-1} \equiv \frac{p+1}{4} \bmod p - 1$. To recover x_0 from c_{t+1}, we need to first compute

$$2^{-(t+1)} \equiv \left(\frac{p+1}{4}\right)^{t+1} \pmod{p-1},$$

$$2^{-(t+1)} \equiv \left(\frac{q+1}{4}\right)^{t+1} \pmod{q-1},$$

and later find x_0 such that

$$x_0 \equiv c_{t+1}^{2^{-(t+1)}} \bmod p,$$
$$x_0 \equiv c_{t+1}^{2^{-(t+1)}} \bmod q,$$

using the Chinese Remainder Theorem.

4.8 Public-Key Encryption Practice

Public-key cryptography traditionally is used to provide confidentiality of data via encryption under a standard assumption that the attacker is an outsider. Experience demonstrates that in many applications the attacker is more likely to be an insider who, apart from the case of public encryption, may have access to the decryption algorithm. In the so-called *lunch-time* or *midnight* attack, an insider can for some time play with the decryption device asking for messages which correspond to a collection of cryptograms chosen by the attacker. The device is assumed to be tamperproof so the attacker is not able to see the secret key.

4.8.1 Taxonomy of Public-Key Encryption Security

It is reasonable to assume that the computational power of an adversary is polynomially bounded. A public-key cryptosystem can be used to provide the following general security goals:

- *One-wayness* (OW) – the adversary who sees a cryptogram is not able to compute the corresponding message (plaintext).
- *Indistinguishability* (IND) – observing a cryptogram, the adversary learns nothing about the plaintext.
- *Nonmalleability* (NM) – the adversary, observing a cryptogram for a message m, cannot derive another cryptogram for a meaningful plaintext m' related to m.

The goals OW and IND relate to the confidentiality of encrypted messages. The IND goal is, however, much more difficult to achieve than the one-wayness. Note that probabilistic encryption presented in Sect. 4.7 provides indistinguishability (also termed *semantic security*). Nonmalleability guarantees that any attempt to manipulate the observed cryptogram to obtain a valid cryptogram will be unsuccessful (with a high probability). For example, the RSA cryptosystem is malleable. The adversary, knowing a cryptogram $c = m^e$, can for the message $m' = 2m$ create the valid cryptogram $c' = c \cdot 2^e$. This allows an adversary to produce valid cryptograms for unknown messages which are smaller or bigger than m (the adversary always wins in electronic bidding).

The power of a polynomial attacker (with polynomial computing resources) very much depends on his/her access to the information about the public-key system. The weakest attacker is an outsider who knows the public encryption algorithm together with other public information about the setup of the system. The strongest attacker seems to be an insider who can access the decryption device in regular intervals (lunch-time and midnight attacks). The access to the decryption key is not possible as the decryption device is assumed to be tamperproof.

A *decryption oracle* is a formalism that mimics an attacker's access to the decryption device. The attacker can experiment with it providing cryptograms and collecting corresponding messages from the oracle (the attacker cannot access the decryption key). In general, the public-key cryptosystem can be subject to the following attacks (ordered in increasing strength):

– *Chosen plaintext attack* (CPA) – the attacker knows the encryption algorithm and the public elements including the public key (the encryption oracle is publicly accessible).
– *Nonadaptive chosen ciphertext attack* (CCA1) – the attacker has access to the decryption oracle before he sees a cryptogram that he wishes to manipulate.
– *Adaptive chosen ciphertext attack* (CCA2) – the attacker has access to the decryption oracle before and after he observes a cryptogram c that he wishes to manipulate (assuming that he is not allowed to query the oracle about the cryptogram c).

The security level that a public-key system achieves can be specified by the pair (goal, attack), where the goal can be either OW, IND, or NM, and the attack can be either CPA, CCA1, or CCA2. For example, the level (NM, CPA) assigned to a public-key system says that the system is nonmalleable under the chosen plaintext attack. There are two sequences of trivial implications

(NM, CCA2) $\Rightarrow$ (NM, CCA1) $\Rightarrow$ (NM, CPA),
(IND, CCA2) $\Rightarrow$ (IND, CCA1) $\Rightarrow$ (IND, CPA),

which are true because the amount of information available to the attacker in CPA, CCA1, and CCA2 grows. Figure 4.3 shows the interrelation among

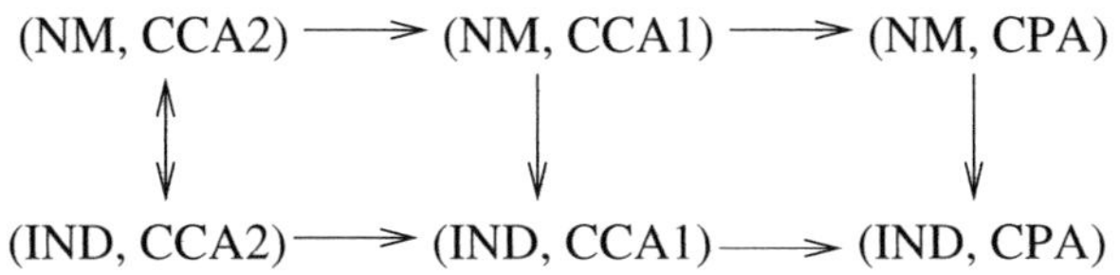

(NM, CCA2) $\longrightarrow$ (NM, CCA1) $\longrightarrow$ (NM, CPA)

(IND, CCA2) $\longrightarrow$ (IND, CCA1) $\longrightarrow$ (IND, CPA)

Fig. 4.3. Relations among security notions

different security notions [22]. Consequently, we can identify the hierarchy of security levels. The top level is occupied by (NM, CCA2) and (IND, CCA2). The bottom level contains (IND, CPA) only as the weakest level of security. If we are after the strongest security level, its enough to prove that our cryptosystem attains the (IND, CCA2) level of security.

4.8.2 Generic OAEP Public-Key Cryptosystem

Most public-key encryption systems exhibit strong algebraic properties which may be exploited by an attacker. For instance, the RSA cryptosystem has a multiplicative property which can be used by an adversary to produce valid cryptograms from a pair of cryptograms created by the sender. Suppose that the attacker knows c_1 and c_2, then he/she is sure that the ciphertext

$$c_1^\alpha \cdot c_2^\beta$$

is a valid one for the message $m_1^\alpha \cdot m_2^\beta$, although he/she does not know the actual values of m_1 and m_2. This could be a security problem in electronic bidding since you can create a valid cryptogram that encrypts a larger (or smaller) message.

Clearly, it would be desirable to "destroy" relations among messages and their cryptograms by the introduction of a redundancy. Bellare and Rogaway [23] introduced the concept of *optimal asymmetric encryption padding*, or OAEP for short. OAEP is a probabilistic encoding of messages before they are encrypted by a public-key cryptosystem. The construction uses random oracles.

A *random oracle* $H : \Sigma^n \to \Sigma^\ell$ is a function which, for an argument $x \in \Sigma^n$, returns a value y which is selected randomly, uniformly, and independently from Σ^ℓ. Random oracle is a theoretical concept that is very useful because its well formulated probabilistic properties allow us to derive conclusions about security. The conclusions are said to be valid in the random oracle (RO) model.

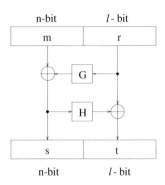

Fig. 4.4. Optimal asymmetric encryption padding

The downside of this approach is that the security conclusions obtained for the RO model may not hold (this happens when the hash function exhibits properties not expected to exist in the random oracle). The following components are used:

- An instance of a public-key cryptosystem with public encryption algorithm E and secret decryption algorithm $D = E^{-1}$ where $E : \Sigma^{n+\ell} \to \Sigma^{n+\ell}$. It is assumed that E is a one-way permutation so a polynomially bounded attacker cannot reverse it.
- Two random oracles $G : \Sigma^{\ell} \to \Sigma^{n}$ and $H : \Sigma^{n} \to \Sigma^{\ell}$.

Encryption of a message $m \in \Sigma^{n}$ proceeds as follows (Fig. 4.4):

1. Generate a random value $r \in_R \Sigma^{\ell}$.
2. Calculate

$$s = m \oplus G(r) \quad \text{and} \quad t = r \oplus H(s).$$

3. Compute the corresponding cryptogram

$$c = E(s, t) \in \Sigma^{n+\ell}.$$

Decryption first recovers the pair $(s, t) = E^{-1}(c)$, the random value $r = t \oplus H(s)$, and the message $m = s \oplus G(r)$. The security of the system meets (IND, CPA).

Note that the OAEP cryptosystem is no longer deterministic. For the same message, the system generates different cryptograms with a high probability. It is expected that cryptograms of two or more messages are not "related" even if the messages are related. OAEP breaks relations among cryptograms by using the Feistel permutation with oracles G and H. Any message is first masked

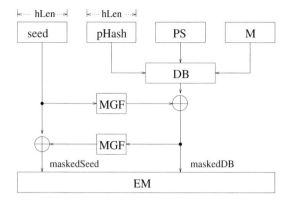

Fig. 4.5. PKCS#1 Version 2.1

by adding $G(r)$ to it. As r_i is likely to be different for each message, then a sequence of $m_i \oplus G(r_i)$ is likely to be a sequence of unrelated numbers. The second oracle H masks r. Both masked strings s and t are concatenated and encrypted.

4.8.3 RSA Encryption Standard

RSA Security developed a public-key encryption standard known as PKCS#1. The early Version 1.5 was shown to be subject to the CCA2 attack [43]. We describe Version 2.1, which can be found in

$$http://www.rsasecurity.com/rsalabs/pkcs$$

This version is also called PKCS-OAEP and is recommended for new applications.

The message M to be encrypted is first encoded using the function EME-OAEP-ENCODE(M,P,emLen) where P indicates encoding parameters specifying the choice of hashing algorithms (random oracles) and emLen gives the requested length of the encoded message (EM) in octets. The encoding procedure is illustrated in Fig. 4.5. The input consists of four strings: seed, pHash, PS, and M. Both seed and pHash are hLen octets long. The message can be at most emLen-1-2hLen octets long. The string seed is randomly chosen. pHash=Hash(P) is a string obtained from transforming P using the chosen Hash function. PS consists of emLen-mLen-2hLen-1 zero octets. The encoding EME-OAEP-ENCODE(M,P,emLen) takes the following steps:

1. Concatenate strings pHash, PS, and M and form the string DB in the form

    DB=(pHash‖ PS ‖ 01 ‖ M).

2. Compute

    maskedDB = DB ⊕ MGF(seed,emLen-hLen),

   where MGF() is the mask generation function (random oracle).
3. Calculate

    maskedSeed = seed ⊕ MGF(maskedDB,hLen).

4. Output EM=(maskedSeed,maskedDB).

The encryption runs through the following steps:

1. Encode the message M by invoking the function EM=EME-OAEP-ENCODE(M, P,emLen).
2. Convert the message EM into an integer representation, i.e., m=OS2IP(EM).
3. Apply the RSA encryption primitive or c=RSAEP((N,K),m) where N is the modulus and K the public key.
4. Convert the cryptogram c into its octet equivalent C and output it.

The decryption reverses the operations and first the encoded message EM is recovered. The decoding procedure allows us to verify the correctness of the cryptogram when:

– The recovered string DB′ does not contain the string PS of zeros separated by the 01 octet.
– The string pHash′ which is a part of DB′ is not equal to the pHash determined by the encoding parameters P.

PKCS-OAEP is a variant of the generic OAEP public-key encryption and its security is believed to be (IND, CCA2) assuming the RO model (if MGF is replaced by random oracles).

4.8.4 Extended ElGamal Cryptosystem

Cramer and Shoup [115] designed a cryptosystem whose security is based on the presumed difficulty of the Diffie-Hellman decision problem.

Name: Diffie-Hellman decision problem.

Instance: Given a group G of large prime order q. Consider the following two distributions:

- the distribution R of random quadruples $(g_1, g_2, u_1, u_2) \in G^4$,
- the distribution D of quadruples $(g_1, g_2, u_1, u_2) \in G^4$ where g_1, g_2 are random and $u_1 = g_1^r$ and $u_2 = g_2^r$ for a random $r \in \mathcal{Z}_q$.

Question: Given a quadruple coming from an unknown distribution (either R or D), does the quadruple belong to R or D?

The cryptosystem is interesting as it allows us to identify cryptograms which have not been created according to the encryption algorithm. Moreover, the identification procedure can be skipped and then the system becomes the original ElGamal.

Extended ElGamal cryptosystem

Problems Used: Diffie-Hellman decision problem.

Given $\mathcal{Z}_q$ for prime q and a hash function $H : \mathcal{Z}_q^3 \to \mathcal{Z}_q$ chosen from the family of universal one-way hash functions.

Message Space: $\mathcal{M} = \mathcal{Z}_q$.

Cryptogram Space: $\mathcal{C} = \mathcal{Z}_q^4$.

Key generation: Random nonzero elements $g_1, g_2, x_1, x_2, y_1, y_2, z \in_R \mathcal{Z}_q$ are chosen. The following elements are computed:

$$c = g_1^{x_1} g_2^{x_2}, \quad d = g_1^{y_1} g_2^{y_2}, \text{ and } h = g_1^z.$$

Public Key: (g_1, g_2, c, d, h, H).

Secret Key: (x_1, x_2, y_1, y_2, z).

Encryption: Given a message $m \in \mathcal{Z}_q$, perform the following steps:

1. Choose random $r \in_R \mathcal{Z}_q$.
2. Compute
$$u_1 = g_1^r, \quad u_2 = g_2^r, \quad e = h^r m, \quad \alpha = H(u_1, u_2, e), \quad v = c^r d^{r\alpha}.$$
   The cryptogram $c = (u_1, u_2, e, v)$.

Decryption: Given a cryptogram $c = (u_1, u_2, e, v)$, do the following:

1. Compute $\alpha = H(u_1, u_2, e)$.

2. Check whether
$$u_1^{x_1+y_1\alpha} u_2^{x_2+y_2\alpha} \stackrel{?}{=} v.$$
If the equation does not hold reject the cryptogram, otherwise continue and output the message
$$m = e \cdot u_1^{-z}.$$

Note that the decryption can be done by the original ElGamal system from the pair (u_1, e). The whole cryptogram is used to verify its validity. The system is provably secure against a CCA2 attack or, more precisely, meets (IND, CCA2), and using the equivalence from Fig. 4.3 satisfies (NM, CCA2).

4.9 Problems and Exercises

1. Name the main components of the public-key cryptosystem and formulate the security requirements. Discuss the use of the system for secrecy and authenticity.
2. Given a modulus $\varphi(N)$ and a public key e, write a C program that calculates a secret key d for the RSA system. Assume that both $\varphi(N)$ and e are long integers.
3. Assume that $p = 467$ and $q = 479$. Calculate the secret key in the RSA system, knowing that the public key is equal to $e = 73443$.
4. Suppose you want to design an RSA system in which the modulus $N = p_1 \cdot p_2 \cdot p_3$ (p_i is prime for $i = 1, 2, 3$). Is it possible? If so, what is the main difference between this modification and the original RSA system? Derive the necessary expressions for encryption, decryption, and keys.
5. Given a Rabin scheme for $p = 179$ and $q = 191$ with the decryption based on the Williams's modification. Compute the deciphering key. What are the cryptograms for the two messages $M_1 = 33001$ and $M_2 = 18344$?
6. Write a primality testing algorithm that incorporates both the test based on Fermat's Little Theorem (see (4.13)) and the Miller-Rabin test.
7. Find all primes from the interval (45700, 45750) using the Miller-Rabin test.
8. Implement the sieve of Eratosthenes as a C language program.
9. Suppose that you have an efficient probabilistic algorithm A which computes square roots (modulo N). More precisely, the algorithm takes an integer x and returns a single integer which is a square root $\sqrt{x}$ mod N. Show how the algorithm can be applied to factor integers.
10. Use the quadratic sieve algorithm to factor $N = 29591$. First do the factorization by hand. Next implement the algorithm in C (or another high-level programming language) assuming that N is a long integer.
11. Apply the iteration attack to recreate the original message for six different pairs (cryptogram, public key) while the RSA system uses the modulus $N = 2773$. The pairs are:
    (a) $c = 1561, e = 573$;

    (b) $c = 1931$, $e = 861$;

    (c) $c = 2701$, $e = 983$;

    (d) $c = 67$, $e = 1013$;

    (e) $c = 178$, $e = 1579$;

    (f) $c = 2233$, $e = 791$.

12. Design the Merkle-Hellman system which encrypts 7-bit messages. Suppose that $w = (w_1, \ldots, w_7) = (2, 3, 6, 12, 24, 49, 100)$, q is the smallest integer which is bigger than $\sum_{i=1}^{7} w_i$ and $r = 119$. What is the cryptogram for the message $M = 1011011$? Show the deciphering process.

13. Consider the easy knapsack vector $w = (1, 2, 4, 8, 16, 32, 64, 128, 256, 512)$. Produce the public key using four iterations defined by the following pairs: (q_1, r_1), (q_2, r_2), (q_3, r_3), and (q_4, r_4). Choose primes q_i, $i = 1, 2, 3, 4$, as small as possible. Accept $(r_1, r_2, r_3, r_4) = (233, 671, 322, 157)$.

14. Given an ElGamal cryptosystem with the modulus $q = 1283$ and $g = 653$, let the receiver choose $k = 977$. Compute the public key and a cryptogram for the message $m = 751$.

15. The ElGamal system works under the assumption that the sender always selects her secret exponent s randomly and independently for each single message. Show how the security of the system can be compromised when the sender has generated two cryptograms (for two different messages) using the same secret s.

16. It is highly recommended for the modulus q to be selected in such a way that $q - 1$ has at least one large factor. Formulate an argument and derive an algorithm which efficiently solves any instance of the discrete logarithm whenever $q - 1$ has small factors only.

    Hint: It is requested to calculate a knowing $g^a \bmod q$ when $q - 1 = p_1 \cdots p_n$. Observe that a can be represented by a vector $(a_1, \ldots, a_n)$, where $a_i \equiv a \bmod p_i$. The component a_i can be readily recovered by computing $(g^a)^{e_i} \bmod q$ where e_i is an integer $e_i \equiv 0 \bmod p_j$ $(i \neq j)$ and $e_i \equiv 1 \bmod p_i$.

17. Suppose that q is a Mersenne number so $q - 1$ is prime. Implement the ElGamal system when $q = 2^{13}$ and $q - 1 = 8191$. Do all computations in $GF(2^{13})$ using the modulus $p(x) = x^{13} + x^{11} + x^8 + x^4 + 1$ ($p(x)$ is an irreducible polynomial over $GF(2)$). Write C programs for addition and multiplication.

18. Assume an elliptic curve $\mathcal{E}_{11}(2, 5)$ with points whose coordinates $P = (x, y)$ satisfy the following congruence $y^2 \equiv x^3 + 2x + 5 \bmod 11$. Given two points $P = (3, 4)$ and $Q = (8, 7)$, what are the points $P + Q$, $P + P$, and $Q + Q$?

19. Let our elliptic curve RSA system apply the group $\mathcal{E}_N(0, b)$ where N is the product of two suitable primes p and q. Decrypt the following cryptograms:

    – $c = (20060, 21121)$ for $p = 257$ and $q = 131$ and the decrypting key $d = 4163$,

    – $c = (1649684061, 291029961)$ for $p = 65537$, $q = 65543$ and the decrypting key $d = 354897809$.

    What are the encrypting keys in the two cases?

20. Implement the RSA encryption on an elliptic curve $\mathcal{E}_N(a, 0)$ using an accessible multi-precision arithmetic system such as MAPLE.

21. Consider the ElGamal cryptosystem on an elliptic curve $\mathcal{E}_p(0, b)$. Assume that $p = 233$, a point P on the curve is $P = (135, 211)$, the secret key is a multiplier $k = 176$, and the public key is $kP = (107, 127)$. Encrypt the following messages:
    - $m = (23, 223)$ for a secret multiplier $s = 97$,
    - $m = (120, 37)$ for a secret multiplier $s = 200$.

    Decrypt the following cryptograms:
    - $c = (R, c_x, c_y) = ((26, 34), 76, 13)$,
    - $c = (R, c_x, c_y) = ((26, 199), 123, 118)$.

22. Design an instance of GM encryption for $p = 101$, $q = 103$, and $u = 5646$.

23. The BG probabilistic encryption uses a BBS pseudorandom-bit generator. Use an instance of the BBS generator for $p = 7$ and $q = 11$ to construct the BG encryption. Make the necessary assumptions. Show the encryption and decryption processes.

5 Pseudorandomness

Most physical processes expose some random behaviour. A good example of such random behaviour is noise in telecommunication channels. A great irony is that when there is a need for a source of random bits or numbers, then the ever-present randomness is in short supply. Generation of a large volume of random bits is usually very expensive and requires special hardware. Also the parameters of truly random generators can fluctuate, so they need to be calibrated and tested from time to time. The major drawback of truly random generators is the lack of reproducibility of the yielded bits and numbers. The reproducibility is crucial in simulations where there is a need to repeat the same experiments many times. It is also necessary in some cryptographic applications when, for instance, two communicating parties want to generate identical sequences from a shared secret (and short) key. From a cryptographic point of view, we are interested in deterministic algorithms that efficiently generate strings of bits and that cannot be distinguished from truly random ones. Readers interested in the subject are referred to Goldreich [205].

5.1 Number Generators

Knuth [282] devotes the whole of Chap. 3 to the generation of "random" numbers. Let us review some of the classical solutions for number generation. The most popular solution applies the *linear congruential method* which generates a sequence of integers $x_1, x_2, \ldots$ according to the congruence

$$x_{i+1} \equiv a \cdot x_i + c \bmod N, \tag{5.1}$$

where N is a positive integer, $0 \leq a, c \leq N$ and $i = 1, 2, \ldots$. The congruence needs the so-called *seed* x_0 which provides a starting point. Note that the sequence of integers is periodic. The choice of the modulus N and the multiplier a forces the length of the period. The maximum length of the period is N.

Consider an instance of the linear congruential generator for $N = 7$, $a = 3$, and $c = 4$. If the starting point is $x_0 = 2$, then we get the following sequence of integers

$x_1 = 3$, $x_2 = 6$, $x_3 = 1$, $x_4 = 0$, $x_5 = 4$, and $x_6 = 2$.

The *quadratic congruential method* is a generalization of the linear one and can be described by

$$x_{i+1} \equiv d \cdot x_i^2 + a \cdot x_i + c \bmod N. \tag{5.2}$$

The maximum length of the period of the sequence is N.

There is a class of number generators based on *linear feedback shift registers* [110, 216]. These generators can be seen as a far fetched generalization of congruential generators. They offer an efficient method of number generation, which can be a very attractive alternative for some applications. Unfortunately, numerous examples show that generators based on linear feedback shift registers are inherently insecure [212, 344].

Observe that the randomness of the sequences obtained is measured by statistical tests. We say that a number generator passes a statistical test if it behaves in the same way as a truly random generator. On the other hand, if a number generator fails a statistical test, the test can be used to distinguish the sequence generated from a truly random one. From a cryptographic point of view, the security of number generators could be determined by the computational efficiency of an algorithm that enables an opponent, Oscar, to find out the seed and other secret parameters from an observed output sequence. There is an intimate relation between the existence of an efficient statistical test (which can be used to distinguish a generator from a truly random one) and the existence of a cryptographic attack that breaks the generator. Informally we can formulate the following proposition:

If a generator G is polynomially indistinguishable from a truly random generator, then there is no efficient algorithm that breaks the generator.

A generator is polynomially indistinguishable if there is no efficient statistical test which can be used to tell apart G from a truly random generator. The proposition can be justified using the contradiction. Assume that there is an efficient algorithm that breaks the generator. Now we can construct a simple test to distinguish the generator from a truly random one. To do that we take a long enough output sequence of the tested generator and feed it to our algorithm.

The algorithm returns the parameters of the generator. We take the computed parameters and determine the next numbers which will be generated. If the observed numbers are equal to the expected ones, we can conclude that this is the generator G. Otherwise, the tested generator is the random generator. This is the requested contradiction which justifies the proposition.

5.2 Polynomial Indistinguishability

The notion of polynomial *indistinguishability* is central in the theory of pseudorandomness [540]. The proof of security of a generator can be reduced to the demonstration that the generator is polynomially indistinguishable from a truly random generator.

An *ensemble* $\mathcal{E} = \{\mathcal{S}_n, \mathcal{P}_n \mid n \in \mathcal{N}\}$ is an infinite family of sets $\mathcal{S}_n; n \in \mathcal{N}$, together with their probability distributions $\mathcal{P}_n = \{p(x) \mid x \in \mathcal{S}_n\}$. For instance, consider an ensemble $\mathcal{E}$ such that $\mathcal{S}_n = \{x_1, \ldots, x_{2^n}\}$ and

$$\mathcal{P}_n = \{p(x) = 2^{-n} \mid x \in \mathcal{S}_n\}. \tag{5.3}$$

For any $n \in \mathcal{N}$, the corresponding ensemble instance generates 2^n strings with uniform probability.

Definition 6. (*Yao* [540]) *Let* $\mathcal{E}_1 = \{\mathcal{S}_n, \mathcal{P}_n^{(1)} \mid n \in \mathcal{N}\}$ *and* $\mathcal{E}_2 = \{\mathcal{S}_n, \mathcal{P}_n^{(2)} \mid n \in \mathcal{N}\}$ *be two ensembles. A distinguisher D for $\mathcal{E}_1, \mathcal{E}_2$ is a probabilistic polynomial-time algorithm such that*

1. *It halts in time $O(n^t)$ and leaves a binary output $D_n(\alpha) \in \{0, 1\}$ for any input (n, α) where n is the size of the instance and $\alpha = (x_1, \ldots, x_{n^\ell})$ is a sequence of n^ℓ elements of $\mathcal{S}_n$. Denote*

$$P_{D_n}(\mathcal{E}_1) = \sum_{\alpha \in \mathcal{S}_n^\ell} p_1(\alpha) p(D_n(\alpha) = 1)$$

and

$$P_{D_n}(\mathcal{E}_2) = \sum_{\alpha \in \mathcal{S}_n^\ell} p_2(\alpha) p(D_n(\alpha) = 1),$$

where $p_1(\alpha)$ and $p_2(\alpha)$ are probabilities induced by $\mathcal{P}_n^{(1)}$ and $\mathcal{P}_n^{(2)}$, respectively.

2. *There exists an infinite sequence of n such that*

$$\mid P_{D_n}(\mathcal{E}_1) - P_{D_n}(\mathcal{E}_2) \mid > \varepsilon \tag{5.4}$$

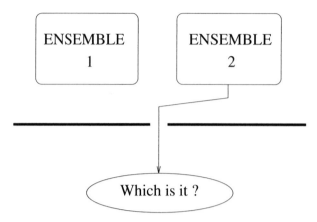

Fig. 5.1. Illustration of the distinguishability problem

for fixed integers t, ℓ, and the number ε > 0.

Consider Fig. 5.1 with two ensembles. Assume that we would like to identify which ensemble is currently used. We can observe the output of the ensemble. A witness algorithm can be used to identify the ensemble. Clearly, the witness algorithm can process only a polynomial samples of output elements as it has to make its decision in polynomial-time. Also its decisions may not always be correct but if it is run for a long enough $\alpha \in \mathcal{S}_n^\ell$, there is a significant (larger than ε) difference between the probabilities $|\ P_{D_n}(\mathcal{E}_1) - P_{D_n}(\mathcal{E}_2)\ |$. If this difference persists for an infinite sequence of n, we say that the witness algorithm distinguishes the two ensembles.

Consider two ensembles over the space $\mathcal{S}_n = \{1, 2, \dots, 2^n\}$:

$$\mathcal{E}_1 = \{\mathcal{S}_n, \{p_1(x) = \frac{1}{2^n} \mid x \in \mathcal{S}_n\} \mid n \in \mathcal{N}\},$$

$$\mathcal{E}_2 = \{\mathcal{S}_n, \{p_2(x) = \frac{x}{2^{n-1}(2^n + 1)} \mid x \in \mathcal{S}_n\} \mid n \in \mathcal{N}\}.$$

Given a polynomial-size sequence α generated by one of the two ensembles (either $\mathcal{E}_1$ or $\mathcal{E}_2$). Assume that we have a probabilistic polynomial-time algorithm D that can be used to identify the ensemble used to generate α. Consider the following two probabilities:

$$P_{D_n}(\mathcal{E}_1) = \sum_{\alpha \in \mathcal{S}_n^\ell} p_1(\alpha)p(D_n(\alpha) = 1),$$

$$P_{D_n}(\mathcal{E}_2) = \sum_{\alpha \in \mathcal{S}_n^\ell} p_2(\alpha)p(D_n(\alpha) = 1).$$

Assuming that $\alpha_i \in \mathcal{S}_n$ are independent we can compute the probabilities $p_1(\alpha) = p_1(\alpha_1) \cdots p_1(\alpha_\ell)$ and $p_2(\alpha) = p_2(\alpha_1) \cdots p_2(\alpha_\ell)$ where $\alpha = (\alpha_1, \ldots, \alpha_\ell)$. Their difference is

$$| P_{D_n}(\mathcal{E}_1) - P_{D_n}(\mathcal{E}_2) |$$
$$= \sum_{\alpha \in \mathcal{S}_n^\ell} | p_1(\alpha_1) \cdots p_1(\alpha_\ell) - p_2(\alpha_1) \cdots p_2(\alpha_\ell) | \, p(D_n(\alpha) = 1).$$

Note that the difference

$$| p_1(\alpha_1) \cdots p_1(\alpha_\ell) - p_2(\alpha_1) \cdots p_2(\alpha_\ell) | \leq \frac{1}{2^{n\ell}}$$

for all $\alpha \in \mathcal{S}_n^\ell$ as $| p_1(x) - p_2(x) | \leq \frac{1}{2^n}$. This implies that

$$| P_{D_n}(\mathcal{E}_1) - P_{D_n}(\mathcal{E}_2) | < \frac{1}{2^{n\ell}} \sum_{\alpha \in \mathcal{S}_n^\ell} p(D_n(\alpha) = 1). \tag{5.5}$$

Note that α goes through all possible sequences of the set $\mathcal{S}_n^\ell$ (there are exponentially many such sequences). As the witness algorithm D is polynomially bounded, it means that for any n it can investigate a polynomial sample of the whole space $\mathcal{S}_n^\ell$. Denote the sample by $\mathcal{S}_{\gamma(n)}^\ell$ where the polynomial $\gamma(n)$ indicates the size of the sample for a given n. Therefore inequality (5.5) becomes

$$| P_{D_n}(\mathcal{E}_1) - P_{D_n}(\mathcal{E}_2) | < \frac{\gamma(n)}{2^{n\ell}}. \tag{5.6}$$

The ratio $\frac{\gamma(n)}{2^{n\ell}}$ can be made as small as required by the selection of a big enough n (see our discussion in Sect. 2.3.2). So the two ensembles are polynomially indistinguishable as inequality (5.6) holds for any witness algorithm D. This kind of indistinguishability is also called *statistical* as it does not depend upon any number theoretic assumptions. In fact, two ensembles are statistically indistinguishable if their probability distributions converge. The statistical indistinguishability implies the polynomial indistinguishability but not vice versa.

Definition 7. *Two ensembles are said to be polynomially indistinguishable if there exists no distinguisher for them.*

To denote that two ensembles $\mathcal{E}_1$, $\mathcal{E}_2$ are polynomially indistinguishable, we simply write $\mathcal{E}_1 \asymp \mathcal{E}_2$. It is easy to verify that the polynomial indistinguishability is an equivalence relation, i.e., it is reflexive, symmetric, and transitive. The relation is reflexive $\mathcal{E} \asymp \mathcal{E}$ as there is no witness algorithm that distinguishes two identical ensembles. It is symmetric as $\mathcal{E}_1 \asymp \mathcal{E}_2 \Rightarrow \mathcal{E}_2 \asymp \mathcal{E}_1$. To show that the relation is transitive, assume that we have three ensembles $\mathcal{E}_1$, $\mathcal{E}_2$, $\mathcal{E}_3$ and (1) $\mathcal{E}_1 \asymp \mathcal{E}_2$, and (2) $\mathcal{E}_2 \asymp \mathcal{E}_3$. Now we have to prove that $\mathcal{E}_1 \asymp \mathcal{E}_3$. From the first two assumptions, we know that for any probabilistic polynomial-time algorithm D

$$| P_{D_n}(\mathcal{E}_1) - P_{D_n}(\mathcal{E}_2) | \leq \varepsilon_1$$

and

$$| P_{D_n}(\mathcal{E}_2) - P_{D_n}(\mathcal{E}_3) | \leq \varepsilon_2,$$

respectively. Take

$$
\begin{aligned}
| P_{D_n}(\mathcal{E}_1) - P_{D_n}(\mathcal{E}_3) | &= | P_{D_n}(\mathcal{E}_1) - P_{D_n}(\mathcal{E}_2) + P_{D_n}(\mathcal{E}_2) - P_{D_n}(\mathcal{E}_3) | \\
&\leq | P_{D_n}(\mathcal{E}_1) - P_{D_n}(\mathcal{E}_2) | + | P_{D_n}(\mathcal{E}_2) - P_{D_n}(\mathcal{E}_3) | \\
&\leq \varepsilon_1 + \varepsilon_2 = \varepsilon.
\end{aligned}
$$

This proves our claim.

Definition 8. *The ensemble $\mathcal{E} = \{\Sigma^n, \mathcal{P}_n \mid n \in \mathcal{N}\}$ which generates binary strings of length n (the set of all n-bit strings is Σ^n) with the uniform probability distributions $\mathcal{P}_n$ is said to be the* reference ensemble *or truly random generator G_R.*

There is a class of ensembles that are polynomially indistinguishable from the truly random generator G_R. As a matter of fact, any member of this class can be used as a reference ensemble.

5.3 Pseudorandom Bit Generators

Bit generators are often defined as deterministic algorithms which produce long bit sequences from random and short seeds [46, 540].

Definition 9. *Given an ensemble $\mathcal{E} = \{\Sigma^n, \mathcal{P}_n \mid n \in \mathcal{N}\}$, a bit generator BG over $\mathcal{E}$ is a deterministic polynomial-time function g that, upon receiving an n-bit input as a seed from $\mathcal{E}$, extends the seed into a sequence of n^ℓ bits where $\ell \in \mathcal{N}$. The seed is selected randomly and uniformly from Σ^n.*

A bit generator consists of two layers. The probabilistic one is given by the uniform ensemble $\mathcal{E} = \{\Sigma^n, \mathcal{P}_n \mid n \in \mathcal{N}\}$ used to produce the seed. The deterministic one defined by the function g which extends an n-bit seed to an n^ℓ-bit output string. The generator induces a new ensemble

$$\mathcal{E}_g = \{\Sigma^{n^\ell}, \mathcal{P}_g \mid n \in \mathcal{N}\},$$

which reflects both the probabilistic and deterministic nature of the bit generator. We simplify the notation of an ensemble to $\mathcal{E}_g$ if the set and the probability
distribution can be derived from the definition of the generator.

Definition 10. *A bit generator g over $\mathcal{E}$ is* pseudorandom *if for a large enough*
n and for any probabilistic polynomial-time (witness) algorithm D

$$\mid P_{D_n}(\mathcal{E}_g) - P_{D_n}(G_R) \mid \leq \frac{1}{\gamma(n)} \tag{5.7}$$

for any polynomial $\gamma(n)$ and for any sufficiently large n.

Pseudorandom bit generators (PBG) cannot be distinguished from a truly random generator G_R by any polynomially bounded attacker. They can be used as
a secure substitute of a truly random generator whenever there is a need. But
how can PBGs be constructed?

The natural candidates for implementation of PBGs are problems from complexity classes higher than **P**. The confirmation of this came when Levin [302]
proved the following important result.

Theorem 19. *A pseudorandom bit generator exists if and only if there exists*
a one-way function.

The problem of PBG construction has been converted into the problem of finding a one-way function. Informally, a one-way function is "easy" (in polynomial-
time) to compute but "hard" to invert. Now we are going to describe some
constructions for PBG. Evidently, the generators are pseudorandom under the
assumption that the underlying function is one-way. That is why all the constructions are conditionally secure.

5.3.1 RSA Pseudorandom Bit Generator

Alexi, Chor, Goldreich, and Schnorr [5] used the RSA exponentiation as a one-
way function.

RSA generator – outputs pseudorandom bits.

Initialization: For an instance n, select at random an instance of exponentiation
function $g \in_R \mathcal{E}_{N,e}$ where N is the product of two random primes $p, q \in_R$

$[2^{n/2-1}, 2^{n/2}]$ and $e \in_R [1, \varphi(N)]$ such that $gcd(e, \varphi(N)) = 1$. The seed $x_0 \in_R [1, N]$. Recall that $\alpha \in_R \mathcal{S}$ means that α is selected randomly and uniformly from $\mathcal{S}$.

Expansion: For an input sequence x_i $(i = 0, 1, \ldots, n^\ell)$, generate

$$x_{i+1} = g(x_i) \equiv x_i^e \bmod N.$$

Output: For $i = 1, 2, \ldots$, extract $\ell(n)$ least-significant bits of x_i, where $\ell(n)$ is a polynomial in n. So the output is $y_i = x_i \rfloor_{\ell(n)}$.

Theorem 20. (*Alexi et al.* [5]) *If the RSA exponentiation is one-way and* $\ell(n) = O(\log n)$, *then the following ensembles are polynomially indistinguishable:*

- $\left(g, x, y = g(x) \rfloor_{\ell(n)}\right)$ *where* $g \in_R \mathcal{E}_{N,e}$, $x \in_R [1, N]$,
- (g, r, z) *where* $g \in_R \mathcal{E}_{N,e}$, $r \in_R [1, N]$, *and* $z \in_R \Sigma^{\ell(n)}$.

Clearly, for a polynomially bounded attacker output bits y_i are indistinguishable from truly random bits $z_i \in_R \Sigma^{\ell(n)}$. The conclusion from this theorem can be formulated as follows:

Corollary 4. (*Alexi et al.* [5]) *If the RSA exponentiation is one-way and* $\ell(n) = O(\log n)$, *then the sequence* $y_1, \ldots, y_{n^\ell}$ *is pseudorandom.*

There are two interesting issues for the RSA generator. The first one is: how to extract more bits per iteration and make the generator more efficient [183]? The second issue is: how to design an RSA generator so the extracted bits are not used in further generation? These issues were studied by Micali and Schnorr in [343].

Consider an instance of the RSA generator for a small $n = 20$. The two primes p, q are chosen at random from $[2^9, 2^{10}]$. Let them be $p = 719$ and $q = 971$. The modulus $N = pq = 698149$. The public exponent $e \in_R [1, \varphi(N) = 348230]$. Let it be $e = 176677$. The random seed $x_0 = 371564$ is chosen from $[1, 698149]$. The first five elements of the sequence are:

$$x_1 = x_0^e \equiv 612281 \bmod 698149,$$
$$x_2 = x_1^e \equiv 421586 \bmod 698149,$$
$$x_3 = x_2^e \equiv 359536 \bmod 698149,$$
$$x_4 = x_3^e \equiv 580029 \bmod 698149,$$
$$x_5 = x_4^e \equiv 210375 \bmod 698149.$$

If we decide to extract 4 least-significant bits from each number x_i ($\log_2 20 > 4$), then the first 20 bits of the output are:

1001 0010 0000 1101 0111

5.3.2 BBS Pseudorandom Bit Generator

Blum, Blum, and Shub [44] studied two-bit generators. One of them based on squaring is pseudorandom provided the quadratic residuosity problem is intractable. The generator is further referred to as the BBS generator.

BBS generator – outputs pseudorandom bits.

Initialization: For an instance n, select at random two primes $p, q \in_R [2^{n/2-1},$
$2^{n/2}]$ such that $p \equiv q \equiv 3 \bmod 4$. The seed $x_0 \in_R [1, N]$ such that its Jacobi
symbols $\left(\frac{x_0}{p}\right) = \left(\frac{x_0}{q}\right) = 1$ (so x_0 is a quadratic residue).

Expansion: For an input sequence x_i ($i = 0, 1, \ldots, n^\ell$), generate

$$x_{i+1} \equiv x_i^2 \bmod N.$$

Output: For $i = 1, 2, \ldots, n^\ell$, extract the least-significant bit (the parity) of x_i,
i.e.,

$$y_i = x_i \bmod 2.$$

First we investigate some algebraic properties of the Jacobi symbol and the BBS generator.

Lemma 11. *Let N be a product of two primes p, q such that $p \equiv q \equiv 3 \bmod 4$. Then $\left(\frac{a}{N}\right) = \left(\frac{-a}{N}\right)$.*

Proof. From the definition of the Jacobi symbol we have

$$\left(\frac{a}{N}\right) = \left(\frac{a}{p}\right)\left(\frac{a}{q}\right)$$

and

$$\left(\frac{-a}{N}\right) = \left(\frac{a}{p}\right)\left(\frac{a}{q}\right)\left(\frac{-1}{p}\right)\left(\frac{-1}{q}\right).$$

Primes p, q can be represented as $p = 4\alpha + 3$ and $q = 4\beta + 3$ for some integers α, β so

$$\left(\frac{-1}{p}\right) = (-1)^{\frac{p-1}{2}} = (-1)^{2\alpha+1} \equiv -1 \bmod p.$$

Similarly, $\left(\frac{-1}{q}\right) = -1$. So $\left(\frac{-1}{p}\right)\left(\frac{-1}{q}\right) = 1$ and the conclusion follows. $\square$

Lemma 12. *Let N be a product of two primes p, q such that $p \equiv q \equiv 3 \mod 4$. Then each quadratic residue modulo N has exactly one square root which is a quadratic residue.*

Proof. Squaring $x^2 \mod N$ where N is a product of two primes, has four roots. To find them, it is enough to find roots of two congruences ($x^2 \mod p$) and ($x^2 \mod q$). Each congruence has two solutions. Let them be $\pm a$ and $\pm b$ for the first and the second congruence, respectively. The Chinese Remainder Theorem allows us to combine them giving the four possible roots: $r_1 = (a \mod p, b \mod q)$, $-r_1 = (-a \mod p, -b \mod q)$, $r_2 = (-a \mod p, b \mod q)$, and $-r_2 = (a \mod p, -b \mod q)$. According to Lemma 11 the Jacobi symbols $\left(\frac{r_1}{N}\right) = \left(\frac{-r_1}{N}\right)$ and and $\left(\frac{r_2}{N}\right) = \left(\frac{-r_2}{N}\right)$. The Jacobi symbols $\left(\frac{r_1}{N}\right) \neq \left(\frac{r_2}{N}\right)$. This is true as

$$\left(\frac{r_1}{N}\right) = \left(\frac{a}{p}\right)\left(\frac{b}{q}\right)$$

and

$$\left(\frac{r_2}{N}\right) = \left(\frac{-a}{p}\right)\left(\frac{b}{q}\right) = \left(\frac{-1}{p}\right)\left(\frac{a}{p}\right)\left(\frac{b}{q}\right).$$

In Lemma 11 we showed that $\left(\frac{-1}{p}\right) = -1$. So we have eliminated two roots, say $\pm r_2$, with their Jacobi symbols with respect to N equal to -1. There is only one root (either r_1 or $-r_1 = N - r_1$) whose two Jacobi symbols (with respect to p and q) are positive. $\qquad\square$

Lemma 12 shows that if the seed is a quadratic residue ($\left(\frac{x_0}{p}\right) = \left(\frac{x_0}{q}\right) = 1$), then there is a one-to-one correspondence of generated elements. Knowledge of the factors of N and a generated x_i allow us to identify the unique predecessor x_{i-1} (which is also a quadratic residue). If the factorization of N is unknown, there are two possible roots, each of which generates a different output bit.

The set of quadratic residues is

$$\mathcal{Z}_N^{Q+} = \{x \in \mathcal{Z}_N \mid \left(\frac{x}{p}\right) = \left(\frac{x}{q}\right) = 1\}$$

and the set

$$\mathcal{Z}_N^{Q-} = \{x \in \mathcal{Z}_N \mid \left(\frac{x}{p}\right) = \left(\frac{x}{q}\right) = -1\}.$$

The set $\mathcal{Z}_N^{Q} = \mathcal{Z}_N^{Q+} \cup \mathcal{Z}_N^{Q-}$ is the set of all integers in $\mathcal{Z}_N$ whose Jacobi symbols with respect to N are equal to 1. The cardinality of $\mathcal{Z}_N^{Q}$ is $\frac{\varphi(N)}{2}$. Both sets $\mathcal{Z}_N^{Q+}$ and $\mathcal{Z}_N^{Q-}$ are of the same size so their cardinality is $\frac{\varphi(N)}{4}$.

The security of a BBS generator depends on how efficiently an opponent can decide which of two possible roots r or $-r$ is the quadratic residue, or whether $r \in \mathcal{Z}_N^{Q+}$ or $-r \in \mathcal{Z}_N^{Q+}$ provided the factors of N are unknown.

Name: Quadratic Residue problem.
Instance: Given a composite integer N with two unknown factors p and q. An integer $x \in \mathcal{Z}_N^{Q}$.
Question: Does x belong to $\mathcal{Z}_N^{Q+}$ (or is x a quadratic residue)?

Definition 11. *Let N and x_0 be selected as in the BBS generator. Given a probabilistic polynomial-time algorithm A which for an input (N, x_0) (of size $2n$) guesses the parity bit of x_{-1} (x_{-1} is a predecessor of x_0), we say that A has an ε-advantage for N in guessing a parity bit of x_{-1} if and only if*

$$\sum_{x_0 \in \mathcal{Z}_N^{Q+}} p(x_0)p\left(A(N, x_0) = (x_{-1} \bmod 2)\right) > \frac{1}{2} + \varepsilon,$$

where $0 < \varepsilon < \frac{1}{2}$.

Note that the space $\mathcal{Z}_N^{Q+}$ has $\frac{\varphi(N)}{4}$ different elements so $p(x_0) = \frac{4}{\varphi(N)}$ for all $x_0 \in \mathcal{Z}_N^{Q+}$.

Definition 12. *Let N be selected as in the BBS generator. Given a probabilistic polynomial-time algorithm B, which for an input (N, x) (of size $2n$) guesses whether $x \in \mathcal{Z}_N^{Q+}$ or $x \in \mathcal{Z}_N^{Q-}$, we say that B has an ε-advantage for N in guessing quadratic residuosity of x if and only if*

$$\sum_{x \in \mathcal{Z}_N^{Q}} p(x)p\left(B(N, x) = 1\right) > \frac{1}{2} + \varepsilon,$$

where $0 < \varepsilon < \frac{1}{2}$ and the algorithm makes a binary decision: $B(N, x) = 1$ if $x \in \mathcal{Z}_N^{Q+}$ or $B(N, x) = 0$ otherwise.

An algorithm A that has an ε-advantage for N in guessing a parity bit of x_{-1} can be converted into an algorithm B which has an ε-advantage for N in guessing the quadratic residuosity of x.

The algorithm B takes as inputs N and $x \in \mathcal{Z}_N^{Q}$ and calls the algorithm A as a subroutine.

$B(N, x)$ {

1. Let $x_0 \equiv x^2 \bmod N$.
2. Call $A(N, x_0) = b \in \{0, 1\}$.
3. If $b \equiv x \bmod 2$ then $x \in \mathcal{Z}_N^{Q+}$,
   otherwise $x \in \mathcal{Z}_N^{Q-}$ }.

Clearly the complexity of B is equivalent to the complexity of A as the overhead involved in the construction is polynomial in n. So we have proved the following lemma.

Lemma 13. [44] *An algorithm A that has an ε-advantage for N in guessing the parity of x_{-1} can be converted efficiently into an algorithm B, which has an ε-advantage for N in guessing the quadratic residuosity of x.*

Lemma 14. [209] *An algorithm B that has an ε-advantage for guessing the quadratic residuosity can be efficiently converted into a probabilistic polynomial-time algorithm C which guesses the quadratic residuosity with an arbitrary small error $\delta > 0$.*

Proof. First we describe the C algorithm, which calls B as a subroutine.

$C(N, x)$ {

1. Let $c_1 \in \mathcal{N}$ and $c_2 \in \mathcal{N}$ be two counters initialized to zero.
2. For $i = 1, \ldots, u$ do {
   - Select a random $r_i \in_R \mathcal{Z}_N^Q$.
   - Compute $r_i^2 \bmod N$ (clearly $r_i^2 \in \mathcal{Z}_N^{Q+}$ and $-r_i^2 \in \mathcal{Z}_N^{Q-}$).
   - Choose at random $\bar{r}_i \in_R \{r_i^2, -r_i^2\}$.
   - Call $B(N, x \cdot \bar{r}_i) = b_i \in \{0, 1\}$ (if $b_i = 1$, then $x \cdot \bar{r}_i \in \mathcal{Z}_N^{Q+}$).
   - If $\bar{r}_i = r_i^2$ and $x \cdot \bar{r}_i \in \mathcal{Z}_N^{Q+}$ or $\bar{r}_i = -r_i^2$ and $x \cdot \bar{r}_i \in \mathcal{Z}_N^{Q-}$, then increment c_1 by 1, otherwise increment c_2 by 1}.
3. If $c_1 > c_2$ then $x \in \mathcal{Z}_N^{Q+}$, otherwise $x \in \mathcal{Z}_N^{Q-}$ }.

Now we discuss the probability of error of the algorithm C assuming that B give correct answers with a probability of at least $\frac{1}{2} + \varepsilon$ and the number of iterations is $u = 2v + 1$. So we have u Bernoulli trials with two probabilities $a = \frac{1}{2} + \varepsilon$ and $b = 1 - a = \frac{1}{2} - \varepsilon$. The probability that j answers are correct in u trials is

$$\binom{u}{j} a^j b^{u-j}.$$

The algorithm C errs if there are more than v incorrect answers of the subroutine B in the sequence of u trials, so

$$p(C \text{ errs}) \leq \sum_{j=0}^{v} \binom{u}{j} a^j b^{2v+1-j}$$

$$= \sum_{j=0}^{v} \binom{u}{j} \frac{a^v}{a^{v-j}} b^{v+1} b^{v-j}$$

$$= a^v b^{v+1} \sum_{j=0}^{v} \binom{u}{j} \frac{b^{v-j}}{a^{v-j}}$$

$$\leq a^v b^{v+1} \sum_{j=0}^{v} \binom{u}{j}$$

$$= a^v b^{v+1} 2^{2v}$$

$$= (1/4 - \varepsilon)^v 4^v b$$

$$\leq \frac{(1 - 4\varepsilon^2)^v}{2}. \tag{5.8}$$

Note that for any fixed ε ($0 < \varepsilon < 0.5$) it is possible to select a big enough $u = 2v + 1 \leq n^t$ so $p(C \text{ errs})$ can be made as small as requested (in particular, smaller than δ). □

Now we can formulate the theorem that asserts the security of the BBS generator.

Theorem 21. [44] *Suppose that the quadratic residuosity problem is intractable (there is no probabilistic polynomial-time algorithm that solves it), then the BBS is pseudorandom (there is no probabilistic polynomial-time distinguisher for it).*

Proof. We need to prove that the ensemble $\mathcal{E}_{\text{BBS}}$ induced by the BBS generator is indistinguishable from the ensemble G_R. The proof proceeds by contradiction. Assume that there is a distinguisher D which tells apart $\mathcal{E}_{\text{BBS}}$ from G_R. It turns out [44] that the distinguisher D can be efficiently converted into a probabilistic polynomial-time algorithm A which guesses the parity of x_{-1} given arbitrary $x_0 \in \mathcal{Z}_N^{Q+}$. Lemma 13 asserts that A can be converted into an algorithm B which guesses the quadratic residuosity. Lemma (14) shows that B can be used to determine a polynomial-time algorithm C which guesses the quadratic residuosity with arbitrary small error δ. This is the contradiction. □

Consider an instance of the BBS generator for $n = 20$. Primes $p, q \in_R$ $[2^9, 2^{10}]$. Let them be $p = 811$ and $q = 967$ ($p \equiv q \equiv 3 \bmod 4$). The modulus is $N = 784237$. Let the seed be $x_0 = 345137$, which is a quadratic residue. The sequence of $x_i \equiv x_{i-1}^2 \bmod N$ is:

$$x_1 = 222365, \quad x_2 = 50375,$$
$$x_3 = 633930, \quad x_4 = 678990,$$
$$x_5 = 367621, \quad x_6 = 774379,$$
$$x_7 = 719013, \quad x_8 = 468688,$$
$$x_9 = 520696, \quad x_{10} = 261487,$$
$$x_{11} = 179850, \quad x_{12} = 167435,$$
$$x_{13} = 359186, \quad x_{14} = 537963,$$
$$x_{15} = 346207, \quad x_{16} = 424954.$$

The first 16 parity bits are $(1,1,0,0,1,1,1,0,0,1,0,1,0,1,1,0)$.

5.4 Next Bit Test

Any witness algorithm applies a (statistical) test. As a witness algorithm has to run in polynomial-time, the statistical test used in the witness algorithm has to be polynomial. The statement "*a bit generator is pseudorandom*" can be equivalently rephrased as "*a bit generator passes all polynomial-time (statistical) tests.*" Among all polynomial-time tests, one can define the subclass of *next-bit tests*.

Definition 13. *Given a bit generator, which produces n^ℓ-bit sequences, let T be a probabilistic polynomial-time test that takes first i bits of an n^ℓ-bit output sequence and guesses the $(i+1)$th bit. The bit generator passes the next-bit test if for any probabilistic polynomial-time test T, for all polynomials $\gamma(n)$, for all sufficiently large n, and for all integers $i \in \{1, \ldots, n^\ell\}$*

$$\mid p\left(T_n(b_1, \ldots, b_i) = b_{i+1}\right) - \frac{1}{2} \mid < \frac{1}{\gamma(n)},$$

where $p\left(T_n(b_1, \ldots, b_i) = b_{i+1}\right)$ is the probability that the test correctly guesses the $(i+1)$th bit of the output sequence $(b_1, \ldots, b_{n^\ell})$.

The importance of next-bit tests is confirmed by the following theorem.

Theorem 22. [540] *Given a bit generator, then the following two statements are equivalent:*

- *The bit generator passes the next-bit test.*
- *The bit generator passes all probabilistic polynomial-time statistical tests for output sequences.*

Blum and Micali defined cryptographically strong pseudorandom bit generators as bit generators that pass the next-bit test. The two notions cryptographically strong pseudorandom bit generators and pseudorandom bit generators (PBG) are equivalent. The next-bit test is universal in the sense that if a PBG passes the next-bit test, it also passes all other probabilistic polynomial-time tests. Some extensions of universal tests can be found in [326, 454].

5.5 Pseudorandom Function Generators

We are going to describe a construction of a pseudorandom function due to Goldreich, Goldwasser, and Micali [206]. The starting ingredient is a *function ensemble*. A function ensemble is $\mathcal{F} = \{\mathcal{F}_n \mid n \in \mathcal{N}\}$, where

$$\mathcal{F}_n = \{f \mid f : \Sigma^n \to \Sigma^n\}$$

is a collection of functions together with the probability distribution. We assume a uniform probability distribution unless another distribution is explicitly given.

Definition 14. *A function ensemble* $\mathcal{F} = \{\mathcal{F}_n \mid n \in \mathcal{N}\}$ *is called polynomial if the ensemble is:*

1. *Polynomial-time sampleable, i.e., there is a probabilistic polynomial-time algorithm that returns a description of a function $f \in_R \mathcal{F}_n$ which is chosen randomly and uniformly from the set $\mathcal{F}_n$. This usually is done by the introduction of indexing (a function is chosen by a random selection of its unique index).*
2. *Polynomial-time computable, i.e., there is a probabilistic polynomial-time algorithm that for the given function f and the input $x \in \Sigma^n$ outputs $f(x)$ for any $f \in \mathcal{F}_n$.*

To clarify the definition, consider the well-known DES encryption algorithm. The DES can be seen as an instance ensemble $\mathcal{F}_{64} = \{f \mid \Sigma^{64} \to \Sigma^{64}\}$. Also note that one can determine different ensembles by defining different keys (possibly with different probability distributions). The polynomial sampling amounts to the requirement that a function can be randomly, uniformly, and efficiently chosen by a random selection of the secret key (index). The polynomial-time computability (or evaluation) requires that the function generates the corresponding cryptogram efficiently for any message (input) and any secret key (index).

A random function ensemble $\mathcal{R} = \{\mathcal{R}_n \mid n \in \mathcal{N}\}$ is an infinite family of functions where $\mathcal{R}_n = \{f \mid f : \Sigma^n \to \Sigma^n\}$ is the collection of all functions on Σ^n. The probability distribution is uniform for a fixed n.

A probabilistic polynomial-time algorithm (Turing machine) can be equivalently defined as a probabilistic polynomial-size acyclic circuit with Boolean gates AND, OR, and NOT, and constant gates 0 and 1. The main difference is that the circuit produces outputs in one step while its Turing counterpart needs a polynomial number of steps. The complexity of computation using the circuit model is expressed by the size of the circuit, which is measured by the total number of connections inside the circuit. Any probabilistic polynomial-size circuit can be implemented by a probabilistic polynomial-time Turing machine, and vice versa.

Definition 15. *A witness circuit C_n is a probabilistic polynomial-size acyclic circuit with Boolean gates AND, OR, and NOT, constant gates 0 and 1, and oracle gates. Oracle gates accept inputs of length n and generate outputs of the same length. Each oracle gate can be evaluated using some function $f : \Sigma^n \to \Sigma^n$.*

Witness circuits can be used to tell apart a polynomial function ensemble $\mathcal{F}$ from the random function ensemble $\mathcal{R}$.

Definition 16. *An infinite sequence of witness circuits $C = \{C_n \mid n \in \mathcal{N}\}$ is called a distinguisher for $\mathcal{F}$ if for two arbitrary constants $t, k \in \mathcal{N}$ and for each large enough parameter n there exists a circuit C_n whose size is bounded by a polynomial n^t and*

$$\mid p_n(\mathcal{F}) - p_n(\mathcal{R}) \mid > \frac{1}{n^\ell},$$

where $p_n(\mathcal{F}) = \sum_{f \in_R \mathcal{F}_n} p_{\mathcal{F}}(f) \left(C_n^f = 1 \right)$ and $p_n(\mathcal{R}) = \sum_{f \in_R \mathcal{R}_n} p_{\mathcal{R}}(f) \left(C_n^f = 1 \right)$ provided that f is used to evaluate the oracle gates.

Definition 17. *A polynomial function ensemble $\mathcal{F}$ is pseudorandom if there is no distinguisher for it (the ensemble $\mathcal{F}$ is also called a pseudorandom function or PRF).*

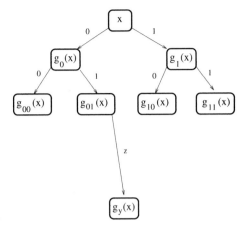

Fig. 5.2. The construction of a function ensemble

An instance witness circuit C_n can query the tested function f using the oracle gates. Oracle gates can be implemented as calls to a subroutine that evaluates the tested function f. C_n can freely choose the input values $x \in \Sigma^n$ for which the function f is to be evaluated. C_n collects the corresponding outputs $f(x) \in \Sigma^n$ from the oracle gates. The number of pairs $(x, f(x))$ is equal to the number of oracle gates and it has to be polynomial in n.

Now we are ready to describe the construction by Goldreich, Goldwasser, and Micali. The construction applies a pseudorandom bit generator that extends an n-bit seed into a $2n$-bit sequence. So the PBG g takes an n-bit seed and produces a $2n$-bit output $g(x) = g_0(x)\|g_1(x)$, where $g_0(x)$ and $g_1(x)$ are n-bit substrings and $\|$ stands for the concatenation of two strings. Strings $g_0(x)$ and $g_1(x)$ are next used as seeds for the second level (Fig. 5.2). After the PBG is used n times, it produces $g_y(x)$ where y is an n-bit string that marks the unique path from the top to the bottom (in Fig. 5.2 $y = 01z$). Our function ensemble is $\mathcal{F}_n = \{f_x \mid f_x(y) = g_y(x); f_x : \Sigma^n \to \Sigma^n\}$ where $g_\alpha(x)$ is defined recursively

$$g(x) = g_0(x)\|g_1(x),$$
$$g_{b_1\ldots b_\ell}(x) = g_{b_1\ldots b_\ell 0}(x)\|g_{b_1\ldots b_\ell 1}(x),$$

for $\ell = 2, \ldots, n-1$, where $b_1 \ldots b_\ell$ is an ℓ-bit string. The parameter x is an index of $\mathcal{F}_n$ as the random selection of a function from $\mathcal{F}_n$ is done by the random choice of $x \in_R \Sigma^n$. It is easy to verify that the ensemble $\mathcal{F}_n$ is polynomial-time sampleable and computable. The next theorem asserts that the ensemble is also pseudorandom.

Theorem 23. *If the underlying PBG g is pseudorandom, then the function ensemble $\mathcal{F} = \{\mathcal{F}_n \mid n \in \mathcal{N}\}$ constructed from g, that is $\mathcal{F}_n = \{f_x \mid f_x(y) = g_y(x); f_x : \Sigma^n \to \Sigma^n\}$, is pseudorandom.*

Proof. (by contradiction) We assume that there is a distinguisher for $\mathcal{F}$, i.e., an infinite sequence of probabilistic polynomial-size witness circuits C_n which can tell apart $\mathcal{F}$ from $\mathcal{R}$ with an arbitrary large probability. We are going to show that this assumption leads us to the conclusion that the underlying bit generator is not pseudorandom. Further, we are going to use a probabilistic polynomial-time algorithm $A_i(n, y)$ where n indicates the current instance size, $y \in \Sigma^n$ is an input (argument) for which a function from A_i is to be evaluated, and $i = 1, \ldots, n$.

$A_i(n, y)$ {

1. If the prefix $(y_1 \ldots y_i, r)$ of $y = y_1 \ldots y_n$ has been used before retrieve the stored pair $(y_1 \ldots y_i, r)$.
2. Otherwise, select $r \in_R \Sigma^n$ and store $(y_1 \ldots y_i, r)$.
3. Return $g_{y_{i+1} \ldots y_n}(r)$ }.

The algorithm A_i operates on a tree $g_y(x)$; see Fig. 5.2. It places random n-bit strings in all nodes on the ith level and returns $g_{y_{i+1} \ldots y_n}(r)$. We use the following notation:

– $p_n(A_i)$ is the probability that the distinguisher C_n outputs 1 when all C_n queries are answered by A_i (or, in other words, oracle gates apply A_i to evaluate their outputs for inputs given by C_n).
– $p_n(\mathcal{F})$ is the probability that the distinguisher C_n outputs 1 when all C_n queries are answered by oracle gates which use $f \in_R \mathcal{F}_n$.
– $p_n(\mathcal{R})$ is the probability that the distinguisher C_n outputs 1 when all C_n queries are answered by oracle gates which use $f \in_R \mathcal{R}_n$.

Observe that $p_n(\mathcal{F}) = p_n(A_0)$ and $p_n(\mathcal{R}) = p_n(A_n)$.

As the ensemble is not pseudorandom, there is a family of probabilistic polynomial-size circuits C_n such that for infinitely many n

$$| p_n(\mathcal{F}) - p_n(\mathcal{R}) | > \frac{1}{n^\ell}.$$

Now we construct a probabilistic polynomial-time witness algorithm D for the underlying bit generator. It calls C_n as a subroutine. The input parameters to the algorithm D are the instance size n and a sequence $U_n = (u_1, u_2, \ldots, u_{n^\ell})$ where each u_i is a $2n$-bit string. It needs to be decided whether the sequence U_n is truly random or comes from the bit generator.

$D(n, U_n)$ {

1. Choose at random $i \in_R \{0, 1, \ldots, n-1\}$.
2. Call the distinguisher C_n.
3. For $j = 1, \ldots, n^\ell$, do {
   - Pick the next $u_j = u_{j_0} \| u_{j_1}$ from the sequence U_n $(u_{j_0}, u_{j_1} \in \Sigma^n)$.
   - C_n queries about the output of the jth oracle gate for an n-bit input $y = y_1 \ldots y_n$ of its choice.
   - Take y and store the pairs $(y_1 \ldots y_i 0, u_{j_0})$ and $(y_1 \ldots y_i 1, u_{j_1})$.
   - If y is the first query with the prefix $y_1 \ldots y_i$ and $y_{i+1} = 0$, return $g_{y_{i+2} \ldots y_n}(u_{j_0})$ to C_n; or
   - if y is the first query with the prefix $y_1 \ldots y_i$ and $y_{i+1} = 1$, return $g_{y_{i+2} \ldots y_n}(u_{j_1})$ to C_n;
   - otherwise, retrieve the pair $(y_1 \ldots y_{i+1}, u)$ and return $g_{y_{i+2} \ldots y_n}(u)$ } to C_n.
4. Return the binary output of C_n as the final guess }.

There are two cases when U_n is

- A string generated by the bit generator g on random selected n-bit seeds so $u_i = g(x_i)$ for $x_i \in_R \Sigma^n$. The probability that $D(n, U_n)$ outputs 1 is

$$\sum_{i=0}^{n-1} \frac{1}{n} p_n(A_i).$$

This case can be illustrated by a tree (Fig. 5.2) with random seeds on the ith level and strings from U_n on the $(i+1)$th level.
- A sequence of randomly selected $2n$ bits. The probability that $D(n, U_n)$ outputs 1 is

$$\sum_{i=0}^{n-1} \frac{1}{n} p_n(A_{i+1}).$$

The function tree in Fig. 5.2 holds random strings on the $(i+1)$th level.

Note that the algorithm D distinguishes random strings from strings generated by the bit generator g as

$$| \sum_{i=0}^{n-1} \frac{1}{n} p_n(A_i) - \sum_{i=0}^{n-1} \frac{1}{n} p_n(A_{i+1}) | = \frac{1}{n} | p_n(A_0) - p_n(A_n) |$$

$$= \frac{1}{n} | p_n(\mathcal{F}) - p_n(\mathcal{R}) | > \frac{1}{n^{k+1}}.$$

This is the contradiction that proves the theorem. □

The construction of pseudorandom function generators is universal and works for any PBG.

5.6 Pseudorandom Permutation Generators

Clearly a one-to-one pseudorandom function is a pseudorandom permutation. Now we are going to describe how pseudorandom permutations can be generated. Recall from Sect. 3.2 the definition of Feistel permutation.

Definition 18. *Given a function $f : \Sigma^n \to \Sigma^n$. A Feistel permutation $F_{2n,f} : \Sigma^{2n} \to \Sigma^{2n}$ associated with the function f is*

$$F_{2n,f}(L, R) = (R \oplus f(L), L),$$

where L and R are n-bit strings.

A truly random permutation is a permutation ensemble $\Pi = \{\Pi_n \mid n \in \mathcal{N}\}$ where Π_n contains all $n!$ permutations and the probability distribution is uniform for all $n \in \mathcal{N}$.

Having a set of functions $f_1, \ldots, f_i \in \mathcal{R}_n$, we can define the composition of the corresponding Feistel permutations as:

$$\psi_{2n}(f_1, \ldots, f_i) = F_{2n,f_i} \circ \ldots \circ F_{2n,f_1}. \tag{5.9}$$

Consider a permutation $\psi_{2n}(f, g)$ for some $f, g \in \mathcal{R}_n$ illustrated in Fig. 5.3. It turns out [307] that $\Psi_R(f, g) = \{\psi_{2n}(f, g) \mid f, g \in_R \mathcal{R}_n, n \in \mathcal{N}\}$ can be told apart from a truly random permutation by a polynomial-size witness circuit C_{2n}. The structure of the circuit is given in Fig. 5.4. The circuit employs two oracle gates O_1 and O_2. In order to decide whether a tested permutation is truly random or is an instance of $\Psi_R(f, g)$, the witness circuit:

– Selects $L_1, L_2, R \in_R \Sigma^n$.
– Queries oracle gates O_1 and O_2 for two strings (L_1, R) and (L_2, R), respectively.

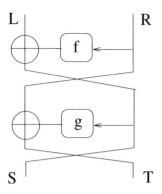

Fig. 5.3. Permutation generator $\Psi_R(f,g)$

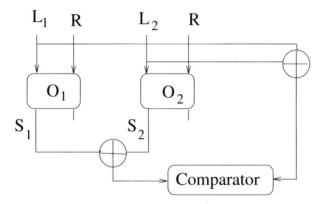

Fig. 5.4. A distinguishing circuit for $\Psi_R(f,g)$

- Collects the answers (S_1, T_1) and (S_2, T_2) from the oracle gates. There are two possible cases:
  1. A tested permutation is an instance of $\Psi_R(f,g)$, then $S_1 = L_1 \oplus f(R)$ and $S_2 = L_2 \oplus f(R)$ so $L_1 \oplus L_2$ is equal to $S_1 \oplus S_2$.
  2. Otherwise S_1 and S_2 are n-bit random string and $L_1 \oplus L_2 \neq S_1 \oplus S_2$ with the probability 2^{-n}.
- Returns the result from the comparator as its guess.

Luby and Rackoff [307] analyzed permutation generators based on Feistel transformations. In particular, they defined a permutation generator $\Psi_R(f,g,h)$ = $\{\psi_{2n}(f,g,h) \mid f,g,h \in_R \mathcal{R}, n \in \mathcal{N}\}$ which uses three Feistel permutations and three random functions. They proved the following theorem.

Theorem 24. *Let $f, g, h \in_R \mathcal{R}$ be three independent random functions and C_{2n} be a probabilistic circuit with $m < 2^n$ oracle gates, then*

$$| p_{2n}(\Pi) - p_{2n}(\Psi_R(f, g, h)) | \leq \frac{m^2}{2^n}. \tag{5.10}$$

As the number m has to be polynomially bounded (the witness circuit has to be of a polynomial-size), the two generators cannot be told apart by any polynomial witness. Note that the permutation generator $\Psi_R(f, g, h)$ can be implemented by no polynomial-time algorithm as it uses three random functions $f, g, h \in_R \mathcal{R}$. But if the functions f, g, h are chosen from a pseudorandom function, then the resulting permutation generator is pseudorandom. Let our pseudorandom function ensemble be $\mathcal{F} = \{\mathcal{F}_n \mid n \in \mathcal{N}\}$. The permutation generator $\Psi(f, g, h) = \{\psi_{2n}(f, g, h) \mid f, g, h \in_R \mathcal{F}, n \in \mathcal{N}\}$.

Theorem 25. [307] *Let $\mathcal{F} = \{\mathcal{F}_n \mid n \in \mathcal{N}\}$ be a pseudorandom function generator. A permutation generator $\Psi(f, g, h) = \{\psi_{2n}(f, g, h) \mid f, g, h \in_R \mathcal{F}, n \in \mathcal{N}\}$ is pseudorandom so for any probabilistic polynomial-size witness circuit C_{2n} (the number of oracle gates is polynomially bounded)*

$$| p_{2n}(\Pi) - p_{2n}(\Psi(f, g, h)) | \leq \frac{1}{n^k} \tag{5.11}$$

for some constant k.

An interesting observation is that the pseudorandom permutation $\Psi(f, g, h)$ is immune against the chosen plaintext attack. Oracle gates allow the circuit to query about cryptograms for messages chosen by the circuit.

Another interesting issue is the number of pseudorandom functions used in the permutation generator. Ohnishi [385] proved that both $\Psi(f, g, g)$ and $\Psi(f, f, g)$ are pseudorandom. Rueppel [437] showed that $\Psi_R(f, f, f)$ can be efficiently distinguished from Π. The distinguisher is depicted in Fig. 5.5. It employs two oracle gates O_1 and O_2 only. The circuit chooses $L, R \in_R \Sigma^n$ and queries the oracle gate O_1. The two n-bit strings of the answer are swapped and the oracle gate O_2 is queried for the swapped answer. If the oracle gates are evaluated using a function from $\Psi_R(f, f, f)$, then O_2 has to return a string that is equal to (L, R) as O_2 undoes the process done by O_1. Otherwise, if the oracle gates are evaluated using a function from Π, O_2 returns a random string that is different from (L, R) with the probability 2^{-2n}. Zheng, Matsumoto, and Imai indexImai, H. showed in [545] that $\Psi(f^i, f^j, f^k)$ is not pseudorandom where $i, j, k \in \mathcal{N}$ and $f^i = \underbrace{f \circ \ldots \circ f^i}$. They gave a construction of a probabilistic

L   R

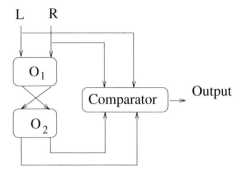

Fig. 5.5. A distinguishing circuit for $\Psi_R(f, f, f)$

polynomial-size witness circuit that efficiently tells apart $\Psi_R(f^i, f^j, f^k)$ from Π. To be pseudorandom, a generator based on a single pseudorandom function needs at least four Feistel permutations. More precisely, $\Psi(f, f, f, f^i)$ is pseudorandom for $i \geq 2$ [406].

5.7 Super Pseudorandom Permutation Generators

One can require that witness circuits not only query about cryptograms (for chosen messages) but also about messages (for chosen cryptograms). The power of such circuits increases as there are two kinds of oracle gates: normal and inverse. For a string x provided by a witness circuit, a normal gate returns $f(x)$. An inverse gate for the same string returns $f^{-1}(x)$ where f is a tested permutation. The notion of pseudorandomness can be extended to super pseudorandomness if a probabilistic polynomial-size witness circuit applies both normal and inverse oracle gates. Luby and Rackoff proved that $\Psi(e, f, g, h)$, where $e, f, g, h \in_R \mathcal{F}$ are pseudorandom functions, is super pseudorandom, so there is no probabilistic polynomial-size witness circuit with normal and inverse oracle gates which can tell apart $\Psi(e, f, g, h)$ from Π. A super pseudorandom permutation generator is immune against both the chosen plaintext and chosen ciphertext attacks.

The number of necessary pseudorandom functions can be reduced to two only as $\Psi(f, f, g, g)$ is super pseudorandom [397]. Now consider the design of a super pseudorandom permutation generator from a single pseudorandom function. A permutation generator $\Psi(f^i, f^j, f^k, f^\ell)$ is not pseudorandom and there is a distinguisher for it. Its construction is given in [440]. Patarin in [397] argued that $\Psi(f, f, f, f \circ \varsigma \circ f)$ is super pseudorandom if ς is a "well chosen" public permutation and f is a pseudorandom function. It turns out [439] that $\Psi(f, 1, f^2, f, 1, f^2)$ is super pseudorandom where f is a pseudorandom function and 1 stands for the identity permutation.

5.8 Problems and Exercises

1. The congruence $x_{i+1} \equiv ax_i + c \bmod N$ is used to generate a sequence of pseudorandom numbers. Compute first 10 numbers assuming the following parameters: $N = 347$, $a = 34$, $c = 23$, and $x_0 = 1$. What is the period of the sequence?

2. Given $\mathcal{S}_n = \{1, \ldots, 2^n\}$ and two ensembles $\mathcal{E}_1 = \{\mathcal{S}_n, \{p_1(x) = \frac{1}{2^n} \mid x \in \mathcal{S}_n\}\}$ and $\mathcal{E}_2 = \{\mathcal{S}_n, \{p_2(x) \mid x \in \mathcal{S}_n\}\}$ where the probability distribution is:

$$p_2(x) = \begin{cases} \frac{3}{2^{n+1}} & \text{for } x \in \mathcal{S}_{n-1}, \\ \frac{1}{2^{n+1}} & \text{for } x \in \mathcal{S}_n \setminus \mathcal{S}_{n-1}. \end{cases}$$

Are the two ensembles statistically indistinguishable?

3. Consider two ensembles:

$$\mathcal{E}_1 = \{\mathcal{S}_n, \{p_1(x) = \frac{1}{2^n} \mid x \in \mathcal{S}_n\}$$

and $\mathcal{E}_2 = \{\mathcal{S}_n, \{p_2(x) \mid x \in \mathcal{S}_n\}$, where the probability distribution is

$$p_2(x) = \begin{cases} \frac{1}{2^{n-1}} & \text{for } x \in \mathcal{S}_{n-1}, \\ 0 & \text{for } x \in \mathcal{S}_n \setminus \mathcal{S}_{n-1}. \end{cases}$$

Are the two ensembles statistically indistinguishable?

4. Compute the first 10 integers using an instance of the RSA pseudorandom bit generator for the following parameters: the modulus $N = 313 \cdot 331$, the seed $x_0 = 83874$, and $e = 23113$. Create a sequence of bits by extracting three less-significant bits from each integer.

5. Discuss the behavior of the period of integers generated from the RSA pseudorandom bit generator. How do you select parameters of the generator to maximize the period?

6. In calculations modulo a prime p, the Jacobi symbol can be used to judge whether a given integer a is a quadratic residue or, in other words, whether there is an integer $x = \sqrt{a}$ such that $x^2 \equiv a \bmod p$. Take $p = 11$ and find all quadratic residues (and quadratic nonresidues). Show that the quadratic residues constitute an algebraic group under multiplication modulo p.

7. The two smallest primes bigger than 3 and congruent to 3 modulo 4 are 7 and 11. Find the set of quadratic residues $\mathcal{Z}_N^{Q+}$ and the set of quadratic nonresidues $\mathcal{Z}_N^{Q-}$. Note that both sets have $\varphi(N)/4 = 15$ elements.

8. Construct an instance of a BBS generator for $p = 7$ and $q = 11$. Generate a sequence of bits for a random selected seed x_0 (x_0 has to be a quadratic residue). What is the period of the sequence?

6 Hashing

In many cryptographic applications, it is necessary to produce a relatively short fingerprint of a much longer message or electronic document. The fingerprint is also called a *digest* of the message. Cryptographic applications of hashing include, among others, the generation of digital signatures.

6.1 Properties of Hashing

A hash function is required to produce a digest of a fixed length for a message of an arbitrary length. Let the hash function be

$$h : \Sigma^* \to \Sigma^n,$$

where $\Sigma^* = \bigcup_{i \in \mathcal{N}} \Sigma^i$. It is said that two different messages m_1, m_2 *collide* if

$$h(m_1) = h(m_2).$$

It is obvious that there are infinitely many collisions for the hash function h. The main requirement of a secure hashing is that it should be collision resistant in the sense that finding two colliding messages is computationally intractable. This requirement must hold not only for long messages but also for short ones. Observe that short messages (for example single bits) must also be hashed to an n-bit digest. In practice, this is done by first padding the message and later by hashing the padded message. Clearly, a padding scheme is typically considered a part of the hash function.

Given a hash function $h : \Sigma^* \to \Sigma^n$. We say that the function is

- *Preimage resistant* if, for (almost) any digest d, it is computationally intractable to find the preimage (message m) such that $d = h(m)$. This means that the function is *one-way*.
- *2nd preimage resistant* if, given the description of the function h and a chosen message m_1, it is computationally intractable to find another message m_2

which collides with m_1, i.e., $h(m_1) = h(m_2)$. 2nd preimage resistance is also equivalently termed *weak collision resistance*.

- *Collision resistant* if, given the description of the function h, it is computationally infeasible to find two distinct messages m_1, m_2 which collide, i.e., $h(m_1) = h(m_2)$. Collision resistance is equivalent to *strong collision resistance*.

There are many different definitions of hash functions depending on what properties are required from them. There are, however, two major classes of hash function, defined as follows:

1. *A one-way hash function* (OWHF) compresses messages of arbitrary length into digests of fixed length. The computation of the digest for a message is easy. The function is preimage and 2nd preimage resistant. Equivalently, the function is termed a *weak one-way hash function*.
2. *A collision-resistant hash function* (CRHF) compresses messages of arbitrary length into digests of fixed length. The computation of the digest for a message is easy. The function is collision resistant. Equivalently, the function is termed *strong one-way hash function*.

Collision-resistant hash functions can be used without special care if the finding collision must be always an intractable task. On the other hand, one-way hash functions do not guarantee that a given selection of two messages is collision resistant.

Note that a collision-resistant hash function must be a one-way function. This statement can be proved by contradiction [496]. Assume that a hash function h is not one-way, i.e., there is a probabilistic polynomial-time algorithm R which for a given digest d returns a message $m = R(d)$ such that $d = h(m)$. The algorithm R can be used to generate collisions in the following way:

- Select at random m and find its digest $d = h(m)$.
- Call the algorithm R which returns $m' = R(d)$ such that $d = h(m')$.
- If $m \neq m'$, then this is a collision. Otherwise select another random message and repeat the process.

6.2 Birthday Paradox

For secure hashing, finding collisions must be intractable. In general, it is assumed that the adversary knows the description of the hashing algorithm. It is also assumed that the adversary can perform an attack, where he/she may choose messages, ask for their digests, and try to compute colliding messages. There are many methods of attack on a hash scheme. The so-called *birthday attack* is a general method and can be applied against any type of hash function. Other methods are applicable against only special groups of hash schemes. Some of these special attacks can be launched against a wide range of hash functions. The so-called *meet-in-the-middle attack* can be launched against any scheme that uses some sort of block chaining. Others can be launched only against smaller groups.

The idea behind the birthday attack originates from a famous problem from Probability Theory, called the *birthday paradox*. The paradox can be stated as follows. What is the minimum number of pupils in a classroom so that the probability that at least two pupils have the same birthday is greater than 0.5? The answer to this question is 23, which is much smaller than the value suggested by intuition. The explanation is as follows: Suppose that the pupils are entering the classroom one at a time. The probability that the birthday of the first pupil falls on a specific day of the year is equal to $\frac{1}{365}$. The probability that the birthday of the second pupil is not the same as the first one is equal to $1 - \frac{1}{365}$. If the birthdays of the first two pupils are different, the probability that the birthday of the third pupil is different from the first one and the second one is equal to $1 - \frac{2}{365}$. Consequently, the probability that t students have different birthdays is equal to $(1 - \frac{1}{365})(1 - \frac{2}{365}) \dots (1 - \frac{t-1}{365})$. So the probability that at least two of them have the same birthday is:

$$P = 1 - \left(1 - \frac{1}{365}\right)\left(1 - \frac{2}{365}\right) \dots \left(1 - \frac{t-1}{365}\right).$$

It can be easily computed that for $t \geq 23$, this probability is bigger than 0.5. In general, the probability of finding at least two pupils with the same birthday is at least 0.5 if the number of pupils is roughly $\sqrt{n}$ and the year has n days.

The birthday paradox can be employed to attack hash functions. Suppose that the number of bits in the digest is n. Any message m can be represented (written) in many different ways. A single representation of the message is called a variant. For instance, the message

On November 5, 1998, I sold my PC to Mr. John Brown for 1000 dollars.

can be equivalently written as

On November 5, 1998, I sold my PC to John Brown for $1000.

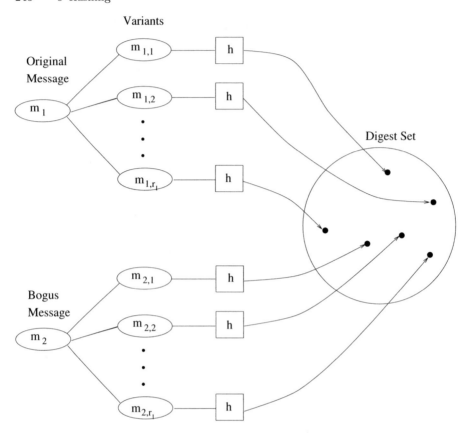

Fig. 6.1. Birthday attack

Due to the natural redundancy of a language, it is always possible to generate many variants of the same message. The variants can be created by adding blanks and empty lines, using equivalent words, abbreviations, and full wording, or removing some words whose existence is not essential. In the attack, an adversary generates r_1 variants of an original message and r_2 variants of a bogus message (Fig. 6.1). The probability of finding a pair of variants (one of the genuine and one of the bogus message) which hashes to the same digest is

$$P \approx 1 - e^{-\frac{r_1 r_2}{2^n}}, \tag{6.1}$$

where $r_2 \gg 1$ [386]. When $r_1 = r_2 = 2^{\frac{n}{2}}$, the above probability is about 0.63. Therefore, any hashing algorithm that produces digests of length around 64 bits is insecure, as the time complexity function for the corresponding birthday attack is $\approx 2^{32}$. It is usually recommended that the hash value should be longer than 128 bits to achieve a sufficient security against the attack.

This method of attack does not take advantage of structural properties of the hash scheme or its algebraic weaknesses. It can be launched against any hash scheme. It is assumed that the hash scheme assigns to a message a value that is chosen with a uniform probability among all the possible hash values. Note that if there is any weakness in the structure or certain algebraic properties of the hash function, so digests do not have a uniform probability distribution, then generally it would be possible to find colliding messages with a better probability and fewer message-digest pairs.

The birthday attack may also be modified to fit a particular structure of the hash scheme. Consider a variant called the *meet-in-the-middle attack*. Instead of comparing the digests, the intermediate results in the chain are compared. The attack can be launched against schemes that employ some sort of block chaining in their structure. In contrast to the birthday attack, the meet-in-the-middle attack enables an attacker to construct a bogus message with a digest selected by the attacker. In this attack the message is divided into two parts. The attacker generates r_1 variants of the first part of a bogus message. He starts from the initial value and goes forward to the intermediate stage. He also generates r_2 variants on the second part of the bogus message. He starts from the desired target digest and goes backwards to the intermediate stage. The probability of a match in the intermediate stage is the same as the probability of success in the birthday attack.

Consider a hash scheme that uses an encryption function $E : \mathcal{K} \times \mathcal{M} \rightarrow \Sigma^n$ where $\mathcal{K} = \mathcal{M} = \Sigma^n$. For a message $m = (m_1, m_2)$, the digest is computed in two steps:

$$h_1 = E(m_1, IV), \text{ and}$$
$$d = h(m) = E(m_2, h_1),$$

where IV is a public initial vector. This scheme can be subject to the meet-in-the-middle attack. Assume the opponent wants to find a bogus message $m^* = (m_1^*, m_2^*)$ that collides with m with digest d. The opponent chooses r_1 variants of m_1^* and r_2 variants of m_2^* (Fig. 6.2). Let the two sets of variants be:

$$\{m_{1,i}^* \mid i = 1, \ldots, r_1\}, \text{ and}$$
$$\{m_{2,j}^* \quad \mid j = 1, \ldots, r_2\}.$$

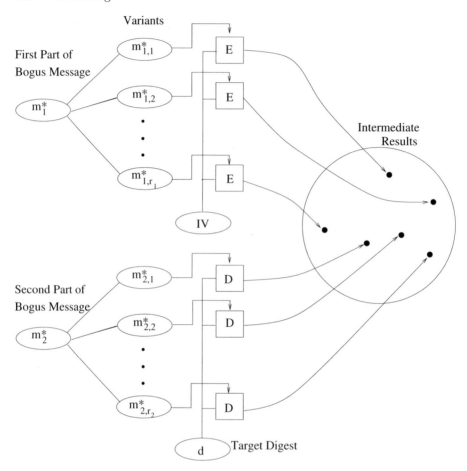

Fig. 6.2. The meet-in-the-middle attack

Next, the opponent computes r_1 variants of $h_{1,i}^* = E(m_{1,i}^*, IV)$ and r_2 variants of $h_{2,j}^* = E^{-1}(m_{2,j}^*, d) = D(m_{2,j}^*, d)$. Note that $D(m_{2,j}^*, d)$ is the decryption function. The probability of a match in the sets $\{h_{1,i}^* \mid i = 1, \ldots, r_1\}$ and $\{h_{2,i}^* \mid i = 1, \ldots, r_2\}$ is the same as the probability of success in the birthday attack if the encryption algorithm E behaves as a truly random function.

The meet-in-the-middle attack was thought to be thwarted when the hashing uses the same chain several times (so-called iterated hashing). Coppersmith [106] showed how the attack can be generalized so it is applicable for iterated hashing.

6.3 Serial and Parallel Hashing

The design of hash functions with arbitrarily long inputs poses some difficulties related to their implementation and evaluation. Arbitrarily long messages can be compressed using a fixed input-size hash function by applying two general methods:

– serial, and
– parallel.

The serial method [120] (also called by Merkle the *meta method* [341]) applies the fixed input-size hash function $h : \Sigma^{2n} \rightarrow \Sigma^n$ (Fig. 6.3). To hash an arbitrarily long message $m \in \Sigma^*$, it is first split into blocks of size n so $m = (m_1, m_2, \ldots, m_k)$ and each $m_i \in \Sigma^n$ for $i = 1, \ldots, k$. If the last block is shorter than n bits, it is padded with zeros to the full length. Next, the function h is used repeatedly:

$$h_1 = h(m_1, m_2), \quad h_2 = h(m_3, h_1), \ldots,$$
$$h_i = h(m_{i+1}, h_{i-1}), \ldots, d = h(m_k, h_{k-2}). \tag{6.2}$$

The result d is the digest of the whole message m. Damgård [120] proved that the hashing induced by the serial method is collision resistant if the underlying fixed-input-size hash function $h : \Sigma^{2n} \rightarrow \Sigma^n$ is collision resistant.

The parallel method is illustrated in Fig. 6.4. The hashing in this method starts from splitting the message $m \in \Sigma^*$ into ℓ blocks of size n, i.e., $m = (m_1, m_2, \ldots, m_\ell)$. The last block is padded to the full length if necessary. Assume that the number of blocks is $2^{k-1} < \ell \leq 2^k$. $2^k - \ell$ blocks all with zero bits are appended to the message m. The resulting message $\tilde{m} = (m_1, \ldots, m_\ell, \ldots, m_{2^k})$ is processed as follows:

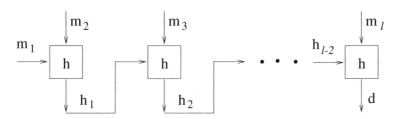

Fig. 6.3. Serial hashing

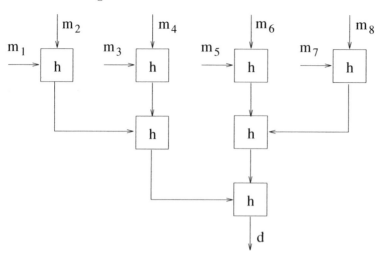

Fig. 6.4. Parallel hashing

$$h_i^1 = h(m_{2i-1}, m_{2i}) \text{ for } i = 1, \ldots, 2^{k-1},$$
$$h_i^j = h(h_{2i-1}^{j-1}, h_{2i}^{j-1}) \text{ for } i = 1, \ldots, 2^{k-i} \text{ and } j = 2, \ldots, k-1, \quad (6.3)$$
$$d(m) = h(h_1^{k-1}, h_2^{k-1}).$$

The final result of hashing is $d(m)$. Again Damgård [120] proved that the parallel hashing is collision resistant if the underlying fixed-input-size hash function $h : \Sigma^{2n} \to \Sigma^n$ is collision resistant.

Needless to say that parallel hashing is faster than serial hashing as the layers of intermediate digests can be generated independently. Also the extra blocks padded with zeros can be preprocessed so their digests enter the hashing process when needed.

6.4 Theoretic Constructions

It is interesting to investigate the relation of hash functions to other cryptographic primitives such as one-way functions (including one-way permutations), signature schemes, and pseudorandom bit generators. The main result in this area was obtained by Rompel [432] who proved that universal one-way hash functions can be constructed from any one-way function.

The notion of a one-way function is central in theoretical computer science. It is the basic cryptographic primitive which can be used to construct other cryptographic primitives. Intuitively, a one-way function f is a family of instance functions f_n indexed by the size of the function domain. The computation of $y = f_n(x)$ is easy, while finding the preimage x knowing $y = f_n(x)$ is difficult. Formally, the instance functions are

$$f_n : \Sigma^n \to \Sigma^{\ell(n)},$$

where $\ell(n)$ is a polynomial in n. The family of functions is a collection $f = \{f_n \mid n \in \mathcal{N}\}$. The family f is said to be polynomially computable if the evaluation of $f_n(x)$, $x \in \Sigma^n$ can be done in time $O(n^t)$ for some $t \in \mathcal{N}$.

Definition 19. *Let the family $f = \{f_n \mid n \in \mathcal{N}\}$ be polynomially computable. We say that f is a* one-way function *if for each probabilistic polynomial-time algorithm A, for each polynomial γ, and for all sufficiently large n, the probability*

$$P\left[f_n(A(f_n(x))) = f_n(x)\right] < \frac{1}{\gamma(n)}, \tag{6.4}$$

where x is chosen randomly and uniformly from the set Σ^n.

Hash functions can now be formally defined. For any index n, there is a collection of hash functions $H_n : \Sigma^{\ell(n)} \to \Sigma^n$ where $\ell(n)$ is a polynomial in n. The family H of hash functions is $H = \{H_n \mid n \in \mathcal{N}\}$. The family H is *accessible* if there is a probabilistic polynomial-time algorithm that on input $n \in \mathcal{N}$ returns a description of $h \in H_n$ chosen randomly and uniformly from all instance functions of H_n. The family H is polynomially computable if there is a polynomial-time algorithm that evaluates any function $h \in H$.

Let F be a *collision finder*, i.e., a probabilistic polynomial-time algorithm F such that for an input $x \in \Sigma^{\ell(n)}$ and for a given hash function $h \in H_n$ returns either '?' (cannot find) or a string $y \in \Sigma^{\ell(n)}$ that collides with x (i.e., $x \neq y$ and $h(x) = h(y)$). The *universal one-way hash function* (UOWHF) is defined as follows.

Definition 20. *Let H be a polynomially computable and accessible hash function compressing an $\ell(n)$-bit input into n-bit output strings and let F be a collision finder. H is a* universal one-way hash function *if for each F, for each polynomial γ, and for all sufficiently large n,*

$$P\left(F(x,h) \neq ?\right) < \frac{1}{\gamma(n)}, \tag{6.5}$$

where $x \in \Sigma^{\ell(n)}$ and $h \in_R H_n$. The probability is computed over all $h \in_R H_n$, $x \in \Sigma^{\ell(n)}$ and the random choice of all finite strings that F could have chosen.

Note that the UOWHF is 2nd preimage resistant. The main difference between UOWHF and OWHF is the way the hash function is chosen. In the case of OWHF, the hash function is fixed. For UOWHF, the hash function is randomly chosen.

Let R be a probabilistic polynomial-time algorithm that for an input $h \in H_n$ returns either '?' (cannot find) or a pair of colliding strings x, y. The algorithm R is called the *collision-pair finder*. The collision-resistant hash function is defined below.

Definition 21. *H is a collision-resistant hash function if for each R, for each polynomial γ, and for sufficiently large n*

$$P\left(R(h) \neq ?\right) < \frac{1}{\gamma(n)}, \tag{6.6}$$

where $h \in_R H_n$. The probability is computed over all $h \in_R H_n$, and the random choice of all finite strings that R could have chosen.

Naor and Yung [365] introduced the concept of an UOWHF and suggested a construction based on a one-way permutation. In their construction, they took advantage of the *universal hash function family with its collision accessibility property* [522]; see the definitions given below.

Definition 22. *Let $G = \{g \mid A \to B\}$ be a family of functions. G is a strongly universal$_r$ hash function family if, given any r distinct elements $a_1, \ldots, a_r \in A$, and any r elements $b_1, \ldots, b_r \in B$, there are $\frac{(\#G)}{(\#B)^2}$ functions that take a_i to b_i, $i = 1, \ldots, r$, where $\#G$ and $\#B$ stand for the cardinality of sets G and B, respectively.*

Definition 23. *A strongly universal$_r$ hash function family G has the* collision accessibility property *if it is possible to generate in polynomial-time a function $g \in G$ that satisfies the equations*

$$g(a_1) = b_1,$$
$$g(a_2) = b_2,$$
$$\vdots$$
$$g(a_r) = b_r,$$

where $a_1, \ldots, a_r$ or $b_1, \ldots, b_r$ are given.

An example of a strongly universal$_r$ family of hash functions with the collision accessibility property is a collection of polynomials of degree $r - 1$ over $GF(q)$.

Naor and Yung showed that the existence of a secure signature scheme reduces to the existence of a UOWHF. They also used the serial method to construct a UOWHF which hashes arbitrarily long messages using a UOWHF with a fixed size input. Their family of UOWHFs is constructed by the composition of a one-way permutation and a family of strongly universal$_2$ hash functions with the collision accessibility property. In Naor and Yung's construction, the one-way permutation provides the one-wayness of the UOWHF, while the strongly universal$_2$ family of hash functions compresses the input. When a member is chosen randomly and uniformly from the family the output is distributed randomly and uniformly over the output space. The construction is given in the following theorem:

Theorem 26. *Let $f : \Sigma^n \to \Sigma^n$ be a one-way permutation and let G_n be a strongly universal$_2$ family $G_n : \Sigma^n \to \Sigma^{n-1}$, then $H_n = \{h = g \circ f \mid g \in G_n\}$ is a UOWHF compressing n-bit input strings into $(n - 1)$-bit output strings.*

The above construction is not very efficient as it compresses a single bit only. This can be improved when a strongly universal$_t$ $(t > 2)$ family of hash functions is used.

Zheng, Matsumoto, and Imai [546] defined a hashing scheme that was based on the composition of a pairwise independent uniformizer and a strongly universal hash function with a quasi-injection one-way function. De Santis and Yung [450] built up a hash function assuming the existence of a one-way function with an almost-known preimage size.

Rompel managed to construct a UOWHF from any one-way function [432]. His construction is rather complicated and elaborate, and a detailed explanation is beyond the scope of this book. However, the idea is to transform any one-way function into a UOWHF through a sequence of complicated procedures. First, the one-way function is transformed into another one-way function such that, for most elements of the domain, it is easy to find a collision, except for a fraction of them. Next another one-way function is constructed such that, for most of the elements, it is hard to find a collision. Subsequently, a length-increasing one-way function is constructed such that it is almost everywhere hard to find any collision. Finally this is turned into a UOWHF, which compresses the input such that it is difficult to find a collision.

In some applications, it may be useful to have a hash scheme with an easy-to-find collection of colliding messages. The calculation of other collisions should be computationally intractable. The construction given in [544] called *sibling intractable function families* or SIFF provides hashing with a controlled number of easy-to-find collisions.

6.5 Hashing Based on Cryptosystems

To minimize the effort, many designers of hash functions tend to base their schemes on existing encryption algorithms. Hashing is done using the serial method by applying the encryption algorithm on blocks of the message. The message block size has to be equal to the input size of the encryption algorithm. If the length of the message is not a multiple of the block size, then the last block is usually padded with some redundant bits. To provide a randomizing element, an initial vector (IV) is normally used. The vector IV is public. The encryption algorithm is $E : \mathcal{K} \times \mathcal{M} \rightarrow \mathcal{C}$. The security of such schemes relies on the collision resistance of the underlying encryption algorithm and the immunity of the scheme against the birthday attack and its variants.

Rabin [423] argued that any private-key cryptosystem $E : \Sigma^{2n} \rightarrow \Sigma^n$ can be used for hashing. The Rabin scheme is depicted in Fig. 6.5. First the message is divided into blocks with n bits. Suppose that we wish to hash a message $m = (m_1, m_2, \ldots, m_\ell)$. The hashing is performed according to

$$h_0 = IV,$$
$$h_i = E(m_i, h_{i-1}) \text{ for } i = 1, 2, \ldots, \ell,$$
$$d = h_\ell,$$

where h_i are intermediate results of hashing, and d is the final digest of m. Note that messages m_i are used in place of the key for the encryption E. Although the Rabin scheme is simple and elegant, it is susceptible to the birthday and

Fig. 6.5. The Rabin hashing scheme

meet-in-the-middle attacks when the size of the hash value is 64 bits. This scheme can be used only if the size of inputs in the encryption algorithm is larger than or equal to 128 bits; see (6.1).

The meet-in-the-middle attack in the Rabin scheme works because it is possible to reverse hashing by using the decryption function. Winternitz [537] suggested designing a one-way function from a block cryptosystem E. The one-way function

$$E^*(k\|m) = E(k,m) \oplus m. \tag{6.7}$$

Davies used the one-way function E^* to design the following hash scheme (Fig. 6.6):

$$h_0 = IV,$$
$$h_i = E(m_i, h_{i-1}) \oplus h_{i-1} \text{ for } i = 1, 2, \ldots, \ell,$$
$$d = h_\ell.$$

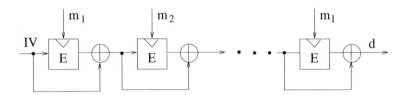

Fig. 6.6. The Davies hashing scheme

The Davies scheme is immune to the meet-in-the-middle attack but may be subject to attacks based on key collision search [419] and weak keys [413].

Based on the one-way function E^*, Merkle proposed several schemes [340, 341, 342]. These schemes use DES and produce digests of size ≈ 128 bits. The construction of these schemes follows the serial method. The message to be hashed is first divided into blocks of 106 bits. Each 106-bit block m_i of data is concatenated with the 128-bit block h_{i-1}. The concatenation $x_i = m_i \| h_{i-1}$ contains 234 bits. Each block x_i is further divided into halves, x_{i1} and x_{i2}. The description of the method is as follows:

$$h_0 = IV,$$
$$x_i = m_i \| h_{i-1},$$
$$h_i = E^*(00 \| \text{first 59 bits of } \{E^*(100 \| x_{i1})\}$$

$\quad\quad$ || first 59 bits of $\{E^*(101 \parallel x_{i2})\})$

$\quad\quad$ || $E^*(01 \parallel$ first 59 bits of $\{E^*(110 \parallel x_{i1})\}$

$\quad\quad$ || first 59 bits of $\{E^*(111 \parallel x_{i2})\})$,

$\quad d = h_\ell.$

In this scheme, E^* is a one-way function defined by (6.7) and the strings 00, 01, 100, 101, 110, and 111 have been included to prevent attacks based on weak keys.

$\quad$ As most encryption algorithms have weak keys and possible colliding keys, the key input of encryption systems E should be used for partial hash values rather than for messages. If we modify the Davies scheme accordingly we get the following scheme:

$$h_0 = IV,$$
$$h_i = E(h_{i-1}, m_i) \oplus m_i \text{ for } i = 1, 2, \ldots, \ell,$$
$$d = h_\ell.$$

Another variant used by Miyaguchi, Ohta, and Iwata [348] in their N-hash algorithm applies a different chaining method $h_i = E(h_{i-1}, m_i) \oplus m_i \oplus h_{i-1}$. Two other possible chaining methods are: $h_i = E(h_{i-1}, m_i \oplus h_{i-1}) \oplus m_i \oplus h_{i-1}$ and $h_i = E(h_{i-1}, m_i \oplus h_{i-1}) \oplus m_i$. For discussion of other less secure chaining methods, the reader is referred to [413].

6.6 MD (Message Digest) Family

Hashing algorithms can also be designed from scratch. Typically, we require the design to be

1. Secure, i.e., collision resistant – this immediately forces the digest to be at least 128 bits long (to protect the design against the birthday attack and its variants).
2. Fast and easy to implement both in software and hardware.

Feistel permutations can be used as the basic component in the design. Clearly, they need to be modified. Let the n-bit input and output be divided into ℓ blocks of r bits such that $\ell \cdot r = n$. Our Feistel permutation modified for hashing is $\mathcal{F}_m : \underbrace{\Sigma^r \times \ldots \times \Sigma^r}_{\ell} \rightarrow \underbrace{\Sigma^r \times \ldots \times \Sigma^r}_{\ell}$ where m is a message (or its

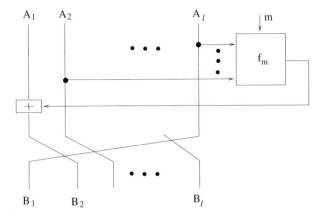

Fig. 6.7. A modified Feistel permutation

part) to be hashed. Let the input $A = (A_1, \ldots, A_\ell) \in \Sigma^n$ and the output $B = (B_1, \ldots, B_\ell) \in \Sigma^n$, then $\mathcal{F}_m(A)$ is described as (Fig. 6.7)

$$B_1 = A_\ell,$$
$$B_2 = A_1 + f_m(A_2, \ldots, A_\ell) \bmod 2^r,$$
$$B_3 = A_2, \ldots, B_\ell = A_{\ell-1}.$$

The function $f_m(A_2, \ldots, A_\ell)$ is indexed by the message m. The hash scheme would employ many rounds, each based on the modified Feistel permutation. To prevent the birthday attack, the size $n \geq 128$. If we use 32-bit machines for a software implementation, it is reasonable to assume that $r = 32$.

Rivest used the above approach to design his MD4 [429] and MD5 [430] hashing algorithms. The other members of the MD family are the Secure Hash Algorithm (SHA), also called the Secure Hash Standard (SHS) [367], RIPEMD [51], and HAVAL [547]. We will describe MD5, SHA-1, RIPEMD-160, and HAVAL.

6.6.1 MD5

MD5 is a strengthened version of MD4. It compresses 512-bit messages into 128-bit digests using the 128-bit chaining input. A message of arbitrary length is first appended bit 1 and enough 0s so it is congruent 448 modulo 512. A 64-bit string $\ell = \ell_1 2^{32} + \ell_0$, which is the binary representation of the length of the original message, is appended to the padded message (Fig. 6.8). Now the message length is a multiple of 512. Hashing is done as in the serial method – block-by-block and each block is 512 bits long.

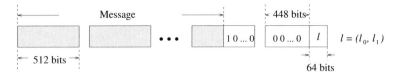

Fig. 6.8. Padding of a message

The hashing of a single message block proceeds as follows. First the message block m is divided into 16 32-bit long words, so $m = (m_0, \ldots, m_{15})$. The chaining input contains four 32-bit registers (A, B, C, D). They are initialized as

$A = 0x67452301,$

$B = 0xefcdab89,$

$C = 0x98badcfe,$

$D = 0x10325476,$

where the strings are written in hexadecimal. Next the four rounds of MD5 are executed (Fig. 6.9). The four outputs of the last round are added modulo 2^{32} to the initial values of the registers A, B, C, D giving the final digest for a 512-bit message m.

MD5 applies four Boolean functions:

$f(x, y, z) = xy \vee \bar{x}z,$

$g(x, y, z) = xz \vee y\bar{z},$

$h(x, y, z) = x \oplus y \oplus z,$

$k(x, y, z) = y \oplus (x \vee \bar{z}),$

where $\vee$ is OR, $\oplus$ is XOR, and xy stands for x AND y. To make the algorithm fast, bitwise operations are used to evaluate the Boolean functions in parallel. The four bitwise functions used in the four rounds are

$F(X, Y, Z) = (X \wedge Y) \vee ((\neg X) \wedge Z),$

$G(X, Y, Z) = (X \wedge Z) \vee (Y \wedge (\neg Z)),$

$H(X, Y, Z) = X \oplus Y \oplus Z,$

$K(X, Y, Z) = Y \oplus (X \vee (\neg Z)),$

where $\wedge$ is bitwise AND, $\vee$ is bitwise OR, $\oplus$ is bitwise XOR, $\neg$ is bitwise complement, and X, Y, Z are 32-bit words. The functions F, H, G, and K are used to define four Feistel permutations FF, GG, HH, and $KK : \Sigma^{128} \rightarrow$

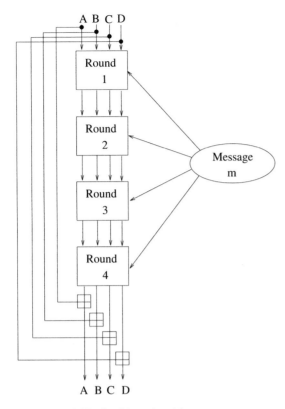

Fig. 6.9. MD5 hashing algorithm

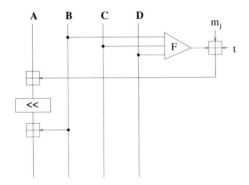

Fig. 6.10. A single iteration in MD5

Σ^{128}. The permutations are identical except for the fact that they use different functions. The permutation based on function F is depicted in Fig. 6.10. The Feistel permutations used in MD5 are

$$FF(A, B, C, D \mid m_j, s, t)$$
$$= (B \boxplus ((A \boxplus F(B, C, D) \boxplus m_j \boxplus t) \lll s), B, C, D),$$
$$GG(A, B, C, D \mid m_j, s, t)$$
$$= (B \boxplus ((A \boxplus G(B, C, D) \boxplus m_j \boxplus t) \lll s), B, C, D),$$
$$HH(A, B, C, d \mid m_j, s, t)$$
$$= (B \boxplus ((A \boxplus H(B, C, D) \boxplus m_j \boxplus t) \lll s), B, C, D),$$
$$KK(A, B, C, D \mid m_j, s, t)$$
$$= (B \boxplus ((A \boxplus K(B, C, D) \boxplus m_j \boxplus t) \lll s), B, C, D),$$

where $(A, B, C, D) \in \Sigma^{128}$ is an input while (m_j, s, t) are current parameters that determine the form of the permutation and $\boxplus$ stands for addition modulo 2^{32}. The first parameter is the current message block m_j, $j = 0, \ldots, 15$. The second parameter s specifies the number of positions in the rotation. The third parameter t is a constant. $(A \lll s)$ means that the binary string A is rotated to the left by s positions. The hashing proceeds through the four rounds:

Round 1:

(1) $FF(A, B, C, D \mid m_0, 7, 0xd76aa478)$,
(2) $FF(D, A, B, C \mid m_1, 12, 0xe8c7b756)$,
(3) $FF(C, D, A, B \mid m_2, 17, 0x242070db)$,
(4) $FF(B, C, D, A \mid m_3, 22, 0xc1bdceee)$,
(5) $FF(A, B, C, D \mid m_4, 7, 0xf57c0faf)$,
(6) $FF(D, A, B, C \mid m_5, 12, 0x4787c62a)$,
(7) $FF(C, D, A, B \mid m_6, 17, 0xa8304613)$,
(8) $FF(B, C, D, A \mid m_7, 22, 0xfd469501)$,
(9) $FF(A, B, C, D \mid m_8, 7, 0x698098d8)$,
(10) $FF(D, A, B, C \mid m_9, 12, 0x8b44f7af)$,
(11) $FF(C, D, A, B \mid m_{10}, 17, 0xffff5bb1)$,
(12) $FF(B, C, D, A \mid m_{11}, 22, 0x895cd7be)$,
(13) $FF(A, B, C, D \mid m_{12}, 7, 0x6b901122)$,
(14) $FF(D, A, B, C \mid m_{13}, 12, 0xfd987193)$,
(15) $FF(C, D, A, B \mid m_{14}, 17, 0xa679438e)$,
(16) $FF(B, C, D, A \mid m_{15}, 22, 0x49b40821)$.

(6.8)

Round 2:

$(17)\ GG(A, B, C, D \mid m_1, 5, 0xf61e2562),$

$(18)\ GG(D, A, B, C \mid m_6, 9, 0xc040b340),$

$(19)\ GG(C, D, A, B \mid m_{11}, 14, 0x265e5a51),$

$(20)\ GG(B, C, D, A \mid m_0, 20, 0xe9b6c7aa),$

$(21)\ GG(A, B, C, D \mid m_5, 5, 0xd62f105d),$

$(22)\ GG(D, A, B, C \mid m_{10}, 9, 0x02441453),$

$(23)\ GG(C, D, A, B \mid m_{15}, 14, 0xd8a1e681),$

$(24)\ GG(B, C, D, A \mid m_4, 20, 0xe7d3fbc8),$

$(25)\ GG(A, B, C, D \mid m_9, 5, 0x21e1cde6),$ (6.9)

$(26)\ GG(D, A, B, C \mid m_{14}, 9, 0xc33707d6),$

$(27)\ GG(C, D, A, B \mid m_3, 14, 0xf4d50d87),$

$(28)\ GG(B, C, D, A \mid m_8, 20, 0x455a14ed),$

$(29)\ GG(A, B, C, D \mid m_{13}, 5, 0xa9e3e905),$

$(30)\ GG(D, A, B, C \mid m_2, 9, 0xfcefa3f8),$

$(31)\ GG(C, D, A, B \mid m_7, 14, 0x676f02d9),$

$(32)\ GG(B, C, D, A \mid m_{12}, 20, 0x8d2a4c8a).$

Round 3:

$(33)\ HH(A, B, C, D \mid m_5, 4, 0xfffa3942),$

$(34)\ HH(D, A, B, C \mid m_8, 11, 0x8771f681),$

$(35)\ HH(C, D, A, B \mid m_{11}, 16, 0x6d9d6122),$

$(36)\ HH(B, C, D, A \mid m_{14}, 23, 0xfde5380c),$

$(37)\ HH(A, B, C, D \mid m_1, 4, 0xa4beea44),$

$(38)\ HH(D, A, B, C \mid m_4, 11, 0x4bdecfa9),$

$(39)\ HH(C, D, A, B \mid m_7, 16, 0xf6bb4b60),$

$(40)\ HH(B, C, D, A \mid m_{10}, 23, 0xbebfbc70),$

$(41)\ HH(A, B, C, D \mid m_{13}, 4, 0x289b7ec6),$ (6.10)

$(42)\ HH(D, A, B, C \mid m_0, 11, 0xeaa127fa),$

$(43)\ HH(C, D, A, B \mid m_3, 16, 0xd4ef3085),$

$(44)\ HH(B, C, D, A \mid m_6, 23, 0x04881d05),$

$(45)\ HH(A, B, C, D \mid m_9, 4, 0xd9d4d039),$

$(46)\ HH(D, A, B, C \mid m_{12}, 11, 0xe6db99e5),$

$(47)\ HH(C, D, A, B \mid m_{15}, 16, 0x1fa27cf8),$

$(48)\ HH(B, C, D, A \mid m_2, 23, 0xc4ac5665).$

Round 4:

$$
\begin{align}
&(49)\ KK(A, B, C, D \mid m_0, 6, 0xf4292244), \\
&(50)\ KK(D, A, B, C \mid m_7, 10, 0x432aff97), \\
&(51)\ KK(C, D, A, B \mid m_{14}, 15, 0xab9423a7), \\
&(52)\ KK(B, C, D, A \mid m_5, 21, 0xfc93a039), \\
&(53)\ KK(A, B, C, D \mid m_{12}, 6, 0x655b59c3), \\
&(54)\ KK(D, A, B, C \mid m_3, 10, 0x8f0ccc92), \\
&(55)\ KK(C, D, A, B \mid m_{10}, 15, 0xffeff47d), \\
&(56)\ KK(B, C, D, A \mid m_1, 21, 0x85845dd1), \\
&(57)\ KK(A, B, C, D \mid m_8, 6, 0x6fa87e4f), \\
&(58)\ KK(D, A, B, C \mid m_{15}, 10, 0xfe2ce6e0), \\
&(59)\ KK(C, D, A, B \mid m_6, 15, 0xa3014314), \\
&(60)\ KK(B, C, D, A \mid m_{13}, 21, 0x4e0811a1), \\
&(61)\ KK(A, B, C, D \mid m_4, 6, 0xf7537e82), \\
&(62)\ KK(D, A, B, C \mid m_{11}, 10, 0xbd3af235), \\
&(63)\ KK(C, D, A, B \mid m_2, 15, 0x2ad7d2bb), \\
&(64)\ KK(B, C, D, A \mid m_9, 21, 0xeb86d391).
\end{align}
$$

(6.11)

MD5 was meant to be fast on machines with a *little-endian* architecture. By the way, for a 32-bit word $(a_0, \ldots, a_{31})$, a machine with little-endian architecture converts the string into integer $a_{31}2^{31} + \ldots + a_1 \cdot 2 + a_0$. In *big-endian* architecture, the same integer is $a_0 2^{31} + \ldots + a_{30} \cdot 2 + a_{31}$.

As MD4 is a weaker version of MD5, it was apparent that the main effort would be concentrated around analysis of MD4. den Boer and Bosselaers [135] successfully analyzed the two last rounds of MD4. Merkle successfully attacked the first two rounds of MD4. In 1996 Dobbertin [156] broke the whole MD4. He also extended his attack to MD5 [157] and showed that MD5 is not collision resistant.

6.6.2 SHA-1

SHA-1 is closely related to MD5 and shares many common features. It is a standard recommended by the US National Institute of Standards and Technology (NIST). SHA-1 hashes arbitrarily long messages using the serial method. The message block of 512 bits is compressed into a 160-bit digest using a 160-bit chaining input.

SHA-1's main features include:

- Padding is identical to that in MD5 except the length of the original message $\ell = (\ell_1 2^{32} + \ell_0)$ is appended as a 64-bit sequence in the order (ℓ_1, ℓ_0) (compare with Fig. 6.8).
- The chaining input is initialized as in MD5 with the additional input $E = 0xc3d2e1f0$.
- The collection of round functions includes

$$f(x, y, z) = xy \vee \bar{x}z,$$

$$g(x, y, z) = xy \vee xz \vee yz,$$

$$h(x, y, z) = x \oplus y \oplus z.$$

Denote by F, G, and H the word equivalents of functions f, g, and h, respectively. The function F is used in the first round (iterations from 0 to 19). The function H is used in rounds 2 and 4 (iterations from 20 to 39 and from 60 to 79). The function G is used in round 3 (iterations 40 to 59).

- The message buffer $(X_0, \ldots, X_{79})$ of 80 words (80×32 bits) is initialized by storing the 512-bit message into the first 16 entries and the remainder words are computed according to

$$X_j = X_{j-3} \oplus X_{j-8} \oplus X_{j-14} \oplus X_{j-16},$$

for $j = 16, \ldots, 79$. Note that the word X_j is used in the ith iteration, $j = 0, \ldots, 79$.

- The jth iteration is based on a Feistel permutation controlled by the message word X_j and the constant t, where

$$t = \begin{cases} 0x5a827999 & \text{Round 1,} \\ 0x6ed9eba1 & \text{Round 2,} \\ 0x8f1bbcdc & \text{Round 3,} \\ 0xca62c1d6 & \text{Round 4.} \end{cases}$$

The Feistel permutation $\mathcal{F}_\alpha : \Sigma^{160} \rightarrow \Sigma^{160}$ takes the 5-word input and outputs the 5-word output, or

$$(A, B, C, D, E) := \mathcal{F}_\alpha(A, B, C, D, E),$$

where α indicates the currently employed round function (either F, G, or H). The form of the iteration is as follows (Fig. 6.11)

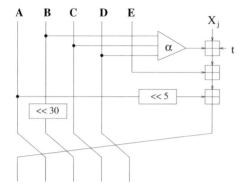

A B C D E

X_j

α

t

<< 5

<< 30

Fig. 6.11. An iteration in SHA-1

$$\mathcal{F}_\alpha(A, B, C, D, E)$$
$$= (\alpha(B, C, D) \boxplus X_j \boxplus t \boxplus E \boxplus (A \lll 5), A, (B \lll 30), C, D),$$

where $(A \lll s)$ stands for rotation s bits to the left and $\boxplus$ is addition modulo 2^{32}.

Hashing of a single message block runs through 4 rounds each containing 20 iterations, as shown in Fig. 6.12. More precisely, round 1 (iterations $j = 0, \ldots, 19$) applies the function F, so

$$(A, B, C, D, E) := \mathcal{F}_F(A, B, C, D, E).$$

Rounds 2 and 4 (iterations $j = 20, \ldots, 39, 60, \ldots, 79$) use the function H. Thus

$$(A, B, C, D, E) := \mathcal{F}_H(A, B, C, D, E).$$

Round 3 (iterations $j = 40, \ldots, 59$) employs the function G, or

$$(A, B, C, D, E) := \mathcal{F}_G(A, B, C, D, E).$$

SHA-1 is believed to be more secure than MD5. Note that the digest space is larger than that offered by MD5 (note the additional word E in the chaining variable).

6.6.3 RIPEMD-160

RIPEMD is an outcome of the European RACE Integrity Primitives Evaluation (RIPE) project. RIPEMD-160 is a strengthened version of the RIPEMD algorithm [158]. It applies 5 rounds (instead of 3 in RIPEMD) and the size of

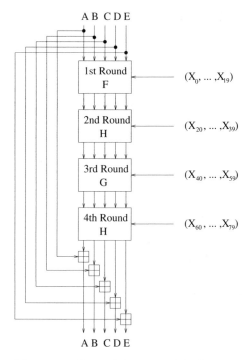

A B C D E

1st Round
F

$(X_0, \ldots, X_{19})$

2nd Round
H

$(X_{20}, \ldots, X_{39})$

3rd Round
G

$(X_{40}, \ldots, X_{59})$

4th Round
H

$(X_{60}, \ldots, X_{79})$

A B C D E

Fig. 6.12. General diagram of SHA-1

the digest (and the chaining variable) is 160 bits (instead of 128 bits). Unlike other algorithms in the MD family, RIPE and RIPE-160 use two parallel lines of executions.

The parameters and structure of RIPE-160 are defined as follows:

– The padding is identical to that in MD5.
– The chaining input is initialized as in MD5.
– The collection of round functions is:

$$f(x, y, z) = x \oplus y \oplus z,$$
$$g(x, y, z) = xy \vee \bar{y}z,$$
$$h(x, y, z) = (x \vee \bar{y}) \oplus z,$$
$$k(x, y, z) = xz \vee y\bar{z}, \text{ and}$$
$$l(x, y, z) = u \oplus (y \vee \bar{z}).$$

Denote by $F, G, H, K,$ and L the word versions of functions $f, g, h, k,$ and l, respectively.

– There are two parallel lines of execution. Both lines use their own message buffers $X[0, \ldots, 79]$ in the left line and $Y[0, \ldots, 79]$ in the right line. The first 16 words of the buffer X are initialized to the 16 words of the message $(m_0, \ldots, m_{15})$, so

$$
\begin{aligned}
X[0, \ldots, 15] &= (0, \ 1, \ 2, \ 3, \ 4, \ 5, \ 6, \ 7, \ 8, 9, 10, 11, 12, 13, 14, 15), \\
X[16, \ldots, 31] &= (7, \ 4, 13, \ 1, 10, \ 6, 15, \ 3, 12, 0, \ 9, \ 5, \ 2, 14, 11, \ 8), \\
X[32, \ldots, 47] &= (3, 10, 14, \ 4, \ 9, 15, \ 8, \ 1, \ 2, 7, \ 0, \ 6, 13, 11, \ 5, 12), \\
X[48, \ldots, 63] &= (1, \ 9, 11, 10, \ 0, \ 8, 12, \ 4, 13, 3, \ 7, 15, 14, \ 5, \ 6, \ 2), \\
X[64, \ldots, 79] &= (4, \ 0, \ 5, \ 9, \ 7, 12, \ 2, 10, 14, 1, \ 3, \ 8, 11, \ 6, 15, 13).
\end{aligned}
$$

The message buffer Y is initialized as follows:

$$
\begin{aligned}
Y[0, \ldots, 15] &= (\ 5, 14, \ 7, 0, 9, \ 2, 11, \ 4, 13, \ 6, 15, \ 8, \ 1, 10, \ 3, 12), \\
Y[16, \ldots, 31] &= (\ 6, 11, \ 3, 7, 0, 13, \ 5, 10, 14, 15, \ 8, 12, \ 4, \ 9, \ 1, \ 2), \\
Y[32, \ldots, 47] &= (15, \ 5, \ 1, 3, 7, 14, \ 6, \ 9, 11, \ 8, 12, \ 2, 10, \ 0, \ 4, 13), \\
Y[48, \ldots, 63] &= (\ 8, \ 6, \ 4, 1, 3, 11, 15, \ 0, \ 5, 12, \ 2, 13, \ 9, \ 7, 10, 14), \\
Y[64, \ldots, 79] &= (12, 15, 10, 4, 1, \ 5, \ 8, \ 7, \ 6, \ 2, 13, 14, \ 0, \ 3, \ 9, 11).
\end{aligned}
$$

– Rounds in the left and right lines apply the following constants:

Round	Left line t_ℓ	Right line t_r
1	0	$0x50a28be6$
2	$0x5a827999$	$0x5c4dd124$
3	$0x6ed9eba1$	$0x6d703ef3$
4	$0x8f1bbcdc$	$0x7a6d76e9$
5	$0xa953fd4e$	0

– The ith iteration (Feistel permutation) is controlled by a message word M (from either X if the iteration is used in the left line, or Y in the right line); see Fig. 6.13. The value

$$
v = ((\alpha(B, C, D) \boxplus M \boxplus A \boxplus t) \lll s) \boxplus E
$$

is generated, and the input (A, B, C, D, E) is transformed according to

$$
(A, B, C, D, E) := \mathcal{F}(A, B, C, D, E, \alpha, t, s) = (E, v, B, C \lll 10, D),
$$

where the constant t is either t_ℓ or t_r.

The hashing process is depicted in Fig. 6.14. The input vector (initialized to the fixed values for the first message block or taking on digests obtained from the previous message block) is used in both lines of execution. Each line includes 5 rounds each round and has 16 iterations. The rounds in the left line of execution apply functions F, G, H, K, and L, while the rounds in the right

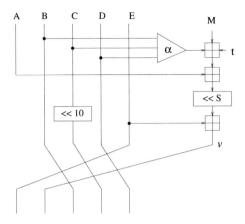

Fig. 6.13. An iteration in RIPEMD-160

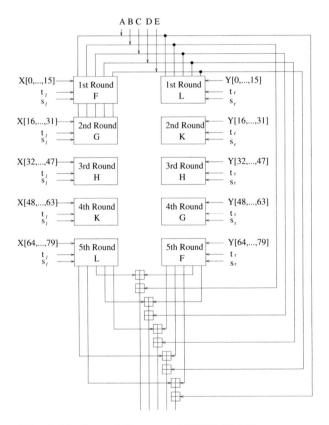

Fig. 6.14. General diagram of RIPEMD-160

line of execution use functions in the reverse order. Constants t_ℓ, t_r and the rotation parameters s_ℓ, s_r are used accordingly. The parameters s_ℓ and s_r are chosen as follows:

Left iterations	Values of s_ℓ
0...15	11, 14, 15, 12, 5, 8, 7, 9, 11, 13, 14, 15, 6, 7, 9, 8
16...31	7, 6, 8, 13, 11, 9, 7, 15, 7, 12, 15, 9, 11, 7, 13, 12
32...47	11, 13, 6, 7, 14, 9, 13, 15, 14, 8, 13, 6, 5, 12, 7, 5
48...63	11, 12, 14, 15, 14, 15, 9, 8, 9, 14, 5, 6, 8, 6, 5, 12
64...79	9, 15, 5, 11, 6, 8, 13, 12, 5, 12, 13, 14, 11, 8, 5, 6
Right iterations	Values of s_r
0...15	8, 9, 9, 11, 13, 15, 15, 5, 7, 7, 8, 11, 14, 14, 12, 6
16...31	9, 13, 15, 7, 12, 8, 9, 11, 7, 7, 12, 7, 6, 15, 13, 11
32...47	9, 7, 15, 11, 8, 6, 6, 14, 12, 13, 5, 14, 13, 13, 7, 5
48...63	15, 5, 8, 11, 14, 14, 6, 14, 6, 9, 12, 9, 12, 5, 15, 8
64...79	8, 5, 12, 9, 12, 5, 14, 6, 8, 13, 6, 5, 15, 13, 11, 11

6.6.4 HAVAL

HAVAL stands for a one-way hashing algorithm with a variable length of output [547]. It compresses an arbitrarily long message into a digest of length either 128, 160, 192, 224, or 256 bits. HAVAL allows us to trade speed versus security by the optional number of passes: 3 (fast and least secure), 4 (moderate speed and security), and 5 (slowest and highly secure). HAVAL uses a 3-bit VERSION field which indicates the version number of HAVAL – the current number is 1. A 3-bit PASS field specifies the number of passes chosen by the user. A 10-bit FPTLEN field defines the requested length of the digest. A 64-bit MSGLEN field is used to store the length of the processed message.

Hashing starts from padding. A message is appended bit 1 followed by enough 0s so it becomes congruent 944 modulo 1024. An 80-bit string (VERSION, PASS,FPTLEN,MSGLEN) is appended to the padded message. The resulting message is a multiple of 1024 bits. The hashing proceeds in a block-by-block fashion (Fig. 6.15). The folding tailors the length of the digest to the requested one.

A 1024-bit message m is divided into 32 32-bit message blocks (words) so $m = (m_0, \ldots, m_{31})$. The general steps executed in HAVAL are depicted in Fig. 6.16. The addition modulo 2^{32} performed on corresponding words completes the process. Each pass H_1, H_2, H_3, H_4, and H_5 employs a Boolean function in seven variables. They are

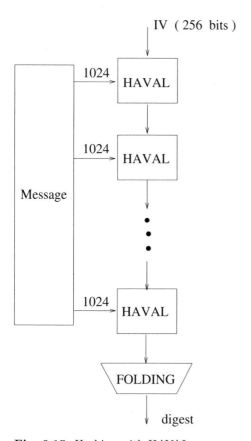

Fig. 6.15. Hashing with HAVAL

$$F_1(X_0, \ldots, X_6) = X_0 \oplus (X_0 \wedge X_1) \oplus (X_1 \wedge X_4) \oplus (X_2 \wedge X_5) \oplus (X_3 \wedge X_6),$$

$$F_2(X_0, \ldots, X_6) = X_0 \oplus (X_0 \wedge X_2) \oplus (X_1 \wedge X_2) \oplus (X_1 \wedge X_4)$$
$$\oplus (X_2 \wedge X_6) \oplus (X_3 \wedge X_5) \oplus (X_4 \wedge X_5)$$
$$\oplus (X_1 \wedge X_2 \wedge X_3) \oplus (X_2 \wedge X_4 \wedge X_5),$$

$$F_3(X_0, \ldots, X_6) = X_0 \oplus (X_0 \wedge X_3) \oplus (X_1 \wedge X_4) \oplus (X_2 \wedge X_5) \oplus (X_3 \wedge X_6)$$
$$\oplus (X_1 \wedge X_2 \wedge X_3),$$

$$F_4(X_0, \ldots, X_6) = X_0 \oplus (X_0 \wedge X_4) \oplus (X_1 \wedge X_4) \oplus (X_2 \wedge X_6) \oplus (X_3 \wedge X_4)$$
$$\oplus (X_3 \wedge X_5) \oplus (X_3 \wedge X_6) \oplus (X_4 \wedge X_5) \oplus (X_4 \wedge X_6)$$
$$\oplus (X_1 \wedge X_2 \wedge X_3) \oplus (X_2 \wedge X_4 \wedge X_5) \oplus (X_3 \wedge X_4 \wedge X_6),$$

$$F_5(X_0, \ldots, X_6) = X_0 \oplus (X_0 \wedge X_5) \oplus (X_1 \wedge X_4) \oplus (X_2 \wedge X_5) \oplus (X_3 \wedge X_6)$$
$$\oplus (X_0 \wedge X_1 \wedge X_2 \wedge X_3).$$

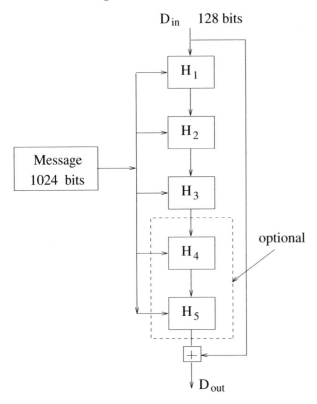

Fig. 6.16. General scheme of HAVAL

Table 6.1. Message word processing order

ord$_2$	5	14	26	18	11	28	7	16	0	23	20	22	1	10	4	8
	30	3	21	9	17	24	29	6	19	12	15	13	2	25	31	27
ord$_3$	19	9	4	20	28	17	8	22	29	14	25	12	24	30	16	26
	31	15	7	3	1	0	18	27	13	6	21	10	23	11	5	2
ord$_4$	24	4	0	14	2	7	28	23	26	6	30	20	18	25	19	3
	22	11	31	21	8	27	12	9	1	29	5	15	17	10	16	13
ord$_5$	27	3	21	26	17	11	20	29	19	0	12	7	13	8	31	10
	5	9	14	30	18	6	28	24	2	23	16	22	4	1	25	15

The Boolean functions chosen are balanced, highly nonlinear, linearly nonequivalent, and all satisfy SAC. For each pass, the message words $(m_0, \ldots, m_{31})$ enter the hashing iterations in a different order, given in Table 6.1. HAVAL uses ϕ permutations to modify functions F_1, F_2, F_3, F_4, and F_5. The aim of the modification is to create 3 "independent" variants of HAVAL depending on the chosen

Table 6.2. HAVAL ϕ permutations

	x_0 x_1 x_2 x_3 x_4 x_5 x_6
$\phi_{3,1}$	x_4 x_2 x_6 x_5 x_3 x_0 x_1
$\phi_{3,2}$	x_6 x_3 x_5 x_0 x_1 x_2 x_4
$\phi_{3,3}$	x_0 x_5 x_4 x_3 x_2 x_1 x_6
$\phi_{4,1}$	x_0 x_3 x_5 x_4 x_1 x_6 x_2
$\phi_{4,2}$	x_4 x_6 x_1 x_0 x_2 x_5 x_3
$\phi_{4,3}$	x_5 x_2 x_0 x_6 x_3 x_4 x_1
$\phi_{4,4}$	x_3 x_1 x_2 x_5 x_0 x_4 x_6
$\phi_{5,1}$	x_6 x_2 x_5 x_0 x_1 x_4 x_3
$\phi_{5,2}$	x_5 x_4 x_3 x_0 x_1 x_2 x_6
$\phi_{5,3}$	x_5 x_1 x_3 x_4 x_0 x_6 x_2
$\phi_{5,4}$	x_6 x_4 x_0 x_2 x_3 x_5 x_1
$\phi_{5,5}$	x_1 x_3 x_4 x_6 x_0 x_5 x_2

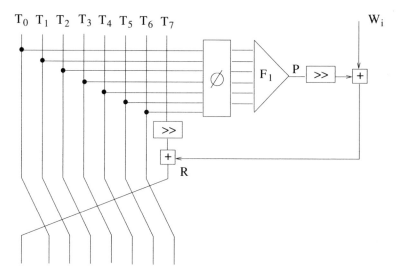

Fig. 6.17. A single pass in HAVAL

number of passes. The permutations are shown in Table 6.2. HAVAL uses the chaining vector $D = (D_0, \ldots, D_7) \in \Sigma^{256}$, where D_i is a 32-bit word. It applies 16 Feistel permutations in each pass.

Pass 1 (Fig. 6.17).

(1) Let $T_i = D_i$ $(i = 0, \ldots, 7)$.
(2) For $j = 0, \ldots, 15$:

$$P = \begin{cases} F_1 \circ \phi_{3,1}(T_0, T_1, T_2, T_3, T_4, T_5, T_6) & \text{if PASS=3,} \\ F_1 \circ \phi_{4,1}(T_0, T_1, T_2, T_3, T_4, T_5, T_6) & \text{if PASS=4,} \\ F_1 \circ \phi_{5,1}(T_0, T_1, T_2, T_3, T_4, T_5, T_6) & \text{if PASS=5,} \end{cases}$$

$$R = (P \gg 7) \boxplus (T_7 \gg 11) \boxplus m_j,$$

$$T_1 = T_0,\ T_2 = T_1,\ T_3 = T_2,\ T_4 = T_3,$$

$$T_5 = T_4,\ T_6 = T_5,\ T_7 = T_6,\ T_0 = R,$$

where $(A \gg s)$ means rotation of A by s positions to the right. The addition $\boxplus$ is modulo 2^{32}.

Pass 2.

(1) The sequence $T_0, \ldots, T_7$ comes from Pass 1.

(2) For $j = 0, \ldots, 15$, repeat the following:

$$P = \begin{cases} F_2 \circ \phi_{3,2}(T_0, T_1, T_2, T_3, T_4, T_5, T_6) & \text{if PASS=3,} \\ F_2 \circ \phi_{4,2}(T_0, T_1, T_2, T_3, T_4, T_5, T_6) & \text{if PASS=4,} \\ F_2 \circ \phi_{5,2}(T_0, T_1, T_2, T_3, T_4, T_5, T_6) & \text{if PASS=5,} \end{cases}$$

$$R = (P \gg 7) \boxplus (T_7 \gg 11) \boxplus m_{\mathrm{ord}_2(j)} \boxplus \pi_{2,j},$$

$$T_1 = T_0,\ T_2 = T_1,\ T_3 = T_2,\ T_4 = T_3,$$

$$T_5 = T_4,\ T_6 = T_5,\ T_7 = T_6,\ T_0 = R,$$

where $\pi = (\pi_{2,0}, \ldots \pi_{2,15})$ are constants generated from the fraction part of π and $m_{\mathrm{ord}_2(j)}$ is the message word defined by Table 6.1.

Pass 3.

(1) The sequence $T_0, \ldots, T_7$ comes from Pass 2.

(2) For $j = 0, \ldots, 15$, repeat the following:

$$P = \begin{cases} F_3 \circ \phi_{3,3}(T_0, T_1, T_2, T_3, T_4, T_5, T_6) & \text{if PASS=3,} \\ F_3 \circ \phi_{4,3}(T_0, T_1, T_2, T_3, T_4, T_5, T_6) & \text{if PASS=4,} \\ F_3 \circ \phi_{5,3}(T_0, T_1, T_2, T_3, T_4, T_5, T_6) & \text{if PASS=5,} \end{cases}$$

$$R = (P \gg 7) \boxplus (T_7 \gg 11) \boxplus m_{\mathrm{ord}_3(j)} \boxplus \pi_{3,j},$$

$$T_1 = T_0,\ T_2 = T_1,\ T_3 = T_2,\ T_4 = T_3,$$

$$T_5 = T_4,\ T_6 = T_5,\ T_7 = T_6,\ T_0 = R,$$

where $\pi = (\pi_{3,0}, \ldots \pi_{3,15})$ are constants generated from the fraction part of π and $m_{\mathrm{ord}_3(j)}$ is the message word defined by Table 6.1.

Pass 4.

(1) The sequence $T_0, \ldots, T_7$ comes from Pass 3.

(2) For $j = 0, \ldots, 15$, repeat the following:

$$P = \begin{cases} F_4 \circ \phi_{4,4}(T_0, T_1, T_2, T_3, T_4, T_5, T_6) & \text{if PASS=4,} \\ F_4 \circ \phi_{5,4}(T_0, T_1, T_2, T_3, T_4, T_5, T_6) & \text{if PASS=5,} \end{cases}$$

$$R = (P \gg 7) \boxplus (T_7 \gg 11) \boxplus m_{\text{ord}_4(j)} \boxplus \pi_{4,j},$$

$$T_1 = T_0, \ T_2 = T_1, \ T_3 = T_2, \ T_4 = T_3,$$

$$T_5 = T_4, \ T_6 = T_5, \ T_7 = T_6, \ T_0 = R,$$

where $\pi = (\pi_{4,0}, \ldots \pi_{4,15})$ are constants generated from the fraction part of π and $m_{\text{ord}_4(j)}$ is the message word defined by Table 6.1.

Pass 5.

(1) The sequence $T_0, \ldots, T_7$ comes from Pass 4.

(2) For $j = 0, \ldots, 15$, repeat the following:

$$P = F_5 \circ \phi_{5,5}(T_0, T_1, T_2, T_3, T_4, T_5, T_6),$$

$$R = (P \gg 7) \boxplus (T_7 \gg 11) \boxplus m_{\text{ord}_5(j)} \boxplus \pi_{5,j},$$

$$T_1 = T_0, \ T_2 = T_1, \ T_3 = T_2, \ T_4 = T_3,$$

$$T_5 = T_4, \ T_6 = T_5, \ T_7 = T_6, \ T_0 = R,$$

where $\pi = (\pi_{5,0}, \ldots \pi_{5,15})$ are constants generated from the fraction part of π and $m_{\text{ord}_5(j)}$ is the message word defined by Table 6.1.

After hashing, the sequence T is shortened to the requested length of digest (for details see [547]). HAVAL is believed to be stronger than MD5. A cryptanalysis of a reduced version of HAVAL can be found in [270].

6.6.5 Hashing Based on Intractable Problems

Gibson [199] based his hashing scheme on the factorization problem. Assume that an integer $N = p \times q$ where p and q are two large enough primes so the factoring N is intractable. Additionally $p - 1 = 2 \times p'$ and $q - 1 = 2 \times q'$ where p', q' are primes. The hashing function $h : \mathcal{Z}_N^* \times \mathcal{Z}_N^* \rightarrow \mathcal{Z}_N^*$ compresses the message m according to the congruence

$$h(m) = g^m \pmod{N}, \tag{6.12}$$

where g is a generator of the cyclic group $\mathcal{Z}_N^*$. The modulus N and the generator g are public. Note that if a collision can be found, then N can be factored. Let $m, m' \in \mathcal{Z}_N^* \times \mathcal{Z}_N^*$ collide, i.e., $g^m = g^{m'} \pmod{N}$ for $m \neq m'$. This implies that $g^{m-m'} = 1 \pmod{N}$ so $m - m'$ is a multiple of the order of the cyclic group $\mathcal{Z}_N^*$ and the factors can be found (see Sect. 4.2.4). On the other hand, knowing factors of N it is easy to produce collisions.

An example of hashing whose collision-freeness relies on intractability of the discrete logarithm problem was given by Chaum, van Heijst, and Pfitzmann in [92]. Assume we have a large enough prime $N \in \mathcal{Z}$ such that $N - 1 = 2 \times p$ (p is prime). The designer of the scheme chooses two primitive elements $g_1, g_2 \in \mathcal{Z}_N^*$ ($g_1 \neq g_2$). The hash function $h : \mathcal{Z}_p \times \mathcal{Z}_p \to \mathcal{Z}_N^*$ translates a message $m = (m_1, m_2)$ into its digest

$$h(m) = g_1^{m_1} \cdot g_2^{m_2} \pmod{N}. \tag{6.13}$$

The generators g_1, g_2 and the modulus N are public. It can be proved that if a collision is found, then the corresponding instance of discrete logarithm can be solved [496].

Knapsack can also be used for hashing. The first such scheme reported in [120] was broken in [74]. Impagliazzo and Naor proposed the scheme that is theoretically sound. The scheme is defined by $h : \Sigma^n \to \Sigma^\ell$ where obviously $\ell < n$. To design a scheme, n integers a_i ($i = 1, \ldots, n$) are chosen randomly and uniformly from the set $\{0, \ldots, 2^\ell\}$ where $\ell < n$. Next, for an n-bit message $m = (b_1, \ldots, b_n)$, a subset $\mathcal{S}_m = \{a_i \mid b_i = 1\}$ is created. The digest of m is:

$$h(m) = \sum_{a \in \mathcal{S}_m} a \pmod{2^\ell}. \tag{6.14}$$

Tillich and Zémor [507] designed a hash scheme based on $SL(2, 2^n)$ that is the group of two-dimensional unimodular matrices with entries in the Galois field $GF(2^n)$. In other words, elements of $SL(2, 2^n)$ are matrices

$$\begin{bmatrix} a & b \\ c & d \end{bmatrix}$$

whose determinant is equal to 1 and $a, b, c, d \in GF(2^n)$. The hash function h operates on arbitrarily long binary messages and returns an element of $SL(2, 2^n)$ so $h : \Sigma^* \to SL(2, 2^n)$. The core elements of the hash scheme are two public elements of $SL(2, 2^n)$, namely

$$A = \begin{bmatrix} x & 1 \\ 1 & 0 \end{bmatrix} \quad \text{and} \quad B = \begin{bmatrix} x & x+1 \\ 1 & 1 \end{bmatrix}.$$

An r-bit message $m = (b_1, \ldots, b_r)$ is first converted into the corresponding sequence of As and Bs according to the function $\pi : \Sigma \to \{A, B\}$, which takes 0 to A and 1 to B. The digest of m is

$$h(m) = \pi(b_1)\pi(b_2)\ldots\pi(b_r). \tag{6.15}$$

Finding collisions in the function h is equivalent to the difficulty of finding short factorizations in the groups $SL(2, 2^n)$, which is known to be intractable. To be collision free, the hash function has to be determined for n in the range 130–170. If $n < 130$, the security may be compromised. On the other hand, schemes with $n > 170$ become slow. To do computations in $GF(2^n)$, the modulus – an irreducible polynomial $p(x)$ (over $GF(2)$) of degree n – is chosen at random and made public.

It was shown in [83] that a careless selection of n or $p(x)$ can result in an instance of the scheme which is not collision free. The order of the group $SL(2, 2^n)$ is $2^{4n}(2^{2n} - 1)(2^{2n} + 1)$. The scheme is believed to be collision free if both $(2^{2n} - 1)$ and $(2^{2n} + 1)$ have very large factors only. Ideally, one would prefer to choose n such that the integers are twin primes. Incidentally, integers p, q are *twins* if $p - q = \pm 2$. There are no twin primes in the recommended range of n.

6.7 Keyed Hashing

A message authentication code (MAC) is a relative short string which is attached to a message to enable a receiver to decide whether the message comes from the original sender. Clearly, to perform this role, the MAC must match the message and the sender. As the message can be long and the MAC is relatively short, it must directly or indirectly employ hashing. Additionally, the pair of communicating parties is uniquely identified by a secret key shared by them. To produce or verify a MAC, the parties must know the message and the shared key. An adversary, on the other hand, knows the message only. Application of MACs allows us to create an authentication channel where the contents of messages are public but the message source can be verified (the sender must share the same secret key with the receiver). Other names for MAC include *integrity check value, cryptographic checksum,* or *authentication tag.*

Keyed hash schemes produce digests that depend on not only messages but also secret keys, which are shared between the sender and receiver. Consequently, hashing can be done only by the holders of the secret key.

Given a family of hash functions:

$$\bar{H}_n = \{h_k : \Sigma^* \rightarrow \Sigma^n \mid k \in \Sigma^n\}.$$

Any instance function h_k is indexed by a secret key k shared by two parties. A *keyed hash function* $H = \{\bar{H}_n \mid n \in \mathcal{N}\}$ is collision resistant if:

1. Any instance function h_k can be applied for messages of arbitrary length.
2. The function H is a *trapdoor one-way* function, that is:
   - Given a key k and message m, it is easy (in polynomial-time) to compute the digest $d = h_k(m)$.
   - For any polynomial-size collection of pairs $(m_i, d_i = h_k(m_i))$, $i = 1, \ldots, \ell(n)$, it is intractable to find the key $k \in \Sigma^n$, where $\ell(n)$ is a polynomial in n.
3. Without knowledge of k, it is computationally difficult to find a collision, that is, two distinct messages $m, m' \in \Sigma^*$ with the same digest $d = h_k(m) = h_k(m')$ (even if given a MAC oracle).

Hashing arbitrarily long messages can be done using either the serial or parallel methods (see Sect. 6.3). For a given n, the family of instance hash functions compresses $\ell \times n$-bit messages into an n-bit digest, so

$$H_n = \{h_k : \Sigma^{\ell \times n} \rightarrow \Sigma^n \mid k \in \Sigma^n\}.$$

Again, finding a collision for $h_k \in \bar{H}_n$ indicates that $h_k \in H_n$ is not collision resistant.

For an ideal collision-resistant keyed hashing scheme, finding a collision could be done by applying either the exhaustive search through the key space which takes on average 2^{n-1} operations, or by employing a variant of the birthday attack which takes $O(2^{n/2})$ steps.

6.7.1 Early MACs

First implementations of keyed hashing were based on encryption algorithms in CBC or CFB modes. An example of keyed hashing in CBC mode is given in Fig. 6.18. For a message $m = (m_1, \ldots, m_r)$, hashing involves r iterations and

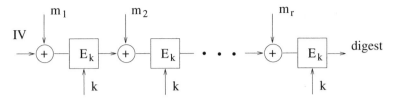

Fig. 6.18. Keyed hashing with CBC

$$h_0 = IV,$$
$$h_i = E_k(h_{i-1} \oplus m_i), \quad i = 1, \ldots, r - 1,$$
$$d = E_k(h_{r-1} \oplus m_r),$$

where IV is an initial value, E_k an encryption function, and d a digest.

The Message Authenticator Algorithm (MAA) is probably the first dedicated MAC which is also an ISO 8731-2 standard. MAA takes a message $m = (m_1, \ldots . m_\ell)$ (m_i is a 32-bit word) and a 64-bit key $k = (k_1, \ldots, k_8)$ and produces a 32-bit digest.

MAA algorithm – produces 32-bit digests.

Key expansion: Take the key k and create six 32-bit words (A, B, C, D, E, F).
Bytes 0x00 and 0xff in k are replaced according to

```
x=0;
for i from 1 to 8 {
        x=2x;
        if kᵢ=0x00 or 0xff then{
                        x=x+1;kᵢ=kᵢ OR x;}
}
```

The key bytes are clustered into 32-bit words. Let $k = (L, R)$ then

$$A = L^4 \pmod{2^{32} - 1} \oplus L^4 \pmod{2^{32} - 2};$$
$$B = (R^5 \pmod{2^{32} - 1} \oplus R^5 \pmod{2^{32} - 2})(1 + x)^2 \pmod{2^{32} - 2});$$
$$C = L^6 \pmod{2^{32} - 1} \oplus L^6 \pmod{2^{32} - 2};$$
$$D = R^7 \pmod{2^{32} - 1} \oplus R^7 \pmod{2^{32} - 2};$$
$$E = L^8 \pmod{2^{32} - 1} \oplus L^8 \pmod{2^{32} - 2};$$
$$F = R^9 \pmod{2^{32} - 1} \oplus R^9 \pmod{2^{32} - 2}.$$

The pairs (A, B), (C, D), and (E, F) are checked to see whether they contain
0x00 or 0xff. If so, they are replaced as shown above.

Message processing: Each block m_i of the message m is subject to the following
transformations

```
h=A; g=B; v=C;
for i from 1 to ℓ {
        v={v≪1}; u={v⊕E};
        t₁={h⊕mᵢ}×₁{{{g⊕mᵢ}+u} OR 0x02040801} AND 0xbfef7fdf};
        t₂={g⊕mᵢ}×₂{{{h⊕mᵢ}+u} OR 0x00804021} AND 0x7dfefbff};
        }
```

where $\times_i$ stands for multiplication modulo $(2^{32} - i)$, and $+$ is addition
modulo 2^{32}. The final result is $h = h \oplus g$.

6.7.2 MACs from Keyless Hashing

Keyless hashing, such as MD5, seems to be an attractive option for MAC generation. Tsudik [511] suggested to use a hashing algorithm which compresses
arbitrarily long messages into n-bit digests under the control of n-bit chaining
blocks, so $H : \Sigma^* \times \Sigma^n \to \Sigma^n$. The hash scheme H uses a hashing function
(such as MD5) $h : \Sigma^\ell \times \Sigma^n \to \Sigma^n$ applied in the serial method. H also pads
the message and appends the length so the resulting message is a multiple of ℓ.
For instance, in MD5 $\ell = 512$ and $n = 128$ bits. For a given message $m \in \Sigma^*$,
keyed hashing can be built on the top of H, using:

– Secret prefix $k \in \Sigma^\ell$. The digest is $d = H(k \parallel m)$.
– Secret suffix $k \in \Sigma^\ell$. The digest is $d = H(m \parallel k)$.
– Secret envelope $k_1, k_2 \in \Sigma^\ell$. The digest is $d = MD(k_1 \parallel m \parallel k_2)$.

Here $\parallel$ stands for concatenation. The secret prefix is equivalent to the keyless
hashing with a secret initial value. For both secret prefix and suffix, if the
underlying hash algorithm is not collision resistant, the keyed hashing scheme
is not collision resistant either [11].

Consider the secret prefix MAC. Let an attacker know a pair, the message
m and its MAC of the form $H(k \parallel m)$. Clearly, she can produce arbitrarily
many valid MACs for the message (m, m') with $H(k \parallel (m, m'))$ where m' is an
arbitrary message selected by the attacker. Even if the padding of the message

includes the length of the message, the security of MACs is determined by the collision resistance of the hash algorithm H rather than the length of the secret prefix.

Again, the security of the secret suffix MAC is determined by the length of the digest rather than by the length of the secret. The attacker knows the message m and the MAC of the form $H(m \parallel k)$. If the hash function is not collision resistant, then she may find second preimages for the chaining variables and produce the valid MAC for arbitrarily many messages.

The secret envelope offers a far smaller profit than expected from the length of the secret key material used in the scheme [415]. Having a message m and a secret $k = (k_p, k_s)$, the MAC is computed as $H(k_p \parallel m \parallel k_s)$. One would expect that the attack on the MAC should involve an exhaustive search of the keys space $\mathcal{K}^2$ if $k_s, k_s \in_R \mathcal{K}$. This is not true and now we show why.

Assume that an attacker can make enquires about the envelope MAC by composing her messages and collecting corresponding digests. The birthday paradox guarantees that if the attacker knows $O(2^{n/2})$ observations $\{(m, H(k_p \parallel m \parallel k_s); m \in \mathcal{M}\}$ where the set $|\mathcal{M}| \approx 2^{n/2}$, then there is at least one internal collision (n is the size of the digest). To identify the pair, the attacker:

- Composes messages (m', r, m''), $m = (m', m'') \in \mathcal{M}$, where r is a random message block, and asks for their MACs.
- Two messages $m_1, m_2 \in \mathcal{M}$ have internal collision if their $H(k_p \parallel m_1', r, m_1'' \parallel k_s) = H(k_p \parallel m_2', r, m_2'' \parallel k_s)$, where $m_i = (m_i', m_i'')$, for $i = 1, 2$.

Having two messages with internal collisions, the attacker now can exhaustively search the key space to identify k_p. If $|\mathcal{K}| = n$, then one pair of such messages is enough to identify k_p with a high probability. In other words, $k = k_p$ if

$$H(k \parallel m_1) = H(k \parallel m_2).$$

Having identified k_p, the second key k_s can be also exhaustively searched through. The overall complexity of the attack is $2^{n/2} + 2^n + 2^n$ which is much smaller than the expected 2^{2n}.

Note that keyed hashing should use the secret key repeatedly throughout the whole hashing process. The keyed hash scheme MDx-MAC [415] uses a modified secret envelope and applies secret keys every time the underlying hashing algorithm is called. MDx-MAC can be based on any hashing algorithm (such as MD4, MD5, HAVAL, or SHA) which uses internal constants (for example,

HAVAL uses π in all iterations in the passes 2, 3, 4, and 5). The secret key is added to the constant in each iteration of the underlying hash algorithm. The advantage of this scheme is that it can be collision free even if the underlying hash algorithm is not. The main drawback of MDx-MAC is its speed. It is always slower than its keyless underlying algorithm.

6.8 Problems and Exercises

1. Explain the difference between a strong and a weak one-way hash function.
2. Prove that the strong collision-freeness of a function implies that the function is one-way.
3. Consider the birthday paradox. Let p be the probability that there are at least two pupils with the same birthday. What is the minimum size of the class so
   - $p = 0.1$,
   - $p = 0.9$.
   What is the probability p when the class has 100 students?
4. To see how the birthday attack works, let us model a hashing function with a probabilistic algorithm. For a given message, the algorithm chooses at random its digest from the set $\mathcal{Z}_N$ where N is an integer. Implement the hash function using the accessible pseudorandom number generator. Prepare two collections of digests (one for the original message, the other for the bogus message). Each collection should have $\sqrt{N}$ random numbers. Run your program several times and count how many times it is possible to find colliding messages.
5. Let the encryption algorithm be based on exponentiation modulo a prime p so $E_k(m) = c^k \bmod p$. Use the algorithm to hash messages $(m_1, m_2) \in \mathcal{Z}_p^2$ according to the following:

   $$h_1 = E_{m_1}(IV) \text{ and } d = E_{m_2}(h_1).$$

   Implement the meet-in-the-middle attack on the scheme using the MAPLE programming environment. To generate variants of bogus messages use a pseudorandom number generator.
6. Suppose a hash function is defined using a good-quality encryption algorithm $E_k(m)$. For an arbitrary message $m = (m_1, \ldots, m_n)$, the digest is computed as $d = E_{m_1}(IV) \oplus \ldots \oplus E_{m_n}(IV)$. Discuss the advantages and drawbacks of the function.
7. In the Gibson scheme, the modulus $N = p \times q$ is public, while its factors are secret. The hashing function is defined as $h(m) = g^m \bmod N$ where g is a generator of the cyclic group $\mathcal{Z}_N^*$. Let $N = 4897$ and $g = 2231$. Compute digests for the following two messages: $m = 132748$ and $m' = 75676$. Assume that you have two colliding messages, show that it is possible to find factors of N. Demonstrate that the knowledge of factors of N allows us to find colliding messages.
8. Define a hash function $h(m_1, m_2) = g_1^{m_1} \times g_2^{m_2} \bmod p$ where p is a prime and $g_1, g_2 \in \mathcal{Z}_p^*$ are two primitive elements such that $\log_{g_1} g_2 \bmod p$ is not known. Assume that $p = 65867$, $g_1 = 11638$, and $g_2 = 22770$. Find digests of the following two messages:
   - $m = (33123, 11789)$,

$- m' = (55781, 9871)$.

Prove that finding collisions is equivalent to solving the corresponding instance of the discrete logarithm problem, i.e., $\alpha \equiv \log_{g_1} g_2 \bmod p$.

9. Consider the knapsack hashing that generates a digest

$$h(m) = \sum_{a \in S_m} a \pmod{2^\ell}$$

for $\ell = 16$ and the vector $A = (a_1, \ldots, a_{20}) = (38434, 29900, 51969, 11915, 44806, 40745, 58466, 34082, 51216, 29628, 45210, 37681, 13804, 57494, 13287, 43391, 28827, 6822, 51901, 3782)$. Produce the digest for $m = (1, 1, 1, 0, 0, 1, 0, 1, 1, 0, 0, 1, 0, 1, 0, 1, 0, 0, 0, 1)$. Write a program which finds collisions. Analyze the efficiency of your program.

10. Implement a hashing scheme based on $SL(2, 2^3)$ which operates on arbitrarily long messages and produces 12-bit digests (four binary polynomials of degree 2).

7 Digital Signatures

Digital signatures should be, in a sense, similar to hand-written ones. Unlike a written one, an electronic document is not tied to any particular storage media. Thus it can be easily copied, transmitted, and manipulated. Digital signatures have to create some sort of digital "encapsulation" for the document, so any interference with either its contents or the signature will be detected with a very high probability. Typically, a signed document must be verifiable by anyone using some publicly accessible information.

Most books on public-key cryptography also include a chapter or section on digital signatures. Stinson in [496], Menezes et al. in [337], and Schneier in [451] provide good texts for introductory reading. The book [401] by Pfitzmann is useful for more advanced study of digital signatures.

7.1 Properties of Digital Signatures

One would expect that digital signatures should be legally binding in the same way as the hand-written ones. To design a signature scheme, it is necessary to determine two algorithms: one for signing and the other for signature verification. The verification algorithm has to be accessible to all potential receivers. The signing algorithm is executed by a signer, Sally, who for a message $m \in \mathcal{M}$ determines a signature $s \in \mathcal{S}$. The signature s is next attached to the message. A verifier, Victor, takes the pair (m, s) and some public information about the alleged signer and performs the corresponding verification algorithm. The algorithm returns a binary result: OK if the signature is Sally's, or FAIL otherwise.

A *digital signature* scheme is a collection of two algorithms.

1. The signing algorithm $SG : \mathcal{K} \cdot \mathcal{M} \rightarrow \mathcal{S}$ assigns a signature s to a pair: the secret key $d \in \mathcal{K}$ of the signer and the message $m \in \mathcal{M}$, i.e., $s = SG(d, m) = SG_d(m)$. The signing algorithm can be also probabilistic.

2. The verification algorithm $VER : \mathcal{K}' \cdot \mathcal{M} \cdot \mathcal{S} \rightarrow \{\text{OK, FAIL}\}$ takes public information $e \in \mathcal{K}'$ of the signer and the message $m \in \mathcal{M}$ and checks whether the pair (e, m) matches the signature $s \in \mathcal{S}$. If there is a match the algorithm returns OK. Otherwise, it outputs FAIL.

3. The signing algorithm executes in polynomial-time when the secret key d is known. For an opponent, Oscar, who does not know the secret key, it should be computationally intractable to forge a signature, that is to find a valid signature for the message.

4. The verification algorithm is public – anyone can use it and check whether the message m matches the signature s. Verification should be easy (takes polynomial-time).

Clearly, a valid signature must pass the verification, or $VER(e, m, SG_d(m)) = $ OK, for any message m and the pair of keys (d, e).

The crucial issue for the security of the signature scheme is the meaning of forged signatures. Clearly, Oscar is successful in forging a signature if the verification algorithm fails to detect the forgery. The verification algorithm takes three variables: the identity of the alleged signer (equivalent to e), the message m, and the signature s. Oscar can tamper with all of them. Consider the identity of the alleged signer. Oscar can always apply the masquerade attack in which he selects the secret key $d \in \mathcal{K}$, sets up the scheme, and tries to register the scheme under Sally's name with the matching public $e \in \mathcal{K}'$. To protect the signature schemes against the masquerade attack, there has to be a trusted registry, PKI, which keeps the list of all signers with their public verification algorithms $VER_e()$ in the public read-only memory. New entries are included after a proper identification of the signer.

If the PKI is set up and works correctly, Oscar can only manipulate messages and signatures. His aim is to find collisions for the verification algorithm so $VER_e(m, s) = VER_e(m', s')$, where m, s are original elements and m', s' are forged $(m \neq m')$. Thus the verification algorithm has to be collision free for any $e \in \mathcal{K}'$. This implies that the signing algorithm has to be collision free too.

Note that the requirement about the public verifiability of signatures many times throughout their lifetime can be satisfied when signatures are generated using *conditionally secure* schemes.

Signature schemes are requested to provide a relatively short signature for a document of arbitrary length. We assume that the document (of arbitrary length) is first hashed, and later the signature is produced for its digest. Clearly, the hashing employed has to be collision free. Moreover, hashing and signing must be analyzed together to avoid attacks which exploit existing algebraic structures in both schemes. For instance, Coppersmith showed that hashing based on squaring together with an RSA-based signature scheme is not collision free [107].

7.2 Generic Signature Schemes

This class of signature schemes can be implemented from any one-way function. Historically, these schemes were first developed using private-key cryptosystems. We will follow the original notation. The applied one-way function is an encryption algorithm. The signer sets up her signature scheme by choosing a one-way function (encryption algorithm). Next she selects an index k (secret key) randomly and uniformly from the set $\mathcal{K}$. The index determines an instance of the one-way function, i.e., $E_k : \Sigma^n \to \Sigma^n$. Note that n has to be large enough to thwart possible birthday attacks. Also the index (secret key) k is known to the signer only.

7.2.1 Rabin Signatures

Rabin [423] designed a scheme in which the signer uses many secret keys (or indices) and later in the verification stage Sally reveals a part of her keys. In the Rabin scheme verification is done with the help of the signer.

Rabin signatures

Initialization: The scheme is set up by Sally who generates $2r$ random keys

$$k_1, k_2, \ldots, k_{2r} \in \Sigma^n.$$

They are secret and known to Sally only. Next, she creates two sequences which are needed in the verification stage. The first sequence is chosen at random:

$$S = (S_1, S_2, \ldots, S_{2r}),$$

where $S_i \in \Sigma^n$ for $i = 1, \ldots, 2r$. The second sequence

$$R = (R_1, R_2, \ldots, R_{2r})$$

consists of cryptograms of the sequence S, i.e.,

$$R_i = E_{k_i}(S_i) \quad \text{for} \quad i = 1, \ldots, 2r.$$

The sequences S and R are stored in the public registry.

Signing: For a message $m \in \Sigma^n$, Sally creates her signature as follows:

$$SG_k(m) = (E_{k_1}(m), \ldots, E_{k_{2r}}(m)). \tag{7.1}$$

Verification: Verifier selects at random a $2r$-bit sequence of r ones and r zeros. A copy of the binary sequence is forwarded to the signer. Using this $2r$-bit sequence, Sally forms an r-element subset of the keys. The key k_i belongs to the subset if the ith element of the $2r$-bit sequence is 1, $i = 1, \ldots, 2r$. The subset of keys is then communicated to Victor. To verify the key subset, Victor generates and compares suitable r cryptograms of S to the originals kept in the public registry.

7.2.2 Lamport Signatures

The scheme invented by Lamport [296] allows verification to be conducted without any help from the signer. This is what is expected from signature schemes. A more efficient version can be found in [50].

Lamport signatures

Initialization: The signer first chooses at random n key pairs, namely,

$$(k_{10}, k_{11}), (k_{20}, k_{21}), \ldots, (k_{n0}, k_{n1}), \tag{7.2}$$

each element $k_{ij} \in \Sigma^n$, $i = 1, \ldots, n$, $j = 0, 1$. The pairs of keys are kept secret and are known to Sally only. Next, she generates a sequence S at random and encrypts it using the secret keys, so

$$S = ((S_{10}, S_{11}), (S_{20}, S_{21}), \ldots, (S_{n0}, S_{n1})),$$
$$R = ((R_{10}, R_{11}), (R_{20}, R_{21}), \ldots, (R_{n0}, R_{n1})),$$

and

$$R_{ij} = E_{k_{ij}}(S_{ij}) \quad \text{for} \quad i = 1, \ldots, n \quad \text{and} \quad j = 0, 1,$$

where $S_{ij}, R_{ij} \in \Sigma^n$ and E_k is the encryption algorithm used. Now S and R are sent to the public registry.

Signing: The signature of an n-bit message $m = (b_1, \ldots, b_n)$, $b_i \in \{0,1\}$ for $i = 1, \ldots, n$ is a sequence of cryptographic keys:

$$SG_k(m) = (k_{1i_1}, k_{2i_2}, \ldots, k_{ni_n}),$$

where $i_j = 0$ if $b_j = 0$, otherwise $i_j = 1$, $j = 1, \ldots, n$.

Verification: Victor validates the signature $SG_k(m)$ by checking whether suitable pairs of S and R match each other for the known keys.

7.2.3 Matyas-Meyer Signatures

Matyas and Meyer [325] designed a signature scheme based on the DES algorithm. Clearly, any one-way function can be used in the scheme. In the description we use $E_k : \Sigma^n \to \Sigma^n$.

Matyas-Meyer signatures

Initialization: Sally first generates a random matrix $U = [u_{i,j}]$, $i = 1, \ldots, 30$, $j = 1, \ldots, 31$, and $u_{i,j} \in \Sigma^n$. Next she constructs a $31 \cdot 31$ matrix $KEY = [k_{i,j}]$, where $k_{i,j} \in \Sigma^n$. The first row of the KEY matrix is chosen at random but the others are generated as follows:

$$k_{i+1,j} = E_{k_{i,j}}(u_{i,j}),$$

for $i = 1, \ldots, 30$ and $j = 1, \ldots, 31$. Finally, Sally communicates the matrix U and the vector $(k_{31,1}, \ldots, k_{31,31})$ (the last row of KEY) to the public registry.

Signing: Sally takes a message $m \in \Sigma^n$ and computes cryptograms

$$c_i = E_{k_{31,i}}(m) \text{ for } i = 1, \ldots, 31.$$

Cryptograms are treated as integers and ordered according to their values, so $c_{i_1} < c_{i_2} < \ldots < c_{i_{31}}$. The signature of m is the sequence of keys

$$SG_k(m) = (k_{i_1,1}, k_{i_2,2}, \ldots, k_{i_{31},31}).$$

Verification: Victor takes the message m recreates the cryptograms c_i, orders them according to increasing order. Next he puts keys of the signature in the "empty" matrix KEY in the places indicated by the ordered sequence of c_is. Victor then repeats Sally's steps and computes all keys below the keys of the signature. He accepts the signature if the last row of KEY is identical to the row stored in the registry.

Note that the Lamport and Matyas-Meyer generic signature schemes can be verified many times. However, signing a new message requires the secret key(s) to be regenerated. This is why they are called *one-time* signatures.

7.3 RSA Signatures

Due to its algebraic structure, the RSA cryptosystem can be easily modified for signing documents [431]. It is enough to let Sally initialize the system. Again PKI keeps the public elements of Sally's RSA scheme.

One-time RSA signatures

Initialization: Sally chooses two strong primes p, q and calculates the modulus $N = p \cdot q$. Next she selects at random a public key $e \in \mathcal{Z}_N$ such that $gcd(e, N) = 1$. The secret key $d \in \mathcal{Z}_N$ satisfies the following congruence

$$e \cdot d \equiv 1 \bmod (p - 1)(q - 1).$$

The signer lodges both the modulus N and the key e with the PKI registry.

Signing: Given a message $m \in \mathcal{Z}_N$, Sally creates

$$s = SG_d(m) = m^d \pmod{N}.$$

The signature is attached to the message.

Verification: Victor looks up the PKI registry for Sally's public entry with her modulus N and public key e. Subsequently, he takes the pair $(\tilde{m}, \tilde{s})$ and checks whether

$$VER_e(\tilde{m}, \tilde{s}) = \left(\tilde{s}^e \stackrel{?}{\equiv} \tilde{m} \pmod{N} \right).$$

If the congruence is satisfied the signature is accepted as authentic.

An opponent, Oscar, can always circumvent potential verifiers using the following attack. He first selects at random a false signature $s' \in \mathcal{Z}_N$. Next he computes the matching false message $m' \equiv s'^e \pmod{N}$. This attack is always successful if there is no redundancy of the message source or all messages in $\mathcal{Z}_N$ are meaningful. The other feature of the attack is that Oscar has no control over forged messages. To protect against the attack, it is enough to introduce a sufficiently large redundancy in the message source so all forged messages will be meaningless with a high probability.

The RSA signature scheme may be subject to a variety of attacks that exploit the commutativity of exponentiation [129, 351] if the RSA signature scheme is meant to be used many times. Assume that Oscar knows two original documents (m_1, s_1) and (m_2, s_2) signed by Sally. He can sign a new document $m = m_1 m_2$ as its valid signature is $s = s_1 s_2$. Even the knowledge of a single document (m, s) signed by Sally can be used to sign message $m' = m^{-1}$ as its valid signature is $s' = s^{-1}$.

Multiple use of the RSA scheme tends to weaken it. The way out is to make subsequent signatures dependent on those previously generated. Cramer and Damgård [113] proposed an RSA scheme for multiple use which is secure against chosen message attacks under the assumption that the factoring is difficult. An additional component is needed to keep track of previous signatures. This component is an algorithm TR that builds up a full ℓ-ary tree of depth d by random selection of its nodes x_i. The root of the tree is an integer x_0. Every time Sally wants to sign a new message, she invokes TR. The algorithm creates a new leaf x_α and returns its full path $(x_1, i_1, \ldots, x_\alpha, i_\alpha)$, where the integer i_j tells us that the node x_j is the i_jth child of x_{j-1}. TR can be used to sign up to ℓ^α messages.

Multiple RSA signatures

Initialization: The scheme is set up as previously; the modulus is $N = p \cdot q$ where p, q are two strong primes. The scheme uses also a set of distinct primes

$$L = \{q, p_0, \ldots, p_{\ell-1}\}.$$

All primes are coprime to $(p-1)(q-1)$. Let β be the smallest integer such that

$$w = q^\beta > N,$$

and β_i be the smallest integer such that

$$v_i = p_i^{\beta_i} > N \text{ for } i = 0, \ldots, \ell - 1.$$

Finally, Sally chooses h and x_0 at random from $\mathcal{Z}_N^*$. The triple (N, h, x_0) is stored in the public registry. Public keys are w and v_{i_j} while their secret versions are w^{-1} and $v_{i_j}^{-1}$. Clearly, the following congruences hold: $w^{-1} \cdot w \equiv 1 \bmod (p-1)(q-1)$, and $v_{i_j}^{-1} \cdot v_{i_j} \equiv 1 \bmod (p-1)(q-1)$.

Signing: The signature generation can be done up to ℓ^α times. For the ith signature, Sally calls $TR(i)$ which returns $(x_1, i_1, \ldots, x_\alpha, i_\alpha)$. Next, she computes

$$y_j \equiv (x_{j-1} h^{x_j})^{v_{ij}^{-1}} \pmod{N} \text{ for } j = 1, \ldots, \alpha. \tag{7.3}$$

and

$$z \equiv (x_\alpha h^m)^{w^{-1}} \pmod{N}. \tag{7.4}$$

Finally, the signature is $SG_{w,v}(m) = (z, y_1, i_1, \ldots, y_\alpha, i_\alpha)$.

Verification: Victor takes $(\tilde{z}, \tilde{y}_1, i_1, \ldots, \tilde{y}_\alpha, i_\alpha)$ and first calculates

$$\tilde{x}_\alpha \equiv \tilde{z}^w h^{-m} \pmod{N}, \tag{7.5}$$

and then goes backwards,

$$\tilde{x}_{j-1} \equiv \tilde{y}_j^{v_{ij}} h^{-\tilde{x}_j} \pmod{N} \text{ for } j = 1, \ldots, \alpha. \tag{7.6}$$

At last, if $\tilde{x}_0 \equiv x_0 \pmod{N}$ the signature is authentic.

Consider (7.3) and (7.4). To get rid of commutativity, the message appears as an exponent and a sequence of random elements x_j is used. Each element plays a double role as a multiplier and exponent.

Victor reverses Sally's computations using public w and v_{ij}. If the signature is authentic, he must always end up with x_0 in the last step of his computations. Victor can also update his copy of the tree from TR. Note that any two valid signatures never traverse through the same path in the tree.

7.4 ElGamal Signatures

The scheme is based on the discrete logarithm problem [163].

ElGamal signatures

Initialization: Sally chooses a finite field $GF(p)$ where p is a long enough prime so that the corresponding instance of a discrete logarithm is intractable. She selects a primitive element $g \in \mathcal{Z}_p^*$ and a random integer $k \in \mathcal{Z}_p^*$. Sally then computes the public key

$$g^k \pmod{p}, \tag{7.7}$$

and communicates g^k, g and p to the public registry. The element k is kept secret.

Signing: For a message $m \in GF(p)$, Sally selects a random integer $r \in \mathcal{Z}_p^*$ such that $gcd(r, p-1) = 1$ and calculates

$$x \equiv g^r \pmod{p}. \tag{7.8}$$

Later, she solves the following congruence

$$m \equiv k \cdot x + r \cdot y \pmod{p-1} \tag{7.9}$$

for y using Euclid's algorithm. The signature is

$$s = SG_k(m) = (x, y).$$

Note that k and r are kept secret by Sally.

Verification: Upon reception of $\tilde{m}$ and $\tilde{s} = (\tilde{x}, \tilde{y})$, Victor checks whether

$$VER(\tilde{m}, \tilde{s}) = \left(g^{\tilde{m}} \stackrel{?}{\equiv} (g^k)^{\tilde{x}} \cdot \tilde{x}^{\tilde{y}} \pmod{p} \right). \tag{7.10}$$

It is worth noting that possessing the pair (x, y), does not allow the message m to be recreated. In fact, there are many pairs that match the message. For every random pair (k, r), there is a pair (x, y).

Oscar may:

1. Try to break the system by solving two instances of discrete logarithm: $k = \log g^k \pmod{p}$ and $r = \log x \pmod{p}$. From our assumption, this is intractable.

2. Choose his own forged message m' and modify y' while keeping x unchanged. This is equivalent to solving the following instance of discrete logarithm $y' \equiv \log_x g^{m'} (g^k)^{-x} \pmod{p}$.

3. Take a forged message m' and try to find x' while keeping the same y. In this attack Oscar has to solve $g^{m'} \equiv (g^k)^{x'} \cdot x'^y \pmod{p}$ for x'. There is no known efficient algorithm to do that.

4. Manipulate with all three elements: m', x', y'. The successful verification is when $g^{m'} \equiv (g^k)^{x'} \cdot x'^{y'} \bmod p$. The congruence can be satisfied if we select $x' \equiv g^\alpha (g^k)^\beta$ as we are going to get powers of g and (g^k) only $(\alpha, \beta \in \mathcal{Z}_p)$. Indeed

$$g^{m'} \equiv (g^k)^{g^\alpha (g^k)^\beta} \cdot g^{\alpha y'} (g^k)^{\beta y'} \pmod{p}.$$

This implies that $y' \equiv -g^\alpha k^\beta \beta^{-1} \pmod{p-1}$ and $m' \equiv \alpha y' \pmod{p-1}$. Clearly, this attack allows us to sign random messages only. To prevent the attack, it is enough to introduce redundancy in the message source.

The elements (g^k, g, p) stored in the public registry are fixed for the lifetime of the scheme. The scheme can be used to sign many signatures. The signer, however, has to select a new secret integer $r \in Z_p^*$ every time she signs. What happens if Sally signs two messages using the same r? Let us consider the repercussions. Suppose Sally has signed two messages: m_1 with (x, y_1) and m_2 with (x, y_2). The two signatures produce (Congruence (7.9)):

$$m_1 \equiv k \cdot x + r \cdot y_1 \pmod{p - 1},$$
$$m_2 \equiv k \cdot x + r \cdot y_2 \pmod{p - 1}.$$

The integer r which was supposed to be secret can now be computed from

$$m_1 - m_2 \equiv r(y_1 - y_2) \pmod{p - 1}$$

(Sect. 2.1.4). If the congruence does not have a unique solution, it can be found by testing possible candidates and calling the verification algorithm. After finding r, it is easy to compute the secret

$$k = (m_1 - ry_1)x^{-1} \pmod{p - 1}.$$

Consider a simple example of the ElGamal signature scheme. First Sally sets up the scheme. She selects a modulus $p = 359$, a random secret $k = 215$, and a primitive element $g = 152$. She computes $g^k = 152^{215} \equiv 293 \pmod{359}$. The triple $(g^k, g, p) = (293, 152, 359)$ is Sally's public registry entry. To sign a message $m = 312$, Sally selects a "one-time" random integer $r = 175$, finds $x = g^r = 152^{175} \equiv 58 \pmod{359}$, and computes y from the following congruence:

$$m \equiv k \cdot x + r \cdot y \pmod{p - 1},$$
$$312 \equiv 215 \cdot 58 + 175 \cdot y \pmod{358}.$$

It is easy to check that $y = 86$. The signature on $m = 312$ is $s = (58, 86)$. Knowing Sally's public elements, Victor verifies the signature by computing first $g^m \equiv 74 \pmod{359}$ and next $(g^k)^x \cdot x^y \equiv 74 \pmod{359}$. So Victor assumes that the signature is authentic.

A modification of the ElGamal signature was proposed as the Digital Signature Standard (DSS) in 1991 [186]. DSS is also known as the Digital Signature Algorithm or DSA.

Digital Signature Standard

Initialization: A large enough prime p is selected as one of the moduli used in the system. The modulus p is recommended to be of length at least 512 bits. The second modulus q is a 160-bit prime factor of $p - 1$. An integer g is a qth root of 1 modulo p, i.e., $g^q \equiv 1 \pmod{p}$ and $g^\alpha \not\equiv 1 \pmod{p}$ for $\alpha < q$. Sally selects her secret $k < q$ and computes the public key $g^k \pmod{p}$. The sequence (g^k, g, p, q) is deposited in the public registry.

Signing: Sally generates a one-time random integer $r < q$ and the corresponding $x \equiv (g^r \bmod p) \bmod q$. For a message $m \in \mathcal{Z}_q^*$, she computes

$$y \equiv r^{-1}(m + k \cdot x) \pmod{q}. \tag{7.11}$$

The signature on the message m is $s = SG_k(m) = (x, y)$.

Verification: Victor takes the signature $\tilde{s} = (\tilde{x}, \tilde{y})$, the message $\tilde{m}$, and Sally's public entry and computes two integers

$$\alpha \equiv \tilde{m} \cdot \tilde{y}^{-1} \pmod{q},$$
$$\beta \equiv \tilde{x} \cdot \tilde{y}^{-1} \pmod{q},$$

and checks whether

$$VER(\tilde{m}, \tilde{s}) = \left(\tilde{x} \stackrel{?}{\equiv} (g^\alpha \cdot (g^k)^\beta \bmod p) \bmod q \right). \tag{7.12}$$

Consider a toy DSS scheme. Sally takes two moduli $p = 2011$ and $q = 67$ ($p - 1 = 67 \cdot 30$). To get an integer g with the required properties, we first choose a primitive element $e = 1570 \in GF(p)$ and next compute $g \equiv e^{(p-1)/q} \pmod{p}$, so $g = 1570^{30} \equiv 948 \pmod{2011}$. It is easy to check that $g^q \equiv 1 \pmod{p}$. Next Sally chooses her secret $k = 37 < 67$ and computes $g^k = 948^{37} \equiv 857 \pmod{2011}$. Sally's public entry is $(g^k, g, p, q) = (857, 948, 2011, 67)$.

To sign, Sally generates a one-time random integer $r = 49 < 67$ and computes

$$x = 60 \equiv (948^{49} \bmod 2011) \bmod 67.$$

For a message $m = 65$, she finds $y = 49^{-1}(65 + 37 \cdot 60) \equiv 48 \pmod{67}$. The signature $SG_k(65) = (60, 48)$.

Victor verifies the signature $s = (60, 48)$ by calculating

$$\alpha = 65 \cdot 48^{-1} \equiv 53 \pmod{67},$$
$$\beta = 60 \cdot 48^{-1} \equiv 18 \pmod{67}.$$

Finally he substitutes values into $g^{\alpha} \cdot (g^k)^{\beta} = 948^{53} 857^{18} \equiv 462 \pmod{2011}$. This result is congruent to 60 modulo 67. Thus the result is equal to $x = 60$, so the signature is authentic.

DSS signatures are shorter than ElGamals. Also messages signed have to be smaller than q. Otherwise, if $m \in \mathbb{Z}_p^*$, any valid signature $SG_k(m) = (x, y)$ can be used to produce a sequence of other valid signatures for messages from the set $\{\tilde{m} \mid \tilde{m} \equiv m \pmod{q}; \tilde{m} < p\}$. Generation of signatures using DSS is substantially faster than using RSA (when both schemes use moduli of the same size). Additionally, the first element of signature x can be precomputed as it does not depend upon the message signed [451].

7.5 Blind Signatures

Sometimes the signer should be prevented from reading messages to be signed. For instance, in a notary system the validation of documents can be done for documents kept in sealed envelopes. Electronic election protocols use a central authority which authenticates voting ballots without being able to read their contents. Chaum developed a cryptographic scheme which can be applied to produce blind signatures [87]. There are three active parties in the scheme. Sally is the signer who has agreed to sign documents blindly. Henry is the holder of the message he wants Sally to sign. Victor is our verifier who checks whether the signature is Sally's.

A blind signature scheme works as follows: Henry takes a message and blinds it. The blinded message is sent to Sally who signs it and sends it back to Henry. Henry unblinds the message. Victor now can verify the signature. A blind signature is a collection of four algorithms: blinding, signing, unblinding, and verifying. Note that blinding and signing operations have to commute. The RSA signature can be used to design a blind signature scheme.

RSA blind signatures

Initialization: Sally sets up an RSA scheme with the public modulus N and the public key e. Primes p, q ($N = p \cdot q$) and key d ($e \cdot d \equiv 1 \bmod (p-1)(q-1)$) are secret.

Blinding: Henry looks up the public registry for Sally's N and e, chooses a random integer $r \in \mathbb{Z}_N^*$, takes his message $m \in \mathbb{Z}_N^*$, and computes the blinded message

$$c \equiv m \cdot r^e \quad (\bmod N).$$

Signing: Sally simply signs the blinded message c as

$$\check{s} = SG_d(c) \equiv c^d \quad (\bmod N).$$

The blind signature $\check{s}$ is sent to Henry.

Unblinding: Henry removes the random integer r using

$$s = SG_d(m) = c \cdot r^{-1} \equiv m^d \quad (\bmod N),$$

and gets Sally's signature.

Verification: Victor takes Sally's public information (N, e), the message $\tilde{m}$, and the signature $\tilde{s}$ and checks whether

$$VER_e(\tilde{m}, \tilde{s}) = \left(\tilde{s}^e \overset{?}{\equiv} \tilde{m} \quad (\bmod N) \right).$$

In applications where messages are long, Harry asks Sally to sign blindly the digest of a message generated from a collision-resistant hash function instead of the message.

7.6 Undeniable Signatures

Chaum and van Antwerpen [89] introduced undeniable signatures. Their main feature is that Victor cannot verify a signature without Sally's cooperation. The cooperation takes the form of a challenge-response interaction. Victor sends a challenge to Sally. Sally answers with her response. Victor takes Sally's response and verifies the signature. If the signature is authentic the process ends.

What happens if the verification fails? There are two possibilities: first, the signature is indeed a fraud, or, second, Sally cheats by giving an "incorrect" response. To eliminate the second case, undeniable signatures have to have a *disavowal protocol* that is run only after verification failures.

Chaum-van Antwerpen signatures

Initialization: The security of the scheme is based on the intractability of the discrete logarithm. Sally selects a large prime modulus p such that $p-1 = 2q$ where q is prime. She also takes an element g which generates the cyclic group G of order q. Next she chooses at random her secret k ($0 < k < q$) and computes the public key g^k (mod p). The triple (g^k, g, p) is Sally's entry stored in the public registry.

Signing: For a message $m \in G$, Sally computes

$$s = SG_k(m) \equiv m^k \quad (\text{mod } p).$$

Verification: Victor and Sally interact, going through the steps given below.

Challenge: Victor selects two random integers $a, b \in \mathcal{Z}_q^*$ and sends the challenge

$$c = s^a (g^k)^b \quad (\text{mod } p)$$

to Sally.

Response: Sally computes k^{-1} ($k \cdot k^{-1} \equiv 1$ (mod q)) and sends back

$$r = c^{k^{-1}} \equiv m^a \cdot g^b \quad (\text{mod } p)$$

to Victor.

Test: Victor checks whether

$$VER(\tilde{m}, \tilde{r}) = \left(\tilde{r} \stackrel{?}{\equiv} \tilde{m}^a g^b \quad (\text{mod } p) \right).$$

If the test fails, Victor runs the disavowal protocol. Otherwise, the signature is accepted.

Disavowal protocol: The protocol is executed only when verification fails.

V→S: Victor selects randomly two $a_1, b_1 \in \mathcal{Z}_q^*$ and sends $c_1 \equiv s^{a_1} (g^k)^{b_1}$ (mod p).

S→V: Sally replies by sending $r_1 = c_1^{k^{-1}}$.

Test: Victor checks whether $r_1 \neq m^{a_1} g^{b_1}$ (mod p). If that is the case, the same process is repeated.

V→S: Victor selects randomly two $a_2, b_2 \in \mathcal{Z}_q^*$ and sends $c_2 \equiv s^{a_2} (g^k)^{b_2}$ (mod p).

S→V: Sally replies by sending $r_2 = c_2^{k^{-1}}$.

Test: Victor checks whether $r_2 \not\equiv m^{a_2}g^{b_2}$ (mod p). He concludes that the
signature is a forgery if
$$(r_1 g^{-b_1})^{a_2} \equiv (r_2 g^{-b_2})^{a_1} \pmod{p}.$$
Otherwise, Sally cheats by giving inconsistent responses.

After signing the message, Sally may have second thoughts and try to modify
either the message or the signature. The next theorem characterizes her chances
of success.

Theorem 27. *If $s \not\equiv m^k$ (mod p), then Sally can provide a valid response
with the probability q^{-1}.*

Proof. We start from an observation that any two pairs (a,b), (a',b'), where
$a \not\equiv a'$ (mod q) or $b \not\equiv b'$ (mod q), create different challenges c and c'. This
statement can be proved by contradiction. Assume that $c \equiv c'$ (mod p). This
implies that $s^a(g^k)^b \equiv s^{a'}(g^k)^{b'}$ (mod p) or $s^{a-a'} \equiv (g^k)^{b'-b}$ (mod p). If we
represent $s = g^\alpha$ and $g^k = g^\beta$, then

$$g^{\alpha(a-a')} \equiv g^{\beta(b'-b)} \pmod{p}$$

and

$$\alpha(a - a') \equiv \beta(b' - b) \pmod{q}.$$

So the above congruence is satisfied if $a \equiv a'$ (mod q) and $b \equiv b'$ (mod q).
This is the requested contradiction.

For the challenge $c \equiv s^a(g^r)^b$ (mod p), Sally has to reply with her response
$r \equiv m^a g^b$ (mod p). Because $s \not\equiv m^k$ (mod p) she cannot use c to produce
the response according to the algorithm. As Sally does not know (a,b), and for
any possible choice of (a,b) the response is different, her best strategy would
be to select a random $x = 0,\ldots,q-1$ and try to send $r \equiv g^x$ (mod p) with
the probability of success q^{-1}. □

Consider the case when Sally follows the algorithm but the signature is a
forgery, that is $s \not\equiv m^k$ (mod p).

Theorem 28. *Let Sally follow the disavowal algorithm, then the following congruence is satisfied*

$$(r_1 g^{-b_1})^{a_2} \equiv (r_2 g^{-b_2})^{a_1} \pmod{p}.$$

Proof. Sally follows the algorithm and for Victor's challenges $c_1 \equiv s^{a_1}(g^k)^{b_1}$ (mod p) and $c_2 \equiv s^{a_2}(g^k)^{b_2}$ (mod p) replies with

$$r_1 \equiv s^{a_1 k^{-1}} g^{b_1} \pmod{p}, \text{ and}$$
$$r_2 \equiv s^{a_2 k^{-1}} g^{b_2} \pmod{p},$$

respectively. After simple transformations we get

$$s^{a_1 k^{-1}} \equiv r_1 g^{-b_1} \pmod{p},$$
$$s^{a_2 k^{-1}} \equiv r_2 g^{-b_2} \pmod{p}.$$

Now if we raise the sides of the first congruence to the power a_2 and the second congruence to the power a_1, we obtain the requested result.   □

Clearly, when Sally cheats by giving an invalid response she may succeed with the probability q^{-1}. So with the probability $(1 - q^{-1})$ she fails and Victor will run the disavowal protocol.

Theorem 29. *Let Sally give responses inconsistent with the algorithm, then Victor will detect the lack of consistency with the probability $(1-q^{-1})$ by running the disavowal protocol.*

Proof. It is enough to note that the first inconsistent response forces Sally to guess the unknown pair of (a_2, b_2) in the second response. Using Theorem 27 the result follows.   □

Consider an example. Sally initializes the scheme by choosing the modulus $p = 983$ with $q = 491$. The primitive element of $GF(983)$ is $e = 7$. This element gives a requested $g = e^{(p-1)/q} = 7^2 = 49$. Finally, Sally randomly selects $k = 375 < 491$, calculates the public key $g^k = 49^{375} \equiv 100$ (mod 983), and puts the triple $(g^k, g, p) = (100, 49, 983)$ into the public registry. To sign, Sally takes her message $m = 413$ and computes $s = SG_k(m) = 413^{375} \equiv 349$ (mod 983). The pair (m, s) is published. To verify the signature, Victor picks up two random numbers $a = 119$ and $b = 227$ smaller than 491 and prepares his challenge $c = s^a(g^k)^b = 349^{119}375^{227} \equiv 884$ (mod 983). Sally follows the algorithm and replies with $r = c^{k^{-1}} = 884^{182} \equiv 32$ (mod 983), where $k^{-1} = 182$. Victor computes $m^a g^b = 413^{119}49^{227} \equiv 32$ (mod 983) which matches Sally's response. The signature is authentic.

7.7 Fail-Stop Signatures

The concept was introduced by Pfitzmann and Waidner in [402]. Fail-stop signatures allow us to protect the signatures against an opponent with unlimited computational power. The trick is that the signature is produced by a signer who has a single secret key. There are, however, many other keys which can be used to produce the same signature and match the public key. Thus there is a high probability that the key computed or guessed by a powerful Oscar will be different from the one held by Sally.

Let x be a secret key known to Sally only and K be the public key. Then Sally's signature is $s = SG_x(m)$ for the message m. A fail-stop signature must satisfy the following conditions:

1. An opponent with unlimited power can forge the signature with a negligible probability. More precisely, if Oscar knows the pair $(s = SG_x(m), m)$ and Sally's public key K, he can create a collection of all keys $\mathcal{K}_{s,m}$ such that $x^* \in \mathcal{K}_{s,m}$ iff $s = SG_{x^*}(m) = SG_x(m)$. The size of $\mathcal{K}_{s,m}$ has to be exponential with the security parameter n. As Oscar does not know the secret x, he may only guess an element from $\mathcal{K}_{s,m}$. Let this element be x^*. Now if Oscar signs another message $m^* \neq m$, it is required that $s^* = SG_{x^*}(m^*) \neq SG_x(m^*)$ with an overwhelming probability.
2. There is a polynomial-time algorithm which, for the input of: a secret key x, a public key K, a message m, a valid signature s, and a forged signature s^*, returns a proof of forgery.
3. Sally with polynomially bounded computing power cannot construct a valid signature which she can later deny by proving it to be a forgery.

Clearly, after Sally has provided a proof of forgery, the scheme is considered to be compromised and is no longer used. That is why it is called "fail-stop."

We are going to discuss a scheme invented by van Heyst and Pedersen [239]. Their scheme can be used to sign a single message and verify the signature many times.

---

van Heyst-Pedersen signature

Initialization: The security of the scheme is based on the intractability of the discrete logarithm. This stage is done jointly by a trusted third party (TTP) and the signer (Sally). The TTP chooses a prime modulus p $(p - 1 = 2q$

where q is prime), an element $g \in \mathcal{Z}_p$ of order q, and a random integer $r \in \mathcal{Z}_q^*$. Next it computes $R = g^r$ and sends (p, q, g, R) to Sally while r is kept secret by the TTP.

Sally chooses at random $x = (a_1, a_2, b_1, b_2) \in \mathcal{Z}_q^5$ and computes:

$$R \equiv g^r \pmod{p},$$
$$A \equiv g^{a_1} R^{a_2} \pmod{p},$$
$$B \equiv g^{b_1} R^{b_2} \pmod{p}.$$

Next she sends $K = (g, p, R, A, B)$ to the public registry while x is kept secret by Sally.

Signing: For a message m, Sally produces

$$s = SG_x(m) = (\beta_1, \beta_2),$$

where $\beta_1 \equiv a_1 + mb_1 \pmod{q}$ and $\beta_2 \equiv a_2 + mb_2 \pmod{q}$.

Verification: Victor takes the signature $\tilde{s} = (\tilde{\beta}_1, \tilde{\beta}_2)$, message $\tilde{m}$, and the public key K and checks whether

$$VERK(\tilde{m}, \tilde{s}) = \left(AB^{\tilde{m}} \stackrel{?}{\equiv} g^{\tilde{\beta}_1} R^{\tilde{\beta}_2} \pmod{p} \right).$$

Proof of forgery: Sally gets a forged signature $s' = (\beta_1', \beta_2')$ on message m. Then she computes

$$PROOF(s') \equiv (\beta_1 - \beta_1')(\beta_2' - \beta_2)^{-1} \pmod{q},$$

where $s = (\beta_1, \beta_2)$ is the original signature for m. After the proof is generated the scheme is no longer used.

Theorem 30. *Let Oscar have an unlimited computational power. Then public information $K = (g, p, R, A, B)$ and the signature $s = (\beta_1, \beta_2)$ on a message m gives a system of four linear equations with q possible solutions for (a_1, a_2, b_1, b_2).*

Proof. Denote $A = g^{e_1}$ and $B = g^{e_2}$, so

$$g^{e_1} \equiv g^{a_1} g^{ra_2} \pmod{p},$$
$$g^{e_2} \equiv g^{b_1} g^{rb_2} \pmod{p},$$

which gives the first two congruences in the system:

$$e_1 \equiv a_1 + r a_2 \pmod q,$$

$$e_2 \equiv b_1 + r b_2 \pmod q,$$

$$\beta_1 \equiv a_1 + m b_1 \pmod q,$$

$$\beta_2 \equiv a_2 + m b_2 \pmod q.$$

The system can be rewritten as

$$
\begin{bmatrix} e_1 \\ e_2 \\ \beta_1 \\ \beta_2 \end{bmatrix}
=
\begin{bmatrix} 1 & r & 0 & 0 \\ 0 & 0 & 1 & r \\ 1 & 0 & m & 0 \\ 0 & 1 & 0 & m \end{bmatrix}
\begin{bmatrix} a_1 \\ a_2 \\ b_1 \\ b_2 \end{bmatrix}.
$$

Clearly, Oscar knows r as he has unlimited power and can solve the corresponding discrete logarithm instance. The coefficient matrix in the system has rank three – this means that Oscar deals with q possible solutions.   □

Theorem 31. *Let* $s = (\beta_1, \beta_2)$ *be a signature on* m *and* $s' = (\beta_1', \beta_2')$ *on a message* m' *(*$m \neq m'$*). Then there is a single solution for* (a_1, a_2, b_1, b_2).

Proof. As before we can get the following system of linear equations over $GF(q)$:

$$
\begin{bmatrix} e_1 \\ e_2 \\ \beta_1 \\ \beta_2 \\ \beta_1' \\ \beta_2' \end{bmatrix}
=
\begin{bmatrix} 1 & r & 0 & 0 \\ 0 & 0 & 1 & r \\ 1 & 0 & m & 0 \\ 0 & 1 & 0 & m \\ 1 & 0 & m' & 0 \\ 0 & 1 & 0 & m' \end{bmatrix}
\cdot
\begin{bmatrix} a_1 \\ a_2 \\ b_1 \\ b_2 \end{bmatrix}.
$$

This time the coefficient matrix has rank 4 and the system has a single solution.
□

Theorem 32. *Let Sally get a forged signature* $s' = (\beta_1', \beta_2')$ *on the message* m *which passes the verification test* $A B^m \equiv g^{\beta_1'} R^{\beta_2'}$ *but* $s' \neq s = S G_x(m)$, *then she can compute* $r = \log_g R$.

Proof. The forged signature s' passes the test

$$A B^m \equiv g^{\beta_1'} R^{\beta_2'} \pmod p,$$

but also the original signature

$$A B^m \equiv g^{\beta_1} R^{\beta_2} \pmod p,$$

so $g^{\beta'_1} R^{\beta'_2} \equiv g^{\beta_1} R^{\beta_2}$ (mod p), which translates to

$$g^{\beta_1 - \beta'_1} \equiv R^{\beta'_2 - \beta_2} \pmod{p}.$$

Note that $\beta_1 - \beta'_1 \not\equiv 0$ (mod q) and $\beta'_2 - \beta_2 \not\equiv 0$ (mod q). This implies that

$$r = \log_g R \equiv (\beta_1 - \beta'_1)(\beta'_2 - \beta_2)^{-1} \pmod{q}$$

and this concludes our proof.   □

Take a simple example. Sally sets up the scheme for $p = 9743$ with $q = 4871$. A primitive element of $GF(9743)$ is $e = 5$ so $g = 5^2 = 25$. Let $r = 3176$, then $R = g^r = 5052$. Further she chooses four random integers from $\mathbb{Z}_q$, so

$$a_1 = 1953, \ a_2 = 2711, \ b_1 = 3998, \ b_2 = 833.$$

The public $A = 25^{1953} 5052^{2711} \equiv 4299$ (mod 9743) and $B = 25^{3998} 5052^{833} \equiv 6058$ (mod 9743). For a message $m = 2164$, Sally computes $s = (\beta_1, \beta_2) = (2729, 3053)$. Victor takes the message, the signature and Sally's public information and checks whether $AB^m = 4299 \cdot 6058^{2164} \equiv 7528$ (mod 9743) is equal to $g^{\beta_1} R^{\beta_2} = 25^{2729} 5052^{3053} \equiv 7528$ (mod 9743). Indeed the expressions are equal so the signature on the message is authentic.

Let Sally be given a forged signature $s' = (1179, 1529)$ on the message $m = 2164$. Note that the signature passes the verification test as $g^{\beta'_1} R^{\beta'_2} = 25^{1179} 5052^{1529} \equiv 7528$ (mod 9743). Sally should now be able to compute her secret key

$$(2729 - 1179)(1529 - 3053)^{-1} \equiv 3176 \pmod{4871}.$$

This constitutes the proof that someone powerful enough has attacked the scheme.

7.8 Timestamping

In practice, legal documents must have clear timestamps to be legally valid. This applies especially when the documents are related to patents, copyrights, or, in general, to cases where the time is an important factor to make a legal or other judgement. Without timestamps, digital signatures can be subject to manipulations either by Oscar or Sally. A simple example of such a manipulation is replay an attack when an original message is repeated by an opponent. Timestamps provide:

- The time when the document was seen, signed, or processed. In this case, timestamps indicate the unique time intervals (time of the day, day, month, and year).
- The logical time when the document was processed in the context of the processing order of other documents. A logical clock provides integers that can be used to recover the correct order of the messages processed. A logical clock can be implemented as a long enough counter that is incremented (or decremented) after processing each document.
- The unique label that can be attached to a document so the receiver always accepts only documents with different labels. Labels can be implemented using truly random number generators or pseudorandom number generators. Labels are also called nouns.

Obviously, the above mentioned classes of timestamps have different characteristics. The first class of timestamps indicates the precise point of time when the message was handled. These timestamps are generated from local clocks. Clearly, in a distributed environment with many local (usually not synchronized) clocks it is difficult to compare two timestamps from two different local clocks.

The second class of timestamps gets around the problem of synchronization by using a single logical clock which is used to mark the correct processing order of documents. In this case all documents have to be handled by a single center, or alternatively a distributed handler of a document has to apply for a timestamp to the center where the logical clock resides.

The third class of timestamps provides the receiver with a noun that can be used to detect copies of a document. Only the first occurrence of a message with a noun is considered to be legal. All other copies are discarded. A random selection of a noun from a large enough population of integers is enough to guarantee with a high probability that a given document will never be assigned the same timestamp. This method of timestamping is very popular in distributed environments. It does not require synchronization. The uniqueness of the timestamp hinges on a probabilistic argument. Nouns provide a convenient tool to distinguish the past from the present, which is sufficient to detect replay attacks.

7.9 Problems and Exercises

1. Let the Rabin signature be produced using the DES encryption algorithm. Discuss the following points:
   - What is the length of signatures for messages $m \in \Sigma^{64}$ and the parameter $r = 80$?
   - What is the probability that all keys will be revealed by the signer after ℓ independent verifications (verifiers select independently and randomly ℓ $2r$-bit sequences)?

2. Consider the Lamport signature which allows us to sign n-bit messages. The signature is the sequence of n secret keys corresponding to the particular pattern of bits in the message. Suppose that the signer was careless and signed two different messages using the same key setting. Show how the opponent, Oscar, can use the two signatures to sign other (forged) messages.

3. Take an instance of the RSA signature scheme with $p = 839$, $q = 983$, and $N = p \cdot q = 824737$. Assume that the secret key is $e = 132111$. Compute the public key d and sign the message $m = 23547$.

4. Assume that signatures are produced using the RSA scheme with the modulus $N = 824737$ and the public key $d = 26959$.
   - Recover the message m from the signature $s = 8798$.
   - Is the pair $(m, s) = (167058, 366314)$ valid?
   - Knowing two pairs $(m, s) = (629489, 445587)$ and $(m', s') = (203821, 229149)$, compute the signatures for $m \cdot m'$.

5. Given an instance of the ElGamal signature scheme for the modulus $p = 45707$ and the primitive element $g = 41382$:
   - Sign the message $m = 12705$ for the secret key $k = 38416$ and the random $r = 3169$.
   - Verify the triple $(m, x, y) = (12705, 16884, 13633)$.

6. Show how Oscar can break the ElGamal signature if Sally has produced two signatures for two different messages using the same random integer r.

7. Consider an instance of the DSS scheme for the following parameters: the modulus $p = 35023$ with $q = 449$ and an integer $g = 4781$ (a qth root of 1 modulo p).
   - Compute the signature for the message $m = 401$ provided $k = 277$ and $r = 168$.
   - Verify that $s = (x, y) = (262, 266)$ is a signature of $m = 401$ for $g^k = 24937$.

8. Given an instance of the RSA blind signature. The public parameters of the signer are the modulus $N = 17869$ and the public key $d = 10117$.
   - What is the secret key if you know that $p = 107$ and $q = 167$?
   - Compute the blinded message $c \equiv m \cdot r^d \bmod N$ for $m = 17040$ and $r = 5593$, sign the blinded message c, and extract the signature $s \equiv m^k \bmod N$ from c.
   - Verify whether $s = 13369$ is the signature of $m = 17040$.

9. Modify the RSA blind signature when the holder of the message computes $c \equiv m \cdot r^{-d} \bmod N$. How does the holder extract the signature?

10. Suppose that Henry (the holder of messages) wishes to obtain RSA blind signatures for a sequence of messages $(m_1, \ldots, m_n)$ where $m_i \in \mathbb{Z}_N^*$. What are the security implications when Henry uses the same blinding integer r for all messages (instead of the prescribed random integer r selected independently for each message m_i)?

11. Consider an instance of the Chaum-van Antwerpen signature for $p = 1019$, $q = 509$, $g = 475$, $k = 200$, and $K = 807 \equiv g^k \bmod p$.
   - Sign the message $m = 555$.
   - Assuming that the message $m = 555$ and its signature is $s = 842$, verify the pair. Generate a challenge c for the random pair $(a, b) = (20, 411)$ and produce a suitable response.

8 Authentication

Authentication is one of the basic cryptographic techniques. Its aim is to provide a receiver with some kind of proof that the information comes from the intended sender. In this chapter we are going to discuss authentication whose security is unconditional, i.e., its security is independent of the computational power of a potential attacker. Simmons wrote a good review on the subject in [475]. Stinson treated authentication in Chap. 10 of his book [496].

8.1 Active Opponents

Authentication systems involve three active parties: the sender (Alice), the receiver (Bob), and the opponent (Oscar). Alice transmits messages to Bob using a communication channel. The opponent, Oscar, controls the channel. Recall that in secrecy systems, Oscar is assumed to eavesdrop the conversation between Alice and Bob. He is a passive attacker who does not modify the stream of cryptograms sent over the channel. It is not difficult to realize that once Oscar has gained the control over the channel, he may become "active." *Active opponents* interfere with the contents of cryptograms transmitted via the channel. Here is a list of threats which may be launched by an active attacker:

1. *Impersonation attack* – Oscar initiates a communication with Bob by sending a forged cryptogram trying to convince Bob that the cryptogram has come from Alice.
2. *Substitution attack* – Oscar intercepts a cryptogram sent by Alice and replaces it with a different cryptogram which is subsequently transmitted to Bob. Again, Oscar tries to deceive Bob by pretending that the forged cryptogram comes from Alice.

3. *Spoofing attack* – Oscar observes r different valid cryptograms sent by Alice and forms a forged cryptogram hoping that the cryptogram will be accepted by Bob as a valid one. This attack is also called *spoofing of order* r.

Authentication is used to thwart the above threats. Being more specific, we are going to investigate authentication systems which enable Bob to detect Oscar's attacks listed above with an overwhelming probability. Note that authentication systems which we are going to consider in this chapter do not allow Bob to detect other possible active attacks, such as replay of valid cryptograms, interference with the order of the transmitted valid cryptograms, duplication of one or more valid cryptograms, deletion of one or more valid cryptograms, or delay of transmission, etc.

Because of the similarity between secrecy and authentication systems, there may be a temptation to use encryption for authentication. Assume that a message source (Alice) generates 64-bit messages and each message occurs with the probability 2^{-64}. Further, let the DES be used for encryption in the electronic codebook mode. The cryptographic key is known to Alice and Bob only. Cryptograms are conveyed via the channel to Bob who decrypts them. Oscar obviously does not know the cryptographic key but can launch either an impersonation, substitution, or spoofing attack. Clearly, Oscar will be successful in any of these attacks – it is enough for him to choose a cryptogram at random and communicate it to Bob. Bob decrypts it and has to accept it as a genuine one! Oscar has attained his goal although he does not know the message that corresponds to the forged cryptogram.

The above scheme can be salvaged if Alice introduces a redundancy to the message source. Given the message source, which generates 64-bit messages, assume that only 2^{32} messages are meaningful. The other $2^{64} - 2^{32}$ messages are meaningless. The meaningful messages occur with a uniform probability. The meaningless messages never occur. Now Oscar faces a harder task. If he applies the same strategy, that is, the random selection of a fraudulent cryptogram from the set of 2^{64} elements, the probability of Oscar's success is 2^{-32}. On the other hand, Bob detects with the probability $1 - 2^{-32}$ that Oscar is cheating.

8.2 Model of Authentication Systems

Authentication theory emerged in the late 1970s as a parallel branch to Shannon's theory of secrecy systems. The model described here follows Simmons' authentication model [477] and deals with authentication *without secrecy*. The set of all source states (messages) generated by the message source is $\mathcal{S}$. The set of all codewords (cryptograms) is denoted by $\mathcal{M}$. The set of all encoding rules (keys) is $\mathcal{E}$. The set of all authentication tags is $\mathcal{T}$.

An *authentication code* or A-code is the collection $\langle \mathcal{S}, \mathcal{M}, \mathcal{E} \rangle$ such that for each source state $s \in \mathcal{S}$, an encoding rule $e \in \mathcal{E}$ assigns a tag $t \in \mathcal{T}$ or simply $t = e(s)$. The cryptogram $m = (s, t)$ so $\mathcal{M} = \mathcal{S} \times \mathcal{T}$. Denote also $\mid \mathcal{S} \mid = S$, $\mid \mathcal{E} \mid = E$, $\mid \mathcal{M} \mid = M$, and $\mid \mathcal{T} \mid = T$. A-codes with $\mathcal{M} = \mathcal{S} \times \mathcal{T}$ are also called *Cartesian* A-codes.

The authentication system described in Fig. 8.1 works as follows. First, Alice and Bob agree on the encoding rule $e \in \mathcal{E}$ they are going to use. The rule is kept secret by the two parties. Assume Alice wants to send a message (state) $s \in \mathcal{S}$ to Bob. She computes the tag $t = e(s)$ and sends the cryptogram $m = (s, t)$ to Bob via the insecure channel. Bob takes $m' = (s', t')$, which may be modified during transmission, computes his tag $t'' = e(s')$ using the message s', and accepts the message s' only if $t'' = t'$.

As the cryptograms are pairs of a clear message and a tag, Oscar can successfully attack the system if he finds the correct tag for a false message. Note that in the impersonation attack, Oscar knows the A-code only. His knowledge

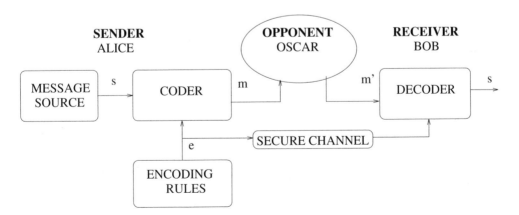

Fig. 8.1. Diagram of authentication system

Table 8.1. Authentication matrix

$\mathcal{E}\backslash\mathcal{S}$	s_1	s_2
e_1	0	0
e_2	1	0
e_3	0	1
e_4	1	1

increases in the substitution attack as he additionally sees a single valid cryptogram. In the spoofing of order r, Oscar knows the A-code and r distinct valid cryptograms. In all these attacks, Oscar's goal is to form a valid cryptogram (or tag) for a false message.

An A-code can be equivalently represented by an *authentication matrix* $B = [b_{ij}]$ with E rows and S columns. Rows are indexed by encoding rules. Columns are labeled by source states (messages). The entry in the intersection of the row e and the column s contains the tag $t = e(s)$. The corresponding cryptogram is $m = (s, t)$.

Consider an A-code with $\mathcal{E} = \{e_1, e_2, e_3, e_4\}$, $\mathcal{S} = \{s_1, s_2\}$, and $\mathcal{T} = \{0, 1\}$. Clearly $\mathcal{M} = \{m_1, m_2, m_3, m_4\}$ with $m_1 = (s_1, 0)$, $m_2 = (s_1, 1)$, $m_3 = (s_2, 0)$, and $m_4 = (s_2, 1)$. The authentication matrix is presented in Table 8.1.

8.2.1 Elements of the Theory of Games

The theory of games [40, 271] investigates possible game strategies for two competing players A and B. Each player can make their move independently. For the player A the collections of moves is $\mathcal{X}$, and for B it is the set $\mathcal{Y}$. The cardinality of sets $\mathcal{X}$ and $\mathcal{Y}$ are n_1 and n_2, respectively. For every pair (x, y), $x \in \mathcal{X}$, $y \in \mathcal{Y}$, there is a value $g(x, y)$ which characterizes how much the player A wins, or equivalently how much the player B loses. The matrix $G = [g_{xy}]$ is the *matrix of the game*.

The game proceeds as follows: The player A selects a row x of the matrix G while B (at the same time) chooses a column y. The value g_{xy} is the gain of A (or the loss of B). Assume that the player A wants to gain as much as possible. If A is prudent he may first compute the smallest entry in each row and select the one that gives the biggest gain, that is, the row with the gain at least:

$$\max_x \min_y g_{xy}. \tag{8.1}$$

On the other hand, B may first calculate the largest value in each column and select the one with the smallest value. This choice guarantees that no matter what A selects, B will never lose more than

$$\min_y \max_x g_{xy}. \tag{8.2}$$

When the matrix of the game G is such that

$$\max_x \min_y g_{xy} = \min_y \max_x g_{xy} = v,$$

then the game has a *point of equilibrium* and the value v is the *value of the game*. A player who applies a *pure strategy* always decides on the single move (row/column).

Players may choose moves in more complex ways using so-called *mixed strategies*. This time players attach probabilities (or weights) to each of their moves and select the current move probabilistically. Assume that the strategy of A is determined by the probability distribution $\pi = \{\pi_{x_1}, \dots, \pi_{x_{n_1}}\}$ and the strategy of Y is determined by $\eta = \{\eta_{y_1}, \dots, \eta_{y_{n_2}}\}$, where $\pi_{x_i} = P(x_i)$ and $\eta_{y_j} = P(y_j)$. It is easy to get an expression for the expected gain/loss

$$\text{payoff}_{\pi\eta} = \sum_{x \in \mathcal{X}} \sum_{y \in \mathcal{Y}} \pi_x \eta_y g_{xy} \tag{8.3}$$

when the players A and B apply their strategies π and η, respectively. Denote

$$v_1 = \max_\eta \min_\pi \text{payoff}_{\pi\eta}$$

and

$$v_2 = \min_\pi \max_\eta \text{payoff}_{\pi\eta}.$$

The fundamental theorem of rectangular games says that if $v_1 = v_2$, then there are two mixed optimal strategies π^* and η^* such that

$$v = \text{payoff}_{\pi^*\eta^*} = v_1 = v_2.$$

The value v is called the *value of the game* and the two strategies (π^*, η^*) are the *saddle point* of the game.

8.2.2 Impersonation Game

An authentication system can be looked at as a game between two players. The first player consists of two communicants Alice and Bob. The second player is Oscar. Alice and Bob can select encoding rules to minimize Bob's chances for deception. On the other hand, Oscar can choose cryptograms according to a strategy which maximizes his chances for a successful deception of Bob. The communicants' strategy for the selection of encoding rules is determined by the probability distribution $\pi = \{\pi_e \mid e \in \mathcal{E}\}$ where π_e is the probability that Alice and Bob choose the encoding rule e (the row of the authentication matrix). Obviously, $\sum_{e \in \mathcal{E}} \pi_e = 1$. Oscar's strategy is described by the probability distribution $\eta = \{\eta_m \mid m \in \mathcal{M}\}$ where η_m is the probability that Oscar selects cryptogram m (where $\sum_{m \in \mathcal{M}} \eta_m = 1$).

After both the communicants and opponent have made their choices about the encoding rule e and the fraudulent cryptogram $m = (s, t)$, Oscar wins only if the tag t' in the row e and the column s of the authentication matrix B are equal to t. While considering the game model of authentication, it is convenient to define the so-called incidence matrix: *An incidence matrix* is a binary matrix $A = [a_{em}]$ ($a_{em} \in \{0, 1\}$) with E rows and M columns ($e \in \mathcal{E}$ and $m \in \mathcal{M}$). The entry $a_{em} = 1$ only if the cryptogram m is valid under the encoding rule e. Otherwise, the entry is zero.

For example, the incidence matrix of the authentication system illustrated in Table 8.1 is given in Table 8.2. Clearly, knowing the authentication matrix it is easy to construct the corresponding incidence matrix and vice versa.

Consider the impersonation attack where Oscar knows the A-code, i.e., the incidence matrix. After the communicants (Alice and Bob) agree on their strategy π, it is possible to compute the conditional probability of Oscar's success provided he has chosen the fraudulent cryptogram m so

$$\text{payoff}_\pi(m) = \sum_{e \in \mathcal{E}} \pi_e a_{em}. \tag{8.4}$$

The probability of Oscar's success never exceeds the values

$$p_0^\pi = \max_\eta \sum_{m \in \mathcal{M}} \eta_m \text{payoff}_\pi(m).$$

Table 8.2. Incidence matrix

$\mathcal{E}\backslash\mathcal{M}$	m_1	m_2	m_3	m_4
e_1	1	0	1	0
e_2	0	1	1	0
e_3	1	0	0	1
e_4	0	1	0	1

Therefore, the optimal strategy π^* for Alice and Bob should minimize p_0^π, that is

$$p_0^{\pi^*} = \min_\pi(\max_\eta \sum_{m \in \mathcal{M}} \eta_m \text{payoff}_\pi(m))$$

$$= \min_\pi(\max_\eta \sum_{m \in \mathcal{M}} \sum_{e \in \mathcal{E}} \pi_e \eta_m a_{em}).$$

Similarly, Oscar can compute the conditional probability of his success provided the communicants have selected the encoding rule $e \in \mathcal{E}$ which is

$$\text{payoff}_\eta(e) = \sum_{m \in \mathcal{M}} \eta_m a_{em}.$$

The probability never drops below the value

$$p_o^\eta = \min_\pi \sum_{e \in \mathcal{E}} \pi_e \text{payoff}_\eta(e).$$

The optimal strategy η^* for Oscar should maximize p_o^η so

$$p_0^{\eta^*} = \max_\eta(\min_\pi \sum_{e \in \mathcal{E}} \pi_e \text{payoff}_\eta(e))$$

$$= \max_\eta(\min_\pi \sum_{m \in \mathcal{M}} \sum_{e \in \mathcal{E}} \pi_e \eta_m a_{em}).$$

Note that $A = [a_{em}]$ is the incidence matrix of the game. According to the fundamental theorem of rectangular games if there is a saddle point of the game then $p_0 = p_0^{\pi^*} = p_0^{\eta^*} = p_0^{\pi^* \eta^*}$.

An A-code is *perfect* under the impersonation if the value p_0 of the impersonation game is independent of Oscar's strategy η.

Theorem 33. (*Simmons* [471, 472]) *An A-code is perfect under the impersonation if and only if there is a communicants' strategy π such that*

$$p_0 = payoff_\pi(m) = \frac{S}{M} = \frac{1}{T}.$$

Consider the A-code given by Table 8.1. Assume that the strategy $\pi = \{\pi_{e_1}, \pi_{e_2}, \pi_{e_3}, \pi_{e_4}\} = \{1/2, 1/4, 1/8, 1/8\}$. The conditional probabilities are equal to:

$$\text{payoff}_\pi(m_1) = 1/2 + 1/8 = 5/8,$$
$$\text{payoff}_\pi(m_2) = 1/4 + 1/8 = 3/8,$$
$$\text{payoff}_\pi(m_3) = 1/2 + 1/4 = 3/4,$$
$$\text{payoff}_\pi(m_4) = 1/8 + 1/8 = 1/4.$$

The probability of success for Oscar is at most 5/8. If the communicants use another strategy, say $\pi^* = \{1/4, 1/4, 1/4, 1/4\}$, then all conditional probabilities $\text{payoff}_{\pi^*}(m_i) = 1/2$ for $i = 1, 2, 3, 4$. Note that the strategy π^* is optimal as the payoff does not depend on Oscar's strategy.

8.2.3 Substitution Game

In the substitution attack, Oscar knows the A-code and a single valid cryptogram m. He tries to deceive Bob by sending him a fraudulent cryptogram m'. The probability of Oscar's success, called the *payoff*, is:

$$
\begin{aligned}
\text{payoff}_{\pi}(m, m') &= P(m' \text{ valid } \mid m \text{ received}) \\
&= \frac{P(m' \text{ valid}, m \text{ received})}{P(m \text{ received})}.
\end{aligned}
\tag{8.5}
$$

For simplicity, denote that $P(m) = P(m \text{ received})$. This probability can be computed as follows:

$$
P(m) = \sum_{e \in \mathcal{E}} P(m, e).
$$

Some pairs (m, e) never happen. This can be conveniently expressed using the entries of the incidence matrix so $P(m) = \sum_{e \in \mathcal{E}} a_{em} P(m, e)$. Note that $P(m, e) = P(e)P(m \mid e) = \pi_e P(m \mid e)$. The probability $P(m \mid e)$ is equal to the probability $P_{\mathcal{S}}(s)$ that the message source has generated a message s such that $m = (s, e(s))$. Therefore $P(m) = \sum_{e \in \mathcal{E}} a_{em} \pi_e P_{\mathcal{S}}(m, e)$. The probability $P(m \mid e) = P_{\mathcal{S}}(m, e)$ as the pair (m, e) uniquely determines the message s.

The probability $P(m' \text{ valid}, m \text{ received})$ can be transformed in similar way, and:

$$
\begin{aligned}
P(m' \text{ valid}, m \text{ received}) &= \sum_{e \in \mathcal{E}} P(m' \text{ valid}, m \text{ received}, e) \\
&= \sum_{e \in \mathcal{E}} \pi_e P(m' \text{ valid}, m \text{ received} \mid e) \\
&= \sum_{e \in \mathcal{E}} \pi_e a_{em} a_{em'} P_{\mathcal{S}}(m, e).
\end{aligned}
$$

Finally, we get

$$
\text{payoff}_{\pi}(m, m') = \frac{\sum_{e \in \mathcal{E}} \pi_e a_{em} a_{em'} P_{\mathcal{S}}(m \mid e)}{P(m)}.
\tag{8.6}
$$

After interception of cryptogram m, Oscar can choose a fraudulent cryptogram m' from $(M-1)$ possibilities. His choice can be described in the form of an assignment $z : \mathcal{M} \to \mathcal{M}$. The assignment can be represented as

intercepted cryptogram		fraudulent cryptogram
m_1	$\to$	$m'_1 (m'_1 \neq m_1)$
$\vdots$		$\vdots$
m_M	$\to$	$m'_M (m'_M \neq m_M)$

or, briefly, $z(m) = m'$. There are $(M-1)^M$ possible assignments. Let the set $\mathcal{Z} = \{ z_i \mid i = 1, \ldots, (M-1)^M \}$ contain all assignments Oscar may ever apply. Obviously, he will have some preferences for some assignments. His strategy (preferences) is determined by the probability distribution

$$\eta = \{ \eta_z \mid z \in \mathcal{Z} \}, \tag{8.7}$$

where η_z is the probability that Oscar chooses z as his substitution assignment (note that $\sum_{z \in \mathcal{Z}} \eta_z = 1$). The probability of Oscar's success when he uses the assignment $z \in \mathcal{Z}$ is

$$p_1^\pi(z) = \sum_{m \in \mathcal{M}} P(m) \, \mathrm{payoff}_\pi(m, m'), \tag{8.8}$$

where $m' = z(m)$. The probability of Oscar's success when he applies the strategy η is:

$$p_1^{\eta\pi} = \sum_{z \in \mathcal{Z}} \eta_z p_1^\pi(z) = \sum_{z \in \mathcal{Z}} \eta_z \sum_{m \in \mathcal{M}} P(m) \, \mathrm{payoff}_\pi(m, m'). \tag{8.9}$$

Substituting the payoff by (8.6), we obtain:

$$p_1^{\eta\pi} = \sum_{z \in \mathcal{Z}} \sum_{m \in \mathcal{M}} \sum_{e \in \mathcal{E}} \eta_z \pi_e a_{em} a'_{em'} P_S(m, e) = \sum_{z \in \mathcal{Z}} \sum_{e \in \mathcal{E}} \eta_z \pi_e \sum_{m \in \mathcal{M}} a_{em} a_{em'} P_S(m, e)$$

Note that $g(e, z) = \sum_{m \in \mathcal{M}} a_{em} a_{em'} P_S(m, e)$ are entries of the game matrix G with E rows and $(M-1)^M$ columns, where $m' = z(m)$ and $A = [a_{em}]$ is the incidence matrix of the A-code. Thus the optimal strategy for Oscar would be η^* such that

$$p_1^{\eta^*} = \max_\eta (\min_\pi \sum_{e \in \mathcal{E}} \sum_{z \in \mathcal{Z}} \pi_e \eta_z g(e, z)). \tag{8.10}$$

On the other hand the optimal Alice and Bob's strategy would be π^* and

$$p_1^{\pi^*} = \min_\pi (\max_\eta \sum_{e \in \mathcal{E}} \sum_{z \in \mathcal{Z}} \pi_e \eta_z g(e, z)). \tag{8.11}$$

If $p_1^{\eta^*} = p_1^{\pi^*}$, then the fundamental theorem of rectangular games assures the existence of two optimal strategies for the players (the saddle point). The value of the game for these two strategies is $p_1 = p_1^{\eta^*} = p_1^{\pi^*}$. The value p_1 expresses also the probability of substitution by Oscar.

An authentication code is *perfect* for the substitution attack if the value of the substitution game for the optimal communicants' strategy does not depend on Oscar's strategy. The next theorem characterizes perfect A-codes.

Theorem 34. (*Massey* [319]) *An A-code is perfect under substitution if and only if there is a communicants' strategy π such that the payoff$_\pi(m, m')$ is constant for every pair $(m, m') \in \mathcal{M}^2$. The value of the substitution game is $p_1 = payoff_\pi(m, m')$.*

As we deal with authentication without secrecy, the requirement that $m \neq m'$ translates to $s \neq s'$ where $m = (s, t)$ and $m' = (s', t')$. It is not difficult to observe that if the payoff function is constant for every pair $s \neq s'$, all tags are equally probable and $p_1 = T^{-1}$.

8.2.4 Spoofing Game

The substitution game can be generalized to a *spoofing game*. In the spoofing game, the communicants, Alice and Bob, play against the opponent Oscar. Oscar knows the A-code applied and sees r different valid cryptograms sent over the channel. He chooses a fraudulent cryptogram m' (the cryptogram has to be different from all cryptograms observed) and tries to deceive Bob so he will accept m' as the valid cryptogram. The spoofing game can be analyzed in a way similar to the analysis of the substitution game. If the spoofing game has a saddle point, then the value of the game denoted by p_r is determined by the following theorem.

Theorem 35. *If the spoofing game is defined by an A-code, then*

$$p_r \geq \frac{1}{T}. \tag{8.12}$$

The equality holds if and only if for any sequence of r observed cryptograms $(m^r \in \mathcal{M}^r)$ and any fraudulent cryptogram m' (m' is different from the observed cryptograms)

$$payoff(m^r, m') = \frac{1}{T}. \tag{8.13}$$

An A-code is r-*fold secure* against spoofing if the game values for impersonation, substitution, and all spoofing games are

$$p_i = \frac{1}{T},$$

where $i = 0, 1, \ldots, r$. Recall that game values are equivalent to the probability of deception or Oscar's success.

8.3 Information Theoretic Bounds

Bounds for probabilities p_i $(i = 0, 1, \ldots, r)$ can be derived using entropies. Let $H(E) = -\sum_{e \in \mathcal{E}} P(e) \log_2 P(e)$ be the entropy of the random variable with the probability distribution $\{P(e) \mid e \in \mathcal{E}\}$ over the set $\mathcal{E}$. Similarly, $H(M)$ and $H(S)$ are entropies of cryptograms and messages, respectively.

Simmons [471] proved that the impersonation probability

$$p_0 \geq 2^{-(H(E)-H(E|M))}. \tag{8.14}$$

This bound was refined by Johansson and Sgarro in [261] and

$$p_0 \geq 2^{-\inf(H(E)-H(E|M))} \tag{8.15}$$

where inf stands for infimum, i.e., the greatest lower bound. The infimum is taken over all source statistics that do not change the set of pairs (m, e) for which $P(m, e) \neq 0$.

In 1974 Gilbert, MacWilliams, and Sloane [200] considered a general class of A-codes without secrecy and proved that the probability of substitution

$$p_1 \geq E^{-1/2}. \tag{8.16}$$

Now we are going to generalize the bound (8.16) for the case of spoofing of order r. To simplify our considerations we assume that

1. The message source generates source states with uniform probability, i.e., $P(s) = 1/S$ for $s \in \mathcal{S}$.
2. Oscar selects the fraudulent cryptogram m' that maximizes the probability $P(m' \text{ is valid} \mid m^r)$. The average probability p_r of Oscar's success is:

$$p_r = \sum_{m^r \in \mathcal{M}^r} P(m^r) \max_{m'} P(m' \text{ is valid} \mid m^r).$$

First, we observe that

$$p_r \geq 2^{-H(M'|M^r)}, \tag{8.17}$$

where $H(M' \mid M^r)$ is the conditional entropy that the fraudulent cryptogram is valid provided r cryptograms have been seen. This follows from the definition of the conditional entropy and the properties of the logarithm:

$$H(M' \mid M^r) = - \sum_{m^r \in \mathcal{M}^r} \sum_{m' \in \mathcal{M}} P(m' \text{ is valid}, m^r) \log_2 P(m' \text{ is valid} \mid m^r)$$

$$\geq - \sum_{m^r \in \mathcal{M}^r} \sum_{m' \in \mathcal{M}} P(m' \text{ is valid}, m^r) \log_2 \max_{m'} P(m' \text{ is valid} \mid m^r)$$

$$\geq - \log_2 \sum_{m^r \in \mathcal{M}^r} \sum_{m' \in \mathcal{M}} P(m' \text{ is valid}, m^r) \max_{m'} P(m' \text{ is valid} \mid m^r)$$

$$= - \log_2 p_r.$$

This sequence produces the requested inequality (8.17).

Second, we will show that:

$$H(M' \mid M^r) \leq \frac{H(E)}{r+1}.$$

Note that $H(E) \geq H(E \mid S^r)$. As the pair, message and encoding rule, assigns the unique cryptogram so $H(E \mid S^r) = H(E, M^r \mid S^r)$, then

$$H(E) \geq H(E, M^r \mid S^r).$$

Using the properties of the entropy, we obtain:

$$H(E, M^r \mid S^r) = H(M^r \mid S^r) + H(E \mid M^r, S^r).$$

The knowledge of r cryptograms is sufficient to determine the corresponding r messages so $H(E \mid M^r, S^r) = H(E \mid M^r)$ and $H(E \mid M^r) \leq H(E) - H(M^r \mid S^r)$. Clearly,

$$H(M' \mid M^r) \leq H(E \mid M^r)$$

as the uncertainty of the encoding rules must be equal to or bigger than the uncertainty associated with the decision about the fraudulent cryptogram. In other words, if the encoding rule is known so is the valid cryptogram. This means that:

$$H(M' \mid M^r) \leq H(E \mid M^r) \leq H(E) - H(M^r \mid S^r). \tag{8.18}$$

The messages are independently and uniformly selected from the set $\mathcal{S}$, so

$$H(M^r \mid S^r) = r H(M \mid S). \tag{8.19}$$

There are two possible cases:

1. $H(M \mid S) \geq \frac{H(E)}{r+1}$, then according to (8.18) and (8.19) we get:

$$H(M' \mid M^r) \leq \frac{H(E)}{r+1}. \tag{8.20}$$

2. $H(M \mid S) \leq \frac{H(E)}{r+1}$, then $H(M' \mid M^r) = H(M' \mid M^r, S) \leq H(M \mid S)$
   $\leq \frac{H(E)}{r+1}$. Note that $H(M' \mid M^r, S) \leq H(M \mid S)$ holds as the knowledge of r
   cryptograms never increases the entropy of M'. This gives the final bound
   for p_r and

$$p_r \geq 2^{-\frac{H(E)}{r+1}}. \tag{8.21}$$

If the inequality (8.21) becomes an equality, then

$-$ $E = 2^{H(E)}$ and all encoding rules are equally probable.
$-$ The probabilities of deception $p_0 = p_1 = \ldots = p_r = \frac{1}{T}$.

More details about entropy bounds for spoofing can be found in [165, 433, 444].

8.4 Constructions of A-codes

Gilbert, MacWilliams, and Sloane [200] demonstrated that A-codes can be constructed using combinatorial designs. Projective spaces are combinatorial objects which may be used to construct A-codes. Also orthogonal arrays and error correcting codes provide tools for the design of A-codes.

8.4.1 A-codes in Projective Spaces

An n-dimensional *projective space* $PG(n, q)$ over a Galois field $GF(q)$ is a collection of points, lines, planes, and subspaces $PG(i, q)$ $(i < n)$ such that

1. The number of all points in the space $PG(n, q)$ is $\kappa(n) = \frac{q^{n+1}-1}{q-1} = q^n$
   $+ q^{n-1} + \ldots + q + 1$.
2. Each subset of $(n-r)$ linearly independent equations constitutes a projective
   subspace $PG(r, q)$. The number of all different subspaces of dimension r
   contained in $PG(n, q)$ is

$$\kappa(r, n) = \frac{\kappa(n)\kappa(n-1)\cdots\kappa(n-r)}{\kappa(r)\kappa(r-1)\cdots\kappa(2)\kappa(1)\kappa(0)}.$$

The implementation of $\langle \mathcal{S}, \mathcal{M}, \mathcal{E} \rangle$ A-code using the projective space $PG(N, q)$ involves the following assignments:

- Messages $s \in \mathcal{S}$ are projective subspaces $PG(N-2, q)$ of $PG(N, q)$. Note that the message spaces are chosen so the intersection of any two arbitrary message spaces is a projective space $PG(N-3, q)$ and in general the intersection of every ℓ message spaces creates a projective space $PG(N - (\ell+1), q)$.
- Encoding rules $e \in \mathcal{E}$ are points.
- Cryptograms $m \in \mathcal{M}$ are projective spaces $PG(N-1, q)$ spanned over the corresponding message space containing the point corresponding to the encoding rule.

The properties of the implementation are:

- The number of encoding rules $E = q^N$.
- The number of tags is $T = q$.
- N different pairs (message, cryptogram) uniquely determine the encoding rule applied and break the A-code.
- The probabilities of deception are $p_0 = p_1 = \ldots = p_r = q^{-1}$ for $r = 1, 2, \ldots, N - 1$.

The projective space $PG(3, 2)$ can be used to construct a simple A-code with four messages, eight cryptograms, and two tags whose incidence matrix is given in Table 8.3. If Oscar sees the cryptogram m_4, he knows that the encoding rule $e \in \{e_3, e_4, e_7, e_8\}$. If he wants to send a fraudulent cryptogram for s_4, he has to choose either m_7 or m_8. Both cryptograms are equally probable. If

Table 8.3. The incidence matrix of an A-code designed in $PG(3, 2)$

$\mathcal{M}$	s_1		s_2		s_3		s_4	
$\mathcal{E} \backslash \mathcal{S}$	m_1	m_2	m_3	m_4	m_5	m_6	m_7	m_8
e_1	1	0	1	0	1	0	1	0
e_2	0	1	1	0	1	0	0	1
e_3	1	0	0	1	1	0	0	1
e_4	0	1	0	1	1	0	1	0
e_5	1	0	1	0	0	1	0	1
e_6	0	1	1	0	0	1	1	0
e_7	1	0	0	1	0	1	1	0
e_8	0	1	0	1	0	1	0	1

Oscar observes the second cryptogram m_5, he knows that the encoding rule is in the set $e \in \{e_3, e_4\}$. This observation does not help him in deciding what is the cryptogram for s_4. He still has two equally probable candidates. Any other third observation breaks the A-code and allows Oscar to determine the encoding rule used.

8.4.2 A-codes and Orthogonal Arrays

Orthogonal arrays (OA) are combinatorial designs that are ideally suited for the design of A-codes without secrecy (Cartesian A-codes). There is also a strong relation between orthogonal arrays and projective spaces. Indeed, one of the general methods used to construct orthogonal arrays applies projective spaces.

Definition 24. *An orthogonal array $OA_\lambda(t, n, k)$ is a $\lambda k^t \times n$ array of k symbols such that for any t columns of the array, every one of the possible k^t ordered t-tuples of symbols occurs in exactly λ rows.*

Assume we assign elements of an A-code to components of OA as follows:

- An encoding rule identifies the unique row.
- A message (source state) labels the unique column.
- A tag is a symbol.

Clearly, we can conclude that for every OA there is a corresponding Cartesian A-code.

Theorem 36. *(Stinson [495]) Given an orthogonal array $OA_\lambda(t, n, k)$, then there is a Cartesian A-code $\langle \mathcal{S}, \mathcal{M}, \mathcal{E} \rangle$ such that $E = \lambda k^t$, $S = n$, $T = k$, $M = nk$, and the probabilities of deception $p_i = T^{-1} = k^{-1}$ for $i = 0, 1, \ldots, t-1$.*

Consider $OA_1(2, 4, 3)$. It can be used to design an A-code of the form given in Table 8.4. If Oscar observes the cryptogram $(s_3, 2)$, he can deduce that the applied encoding rule $e \in \{e_3, e_5, e_7\}$. His chances of success are no better than random selection of a tag from the set $\{0, 1, 2\}$ for any fraudulent cryptogram. Any other second observation breaks the A-code.

Theorem (36) asserts that any orthogonal array corresponds to an A-code. In many practical situations we would like to know whether a given A-code can be obtained from an orthogonal array. More precisely, we know the set of source states $\mathcal{S}$ and require the deception probabilities to be smaller than ε ($p_i \leq \varepsilon$ for

Table 8.4. The authentication matrix of an A-code based on $OA_1(2, 4, 3)$

$\mathcal{E} \backslash \mathcal{M}$	s_1	s_2	s_3	s_4
e_1	0	0	0	0
e_2	0	1	1	2
e_3	0	2	2	1
e_4	1	0	1	1
e_5	1	1	2	0
e_6	1	2	0	2
e_7	2	0	2	2
e_8	2	1	0	1
e_9	2	2	1	0

$i = 0, 1, \ldots, r$). We are looking for an OA which produces an A-code whose construction is in a sense "minimal," i.e., contains the smallest possible collection of tags and encoding rules and satisfies the imposed conditions. This problem can be translated into the language of combinatorics. Given the parameter n and conditions $t \geq r + 1$ and $k \geq \varepsilon^{-1}$, what is the "smallest" $OA_\lambda(t, n, k)$? A discussion of this problem can be found in [496].

8.4.3 A-codes Based on Error Correcting Codes

Error correcting codes (E-codes) were invented to detect and hopefully correct errors that occurred during the transmission of messages via a noisy channel [317].

Given a vector space $\mathcal{V}_n$ over $GF(q)$, a vector $v = (v_1, \ldots, v_n) \in \mathcal{V}_n$ contains n coordinates from $GF(q)$ ($v_i \in GF(q)$ for $i = 1, \ldots, n$). The *Hamming distance* between two vectors $x, y \in \mathcal{V}_n$ is the number of coordinates in which the two vectors differ. The number is denoted by $d(x, y)$.

An (n, ℓ, d) E-code is a set of ℓ vectors from $\mathcal{V}_n$ such that the Hamming distance between any two vectors is at least d. The set of all codewords is denoted using $\mathcal{C}$. Clearly $| \mathcal{C} | = \ell$.

Johansson, Smeets, and Kabatianskii [262] investigated the relation between A-codes and E-codes. Their observations are summarized in the following two theorems. The first theorem indicates how A-codes with the requested probability of substitution p_1 can be implemented using E-codes.

Theorem 37. *Given an $\langle \mathcal{S}, \mathcal{M}, \mathcal{E} \rangle$ A-code with uniform selection of both messages and encoding rules and with the probabilities $p_0 = T^{-1}$ and $p_1 = \varepsilon$, then there exists a corresponding (n, ℓ, d) E-code with the parameters $n = E$, $\ell = q(q-1)S + q$, and $d = E(1 - \varepsilon)$.*

The next theorem identifies a class of E-codes which corresponds to A-codes with protection against substitution.

Theorem 38. *Assume there is an E-code $\mathcal{C}$ over $GF(q)$ with parameters (n, ℓ, d) such that if $c \in \mathcal{C}$ then $c + \lambda \mathbf{1} \in \mathcal{C}$ for all $\lambda \in GF(q)$. Then there exists a corresponding Cartesian A-code $\langle \mathcal{S}, \mathcal{M}, \mathcal{E} \rangle$ with parameters $S = \ell q^{-1}$, $E = nq$, and probabilities $p_0 = q^{-1}$, $p_1 = 1 - \frac{d}{n}$.*

In contrast to combinatorial designs, E-codes offer a relatively efficient implementation tool for A-codes that are perfect under substitution.

8.5 General A-codes

If we drop the restriction on the set of cryptograms, then the general A-code is a collection $\langle \mathcal{S}, \mathcal{M}, \mathcal{E} \rangle$ with $M \geq S$. As previously, the active opponent Oscar has access to the communication channel. Alice sends to Bob a pair consisting of a message s and the corresponding cryptogram m. After receiving the pair (s', m') from the channel and knowing the secret encoding rule, Bob recovers the message from the cryptogram m' and compares it with the message s'. If they are equal, he accepts the pair as genuine. Oscar may try impersonation, substitution, or spoofing attacks. General A-codes can also be analyzed using the game model. As previously, the spoofing game (which covers also impersonation and substitution) is played between communicants (Alice and Bob) and the opponent (Oscar). Oscar knows the A-code (the authentication matrix is public) and observes r pairs of (message, cryptogram).

An A-code is *r-fold secure* against spoofing if the values of the games p_i (or probabilities of deception) are

$$p_i = \frac{S - i}{M - i}$$

for $i = 0, \ldots, r$. Readers interested in details of the game model are referred to [471, 472, 475]. The combinatorial nature of A-codes is studied in [443, 491, 492, 493]. Bounds for probabilities of deception are investigated in [31, 261, 260,

433, 481, 517]. A-codes and their resistance against spoofing are examined in
[441, 442, 508].

8.6 Problems and Exercises

1. Given an A-code in the form of its authentication matrix shown in Table 8.5, determine
   the set of encoding rules $\mathcal{E}$, the set of tags $\mathcal{T}$, the set of source states $\mathcal{S}$, and the set of
   cryptograms $\mathcal{M}$. Assume that the communicants have agreed to use the encoding rule e_3.
   What are the cryptograms for all possible messages? Is the cryptogram $(s_1, 2)$ valid?

2. Write an incidence matrix for the A-code given in Table 8.5.

3. Consider again the code in Table 8.5. Suppose that an attacker, Oscar, knows that the
   communicants use the strategy

   $$\pi = (\pi_{e_1}, \ldots, \pi_{e_6}) = (\frac{1}{12}, \frac{3}{12}, \frac{1}{12}, \frac{4}{12}, \frac{2}{12}, \frac{1}{12}).$$

   What are the conditional probabilities $\text{payoff}_\pi(m_i)$ for all possible cryptograms m_i? What
   are the conditional probabilities $\text{payoff}_{\pi^*}(m_i)$ when Alice and Bob select encoding rules
   with uniform probabilities (so $\pi^* = (\frac{1}{6}, \frac{1}{6}, \frac{1}{6}, \frac{1}{6}, \frac{1}{6}, \frac{1}{6})$)? Discuss the results in the context
   of the impersonation attack.

4. Table 8.2 shows an A-code with four cryptograms and four encoding rules. Analyze the
   code under the substitution attack. In particular, compute the conditional probabilities
   $\text{payoff}_\pi(m, m')$ for the two following strategies: $\pi = (\frac{1}{8}, \frac{1}{8}, \frac{2}{8}, \frac{4}{8})$ and $\pi^* = (\frac{1}{4}, \frac{1}{4}, \frac{1}{4}, \frac{1}{4})$.
   Discuss possible strategies for Oscar.

5. The incidence matrix in Table 8.6 shows an A-code with 14 encoding rules and six cryptograms. Analyze the code under the spoofing attack of order 2. Compute the conditional
   probabilities $\text{payoff}_\pi(m, m', m'') = P(m'' \text{valid} \mid (m, m') \text{ received})$ for the strategy π^* in
   which the communicants choose an encoding rule randomly and uniformly from all the
   candidates. Discuss Oscar's chances in the attack.

6. Design an A-code over the projective plane $PG(2, 2)$. Note that the number of points is
   7 in $PG(2, 2)$. Points are used as messages and encoding rules. If the number of encoding
   rules is 4, the number of messages must be 3. Represent the A-code as the authentication

Table 8.5. Authentication matrix

$\mathcal{E}\backslash\mathcal{S}$	s_1	s_2	s_3
e_1	1	2	3
e_2	2	3	1
e_3	3	1	2
e_4	1	3	2
e_5	3	2	1
e_6	2	1	3

Table 8.6. Incidence matrix

$\mathcal{E}\backslash\mathcal{M}$	m_1	m_2	m_3	m_4	m_5	m_6
e_1	0	0	0	1	1	1
e_2	0	0	1	0	1	1
e_3	0	0	1	1	0	1
e_4	0	1	0	0	1	1
e_5	0	1	0	1	0	1
e_6	0	1	1	0	1	0
e_7	0	1	1	1	0	0
e_8	1	0	0	1	1	0
e_9	1	0	1	0	0	1
e_{10}	1	0	1	0	1	0
e_{11}	1	0	1	1	0	0
e_{12}	1	1	0	0	0	1
e_{13}	1	1	0	0	1	0
e_{14}	1	1	0	1	0	0

and incidence matrices. Discuss the properties of the code for the impersonation and substitution attacks. How many observations allow Oscar to find out the encoding rule applied?

7. Show that it is always possible to design an orthogonal array $OA_1(2, p, p)$ with p^2 rows and p columns.

   Hint: Let a row be labeled by a pair $(a, b) \in \mathcal{Z}_p^2$ and a column by an integer $c \in \mathcal{Z}_p$. For the row (a, b) and column c, define the array entry $a \cdot c + b$. Prove that the array is orthogonal (see [496] p. 317). Design an orthogonal array $OA_1(2, 5, 5)$ and investigate its properties in the context of impersonation, substitution, and spoofing attacks.

9 Secret Sharing

Secret sharing becomes indispensable whenever secret information needs to be kept collectively by a group of participants in such a way that only a qualified subgroup is able to reconstruct the secret. An example of such a scheme is a (t, n) threshold secret sharing in which there are n participants holding their shares of the secret and every t $(t \leq n)$ participants can collectively recreate the secret while any $(t-1)$ participants cannot get any information about the secret. The need for secret sharing arises if the storage system is not reliable, so there is a high likelihood that some pieces of information will be lost. Secret sharing is also useful if the owner of the secret does not trust any single person. Instead, the owner can deposit the secret with a group so that only a sufficiently large subgroup of members can reconstruct the secret. Threshold schemes were independently proposed by Blakley [41] and Shamir [464].

9.1 Threshold Secret Sharing

A (t, n) *threshold secret sharing scheme* distributes a secret among n participants in such a way that any t of them can recreate the secret, but any $t-1$ or fewer members gain no information about it. The piece held by a single participant is called a *share* of the secret. Secret sharing schemes are normally set up by a trusted authority who computes all shares and distributes them to participants via secure channels. The trusted authority who sets up the scheme is called a *dealer*. The participants hold their shares until some of them decide to pool their shares and recreate the secret. The recovery of the secret is done by the so-called *combiner* who on behalf of the cooperating group computes the secret. The combiner is successful only if the cooperating group has at least t members. The combiner can be collective, i.e., all active participants show to each other their shares so that any active participant can calculate the secret.

The combiner can also be a mutually trusted participant who collects all shares, calculates the secret, and distributes it secretly to the active participants.

Assume that secrets belong to the set $\mathcal{K}$ and shares are from the set $\mathcal{S}$. Let $\mathcal{S}_i$ be the set from which the dealer draws shares for the participant P_i, $i = 1, \ldots, n$. The set of all participants $\mathcal{P} = \{P_1, \ldots, P_n\}$.

Definition 25. *A (t, n) threshold scheme is a collection of two algorithms. The first algorithm called the dealer*

$$D : \mathcal{K} \to \mathcal{S}_1 \times \mathcal{S}_2 \times \cdots \times \mathcal{S}_n$$

assigns shares to the participants for a secret $k \in \mathcal{K}$. The share $s_i \in \mathcal{S}_i$ is communicated via a secure channel to the participant P_i. If all share sets $\mathcal{S}_i$ are equal we simply say that $s_i \in \mathcal{S}$.

The second algorithm (the combiner)

$$C : \mathcal{S}_{i_1} \times \mathcal{S}_{i_2} \times \cdots \times \mathcal{S}_{i_j} \to \mathcal{K}$$

takes an arbitrary collection of shares and attempts to compute the secret. The combiner recovers the secret successfully only if the number j of different shares is greater or equal to t ($j \geq t$). It fails if the number j of shares is smaller than t ($j < t$).

A (t, n) threshold scheme is *perfect* if any $(t-1)$ shares provide no information about the secret. Note that secret sharing schemes are normally intended to be used one time only. Once the secret has been recreated the scheme is effectively no longer in existence.

9.1.1 (t, t) Threshold Schemes

Karnin, Greene, and Hellman [268] studied (t, t) threshold sharing. The secret can be recovered only when all participants cooperate. The implementation of (t, t) schemes can be done as follows.

Let the secret integer k be given. The dealer chooses a modulus p that can be any integer bigger than k. Its value determines the security parameter. Next the dealer Don selects randomly, uniformly, and independently $(t-1)$ elements $s_1, \ldots, s_{t-1}$ from $\mathcal{Z}_p$. The share s_t is

$$s_t = k - \sum_{i=1}^{t-1} s_i \pmod{p}. \tag{9.1}$$

The shares are distributed securely to the participants from the set $\mathcal{P} = \{P_1, \ldots, P_t\}$.

At the pooling time, the combiner Clara can reconstruct the secret only if she is given all shares as

$$k = \sum_{i=1}^{t} s_i \pmod{p}.$$

Obviously, any $(t-1)$ or fewer shares provide no information about the secret k.

9.1.2 Shamir Scheme

Shamir [464] used Lagrange polynomial interpolation to design (t, n) threshold schemes. All calculations are done in $GF(p)$ where the prime p is a big enough integer (so the secret is always smaller than p).

A (t, n) Shamir scheme is constructed by the dealer Don. First Don chooses n different points $x_i \in GF(p)$ for $i = 1, \ldots, n$. These points are public. Next Don selects at random coefficients $a_0, \ldots, a_{t-1}$ from $GF(p)$. The polynomial $f(x) = a_0 + a_1 x + \ldots + a_{t-1} x^{t-1}$ is of degree at most $(t-1)$. The shares are $s_i = f(x_i)$ for $i = 1, \ldots, n$, and the secret is $k = f(0)$. The share s_i is distributed to the participant $P_i \in \mathcal{P}$ via a secure channel and is kept secret.

When t participants agree to cooperate, the combiner Clara takes their shares and tries to recover the secret polynomial $f(x)$. She knows t points on the curve $f(x)$

$$(x_{i_j}, f(x_{i_j})) = (x_{i_j}, s_{i_j}) \text{ for } j = 1, \ldots, t.$$

These points produce the following system of equations:

$$\begin{aligned} s_{i_1} &= a_0 + a_1 x_{i_1} + \ldots + a_{t-1} x_{i_1}^{t-1}, \\ s_{i_2} &= a_0 + a_1 x_{i_2} + \ldots + a_{t-1} x_{i_2}^{t-1}, \\ &\vdots \\ s_{i_t} &= a_0 + a_1 x_{i_t} + \ldots + a_{t-1} x_{i_t}^{t-1}. \end{aligned} \qquad (9.2)$$

The system (9.2) has a unique solution for $(a_0, \ldots, a_t)$, since

$$\Delta = \begin{vmatrix} 1 & x_{i_1} & \cdots & x_{i_1}^{t-1} \\ 1 & x_{i_2} & \cdots & x_{i_2}^{t-1} \\ \vdots & \vdots & \ddots & \vdots \\ 1 & x_{i_t} & \cdots & x_{i_t}^{t-1} \end{vmatrix}$$

is a Vandermonde determinant different from zero. The Lagrange interpolation formula allows us to determine the polynomial $f(x)$ of degree $(t-1)$ from the t different points (x_{i_j}, s_{i_j}), thus

$$f(x) = \sum_{j=1}^{t} s_{i_j} \prod_{\substack{1 \leq \ell \leq t \\ \ell \neq j}} \frac{x - x_{i_\ell}}{x_{i_j} - x_{i_\ell}}.$$

The secret $k = f(0)$, therefore we obtain

$$k = a_0 = \sum_{j=1}^{t} s_{i_j} b_j,$$

where,

$$b_j = \prod_{\substack{1 \leq \ell \leq t \\ \ell \neq j}} \frac{x_{i_\ell}}{x_{i_\ell} - x_{i_j}}.$$

If Clara knows $(t-1)$ shares, she cannot find the unique solution for $k = a_0$ as the system (9.2) contains $(t-1)$ equations with t unknowns. The security is discussed later.

Consider a simple $(3, 6)$ Shamir scheme over $GF(7)$. The dealer selects six public numbers, say $x_i = i$ for $i = 1, \ldots, 6$, and a random polynomial of degree at most 2. Let it be $f(x) = 5 + 3x + 2x^2$. The shares are

$$s_1 = f(x_1) = 3; \quad s_2 = f(x_2) = 5;$$
$$s_3 = f(x_3) = 4; \quad s_4 = f(x_4) = 0;$$
$$s_5 = f(x_5) = 0; \quad s_6 = f(x_6) = 4.$$

The shares are sent to the corresponding participants in a secure way.

Assume that three participants P_1, P_3, and P_6 cooperate and have revealed their shares to the combiner. Clara solves the following system of equations:

$$3 = a_0 + a_1 + a_2,$$
$$4 = a_0 + 3a_1 + 2a_2,$$
$$4 = a_0 + 6a_1 + a_2.$$

According to the Lagrange interpolation formula, the coefficients $b_1 = 6$, $b_2 = 6$, and $b_3 = 3$ and the secret $k = a_0 = b_1 s_1 + b_2 s_3 + b_3 s_6 = 5$.

9.1.3 Blakley Scheme

Blakley [41] used projective spaces to construct a (t, n) threshold scheme. The dealer chooses a projective space of dimension t over $GF(q)$. Denote the space by $PG(t, q)$. Next Don selects at random a point $p \in PG(t, q)$. There are $\frac{(q^t - 1)}{(q - 1)}$ subspaces of dimension $(t - 1)$. A subspace of dimension $(t - 1)$ is called a hyperplane. Shares are different hyperplanes $PG(t - 1, q)$ that contain the point p. The shares are distributed to all participants.

At the pooling time, the combiner takes the provided collection of hyperplanes and finds their intersection, the point p. The secret cannot be reconstructed when Clara has $t - 1$ or fewer hyperplanes as the intersection is a subspace containing p.

A modification of the scheme based on affine spaces was suggested by Simmons in [474].

9.1.4 Modular Scheme

Asmuth and Bloom used congruence classes to define threshold schemes [9].

Assume that every participant $P_i \in \mathcal{P}$ is assigned a public modulus p_i, $i = 1, \ldots, n$. The moduli can be primes or mutually coprimes. The secret k belongs to $\mathcal{Z}_{p_0}$ where the modulus p_0 is public and mutually coprime to p_i, $i = 1, \ldots, n$. Let the moduli be such that $p_0 < p_1 < \ldots < p_n$. The dealer selects at random an integer s such that $0 < s < \prod_{i=1}^{t} p_i$. The secret $k \equiv s \pmod{p_0}$. Next the dealer distributes shares

$$s_i \equiv s \pmod{p_i}$$

to the participants P_i $(i = 1, \ldots, n)$ via secure channels.

Assume that there are t or more participants who want to recreate the secret. The combiner takes their shares $s_{i_1}, \ldots, s_{i_t}$ and solves the following system of congruences:

$$s_{i_1} \equiv s \pmod{p_{i_1}},$$
$$\vdots \tag{9.3}$$
$$s_{i_t} \equiv s \pmod{p_{i_t}}.$$

According to the Chinese Remainder Theorem, the system (9.3) has a unique solution, i.e., $0 < s < \prod_{j=1}^{t} p_{i_j}$. The secret is $k \equiv s \pmod{p_0}$.

Note that the condition $0 < s < \prod_{i=1}^{t} p_i$ is necessary for the combiner to be able to recompute the unique s and find the correct secret k. Note also that s is always smaller than any product of t moduli as $p_1 < \ldots < p_n$. The security of the scheme is discussed in [420].

Let us build a $(2,4)$ threshold scheme. First we select public moduli: $p_0 = 17$, $p_1 = 19$, $p_2 = 23$, $p_3 = 29$, and $p_4 = 31$. The dealer selects a secret number s randomly from $\mathcal{Z}_{19 \times 23} = \mathcal{Z}_{437}$. Let it be $s = 241$. Then the secret $k = 3 \equiv 241$ (mod 17). The shares are $s_1 = 13 \equiv 241$ (mod 19), $s_2 = 11 \equiv 241$ (mod 23), $s_3 = 9 \equiv 241$ (mod 29), and $s_4 = 24 \equiv 241$ (mod 31). The shares are communicated securely to all four participants. Assume that the combiner has received two shares from P_2 and P_4. Clara can easily solve the following system of congruences:

$$11 \equiv s \quad (\text{mod } 29),$$
$$24 \equiv s \quad (\text{mod } 31).$$

According to the Chinese Remainder Theorem, there is a solution $s = 241$. Clearly, the secret $k = 3 \equiv 241$ (mod 17).

The modular scheme can be modified to work with polynomials instead of integers.

9.2 General Secret Sharing

A (t,n) threshold scheme allows any group of t or more participants to access the secret. The *access structure* Γ is the collection of all subsets of participants who are able to access the secret. In other words, the access structure of (t,n) threshold schemes is

$$\Gamma = \{ \mathcal{A} \in 2^{\mathcal{P}} : |\mathcal{A}| \geq t \},$$

where $2^{\mathcal{P}}$ is the class of all subsets of $\mathcal{P}$ (or $2^{\mathcal{P}}$ consists of all possible groups which can be created from $\mathcal{P}$). The access structure, in this case, consists of all groups whose cardinality is at least t. These groups are also called *authorized subsets*. On the other hand, an *unauthorized subset* is a group that does not belong to Γ or whose cardinality is smaller than t.

In general, however, secret sharing may have a far more complicated access structure than those from the (t,n) threshold scheme. Let the set of all participants be $\mathcal{P} = \{P_1, \ldots, P_n\}$. We split the class $2^{\mathcal{P}}$ of all subsets of $\mathcal{P}$ into two disjoint subclasses: the class Γ of all *authorized subsets* of $\mathcal{P}$ and the class $2^{\mathcal{P}} \setminus \Gamma$ of all *unauthorized subsets* of $\mathcal{P}$. An authorized subset of participants is the one that is able to recover the secret $k \in \mathcal{K}$ while any unauthorized subset cannot. The *access structure* Γ is the class of all authorized subsets of $\mathcal{P}$.

Benaloh and Leichter observed in [24] that any reasonable access structure should be *monotone*, which means that an authorized group remains authorized if additional users join.

Definition 26. *An access structure Γ is monotone if for any subset $\mathcal{A} \in \Gamma$ all its supersets $\mathcal{B}$ are contained in Γ, that is*

if $\mathcal{A} \in \Gamma$ and $\mathcal{A} \subseteq \mathcal{B}$, then $\mathcal{B} \in \Gamma$.

Take a closer look at Γ. Among the elements (subsets) of Γ we can identify *minimal* subsets. A subset $\mathcal{A} \in \Gamma$ is minimal if for all $\mathcal{B} \subset \mathcal{A}$, the subset $\mathcal{B}$ does not belong to the access structure Γ. The collection of all minimal subsets of Γ is called the *access structure basis* Γ_0, and

$$\Gamma_0 = \{\mathcal{A} \in \Gamma \mid \forall_{\mathcal{B} \subset \mathcal{A}} \mathcal{B} \notin \Gamma\}.$$

The basis Γ_0 of a (t, n) threshold scheme is

$$\Gamma_0 = \{\mathcal{A} \in 2^{\mathcal{P}} : |\mathcal{A}| = t\}.$$

Because of the monotone property, the access structure basis Γ_0 can always be expanded to Γ by including all supersets generated from the sets of Γ_0, i.e.,

$$\Gamma = cl(\Gamma_0) = \{\mathcal{A} : \mathcal{A} \supseteq \mathcal{B}; \mathcal{B} \in \Gamma_0\},$$

where $cl(\Gamma_0)$ is the *closure* of Γ_0.

A general secret sharing over the access structure Γ is defined as follows.

Definition 27. *A secret sharing scheme over a (monotone) access structure Γ with n participants is a collection of two algorithms. The first algorithm, called the dealer,*

$$D : \mathcal{K} \to \mathcal{S}_1 \times \mathcal{S}_2 \times \cdots \times \mathcal{S}_n$$

assigns shares to the participants for a secret $k \in \mathcal{K}$. The share $s_i \in \mathcal{S}_i$ is communicated via a secure channel to the participant P_i.

The second algorithm (the combiner)

$$C : \mathcal{S}_{i_1} \times \mathcal{S}_{i_2} \times \cdots \times \mathcal{S}_{i_j} \to \mathcal{K}$$

takes an arbitrary collection of shares and attempts to compute the secret. The combiner recovers the secret only if the set of cooperating participants $\{P_{i_1}, P_{i_2}, \ldots, P_{i_j}\} \in \Gamma$. It fails if the set of active participants is not in Γ.

9.2.1 Cumulative Array Construction

Ito, Saito, and Nishizeki showed how a monotone access structure can be realized as a perfect secret sharing scheme [255]. We are going to illustrate their method by using the so-called *cumulative array*.

First note that for every access structure Γ, there is a unique collection of *maximal unauthorized subsets*. More formally, for a given Γ, we define

$$\mathcal{M} = \{\mathcal{B}_1, \ldots, \mathcal{B}_m\}$$

such that each $\mathcal{B}_i \notin \Gamma$, but

$$\mathcal{B}_i \cup P_j \in \Gamma$$

for any $P_j \notin \mathcal{B}_i$. The collection $\mathcal{M}$ contains all possible maximal unauthorized subsets.

Consider an example for the following access structure

$$\Gamma = cl(\{\{P_1, P_2\}, \{P_3, P_4\}\}),$$

where $\mathcal{P} = \{P_1, P_2, P_3, P_4\}$. The collection $\mathcal{M} = \{\mathcal{B}_1, \mathcal{B}_2, \mathcal{B}_3, \mathcal{B}_4\} = \{\{P_1, P_3\}, \{P_1, P_4\}, \{P_2, P_3\}, \{P_2, P_4\}\}$. Consider the subset $\{P_2, P_3\}$. Any extra element, either P_1 or P_4 added to it, converts it to an authorized subset.

Every access structure Γ can be associated with a Boolean function $\Gamma(P_1, \ldots, P_n)$ that becomes 1 for any subset $\mathcal{A} \in \Gamma$, and 0 otherwise. The subset $\mathcal{A}$ can be equivalently represented by the assignment $(P_1 = p_1, \ldots, P_n = p_n)$ for which $P_i \in \mathcal{A}$ iff $p_i = 1$. More formally, the Boolean function $\Gamma(P_1, \ldots, P_n)$ is defined as follows:

$$\Gamma(P_1 = p_1, \ldots, P_n = p_n) = \begin{cases} 1 \text{ if } \{P_i \mid p_i = 1; i = 1, \ldots, n\} \in \Gamma, \\ 0 \qquad\qquad \text{otherwise.} \end{cases}$$

For instance, if $\Gamma = cl(\{\{P_1, P_2\}, \{P_3, P_4\}\})$ the corresponding Boolean function is $\Gamma(P_1, P_2, P_3, P_4) = P_1 P_2 + P_3 P_4$.

From now on, we assume that the function $\Gamma(P_1, \ldots, P_n)$ is always in the canonical sum-of-product form (or disjunctive normal form).

Given a Boolean function $\Gamma(P_1, \ldots, P_n)$, define the *dual Boolean function* $\Gamma^*(P_1, P_2, \ldots, P_n)$ that is generated from $\Gamma(P_1, P_2, \ldots, P_n)$ by swapping OR with AND operators. The function is also associated with the corresponding access structure Γ^*. We call it the *dual access structure*.

For instance, for $\Gamma(P_1, P_2, P_3, P_4) = P_1 P_2 + P_3 P_4$ its dual function

$$\Gamma^*(P_1, P_2, P_3, P_4) = (P_1 + P_2)(P_3 + P_4) = P_1 P_3 + P_1 P_4 + P_2 P_3 + P_2 P_4.$$

The dual access structure is $\Gamma^* = cl(\{\{P_1, P_3\}, \{P_1, P_4\}, \{P_2, P_3\}, \{P_2, P_4\}\})$.

Now we follow the observation made in [476] which links duality with the collection $\mathcal{M}$ of maximal unauthorized subsets.

Theorem 39. *Given an access structure Γ with a collection of maximal unauthorized subsets $\mathcal{M} = \{\mathcal{B}_1, \ldots, \mathcal{B}_m\}$ and its dual $\Gamma^* = \{\mathcal{A}_1, \ldots, \mathcal{A}_m\}$, where $\mathcal{A}_i \subset \mathcal{P}$, then*

$$\mathcal{B}_i = \mathcal{P} \setminus \mathcal{A}_i$$

for $i = 1, \ldots, m$.

Now we are ready to define the notion of cumulative array.

Definition 28. *Given $\Gamma = cl(\Gamma_0)$ for n participants with the corresponding collection $\mathcal{M} = \{\mathcal{B}_1, \ldots, \mathcal{B}_m\}$ of maximal unauthorized subsets, let $\mathcal{T}$ be a set of integers from which share tokens are chosen. Then the cumulative array C_Γ is the assignment of m share tokens $s_i \in \mathcal{T}$ to each participant $P_i \in \mathcal{P}$ according to the following table:*

$\mathcal{M}$	$\mathcal{B}_1$	$\mathcal{B}_2$	$\cdots$	$\mathcal{B}_m$
Γ^*	$\mathcal{A}_1$	$\mathcal{A}_2$	$\cdots$	$\mathcal{A}_m$
	s_1	s_2	$\cdots$	s_m
P_1	$b_{1,1}$	$b_{1,2}$	$\cdots$	$b_{1,m}$
P_2	$b_{2,1}$	$b_{2,2}$	$\cdots$	$b_{2,m}$
			$\vdots$	
P_n	$b_{n,1}$	$b_{n,2}$	$\cdots$	$b_{n,m}$

The entries $b_{i,j}$ are binary and

$$b_{i,j} = \begin{cases} 1 & \text{if } P_i \in \mathcal{A}_j, \\ 0 & \text{otherwise} . \end{cases}$$

The participant P_i gets a share $S_i = \{s_j | b_{i,j} = 1\}$ for $i = 1, \ldots, n$.

In our example $\Gamma(P_1, P_2, P_3, P_4) = cl(P_1 P_2 + P_3 P_4)$ and its dual access structure is $\Gamma^* = cl(\{\{P_1, P_3\}, \{P_1, P_4\}, \{P_2, P_3\}, \{P_2, P_4\}\})$. A Boolean function associated with Γ^* is $\Gamma^*(P_1, P_2, P_3, P_4) = P_1 P_3 + P_1 P_4 + P_2 P_3 + P_2 P_4$. The cumulative matrix C_Γ takes the following form:

Γ^*	P_1P_3	P_1P_4	P_2P_3	P_2P_4
	s_1	s_2	s_3	s_4
P_1	1	1	0	0
P_2	0	0	1	1
P_3	1	0	1	0
P_4	0	1	0	1

which assigns P_1 the share $\{s_1, s_2\}$, P_2 the share $\{s_3, s_4\}$, P_3 the share $\{s_1, s_3\}$, and finally P_4 gets the share $\{s_2, s_4\}$.

An implementation of secret sharing with the access structure Γ over the set $\mathcal{P}$ can be done in two steps:

1. Design a cumulative array C_Γ. The number m of products in the minimal form of $\Gamma^*(P_1, \ldots, P_n)$ gives the number of share tokens.
2. For a given m, we design an (m, m) threshold scheme and the share tokens are distributed to the participants according to the cumulative array.

Clearly, for a given access structure, one would like to be sure that the cumulative array gives the smallest number of share tokens. This can be taken care of by finding the minimal form of the Boolean function associated with Γ^* [197]. It is also reasonable to expect a single participant to be given as few share tokens as possible.

In general, the cumulative array does not guarantee that the resulting secret sharing gives short shares. To illustrate the point, consider a $(2, 3)$ threshold scheme. $\Gamma = cl(\{\{P_1, P_2\}, \{P_1, P_3\}, \{P_2, P_3\}, \{P_1, P_2, P_3\}\})$. The Boolean functions are

$$\Gamma(P_1, P_2, P_3) = P_1P_2 + P_1P_3 + P_2P_3 + P_1P_2P_3 = P_1P_2 + P_1P_3 + P_2P_3$$

and

$$\Gamma^*(P_1, P_2, P_3) = (P_1 + P_2)(P_1 + P_3)(P_2 + P_3) = P_1P_2 + P_1P_3 + P_2P_3.$$

The cumulative array C_Γ is:

Γ^*	P_1P_2	P_1P_3	P_2P_3
	s_1	s_2	s_3
P_1	1	1	0
P_2	1	0	1
P_3	0	1	1

Clearly, any two participants are able to recover all three tokens (and the secret). Any single one cannot as there is always a missing token. Note that for each participant, the share consists of two tokens. In contrast, the Shamir scheme that implements $(2,3)$ sharing requires a single share for each participant.

9.2.2 Benaloh-Leichter Construction

Benaloh and Leichter [24] also gave a simple construction for arbitrary monotone access structures. Their construction applies (t,t) threshold schemes.

Given a monotone access structure Γ over the set $\mathcal{P} = \{P_1, \ldots, P_n\}$ of n participants, a Boolean function $\Gamma(P_1, \ldots, P_n)$ associated with the access structure is first represented in the minimal disjunctive normal form. Let

$$\Gamma(P_1, \ldots, P_n) = \sum_{i=1}^{\alpha} \gamma_i,$$

where γ_i is a monomial of degree t_i. The construction uses α threshold schemes (each for the given monomial γ_i). All threshold schemes share the same secret $k \in \mathcal{K}$. The shares in α threshold schemes are selected independently.

Consider an example. Let $\Gamma = cl(\{\{P_1, P_2, P_3\}, \{P_1, P_4\}, \{P_2, P_4\}\})$. The Boolean function $\Gamma(P_1, P_2, P_3, P_4) = P_1 P_2 P_3 + P_1 P_4 + P_2 P_4$. The first monomial $P_1 P_2 P_3$ is of degree 3 so the corresponding threshold scheme is $(3,3)$. P_1 is assigned a share $s_{1,1}$, P_2 a share $s_{1,2}$, and P_3 a share $(k - s_{1,1} - s_{1,2})$. The second and third monomials are of degree 2 each so their threshold schemes are $(2,2)$. For the second threshold scheme, P_1 gets a share $s_{2,1}$ and P_4 a share $(k - s_{2,1})$. For the third threshold scheme, P_2 obtains a share $s_{3,1}$ and P_4 a share $(k - s_{3,1})$. In summary, the participants hold the following shares:

$$P_1 \mapsto \{s_{1,1}, s_{2,1}\},$$
$$P_2 \mapsto \{s_{1,2}, s_{3,1}\},$$
$$P_3 \mapsto \{k - s_{1,1} - s_{1,2}\},$$
$$P_4 \mapsto \{k - s_{2,1}, k - s_{3,1}\}.$$

Note that P_i possesses many shares (each share for a different scheme to which P_i belongs). At the pooling time, participants submit their whole shares to the combiner who, knowing the ordering of partial shares, is able to recreate the secret.

9.3 Perfectness

The notion of perfect secret sharing is defined as follows.

Definition 29. *A secret sharing scheme over the access structure Γ is perfect if for any subset of participants $\mathcal{A}$ the entropy of the secret is*

$$H(K \mid S_\mathcal{A}) = \begin{cases} H(K) & \text{if } \mathcal{A} \notin \Gamma, \\ 0 & \text{otherwise,} \end{cases}$$

where $S_\mathcal{A}$ is a random variable representing the shares assigned to the set $\mathcal{A}$ of participants.

For a perfect secret sharing, shares held by participants must be at least as long as the secret, as the following theorem asserts. Before we formulate the theorem, we simplify the notation for entropy. Given a set $\mathcal{B} \subset \mathcal{P}$, then the entropy of their shares is denoted as $H(\mathcal{B})$ instead of the more precise $H(S_\mathcal{B})$ where $S_\mathcal{B}$ is the random variable representing shares held by $\mathcal{B}$.

Theorem 40. *Given a perfect secret sharing, then*

$$H(P) \geq H(K),$$

where $H(P)$ is the entropy of the share held by a participant $P \in \mathcal{P}$.

Proof. Take a maximal unauthorized set $\mathcal{B} \notin \Gamma$ that does not contain P or $P \notin \mathcal{B}$. Clearly, $\mathcal{B} \cup P \in \Gamma$ so the following two equations are true

$$H(K|\mathcal{B}) = H(K) \text{ and } H(K|\mathcal{B}, P) = 0.$$

Now we use the two equations to derive the requested inequality. We start with:

$$
\begin{aligned}
H(P) &\geq H(P|\mathcal{B}) && \text{any side information decreases the entropy} \\
&= H(P, \mathcal{B}) - H(\mathcal{B}) && \text{as } H(P, \mathcal{B}) = H(\mathcal{B}) + H(P|\mathcal{B}) \\
&= H(K, P, \mathcal{B}) - H(K|\mathcal{B}, P) - H(\mathcal{B}) && \text{as } H(K, P, \mathcal{B}) = H(\mathcal{B}, P) + H(K, B, P) \\
&= H(K, P, \mathcal{B}) - H(\mathcal{B}) && \text{as } H(K|\mathcal{B}, P) = 0 \\
&= H(K, P, \mathcal{B}) - H(K, \mathcal{B}) + H(K|\mathcal{B}) && \text{as } H(K, \mathcal{B}) = H(\mathcal{B}) + H(K|\mathcal{B}) \\
&= H(K, P, \mathcal{B}) - H(K, \mathcal{B}) + H(K) && \text{since } H(K|\mathcal{B}) = H(K) \\
&\geq H(K) && \text{note that } H(K, P, \mathcal{B}) - H(K, \mathcal{B}) \geq 0
\end{aligned}
$$

The above sequence establishes the result.   □

Theorem 41. *The (t, t) Karnin-Greene-Hellman threshold scheme is perfect.*

Proof. Recall that $(t-1)$ shares are selected randomly, uniformly, and independently from $\mathcal{Z}_p$, i.e., $P(S_i = s_i) = \frac{1}{p}$ for $i = 1, \ldots, t-1$ and $S_1, \ldots, S_{t-1}$ are independent random variables. The random variable $S_t = K - \sum_{i=1}^{t-1} S_i$. Without loss of generality, assume that we have $t-1$ random variables $S_1, S_2, \ldots, S_{t-2}, S_t$. Clearly, the first $(t-2)$ variables are independent. S_t is independent as $S_t = K - \sum_{i=1}^{t-2} S_i - S_{t-1}$ includes S_{t-1} that is independent of $S_1, S_2, \ldots, S_{t-2}$. □

From Theorem 41, it is possible to conclude that both the cumulative array and the Benaloh-Leichter constructions produce perfect secret sharing schemes.

Consider the Shamir scheme. In our definition, the dealer selects at random a polynomial $f(x)$ of degree at most $(t-1)$, that is Don chooses independently and uniformly at random coefficients $a_0, \ldots, a_{t-1}$ from $GF(p)$.

Theorem 42. *The Shamir scheme based on a random polynomial* $f(x) = a_0 + a_1 x + \ldots + a_{t-1} x^{t-1}$ *of degree at most* $(t-1)$ *with* $a_i \in_R GF(p)$ *for* $i = 0, \ldots, t-1$ *is perfect (the secret is* $a_0 = k$*).*

Proof. Assume that $(t-1)$ shares have been made public. Without loss of generality, we assume that these shares are $s_1, \ldots, s_{t-1}$. Thus the following system of equations can be written:

$$s_1 = f(x_1) = a_0 + a_1 x_1 + \ldots + a_{t-1} x_1^{t-1},$$
$$s_2 = f(x_2) = a_0 + a_1 x_2 + \ldots + a_{t-1} x_2^{t-1},$$
$$\vdots$$
$$s_{t-1} = f(x_{t-1}) = a_0 + a_1 x_{t-1} + \ldots + a_{t-1} x_{t-1}^{t-1}.$$

The system includes $(t-1)$ linear equations with t unknowns. The best we can do is to select one of the unknowns, say a_0, and express other unknowns as linear combinations of a_0. The uncertainty about the secret is not diminished. This means that the Shamir secret sharing is perfect. □

The Blakley (t, n) threshold scheme is also perfect. A set of $(t-1)$ participants can identify collectively a line containing the secret (a point on the line). On the other hand, a single participant may try to guess the line and then find the secret. In both cases, the chances of getting the correct secret (point) are the same.

Secret sharing schemes can be constructed using geometrical, algebraic, or combinatorial structures for which there is a well-defined critical set of elements which allows us to recover the whole structure (and the secret). It could be argued that perfect secret sharing schemes are equivalent to orthogonal arrays (for a definition consult [498]). There are also nonperfect schemes that can be constructed using such combinatorial structures such as Latin squares, room squares, cycle systems, etc.

9.4 Information Rate

Recall that, in perfect secret sharing, any participant must hold a share at least as long as the secret. Participants typically insist on having shares that are short as possible. Clearly, shorter shares are easier to manipulate, require less storage, and consume a smaller communication overhead. Also shorter shares are easier to protect. Therefore, the lengths of shares assigned to each participant by the dealer are widely considered as the most important efficiency measures of secret sharing. These measures are also called the *information rates*.

Definition 30. *Assume there is a secret sharing scheme with its dealer function* $D : \mathcal{K} \to \mathcal{S}_1 \times \mathcal{S}_2 \times \cdots \times \mathcal{S}_n$ *over the access structure* Γ. *The information rate for* $P_i \in \mathcal{P}$ *is*

$$\rho_i = \frac{H(K)}{H(S_i)},$$

where $H(S_i)$ *is the entropy of the share of* P_i *(or, more precisely, the entropy of a random variable* S_i *that represents the uncertainty of the share assigned to* P_i*). The average information rate of the scheme is*

$$\tilde{\rho} = \frac{1}{n} \sum_{i=1}^{n} \rho_i.$$

The information rate of the scheme is

$$\rho = \min_{i=1,\ldots,n} \rho_i.$$

According to Theorem 40, we can say that $\rho_i \leq 1$ for every participant $P_i \in \mathcal{P}$. As $\tilde{\rho}$ is the average over all participants, then obviously $\tilde{\rho} \leq 1$. The information rates satisfy the relation

$$0 \leq \rho \leq \tilde{\rho} \leq 1.$$

Shamir threshold schemes assign shares and the secret from the same set (normally from $GF(p)$) so their information rate is one. On the other hand, secret sharing based on cumulative arrays tends to produce much longer shares. Threshold schemes are the ultimate example of the inefficiency of cumulative arrays.

Definition 31. *A perfect secret sharing scheme is ideal if $\rho_i = 1$; so the length of the secret equals the length of a share held by a participant. In this case, $\rho = \tilde{\rho} = 1$.*

9.4.1 Upper Bounds

It is interesting to find secret sharing schemes whose information rates are higher than those obtained using Ito-Saito-Nishizeki or Benaloh-Leichter constructions for general access structures. There is also a more fundamental question about the existence of perfect secret sharing for a given information rate or, more precisely, what are the upper bounds on information rates beyond which perfect secret sharing simply does not exist. Secret sharing that attains the upper bounds on information rates is called *optimal*. The nonexistence argument is developed by using tools (entropy) from Information Theory. Upper bounds are important for designers of secret sharing schemes. Knowing the bounds, the designers may in the first attempt obtain the optimal scheme. If, however, this turns out to be difficult, the designers may be satisfied with a scheme whose information rates are "close enough" to the upper bounds.

Benaloh and Leichter [24] observed that there are access structures for which there is no ideal scheme. The access structure with the base $\Gamma_0 = \{\{P_1, P_2\}, \{P_2, P_3\}, \{P_3, P_4\}\}$ is in this category. Capocelli, De Santis, Gargano, and Vaccaro first showed in [75] how to get upper bounds on information rates. To simplify our notation, we are going to denote the entropy of the random variable that represents the share associated with the participant $P \in \mathcal{P}$ by $H(P)$ instead of $H(S_P)$. The entropy of the secret is $H(K)$. First we prove two lemmas.

Lemma 15. *Let $\mathcal{Y} \notin \Gamma$ and $\mathcal{X} \cup \mathcal{Y} \in \Gamma$. Then*

$$H(\mathcal{X} \mid \mathcal{Y}) = H(K) + H(\mathcal{X} \mid \mathcal{Y}, K).$$

Proof. Note that $H(\mathcal{X}, K \mid \mathcal{Y})$ can be written in two ways (Sect. 2.4.1):

$$H(\mathcal{X}, K \mid \mathcal{Y}) = H(\mathcal{X} \mid \mathcal{Y}) + H(K \mid \mathcal{X}, \mathcal{Y})$$

or

$$H(\mathcal{X}, K \mid \mathcal{Y}) = H(K \mid \mathcal{Y}) + H(\mathcal{X} \mid \mathcal{Y}, K).$$

Thus we get the following sequence:

$$H(\mathcal{X} \mid \mathcal{Y}) + H(K \mid \mathcal{X}, \mathcal{Y}) = H(K \mid \mathcal{Y}) + H(\mathcal{X} \mid \mathcal{Y}, K),$$

$$H(\mathcal{X} \mid \mathcal{Y}) = H(K \mid \mathcal{Y}) + H(\mathcal{X} \mid \mathcal{Y}, K) - H(K \mid \mathcal{X}, \mathcal{Y}). \tag{9.4}$$

As $\mathcal{X} \cup \mathcal{Y} \in \Gamma$ so $H(K \mid \mathcal{X}, \mathcal{Y}) = 0$. On the other hand, the scheme is perfect and $\mathcal{Y} \notin \Gamma$ so $H(K \mid \mathcal{Y}) = H(K)$ and the final result follows.   □

Lemma 16. *Let* $\mathcal{X} \cup \mathcal{Y} \notin \Gamma$, *then*

$$H(\mathcal{Y} \mid \mathcal{X}) = H(\mathcal{Y} \mid \mathcal{X}, K).$$

Proof. According to (9.4) from Lemma 15 we have

$$H(\mathcal{X} \mid \mathcal{Y}) = H(K \mid \mathcal{Y}) + H(\mathcal{X} \mid \mathcal{Y}, K) - H(K \mid \mathcal{X}, \mathcal{Y}).$$

Note that $H(K \mid \mathcal{Y}) = H(K)$ and $H(K \mid \mathcal{X}, \mathcal{Y}) = H(K)$ so $H(\mathcal{Y} \mid \mathcal{X}) = H(\mathcal{Y} \mid \mathcal{X}, K)$.   □

Now we are ready to prove the main result.

Theorem 43. [75] *Given the access structure*

$$\Gamma = cl(\{\{P_1, P_2\}, \{P_2, P_3\}, \{P_3, P_4\}\})$$

for four participants P_1, P_2, P_3, P_4, *then the inequality*

$$H(P_2) + H(P_3) \geq 3H(K)$$

has to be satisfied for any perfect secret sharing over Γ.

Proof. First observe that secret sharing is perfect, so the following equations are true:

1. $H(K|P_1, P_2) = H(K|P_2, P_3) = H(K|P_3, P_4) = 0$.
2. $H(K|P_1) = H(K|P_2) = H(K|P_3) = H(K|P_1, P_3) = H(K|P_1, P_4)$
   $= H(K|P_2, P_4) = H(K)$.

Consider the set $\{P_1, P_3, P_4\} \in \Gamma$. The set $\{P_1, P_4\} \notin \Gamma$, so from Lemma 15 we have

$$H(P_3 \mid P_1, P_4) = H(K) + H(P_3 \mid P_1, P_4, K).$$

This is a starting point for the following sequence of inequalities:

$$
\begin{aligned}
H(K) &= H(P_3 \mid P_1, P_4) - H(P_3 \mid P_1, P_4, K) \\
&\leq H(P_3 \mid P_1, P_4) && \text{entropy is non-negative} \\
&\leq H(P_3 \mid P_1) && \text{as } H(P_3 \mid P_1, P_4) \leq H(P_3 \mid P_1) \\
&= H(P_3 \mid P_1, K) && \text{from Lemma 16} \\
&= H(P_2, P_3 \mid P_1, K) - H(P_2 \mid P_1, P_3, K) \\
&\leq H(P_2, P_3 \mid P_1, K) && \text{entropy is non-negative} \\
&= H(P_2 \mid P_1, K) + H(P_3 \mid P_1, P_2, K) \\
&\leq H(P_2 \mid P_1, K) + H(P_3 \mid P_2, K) && \text{as } H(P_3 \mid P_1, P_2, K) \leq H(P_3 \mid P_2, K) \\
&= H(P_2 \mid P_1) - H(K) + H(P_3 \mid P_2) - H(K) && \text{from Lemma 15} \\
&\leq H(P_2) + H(P_3 \mid P_2) - 2H(K) && \text{as } H(P_2 \mid P_1) \leq H(P_2) \\
&= H(P_2) + H(P_2, P_3) - H(P_2) - 2H(K) && \text{as } H(P_2, P_3) = H(P_2) + H(P_3 \mid P_2) \\
&= H(P_2, P_3) - 2H(K)
\end{aligned}
$$

Thus we have

$$
3H(K) \leq H(P_2, P_3) = H(P_2) + H(P_3 \mid P_2) \leq H(P_2) + H(P_3)
$$

which concludes our proof.   □

Corollary 5. *Given access structure* $\Gamma = cl(\{\{P_1, P_2\}, \{P_2, P_3\}, \{P_3, P_4\}\})$, *then for any secret sharing, the information rate* $\rho \leq \frac{2}{3}$ *and* $\tilde{\rho} \leq \frac{5}{6}$.

Proof. Note that $H(P_1) \geq H(K)$ and $H(P_4) \geq H(K)$ must hold according to Theorem 40. Clearly,

$$
\frac{H(P_2)}{H(K)} \leq \rho^{-1} \text{ and } \frac{H(P_3)}{H(K)} \leq \rho^{-1}.
$$

Adding the two inequalities, we obtain

$$
\frac{H(P_2) + H(P_3)}{H(K)} \leq 2\rho^{-1}.
$$

From Theorem 43 we have that $H(P_2) + H(P_3) \geq 3H(K)$, so

$$
\rho \leq \frac{2}{3}.
$$

This also means that $\rho_2 \leq \frac{2}{3}$ and $\rho_3 \leq \frac{2}{3}$. As we noted above, $\rho_1 \leq 1$ and $\rho_4 \leq 1$. Consequently, $\tilde{\rho} \leq \frac{5}{6}$.   □

Consider the following collection of access structures:

$$\Gamma_1 = cl(\{\{P_1, P_2\}, \{P_2, P_3\}, \{P_3, P_4\}, \{P_2, P_4\}\}),$$
$$\Gamma_2 = cl(\{\{P_1, P_2\}, \{P_2, P_3\}, \{P_1, P_3, P_4\}\}),$$
$$\Gamma_3 = cl(\{\{P_1, P_2\}, \{P_2, P_3\}, \{P_1, P_3, P_4\}, \{P_2, P_4\}\}).$$

In a similar way to Theorem 43, it can be shown that the hypothesis of Theorem 43 is also valid for the access structures $\Gamma_1, \Gamma_2, \Gamma_3$. So their information rates are also smaller than or equal to $\frac{2}{3}$ and $\tilde{\rho} = \frac{5}{6}$.

9.4.2 Ideal Schemes

Ideal secret sharing attains the best possible information rate $\tilde{\rho} = \rho = 1$. Now we are going to discuss the construction of ideal schemes using a linear vector space described by Brickell [66] (this idea is also credited to Simmons [473]).

Recall the Shamir scheme with the polynomial $f(x) = a_0 + a_1 x + \ldots + a_{t-1} x^{t-1}$ over $GF(p)$. The share is

$$s_i = f(x_i) = a_0 + a_1 x_i + \ldots + a_{t-1} x_i^{t-1}.$$

This can be equivalently rewritten as

$$s_i = (a_0, a_1, \ldots, a_{t-1}) \cdot (1, x_i, \ldots, x_i^{t-1}) = \bar{a} \cdot \bar{x}_i,$$

where vectors $\bar{a}$ and $\bar{x}_i$ belong to the vector space $GF(p^t)$. Each participant P_i is assigned the public vector $\bar{x}_i$ and the secret share $s_i = \bar{a} \cdot \bar{x}_i$, the inner product of the two vectors.

Brickell [66] observed that ideal secret sharing schemes can be designed in a vector space $GF(p^t)$. His method generalizes the Shamir approach. Given a vector space $GF(p^t)$:

1. Let a function $\tau : \mathcal{P} \to GF(p^t)$ assign a public vector $\bar{x}_i$ to $P_i \in \mathcal{P}$ in such a way that

$$\forall_{\mathcal{B} \in \Gamma} \; (1, 0, \ldots, 0) = b_1 \bar{x}_1 + b_2 \bar{x}_2 + \ldots + b_t \bar{x}_t \tag{9.5}$$

for some public vector $\bar{b} = (b_1, b_2, \ldots, b_t) \in GF(p^t)$.
2. The vector $(1, 0, \ldots, 0)$ cannot be expressed as a linear combination of vectors $\bar{x}_i$ if the subset $\mathcal{B} \notin \Gamma$.

The dealer first determines the vector space, the function τ, and the collection of public vectors $\bar{x}_1 = \tau(P_1), \ldots, \bar{x}_n = \tau(P_n)$, where $n = |\mathcal{P}|$. Don also selects at random t elements of $GF(p)$ – let them be $a_1, \ldots, a_t$. The vector

$\bar{a} = (a_1, a_2, \ldots, a_t)$ and the secret $k = \bar{a} \cdot (1, 0, \ldots, 0) = a_1$. The share assigned to P_i is

$$s_i = \bar{a} \cdot \bar{x}_i \tag{9.6}$$

for $i = 1, \ldots, n$.

At the pooling time, participants submit their shares to the combiner.

1. If the subset $\mathcal{B} \in \Gamma$, Clara takes the public vector $\bar{b} = (b_1, \ldots, b_t)$ such that

$$(1, 0, \ldots, 0) = b_1 \bar{x}_1 + b_2 \bar{x}_2 + \ldots + b_t \bar{x}_t.$$

She multiplies both sides of the equation by the vector $\bar{a}$ and using (9.6) she calculates the secret

$$k = \sum_{i=1}^{t} b_i \bar{a} \cdot \bar{x}_i = \sum_{i=1}^{t} b_i s_i.$$

2. If the subset $\mathcal{B} \notin \Gamma$ and $|\mathcal{B}| = r$ $(r < t)$, then Clara gets r linear equations

$$\bar{x}_i \cdot \bar{a} = s_i \text{ for } P_i \in \mathcal{B}$$

in the t unknowns $(a_1, \ldots, a_t)$. The secret $k = a_1$ cannot be found as $(1, 0, \ldots, 0) \neq b_1 \bar{x}_1 + b_2 \bar{x}_2 + \ldots + b_t \bar{x}_t$ for any vector $\bar{b} = (b_1, \ldots, b_t)$.

The vector space construction is easy to implement if a suitable function τ can be found. Unfortunately, for a general access structure, there is no general algorithm known which would allow us to find suitable functions τ efficiently.

Consider the access structure $\Gamma = cl(\{\{P_1, P_2, P_3\}, \{P_1, P_4\}\})$ over four participants. Let $GF(p^t)$ be selected for $t = 3$ and for some big enough p. Assume the following assignment of public vectors:

$$\tau(P_1) = \bar{x}_1 = (0, 1, 1),$$
$$\tau(P_2) = \bar{x}_2 = (0, 1, 0),$$
$$\tau(P_3) = \bar{x}_3 = (1, 0, 1),$$
$$\tau(P_4) = \bar{x}_4 = (-1, -1, -1).$$

First we check whether any minimal authorized set $\mathcal{B} \in \Gamma$ can get the vector $(1, 0, 0)$ by a linear combination of its public vectors.

− If $\mathcal{B} = \{P_1, P_2, P_3\}$, then

$$(1, 0, 0) = \bar{x}_3 + \bar{x}_2 - \bar{x}_1 = (1, 0, 1) + (0, 1, 0) - (0, 1, 1).$$

- If $\mathcal{B} = \{P_1, P_4\}$, then

$$(1, 0, 0) = -\bar{x}_4 - \bar{x}_1 = (1, 1, 1) - (0, 1, 1).$$

Next we have to verify that any $\mathcal{B} \notin \Gamma$ is not able to determine the vector $(1, 0, 0)$. We choose the maximal unauthorized subsets, i.e., those which become authorized after adding any single participant to them. These subsets are $\{P_1, P_2\}$, $\{P_1, P_3\}$, and $\{P_2, P_3, P_4\}$.

- If $\mathcal{B} = \{P_1, P_2\}$, then we are looking for $b_1, b_2 \in GF(p)$ such that

$$b_1 \bar{x}_1 + b_2 \bar{x}_2 = b_1 (0, 1, 1) + b_2 (0, 1, 0) \stackrel{?}{=} (1, 0, 0),$$

which clearly has no solution.
- If $\mathcal{B} = \{P_1, P_3\}$, then we are looking for $b_1, b_3 \in GF(p)$ such that

$$b_1 \bar{x}_1 + b_3 \bar{x}_3 = b_1 (0, 1, 1) + b_3 (1, 0, 1) = (b_3, b_1, b_1 + b_3) \stackrel{?}{=} (1, 0, 0).$$

To satisfy the equation, $b_3 = 1$ and $b_1 = 0$ so the third component $b_1 + b_3 = 1 \neq 0$. So there is no such pair.
- If $\mathcal{B} = \{P_2, P_3, P_4\}$, then we have to find $b_2, b_3, b_4 \in GF(p)$ such that

$$b_2 \bar{x}_2 + b_3 \bar{x}_3 + b_4 \bar{x}_4 \stackrel{?}{=} (1, 0, 0).$$

This is equivalent to the system

$$b_3 - b_4 = 1,$$
$$b_2 - b_4 = 0,$$
$$b_3 - b_4 = 0,$$

which has no solution.

Finally, knowing the public vectors $\bar{x}_i$, the dealer selects at random a vector $\bar{a}$. Let it be $\bar{a} = (12, 17, 6)$ over $GF(19)$. The collection of shares is:

$$s_1 = \bar{a} \cdot \bar{x}_1 = (12, 17, 6)(0, 1, 1) = 23,$$
$$s_2 = \bar{a} \cdot \bar{x}_2 = (12, 17, 6)(0, 1, 0) = 17,$$
$$s_3 = \bar{a} \cdot \bar{x}_3 = (12, 17, 6)(1, 0, 1) = 18,$$
$$s_4 = \bar{a} \cdot \bar{x}_4 = (12, 17, 6)(-1, -1, -1) = 3.$$

The secret $k = \bar{a} \cdot (1, 0, 0) = 12$. Recovery of the secret is possible only when the vector $(1, 0, 0)$ is a linear combination of public vectors $\bar{x}_i$ for some i. So for $\mathcal{B} = \{P_1, P_2, P_3\}$ we know that $(1, 0, 0) = \bar{x}_3 + \bar{x}_2 - \bar{x}_1$. If a combiner knows the shares $s_1, s_2,$ and s_3, the secret $k = \bar{a}(1, 0, 0) = \bar{a}(\bar{x}_3 + \bar{x}_2 - \bar{x}_1) = s_3 + s_2 - s_1 = 18 + 17 - 23 \equiv 12 \bmod 19.$

9.4.3 Non-ideal Optimal Secret Sharing

Consider secret sharing over the access structure Γ whose upper bounds on information rates are different from 1. Clearly, it is impossible to design ideal schemes (as they do not exist). It makes sense, however, to investigate how the optimal scheme can be constructed.

Consider the access structure $\Gamma = cl(\{\{P_1, P_2\}, \{P_2, P_3\}, \{P_3, P_4\}\})$ whose upper bound on information rate is $\rho \leq 2/3$. Using the Ito-Saito-Nishizeki construction, we get:

	s_1 s_2 s_3
P_1	1 0 0
P_2	0 1 1
P_3	1 1 0
P_4	0 0 1

In other words, the participants hold the following shares:

$$P_1 \rightarrow \{s_1\},$$
$$P_2 \rightarrow \{s_2, s_3\},$$
$$P_3 \rightarrow \{s_1, s_2\},$$
$$P_4 \rightarrow \{s_3\},$$

where $s_i \in \mathcal{T}$ are share tokens, $i = 1, 2, 3, 4$. Note that for any $\mathcal{B} \in \Gamma$ the members of $\mathcal{B}$ have the complete collection $\{s_1, s_2, s_3, s_4\}$ that allows them to recover the secret

$$k = \sum_{i=1}^{3} s_i,$$

as in the Karnin-Greene-Hellman scheme where $k, s_i \in GF(p)$. The information rate of the scheme is $\rho = \frac{1}{2}$, which is smaller than optimal.

The information rates of the scheme can be improved if we give the participant P_3 a single share token $s_1 + s_2$ so the distribution of tokens is as follows:

	s_1 s_2 s_3 $s_1 + s_2$
P_1	1 0 0 0
P_2	0 1 1 0
P_3	0 0 0 1
P_4	0 0 1 0

There is also a second variant with the same information rates for which P_2 gets a single token. This variant can be represented as:

	s_1 s_2 s_3 $s_2 + s_3$
P_1	1 0 0 0
P_2	0 0 0 1
P_3	1 1 0 1
P_4	0 0 1 0

Assume that our scheme is used for the secret $k = (k_1, k_2) \in GF(p) \times GF(p)$. Now we use the first variant for $k_1 \in GF(p)$ and the second for $k_2 \in GF(p)$. The secret sharing is illustrated below.

	s_{11} s_{12} s_{13} $s_{11} + s_{12}$	s_{21} s_{22} s_{23} $s_{22} + s_{23}$
P_1	1 0 0 0	1 0 0 0
P_2	0 1 1 0	0 0 0 1
P_3	0 0 0 1	1 1 0 0
P_4	0 0 1 0	0 0 1 0

In other words, the participants hold the following shares (collections of tokens):

$$P_1 \rightarrow \{s_{11}, s_{21}\},$$
$$P_2 \rightarrow \{s_{12}, s_{13}, s_{22} + s_{23}\},$$
$$P_3 \rightarrow \{s_{11} + s_{12}, s_{21}, s_{22}\},$$
$$P_4 \rightarrow \{s_{13}, s_{23}\}.$$

The information rates are $\rho_1 = \rho_4 = 1$ and $\rho_2 = \rho_3 = \frac{2}{3}$. So $\rho = \frac{2}{3}$ and $\tilde{\rho} = \frac{5}{6}$. This is an optimal scheme. The approach presented is taken from [84]. Some other methods for optimal secret sharing are based on ideal decomposition and linear programming [494].

9.5 Extended Capabilities

So far we have studied fundamental properties and constructions of secret sharing. In many circumstances, secret sharing is expected to provide extra functionality. Here is a list that shows some examples:

– The scheme is set up collectively by all participants (there is no single entity called the dealer).
– The parameters of secret sharing need to be modified. The modification typically includes admission of a new participant to the group (enrollment), removal of a participant from the group (disenrollment), and change of the access structure (say increment or decrement of the threshold parameter).

– Shares in long-lived secret sharing are subject to numerous risks related to their loss or corruption. These risks, although negligible for secret sharing whose life span is short (say a week/month), tend to cumulate over time and cannot be ignored for long-lived secret sharing (life spans of years or tens of years). *Proactive secret sharing* allows us to recover lost shares by running (collectively) a share refreshment protocol.

– Verifiable secret sharing allows participants to check whether shares they are given by the dealer are consistent with other shares and the secret.

– Cheating prevention, where a dishonest participant intentionally modifies shares in such a way that after the combiner announces the secret the cheating participant is able to compute it.

Let us consider the cheating problem. So far we have assumed that all participants are honest and follow the recovery protocol of the secret. Tompa and Woll [509] studied the problem of cheaters who do not obey the protocol. Although they analyzed the susceptibility of the Shamir scheme to cheating, their results can be easily extended to many other implementations of secret sharing.

Given a (t,n) Shamir scheme with a polynomial $f(x) = a_0 + a_1 x + \ldots, a_{t-1} x^{t-1}$ over $GF(p)$, assume that at the pooling time there are t co-operating participants $P_1, \ldots, P_t$ who wish to reconstruct the secret. Among them there is a cheater, say P_1, who wants to submit a false share. The share is modified in a such way that after the combiner announces the reconstructed (incorrect) secret, P_1 can correct it and recreate the correct value of the secret.

How can the cheater P_1 modify his share? Assume that P_1 knows all cooperating participants so he knows the set $\{P_1, P_2, \ldots, P_t\}$. P_1 can now use the public information to determine a polynomial $\Delta(x)$ such that

$$\Delta(0) = \delta, \ \Delta(x_2) = 0, \ldots, \Delta(x_t) = 0.$$

This can be easily done using Lagrange interpolation. The cheater computes $\Delta(x_1)$ and creates his false share

$$\tilde{s}_1 = s_1 + \Delta(x_1).$$

P_1 submits $\tilde{s}_1$ to the combiner. Clara takes all shares $\tilde{s}_1, s_2, \ldots, s_t$ and determines the polynomial $f(x) + \Delta(x)$ and the secret $\tilde{k} = f(0) + \Delta(0) = k + \delta$ that is clearly different from the original. Nobody except the cheater can get the true secret $k = \tilde{k} - \delta$. Cheating will be undetected.

How can the Shamir scheme be modified so it is immune against this type of cheating ? One solution is that the points $x_1, \ldots, x_n$ be made secret as well. So the share is the pair $s_i = (x_i, f(x_i))$ and is kept secret by P_i. The selection of $x_1, \ldots, x_n$ is done by the dealer at random from all permutations of n distinct elements from $GF(p) \setminus \{0\}$. Now if ℓ participants cheat ($\ell \le t - 1$), there is an overwhelming probability that the recovered secret is a random value that cannot be corrected by the cheaters. Note that the cost is the increase in share size.

9.6 Problems and Exercises

1. Design a $(4, 5)$ Shamir threshold scheme over $GF(787)$. Choose at random all coefficients of the polynomial $f(x)$ and determine shares for the participants. Assume that you are a combiner. Three participants, P_2, P_4, and P_5, provided their shares so you know three points on the parabola. Let them be $(2, 123)$, $(4, 345)$, and $(5, 378)$. Find the polynomial and the secret, assuming that the threshold is 3 and arithmetic is done in $GF(787)$.

2. Consider the modular threshold scheme with the parameters $p_0 = 97$, $p_1 = 101$, $p_2 = 103$, $p_3 = 107$, and $p_4 = 109$.
   - Given the secret $k = 72$ and $s_1 = 54$, compute the other shares providing the threshold $t = 2$ ($n = 4$).
   - A combiner is given two shares $s_2 = 51$ and $s_4 = 66$, and the threshold is 2. What is the secret?

3. Take an instance of the Karnin-Greene-Hellman scheme.
   - Design a system for $t = 7$ over $GF(101)$.
   - What is the secret if $t = 5$ and the shares are $s_1 = 23$, $s_2 = 75$, $s_3 = 13$, $s_4 = 86$, and $s_5 = 56$ in $GF(101)$?

4. Suppose that $\mathcal{P} = \{A, B, C, D\}$ and the access structure basis $\Gamma_0 = \{\{A, B\}, \{B, C\}, \{C, D\}\}$. Write down a full expression for the access structure Γ (or $\Gamma = cl(\Gamma_0)$).

5. Given the access structure bases
   $\Gamma_0 = \{\{A, B\}, \{B, C\}, \{B, D\}, \{C, D\}\}$,
   $\Gamma_0 = \{\{A, B\}, \{B, C\}, \{C, D\}\}$, and
   $\Gamma_0 = \{\{A, B, C\}, \{A, B, D\}\}$,
   construct the corresponding cumulative arrays. Using the share assignments provided by the corresponding cumulative arrays and the Karnin-Greene-Hellman scheme, show how to design secret sharing schemes for the above access structures.

   Design secret sharing for the above access structures using the Benaloh-Leichter construction. Compare the resulting schemes with the schemes obtained using cumulative arrays.

6. The Brickell vector space construction allows us to design ideal secret sharing schemes. Let us $\mathcal{P} = \{A, B, C, D\}$. Use the Brickell method to design ideal schemes for the following access structures:

- $\Gamma_0 = \{\{A, B, C\}, \{A, B, D\}\}$. *Hint:* Apply a function $\tau : \mathcal{P} \rightarrow GF^3(103)$. $\tau(A)$ and $\tau(B)$ must assign two linear independent vectors, while $\tau(C)$ and $\tau(D)$ must assign two linear dependent vectors (try $\tau(C) = \tau(D)$). Check whether the vector $(1, 0, 0)$ can be expressed by a linear combination of the vectors assigned to participants from the access structure while the vector $(1, 0, 0)$ is not a linear combination of vectors assigned to participants from unauthorized subsets.
- $\Gamma_0 = \{\{A, B, D\}, \{A, C, D\}, \{B, C\}\}$. *Hint:* Consider the following vectors $(0, 0, 1)$, $(0, 1, 0)$, $(1, 1, 0)$, and $(1, 2, 1)$. Can you find an assignment τ that satisfies the necessary conditions?

What are the shares for $\bar{a} = (45, 3, 56)$ over $GF(57)$?

7. Take the access structure $\Gamma = cl(\{\{P_1, P_2\}, \{P_2, P_3\}, \{P_3, P_4\}, \{P_2, P_4\}\})$ whose information rate is no better that $2/3$:
   - Find a cumulative array for Γ.
   - Combine variants of the cumulative array and compute information rates for the resulting secret sharing scheme.

8. Consider a $(3, 6)$ Shamir threshold scheme over $GF(47)$. A dishonest participant P_1 can cheat the other cooperating participants by providing a modified share $\tilde{s}_1$. Assume that the participant holds his share $s_1 = 24$ and modifies it in such a way that $\Delta(0) = 13$, $\Delta(2) = 0, \ldots, \Delta(6) = 0$. What is the modified share $\tilde{s}_1$?

9. Elaborate on how a dishonest participant can cheat in the Karnin-Greene-Hellman scheme.

10. Given a (t, n) modular threshold scheme. Derive appropriate equations that can be used by a dishonest participant to cheat. How can cheating be prevented in the modular scheme?

10 Group-Oriented Cryptography

It may be required that the power to execute some operations is to be shared among members of a group. The recognition of such needs came when NIST tried to introduce the controversial Clipper Chip [368] with key escrowing to achieve legal wiretapping. The proposed escrowed encryption algorithm used two parties (called Key Escrow Agencies) to deposit the valid cryptographic key. Only if the two parties pooled their partial keys together, could ciphertext be decrypted.

This chapter is devoted to group-oriented (also called society-oriented) cryptography. The security of the solutions presented is conditional as it depends on the assumption of the intractability of the underlying numerical problems. Group-oriented cryptography emerged as a natural consequence of embedding secret sharing schemes into a single-user cryptography. Unlike in secret sharing, the secret shares held by participants should never be given to the combiner – shares are used to produce partial results. The combiner collects partial results and merges them into the final result.

Readers who want to study the subject are referred to a review by Desmedt [147].

10.1 Conditionally Secure Shamir Scheme

The Shamir scheme described previously is one-time. Once shares have been pooled, the secret is recovered and used. The scheme dies. Also if a participant loses his share, the whole scheme needs to be regenerated and new shares redistributed. This can be avoided if the Shamir scheme is combined with exponentiation in $GF(q)$ in which discrete logarithm instances are intractable.

10.1.1 Description of the Scheme

The conditionally secure Shamir scheme is defined by two algorithms: dealer and combiner. The dealer, Don, selects at random a polynomial $f(x) = a_0 + a_1 x + \ldots + a_{t-1} x^{t-1}$ of degree at most $(t-1)$ and distributes *permanent shares* $s_i = f(x_i)$ to participants P_i $(i = 1, \ldots, n)$ via a secure channel. The values $x_i \in GF(q)$ are public. Don also chooses at random a primitive element $g \in GF(q)$, a generator of the cyclic group of the field, and broadcasts it to all participants via a public channel. We also require that $q = 2^\ell$ so that $q - 1 = p$ is a prime, i.e., p is a *Mersenne prime*. Note that if p is prime then all nonzero elements of $GF(q)$ have their multiplicative inverses. The secret is

$$k = g^{f(0)}$$

and each participant P_i can easily calculate his *transient share*

$$c_i = g^{s_i} = g^{f(i)}.$$

The transient shares c_i in our scheme are like the public communications in the Diffie-Hellman [152] protocol. The scheme is based on the function

$$F(x) = g^{f(x)} = g^{a_0} (g^{a_1})^x \; \cdots \; (g^{a_{t-1}})^{x^{t-1}}$$
$$= g_0 \, g_1^x \; \cdots \; g_{t-1}^{x^{t-1}},$$

where $g_i = g^{a_i}$ for $i = 0, \ldots, (t-1)$ and $k = F(0)$.

At the pooling time, the combiner, Clara, collects t transient shares $(c_{i_1} = g^{f(x_{i_1})}, \ldots, c_{i_t} = g^{f(x_{i_t})})$ from participants $(P_{i_1}, \ldots, P_{i_t})$, and sets up the following system of equations in $GF(q)$:

$$c_{i_1} = g_0 \, g_1^{x_{i_1}} \; \cdots \; g_{t-1}^{x_{i_1}^{t-1}},$$
$$c_{i_2} = g_0 \, g_1^{x_{i_2}} \; \cdots \; g_{t-1}^{x_{i_2}^{t-1}},$$
$$\vdots \qquad\qquad\qquad\qquad (10.1)$$
$$c_{i_t} = g_0 \, g_1^{x_{i_t}} \; \cdots \; g_{t-1}^{x_{i_t}^{t-1}}.$$

The following theorem asserts that the system of equations (10.1) has a unique solution.

Theorem 44. [85] *The system of equations (10.1) has a unique solution for the variables g_i in Galois fields $GF(q)$ for $q = 2^\ell$, such that $q - 1 = p$ is a prime and $p > 3$. The secret*

$$k = g^{f(0)} = \prod_{j=1}^{t} (c_{i_j})^{b_j}, \tag{10.2}$$

where $c_i = g^{s_i}$ and

$$b_j = \prod_{\substack{1 \le \ell \le t \\ \ell \ne j}} \frac{x_{i_\ell}}{x_{i_\ell} - x_{i_j}} \pmod{p}.$$

Equation (10.2) is equivalent to the Lagrange interpolation formula for polynomials.

Note that the permanent shares are never revealed to the combiner by their owners. They are used to generate transient shares by participants. The combiner never sees the polynomial $f(x)$. Instead she works with the function $F(x)$ in order to recalculate the secret k. This is certainly true only if the corresponding instances of discrete logarithm are intractable.

10.1.2 Renewal of the Scheme

Suppose that some transient shares have been compromised so there is a possibility that they could be used by unauthorized persons. We also assume that the permanent shares remain secret and unknown to the other participants throughout the life-time of the scheme. If a transient share c_j is invalidated, the owner, the participant P_j, notifies the combiner. The combiner invalidates all the shares of the participants, and distributes to the participants a new primitive element $\hat{g}$ via a public channel. This channel has the property that anyone can read it, but the transmitted messages cannot be modified without detection of such modifications. After authentication of the new primitive element, the participants use $\hat{g}$ to regenerate his transient shares using

$$\hat{c}_i = \hat{g}^{s_i} \text{ for } i = 1, \ldots, n.$$

Renewal algorithm – regenerates lost transient shares.

R1. Participant P_i notifies the combiner that his share c_i has been compromised. At this stage the combiner ignores requests from other participants to reconstruct the secret key.

R2. The combiner generates at random a R $(1 < R < q - 1)$ such that $\hat{g} = g^R$ is another primitive element. The element $\hat{g}$ is distributed via a public channel to all participants, and the pair (R, R^{-1}) is kept by the combiner for further reference. The combiner now accepts requests from participants who would like to reconstruct the secret key.

R3. The participants who would like to reconstruct the secret calculate their new transient shares

$$\hat{c}_i = \hat{g}^{s_i} = g^{Rs_i},$$

and send these to the combiner.

R4. The combiner computes $\hat{k} = \hat{g}^{f(0)}$ using (10.2). Now $k = g^{f(0)}$ can be readily recovered from $\hat{k}$ since

$$k = g^{f(0)} = g^{Rf(0)R^{-1}} = (\hat{k})^{R^{-1}}.$$

Only the combiner knows the pair (R, R^{-1}), hence only the combiner can recreate the secret.

Assuming that solving an instance of the discrete logarithm problem is intractable, the above algorithm will regenerate the shares securely provided that R is chosen randomly by the combiner.

The combiner can recreate the secret only if she knows t transient shares (t is the threshold value of the scheme). On the other hand, an opponent who knows only r shares ($r < t$) cannot solve the suitable system of equations and is unable to recreate the secret.

Once the scheme is created by the dealer, the secret $k = g^{f(0)}$ remains the same for the lifetime of the scheme. New primitive elements are generated from the initial primitive element by the combiner at the time when there is a group of participants who are willing to cooperate to recreate the secret.

10.1.3 Noninteractive Verification of Shares

We now describe a verification protocol that allows all participants to check whether the secret sharing scheme parameters are consistent, i.e., the shares s_i are consistent with the polynomial $f(x)$. The verification protocol due to Pedersen [399] is based on the commitment function

$$E(s, u) = g^s h^{s+u},$$

where g is a randomly chosen primitive element in $GF(q)$, and h is a randomly selected integer such that $\log_g h$ is unknown.

Definition 32. *A secret sharing with verification protocol has to satisfy the following two conditions:*

1. *If all parties, the dealer and participants, follow the protocol, then each participant P_i accepts his share s_i with probability 1 $(i = 1, \ldots, n)$.*
2. *Any subset $\mathcal{A}_i \in \Gamma$ of t or more different participants who have accepted their shares using the verification protocol recovers the secret $k = f(0)$.*

Verification protocol – checks consistency of shares.

V1. The dealer first designs a (t, n) Shamir scheme with a polynomial $f(x) = a_0 + a_1 x + \ldots + a_{t-1} x^{t-1}$ of degree at most $(t - 1)$ with shares $s_i = f(x_i)$ assigned to participants P_i $(i = 1, \ldots, n)$. The secret $k = f(0)$. Shares are communicated to corresponding participants secretly. The dealer publishes two random integers $g, h \in GF(q)$ where g is a primitive element and $\log_g h$ is not known.

V2. Don calculates $E_0 = E(k, u)$ for a random $u \in_R GF(q)$. E_0 is a commitment to the secret k. Next he chooses at random a sequence of $t - 1$ elements $b_1, \ldots, b_{t-1} \in GF(q)$ and computes commitments $E_i = E(a_i, b_i)$ to coefficients of the polynomial $f(x)$ for $i = 1, \ldots, t - 1$. All commitments E_i are broadcast.

V3. Don creates a polynomial $B(x) = u + b_1 x_1 + \ldots + b_{t-1} x^{t-1}$ and sends $u_i = B(x_i)$ to the participant P_i via a secure channel $(i = 1, \ldots, n)$.

V4. Each participant P_i verifies whether

$$E(s_i, u_i) \equiv \prod_{j=0}^{t-1} E_j^{x_i^j} \bmod q. \tag{10.3}$$

Equation (10.3) is true for each index $i = 1, \ldots, n$ as the left side of the equation can be derived from the right one, as:

$$\prod_{j=0}^{t-1} E_j^{x_i^j} \equiv E_0 \prod_{j=1}^{t-1} (g^{a_j} h^{a_j + b_j})^{x_i^j}$$

$$\equiv g^k h^{k+u} \cdot g^{a_1 x_i} h^{(a_1 + b_1) x_i} \ldots g^{a_{t-1} x_i^{t-1}} h^{(a_{t-1} + b_{t-1}) x_i^{t-1}}$$

$$\equiv g^{k + a_1 x_i + \ldots + a_{t-1} x_i^{t-1}} h^{k + a_1 x_i + \ldots + a_{t-1} x_i^{t-1} + u + b_1 x_i + \ldots + b_{t-1} x_i^{t-1}}$$

$$\equiv g^{f(x_i)}h^{f(x_i)+B(x_i)}$$

$$\equiv g^{s_i}h^{s_i+u_i}$$

$$\equiv E(s_i, u_i) \bmod q.$$

The above transformations prove that the first condition of Definition 32 is satisfied. The proof of the second condition is left as an exercise.

10.1.4 Proactive Secret Sharing

Herzberg, Jarecki, Krawczyk, and Yung came up with a concept of proactive secret sharing [238]. It is expected that throughout the lifetime of the system shares may be either compromised, lost, or corrupted. Clearly, disclosure of a share results in the effective threshold parameter in a (t, n) threshold scheme dropping by one. If more than $(n - t)$ shares are lost, then the secret cannot be recovered. If we assume that shares are being compromised (revealed or lost) gradually, then it is possible to divide the lifetime of the system into relatively short periods of time. At the beginning of each consecutive period, a share renewal protocol is run. The protocol is always successful if the deterioration of shares does not exceed the bounds for revealed and lost shares. As a result, all compromised (lost or revealed) shares are regenerated, while the secret stays the same. An important characteristic of proactive secret sharing is that the share renewal protocol does not change the value of the secret.

Definition 33. *A proactive secret sharing is a collection of two algorithms: dealer and combiner with a share renewal protocol that keeps the secret unchanged throughout the lifetime of the scheme.*

Consider an implementation of proactive secret sharing using the Shamir (t, n) threshold scheme. The scheme is initialized by the dealer. Shares are $s_i^{(0)} = f^{(0)}(x_i)$ for $i = 1, \ldots, n$ and the secret is $k = f^{(0)}(0)$ for some polynomial $f^{(0)}(x)$. The share renewal protocol run at the beginning of the ℓth period switches the scheme from the polynomial $f^{(\ell-1)}(x)$ to $f^{(\ell)}(x)$. New shares are $s_i^{(\ell)} = f^{(\ell)}(x_i)$, but the secret stays the same $k = f^{(\ell)}(0)$. The switch between two polynomials is done by using a polynomial $\delta(x)$ such that $\delta(0) = 0$. In other words, $f^{(\ell)}(x) = f^{(\ell-1)}(x) + \delta(x)$ for $\ell = 1, 2, \ldots$.

We now assume that all participants are honest or, in other words, they follow the protocol and the opponents are passive. The share renewal protocol is run concurrently by all participants P_i, $i = 1, \ldots, n$ at the beginning of each time period ℓ. Each participant P_i executes the following steps:

1. P_i chooses at random a polynomial $\delta_i(x) = d_{i,1}x + \ldots + d_{i,t-1}x^{t-1}$ in $\mathbb{Z}_q[x]$ ($d_{i,j} \in_R \mathbb{Z}_q$ for $j = 1, \ldots, t-1$). Note that $\delta_i(0) = 0$.
2. P_i communicates to each P_j ($j \neq i$) a correction $c_{ij} = \delta_i(x_j)$. Communication is done via secure channels (providing secrecy).
3. P_i collects all corrections $\delta_j(x_i)$ for $j = 1, \ldots, n$ and computes his new share $s_i^\ell = s_i^{\ell-1} + \sum_{j=1}^n \delta_j(x_i)$. The old share is discarded.

Let us illustrate the protocol on a simple example. Given a $(3, 4)$ threshold scheme with the polynomial $f^{(0)}(x) = 3 + 5x + 12x^2$ over $GF(13)$, after the initialization the collection of shares is $s_1^0 = f^{(0)}(1) = 7$, $s_2^0 = f^{(0)}(2) = 9$, $s_3^0 = f^{(0)}(3) = 9$, and $s_4^0 = f^{(0)}(4) = 7$. The participants P_1, P_2, P_3, and P_4 generate their random polynomials $\delta_1(x) = 2x + 6x^2$, $\delta_2(x) = x$, $\delta_3(x) = 5x + 7x^2$, and $\delta_4(x) = 9x^2$, respectively. Next they compute values c_{ij}. In particular, P_1 calculates $c_{11} = \delta_1(1) = 8$, $c_{12} = \delta_1(2) = 2$, $c_{13} = \delta_1(3) = 8$, $c_{14} = \delta_1(4) = 0$, P_2 computes $c_{21} = \delta_2(1) = 1$, $c_{22} = \delta_2(2) = 2$, $c_{23} = \delta_2(3) = 3$, $c_{24} = \delta_2(4) = 4$, P_3 obtains $c_{31} = \delta_3(1) = 12$, $c_{32} = \delta_3(2) = 12$, $c_{33} = \delta_3(3) = 0$, $c_{34} = \delta_3(4) = 2$, and P_4 finds out $c_{41} = \delta_4(1) = 9$, $c_{42} = \delta_4(2) = 10$, $c_{43} = \delta_4(3) = 3$, $c_{44} = \delta_4(4) = 1$. The participant P_i forwards the corrections c_{ij} to the corresponding participants P_j via secure channels. The value c_{ii} stays with P_i. The new shares are $s_1^1 = s_1^0 + c_{11} + c_{21} + c_{31} + c_{41} = 11$, $s_2^1 = s_2^0 + c_{12} + c_{22} + c_{32} + c_{42} = 9$, $s_3^1 = s_3^0 + c_{13} + c_{23} + c_{33} + c_{43} = 10$, and $s_4^1 = s_4^0 + c_{14} + c_{24} + c_{34} + c_{44} = 1$. It is easy to check that the secret stays the same.

The share renewal protocol needs to be modified if potential opponents are assumed to be active. After the exchange of shares, all participants engage themselves in a noninteractive verification of shares, described in Sect. (10.1.3). The initialization of secret sharing includes also the calculation and announcement of the public parameters necessary for verification of the shares. The commitment function used is $E(s, u) = g^s h^{s+u}$, where g is a primitive element and h is a random integer whose $\log_g h$ is unknown ($g, h \in GF(p)$). The public elements are: the function $E()$ and integers g, h, p. The protocol runs at the beginning of the ℓth time period and consists of the following steps:

1. P_i chooses at random a polynomial $\delta_i(x) = d_{i,1}x + \ldots + d_{i,t-1}x^{t-1}$ in $\mathbb{Z}_q[x]$ ($d_{i,j} \in_R \mathbb{Z}_q$ for $j = 1, \ldots, t-1$). Note that $\delta_i(0) = 0$. Next the participant generates a collection of parameters for verification of the corrections $c_{ij} =$

$\delta_i(x_j)$. They are $E_{i,j} = E(d_i, b_{i,j})$, where $B_i(x) = b_{i,0} + b_{i,1}x + \ldots + b_{i,t-1}x^{t-1}$ is a random polynomial selected by P_i and $j = 1, \ldots, t-1$.

2. P_i calculates the corrections $c_{ij} = \delta_i(x_j)$, $j = 1, \ldots, n$ $(j \neq i)$, and a proper share of the polynomial $B_i(x)$, that is, $u_{i,j} = B_i(x_j)$. The pair $(c_{ij}, u_{i,j})$ is encrypted using public-key cryptosystems of the corresponding participants P_j, i.e., $v_{ij} = E_{K_j}(c_{ij}, u_{i,j})$, where K_j is the authentic public key of P_j.

3. P_i broadcasts the message $(P_i, \ell, \{E_{i,j} \mid j = 0, \ldots, t-1\}, \{v_{ij} \mid j = 1, \ldots, n, j \neq i\})$ and appends the signature to eliminate tampering with the contents of the message.

4. After all participants have finished broadcasting, P_i decrypts the cryptograms v_{ji}, where $j = 1, \ldots, n$, $j \neq i$, and verifies the correctness of the shares c_{ji} and $u_{j,i}$ generated by P_j by checking

$$E(c_{ji}, u_{j,i}) \stackrel{?}{\equiv} \prod_{\alpha=0}^{t-1} E_{j,\alpha}^{x_i^{\alpha}} \pmod{p},$$

where $E_{j,0} = E(0, b_{i,0})$. Note that P_i has to verify $n-1$ shares (corrections) generated by other participants. If all checks are OK, P_i broadcasts a signed acceptance message. If P_i discovers that some checks have failed, P_i sends a signed accusation in which he specifies misbehaving participants.

5. If all participants have sent their acceptance messages, then each participant P_i updates his shares to $s_i^{\ell} = s_i^{\ell-1} + \sum_{j=1}^{n} c_{ji}$. The old share is discarded.

6. If there are some accusations, then the protocol resolves them (for details see [238]). As all messages are broadcast, it is reasonable to assume that all honest participants will come up with the same list of misbehaving participants. Honest participants update their shares ignoring corrections from misbehaving participants.

The above protocol has no provision for dealing with lost shares. We have assumed that at any point in time there must be a large enough set $\mathcal{D}$ of participants whose shares are valid ($|\mathcal{D}| \geq t$). The other participants $\mathcal{P} \setminus \mathcal{D}$ either lost their shares or hold invalid ones. To determine the set $\mathcal{D}$, participants employ a noninteractive verification of shares (Sect. 10.1.3). As the verification may be triggered by any participant at any time, the verification parameters must be generated at the initialization stage and updated after each renewal of shares. The next protocol allows us to recover shares, and it is run concurrently by all participants $P_i \in \mathcal{D}$. Before we describe the protocol, first note that the participants from $\mathcal{D}$ want to recover a share $s_r^{(\ell)} = f^{(\ell)}(x_r)$ of participant

$P_r \in \mathcal{P} \setminus \mathcal{D}$. Instead of revealing their shares to P_r (and compromising the secret), they randomize the polynomial $f^{(\ell)}(x)$ so $s_r^{(\ell)}$ stays the same. Finally, they supply their shares of the randomized polynomial to P_r so P_r can recover $s_r^{(\ell)}$ using the Lagrange interpolation formula.

The share recovery protocol has to be run for each lost share and involves all participants from the set $\mathcal{D}$. It takes the following steps:

1. Each $P_i \in \mathcal{D}$ selects a random polynomial $\delta_i(x)$ of degree $(t-1)$ over $\mathcal{Z}_q$ such that $\delta_i(x_r) = 0$.
2. P_i broadcasts shares to other participants from $\mathcal{D}$, i.e., sends $E_{K_j}(\delta_i(x_j))$ for $P_j \in \mathcal{D}$.
3. P_i ensembles his new share of the lost share, i.e., $s_i' = s_i^{(\ell)} + \sum_{P_j \in \mathcal{D}} \delta_i(x_j)$ and broadcasts it to P_r (for instance by cryptogram $E_{K_r}(s_i')$).
4. P_r decrypts the cryptograms and uses the Lagrange interpolation to reconstruct $s_r^{(\ell)}$ from the shares s_i' of all participants from $\mathcal{D}$.

10.2 Threshold Decryption

The (t, n) threshold decryption allows a group of n participants to extract the message from a cryptogram only if the active subgroup $\mathcal{B}$ consists of t or more participants or $\mathcal{B} \in \Gamma$. If the collaborating subgroup is smaller, it learns nothing about the message. The cryptogram is generated by a single sender and is assumed to be public.

10.2.1 ElGamal Threshold Decryption

The group decryption based on the ElGamal system was described by Desmedt and Frankel in [148]. The system is set up by the dealer, Don, who first chooses a proper Galois field $GF(p)$ such that $(q = p-1)$ is a *Mersenne prime*, $p = 2^\ell$, and discrete logarithm instances are intractable. Further, Don selects a primitive element $g \in GF(p)$ and a nonzero random integer $k \in GF(p)$. Next, Don computes $y = g^k$ and publishes the triple (g, p, y) as the public parameters of the system. The triple is stored in read-only White Pages so any potential sender has access to the authentic parameters of the given receiver. Here the receiver is a group $\mathcal{P}$ of n participants. The dealer then uses the Shamir (t, n) threshold scheme over $GF(p)$ to distribute the secret k among the participants.

The scheme uses $f(x)$ with the public sequence of $x_1, \ldots, x_n$. The shares are $s_i = f(x_i)$ for $i = 1, \ldots n$, and the secret $k = f(0)$.

Suppose that a sender Sue wants to send a message $m \in GF(p)$ to the group $\mathcal{P}$. Sue first collects the public parameters from the White Pages, chooses at random an integer $r \in \mathcal{Z}_q^*$ and computes the cryptogram $c = (g^r, my^r)$ for the message m.

Assume that $\mathcal{B} \in \Gamma$ is the authorized subset so it contains at least t participants. Let it be $\mathcal{B} = \{P_1, \ldots, P_t\}$. The first stage of decryption is executed separately by each participant $P_i \in \mathcal{B}$. P_i takes the first part of the cryptogram and computes $(g^r)^{s_i}$ in $GF(p)$. The results are sent to the combiner.

Having t values g^{rs_i}, Clara "corrects" the values by computing

$$(g^{rs_i})^{b_i},$$

where the b_is are computed from the public elements x_j of the active set $\mathcal{B}$, and

$$b_i \equiv \prod_{P_j \in \mathcal{B}; j \neq i} \frac{x_j}{x_j - x_i} \bmod q.$$

Then Clara computes $\prod_{P_i \in \mathcal{B}}(g^{rs_i})^{b_i} = g^{kr} = y^r$, and decrypts the cryptogram

$$m \equiv my^r \times y^{-r}$$

using the multiplicative inverse y^{-r} in $GF(p)$.

Note that shares are never communicated in clear to the combiner. Instead values $(g^r)^{s_i}$ are transmitted via a public channel to Clara. The scheme can be used repeatedly. Assuming that the ElGamal system is secure, the threshold ElGamal is also secure.

(t, n) ElGamal threshold decryption

Initialization: 1. The dealer selects a big enough integer $p = 2^\ell$ so $q = p-1$ is a Mersenne prime. Next, Don chooses two nonzero integers $g, k \in_R GF(q)$, and computes $y = g^k$. Don deposits (p, g, y) in the White Pages.

  2. Don designs a (t, n) Shamir scheme over $GF(p)$ with a polynomial $f(x)$ of degree at most $(t - 1)$. The secret $k = f(0)$. Shares $s_i = f(x_i)$ are communicated to $P_i \in \mathcal{P}$ secretly (x_i are public $i = 1, \ldots, n$).

Encryption: Sue takes the triple of the authentic elements from the White Pages. For a message $m \in \mathcal{Z}_q^*$, she prepares the cryptogram $C = (g^r, my^r)$, where $r \in_R \mathcal{Z}_q^*$.

Decryption: 1. Each participant $P_i \in \mathcal{B}$, $|\mathcal{B}| = t$, calculates $(g^r)^{s_i}$ and sends the result to the combiner.

2. The combiner first finds out $y^r \equiv \prod_{P_i \in \mathcal{B}} (g^{rs_i})^{b_i}$ and $m \equiv my^r \times y^{-r}$.

The above scheme can be modified to work in $GF(p)$ where p is a large prime with $p - 1 = 2q$, where q is prime.

Let us consider an example. Suppose the modulus is $p = 263$ with $q = 131$ and a primitive element is $g = 193$. Assume further that the secret $k = 161$ and $y = g^k \equiv 257 \bmod p$. The triple (g, p, y) is public. An instance of the $(3, 4)$ Shamir secret sharing is defined by the polynomial $f(x) = 161 + 88x + 211x^2$ over $GF(p)$. Participants are $\mathcal{P} = \{P_1, P_2, P_3, P_4\}$ with public coordinates $x_1 = 1$, $x_2 = 2$, $x_3 = 3$, and $x_4 = 4$. Their shares are $s_1 = f(1) = 197$, $s_2 = f(2) = 129$, $s_3 = f(3) = 220$, and $s_4 = f(4) = 207$, and $k = f(0) = 161$. To send a message $m = 157$, Sue selects a random integer $r = 95$ and forwards the cryptogram $c = (g^r, my^r) = (247, 139)$ over $GF(p)$.

Assume that our active set is $\mathcal{B} = \{P_1, P_2, P_4\}$. On arrival of the cryptogram c, each participant $P_i \in \mathcal{B}$ computes their correction b_i. The corrections are: $b_1 = \frac{x_2}{x_2 - x_1} \frac{x_4}{x_4 - x_1} = 178 \bmod 263$, $b_2 = \frac{x_1}{x_1 - x_2} \frac{x_4}{x_4 - x_2} = 261 \bmod 263$, and $b_4 = \frac{x_1}{x_1 - x_4} \frac{x_2}{x_2 - x_4} = 88 \bmod 263$. Next each $P_i \in \mathcal{B}$ takes the first part of the cryptogram and finds $g^{rs_i b_i}$, so

$$g^{rs_1 b_1} \equiv 233 \pmod{p}, \quad g^{rs_2 b_2} \equiv 169 \pmod{p}, \quad g^{rs_4 b_4} \equiv 30 \pmod{p}.$$

The above integers are communicated to Clara who multiplies them, finds $y^r \equiv 155 \bmod p$, and retrieves the message $m = 157$.

10.2.2 RSA Threshold Decryption

Desmedt and Frankel [149] showed how the RSA public key cryptosystem can be combined with the Shamir scheme for group decryption.

All public computations in RSA are done modulo N where $N = pq$ (p, q are strong primes, i.e., $p - 1 = 2p'$ and $q - 1 = 2p'$, where p' and q' are primes). The secret computations are done in the multiplicative (cyclic) group of invertible elements of the ring $\mathcal{Z}_N$, and can be performed when $\lambda(N) = lcm(p-1, q-1) = 2p'q'$ is known. Suppose we use a (t, n) Shamir threshold scheme defined by a polynomial $f(x)$ of degree at most $(t-1)$. The polynomial can be reconstructed by every subset $\mathcal{B}$ of t participants using the Lagrange interpolation formula

$$f(x) = \sum_{P_i \in \mathcal{B}} f(x_i) \prod_{\substack{j \neq i \\ P_j \in \mathcal{B}}} \frac{(x - x_j)}{(x_i - x_j)} \mod \lambda(N). \tag{10.4}$$

Computations modulo $\lambda(N)$ can be done by applying the Chinese Remainder Theorem. This involves calculations for the following three moduli: 2, p', and q'. Multiplicative inverses of $(x_i - x_j)$ in (10.4) exist only if they are coprime to $\{2, p', q'\}$. It is impossible to satisfy these conditions when the number of participants is greater than two. For example, it is impossible to select three x_1, x_2, x_3 such that all their differences are odd. The way out is to set $f(x_i)$ $(i = 1, \ldots, n)$ and all differences (x_i, x_j) $(i \neq j)$ to even numbers, so that all computations yield integers that can be represented as vectors: $a = (0 \mod 2, a \mod p', a \mod q')$. This implies that all x_i $(i = 1, \ldots, n)$ have to be odd (including the coordinate for the secret). Therefore we assume that the secret is $f(-1)$, instead of the usual 0.

Consider the denominator of (10.4)

$$\prod_{P_j \in \mathcal{B}; j \neq i} \frac{1}{(x_i - x_j)} = \frac{\prod_{P_j \in \mathcal{P} \backslash \mathcal{B}; j \neq i}(x_i - x_j)}{\prod_{P_j \in \mathcal{P}; j \neq i}(x_i - x_j)}.$$

Note that $\alpha_i = \prod_{P_j \in \mathcal{P}; j \neq i}(x_i - x_j)$ does not depend upon the currently active set of participants $\mathcal{B}$ and is known to the dealer at the setup time. So (10.4) can be equivalently represented as

$$f(x) = \sum_{P_i \in \mathcal{B}} \frac{f(x_i)}{\alpha_i} \prod_{P_j \in \mathcal{P} \backslash \mathcal{B}; j \neq i} (x_i - x_j) \prod_{P_j \in \mathcal{B}; j \neq i} (x - x_j) \mod \lambda(N). \tag{10.5}$$

Now we are ready to describe the RSA threshold decryption. The dealer first designs an RSA system with public elements: the modulus N and the public exponent e. The secret key is d and $e \cdot d = 1 \mod \lambda(N)$. Don next sets up a Shamir (t, n) threshold scheme with polynomial $f(x)$. All public coordinates x_i are odd numbers. The secret $d - 1 = f(-1)$ and all shares $s_i = \frac{f(x_i)}{\alpha_i}$ are even numbers. The shares are distributed to participants of $\mathcal{P}$ secretly.

For a message $m \in \mathcal{Z}_N$, a sender creates the cryptogram $c = m^K \pmod{N}$ and broadcasts it to the group. On receipt, each participant P_i of a subgroup $\mathcal{B} = \{P_1, \ldots, P_t\} \in \Gamma$ computes

$$c_i \equiv c^{s_i} \mod N$$

and dispatches the result to a trusted combiner.

Clara collects partial cryptograms $c_i, i = 1, \ldots, t$ and, knowing the currently active subset $\mathcal{B} = \{P_1, \ldots, P_t\}$, modifies them:

$$\hat{c}_i \equiv c_i^{\prod_{P_j \in \mathcal{P} \backslash \mathcal{B}; j \neq i}(x_i - x_j) \prod_{P_j \in \mathcal{B}; j \neq i}(-1-x_j)} \mod N. \tag{10.6}$$

Finally, she recovers the message

$$\prod_{P_i \in \mathcal{B}} \hat{c}_i \cdot c = c^{f(-1)+1} = c^d \equiv m \pmod{N}.$$

(t, n) RSA threshold decryption

Initialization: 1. The dealer designs an RSA system with the modulus N, the public key e, and the secret key d. Public elements (N, e) are deposited with the White Pages.

2. Don sets up a (t, n) Shamir scheme with a polynomial $f(x)$ of degree at most $(t - 1)$ over $\mathcal{Z}_{\varphi(N)}$. The coordinates x_i are odd and public. Shares $s_i = \frac{f(x_i)}{\alpha_i}$ are even, where $\alpha_i = \prod_{P_j \in \mathcal{P}; j \neq i}(x_i - x_j)$. The secret $f(-1) = d - 1$.

Encryption: Sue takes public elements N, e from the White Pages. For a message $m \in \mathcal{Z}_N$, the cryptogram $c \equiv m^e \mod N$.

Decryption: 1. Each participant $P_i \in \mathcal{B}, |\mathcal{B}| = t$, computes $c_i \equiv c^{s_i} \mod N$.

2. The combiner corrects the partial decryptions, getting $\hat{c}_i$ according to Congruence (10.6) and recovers the message m.

Let us illustrate the scheme on a simple example. The dealer selects two primes $p = 11$ and $q = 23$. The modulus $N = pq = 253$ and $\lambda(N) = 110$. The dealer also creates an instance of Shamir secret sharing for four participants $\mathcal{P} = \{P_1, P_2, P_3, P_4\}$ with the threshold $t = 3$ using a random polynomial of degree at most 2 over $\mathcal{Z}_{\lambda(N)}$. Let it be $f(x) = 6 + 15x + 81x^2$. The public coordinates are $x_1 = 1$, $x_2 = 3$, $x_3 = 5$, and $x_4 = 7$. The secret key $d = f(-1) + 1 = 73$ and the public key $e = 107$. The public information is (e, N) and coordinates x_i for $P_i \in \mathcal{P}$. Don computes parameters α_i and:

$$\begin{aligned}
\alpha_1 &= (x_1 - x_2)(x_1 - x_3)(x_1 - x_4) \equiv 62 \pmod{110}, \\
\alpha_2 &= (x_2 - x_1)(x_2 - x_3)(x_2 - x_4) \equiv 16 \pmod{110}, \\
\alpha_3 &= (x_3 - x_1)(x_3 - x_2)(x_3 - x_4) \equiv 94 \pmod{110}, \\
\alpha_4 &= (x_4 - x_1)(x_4 - x_2)(x_4 - x_3) \equiv 48 \pmod{110}.
\end{aligned}$$

Clearly, α_i does not have its inverse modulo 110 as they are even and divisible by 2. Take α_1. It can be represented in the vector form as $\alpha_1 = (0 \bmod 2, 2 \bmod$

$5, 7 \bmod 11$). We compute $\beta_1 = (0 \bmod 2, 2^{-1} \bmod 5, 7^{-1} \bmod 11) = (0, 3, 8) = 8$ and:

$$\beta_2 = (0 \bmod 2, 1 \bmod 5, 9 \bmod 11) = 86,$$
$$\beta_3 = (0 \bmod 2, 4 \bmod 5, 2 \bmod 11) = 24,$$
$$\beta_4 = (0 \bmod 2, 2 \bmod 5, 3 \bmod 11) = 102.$$

Don prepares shares for participants

$$s_1 = f(x_1)\beta_1 \equiv 46 \quad (\bmod \ 110),$$
$$s_2 = f(x_2)\beta_2 \equiv 90 \quad (\bmod \ 110),$$
$$s_3 = f(x_3)\beta_3 \equiv 54 \quad (\bmod \ 110),$$
$$s_4 = f(x_4)\beta_4 \equiv 30 \quad (\bmod \ 110),$$

and sends them to corresponding participants via secret channels.

A sender, Sue, takes her message $m = 67$ and public elements and computes the cryptogram $c = m^e = 67^{107} \equiv 89 \bmod 253$. The cryptogram is broadcast to all participants. Let an active set be $\mathcal{B} = \{P_1, P_3, P_4\}$. Each participant from $\mathcal{B}$ computes his partial cryptogram, and

$$c_1 = c^{s_1} \equiv 78 \quad (\bmod \ 253),$$
$$c_3 = c^{s_3} \equiv 100 \quad (\bmod \ 253),$$
$$c_4 = c^{s_4} \equiv 144 \quad (\bmod \ 253).$$

The partial cryptograms are sent to the combiner. Clara corrects the cryptograms

$$\hat{c}_1 = c_1^{(x_1-x_2)(-1-x_3)(-1-x_4)} \equiv 177 \quad (\bmod \ 253),$$
$$\hat{c}_3 = c_3^{(x_3-x_2)(-1-x_1)(-1-x_4)} \equiv 210 \quad (\bmod \ 253),$$
$$\hat{c}_4 = c_4^{(x_4-x_2)(-1-x_1)(-1-x_3)} \equiv 100 \quad (\bmod \ 253),$$

and recovers the message

$$m = \prod_{P_i \in \mathcal{B}} \hat{c}_i \cdot c = \hat{c}_1 \hat{c}_3 \hat{c}_4 c \equiv 67 \quad (\bmod \ 253).$$

10.2.3 RSA Decryption Without Dealer

It may happen that participants fail to agree on who can be a trusted dealer. The way out is to allow the sender to set up the system and to compose the requested group of receivers at the time when there is a need for communication. Also the sender can exercise her discretion in the selection of the threshold parameter t. The scheme we describe here is taken from [198].

Suppose that all participants have established their own RSA public key cryptosystems and registered their systems with the White Pages. The registry provides the authentic public parameters of all registered RSA systems. Now we will show how the sender constructs a group decryption system on top of the single-user RSA systems. The sender, Sue, creates the group $\mathcal{P} = \{P_1, \ldots, P_n\}$ and looks up the White Pages for its public parameters. Let them be N_i and e_i for $i = 1, \ldots, n$, ordered in the increasing order so $N_i < N_{i+1}$. Next, Sue selects at random a polynomial $f(x)$ of degree at most $(t-1)$ over $GF(p)$ where $p < N_1$. She further computes the collection of shares

$$s_i = f(x_i)$$

for public coordinates x_i, $i = 1, \ldots, n$ and the secret $d = f(0)$. The shares are hidden using RSA encryption, so

$$c_i = s_i^{e_i} \bmod N_i.$$

The first part of the cryptogram C_1 is the merge of all encrypted shares using the Chinese Remainder Theorem:

$$C_1 = (c_1 \bmod N_1, \ldots, c_n \bmod N_n).$$

For a message m ($m \leq \prod_{i=1}^{t} N_i$), the sender computes $m_i \equiv m \bmod N_i$ and $m_i^d \bmod N_i$ and creates

$$C_2 = (m_1^d \bmod N_1, \ldots, m_n^d \bmod N_n).$$

The cryptogram $C = (\mathcal{P}, p, t, C_1, C_2)$ is broadcast.

Each participant $P_i \in \mathcal{P}$ performs the following operations: First, P_i gets $c_i \equiv C_1 \bmod N_i$ and $m_i^d \equiv C_2 \bmod N_i$. Next, using his secret key d_i recovers the share $s_i \equiv c_i^{d_i} \bmod N_i$. The share s_i is broadcast to all other participants. After receiving $t - 1$ shares, each participant in the group can reconstruct the secret $d \in GF(p)$ and compute

$$m_i \equiv (m_i^d)^{d^{-1}} \bmod N_i.$$

Although d is public, only the participant P_i is able to find the inverse d^{-1} as P_i knows the factors of N_i and can calculate $d \cdot d^{-1} \equiv 1 \bmod \lambda(N_i)$. Now, if t participants have sent their partial messages m_i, the combiner can recreate the message m using the Chinese Remainder Theorem.

The decryption process involves two stages: the recovery of the secret d and the reconstruction of the message. If at least t participants have collaborated at each stage, the message m is reconstructed. If fewer than $t - 1$ participants broadcast their shares s_i at the first stage, then the exponent d is unknown and the message cannot be recovered. An interesting case is when the requested number of $t - 1$ participants have broadcast their shares but fewer than t deposited their partial message to the combiner. More formally, let the combiner know $(m_1, \ldots, m_{t-1})$. Then the recovery of the message m is reduced to a guess of a single partial message, say m_t.

(t, n) RSA threshold decryption without dealer

Initialization: 1. The sender creates a group $\mathcal{P} = \{P_1, \ldots, P_n\}$. She collects the public parameters of their RSA systems $(e_i, N_i), i = 1, \ldots, n$ from the White Pages.

2. Sue constructs a (t, n) Shamir scheme with a polynomial $f(x)$ over $GF(p)$ where $p < N_1$. The secret $d = f(0)$ and shares $s_i = f(x_i)$. The coordinates x_i are public.

Encryption: 1. Sue computes $c_i \equiv s_i^{d_i} \bmod N_i$, $i = 1, \ldots, n$. The first part of the cryptogram is $C_1 = (c_1 \bmod N_1, \ldots, c_n \bmod N_n)$.

2. For a message $m \leq \prod_{i=1}^t N_i$, she creates $C_2 = (m_1^d \bmod N_1, \ldots, m_n^d \bmod N_n)$.

3. The cryptogram $C = (\mathcal{P}, p, t, C_1, C_2)$ is broadcast.

Decryption: 1. Each participant $P_i \in \mathcal{B}$, $|\mathcal{B}| = t$, gets c_i and m_i^d. Next P_i recovers $s_i = c_i^{d_i} \bmod N_i$. The shares s_i are broadcast.

2. After receiving $t - 1$ shares, participant P_i reconstructs $d \in GF(p)$ and computes his partial messages m_i.

3. The combiner recreates the message m having any t partial messages.

10.3 Threshold Signatures

Group signatures appeared as so-called multisignatures. The concept of multisignatures was introduced independently by Boyd in [53] and Okamoto [387]. A group of n participants generates a multisignature if all n members have to contribute to sign documents. Desmedt and Frankel in [148] generalized the concept of multisignatures to the case when each t out of n participants are able to sign a document – these are threshold signatures. Note that any $(t - 1)$

or fewer participants fail to sign a document. The verification of signatures can be done by any single person who knows the document and the signature (and perhaps some additional public information). The threshold signature system is initialized by a trusted dealer who creates all the necessary secret parameters used by the participants. The signing algorithm is executed independently by the participants. The results are given to a not necessarily trusted combiner who generates the signature. The signature is attached to the message. The verification algorithm can be executed by anybody.

10.3.1 RSA Threshold Signatures

An RSA group signature can be implemented in a similar fashion to the RSA threshold decryption. The group of signers is $\mathcal{P} = \{P_1, \ldots, p_n\}$ and the threshold parameter is t. The necessary adjustments are presented below.

(t, n) RSA threshold signature

Initialization: 1. The dealer designs an RSA system with the modulus N, the public key e, and the secret key d. The collection of public elements is stored in the White Pages.

2. Don sets up a (t, n) Shamir scheme with a polynomial $f(x)$ of degree at most $(t - 1)$ over $\mathcal{Z}_{\lambda(N)}$. The coordinates x_i are odd and public. Shares $s_i = \frac{f(x_i)}{\alpha_i}$ are even, where $\alpha_i = \prod_{P_j \in \mathcal{P}; j \neq i}(x_i - x_j)$. The secret $f(-1) = d - 1$. The shares are secretly communicated to $\mathcal{P}$.

Signing: For a given message $m \in \mathcal{Z}_N$, the group $\mathcal{B} \subset \mathcal{P}$ of t participants wants to sign the message.

1. Each participant $P_i \in \mathcal{B}$ computes his partial signature
$$c_i \equiv m^{s_i} \bmod N.$$

2. The combiner, Clara, collects t partial signatures and modifies them according to the currently active group $\mathcal{B}$
$$\hat{c}_i \equiv c_i^{\prod_{P_j \in \mathcal{P} \setminus \mathcal{B}; j \neq i}(x_i - x_j) \prod_{P_j \in \mathcal{B}; j \neq i}(-1 - x_j)} \bmod N.$$

3. Clara assembles the signature
$$\sigma = \prod_{P_i \in \mathcal{B}} \hat{c}_i = m^{f(-1)} \equiv m^{d-1} \bmod N.$$

Verification: The verifier, Victor, looks up the White Pages for the public parameters (N, e) of the RSA system used by the group $\mathcal{P}$. Next Victor takes a pair $(\tilde{m}, \tilde{\sigma})$ and checks whether

$$\text{VER}(\tilde{m}, \tilde{\sigma}) = \left((\tilde{\sigma} \cdot \tilde{m})^e \stackrel{?}{\equiv} \tilde{m} \bmod N \right). \tag{10.7}$$

If the congruence is true the signature is accepted, otherwise it is rejected.

Note that the signature is anonymous, as the currently active subset $\mathcal{B}$ of t cosigners cannot be identified by the verifier.

Recall the example from Sect. 10.2.2. We are going to use the setting to illustrate the RSA threshold signature. The primes $p = 11$ and $q = 23$, the modulus $N = 253$, and $\lambda(N) = 110$. The set of participants is $\mathcal{P} = \{P_1, P_2, P_3, P_4\}$ with the $(3, 4)$ threshold secret sharing based on the polynomial $f(x) = 6 + 15x + 81x^2$ over $\mathcal{Z}_{\lambda(N)}$. The public coordinates are $x_1 = 1$, $x_2 = 3$, $x_3 = 5$, and $x_4 = 7$. The secret key $d = f(-1) + 1 = 73$ and the public key $e = 107$. The public information is (e, N) and the coordinates x_i for $P_i \in \mathcal{P}$. Don computes parameters $\alpha_1 = 62$, $\alpha_2 = 16$, $\alpha_3 = 94$, and $\alpha_4 = 48$. Their "false" inverses are $\alpha_1^{-1} = 8$, $\alpha_2^{-1} = 86$, $\alpha_3^{-1} = 24$, and $\alpha_4^{-1} = 102$. The shares are $s_1 = 46$, $s_2 = 90$, $s_3 = 54$, and $s_4 = 30$. The shares are held by corresponding participants.

Assume that the active set of participants who collectively want to sign a message $m = 67$ is $\mathcal{B} = \{P_1, P_3, P_4\}$. Their partial signatures are:

$$c_1 = m^{s_1} \equiv 188 \pmod{253},$$
$$c_3 = m^{s_3} \equiv 12 \pmod{253},$$
$$c_4 = m^{s_4} \equiv 210 \pmod{253}.$$

The combiner collects the partial signatures and modifies them accordingly, i.e.,

$$\hat{c}_1 = c_1^{(x_1 - x_2)(-1 - x_3)(-1 - x_4)} \equiv 177 \pmod{253},$$
$$\hat{c}_3 = c_3^{(x_3 - x_2)(-1 - x_1)(-1 - x_4)} \equiv 210 \pmod{253},$$
$$\hat{c}_4 = c_4^{(x_4 - x_2)(-1 - x_1)(-1 - x_3)} \equiv 100 \pmod{253},$$

and creates the signature

$$\sigma = \prod_{P_i \in \mathcal{B}} \hat{c}_i = \hat{c}_1 \hat{c}_3 \hat{c}_4 c \equiv 133 \pmod{253}.$$

A verifier, Victor, takes the pair $(\tilde{m}, \tilde{\sigma}) = (67, 133)$ and the public key $e = 107$ and computes

$$(\tilde{\sigma}\tilde{m})^e = (133 \cdot 67)^{107} \equiv 67 \pmod{253}.$$

The result is equal to the message $m = 67$ so the signature is considered to be valid.

10.3.2 ElGamal Threshold Signatures

The scheme we present is due to Li, Hwang, and Lee [303]. The signature scheme is set up by a trusted dealer, Don, who on behalf of the group $\mathcal{P} = \{P_1, \ldots, P_n\}$ sets up the scheme. The scheme allows us to sign a message by every subset $\mathcal{B} \subset \mathcal{P}$ of t participants (cosigners).

Don first chooses a collision-resistant one-way function H, a big enough prime modulus p (say bigger than 512 bits), and a large prime divisor q of $p - 1$ (q should be not smaller than 160 bits). Also Don selects at random a generator g of the cyclic group of order q. Next, Don determines a polynomial $f(x) = a_0 + a_1 x + \ldots + a_{t-1} x^{t-1}$ with $a_i \in_R GF(q)$.

The group secret is $k = f(0)$ and the group public key is $y = g^k \bmod p$. The shares are

$$s_i = u_i + f(x_i),$$

where $u_i \in_R GF(q) \setminus 0$ and the coordinates x_i are public ($i = 1, \ldots, n$). Further, Don calculates the public elements associated with each participant $P_i \in \mathcal{P}$. They are $y_i \equiv g^{s_i} \bmod p$ and $z_i \equiv g^{u_i} \bmod p$. The parameters (H, p, q, g, y) together with $\{(y_i, z_i) \mid P_i \in \mathcal{P}\}$ are public and accessible for authentication purposes from the White Pages.

To sign a message, each participant P_i first chooses his secret integer $k_i \leq q-1$ and computes $r_i \equiv g^{k_i} \bmod p$. The element r_i is broadcast. Once the active subset $\mathcal{B}$ of t participants is known, each P_i computes:

$$R = \prod_{P_i \in \mathcal{B}} r_i \equiv g^{\sum_{P_i \in \mathcal{B}} k_i} \bmod p, \tag{10.8}$$

$$E \equiv H(m, R) \bmod q. \tag{10.9}$$

Having their (s_i, k_i), P_i generates their partial signature:

$$c_i \equiv s_i \prod_{P_j \in \mathcal{B}; j \neq i} \frac{-x_j}{x_i - x_j} + k_i E \bmod q. \tag{10.10}$$

The partial signatures (m, c_i) are sent to the combiner.

The combiner can verify partial signatures by checking whether

$$g^{c_i} \overset{?}{\equiv} y_i^{\prod_{P_j \in \mathcal{B}; j \neq i} \frac{-x_j}{x_i - x_j}} \cdot r_i^E \bmod p. \tag{10.11}$$

If all partial signatures are genuine, Clara creates the signature as:

$$\sigma \equiv \sum_{P_i \in \mathcal{B}} c_i \bmod q.$$

The triple $(\mathcal{B}, R, \sigma)$ is the signature of m.

The verifier, Victor, takes $(\mathcal{B}, \tilde{R}, \tilde{\sigma}, \tilde{m})$ and computes:

$$T \equiv \prod_{P_i \in \mathcal{B}} \tilde{z}_i^{\prod_{P_j \in \mathcal{B}; j \neq i} \frac{-x_j}{x_i - x_j}} \mod p, \tag{10.12}$$

$$\tilde{E} \equiv H(\tilde{m}, \tilde{R}) \mod q. \tag{10.13}$$

Next, Victor looks up the White Pages for the public parameters of the group and checks:

$$g^{\tilde{\sigma}} \stackrel{?}{\equiv} \tilde{y} T \tilde{R}^{\tilde{E}}.$$

If the congruence holds then the signature is valid.

(t, n) ElGamal threshold signature

Initialization: 1. The dealer selects: a collision-resistant hashing algorithm H, a prime modulus p with its prime factor q, the generator g of a cyclic group of order q, and the polynomial $f(x)$ of degree at most $(t - 1)$ with public coordinates associated with each $P_i \in \mathcal{P}$.

2. The secret of the group is $k = f(0)$. The public key of the group is $y \equiv g^k \mod p$. The shares assigned to the participants are $s_i = u_i + f(x_i)$.

3. Don publishes (H, p, q, g, y) together with $\{(y_i, z_i) \mid P_i \in \mathcal{P}\}$ where $y_i \equiv g^{s_i} \mod p$ and $z_i \equiv g^{u_i} \mod p$.

Signing: 1. Each active participant P_i chooses a secret key $k_i \leq q - 1$ and computes $r_i \equiv g^{k_i} \mod p$. The element r_i is broadcast.

2. Once the active subset $\mathcal{B} \subset \mathcal{P}$ is known, each participant $P_i \in \mathcal{B}$ computes R and E according to Congruences (10.8) and (10.9), respectively.

3. P_i computes his partial signature c_i by using (10.10) and sends (m, c_i) to the combiner.

4. The combiner, Clara, verifies the partial signatures by checking Congruence (10.11). If the congruence holds for all participants, she computes $\sigma = \sum_{P_i \in \mathcal{B}} c_i \mod p$. The triple $(\mathcal{B}, R, \sigma)$ is the signature of m.

Verification: A verifier, Victor, checks whether

$$g^{\tilde{\sigma}} \stackrel{?}{\equiv} \tilde{y} T \tilde{R}^{\tilde{E}},$$

where T is defined by Congruence (10.12) and $\tilde{E}$ by (10.13). If the check is true the signature is accepted.

The verifier accepts always a genuine signature. This observation flows from the following sequence of congruences:

$$g^{\tilde{\sigma}} \equiv g^{\sum_{P_i \in \mathcal{B}} \tilde{c}_i}$$
$$\equiv g^{\sum_{P_i \in \mathcal{B}} \tilde{s}_i \prod_{P_j \in \mathcal{B}; j \neq i} \frac{-x_j}{x_i - x_j} + \tilde{k}_i \tilde{E}}$$
$$\equiv g^{\sum_{P_i \in \mathcal{B}} (\tilde{u}_i + \tilde{f}(x_i)) \prod_{P_j \in \mathcal{B}; j \neq i} \frac{-x_j}{x_i - x_j}} g^{\sum_{P_i \in \mathcal{B}} \tilde{k}_i \tilde{E}}$$
$$\equiv g^{\sum_{P_i \in \mathcal{B}} \tilde{u}_i \prod_{P_j \in \mathcal{B}; j \neq i} \frac{-x_j}{x_i - x_j}}$$
$$\times g^{\sum_{P_i \in \mathcal{B}} \tilde{f}(x_i)) \prod_{P_j \in \mathcal{B}; j \neq i} \frac{-x_j}{x_i - x_j}} \times \prod_{P_i \in \mathcal{B}} \tilde{r}_i^{\tilde{E}}$$
$$\equiv \prod_{P_i \in \mathcal{B}} \tilde{z}_i^{\prod_{P_j \in \mathcal{B}; j \neq i} \frac{-x_j}{x_i - x_j}} \times g^{\tilde{f}(0)} \times \tilde{R}^{\tilde{E}}$$
$$\equiv \tilde{T} \tilde{y} \tilde{R}^{\tilde{E}} \bmod p.$$

The scheme has some interesting properties:

- The signature is not anonymous. The currently active subset $\mathcal{B}$ must be known to a verifier and the specification of $\mathcal{B}$ is attached to the signature. That is why the signature resembles a multisignature.
- Partial signatures c_i can be verified by a combiner. This allows us to detect and disregard faulty partial signatures.
- The length of the string σ is determined by the value of the prime q and is no longer than 160 bits.

The security depends on the intractability of the discrete logarithm. Some possible attacks are discussed in [303]. Also the authors studied a variant of their signature, which works with no dealer.

10.3.3 Threshold DSS Signatures

Gennaro, Jarecki, Krawczyk, and Rabin designed a threshold DSS signature in [196]. Recall that the regular DSS signature was described in Sect. 7.4. The signature uses two prime moduli p and q, where q is a large enough factor of $(p - 1)$. The integer $g \in GF(p)$ is an element of order q. The secret key is k $(1 \leq k \leq q)$ and the public key is $\beta = g^k$. The elements (β, g, p, q) are public. To generate a signature for a message m, the signer picks up a random integer r $(1 \leq r \leq q)$ and computes $x \equiv (g^{r^{-1}} \bmod p) \bmod q$ and $y = r(m + k \cdot x) \bmod q$. The signature of m is the pair (x, y). Note a slight modification in the definition of x for which we use r^{-1} instead of the prescribed r. To verify the triple $(\tilde{m}, \tilde{x}, \tilde{y})$, we check whether $\tilde{x} \stackrel{?}{\equiv} (g^{my^{-1}} \beta^{xy^{-1}} \bmod p) \bmod q$.

Before we describe a distributed version of the DSS signature scheme, we show how to compute $r^{-1} \bmod q$ collectively using participants $\mathcal{P} = \{P_1, \ldots, P_n\}$ when they know shares of r (each P_i knows his share r_i). To simplify our notation, we are going to use

$$(r_1, \ldots, r_n) \overset{(t,n)}{\leftrightarrow} r$$

to indicate that integer r is shared by $\mathcal{P}$ with the threshold t. The algorithm for computing reciprocals of r when its shares are distributed among participants from $\mathcal{P}$ is:

1. Participants collectively generate a (t, n) secret sharing of a random element $a \in \mathcal{Z}_q$. In other words, each participant P_i selects a random polynomial $\delta_i(x)$ of degree at most $(t - 1)$ and sends corresponding shares via a secret channel to the other participants so every P_j gets $\delta_i(x_j)$ $(i \neq j)$. The polynomial $A(x) = \sum_{i=1}^{n} \delta_i(x)$ defines our requested (t, n) secret sharing with $A(0) = a$ and shares $a_j = A(x_j) = \sum_{i=1}^{n} \delta_i(x_j)$, or $(a_1, \ldots, a_n) \overset{(t,n)}{\leftrightarrow} a$.

2. Participants collectively generate a $(2t, n)$ secret sharing of 0, that is, each participant P_i selects a random polynomial $\delta_i(x)$ (such that $\delta_i(0) = 0$) of degree at most $(2t - 1)$ and sends corresponding shares via secret channels to the other participants. The polynomial $B(x) = \sum_{i=1}^{n} \delta_i(x)$ defines the requested $(2t, n)$ secret sharing, and each P_i holds the share $b_i = B(x_i)$. Shortly, $(b_1, \ldots, b_n) \overset{(2t,n)}{\leftrightarrow} 0$.

3. Participants broadcast their values $r_i a_i + b_i$, and each participant recreates the value $\nu = ra$. Observe that, assuming that $R(x)$ is the polynomial that distributes r among $\mathcal{P}$, then the polynomial $R(x)A(x) + B(x)$ becomes ra for $x = 0$.

4. P_i computes ν^{-1} in $GF(q)$ and sets his share $u_i \equiv \nu^{-1} a_i$. It can be shown that $(u_1, \ldots, u_n) \overset{(t,n)}{\leftrightarrow} r^{-1}$.

An algorithm for a distributed DSS signature is described below. The signature is secure under the assumption that the opponent is passive (can eavesdrop only) and can prevent up to a third of the participants collaborating in the signing process. To simplify the description, we denote using *Joint-Shamir-RSS* a protocol in which all participants collectively generate a (t, n) Shamir secret sharing with a random secret. Each participant P_i chooses his random polynomial $\delta_i(x) = d_{i,0} + d_{i,1}x + \ldots + d_{i,t-1}x^{t-1}$, where $d_{i,j} \in_R GF(q)$. Each P_i communicates secretly shares of the polynomial $\delta_i(x)$ to other participants. Finally, the participant P_j holds a share $\sum_{i=1}^{n} \delta_i(x_j)$ of the polynomial $f(x) = \sum_{i=1}^{n} \delta_i(x)$. We denote using *Joint-Zero-SS* a protocol similar to *Joint-Shamir-RSS* except that all participants select their polynomials such that $\delta_i(0) = 0$.

(t, n) DSS signature

Initialization: 1. The dealer distributes shares of the group secret k, i.e., $(k_1, \ldots, k_n) \overset{(t,n)}{\leftrightarrow} k$ using a polynomial $f(x)$.

2. The dealer announces the public information (β, g, p, q) where $\beta = g^k$ is the public key, $g \in GF(p)$ is an element of order q, and p, q are two primes such that q is a large factor of $p - 1$.

Signing: 1. Participants $\mathcal{P}$ collectively generate a random integer r $(1 \geq r \geq q)$ by running the *Joint-Shamir-RSS* protocol, i.e., $(r_1, \ldots, r_n) \overset{(t,n)}{\leftrightarrow} r$.

2. Participants run the *Joint-Zero-SS* protocol twice and obtain two schemes:
$$(b_1, \ldots, b_n) \overset{(2t,n)}{\leftrightarrow} b \text{ and } (c_1, \ldots, c_n) \overset{(2t,n)}{\leftrightarrow} c.$$

3. Participants jointly compute $x = g^{r^{-1}} \bmod q$.

   (a) Participants collectively execute *Joint-Shamir-RSS* so
   $$(a_1, \ldots, a_n) \overset{(t,n)}{\leftrightarrow} a.$$

   (b) Participant P_i broadcasts $v_i \equiv r_i a_i + b_i \bmod q$ and $w_i \equiv g^{a_i} \bmod p$. The elements v_i, w_i are public for $i = 1, \ldots, n$.

   (c) P_i calculates the secret $v = ra \bmod q$ using the Lagrange interpolation of $(v_1, \ldots, v_n)$. Similarly, P_i computes $g^a \bmod p$ using $(w_1, \ldots, w_n)$. Clearly, $x \equiv (g^a)^{v^{-1}} \bmod p \bmod q$. The first part of signature x is published.

4. Participants collectively calculate $y \equiv r(m + k \cdot x) \bmod q$.

   (a) P_i broadcasts $y_i \equiv r_i(m + k_i x) + c_i \bmod q$. Note that
   $$(y_1, \ldots, y_n) \overset{(2t,n)}{\leftrightarrow} y = r(m + kx).$$

   (b) P_i individually interpolates y from public y_i, $i = 1, \ldots, n$.

5. The signature of message m is (x, y).

Verification: This proceeds as for the regular DSS signature. To verify the triple $(\tilde{m}, \tilde{x}, \tilde{y})$, Victor checks whether

$$\tilde{x} \overset{?}{\equiv} (g^{my^{-1}} \beta^{xy^{-1}} \bmod p) \bmod q.$$

The above signature tolerates up to $(t-1)$ lost shares with the total number of $n \geq 2t + 1$ participants.

A version of the threshold DSS signature that allows us to sign messages in the presence of malicious opponents is described in [196].

10.4 Problems and Exercises

1. Given a $(2,3)$ conditionally secure Shamir scheme over $GF(23)$ with $f(x)$ where P_i is assigned $x_i = i$ for $i = 1, 2, 3$. Assume some primitive element $g \in GF(23)$ and take $s_1 = f(1) = 4$ and $s_2 = f(2) = 19$. What is the missing s_3? Retrieve the secrets $k = f(0)$ and $k' = g^k$. Show how the computation of k' can be done when participants pool their transient shares g^{s_i}.

2. Design a $(2,3)$ conditionally secure Shamir scheme over $GF(2^3)$. Show the reconstruction process of the secret when transient shares are pooled by participants.

3. Feldman [170] suggested a noninteractive verification of shares for a (t, n) Shamir scheme with the polynomial $f(x) = a_0 + a_1 x + \ldots + a_{t-1} x^{t-1}$ over $GF(p)$ such that $p = \alpha q + 1$ (α is a small integer while q is a large prime). The dealer, after distribution of the shares $s_i = f(x_i)$ to the corresponding participants via secret channels, broadcasts public elements $g^{a_i} \bmod p$ for $i = 0, 1, \ldots, t-1$. Show how P_i can use his secret s_i together with the public information to verify the consistency of the share with the public information.

4. Prove that the noninteractive verification of shares in Sect. 10.1.3 fails with a negligible probability.

5. The concept of proactive secret sharing employs a protocol that allows participants to jointly share 0. First each participant P_i generates his own random polynomial $\delta_i(x)$ such that $\delta(0) = 0$. Next P_i plays the role of the dealer and distributes shares $\delta_i(x_j)$ to other participants. Prove that the polynomial $\delta(x) = \sum_{i=1}^{n} \delta_i(x)$ becomes 0 for $x = 0$. Show that $\sum_{i=1}^{n} \delta_i(x_j)$ is a share of 0 of P_j.

6. Given the modular secret sharing, demonstrate how participants can collectively share "0" by random selection of individual schemes and by distribution of the corresponding shares via secret channels to other participants. Generalize the concept for any linear code.

7. Consider the sequence of threshold schemes indexed by their polynomials $\{f^\ell(x) \mid \ell = 1, 2, \ldots\}$ in the proactive secret sharing. Discuss the perfectness of secret sharing for consecutive periods of time.

8. A $(3,5)$ Shamir secret sharing is defined by the polynomial $f(x) = 38 + 57x + 112x^2$ over $GF(131)$ with public coordinates assigned in a typical way, $x_i = i$ for $i = 1, 2, 3, 4, 5$. Assume that an active set of participants is $\mathcal{B} = \{P_2, P_3, P_5\}$. Compute shares s_i and corrections b_i for $i = 2, 3, 5$. Show encryption and $(3, 5)$ ElGamal threshold decryption by the active set $\mathcal{B}$ for $q = 263$, $p = 131$, and $g = 166$ (g is an element of order 131).

9. Consider an instance of the $(3,4)$ ElGamal threshold decryption scheme. Public computations should be performed over $GF(2^3)$ while secret computations (including secret sharing) should be executed modulo $p = 7$. Make all the necessary assumptions.

10. In the ElGamal threshold decryption, the final retrieval of the message from a cryptogram is done by the combiner. Discuss how the combiner can handle participants who, instead of the prescribed g^{rs_i}, have sent $g^{rs_ib_i}$.

11. In Sect. 10.2.2, the RSA threshold decryption is presented for small parameters where the modulus $N = 253$ and any 3 out of 4 participants can jointly decrypt a cryptogram. Show how the following active sets $\mathcal{B}$ can decrypt the cryptogram when
    - $\mathcal{B} = \{P_2, P_3, P_4\}$,
    - $\mathcal{B} = \{P_1, P_2, P_3\}$,
    - $\mathcal{B} = \{P_1, P_2, P_4\}$.

12. Design an instance of the RSA threshold decryption where every 2 out of 5 participants can jointly decrypt a cryptogram. Select two strong primes p and q smaller than 100. Make the necessary assumptions.

13. The RSA threshold decryption uses the Shamir secret sharing to allow us to construct any (t, n) threshold decryption. The system can be considerably simplified for (n, n) threshold decryption. Modify the general (t, n) RSA threshold decryption for the case when $t = n$. *Hint*: Apply the Karnin-Greene-Hellman secret sharing.

14. Reconsider the example from Sect. 10.3.1. Show how the combiner assembles the signature for the active sets
    - $\mathcal{B} = \{P_2, P_3, P_4\}$,
    - $\mathcal{B} = \{P_1, P_2, P_3\}$,
    - $\mathcal{B} = \{P_1, P_2, P_4\}$.

15. Simplify the ElGamal threshold signature when $t = n$ by using the Karnin-Greene-Hellman secret sharing.

11 Key Establishment Protocols

So far we have tacitly assumed that all cryptographic algorithms can be readily used assuming that a suitable collection of secret and public keys is already distributed and known to the parties. For instance, secrecy systems based on secret key encryption require the same key to be shared by both the sender and receiver. In this chapter we focus our attention on how keys that are needed to enable cryptographic protection can be exchanged among the parties. The key establishment becomes a major hurdle in computer networks with many users. To show the scale of the problem, assume that a computer network encompasses n users. If we allow any pair of users to communicate in a secure way using private key encryption, then we may need to generate and distribute

$$\binom{n}{2} = \frac{n(n-1)}{2}$$

different keys. If some network (cryptographic) services involve more than two users (for example a secure conferencing with i users where $i = 2, \ldots, n$), the number of possible keys to be distributed can grow exponentially in n

$$2^n = \sum_{i=0}^{n} \binom{n}{i}.$$

If we cannot predistribute keys, then we have to establish them on request whenever there is a collection of parties who want to share the same key.

There are two major categories of key establishment protocols:

– *key transport protocols*, and
– *key agreement protocols*.

In the first category, there is, typically, a trusted authority TA (also called a server) that generates the requested key material and distributes it among the parties. This category is also called *key distribution protocols*. The important ingredient of any TA is trust. For our purposes, trust can be translated into an assumption that a TA will follow the course of action prescribed by the key distribution protocol and will not divulge any secret information to unauthorized users. In particular, we exclude any hostile activity by a TA towards any user. Also any potential attacker is not able to corrupt or collude with TA.

Normally, in key agreement protocols, a key is established collectively as a result of some prescribed interaction among the parties involved in the protocol. This is the class of decentralized key establishment protocols where there is, typically, no need for a trusted authority to generate and distribute cryptographic keys.

The design of key establishment protocols has to be done with extreme caution mainly because the interaction is being done via an insecure public network. Usually the interaction involves the transmission of several messages or protocol passes. It is assumed that a potential attacker can:

– record messages and replay them later,
– change their order,
– modify a part of or the whole message,
– repeat some messages, or
– delete some messages.

Apart from an abundance of potential threats, large computer networks provide no global public trusted read-only registry (White Pages), which could be used to verify identities of the parties involved. The parties are usually called principals. A *principal* is understood to be any active entity. So it can be a user, a computer process, a terminal, a node in a computer network, etc.

The main goal of key establishment protocols is to enable two or more principals to obtain some cryptographic key. Some other desirable goals may include:

– key freshness,
– entity authentication,
– key confirmation,
– implicit key authentication, and
– explicit key authentication.

A key is *fresh* if it has never been generated and used before. *Entity authentication* is a corroboration process that allows one principal to correctly identify the other involved in the protocol. Typically, it allows a party to check whether the other party is active (alive) at the time when the protocol is being executed.

Key confirmation is a property of a protocol that allows one principal to make sure that the other party possesses a given key. *Implicit key authentication* provides an assurance to one principal that no one except a specific other party could have gained access to a given key. Implicit key authentication can also be viewed as *key confidentiality*. By *explicit key authentication* we mean that both implicit key authentication and key confirmation hold.

A treatment of key establishment protocols can be found in [496] and [337]. For a variety of other interpretations of entity authentication see [213].

11.1 Classical Key Transport Protocols

An elementary event in a key establishment protocol is a single transmission of a message from one principal to another. This is also called a pass of a protocol. To indicate that a principal A sends a message m to a principal B, we write $(A \rightarrow B : m)$. Note that m may consist of plaintext or ciphertext or both. For example, if A wants to use encryption to ensure the confidentiality of a plaintext $ptxt$ the transmission would be written as $(A \rightarrow B : \{ptxt\}_{k_{AB}})$, where $\{ptxt\}_{k_{AB}}$ denotes the message obtained by encrypting $ptxt$ using a (secret) cryptographic key k_{AB} shared by A and B.

In 1978 Needham and Schroeder [370] published their key exchange protocols. The aim of the protocol is to establish a secret key between two principals A and B with the help of a trusted server S.

Needham-Schroeder protocol (private key case)

Goal: To distribute a fresh secret key to A and B using a trusted server S.

Assumptions: S shares a common secret key k_{AS} with A and a common secret key k_{BS} with B. A and B choose two random challenges (nonces) r_A and r_B, respectively.

Message Sequence: The protocol consists of the following sequence of messages:

1. $A \rightarrow S : A, B, r_A$.
2. $S \rightarrow A : \{r_A, B, k_{AB}, \{k_{AB}, A\}_{k_{BS}}\}_{k_{AS}}$.
3. $A \rightarrow B : \{k_{AB}, A\}_{k_{BS}}$.
4. $B \rightarrow A : \{r_B\}_{k_{AB}}$.
5. $A \rightarrow B : \{r_B - 1\}_{k_{AB}}$.

The protocol is initiated by A who sends its name A, B's name, and its challenge r_A in clear to the server S. The server replies with the cryptogram $\{r_A, B, k_{AB}, \{k_{AB}, A\}_{k_{BS}}\}_{k_{AS}}$, where k_{AB} is the shared key to be used by A and B (also called a session key). A decrypts the cryptogram and checks whether r_A and B match the originals. This check enables A to make sure that the message has come from the holder of the secret key k_{AS} in response to A's request. If the check is successful, A accepts k_{AB} and forwards $\{k_{AB}, A\}_{k_{BS}}$ to B.

B decrypts the cryptogram, learns who wants to talk to it, and stores the key k_{AB}. The last two steps allow B to verify whether A knows the key k_{AB}. B takes his random challenge r_B and encrypts it using k_{AB}. Since A knows the key, she extracts r_B from the cryptogram, decrements r_B by 1, encrypts the result, and communicates $\{r_B - 1\}_{k_{AB}}$ to B. B decrypts the cryptogram and verifies whether the challenge has been decremented as required.

First, some general observations. The protocol uses three secure channels (each channel provides both the confidentiality and authentication). The two channels between the server and A (k_{AS}) and between the server and B (k_{BS}) are set up beforehand. The third one is created as a result of the protocol execution. All communication is done via these three channels, except the first message that is sent in clear.

Suppose that an opponent, Oscar, copies the message forwarded by A to B in the above protocol [138] and that somehow he obtains the corresponding session key k_{AB}. Perhaps, this key was used some time ago and was carelessly discarded. Now he can trick B to accept an old session key k_{AB}. Oscar replays the copied message in step 3 and successfully completes the rest of the protocol. B cannot detect Oscar's impersonation. Observe that the attack shows that the protocol fails to provide key freshness from the point of view of B. Denning and Sacco [138] suggest using timestamps to thwart the attack.

Needham-Schroeder protocol with timestamps [138]

Goal: To distribute a fresh secret key to A and B using a trusted server S.

Assumptions: S shares a common secret key k_{AS} with A and a common secret key k_{BS} with B. T denotes a timestamp value generated at S.

Message Sequence: The parties exchange the following sequence of messages:

1. $A \to S : A, B$.

2. $S \rightarrow A : \{B, k_{AB}, T, \{A, k_{AB}, T\}_{k_{BS}}\}_{k_{AS}}$.
3. $A \rightarrow B : \{A, k_{AB}, T\}_{k_{BS}}$.

A and B can make sure that messages are fresh by checking whether the transmission is within the permitted time interval.

In public key cryptography, users need to know authentic public keys. The server S distributes authentic public keys provided that every user within the server domain knows the authentic public key K_S of the server S. The original Needham-Schroeder protocol consists of seven steps. The version given below is a modification with timestamps by Denning and Sacco [138]. The protocol does not use confidentiality channels at all. All messages are transmitted in clear or in the form of public timestamped certificates (signatures). A certificate $\langle m \rangle_k$ signed using a secret key k allows anybody who knows the matching public key K to recover the message m. This is a typical way of providing an authentication channel under the assumption that K is an authentic public key of the sender and matches its secret key k.

Modified Needham-Schroeder protocol (public key case)

Goal: To distribute the authentic public keys K_A and K_B of A and B, respectively.

Assumptions: A and B know the authentic public key K_S of the server. The timestamp is T. The key k_S is the secret key of S.

Message Sequence: The protocol consists of the following sequence of messages:
    1. $A \rightarrow S : A, B$.
    2. $S \rightarrow A : \langle A, K_A, T \rangle_{k_S}, \langle B, K_B, T \rangle_{k_S}$.
    3. $A \rightarrow B : \langle A, K_A, T \rangle_{k_S}, \langle B, K_B, T \rangle_{k_S}$.

11.2 Diffie-Hellman Key Agreement Protocol

Diffie and Hellman [152] in their seminal paper made several breakthroughs in cryptology. Apart from introducing the notion of public key cryptography, they showed how two parties A and B can establish a secret key via an insecure network using a public discussion.

Diffie-Hellman key agreement protocol

Goal: To establish a secret key k between A and B.

Assumptions: A and B use a modulus p (p is a large enough prime) and a primitive element $g \in Z_p^*$. Both integers p and g are public. The integers α and β are randomly chosen from Z_{p-1} by A and B, respectively.

Message Sequence: The parties exchange the following sequence of messages:

1. $A \rightarrow B : g^\alpha \bmod p$.
2. $B \rightarrow A : g^\beta \bmod p$.

A and B compute a common secret key

$$k = \left(g^\beta\right)^\alpha = (g^\alpha)^\beta = g^{\alpha\beta} \bmod p.$$

Consider a toy example. Let the modulus $p = 2447$ and the primitive element $g = 1867$. A and B choose their secret elements at random from Z_{2446}. Let $\alpha = 1347$ and $\beta = 2186$. In step 1, A communicates to B the integer $g^\alpha = 1867^{1347} \equiv 1756 \bmod 2447$. In step 2, B sends to A the integer $g^\beta = 1867^{2186} \equiv 848 \bmod 2447$. A computes the secret key $k = (g^\beta)^\alpha = 848^{1347} \equiv 2177 \bmod 2447$. B calculates the key $k = (g^\alpha)^\beta = 1756^{2186} \equiv 2177 \bmod 2447$.

The protocol suffers from the *intruder-in-the-middle attack*. Suppose that our attacker, Oscar, sits between A and B. The attack proceeds as follows:

1. A sends B a message $(g^\alpha \bmod p)$.
2. Oscar intercepts it and forwards to B his own message $(g^\gamma \bmod p)$, where $\gamma \in Z_{p-1}$ is an integer chosen by Oscar.
3. B responds by conveying the message $(g^\beta \bmod p)$ to A.
4. Again, Oscar intercepts the message and sends $(g^\gamma \bmod p)$ to A.
5. Finally, A computes its secret key $k_A = (g^\gamma)^\alpha$ and B calculates its $k_B = (g^\gamma)^\beta$. Clearly, the secret keys computed by A and B are different. Note that Oscar knows both keys k_A and k_B and controls the message exchange between A and B.

Another manifestation of the same security problem emerges when A receives two (or more) replies g^{β_1}, g^{β_2} from two different persons. A cannot identify the senders of these messages. The parties can establish a secret key but they do not know with whom they share it! The protocol provides no key authentication and no key confirmation.

11.2.1 DH Problem

The security of the Diffie-Hellman key exchange depends upon the difficulty of finding $g^{\alpha\beta}$ from two public messages g^α and g^β. This is known as the Diffie-Hellman problem.

Name: DH search problem.
Instance: Given a prime modulus p, a primitive element $g \in Z_p^*$, and two integers a and b such that $a \equiv g^\alpha \bmod p$ and $b \equiv g^\beta \bmod p$.
Question: What is the integer c such that $c \equiv g^{\alpha\beta} \bmod p$?

Let us recall the definition of the discrete logarithm (search) problem.

Name: DL problem.
Instance: Integers (g, s) that belong to $GF(p)$ determined by a prime p.
Question: What is the integer $h \in Z_{p-1}$ such that $h = \log_g s \pmod{p}$ (or equivalently $g^h \equiv s \bmod p$)?

Note that the DL problem is not easier than the DH problem. In other words, the DL problem could be harder or as hard as the DH problem. To see this, it is enough to assume the existence of an algorithm that solves the DL problem. This algorithm also solves all instances of the DH problem. It is unknown what would have happened with the complexity of the DL problem if the DH problem had been shown to be solvable in polynomial time.

It is easy to show that inverting the ElGamal encryption is equivalent to solving the DH problem (see [496]). For further study of the DH problem, the reader is referred to [327] and [328].

One of the security goals we have not mentioned is *forward secrecy*. It is relevant to mention it in the context of the DH key agreement protocol as it is one of the few that actually provides it. Forward secrecy is achieved if disclosure of long-term keys does not compromise session keys generated before the disclosure.

11.3 Modern Key Distribution Protocols

Modern key distribution protocols are assumed to pass some sort of security scrutiny. Verification proceeds using formal methods. The algebraic approach to protocol verification applies a finite state machine analysis with a definition of bad states (a protocol failure) [274]. Burrows, Abadi, and Needham have developed a logic that can analyze the evolution of beliefs during the execution of cryptographic protocols [71]. This is the well-known BAN logic. Gong, Needham, and Yahalom have extended the BAN logic [217]. Their extension is often referred to as the GNY logic. A comprehensive review of formal verification methods for cryptographic protocols can be found in a survey paper by Meadows [334].

A different approach to the design of key distribution protocols has been suggested by Boyd and Mao [55, 56]. They argue that instead of verifying the protocol security after the design stage, it is better to formulate a rigorous design procedure so that the final product is always a secure protocol. To achieve this, the designer needs to establish the minimum cryptographic requirements imposed on a protocol and identify how these requirements are to be realized.

Otway and Rees [396] designed a protocol that was intended to provide a secure alternative for the Needham and Schroeder protocol. The protocol presented below is a modification of the original (see [56] for further details). Challenges r_A and r_B play the role of timestamps and are used to prevent the replay attack.

Modified Otway-Rees protocol (Boyd and Mao [56])

Goals: 1. Establishment of a fresh secret key k_{AB} between two principals A and B.

2. Mutual key authentication.

Assumptions: S shares a common secret key k_{AS} with A and a common key k_{BS} with B. A and B choose two random challenges (nonces) r_A and r_B, respectively.

Message Sequence: The parties send the following sequence of messages:

1. $A \rightarrow B : A, r_A$.
2. $B \rightarrow S : A, B, r_A, r_B$.
3. $S \rightarrow B : \{A, B, r_B, k_{AB}\}_{k_{BS}}, \{A, B, r_A, k_{AB}\}_{k_{AS}}$.
4. $B \rightarrow A : \{A, B, r_A, k_{AB}\}_{k_{AS}}$.

The Otway-Rees protocol uses the secure channels (defined by two secret keys k_{AS} and k_{BS}) for both message confidentiality and authentication. These two roles can be clearly separated as is shown in the following alternative protocol designed by Boyd and Mao [56].

Boyd-Mao split channel protocol

Goals: 1. Establishment of a fresh secret key k_{AB} between two principals A and B.

2. Mutual key authentication.

Assumptions: S shares a common secret key k_{AS} with A and a common key k_{BS} with B. A and B choose two random challenges (nonces) r_A and r_B, respectively. $MAC_k\{m\}$ stands for the message authentication code of the message m generated under the control of the secret key k.

Message Sequence: The parties send the following sequence of messages:

1. $A \rightarrow B : A, r_A$.
2. $B \rightarrow S : A, B, r_A, r_B$.
3. $S \rightarrow B : \{k_{AB}\}_{k_{BS}}, MAC_{k_{BS}}\{A, B, r_B, k_{AB}\},$
   $\{k_{AB}\}_{k_{AS}}, MAC_{k_{AS}}\{A, B, r_A, k_{AB}\}.$
4. $B \rightarrow A : \{k_{AB}\}_{k_{AS}}, MAC_{k_{AS}}\{A, B, r_A, k_{AB}\}.$

Note that $MAC_k\{m\}$ provides an authentication channel, whereas $\{m\}_k$ provides a confidentiality channel. $MAC_k\{m\}$ can also be generated using a keyed hashing algorithm. Only those messages that need to be recovered are encrypted. Messages sent over the authentication channel are short and of a fixed length (as determined by the length of the MAC). The advantage of the above protocol is that messages are relatively short.

11.3.1 Kerberos

Kerberos is an authentication system developed at the Massachusetts Institute of Technology (MIT) as part of the Athena project [489]. The aim of the project was to provide a broad range of computing services to students across the campus. Kerberos provides authentication services for principals over an open computer network. There are two trusted authorities: the authentication server AS and the ticket granting server TGS. The predistributed cryptographic key between a principal A and the authentication server is computed from A's password (passwd$_A$) using a one-way function f as $k_{A,AS} = f(\text{passwd}_A)$. The password and the secret key $k_{A,AS}$ are stored in the Kerberos database. The system is based on a private-key encryption, such as DES.

Kerberos uses two main protocols: credential initialization and client-server authentication. The first protocol is executed every time a principal A logs on to a host H. Note that the exchange of messages between A and the host H is performed via a secure channel.

Kerberos credential initialization protocol (Version V)

Goals: 1. Verification of password of a principal A who logs on to a host H.

2. Distribution of a fresh secret key to host H (acting on behalf of the principal A) for use with TGS.

Assumptions: The principal A and the authentication server AS share the secret key $k_{A,AS}$. The authentication server AS and TGS share k_{TGS}.

Message Sequence: The parties exchange the following sequence of messages:

1. $A \to H : A$.
2. $H \to AS : A, TGS, L_1, N_1$.

   L_1 is a life span of the ticket and N_1 is a nonce. The authentication server AS undertakes the following steps:

   – retrieves the keys $k_{A,AS}$ and k_{TGS} from the database.

   – generates a fresh session key k and composes a ticket$_{TGS} = \{A, H, TGS, k, T, L\}_{k_{TGS}}$, where T is a timestamp and L is the lifetime of the ticket.

3. $AS \to H : A$, ticket$_{TGS}, \{TGS, k, T, L, N_1\}_{k_{A,AS}}$.
4. $H \to A :$ request for password.
5. $A \to H :$ passwd.

   H computes $\tilde{k}_{A,AS} = f(\text{passwd})$ and uses the computed key to decrypt the message $\{TGS, k, T, L, N_1\}_{k_{A,AS}}$. If the decryption is successful, H concludes that the keys $k_{A,AS} = \tilde{k}_{A,AS}$ and the password provided by A is valid. In this case, H stores the session key k, the timestamp T, the ticket lifetime L, and the ticket$_{TGS}$. If the decryption fails ($k_{A,AS} \neq \tilde{k}_{A,AS}$), and the login is aborted.

The next protocol is executed between a client C and a server S. The client C is a process run by a principal A on a host H. The server S provides computing resources to C. The client C runs the protocol to establish a secure channel with the server S. It is assumed that the host and the principal who resides in it have successfully completed a run of the credential initialization protocol.

Kerberos client-server authentication protocol (Version V)

Goal: To distribute a fresh session key k_{CS} generated by TGS for use between a client C and a server S. To confirm the key k_{CS}.

Assumptions: The client C holds a valid ticket$_{TGS}$ and shares a key k with TGS. The server S shares k_S with TGS.

Message Sequence: The parties exchange the following sequence of messages:

1. $C \rightarrow TGS : S, N, L, \text{ticket}_{TGS}, \{C, T_1\}_k,$

   where N is a nonce, L is a life span of the ticket, and T_1 is a timestamp. The ticket granting server TGS:

   − retrieves the key k from ticket$_{TGS}$,

   − checks the timeliness of the ticket,

   − recovers the timestamp T_1 from $\{C, T_1\}_k$,

   − checks the timeliness of T_1,

   − generates a fresh session key k_{CS},

   − creates a server ticket$_S = \{A, C, S, k_{CS}, T_s, L_s\}_{k_S}$, where T_s is a timestamp and L_s is a lifetime of the ticket.

2. $TGS \rightarrow C : A, \text{ticket}_S, \{S, k_{CS}, T_s, L_s, N\}_k.$

   The client C

   − extracts k_{CS}, timestamp T_s, the lifetime L_s, and the nonce N,

   − checks the timeliness of the message.

3. $C \rightarrow S : \text{ticket}_S, \{C, T_2\}_{k_{CS}}.$

   The server S

   − retrieves k_{CS} from ticket$_S$,

   − checks the timeliness of the ticket,

   − recovers the timestamp T_2 from $\{C, T_2\}_{k_{CS}}$,

   − checks the timeliness of T_2.

4. $S \rightarrow C : \{T_2\}_{k_{CS}}$

An authentication server is responsible for a single domain (in Kerberos called a *realm*). To support authentication services across different realms, authentication servers need to hold inter-realm keys that provide secure inter-realm communication channels. A principal A can obtain a granting ticket to contact a remote TGS from its local TGS [394].

11.3.2 SPX

SPX is an authentication system for large distributed systems [502]. It is a part of the Digital Distributed System Security Architecture [195]. SPX uses both secret and public key cryptography. We are going to use the following notation:

- $\{m\}_k$ – message m encrypted under a secret key k using a private-key cryptosystem; it is assumed that encryption preserves both the confidentiality and integrity of m.
- $\langle m \rangle_k$ – message m signed using a private key k; anyone who knows the matching public key K can verify the signed message m.
- $[m]_K$ – message m encrypted using a public key K; only the holder of the matching secret key k can read the message m.

There are two authentication servers: a login enrollment agent facility ($LEAF$) and a certificate distribution center (CDC). There is also a collection of certification authorities (CA) organized in a hierarchical structure. A single CA has jurisdiction over a subset of principals and is assumed to be trusted. The main goal of a CA is to issue public key certificates. $LEAF$ is a trusted authority, whereas CDC does not need to be trusted as all the information stored in the CDC is encrypted. Like Kerberos, SPX provides several authentication protocols. We are going to describe two basic ones: credential initialization and client-server authentication. The credential initialization protocol is initiated by a principal A who wants to login to his host H. The host exchanges messages with its local $LEAF$ and CDC.

SPX credential initialization protocol

Goals: 1. Delivery of the public key K_{CA} of the local CA to host H of the principal A.
  2. Verification of A's password.
Assumptions: Principal A holds a valid password (passwd$_A$). $LEAF$ has generated its pair of secret and public keys (k_{LEAF}, K_{LEAF}). Every host knows the authentic public key K_{LEAF} of its local $LEAF$. CDC keeps the secret key k_A of principal A in the form of a record ($\{k_A\}_{h_2(\text{passwd}_A)}, h_1(\text{passwd}_A)$), where h_1 and h_2 are two suitably chosen one-way functions.
Message Sequence: The parties exchange the following sequence of messages:
  1. $A \rightarrow H : A, \text{passwd}$.

2. $H \rightarrow LEAF : A, [T, r, h_1(\text{passwd})]_{K_{LEAF}}$,
   where r is a nonce and T is a timestamp.
3. $LEAF \rightarrow CDC : A$.
   CDC
   - retrieves the record for A,
   - chooses a fresh key k,
   - uses a private-key encryption to create
     $$\{\{k_A\}_{h_2(\text{passwd}_A)}, h_1(\text{passwd}_A)\}_k,$$
   - encrypts k using K_{LEAF} for confidentiality.
4. $CDC \rightarrow LEAF : \{\{k_A\}_{h_2(\text{passwd}_A)}, h_1(\text{passwd}_A)\}_k, [k]_{K_{LEAF}}$.
   LEAF now proceeds as follows:
   - LEAF retrieves the key k from $[k]_{K_{LEAF}}$,
   - extracts $\{k_A\}_{h_2(\text{passwd}_A)}$ and $h_1(\text{passwd}_A)$,
   - verifies whether $h_1(\text{passwd}) = h_1(\text{passwd}_A)$,
   - aborts A's login attempt if the two passwords are different.
5. $LEAF \rightarrow H : \{\{k_A\}_{h_2(\text{passwd}_A)}\}_r$.
   The host H
   - decrypts the message using the key (nonce) r,
   - recovers the secret key k_A,
   - generates a pair of RSA delegation keys (d, e),
   - creates a ticket $tick_A = \langle L, A, d \rangle_{k_A}$ (a certificate of d).
6. $H \rightarrow CDC : A$.
7. $CDC \rightarrow H : \langle CA, K_{CA} \rangle_{k_A}$.

Now A can run a client program C that may wish to establish a secure channel (a secret key) to a server S. It is assumed that the client C has already completed a successful run of the credential initialization protocol.

SPX client-server authentication protocol

Goals: To distribute a fresh session key k to a client C and the server S for use in a private-key cryptosystem.

Assumptions: The CA of the client C keeps C's public key K_C. The client C holds a ticket $tick_C = \langle L, C, d \rangle_{k_C}$. The client knows the valid public key of its CA, i.e., K_{CA_C}, and the server knows the valid public key of its CA, i.e., K_{CA_S}.

Message Sequence: 1. $C \rightarrow CDC : S$.

CDC retrieves the public-key certificate of K_S.

2. $CDC \rightarrow C : \langle S, K_S \rangle_{k_{CAC}}$.

The client C

- recovers the public key K_S of S from the certificate using the public key K_{CAC},
- generates a fresh session key k to be shared with S,
- encrypts the session key using the public key K_S of the server,
- encrypts the delegation key e using the session key.

3. $C \rightarrow S : C, [k]_{K_S}, tick_C = \langle L, C, d \rangle_{k_C}, \{e\}_k$.

4. $S \rightarrow CDC : C$.

5. $CDC \rightarrow S : \langle C, K_C \rangle_{k_{CAS}}$.

The server S

- retrieves the key k from $[k]_{K_S}$ using its private key k_S,
- recovers e from $\{e\}_k$,
- gets the public key K_C from the certificate $\langle C, K_C \rangle_{k_{CAS}}$,
- extracts L, C, d from the ticket $tick_C$ using the public key K_C,
- checks whether e and d form a valid pair of delegation keys (i.e., for a random number α, $(\alpha^e)^d \equiv \alpha$ using the RSA system or, alternatively, checking $e \cdot d \equiv 1 \pmod{\varphi(N)}$).

6. $S \rightarrow C : \{T + 1\}_k$.

11.3.3 Other Authentication Services

SELANE (SEcure Local Area Network Environment) was developed at the European Institute for System Security (EISS) in Karlsruhe, Germany as an authentication service for distributed systems [18, 215]. Security operations are based on modular exponentiation. In particular, the signature scheme is based on on the ElGamal scheme. Trusted authorities called SKIAs (Secure Key Issuing Authorities) supply certificates that are used by principals to establish a common secret session key. The key can be used later to ensure confidentiality or authentication.

The RHODOS distributed operating system incorporates a number of authentication services that allow us to verify user passwords at the login stage (similar to the Kerberos credential initialization protocol). One-way (unilateral) and two-way (mutual) authentication of principals is also provided [519].

KryptoKnight, or the network security program (NetSP), is an authentication service designed by IBM. Protocols in KryptoKnight make extensive use of collision-free hash functions and MACs to provide authentication channels [37, 38, 39].

Some other authentication systems are the SESAME project (a secure European system for applications in a multivendor environment), the Open Software Foundation's (OSF) distributed computing environment [394], and Kuperee [230, 231].

11.4 Key Agreement Protocols

The basic Diffie-Hellman (DH) key agreement protocol was discussed in Sect. 11.2. The protocol provides no entity authentication. This problem is partially fixed in a modification of the DH protocol due to ElGamal [163]. It is assumed that there is a trusted authority TA, which keeps authentic (certified) public keys of principals. A principal P generates its secret $\gamma \in \mathcal{Z}_{p-1}$ and deposits its public key $g^{\gamma} \bmod p$ with TA, where p is a large enough prime and g is a primitive element $g \in \mathcal{Z}_p^*$.

ElGamal key agreement protocol

Goal: Agreement of A and B on a secret key k.

Assumptions: TA keeps a certified public key of B. The modulus p is a large enough prime and a primitive element $g \in \mathcal{Z}_p^*$. Both integers p and g are public.

Message Sequence: A collects an authentic copy of B's public key (g^{β}) from TA, generates a random integer $\alpha \in_R \mathcal{Z}_{p-1}$, and sends

1. $A \rightarrow B : g^{\alpha} \bmod p$.

A calculates the secret key $k \equiv (g^{\beta})^{\alpha} \bmod p$ and B derives $k \equiv (g^{\alpha})^{\beta} \bmod p$.

The protocol takes a single pass and both A and B can establish the common secret key. A knows that the key can be shared with B only, so the protocol ensures implicit key authentication of B. There is no provision for key confirmation. A can be sure of key freshness as long as A selected a fresh α. On the other side, B derives a key but B does not know with whom it is shared.

The ElGamal protocol can be upgraded to a protocol where both A and B obtain their corresponding certified public keys from TA. This protocol involves no exchange of message between A and B at all and is called the DH key predistribution. It provides mutual implicit key authentication. There is no entity authentication or key confirmation as there is no interaction between A and B.

11.4.1 MTI Protocols

Matsumoto, Takashima, and Imai designed a family of key agreement protocols [324]. Their main idea is to use the DH predistribution protocol with two passes.

MTI protocol (version A0)

Goal: Agreement of A and B on a fresh secret key k.

Assumptions: TA keeps certified public keys $K_A \equiv g^\alpha \bmod p$ and $K_B \equiv g^\beta \bmod p$ of A and B, respectively. The modulus p is a large enough prime and a primitive element $g \in \mathcal{Z}_p^*$. Both integers p and g are public.

Message Sequence: A selects a random integer $a \in_R \mathcal{Z}_{p-1}$.

1. $A \to B : g^a \bmod p$.

   B chooses its own random integer $b \in_R \mathcal{Z}_{p-1}$.

2. $B \to A : g^b \bmod p$.

A can compute a common secret key

$$k \equiv K_B^a \cdot \left(g^b\right)^\alpha \bmod p.$$

B can compute the same key

$$k \equiv K_A^b \cdot (g^a)^\beta \bmod p.$$

The protocol provides mutual implicit key authentication and key freshness. There is no provision for entity authentication or key confirmation. Readers interested in other versions of MTI protocols are referred to the original paper [324].

11.4.2 Station-to-Station Protocol

The station-to-station (STS) protocol was designed by Diffie, Van Oorschot, and Wiener [154]. The protocol combines the basic Diffie-Hellman protocol with certificates. Recall that a certificate $\langle m \rangle_{k_A}$ denotes message m signed using the secret key of A. Anyone who knows the matching public key K_A can read the message m.

STS protocol

Goals: 1. Agreement of A and B on a fresh secret key k.

    2. Mutual entity authentication.

    3. Explicit key authentication.

Assumptions: TA keeps certified public keys K_A and K_B of A and B, respectively. The modulus p is a large enough prime and $g \in \mathcal{Z}_p^*$ is a primitive element. Both integers p and g are public. H denotes a public one-way hash algorithm.

Message Sequence: A collects a certified copy of B's public key K_B from TA, and generates a random integer $\alpha \in_R \mathcal{Z}_{p-1}$. B collects a certified copy of A's public key K_A from TA, and generates a random integer $\beta \in_R \mathcal{Z}_{p-1}$.

  1. $A \rightarrow B : g^\alpha \bmod p$.

    Principal B chooses at random $\beta \in_R \mathcal{Z}_{p-1}$ and computes

      $k = (g^\alpha)^\beta \bmod p$.

  2. $B \rightarrow A : g^\beta, \{\langle H(g^\beta, g^\alpha)\rangle_{k_B}\}_k$.

    Principal A computes its version of the shared key $\tilde{k} = (g^\beta)^\alpha$, decrypts the cryptogram and uses K_B to retrieve $\tilde{H}(g^\beta, g^\alpha)$ from the certificate. Next, A calculates the hash value $H(g^\beta, g^\alpha)$. If $H = \tilde{H}$, A accepts the key k.

  3. $A \rightarrow B : \{\langle H(g^\alpha, g^\beta)\rangle_{k_A}\}_k$.

    B verifies the hash values in a similar way.

The protocol also provides forward secrecy because if the long-term keys k_A and k_B are compromised then the past session keys are unaffected. This is due to the fact that the long-term keys are used for authentication but not for confidentiality.

The protocol can be simplified by dropping hashing at the expense of efficiency [496]. Some other variants are discussed in [154]. In some definitions of entity authentication, there is an attack that can be prevented by inclusion of the recipient identity in the signature (see [305]).

11.4.3 Protocols with Self-certified Public Keys

Girault [202] suggested a family of key agreement protocols using so-called self-certified public keys. Let a trusted authority TA set up an RSA cryptosystem with the public modulus $N = p \cdot q$ (p and q are strong primes). An integer g generates the multiplicative group $\mathbb{Z}_N^*$. TA generates a pair of keys (k_{TA}, K_{TA}).

Any principal is assumed to possess its identifying string. For instance, the identifying string ID_A is A's name and address. The principal A selects its secret key k_A and computes the public key $K_A \equiv g^{-k_A} \bmod N$. The public integer g^{-k_A} and ID_A are communicated to TA via an authentication channel. TA computes A's public-key certificate

$$\sigma_A \equiv \left(g^{-k_A} - ID_A\right)^{k_{TA}} \quad (\bmod\ N).$$

Anyone who knows the public key K_{TA}, ID_A, and A's certificate σ_A can compute the public key of A as

$$K_A \equiv \sigma_A^{K_{TA}} + ID_A \quad (\bmod\ N).$$

Key predistribution with self-certified keys

Goal: Agreement of A and B on a secret key k.

Assumptions: TA applies an RSA cryptosystem with public modulus N and a
primitive element $g \in \mathbb{Z}_N^*$. TA keeps public key certificates σ_A and σ_B of
A and B, respectively. Both A and B hold their pairs of keys (k_A, K_A) and
(k_B, K_B), respectively.

Message Sequence: A and B independently compute the common secret key. A
calculates

$$k \equiv \left(\sigma_B^{K_{TA}} + ID_B\right)^{k_A} \bmod N$$

and B computes

$$k \equiv \left(\sigma_A^{K_{TA}} + ID_A\right)^{k_B} \bmod N.$$

This protocol needs no interaction between principals A and B. It provides mutual implicit key authentication but not key freshness.

Two-pass protocol with self-certified keys

Goal: Agreement of A and B on a fresh secret key k.

Assumptions: TA applies an RSA cryptosystem with public modulus N and a
primitive element $g \in \mathbb{Z}_N^*$. TA keeps public-key certificates σ_A and σ_B of
A and B, respectively. Both A and B hold their pairs of keys (k_A, K_A) and
(k_B, K_B), respectively.

Message Sequence: A selects at random integer $\alpha < N$.

   1. $A \rightarrow B : g^\alpha \bmod N$.

      B chooses its own random integer $\beta < N$.

   2. $B \rightarrow A : g^\beta \bmod N$.

   A calculates

$$k \equiv (g^\beta)^\alpha \left(\sigma_B^{K_{TA}} + ID_B\right)^{k_A} \bmod N$$

and B calculates

$$k \equiv (g^\alpha)^\beta \left(\sigma_A^{K_{TA}} + ID_A\right)^{k_B} \bmod N.$$

The protocol provides mutual implicit key authentication as well as key freshness.

11.4.4 Identity-Based Protocols

Günter [224] proposes identity-based protocols in which a trusted authority TA is assumed to set up all the required parameters. All secret elements are generated by TA and communicated to the corresponding principals via confidentiality channels.

During the setup phase, TA selects a large enough prime modulus p and a generator g of $\mathcal{Z}_p^*$ (p and g are public). It chooses a secret key k_{TA} and computes its public key $K_{TA} \equiv g^{k_{TA}} \bmod p$. For each principal A, TA assigns a unique identity ID_A, generates a random integer r_A ($\gcd(r_A, p-1) = 1$), and calculates A's certificate $\sigma_A \equiv g^{r_A} \bmod p$. Next TA finds a value k_A satisfying the following congruence:

$$H(ID_A) \equiv \sigma_A \cdot k_{TA} + r_A \cdot k_A \pmod{p-1},$$

where H is a collision-free one-way hash function. The pair (σ_A, k_A) is sent via a confidentiality channel to A. The certificate σ_A is made public, whereas k_A serves as the secret key of A. Further, the public-key of A is $\sigma_A^{k_A} \equiv g^{r_A k_A} \bmod p$.

Anyone can reconstruct A's public key from the public information. First note that $k_A \equiv (H(ID_A) - \sigma_A \cdot k_{TA}) r_A^{-1} \bmod (p-1)$, which implies that

$$\sigma_A^{k_A} \equiv g^{H(ID_A)} \cdot K_{TA}^{-\sigma_A} \bmod p.$$

Identity-based key agreement protocol

Goal: Agreement of A and B on a fresh secret key k.

Assumptions: TA publishes the prime modulus p, a generator g of $\mathbb{Z}_p^*$, and its
   public key K_{TA}. Any principal A with identity ID_A holds its secret key k_A
   and public certificate σ_A.

Message Sequence: A starts the protocol.

   1. $A \rightarrow B : ID_A, \sigma_A$.

      B chooses a random integer β.

   2. $B \rightarrow A : ID_B, \sigma_B, (\sigma_A)^\beta \bmod p$.

      A selects its fresh integer α.

   3. $A \rightarrow B : (\sigma_B)^\alpha \bmod p$.

   A calculates

   $$k \equiv (\sigma_A^\beta)^{k_A} (\sigma_B^{k_B})^\alpha \bmod p$$

   and similarly B computes

   $$k \equiv (\sigma_A^{k_A})^\beta (\sigma_B^\alpha)^{k_B} \bmod p.$$

The protocol guarantees mutual implicit key authentication and key freshness. Other variants of the protocols are discussed in [337, 438].

11.5 Conference-Key Establishment Protocols

In multiuser cryptography, there are more than two principals who may need
to establish a common secret key. Conference-key establishment is an um-
brella name for these applications. Burmester and Desmedt [70] describe several conference-key distribution protocols. Assume that there are n principals
$P_1, \ldots, P_n$ who wish to establish a common secret key. The principal P_1 plays
the role of a trusted authority and after an initial interaction with the other
principals creates a fresh key and distributes it among them.

Star-based protocol

Goal: Distribution of a (fresh) secret key among n principals $P_1, \ldots, P_n$.

Assumptions: There is a public prime modulus p and a generator g of $\mathbb{Z}_p^*$ commonly known to all principals. P_1 is a trusted authority.

Message Sequence: Each P_i selects a random integer $r_i \in_R \mathbb{Z}_{p-1}$ and computes
   $z_i = g^{r_i} \bmod p$ for $i = 1, \ldots, n$.

   1. $P_1 \rightarrow P_i : z_1$ for $i = 2, \ldots, n$.

2. $P_i \rightarrow P_1 : z_i$ for $i = 2, \ldots, n$.

Now P_1 computes common secret keys $k_i \equiv z_i^{r_1} \bmod p$ between P_1 and P_i. P_1 chooses at random a fresh key $k \in_R \mathbb{Z}_p$.

3. $P_1 \rightarrow P_i : y_i \equiv k \cdot k_i \bmod p$.

Each principal computes its secret key $k_i \equiv z_1^{r_i} \bmod p$ and finds $k \equiv y_i \cdot k_i^{-1} \bmod p$, $i = 2, \ldots, n$.

The next protocol needs no trusted principal.

Broadcast protocol

Goal: Agreement on a (fresh) secret key by n principals $P_1, \ldots, P_n$.

Assumptions: There is a public prime modulus p and a generator g of $\mathbb{Z}_p^*$ agreed for use by all principals.

Message Sequence: Each P_i selects a random integer $r_i \in_R \mathbb{Z}_{p-1}$, computes $z_i = g^{r_i} \bmod p$, and broadcasts

1. $P_i \rightarrow \star : z_i$, $i = 1, \ldots, n$.

Each P_i computes $x_i \equiv \left(\frac{z_{i+1}}{z_{i-1}} \right)^{r_i} \bmod p$.

2. $P_i \rightarrow \star : x_i$, $i = 2, \ldots, n$.

Each principal P_i computes the secret key

$$k \equiv z_{i-1}^{n r_i} \cdot x_i^{n-1} \cdot x_{i+1}^{n-2} \cdots x_{i-2} \bmod p.$$

Note that $P_i \rightarrow \star$ means that principal P_i uses a broadcast channel.

Chen and Hwang [93] proposed an identity-based conference-key distribution using a broadcast channel. As in the identity-based setting, a trusted authority TA generates all secrets for all principals. TA uses the RSA system with modulus $N = p_1 p_2 p_3 p_4$, where p_i are distinct strong primes for $i = 1, 2, 3, 4$. It has a pair (e, d) of secret and public keys, respectively. Clearly,

$$e \cdot d \equiv 1 \pmod{lcm(p_1 - 1, p_2 - 1, p_3 - 1, p_4 - 1)}.$$

TA publishes $K \equiv g^{-d} \bmod N$, where g is a generator of $\mathbb{Z}_N^*$. Further, TA computes a secret key k_i for principal P_i according to the congruence

$$g^{k_i} \equiv ID_i^2 \bmod N,$$

using CRT, where ID_i is the identity of principal P_i, $i = 1, \ldots n$. The secret key k_i is communicated to P_i via a confidentiality channel. One principal from the group plays the role of a chair who generates a fresh conference-key. Let this principal be P_1.

Identity-based conference-key distribution protocol

Goal: Distribution of a (fresh) secret key among n principals.

Assumptions: TA sets up an RSA cryptosystem. The modulus N, the key e, a primitive element $g \in \mathcal{Z}_N^*$, $K \equiv g^{-d} \bmod N$, and a one-way hashing function H are public. The key d and the factorization of N are secret. Each principal P_i has its secret key k_i, $i = 1, \ldots, n$. Anybody knows the identity ID_i of principal P_i. P_1 is trusted.

Message Sequence: P_1 chooses a fresh conference-key $k \in_R \mathcal{Z}_{N-1}$, an element $r \in_R \mathcal{Z}_{N-1}$, and computes a hash value $H(t)$ of the current time and date t. Further, P_1 calculates

$$\sigma_1 \equiv \left(K^{k_1} \right)^{H(t)} g^r \bmod N$$

and

$$\alpha_{1,i} \equiv \left(ID_i^2 \right)^{re} \equiv g^{k_i re} \bmod N$$

for $i = 2, \ldots, n$. Subsequently, P_1 constructs a polynomial $p(x)$ of degree at most $(n-2)$ and

$$p(x) \equiv \sum_{i=1}^{n}(k + ID_i) \prod_{j=2;j\neq i}^{n} \frac{x - \alpha_{1,j}}{\alpha_{1,i} - \alpha_{1,j}} \bmod N.$$

1. $P_1 \rightarrow \star : (\sigma_1, p(x), t)$.

Each principal P_i performs the following transformations:

$$\alpha_{1,i} \equiv \left(\sigma_1^e (ID_1^2)^{H(t)} \right)^{k_i}$$
$$\equiv g^{-dk_1 H(t) ek_i} \cdot g^{rek_i} \cdot (ID_1^2)^{H(t)k_i}$$
$$\equiv ID_1^{-2H(t)k_i} \cdot g^{rek_i} \cdot (ID_1^2)^{H(t)k_i}$$
$$\equiv g^{rek_i} \bmod N,$$

and recovers the conference-key

$$k \equiv p(\alpha_{1,i}) - ID_i \bmod N.$$

Other conference-key distribution protocols were also investigated, see [254] and [287].

11.6 BAN Logic of Authentication

Burrows, Abadi, and Needham [71] have developed a formalism for analyzing authentication protocols. The formalism is referred to as the BAN logic. It investigates the evolution of principal beliefs throughout the execution of the protocol. The BAN logic operates on

– principals,
– cryptographic keys, and
– statements (or formulas).

Typically, the symbols P, Q range over principals; X, Y range over statements; and K ranges over keys. The BAN logic uses the following constructs:

1. P **believes** X – P is persuaded of the truth of X. This construct is central to the logic.
2. P **sees** X – P receives a message containing X. P can read and repeat X.
3. P **said** X – some time ago, P sent a message X.
4. P **controls** X – P has jurisdiction over X; i.e., P is an authority on X. Typically, a server is assumed to have jurisdiction over the generation of fresh session keys.
5. **fresh**(X) – X has never been sent in any message in the past (nonces are fresh; timestamped messages are also fresh for their lifetime).
6. $P \overset{K}{\leftrightarrow} Q$ – two principals P and Q share a secret key K (K is known to P and Q and other principals trusted by them only).
7. $\overset{K}{\mapsto} P$ – K is the public key of P (the matching secret key K^{-1} is not known to anyone except P).
8. $P \overset{X}{\rightleftharpoons} Q$ – the statement X is known to P, Q and other principals trusted by them but is secret to the others. The formula X can be used as a token (password) to verify the identities of P and Q.
9. $\{X\}_K$ – X is encrypted using K.
10. $\langle X \rangle_Y$ – X is authenticated using Y. Y serves as a proof of origin for X. For example, $\langle X \rangle_Y$ can be a concatenation of X and a password Y.

11.6.1 BAN Logical Postulates

The BAN logic is based on logical postulates (or deduction rules) that allow us to derive conclusions from the assumptions and statements of the current run of a protocol. The notation $\frac{X,Y}{Z}$ reads: given that X and Y hold, Z holds as well. The conjunction operator is denoted by ','. Although the list given below does not exhaust the collection of rules provided by the creators of the BAN logic, it conveys most of the flavor of the logic.

1. *The message meaning rule.* There are three versions of the rule depending on the secret involved.
   - For a shared key, the rule takes the following form:
     $$\frac{P \text{ believes } Q \overset{K}{\leftrightarrow} P, P \text{ sees } \{X\}_K}{P \text{ believes } Q \text{ said } X}$$
     If P believes that the key K is shared with Q and P sees a statement encrypted under the key K, then P believes that Q once said X.
   - For a public key, the rule can be represented by the following expression:
     $$\frac{P \text{ believes } \overset{K}{\mapsto} Q, P \text{ sees } \{X\}_{K^{-1}}}{P \text{ believes } Q \text{ said } X}$$
     If P believes that the public key K belongs to Q and P sees a statement encrypted under the secret key K^{-1}, then P believes that Q once said X.
   - For shared secrets, the rule can be expressed using the following form:
     $$\frac{P \text{ believes } Q \overset{Y}{\rightleftharpoons} P, P \text{ sees } \langle X \rangle_Y}{P \text{ believes } Q \text{ said } X}$$
     If P believes that the statement Y is shared with Q and P sees a statement $\langle X \rangle_Y$, then P believes that Q once said X.

2. *The nonce verification rule:*
   $$\frac{P \text{ believes } \mathbf{fresh}(X), P \text{ believes } Q \text{ said } X}{P \text{ believes } Q \text{ believes } X}$$
   If P believes that X is fresh and P believes that Q once said X, then P believes that Q believes X.

3. *The jurisdiction rule:*
   $$\frac{P \text{ believes } Q \text{ controls } X, P \text{ believes } Q \text{ believes } X}{P \text{ believes } X}$$
   If P believes that Q has jurisdiction over X and P believes that Q believes that X is true, then P believes that X is true.

4. *Other rules.* These rules allow us to infer about the components of a statement.
   (4.1) If P sees a compound statement (X, Y), then P also sees its component X, that is:
   $$\frac{P \text{ sees } (X, Y)}{P \text{ sees } X}$$

This rule applies also to the component Y, so the following rule also holds:

$$\frac{P \textbf{ sees } (X,Y)}{P \textbf{ sees } Y}$$

(4.2) If P sees $\langle X \rangle_Y$, then P sees X, that is:

$$\frac{P \textbf{ sees } \langle X \rangle_Y}{P \textbf{ sees } X}$$

(4.3) If P and Q share a key K then P can decrypt $\{X\}_K$ and see X. This can be formalized as

$$\frac{P \textbf{ believes } Q \overset{K}{\leftrightarrow} P, P \textbf{ sees } \{X\}_K}{P \textbf{ sees } X}$$

(4.4) If P believes that its public key is K and P sees a cryptogram $\{X\}_K$, then P sees the message X

$$\frac{P \textbf{ believes } \overset{K}{\mapsto} P, P \textbf{ sees } \{X\}_K}{P \textbf{ sees } X}$$

(4.5) If P believes that K is a public key of Q and sees a cryptogram $\{X\}_{K^{-1}}$, then P sees the message X

$$\frac{P \textbf{ believes } \overset{K}{\mapsto} Q, P \textbf{ sees } \{X\}_{K^{-1}}}{P \textbf{ sees } X}$$

(4.6) If P believes that a part X of a compound statement is fresh, then P believes that the whole statement (X,Y) if fresh. This rule is expressed as:

$$\frac{P \textbf{ believes } \textbf{fresh}(X)}{P \textbf{ believes } \textbf{fresh}(X,Y)}$$

(4.7) If P believes that Q believes in (X,Y), then P believes that Q believes in X and

$$\frac{P \textbf{ believes } (Q \textbf{ believes } (X,Y))}{P \textbf{ believes } (Q \textbf{ believes } X)}$$

If P believes that Q believes in (X,Y), then P believes that Q believes in Y and

$$\frac{P \textbf{ believes } (Q \textbf{ believes } (X,Y))}{P \textbf{ believes } (Q \textbf{ believes } Y)}$$

11.6.2 Analysis of the Needham-Schroeder Protocol

The BAN logic can be used to investigate the evolution of beliefs during the execution of a protocol. We show how the Needham-Schroeder protocol can be analyzed using the logic. First the protocol description (Sect. 11.1) needs to be rewritten in the BAN logic language [112].

Idealized Needham-Schroeder protocol

Goals: 1. Beliefs for A:

    (a) $A \overset{K_{AB}}{\leftrightarrow} B$.

    (b) B **believes** $(A \overset{K_{AB}}{\leftrightarrow} B)$.

  2. Beliefs for B:

    (a) $A \overset{K_{AB}}{\leftrightarrow} B$.

    (b) A **believes** $(A \overset{K_{AB}}{\leftrightarrow} B)$.

Assumptions: 1. Principal A believes:

    (a) $A \overset{K_{AS}}{\leftrightarrow} S$ – the key K_{AS} is shared with S,

    (b) S **controls** $A \overset{K_{AB}}{\leftrightarrow} B$ – S has a jurisdiction over the shared key K_{AB},

    (c) S **controls** **fresh**$(A \overset{K_{AB}}{\leftrightarrow} B)$ – S has jurisdiction over the freshness of the key K_{AB},

    (d) **fresh**(r_A) – r_A is fresh.

  2. Principal B believes:

    (a) $B \overset{K_{BS}}{\leftrightarrow} S$ – the key K_{BS} is shared with S,

    (b) S **controls** $A \overset{K_{AB}}{\leftrightarrow} B$ – S has jurisdiction over the shared key K_{AB},

    (c) **fresh**(r_B) – r_B is fresh.

  3. Principal S believes:

    (a) $A \overset{K_{AS}}{\leftrightarrow} S$ – the key K_{AS} is shared with A,

    (b) $B \overset{K_{BS}}{\leftrightarrow} S$ – the key K_{BS} is shared with B,

    (c) $A \overset{K_{AB}}{\leftrightarrow} B$ – the key K_{AB} is shared between A and B,

    (d) **fresh**$(A \overset{K_{AB}}{\leftrightarrow} B)$ – the key K_{AB} is fresh.

Message Sequence: 1. $A \rightarrow S : A, B, r_A$ (this step is usually omitted in the BAN idealization).

  2. $S \rightarrow A : \{r_A, (A \overset{K_{AB}}{\leftrightarrow} B), \mathbf{fresh}(A \overset{K_{AB}}{\leftrightarrow} B), \{A \overset{K_{AB}}{\leftrightarrow} B\}_{K_{BS}}\}_{K_{AS}}$.

  3. $A \rightarrow B : \{A \overset{K_{AB}}{\leftrightarrow} B\}_{K_{BS}}$.

  4. $B \rightarrow A : \{r_B, (A \overset{K_{AB}}{\leftrightarrow} B)\}_{K_{AB}}$.

  5. $A \rightarrow B : \{r_B, (A \overset{K_{AB}}{\leftrightarrow} B)\}_{K_{AB}}$.

The aim of the analysis is to determine whether the statements formulated as the goals of the protocol can be derived from the assumptions and passes of the protocol by applying the BAN rules (postulates). We start from pass (2) of the protocol. Let

$$X = \left(r_A, (A \overset{K_{AB}}{\leftrightarrow} B), \mathbf{fresh}(A \overset{K_{AB}}{\leftrightarrow} B), \{A \overset{K_{AB}}{\leftrightarrow} B\}_{K_{BS}} \right).$$

The statements $(A \overset{K_{AB}}{\leftrightarrow} B)$ and $\mathbf{fresh}(A \overset{K_{AB}}{\leftrightarrow} B)$ inserted in the idealized protocol above do not appear in the original protocol but are apparent from the context of the protocol. According to the message meaning rule

$$\frac{A \text{ believes } A \overset{K_{AS}}{\leftrightarrow} S, A \text{ sees } \{X\}_{K_{AS}}}{A \text{ believes } S \text{ said } X}$$

According to the rule (4.6)

$$\frac{A \text{ believes } \mathbf{fresh}(r_A)}{A \text{ believes } \mathbf{fresh}(X)}$$

That is, A believes that the compound statement X is fresh. From the nonce verification rule

$$\frac{A \text{ believes } \mathbf{fresh}(X), A \text{ believes } S \text{ said } (r_A, (A \overset{K_{AB}}{\leftrightarrow} B), \mathbf{fresh}(A \overset{K_{AB}}{\leftrightarrow} B))}{A \text{ believes } (S \text{ believes } r_A, (A \overset{K_{AB}}{\leftrightarrow} B), \mathbf{fresh}(A \overset{K_{AB}}{\leftrightarrow} B))}$$

we can derive the conclusion that

A **believes** $(S$ **believes** $r_A, (A \overset{K_{AB}}{\leftrightarrow} B), \mathbf{fresh}(A \overset{K_{AB}}{\leftrightarrow} B))$

The rule (4.7) gives us

$$\frac{A \text{ believes } (S \text{ believes } (r_A, A \overset{K_{AB}}{\leftrightarrow} B, \mathbf{fresh}(A \overset{K_{AB}}{\leftrightarrow} B)))}{A \text{ believes } (S \text{ believes } A \overset{K_{AB}}{\leftrightarrow} B)} \tag{11.1}$$

and by the same rule

$$\frac{A \text{ believes } (S \text{ believes } (r_A, A \overset{K_{AB}}{\leftrightarrow} B, \mathbf{fresh}(A \overset{K_{AB}}{\leftrightarrow} B)))}{A \text{ believes } (S \text{ believes } \mathbf{fresh}(A \overset{K_{AB}}{\leftrightarrow} B))} \tag{11.2}$$

Take the assumption (1b) and the conclusion (11.1). From the jurisdiction rule

$$\frac{A \text{ believes } (S \text{ controls } A \overset{K_{AB}}{\leftrightarrow} B), A \text{ believes } (S \text{ believes } A \overset{K_{AB}}{\leftrightarrow} B)}{A \text{ believes } A \overset{K_{AB}}{\leftrightarrow} B}$$

Take the assumption (1c) and the conclusion (11.2). Again from the jurisdiction rule

$$\frac{A \text{ believes } (S \text{ controls } \mathbf{fresh}(A \overset{K_{AB}}{\leftrightarrow} B)), A \text{ believes } (S \text{ believes } \mathbf{fresh}(A \overset{K_{AB}}{\leftrightarrow} B))}{A \text{ believes } \mathbf{fresh}(A \overset{K_{AB}}{\leftrightarrow} B)}$$

The principal A has achieved its goal after pass (2), i.e., A believes that the key K_{AB} has been generated by S for use between A and B and is fresh.

Use assumption (2a) and message (3) of the protocol. We can apply the message meaning rule

$$\frac{B \text{ believes } B \overset{K_{BS}}{\leftrightarrow} S, B \text{ sees } \{A \overset{K_{AB}}{\leftrightarrow} B\}_{K_{BS}}}{B \text{ believes } (S \text{ said } A \overset{K_{AB}}{\leftrightarrow} B)}$$

So B knows that S once said $A \overset{K_{AB}}{\leftrightarrow} B$ but B does not know whether the statement $A \overset{K_{AB}}{\leftrightarrow} B$ is fresh. To derive the goal (2a), we make the dubious assumption that B **believes** **fresh**$(A \overset{K_{AB}}{\leftrightarrow} B)$, the nonce verification rule would then allow us to infer that B **believes** $(S$ **believes** $A \overset{K_{AB}}{\leftrightarrow} B)$, and, further, by the jurisdiction rule, we could conclude $(B$ **believes** $A \overset{K_{AB}}{\leftrightarrow} B)$.

A believes $(A \overset{K_{AB}}{\leftrightarrow} B)$ and sees the corresponding message (4). From the message meaning rule, we can deduce that

A **believes** B **said** $A \overset{K_{AB}}{\leftrightarrow} B$

A believes that K_{AB} is fresh, so by the nonce verification rule

A **believes** B **believes** $A \overset{K_{AB}}{\leftrightarrow} B$

If we make the additional assumption that B **believes** **fresh**$(A \overset{K_{AB}}{\leftrightarrow} B)$, we can repeat the same deduction process and derive

B **believes** A **believes** $A \overset{K_{AB}}{\leftrightarrow} B$

To conclude the above protocol analysis, it is worth noting that the BAN logic provides a useful tool for detecting some security flaws in key distribution protocols. The analysis presented above allows us to detect a flaw in the Needham-Schroeder protocol that was first pointed out by Denning and Sacco [138]. There are some drawbacks of the BAN logic. An obvious one is the lack of a precise formalism for converting a concrete protocol into its idealized form. For instance, message (4) in the idealized Needham-Schroeder protocol is open to different interpretations. If we correct message (4) from $\{r_B, (A \overset{K_{AB}}{\leftrightarrow} B)\}_{K_{AB}}$ to $\{r_B\}_{K_{AB}}$, then the deduction process shown above collapses and A is not able to derive the conclusion A **believes** B **believes** $A \overset{K_{AB}}{\leftrightarrow} B$. Additionally, B selects at random a nonce r_B so A after decryption sees a meaningless number. Some other properties of the BAN logic that may be seen as drawbacks relate to the lack of an independently motivated semantics and are discussed in [334].

11.7 Problems and Exercises

1. Generalize the Needham-Schroeder protocol for a multidomain environment. Assume that there are two domains $\mathcal{D}_1$ and $\mathcal{D}_2$ with two trusted servers S_1 and S_2, respectively. There is also a server S who keeps secret channels $(S \overset{k_{SS_1}}{\leftrightarrow} S_1)$ and $(S \overset{k_{SS_2}}{\leftrightarrow} S_2)$. Implement a protocol that can be used by two principals $A \in \mathcal{D}_1$ (so there is $(A \overset{k_{AS_1}}{\leftrightarrow} S_1)$) and $B \in \mathcal{D}_2$ (so $(B \overset{k_{BS_2}}{\leftrightarrow} S_2)$) to establish a secret channel $(A \overset{k_{AB}}{\leftrightarrow} B)$.

2. Modify the Needham-Schroeder protocol with timestamps so it can be used to establish a secret key among more than two principals.

3. Consider the Needham-Schroeder protocol with timestamps for public key distribution. Make the necessary modifications so the protocol is applicable for multidomain environments (domains are arranged in a hierarchical structure).

4. Show how the common secret key can be agreed upon between two principals A and B using the Diffie-Hellman protocol. Select a prime $p \leq 10000$. Exemplify the intruder-in-the-middle attack.

5. Two principals A and B wish to use the Diffie-Hellman protocol to agree on a common key. At the same time A and B share with their trusted server S their secret channels $(A \overset{k_{AS}}{\leftrightarrow} S)$ and $(B \overset{k_{BS}}{\leftrightarrow} S)$. The server S has agreed to generate a primitive element g and the modulus p and send the pair (g, p) secretly to A and B using the Otway-Rees protocol. Present the overall protocol that allows A and B to establish their secret key which applies the Otway-Rees protocol (to distributed parameters g and N) and the Diffie-Hellman protocol to agree on the secret key.

6. Take the Otway-Rees and Boyd-Mao protocols. Discuss their properties and emphasize their differences.

7. Consider the following key agreement protocols: Diffie-Hellman, ElGamal, MTI, and STS. Compare the protocols and contrast them taking their security as the basis for discussion.

8. Demonstrate on simple numerical examples how two principals can agree on a secret key using
   – key predistribution with self-certified keys,
   – a two-pass protocol with self-certified keys.
   Construct a suitable instance of the RSA cryptosystem.

9. Show how three principals P_1, P_2, and P_3 execute the star-based protocol to establish a common secret key. Assume that the modulus $p = 1879$ and $g = 1054$.

10. The star-based protocol can be seen as a variant of the Diffie-Hellman protocol. Show that the protocol is subject to the intruder-in-the-middle attack. In particular, demonstrate how the intruder who sits between P_2 and P_1 (P_1 plays the role of a trusted authority) can obtain the common secret key and then control the traffic coming to and going from P_2.

11. Use the broadcast protocol to establish a common secret key among three principals P_1, P_2, and P_3. Accept the modulus $p = 1879$ and the primitive element $g = 1054$.

12. Rewrite the Diffie-Hellman key agreement protocol into its idealized form and analyze it using the BAN logic.

12 Zero-Knowledge Proof Systems

Zero-knowledge (also called minimum disclosure) proof systems are indispensable wherever there is a necessity to prove the truth of a statment without revealing anything more about it. Zero-knowledge proofs involve two parties: the prover who claims that a statement is true, and the verifier who would like to be convinced that the statement is indeed true. The proof is conducted via an interaction between the parties. At the end of the protocol, the verifier is convinced only when the statement is true. If, however, the prover lies about the statement, the verifier will discover the lie with an overwhelming probability. The idea sprang out of interactive proof systems. Interactive proofs have gained a quite independent status as a part of computational complexity theory.

Most books on cryptography contain some discussion of the topic. Schneier's book [451] discusses the idea of zero-knowledge proofs and describes some zero-knowledge protocols. An encyclopedic treatment of the subject can be found in [337]. Stinson's book [496] contains a comprehensive introduction to zero-knowledge proofs. An entertaining exposure of the idea of zero-knowledge was presented by Quisquater and Guillou at Crypto '89 [418]. Most of the results presented in this chapter can be found in the papers [61, 208, 210].

12.1 Interactive Proof Systems

The class **NP** can be seen as a class of problems for which there is a polynomial time proof of membership. An interactive proof system is a protocol which involves two parties: the prover P and verifier V. Sometimes P and V are called, mnemonically, Peggy and Vic, respectively. The verifier is assumed to be a polynomial-time probabilistic algorithm. The prover, however, is a probabilistic algorithm with an unlimited computational power. Their interactions consist of a (polynomial) number of rounds. In each round, the verifier sends a challenge to the prover via a communication channel. The prover replies to the verifier.

At the end of the interaction, the verifier is either convinced and stops in an accept state or is not convinced and halts in a reject state.

Given a decision problem Q (not necessarily in **NP**), it has an *interactive proof system* if there is a protocol which satisfies

- *Completeness* – for each yes-instance x of Q, V accepts x with a probability no smaller than $1 - n^{-c}$ for every constant $c > 0$ (n means the size of the instance x),
- *Soundness* – for each no-instance, V rejects x with a probability no smaller than $1 - n^{-c}$ for any prover (honest or otherwise),

whenever V follows the protocol. It turns out [207] that the error probability in the completeness condition can be reduced to zero with no consequences for the protocol. In other words, V always accepts any yes-instance.

Consider an interactive proof based on the quadratic residue problem. Recall that Z_N^Q is the set of all integers in Z_N whose Jacobi symbol with respect to N is equal to 1. The set $Z_N^Q = Z_N^{Q+} \cup Z_N^{Q-}$. An integer $x \in Z_N^Q$ is a quadratic residue modulo N if there is an integer $y \in Z_N^*$ such that $y^2 \equiv x \bmod N$. We simply say that $x \in Z_N^{Q+}$. Otherwise, the integer x is a quadratic nonresidue or simply $x \in Z_N^{Q-}$. To decide whether $x \in Z_N^Q$ is a quadratic residue modulo N or not, one would need to find the factorization of N and compute Jacobi symbols of x with respect to all (nontrivial) factors of N.

Name: Quadratic residue (QR) problem.
Instance: Given a composite integer N, the integer $x \in Z_N^Q$.
Question: Does x belong to Z_N^{Q+} (or is x a quadratic residue)?

An interactive proof for the QR problem proceeds as follows [210]. Both the prover and verifier know an instance (x, N) where x is an integer which may or may not be a quadratic residue modulo N. The interaction takes $t(n)$ rounds. A round is started by P who picks up at random a quadratic residue u and sends it to V. V selects a random bit b and forwards it to P. If $b = 0$, the prover shows a random square root w of u to V. Otherwise, P shows a random square root w of $(x \cdot u)$. As P is assumed to be of unlimited power, the computations of square roots can be done instantly. The verifier checks whether w^2 is either $u \bmod N$ if $b = 0$ or $u \cdot x \bmod N$ if $b = 1$.

QR interactive proof – $QR_{\leftrightarrow}$

Common Knowledge: an instance (x, N) of the QR problem (n is the size of the instance).

Description: Given a polynomial $t(n)$ in n, P and V repeat the following steps $t(n)$ times.

1. P selects at random $u \in_R \mathcal{Z}_N^{Q+}$.
2. $P \to V : u$.
3. $V \to P : b$, where $b \in_R \{0, 1\}$.
4. $P \to V : w$, where w is a random square root of either u if $b = 0$ or $x \cdot u$ if $b = 1$.
5. V checks whether
$$w^2 \stackrel{?}{\equiv} \begin{cases} u \bmod N & \text{if } b = 0, \\ ux \bmod N & \text{otherwise.} \end{cases}$$
If the condition fails, V stops and rejects. Otherwise, the interaction continues.

Finally, after $t(n)$ rounds, V halts and accepts.

The proof satisfies the completeness property, as for any yes-instance of QR (or $x \in \mathcal{Z}_N^{Q+}$) V always accepts P's proof. For any b, the prover can always compute the correct response w. Note that for a no-instance (or $x \in \mathcal{Z}_N^{Q-}$), if P follows the protocol than u is a quadratic residue modulo N but $x \cdot u$ is a quadratic nonresidue modulo N. If P cheats then u is a quadratic nonresidue but $x \cdot u$ is a quadratic residue. Once P committed herself to u and sent it to V (it does not matter if P cheats or not), the probability that V rejects (or accepts) x is $1/2$. As the protocol is executed $t(n)$ times, the cheating prover can succeed and convince V to accept a no-instance with a probability of at most $2^{-t(n)}$. The proof system satisfies the soundness property.

The next interactive proof system is based on the graph isomorphism (GI) problem. Let $\mathcal{V}$ be a set of n elements. $Sym(\mathcal{V})$ denotes the group of permutations over the set $\mathcal{V}$. The composition of two permutations $\pi, \tau \in Sym(\mathcal{V})$ is denoted by $\pi \circ \tau$. Let $G_0 = (\mathcal{V}_0, \mathcal{E}_0)$ and $G_1 = (\mathcal{V}_1, \mathcal{E}_1)$ be two graphs where $\mathcal{V}_i$ is the set of vertices and $\mathcal{E}_i$ is the set of edges ($i = 0, 1$).

Name: Graph isomorphism (GI) problem.
Instance: Given two graphs $G_0 = (\mathcal{V}_0, \mathcal{E}_0)$ and $G_1 = (\mathcal{V}_1, \mathcal{E}_1)$ with $|\mathcal{V}_0| = |\mathcal{V}_1| = n$.

Question: Is there a permutation $\pi : \mathcal{V}_0 \to \mathcal{V}_1$ such that an edge $(u, v) \in \mathcal{E}_0$ if and only if $(\pi(u), \pi(v)) \in \mathcal{E}_1$?

An interactive proof system for GI is presented below [208]. The interaction takes $t(n)$ rounds. At each round, the prover selects a random permutation $\pi \in_R Sym(\mathcal{V}_0)$, computes an isomorphic copy of G_0, i.e., $h = \pi(G_0)$, and forwards h to the verifier. V selects at random a bit b and communicates it to P. P responds by sending π if $b = 0$, or $\pi \circ \tau$ otherwise. The permutation τ establishes the isomorphism between G_0 and G_1 or $G_0 = \tau(G_1)$ and exists for yes-instances only. V checks whether the provided permutation forces the isomorphism between h and G_b. If the check is satisfied, V continues. Otherwise, V stops and rejects.

GI interactive proof – $GI_{\leftrightarrow}$

Common Knowledge: An instance of GI, i.e., two graphs $G_0 = (\mathcal{V}_0, \mathcal{E}_0)$ and $G_1 = (\mathcal{V}_1, \mathcal{E}_1)$ (n is the number of vertices in $\mathcal{V}_0$ and $\mathcal{V}_1$).
Description: Given a polynomial $t(n)$ in n. P and V repeat the following steps $t(n)$ times.
  1. P selects $\pi \in_R Sym(\mathcal{V}_0)$ and computes an isomorphic copy h of G_0 (i.e., $h = \pi(G_0)$).
  2. $P \to V : h$.
  3. $V \to P : b$ where $b \in_R \{0, 1\}$.
  4. P responds to the V challenge and
  $$P \to V : \begin{cases} \pi & \text{if } b = 0, \\ \pi \circ \tau & \text{otherwise}, \end{cases}$$
    where τ is the permutation that asserts the isomorphism between G_0 and G_1 or $G_0 = \tau(G_1)$ (τ always exists for any yes-instance).
  5. V checks whether the provided permutation establishes the isomorphism between h and G_b. V halts and rejects the instance whenever the check fails. Otherwise, the interaction continues.
  If all $t(n)$ rounds have been successful, V stops and accepts.

Assume that both P and V share a yes-instance. No matter how V has chosen the bit b, P always can arbitrarily select either π or $\pi \circ \tau$ as both graphs G_0 and G_1 are isomorphic to h. So the proof satisfies the completeness property. What happens when P and V share a no-instance and the prover wants to cheat? P has to choose a random h that can be isomorphic to either G_0 ($h \sim G_0$) or

G_1 ($h \sim G_1$). Once h has been sent to V, P is committed to either $h \sim G_0$ or $h \sim G_1$ (but not to both). V randomly selects b and asks P to show the appropriate permutation. There is a probability of $1/2$ that P will be caught. As the interaction takes $t(n)$ rounds, the probability that V stops in an accept state is $2^{-t(n)}$. So the soundness of the proof holds.

The class **IP** (interactive polynomial time) contains all decision problems for which there exist interactive proof systems. Clearly, $\mathbf{NP} \subseteq \mathbf{IP}$.

12.2 Perfect Zero-Knowledge Proofs

Informally, an interactive proof system is zero-knowledge if during the interaction the verifier gains no information from the prover. In particular, having a transcript of an interaction with P, V is not able to play later the role of the prover for somebody else.

To make our discussion more formal we need some definitions. A view is a transcript that contains all messages exchanged between the prover and verifier. Assume that during the ith round, P sends a random commitment A_i, V responds by sending a random challenge bit B_i and P forwards her proof C_i. The triple (A_i, B_i, C_i) are random variables. The view is a sequence of all messages $(A_1, B_1, C_1, \ldots, A_{t(n)}, B_{t(n)}, C_{t(n)})$ exchanged by P and V during the interaction. For an honest V all B_i are uniform and independent random variables $(i = 1, \ldots, t(n))$. Note that the view is defined for a yes-instance only. All no-instances are not of interest to us as the prover does not know the truth (or secret). She may merely pretend to know it but she will be caught with a high probability.

The behavior of a cheating verifier V^* can significantly deviate. First the random variables B_i may not be statistically independent. Moreover, the verifier can use some transcripts from previous interactions hoping that they can help him extract some information from P. So the view should also include the past interactions $\hbar$ (history). For an instance $x \in Q$ and an arbitrary verifier V^*, the view is

$$View_{P,V^*}(x, \hbar) = (x, \hbar, A_1, B_1, C_1, \ldots, A_{t(n)}, B_{t(n)}, C_{t(n)}).$$

Random variables B_i are calculated by a cheating V^* using a polynomial-time probabilistic function F so $B_i = F(x, \hbar, A_1, B_1, C_1, \ldots, A_{i-1}, B_{i-1}, C_{i-1}, A_i)$.

The view is a probabilistic ensemble with a well-defined set of possible values and associated probabilities (Sect. 5.2).

A transcript simulator $S_{V^*}(x, \hbar)$ is an expected polynomial-time probabilistic algorithm that uses all the information accessible to V^* (i.e., previous transcripts $\hbar$ and the function F) and generates a transcript for an instance $x \in Q$ without an interaction with the prover P. Note that the simulator can be seen as an ensemble generator.

An interactive proof system is perfect zero-knowledge if there is a transcript simulator $S_{V^*}(x, \hbar)$ such that its ensemble is identical to the view ensemble. In other words, the knowledge extracted from P by V^* could be obtained without interaction with P. Instead, V^* could run the corresponding transcript simulator. A more formal definition can be formulated as follows.

Definition 34. *An interactive proof system for a decision problem Q is perfect zero-knowledge if the ensemble $View_{P,V^*}(x, \hbar)$ is identical to the ensemble generated by an expected polynomial-time probabilistic simulator $S_{V^*}(x, \hbar)$ for any yes-instance of Q and any $\hbar$.*

Now we can go back to the first interactive proof system $QR_{\leftrightarrow}$.

Theorem 45. (*Goldwasser, Micali, Rackoff* [210]) $QR_{\leftrightarrow}$ *is perfect zero-knowledge.*

Proof. Let (x, N) be a yes-instance of QR. The ith round involves the following random variables: U_i, a quadratic residue generated by P; B_i, a bit generated by V^*; and W_i, a proof of P. So the view for an arbitrary verifier V^* is

$$View_{P,V^*}(x, N, \hbar) = (x, N, \hbar, U_1, B_1, W_1, \ldots, U_{t(n)}, B_{t(n)}, W_{t(n)}).$$

For simplicity, we denote $V_i = (U_1, B_1, W_1, \ldots, U_i, B_i, W_i)$. Note that if V^* is honest, all B_i are independent and uniform random variables over $\{0, 1\}$. However, if V^* cheats, he uses some polynomial-time probabilistic algorithm F that generates $b_{i+1} = F(x, N, \hbar, v_i, u_{i+1})$, where $V_i = v_i$. Now we can use the algorithm F to construct a simulator $S_{V^*}(x, N, \hbar)$ as follows.

Transcript simulator $S_{V^*}(x, N, \hbar)$ for $QR_{\leftrightarrow}$

Input: (x, N), a yes-instance of QR; $\hbar$, past transcripts; v_i, transcript of the current interaction (i rounds).

Description: Repeat the following steps for $i + 1 \leq t(n)$.

1. Select $b_{i+1} \in_R \{0, 1\}$.
2. Choose $w_{i+1} \in_R \mathcal{Z}_N^*$.
3. If $b_{i+1} = 0$, then $u_{i+1} \equiv w_{i+1}^2 \bmod N$
   else $u_{i+1} \equiv w_{i+1}^2 \cdot x^{-1} \bmod N$.
4. If $b_{i+1} = F(x, N, \hbar, v_i, u_{i+1})$, then
   return $(u_{i+1}, b_{i+1}, w_{i+1})$
   else go to (1).

Some comments about the simulator. Instead of selecting first a quadratic residue u_{i+1}, the simulator chooses w_{i+1} and b_{i+1} at random and computes u_{i+1}. Having u_{i+1}, the simulator can recompute b_{i+1} using the function F where u_{i+1} is a part of an input. There is a probability of $1/2$ that a randomly selected b_{i+1} will match the correct value indicated by $F(x, N, \hbar, v_i, u_{i+1})$. On average, the simulator will need two rounds per single output $(u_{i+1}, b_{i+1}, w_{i+1})$. So the simulator runs in an expected polynomial time. Note also that for an honest verifier, the function F simplifies to a single toss of an unbiased coin.

Now we prove that the view ensemble

$$View_{P, V^*}(x, N, \hbar) = (x, N, \hbar, U_1, B_1, W_1, \ldots, U_{t(n)}, B_{t(n)}, W_{t(n)})$$

is identical to the simulator ensemble

$$S_{V^*}(x, N, \hbar) = (x, N, \hbar, U_1', B_1', W_1', \ldots, U_{t(n)}', B_{t(n)}', W_{t(n)}').$$

The proof proceeds by induction on i. The case when $i = 0$ is trivial as both ensembles are constant. In the inductive step, we assume that the ensemble

$$View_{P, V^*}(x, N, \hbar) = (x, N, \hbar, U_1, B_1, W_1, \ldots, U_{i-1}, B_{i-1}, W_{i-1})$$

is identical to

$$S_{V^*}(x, N, \hbar) = (x, N, \hbar, U_1', B_1', W_1', \ldots, U_{i-1}', B_{i-1}', W_{i-1}').$$

The next part of the view transcript consists of the triple (U_i, B_i, W_i). The variable U_i is independent. B_i depends on U_i, V_{i-1}, and $\hbar$. W_i depends on both previous variables so

$$P(U_i = u, B_i = b, W_i = w)$$
$$= P(U_i = u) \cdot P(B_i = b | V_{i-1} = v, U_i = u, \hbar) \cdot P(W_i = w | U_i = u, B_i = b).$$

The probability $P(U_i = u) = \alpha^{-1}$ where $\alpha = |\mathcal{Z}_N^{Q+}|$. Denote the probability $P(B_i = b | V_{i-1} = v, U_i = u, \hbar) = p_b$. Assume that Ω_u and Ω_{xu} are sets of all square roots of u and xu, respectively. There is an integer β such that $|\Omega_u| = |\Omega_{xu}| = \beta$. The probability $P(W_i = w | U_i = u, B_i = 0) = \beta^{-1}$ for all $w \in \Omega_u$ and $P(W_i = w | U_i = u, B_i = 1) = \beta^{-1}$ for all $w \in \Omega_{xu}$. So $P(U_i = u, B_i = b, W_i = w) = \frac{p_b}{\alpha\beta}$.

The ith part of the simulator transcript is (U_i', B_i', W_i'). Considering the order the variables are generated in, we can write that the probability

$$P(U_i' = u, B_i' = b, W_i' = w)$$
$$= P(U_i' = u | W_i' = w, B_i' = b) \cdot P(B_i' = b | U_i' = u) \cdot P(W_i' = w).$$

The random variable W_i is chosen independently from the set $\mathcal{Z}_N^*$ so $P(W_i' = w) = \frac{1}{\alpha\beta}$. The probability

$$P(U_i' = u) = P(U_i' = u, W_i' \in \Omega_u \cup \Omega_{xu}, B_i' \in \{0,1\})$$
$$= \sum_{w \in \Omega_u} P(U_i' = u, W_i' = w, B_i' = 0)$$
$$+ \sum_{w \in \Omega_{xu}} P(U_i' = u, W_i' = w, B_i' = 1)$$
$$= \sum_{w \in \Omega_u} P(W_i' = w)P(B_i' = 0) + \sum_{w \in \Omega_{xu}} P(W_i' = w)P(B_i' = 1)$$
$$= \frac{\beta}{\alpha\beta}(P(B_i' = 0) + P(B_i' = 1))$$
$$= \frac{1}{\alpha}.$$

The random variable U_i' has the same probability distribution as U_i. Consequently, B_i' has the identical probability distribution to B_i. So, both the view and simulator probability distributions for i rounds are identical and the corresponding ensembles are the same. Finally, we conclude that $QR_\leftrightarrow$ is perfect zero-knowledge.   □

Consider our second interactive proof system $GI_\leftrightarrow$ for graph isomorphism.

Theorem 46. (*Goldreich, Micali, Wigderson* [208]) $GI_\leftrightarrow$ *is perfect zero-knowledge.*

Proof. The proof proceeds in a similar manner to the previous one. The core of the proof is the construction of an expected polynomial-time simulator that generates an ensemble identical to the view ensemble. An honest verifier is V while a verifier who deviates arbitrarily from the protocol is denoted by V^*.

Let (G_0, G_1) be a yes-instance of GI. The view of interaction between P and V^* is an ensemble

$$View_{P,V^*}(G_0, G_1, \hbar) = (G_0, G_1, \hbar, H_1, B_1, \Phi_1, \ldots, H_{t(n)}, B_{t(n)}, \Phi_{t(n)}),$$

where (H_i, B_i, Φ_i) are random variables used in the ith round of the protocol. H_i represents an isomorphic copy of G_0, B_i is a binary random variable generated by V^*, and Φ_i is a random permutation sent by P. Again $\hbar$ indicates the additional information accessible to V^* from previous interactions with the prover P. Note that instead of a random selection of his bit, a cheating V^* may use a polynomial-time probabilistic algorithm F to generate his bits. Having F, the verifier V^* can design a simulator $S_{V^*}(G_1, G_2, \hbar)$ that works as follows.

Transcript simulator $-\ S_{V^*}(G_0, G_1, \hbar)$ **for** $GI_\leftrightarrow$

Input: (G_0, G_1), a yes-instance of QR; $\hbar$, past transcripts; v_i, transcript of the
   current interaction (first i rounds).
Description: Repeat the following steps for $(i + 1) \le t(n)$.
   1. Choose $b_{i+1} \in_R \{0, 1\}$.
   2. Select $\pi \in_R Sym(\mathcal{V}_1)$ and compute $h_{i+1} = \pi(G_{b_{i+1}})$.
   3. If $b_{i+1} = F(G_1, G_2, \hbar, v_i, h_{i+1})$, then
         return $(h_{i+1}, b_{i+1}, \pi_{i+1})$
         else go to (1).

Note that all computations can be done in polynomial time except that b_{i+1} generated at step (1) may not match the value calculated in step (3). The probability that they match in a single round is $1/2$. On average it is necessary to run two rounds of the simulator to produce a single output. So the simulator runs in expected polynomial time.

Now we prove that the view ensemble $View_{P,V^*}(G_0, G_1, \hbar)$ is identical to the ensemble $S_{V^*}(G_0, G_1, \hbar)$. The proof proceeds by induction on the number of rounds i. When $i = 0$, both the simulator and the view consist of constants so their probability distributions are identical. Now we assume that both probability distributions are identical for $(i - 1)$ rounds, i.e.,

$$P(View_{P,V^*}(V_{i-1}) = v_{i-1}) = P(S_{V^*} = v_{i-1}).$$

Consider a triple of random variables (H_i, B_i, Φ_i), which is the transcript of the ith round of the protocol. The probability that

$$P(H_i = h, B_i = b, \Phi_i = \pi)$$
$$= P(\Phi_i = \pi) \cdot P(B_i = b | \Phi_i = \pi) \cdot P(H_i = h | \Phi_i = \pi, B_i = b).$$

As the permutation is selected at random, $P(\Phi_i = \pi) = \frac{1}{n!}$. The random variable $B_i = F(\hbar, V_i, H_i)$ so we can assume that $P(B_i = b) = p_b$. The probability $P(H_i = h | \Phi_i = \pi, B_i = b) = 1$ for the matching h and $P(H_i = h, B_i = b, \Phi_i = \pi) = \frac{p_b}{n!}$.

Consider a triple (H'_i, B'_i, Φ'_i) that is the ith part of the simulator transcript. The random variable $P(\Phi'_{i+1} = \pi) = \frac{1}{n!}$. As the simulator uses the same polynomial-time probabilistic algorithm F, the random variable B_{i+1} has the same probability distribution as for the view. So the probability distributions of the view and the simulator are identical, and consequently $GI_{\leftrightarrow}$ is perfect zero-knowledge. □

The complement of GI is the graph non-isomorphism problem. The problem is stated below.

Name: Graph nonisomorphism (GNI) problem.
Instance: Given two graphs $G_0 = (V_0, \mathcal{E}_0)$ and $G_1 = (V_1, \mathcal{E}_1)$ with $|V_0| = |V_1| = n$.
Question: Are the two graphs nonisomorphic? (So there is no permutation $\pi : V_0 \to V_1$ such that an edge $(u, v) \in \mathcal{E}_0$ if and only if $(\pi(u), \pi(v)) \in \mathcal{E}_1$.)

An interactive proof system for GNI is more complex than for its relative GI and each round takes five transmissions. The main idea is to allow the verifier to construct pairs of graphs in every round. Each pair contains an isomorphic copy of G_0 and G_1 in a random order. The powerful prover can tell apart those copies for every yes-instance (because G_0 and G_1 are not isomorphic), while for any no-instance P can only guess the order.

GNI interactive proof – $GNI_{\leftrightarrow}$

Common Knowledge: an instance of GNI, i.e., two graphs $G_0 = (V_0, \mathcal{E}_0)$ and $G_1 = (V_1, \mathcal{E}_1)$. The parameter n is the number of vertices in V_0 and V_1. Denote $V = V_0 = V_1$.

Description: Given a polynomial $t(n)$ in n. P and V repeat the following steps $t(n)$ times.

1. V chooses $b \in_R \{0, 1\}$, a permutation $\pi \in_R Sym(V)$, and computes $h = \pi(G_b)$. The graph h is called a question. Further, V prepares n^2 pairs

of graphs such that each pair contains an isomorphic copy of G_0 and G_1 in a random order. So for $j = 1, \ldots, n^2$, V chooses $a_j \in_R \{0,1\}$ and two permutations $\tau_{j,0}, \tau_{j,1} \in_R Sym(\mathcal{V})$ and computes $T_{j,0} = \tau_{j,0}(G_{a_j})$ and $T_{j,1} = \tau_{j,1}(G_{a_j+1 \bmod 2})$. So

$$V \to P : h, (T_{1,0}, T_{1,1}), \ldots, (T_{n^2,0}, T_{n^2,1}).$$

2. P chooses uniformly at random a subset $I \subseteq \{1, \ldots, n^2\}$ and

$$P \to V : I.$$

3. If I is not a subset of $\{1, \ldots, n^2\}$, then V stops and rejects. Otherwise,

$$V \to P : \{(a_j, \tau_{j,1}, \tau_{j,0}) | j \in I\},$$

$$\{(b + a_j \bmod 2, \tau_{j,(b+a_j) \bmod 2} \circ \pi^{-1}) | j \in \bar{I}\}$$

where $\bar{I} = \{1, \ldots, n^2\} \setminus I$.

4. P checks whether $\tau_{j,0}$ is the isomorphism between $T_{j,0}$ and G_{a_j}, and whether $\tau_{j,1}$ is the isomorphism between $T_{j,1}$ and $G_{a_j+1 \bmod 2}$ for $j \in I$. Also, P verifies that $\tau_{j,(b+a_j) \bmod 2} \circ \pi^{-1}$ is an isomorphism between $T_{j,(b+a_j) \bmod 2}$ and h for every $j \in \bar{I}$. If the checks fail, the prover stops. Otherwise, P answers $\beta \in \{0,1\}$ such that h is isomorphic to G_β.

5. V checks whether $b = \beta$. If the condition is not satisfied, V stops and rejects. Otherwise, the interaction continues.

After passing through $t(n)$ rounds without rejection, V halts and accepts.

It is easy to verify that the interactive proof satisfies both the completeness and soundness properties. It is also perfect zero-knowledge (for details consult [208]).

Consider the complementary problem to the quadratic residue problem. This is the quadratic nonresidue problem and is defined as follows.

Name: Quadratic nonresidue (QNR) problem.
Instance: Given a composite integer N. The integer $x \in \mathcal{Z}_N^Q$.
Question: Does x belong to $\mathcal{Z}_N^{Q-}$ (or is x a quadratic nonresidue)?

An interactive proof system for QNR is given below. At each round, the verifier forwards to the prover two types of elements: quadratic residues $r^2 \bmod N$ and products $r^2 x \bmod N$. If (x, N) is a yes-instance, the prover can easily tell apart the type of an element. If (x, N) is a no-instance (i.e., x is a quadratic residue), the prover cannot distinguish elements as they belong to the same class of quadratic residues.

QNR interactive proof – $QNR_{\leftrightarrow}$

Common Knowledge: an instance (x, N) of the QNR problem (n is the size of the instance).

Description: Given a polynomial $t(n)$ in n. P and V repeat the following steps $t(n)$ times.

1. V picks up $r \in_R Z_N^*$ and $\beta \in_R \{0, 1\}$.
2. $V \rightarrow P : w \equiv r^2 \cdot x^\beta \bmod N$.
3. For $1 \leq j \leq n$, V selects $r_{j1}, r_{j2} \in_R Z_N^*$ and $b_j \in_R \{0, 1\}$. V creates $a_j \equiv r_{j1}^2 \bmod N$ and $b_j \equiv xr_{j2}^2 \bmod N$. Next

$$V \rightarrow P : \begin{cases} (a_j, b_j) & \text{if } b_j = 1, \\ (b_j, a_j) & \text{if } b_j = 0. \end{cases}$$

4. $P \rightarrow V : (\alpha_1, \ldots, \alpha_n)$ where $\alpha_j \in_R \{0, 1\}$ for $1 \leq j \leq n$.
5. $V \rightarrow P : v = (v_1, \ldots, v_n)$ where $v_j = (r_{j1}, r_{j2})$ if $\alpha_j = 0$. If $\alpha_j = 1$ and $\beta = 0$, then $v_j \equiv rr_{j1} \bmod N$ (or a square root of $wa_j \bmod N$). If $\alpha_j = 1$ and $\beta = 1$, $v_j \equiv xrr_{j2} \bmod N$ (or a square root of $wb_j \bmod N$).
6. P verifies that the sequence v is correct. If not, P terminates the interaction. Otherwise, $P \rightarrow V : \gamma$ where $\gamma = 0$ if w is quadratic residue modulo N, or $\gamma = 1$ otherwise.
7. V checks whether $\beta = \gamma$. If the condition fails, V stops and rejects. Otherwise, the interaction continues.

After passing through $t(n)$ rounds without rejection, V halts and accepts.

Both completeness and soundness of the interactive proof can be asserted by a careful examination of the protocol. An interesting feature of the proof system is that it satisfies a weaker zero-knowledge property called the *statistical zero-knowledge*. Consider two probabilistic ensembles: a view (transcript of interaction between the prover P and arbitrary verifier V^*) and a simulator S_{V^*} that is used by V^* to generate transcripts without interaction with P. Perfect zero-knowledge requires the equality of two ensembles, i.e., $View_{P,V^*}(x, N, \hbar) = S_{V^*}(x, N, \hbar)$ for any yes-instance of the problem QNR. Statistical zero-knowledge is weaker as we request that

$$\lim_{n \to \infty} View_{P,V^*}(x, N, \hbar) = \lim_{n \to \infty} S_{V^*}(x, N, \hbar)$$

for any yes-instance of the problem QNR, where n is the size of instance (x, N). Details of the proof can be found in [210].

12.3 Computational Zero-Knowledge Proofs

Perfect or statistical zero-knowledge may still seem to be too restrictive for our polynomially bounded verifier V. An interactive proof is *computational zero-knowledge* if there is a simulator S_{V^*} that is polynomially indistinguishable from the view $View_{P,V^*}$ for an arbitrary verifier and any yes-instance.

Goldreich, Micali, and Wigderson in [208] showed that there is a computational zero-knowledge proof system for the graph 3-colorability (G3C) problem. As the G3C problem is known to belong to the **NPC** class, this result asserts that any **NPC** problem has a computational zero-knowledge proof. The G3C problem is defined as follows [191].

Name: Graph 3-colorability (G3C) problem.
Instance: Given graph $G = (\mathcal{V}, \mathcal{E})$.
Question: Is G 3-colorable, that is, does there exist a function $\phi : \mathcal{V} \to \{1, 2, 3\}$ such that $\phi(u) \neq \phi(v)$ whenever $(u, v) \in \mathcal{E}$?

This time we need to make an additional assumption that there is a secure probabilistic encryption (Sect. 4.7). Assume that the message space is $\mathcal{M} = \{0, 1, 2, 3\}$ and the key space is $\mathcal{K}$. An encryption function

$$E : \mathcal{M} \times \mathcal{K} \to \mathcal{C}$$

runs in polynomial time and for any $r, s \in \mathcal{K}$ and $E(x, r) \neq E(y, s)$ as long as $x \neq y$ where $x, y \in \{0, 1, 2, 3\}$ and $\mathcal{C}$ is the cryptogram space. Note that for any message $x \in \mathcal{M}$, we can define an ensemble $\mathcal{C}_x = E(x, \mathcal{K})$. The encryption function E is secure if any two ensembles $E(x, \mathcal{K})$, $E(y, \mathcal{K})$ are polynomially indistinguishable for $x, y \in \mathcal{M}$.

An interactive proof system for G3C is presented below. We use the following notations: $n = |\mathcal{V}|$ and $m = |\mathcal{E}|$ (note that $m \leq n^2/2$). P chooses a random permutation of colors π and encrypts colors of all vertices using a secure probabilistic encryption. The cryptograms of the random colors of vertices are revealed to V. The verifier selects a random edge (u, v) for which the prover must show the colors that were used in encryption. V recomputes cryptograms for vertices u and v and checks whether they are valid (or appear in the collection of cryptograms computed by P). This process is repeated many times.

G3C interactive proof – $G3C_{\hookrightarrow}$

Common Knowledge: an instance of G3C, i.e., a graph $G = (\mathcal{V}, \mathcal{E})$ (n is the number of vertices in $\mathcal{V}$).

Description: P and V repeat the following steps m^2 times.

1. P picks up $\pi \in_R Sym(\{1,2,3\})$ and an n-bit random vector $r_j \in_R \mathcal{K} = \{0,1\}^n$ for each vertex $v_j \in \mathcal{V}$, $j = 1,\ldots,n$. The prover computes $E_j = E(\pi(\phi(v_j)), r_j)$ and
$$P \to V : E_1, \ldots, E_n$$
where $\phi : \mathcal{V} \to \{1,2,3\}$ is a 3-coloring (always exists for a yes-instance).

2. V selects an edge $(u,v) \in_R \mathcal{E}$ and
$$V \to P : (u,v).$$

3. If $(u,v) \in \mathcal{E}$, then P reveals the coloring of u and v, or in other words
$$P \to V : (\pi(\phi(u)), r_u), (\pi(\phi(v)), r_v).$$

4. V checks whether the coloring
$$E_u \stackrel{?}{=} E(\pi(\phi(u)), r_u) \text{ and } E_v \stackrel{?}{=} E(\pi(\phi(v)), r_v),$$
makes sure that two vertices are assigned different colors $\pi(\phi(u)) \neq \pi(\phi(v))$, and confirms that the colors are valid, i.e., $\pi(\phi(u)), \pi(\phi(v)) \in Sym(\{1,2,3\})$. If any of these checks fail, V stops and rejects. Otherwise, the interaction continues.

After a successful completion of m^2 rounds, V halts and accepts.

Observe that the interactive proof satisfies the completeness property. For any yes-instance, the prover who knows the requested 3-coloring of the graph and follows the protocol can always convince the verifier. For any no-instance, at each round the prover can convince V with probability at most $1 - \frac{1}{m}$ as there must be at least one edge $(u,v) \in \mathcal{E}$ such that $\phi(u) = \phi(v)$. After m^2 rounds, V accepts with the probability $(1 - \frac{1}{m})^{m^2} \leq e^{-m}$. The soundness of the proof system holds. To assert that the interactive protocol is computationally zero-knowledge, we need to show that there is a polynomial-time transcript simulator $S_{V^*}(G, \hbar)$ that is polynomially indistinguishable from the view $View_{P,V^*}(G, \hbar)$ for any yes-instance and an arbitrary verifier V^*. As previously, the verifier uses a polynomial-time probabilistic algorithm F to choose an edge for verification.

Transcript simulator – $S_{V^*}(G, \hbar)$ for $G3C_{\hookleftarrow}$

Input: A graph $G(\mathcal{V}, \mathcal{E})$, a yes-instance of G3C; $\hbar$, past transcripts; v_{i-1}, transcript of the current interaction.

Description: Repeat the following steps until the transcript contains m^2 entries.

1. Choose an edge $e = (u, v) \in_R \mathcal{E}$ and its colors, i.e., a pair of integers $(a, b) \in_R \{(\alpha, \beta) | \alpha \neq \beta \text{ and } \alpha, \beta \in \{1, 2, 3\}\}$.

2. Select n random integers $r_j \in \mathcal{K}$ for $j = 1, \ldots, n$.

3. For $j = 1, \ldots, n$, compute the encryption

$$E_j = \begin{cases} E(a, r_j) & \text{if } j = u, \\ E(b, r_j) & \text{if } j = v, \\ E(0, r_j) & \text{otherwise.} \end{cases}$$

4. If $e = F(G, \hbar, v_{i-1}, E_1, \ldots, E_n)$, then

    return $(E_1, \ldots, E_n, e, a, b, r_u, r_v)$

    else go to (1).

A single round of the simulator is successful whenever the edge chosen in step (1) equals the edge indicated by the algorithm F. This event happens with the probability $\frac{1}{m}$. The analysis in [208] shows that the simulator runs in expected polynomial time and the expected number of rounds (to generate a single output) is bounded from below by $2m$. In the same paper, the authors also demonstrated that the ensemble generated by the simulator is polynomially indistinguishable from the view ensemble of $G3C_{\hookleftarrow}$.

Note that the prover has never used her unlimited power during the execution of $G3C_{\hookleftarrow}$. In fact, it is enough to assume that the prover P is polynomially bounded provided that she knows a 3-coloring of a yes-instance. In this context, computational zero-knowledge of $G3C_{\hookleftarrow}$ assures the prover that her secret (the 3-coloring) will not be divulged to the verifier V during the execution of the protocol. What V gains is the assertion that P knows a 3-coloring without revealing any details about it.

Brassard, Chaum, and Crepeau [61] independently showed that the satisfiability (SAT) problem has a computational zero-knowledge protocol. Instead of probabilistic encryption, they used a bit commitment scheme.

12.4 Bit Commitment Schemes

Consider again the protocol $G3C_\hookleftarrow$. The probabilistic encryption E was used there to hide the known 3-coloring into a sequence of n cryptograms $E_i = E(\pi(\phi(v_i)), r_i)$ $(i = 1, \ldots, n)$. A single cryptogram can be seen as a locked box with a single (permuted) color $\pi(\phi(v_i))$ of the vertex v_i. The lock can be opened by a holder of the key r_i. After sending a box, the prover commits herself to the particular color. P cannot change the contents of the box. Later the verifier may ask P to open the box and reveal the color.

A bit commitment scheme is a necessary ingredient for the design of computational zero-knowledge protocols for all problems from **NPC**. It provides a tool to hide the structure of a yes-instance and pins down the prover's choice before getting the verifier's challenge. Having a bit commitment scheme we can encrypt bit by bit the structure or put these bits into locked boxes. The boxes can be treated as pieces of paper covering bits of the yes-instance structure. Obviously, the prover reveals a small part of the structure only so the verifier learns nothing about the structure itself but this is enough for V to be convinced (after several rounds) that the prover indeed knows the structure.

Definition 35. *A bit commitment scheme is a pair of polynomial-time functions* (f, v). *The function*

$$f : \{0, 1\} \times \mathcal{Y} \to \mathcal{X}$$

transforms binary messages $b \in \{0, 1\}$ *using a random* $y \in \mathcal{Y}$. *The number* $x = f(b, y)$ *is called a blob. The verification function*

$$v : \mathcal{X} \times \mathcal{Y} \to \{0, 1, \bullet\}$$

is used to open a blob and reveal the bit ($\bullet$ stands for "undefined"). The functions have to satisfy the following conditions:

1. *Binding – for any blob* $x = f(b, y)$, *the prover is not able to find* $y' \neq y$ *such that the blob can be opened to the different bit, i.e.,*

   $$v(x, y) \neq v(x, y').$$

2. *Secrecy – two ensembles* $\{f(0, \mathcal{Y})\}$ *and* $\{f(1, \mathcal{Y})\}$ *are indistinguishable.*

Condition (1) says that once P has committed herself to a bit b by presenting a blob $x = f(b, y)$ to the verifier, she is later unable to change the bit. Condition

(2) ensures that there is no leakage of information about the committed bits from the blobs that are not opened by the prover.

Commitment schemes can be divided into two major classes:

– schemes with unconditional binding,
– schemes with unconditional secrecy.

If binding holds unconditionally, unambiguity of the committed bit is unconditional. If secrecy holds unconditionally, the verifier can learn nothing about the committed bit in the information theoretical sense (the entropy of the bit stays 1).

12.4.1 Blobs with Unconditional Secrecy

Brassard, Chaum, and Crepeau [61] gave a list of such schemes. We start from a scheme based on the factorization problem. The scheme is initialized by the verifier who chooses at random two large enough primes p and q and creates the modulus $N = pq$. Next, V picks up at random $t \in_R \mathbb{Z}_N^*$ and computes $s = t^2 \bmod N$. The pair (s, N) is made public and is used by P. The encryption and verification is described below.

Bit commitment based on factoring

Setup: V selects two large enough primes p and q, creates the modulus $N = pq$, picks up at random $t \in_R \mathbb{Z}_N^*$, and computes $s = t^2 \bmod N$. The set of blobs $\mathcal{X} = \mathbb{Z}_N^{Q+}$ and the set $\mathcal{Y} = Z_N^*$. V sends the public parameters of the scheme to P, that is $V \rightarrow P : s, N$.

Hiding: To hide a bit b, P chooses at random $y \in \mathbb{Z}_N^*$ and creates a blob

$$x = f(b, y) = s^b y^2 \bmod N.$$

Opening: P reveals her random y and V checks

$$v(x, y) = \begin{cases} 0 \text{ if } x \equiv y^2 \bmod N, \\ 1 \text{ if } x \equiv sy^2 \bmod N, \\ \bullet \text{ otherwise.} \end{cases}$$

Binding holds under the assumption that the factorization problem is intractable (clearly P has to be polynomially bounded). Secrecy is satisfied unconditionally as the ensembles $\{f(0, \mathcal{Y})\}$ and $\{f(1, \mathcal{Y})\}$ are identical.

Under the assumption that the discrete logarithm is intractable, it is possible to build a bit commitment scheme that uses exponentiation as a one-way function.

Bit commitment based on discrete logarithm

Setup: P and V agree on a large enough prime p and a primitive element $g \in \mathbb{Z}_p^*$. The set $\mathcal{X} = \mathbb{Z}_p^*$ and $\mathcal{Y} = \{0, 1, \ldots, p-2\}$. V chooses $s \in \mathbb{Z}_{p-1}$ and forwards it to P.

Hiding: To hide a bit b, P chooses at random $y \in \mathcal{Y}$ and creates a blob

$$x = f(b, y) = s^b g^y \bmod p.$$

Opening: P reveals her random y and V checks

$$v(x, y) = \begin{cases} 0 \text{ if } x \equiv g^y \bmod p, \\ 1 \text{ if } x \equiv sg^y \bmod p, \\ \bullet \text{ otherwise.} \end{cases}$$

Binding is satisfied conditionally if the discrete logarithm is intractable. Again secrecy is satisfied unconditionally as the ensembles $\{f(0, \mathcal{Y})\}$ and $\{f(1, \mathcal{Y})\}$ are identical.

The GI problem can also be used to construct bit commitment schemes assuming that instances applied are intractable.

Bit commitment based on GI

Setup: P and V agree on a graph $G = (\mathcal{V}, \mathcal{E})$ $(n = |\mathcal{V}|)$. V selects a random permutation $\pi \in_R Sym(\mathcal{V})$ and defines $H = \pi(G)$. The pair (G, H) of graphs is known to both P and V (while the permutation π is kept secret by V). The set $\mathcal{X} = \{H | H = \pi(G), \pi \in_R Sym(\mathcal{V})\}$ and $\mathcal{Y} = Sym(\mathcal{V})$.

Hiding: To hide a bit b, P chooses at random $\gamma \in \mathcal{Y}$ and creates a blob (a graph)

$$X = f(b, \gamma) = \begin{cases} \gamma(G) \text{ if } b = 0, \\ \gamma(H) \text{ if } b = 1. \end{cases}$$

Opening: P reveals her random γ and V checks

$$v(X, \gamma) = \begin{cases} 0 \text{ if } \gamma(G) = X, \\ 1 \text{ if } \gamma(H) = X, \\ \bullet \text{ otherwise.} \end{cases}$$

Note that a blob cannot be opened to a different bit under the assumption that P is not able to find the isomorphism π used by V (intractability of GI instances) to generate H that is an isomorphic copy of G. The ensembles $\{f(0, \mathcal{Y})\}$ and $\{f(1, \mathcal{Y})\}$ are identical, so secrecy holds unconditionally.

12.4.2 Blobs with Unconditional Binding

Consider the quadratic residue problem. It is assumed that for a composite modulus $N = pq$, the sets $\mathcal{Z}_N^{Q+}$ and $\mathcal{Z}_N^{Q-}$ are polynomially indistinguishable. This property can be exploited in the design of bit commitment schemes. This time the scheme is set up by the prover who chooses two random and big enough primes p and q and a quadratic nonresidue $s \in \mathcal{Z}_N^{Q-}$.

Bit commitment based on QR

Setup: P selects two large enough primes p and q, creates the modulus $N = pq$, and picks up at random $s \in_R \mathcal{Z}_N^{Q-}$. The set of blobs $\mathcal{X} = \mathcal{Z}_N^Q$ and the set $\mathcal{Y} = \mathcal{Z}_N^*$. P sends the public parameters of the scheme to V, that is $P \to V : s, N$.

Hiding: To hide a bit b, P chooses at random $y \in \mathcal{Z}_N^*$ and creates a blob

$$x = f(b, y) = s^b y^2 \bmod N.$$

Opening: P reveals her random y and V checks

$$v(x, y) = \begin{cases} 0 \text{ if } x \equiv y^2 \bmod N, \\ 1 \text{ if } x \equiv sy^2 \bmod N, \\ \bullet \text{ otherwise.} \end{cases}$$

The prover is unable to cheat and open a blob to the different bit as there exists no $y' \in \mathcal{Z}_N^*$ which would give the same blob for the different bit. This is the consequence of the fact that $\mathcal{Z}_N^{Q-} \cap \mathcal{Z}_N^{Q+} = \emptyset$. Binding is unconditional. The two ensembles $\{f(0, \mathcal{Y})\}$ and $\{f(0, \mathcal{Y})\}$ are polynomially indistinguishable. Secrecy holds under the assumption that the testing quadratic residuosity is intractable.

The discrete logarithm can also be used. Let p be a large enough Blum prime and g be a primitive element of $\mathcal{Z}_p^*$.

Bit commitment based on discrete logarithm

Setup: P and V agree on a large enough Blum prime p ($p \equiv 3 \bmod 4$) and a primitive element $g \in \mathcal{Z}_p^*$. The set $\mathcal{X} = \mathcal{Z}_p^*$ and $\mathcal{Y} = \mathcal{Z}_{p-1}$.

Hiding: To lock a bit b, P chooses at random $y \in \mathcal{Y}$. Observe that the second least significant bit of y is b, or for short $b = SLB(y)$, or equivalently $y \bmod 4 \in \{0, 1\}$ if $b = 0$ and $y \bmod 4 \in \{2, 3\}$ if $b = 1$. P creates a blob

$$x = f(b, y) = \begin{cases} g^y \bmod p & \text{if } SLB(y) = b, \\ g^{-y} \bmod p & \text{if } SLB(y) = \bar{b}. \end{cases}$$

Opening: P reveals her random y and V checks

$$v(x, y) = \begin{cases} b = SLB(y) \text{ if } x \equiv g^y \bmod p, \\ \bar{b} = SLB(y) \text{ if } x \equiv g^{p-y} \bmod p, \\ \bullet \text{ otherwise.} \end{cases}$$

Once the prover has committed herself to a blob, the hidden bit cannot be changed – binding is unconditional. On the other hand, secrecy holds under the assumption that an instance of DL is intractable.

Another example of a bit commitment is a probabilistic encryption discussed in Sect. 4.7 and applied in Sect. 12.3.

12.4.3 Multivalued Blobs

A string commitment scheme is a generalization of bit commitment schemes. Unlike in a bit commitment, the prover can hide a string of bits in a single blob. An advantage of these schemes is that they can be tailored to a particular zero-knowledge protocol making the interactions more efficient. We need to adjust our definition. The function $f : \{0, 1\}^n \times \mathcal{X} \to \mathcal{Y}$ operates on n-bit sequences. The function $v : \mathcal{X} \times \mathcal{Y} \to \{0, 1, \dots, 2^{n-1}, \bullet\}$.

Consider a multivalued blob that constitutes a commitment to an n-bit string $s = (b_1, \dots, b_n)$ [399].

String commitment based on discrete logarithm

Setup: P and V agree on a large enough prime p, a primitive element $g \in \mathcal{Z}_p^*$ and an integer h such that $\log_g h$ is unknown. The set $\mathcal{X} = \mathcal{Z}_p^*$ and $\mathcal{Y} = \mathcal{Z}_p^*$.

Hiding: To lock an n-bit string s, P chooses at random $y \in \mathcal{Y}$ and creates a blob

$$x = f(s,y) = g^s h^y \bmod p.$$

Opening: P reveals the pair (s', y') and V checks

$$v(x,y) = \begin{cases} s' & \text{if } x \overset{?}{\equiv} g^{s'} h^{y'} \bmod p, \\ \bullet & \text{otherwise.} \end{cases}$$

Blobs in the scheme are secret unconditionally. Binding is conditional as it depends on the assumption that the discrete logarithm is intractable.

Claw-free permutation pairs studied in [211] can be used to build a string commitment scheme [228]. Given two large primes p and q such that $p \equiv 3 \bmod 8$ and $q \equiv 7 \bmod 8$, the modulus $N = pq$. Define a function $g_b(x) \equiv 4^b x \bmod N$ where b is a bit.

String commitment based on claw-free permutations

Setup: V selects two primes p and q such that $p \equiv 3 \bmod 8$ and $q \equiv 7 \bmod 8$.
   V communicates N to P. The set $\mathcal{X} = \mathcal{Z}_N^{Q+}$ and $\mathcal{Y} = \mathcal{Z}_N^*$.
Hiding: To lock an n-bit string s, P chooses at random $y \in \mathcal{Y}$ and creates a blob

$$x = f(s,y) = g_{b_1} \circ g_{b_1} \circ \ldots \circ g_{b_n}(y),$$

   where $s = (b_1, \ldots, b_n)$.
Opening: P reveals the pair (s', y') and V checks

$$v(x,y) = \begin{cases} s' & \text{if } x \overset{?}{\equiv} g_{b_1'} \circ \ldots \circ g_{b_n'}(y), \\ \bullet & \text{otherwise.} \end{cases}$$

   where $s' = (b_1', \ldots, b_n')$.

Secrecy is unconditional, binding is conditional if the factorization of N is intractable.

Let us discuss the implications of this type of bit commitment scheme on a zero-knowledge proof in which the scheme is being used. A bit commitment scheme with unconditionally secure blobs for the verifier was used to design a zero-knowledge proof for G3C. The protocol works correctly for the prover who may or may not be polynomially bounded. Moreover, the prover is not able to cheat the verifier when P opens some blobs. An evident disadvantage is that the security of unopened blobs depends on the assumption of intractability. After completion of the protocol, if the verifier is able to break the bit commitment scheme, the secret structure of yes-instance (in the case of $G3C_{\hookrightarrow}$, a 3-coloring) can be easily revealed.

What happens when a zero-knowledge proof employs a bit commitment with unconditional secrecy? P cannot open a blob to two different bits under some intractability assumption. Clearly, P has to be polynomially bounded. Otherwise, P could cheat. To make the point clearer, consider a bit commitment based on factoring. If a blob is x, then an "all powerful" prover can easily find factors of the modulus N and open x as bit 0 (for this she needs to find a square root of x) or as bit 1 (she computes a square root of xs^{-1}). Unlike in the first case, however, the prover has a limited time for computations that may help her to cheat. After the execution of the protocol, even if P gains some additional computational power (either by progress in computing technology or the development of new more powerful algorithms), it is too late for cheating. Unopened blobs are unconditionally secure and the security does not depend on the computational power of the verifier. In the literature, protocols that use this type of bit commitment are called *zero-knowledge arguments*.

12.5 Problems and Exercises

1. Consider the following interactive proof system.

QNR interactive proof – $QNR_{\hookrightarrow}$

Common Knowledge: an instance (x, N) of the QNR problem (n is the size of the instance).

Description: Given a polynomial $t(n)$ in n. P and V repeat the following steps $t(n)$ times.
  (a) V picks up $r \in_R Z_N^*$ and $\beta \in_R \{0, 1\}$.
  (b) $V \to P : w \equiv r^2 \cdot x^\beta \bmod N$.
  (c) The prover sends to V
  $$P \to V : \alpha = \begin{cases} 0 & \text{if } w \in Z_N^{Q+}, \\ 1 & \text{otherwise.} \end{cases}$$
  (d) V checks whether $\alpha = \beta$. If the check fails, V stops and rejects. Otherwise V continues.

  After passing through $t(n)$ rounds without rejection, V halts and accepts.

   Prove that the protocol is complete and sound. Is the protocol zero-knowledge? Justify your answer [210].
2. Consider two protocols $QR_{\hookrightarrow}$ and $GI_{\hookrightarrow}$. Assume that the verifier follows strictly the protocol. Modify the corresponding transcript simulators and show that both protocols are zero-knowledge.

3. Consider two protocols $GNI_{\hookleftarrow}$ and $QNR_{\hookleftarrow}$. Show that the two protocols are complete and sound.

4. Consider the following decision problem [496].

   Name: Subgroup membership problem.

   Instance: Given a composite integer N. Two integers $g, x \in \mathcal{Z}_N^*$ where g generates a subgroup of order α.

   Question: Is $x \equiv g^k \bmod N$ for some $k \leq \alpha$?

   Consider the following interactive proof based on the problem.

   Subgroup membership interactive proof

   Common Knowledge: an instance of the subgroup membership problem, i.e., a modulus N and two integers $g, x \in \mathcal{Z}_N^*$ where g has order α in $\mathcal{Z}_N^*$.

   Description: Given a polynomial $t(n)$ in n (n is the size of the instance). For $i = 1, \ldots, t(n)$, P and V repeat the following steps

   (a) P picks up j at random ($0 \leq j \leq \alpha$) and evaluates $\beta \equiv g^j \bmod N$.

   (b) $P \rightarrow V : \beta$.

   (c) V chooses at random a bit b and sends it to P.

   (d) P finds out $h \equiv j + bk \bmod \alpha$ where $k = \log_g x$ and sends h to V.

   (e) V stops and rejects when $g^h \overset{?}{\not\equiv} x^b \beta \bmod N$.

   After passing through $t(n)$ rounds without rejection, V halts and accepts.

   Show that the protocol is complete and sound.

5. Consider the $G3C_{\hookleftarrow}$ protocol. It is assumed that the verifier strictly obeys the protocol. Modify the corresponding transcript simulator. What is the time complexity of the modified simulator?

6. Take the bit commitment scheme based on DL. Prove that the secrecy is unconditional. Is this still true if the verifier knows that the prover chooses $y < \frac{p}{2}$?

7. Let us consider the bit commitment based on the GI problem. Show how the prover can cheat if she knows the permutation π that establishes the isomorphism between public graphs H and G.

8. Given the bit commitment scheme based on QR. Assume that P cheats and sends s that belongs to $\mathcal{Z}_N^{Q+}$ (instead of to $\mathcal{Z}_N^{Q-}$ as prescribed). P also knows a square root of s. Is binding still satisfied?

9. Recall the string commitment scheme based on DL. Prove that the secrecy is unconditional. Show that if a particular instance of DL is easy, then P can always open a blob to a different string.

10. Consider the bit commitment based on claw-free permutations. Prove that binding is conditional and the secrecy holds unconditionally.

13 Identification

Identification is usually one of the first safeguards that is used to protect computer resources against an unauthorized access. Any access control that governs how the computer resources are accessed and by whom assumes that there is an identification mechanism that works reliably.

There is a large volume of literature that covers different aspects of entity identification. Good overviews of the topic can be found in [337, 496].

13.1 Basic Identification Techniques

Identification of a person, host, intelligent terminal, program, system, etc. can be seen as a two-party protocol. The two players involved are: the prover and the verifier. The prover P, also mnemonically called Peggy, wishes to introduce herself to the verifier V, Victor, in such a way that Victor is convinced that he is indeed dealing with Peggy. An identification protocol can go wrong in two different ways. First, the failure can occur when an opponent, Oscar, manages to convince Victor that he is Peggy. This is a *false acceptance*. Secondly, a failure may occur if Peggy fails to convince Victor about her identity. This is a *false rejection*. An identification protocol is characterized by two probabilities (also called rates). The probability of a false acceptance P_{fa} and the probability of a false rejection P_{fr}.

Consider two trivial identification protocols. In the first protocol, Victor asks Peggy for her name and always accepts her under the given name. The probability of false acceptance $P_{fa} = 1$ and the probability of false rejection $P_{fr} = 0$. In the second protocol, Victor always rejects Peggy's proofs of identity. The probabilities of false acceptance $P_{fa} = 0$ and false rejection $P_{fr} = 1$. A "good" identification protocol should achieve both P_{fa} and P_{fr} values as small as possible.

Identity of an entity (person, host, intelligent terminal, program, etc.) can be asserted by the verification of what the entity

– is,
– has, or
– knows.

The verification of "what the entity is" is traditionally referred to as *user identification* mainly because in a computer environment, hardly any entity displays unique and nontransferable identification characteristics. On the contrary, due to the ease of copying, all digital information can be duplicated making it impossible to distinguish copies from the original. Typically, a user identification mechanism uses unique and nontransferable characteristics such as fingerprints, retinal prints, hand signature, etc.

The verification of "what the entity has" makes sure that the entity has a unique token such as a smart card with some secret information, which can be used to prove the identity of the holder. The proof of identity is based on the assumption that the owner never loses its token. If a token is lost, it can be used by some other entity to falsely claim the identity of the owner of the token.

The verification of "what the entity knows" exploits a piece of secret information that is known to a given entity only. A common identification mechanism in this class uses passwords. The security of the identification relies on the security of the secret. Secrets that are compromised (revealed) can be used by unauthorized entities. On the other hand, forgotten secrets cannot be used by an authorized entity.

The identification based on what the entity has and knows uses a secret and unique piece of information. The difference is in the storage of the information. The secret can be stored away from the entity on a token (the token is owned by the entity) or just be stored within the entity (the entity knows the secret).

13.2 User Identification

Fingerprints are commonly considered as a unique characteristic of a person. The reliability of fingerprint identification is so high that it is legally admissible in court. Fingerprint identification systems use ridge and valley patterns. The patterns are classified into a collection of *minutiae*. The minutiae are stored as an individual fingerprint template. Currently available automated fingerprint identification machines (AFIMs) verify persons with false acceptance/rejection probabilities approximately 10^{-3} or better. The enrollment time necessary to store an individual fingerprint template is usually below 10 seconds and requires about 1 kbyte memory storage. The verification time typically takes around a few seconds. However, AFIMs are still expensive and their prices range close to or above US\$1000. Because of the cost and the relatively high error rates, their application in the computer environment is limited.

Similarly, both the iris and retina can be used as the base for identification. Retinal scan technology applies the capillary pattern of the retina and converts it to a digital pattern template. The template takes about 40 bytes of storage. The probability of false acceptance/rejection is smaller than 10^{-6}. The enrollment time is approximately 30 seconds and the verification can be done in less than 2 seconds. Again this technology requires dedicated hardware and is expensive.

Hand geometry and face images fall into the same category of biometric identification. Hand geometry identification uses key geometric features of the topography of a hand. The features are encoded into a template that needs 10 bytes only. Face recognition is rapidly growing due to the noninvasive nature of the method. It can also be used for massive scanning, for instance in the search for terrorists in airports. The false acceptance/rejection probabilities are smaller than 10^{-4}.

The handwritten signature is a common method of authenticating paper documents. There are some features of the signature that tend to be different for each signature. More importantly, there are also features that do not change at all. They are related to habitual aspects of signing. To capture these unique signing patterns, signature verification systems use analysis of the pen pressure, style, stroke direction, acceleration, and speed. A typical template that characterizes the unique signing features of an individual takes up about 1 kbyte. To create a template for a new person, the person is required to sign from five to eight times. The verification time is less than 1 second. An attractive characteristic of a signature is that a simple verification system can be implemented for all computer systems with a mouse with no additional hardware. The mouse can be used as a pen.

Voice verification can also be an option for person identification. Voice recognition devices are probably the least reliable in terms of their high false acceptance/rejection probabilities. Their useful feature is, however, that a voice sample can be taken remotely using a telephone only (no additional hardware).

When a person types on a keyboard, the keystroke characteristics (typing rhythms) also contain some unique features of the person. This verification method is the most "computer" friendly. Experiments have shown that the false acceptance/rejection rate is still too high for any practical and reliable identification. To make this technique reliable for identification, keyboards will need to be equipped with special sensors to measure not only the typing rhythm but also some other typing features such as speed, acceleration, key pressure, etc.

For the sake of completeness, DNA identification needs to be added to the list of available identification methods. In theory, this method offers a false acceptance/rejection rate equal to zero. The only exception is when the method is used to identify one of two identical twins. In practice, the identification service is provided by specialized laboratories only. The verification is time consuming and requires a sample of the tested person's genetic material. Because of these properties, the method is not used for personal identification in the computer environment.

Biometric identification is vulnerable to all kinds of replay attacks. For example, a voice pattern could be recorded and later replayed unless the tested person has to repeat a randomly selected sentence.

13.3 Passwords

The most popular single identification technique used in computer environments is via what a person knows. The piece of information memorized by a person is a *password* or personal identification number (PIN). PINs are passwords that are sequences of digits. This restriction is imposed by a specific technology used in, for example, automated teller machines (ATMs) where the keypad has digit keys only. As the main requirement for passwords is that they have to be memorized by persons, their length has to restricted. Typically, the length varies from 4 to 9 alphanumeric characters.

Given a password of n characters, if the number of letters is 26 (upper and lower case letters are considered to be identical), the probability of guessing the password is 26^{-n}, provided the password is selected independently and uniformly from the set of 26^n possible words. If upper and lower case letters are considered different, the guessing probability drops to 52^{-n}. Further reduction can be achieved if a password can contain not only letters but also digits, and other printable characters such as \$, %, <, {, ;, ", etc.

Typically password identification takes place every time a user, Peggy, wishes to login to a host computer V. Peggy knows her password while the host V maintains a password file in which V stores the passwords of all registered users. Peggy types her login name and her password. Having the pair: login name, password, the host V checks whether there is an entry for Peggy and, if so, compares the password submitted by Peggy with the one stored in the password file. If there is a match, Peggy can access the host, otherwise Peggy is identified as an illegal user and the access is denied. Note that the password file in the host has to be protected not only against users but, preferably, against a superuser as well. Usually, password files are protected by storing either encrypted or hashed passwords. The verification process would involve the same steps except that a password provided by Peggy is first encrypted (or hashed) and then compared. Hashing has an advantage over encryption as it applies no cryptographic key.

Every time a password is used, its security decreases. The simple remedy would be to introduce *password aging*. A password is valid for its lifetime, which is usually any time between 20 days and 3 months. In the extreme, the lifetime of a password can be a single login attempt. These passwords are called *one-time passwords*. Implementation of one-time passwords can be done simply by generating a list of passwords and applying them in some order. The main problem is now having them memorized by a user. A way out would be to store passwords on a token. This obviously shifts the identification from what a person knows to what a person possesses. One-time passwords could be created by repetitive application of a one-way function. Given a one-way function f and a password p_0, the sequence of passwords is $p_i = f(p_{i-1})$ for $i = 1, \ldots, n$. The passwords are used by their holder in reverse order so the first password to be used is p_n and the last one is p_0.

13.3.1 Attacks on Passwords

A password can be compromised every time it is used. An outsider may look over Peggy's shoulder when she is typing her password and learn it. To thwart the attack requires putting a keyboard in such a position that the movement of hands cannot be observed. Also, the use of a one-time password may be a possibility. After Peggy has typed her password, the password needs to be verified by the host. If Peggy accesses her host via remote terminal, her password may travel via unprotected communication channels to the host. The security risk becomes even higher if Peggy uses the Internet for a remote login.

The selection of passwords is crucial. Ideally, Peggy should choose her password at random. The problem with this is that random passwords are difficult to learn by heart. Consequently, users tend to choose passwords in a nonrandom way, making their passwords vulnerable to an exhaustive search attack. Knowing Peggy's habits, favourite movies, songs, etc., a potential attacker Oscar may restrict the search for Peggy's password to: her name, names of her friends, names of her relatives, names of her pets, names of her favourite actors, singers, and sportswomen. If this fails, Oscar may try the name of Peggy's host computer, her phone numbers, her car registration number, the number of her passport, her address details, her birthday, and so on. Oscar may also try some easy-to-memorize combination of digits/letters such as a sequence of zeros. In general, Oscar may apply the so-called *dictionary attack*. In this attack, Oscar tries all words (in lower and upper cases, written also backwards) in a typical (around 100,000 words) dictionary. To limit the efficiency of the dictionary attack, it is desirable to put an upper bound on the number of unsuccessful password guesses after which the system terminates the login session with extra delays between subsequent attempts. This may not work if Oscar can access the encrypted password file.

Passwords may be easier to memorized and more difficult to guess if Peggy obeys the following rules when she selects her password:

1. Passwords should use the full allowed length of the password.
2. Passwords should contain special characters such as $, %, &, @, {, [, (, etc., digits, and lower and upper case letters.
3. Words in passwords should not be part of any dictionary (words should be composed from parts of an easy-to-memorize and long sequence with inserted digits and special characters).

Again we emphasize that only long and truly random passwords are immune to the exhaustive search or any dictionary attack.

13.3.2 Weaknesses of Passwords

Identification based on passwords suffers from the following inherent weaknesses:

– The password verification process requires Peggy to show her password to Victor. After learning her password, Victor can try to impersonate Peggy.
– Victor never proves his identity to Peggy. Oscar may try to impersonate Victor to learn Peggy's password.
– The password communicated by Peggy to Victor does not depend on the current time. Oscar may use the replay attack.

The impact of the first weakness can be reduced by encrypting or hashing passwords at the point of entry and handling them in an encrypted or hashed form. Typing passwords on a keyboard is itself still a potential hazard for the security of a password. This weakness also raises the following question: is it possible to verify a piece of secret information without telling the secret? The answer is affirmative, and examples of such verification techniques are given in the next sections.

The prover-verifier relation is highly asymmetrical. Victor verifies Peggy's credentials but Peggy knows nothing about Victor's identity. The lack of mutual authentication is a major hurdle for extending the password-based identification to peer entities such as collaborating concurrent processes. Moreover, the two first weaknesses can be used to launch a variety of masquerade attacks. Typically in the attack, an intelligent remote terminal (disconnected from the host) is applied to collect passwords from unsuspecting users who want to login to the host. After the prescribed user name and password have been typed by a user, the terminal aborts the session displaying a message

```
the host is temporarily unavailable due to scheduled maintenance,
                    try again in 30 minutes
```

The attacker may even connect the terminal back to its host after 30 minutes making users believe that the message was true. Some other variants of the above attack may include a forged login program. The program asks a user for their name and password, stores the pair (user name, password) and displays

```
                    wrong password, try again
```

After that it calls the original login program making the user believe that he or she has made a typing mistake. In these attacks, most users will not even realize that their passwords have been compromised.

Notice that passwords do not depend on time so, consequently, Victor does not know whether the current password has been sent now or perhaps it is a copy of a password sent some time ago. This property can also be exploited to design an attack on the password identification mechanism.

13.4 Challenge-Response Identification

Challenge-response identification is also called a *strong entity authentication* or *handshaking protocol.* The identification takes the form of a dialog between Peggy and Victor in which the password is never exchanged between them. Instead the password known to both P and V is used to generate "proper" responses to random challenges. In this context, passwords play the role of secret cryptographic keys used to perform computations on challenges. The challenge-response protocol can also be used by P and V to assert that they have been successful in running their key establishment protocol. In other words, P and V wish to verify whether they possess the right collection of keys.

13.4.1 Authentication of Shared Keys

Assume that two peer entities A and B (mnemonically Alice and Bob) are supposed to know the same cryptographic key k. Now they would like to verify whether they indeed share the same key. A typical challenge-response dialog for this case may proceed as follows.

Challenge-response protocol (a shared key)

Goal: Mutual authentication of A and B by checking whether they share a key k.

Assumptions: A and B choose two random challenges (nonces) r_A and r_B, respectively, and they use the same encryption algorithm.

Message Sequence: The protocol consists of the following sequence of messages:

    1. $A \rightarrow B : r_A$.

    2. $B \rightarrow A : \{A, r_A, r_B\}_k$.

3. $A \rightarrow B : \{B, r_B\}_k$.

where $\{A, r_A, r_B\}_k$ is the cryptogram for message (A, r_A, r_B) under the key k.

The protocol works as follows. First, A sends her challenge to B in clear. In response, B takes the name of A, her challenge r_A, and concatenates it with his challenge r_B. The triplet is encrypted using the key k. The cryptogram $\{A, r_A, r_B\}_k$ is sent to A. A decrypts the cryptogram, retrieves the pair of nonces and checks whether the second element is equal to her nonce r_A. If there is a match, A knows that B holds the same key. Now, A encrypts B's challenge and forwards $\{B, r_B\}_k$ to B. Now B verifies the validity of A's response by first checking whether there is B in it and next comparing the nonce recovered from the cryptogram with the original r_B. If there is a match, B is convinced that A applied the correct key for encryption so she knows the key. The security of the challenge-response protocol depends on the length of the key k, the strength of the encryption algorithm, and the freshness of the challenges. The protocol can be easily adopted for a unilateral authentication where A authenticates B only.

The encryption algorithm can be replaced by any one-way function including a collision-free hash function. If both A and B decide to used the same hash function h, then the message exchange in the above protocol may proceed as follows:

1. $A \rightarrow B : r_A$.
2. $B \rightarrow A : r_B, h(A, r_A, r_B, k)$.
3. $A \rightarrow B : h(k, B, r_B, r_A)$.

A first communicates r_A to B in clear. B hashes the tuple A, r_A, r_B, k and forwards the pair $(r_B, h(A, r_A, r_B, k))$ to A. A verifies the hash value and sends $h(k, B, r_B, r_A)$ to B. Note that A changes the order of elements to make the protocol immune against the replay attack.

13.4.2 Authentication of Public Keys

Suppose that A and B know each other's authentic public key. So A knows K_B and B knows K_A. Clearly, A has to know her own secret key k_A and B has to know his secret key k_B. Assume that they wish to verify whether the other entity indeed holds the corresponding secret key. Note that a public-key cryptosystem can be used for confidentiality or authenticity (signature). A challenge-response protocol for unilateral authentication of B by A when B uses his public key for confidentiality is described below.

Challenge-response protocol (public encryption)

Goal: A identifies B by checking whether B holds the secret key k_B that matches his public key K_B.

Assumptions: A chooses a random challenge (nonce) r_A. B applies his public-key system for confidentiality.

Message Sequence: The protocol consists of the following sequence of messages:

1. $A \rightarrow B : [r_A, A]_{K_A}$.
2. $B \rightarrow A : r_A$.

where $[r_A, A]_{K_A}$ stands for the cryptogram of (r_A, A) obtained using the key K_B.

A knowing the public key of B encrypts her nonce r_A together with her name A and sends the cryptogram to B. Only B can recover the nonce and the name of A from the cryptogram. B communicates r_A to A. If the returned nonce is equal to r_A, A accepts that she is dealing with B.

The protocol needs some modifications when B uses his public-key cryptosystem for authentication.

Challenge-response protocol (authentication)

Goal: A identifies B by checking whether B holds the secret key k_B that matches the public key K_B.

Assumptions: A chooses a random challenge (nonce) r_A, B uses his random nonce r_B. B applies his public-key system for authentication.

Message Sequence: The protocol consists of the following sequence of messages:

1. $A \rightarrow B : r_A$.
2. $B \rightarrow A : r_B, \langle r_A, r_B \rangle_{k_B}$.

A sends her random challenge to B. B takes a fresh nonce r_B and signs the pair. The signature $\langle r_A, r_B \rangle_{k_B}$ is sent to A who verifies its validity in the usual way. Note that the nonce r_B may not need to be transmitted in clear if the signature $\langle r_A, r_B \rangle_{k_B}$ allows the recovery of the message.

13.5 Identification Protocols

Recall that zero-knowledge proof systems considered in Chap. 12 allow the prover P to demonstrate to the verifier V the knowledge of her secret without revealing any information about it. Clearly, they are ideal vehicles for identification. Note that a direct use of a zero-knowledge proof system allows unilateral authentication of P (Peggy) by V (Victor) and the identification protocol will need to consist of a large enough number of iterations. The *completeness*, *soundness*, and *zero-knowledge* properties defined for interactive proof systems, have their own interpretation in the context of identification. An identification protocol is *complete* if a legitimate prover (who follows the protocol) is always correctly identified by V. In other words, the probability of false rejection is zero. An identification protocol is *sound* if the verifier detects an impostor with an overwhelming probability. This can be translated into the requirement that the probability of false acceptance be 2^{-t}, where t is the number of iterations. A zero-knowledge identification protocol reveals no information about the secret held by the prover under some reasonable computational assumptions.

In this section we are going to discuss the Fiat-Shamir identification protocol and its more efficient variant given by Feige, Fiat, and Shamir. We next study an identity-based identification protocol by Guillou and Quisquater. Schnorr presented a very efficient identification protocol designed especially for smart card applications. We describe the Schnorr scheme together with its variant given by Okamoto. Other identification protocols not discussed here include several variants based on error correcting codes [490, 94]. One of the more exotic intractable problems used to design identification protocols is an **NPC** problem from learning machines, called the perceptrons problem [409].

13.5.1 Fiat-Shamir Identification Protocol

Fiat and Shamir [181] designed an identification protocol whose security hinges on the assumption that finding square roots modulo N is difficult provided the factorization of N is unknown. This is equivalent to the difficulty of factoring N. The FS protocol is described here.

FS identification protocol

TA Precomputations: A trusted authority TA holds its public modulus N where $N = pq$ and primes p and q are secret.

Registration: P selects her secret $s \in_R \mathbb{Z}_N^*$. P registers the integer $\sigma \equiv s^2$ (mod N) with TA as her public identification information.

Message Sequence: P proves to V that she knows the secret s by performing the following iterations t times:

1. $P \to V : u \equiv r^2 \bmod N$ where $r \in_R \mathbb{Z}_N^*$.
2. $V \to P : b \in_R \{0,1\}$.
3. $P \to V : v \equiv r \times s^b \bmod N$.
4. Verification: V checks whether
$$v^2 \stackrel{?}{\equiv} u \times \sigma^b \bmod N.$$
   V stops on failure or continues otherwise.

After t successful iterations V accepts.

TA keeps the identification information of all registered users. The registration of P has to be performed at the setup stage. Registration has to proceed after the mutual authentication of TA and P, which is typically done by physical exchange of their credentials (passports, identification cards with photos, etc.). This step is crucial from a security point of view.

Assume that a verifier V would like to make sure that P is indeed the same person whose public information σ is published by TA. V asks P to prove herself to him. The identification protocol takes t iterations. Each iteration is independent of the other in the sense that an iteration starts from selection of a random r by Peggy, who then squares it and forwards the commitment u to Victor. Next, V chooses his binary challenge b and communicates it to P. Peggy replies by sending $v = r \times s^b$. Finally, Victor squares the response v and verifies whether the result is equal to $u \times \sigma^b$. If the check fails, V stops and rejects P's identity, otherwise the protocol continues. If P and V passed t iterations without rejection, then V accepts P.

An impostor, Oscar, may cheat Victor if he is able to guess his binary challenge. Let $g \in \{0,1\}$ be Oscar's guess of Victor's challenge. Oscar selects at random r and sends his commitment

$$u \equiv r^2 \sigma^{-g} \bmod N.$$

Victor replies by sending his challenge $b \in_R \{0,1\}$. Oscar now has to dispatch

$$v \equiv r \times s^{b-g} \bmod N$$

to pass the check $v^2 \stackrel{?}{\equiv} u \times \sigma^b \bmod N$. The verification can be rewritten as

$$v^2 = r^2\sigma^{b-g} \stackrel{?}{\equiv} u \times \sigma^{b-g}.$$

Note that when $g \neq b$ then Oscar is unable to produce the proper $v \equiv r \times s^{b-g} \bmod N$ as he needs to know either s or s^{-1}. So he will fail each iteration with probability $1/2$. If the protocol is run for t iterations, Oscar is detected as an impostor by Victor with probability $1 - 2^{-t}$. The probability of false acceptance is 2^{-t}.

Consider an example. TA has published the modulus $N = 46161041$ ($p = 4787$ and $q = 9643$). The prover has selected her secret $s = 21883917$ and registered her public information $\sigma = s^2 \equiv 25226214 \pmod{46161041}$. The identification protocol runs t times. At each run, P selects at random r. Let it be $r = 41435437$ in the first round. P sends her commitment

$$P \rightarrow V : u = r^2 \equiv 6360246 \pmod{46161041}.$$

V replies by sending his random challenge $b = 1$. P sends the response

$$P \rightarrow V : v = rs \equiv 39085596 \pmod{46161041}.$$

V checks whether $v^2 \equiv 42178320 \pmod{46161041}$ is equal to $u\sigma \equiv 42178320 \pmod{46161041}$. Indeed two integers are the same, so P continues the protocol.

13.5.2 Feige-Fiat-Shamir Identification Protocol

The FS identification protocol requires a large number of iterations, consequently the identification process is slow and computationally expensive for both the prover and verifier. Feige, Fiat, and Shamir came up with a more efficient protocol [167]. The security of the protocol relies on the assumption that factoring is difficult.

FFS identification protocol

TA Precomputations: TA holds its public modulus N where $N = pq$ and primes
    $p \equiv 3 \bmod 4$ and $q \equiv 3 \bmod 4$ are kept secret.
Registration: P performs the following steps:
1. selects at random ℓ integers $s_1, \ldots, s_\ell \in_R \mathcal{Z}_N^*$,
2. chooses a binary vector $(e_1, \ldots, e_\ell)$ at random,
3. computes $w_i \equiv (-1)^{e_i} s_i^{-2} \pmod{N}$ for $i = 1, \ldots, \ell$, and
4. registers $(w_1, \ldots, w_\ell)$ with TA as P's identification public information while keeping integers $(s_1, \ldots, s_\ell)$ secret.

Message Sequence: P proves to V that she knows the secret vector $s_1, \ldots, s_\ell$
by performing the following iterations t times.

1. $P \to V : u \equiv r^2 \pmod{N}$ where $r \in_R \mathcal{Z}_N^*$.
2. $V \to P : (b_1, \ldots, b_\ell) \in_R \{0, 1\}^\ell$.
3. $P \to V : v \equiv r \prod_{i=1}^\ell s_i^{b_i} \pmod{N}$.
4. Verification: V checks whether

$$u \overset{?}{\equiv} \pm v^2 \prod_{i=1}^\ell w_i^{b_i} \pmod{N}.$$

V stops on failure or continues otherwise.

After t successful iterations, V accepts.

Oscar, who would like to impersonate P, can succeed if he can guess V's
challenge. Denote Oscar's guess by $(g_1, \ldots, g_\ell)$. Oscar generates a random $r \in_R$
$\mathcal{Z}_N^*$ and sends his commitment modified according to the guessed challenge
$(g_1, \ldots, g_\ell)$ as

$$u \equiv r^2 \prod_{i=1}^\ell w_i^{g_i} \pmod{N}.$$

Now V sends his challenge. If the challenge $(b_1, \ldots, b_\ell) = (g_1, \ldots, g_\ell)$, Oscar now
replies by sending simply $v = r$. V now checks whether $u \equiv v^2 \prod_{i=1}^\ell w_i^{b_i} \bmod N$
holds.

Assume that Oscar has made his guess $(g_1, \ldots, g_\ell)$ and sent his commitment
$u \equiv r^2 \prod_{i=1}^\ell w_i^{g_i} \pmod{N}$. In response, V sends his challenge $(b_1, \ldots, b_\ell)$ such
that $b_i = g_i$ for all i except for $i = 1$. It means that Oscar has failed to guess b_1
and g_1 is its negation. Oscar now has to respond by sending rs_1 if $(g_1 = 0$ and
$b_1 = 1)$ or rs_1^{-1} if $(g_1 = 1$ and $b_1 = 0)$. In either case, Oscar has to know s_1. As
s_1 is secret and it is computationally intractable to compute it from w_1, Oscar
will be detected as an impostor. The probability of false acceptance is $2^{-\ell t}$.

Consider an example. TA selects $p = 1367$ and $q = 1103$ ($p \equiv 3 \bmod 4$ and
$q \equiv 3 \bmod 4$). The modulus $N = 1507801$. Let $\ell = 4$ so P selects four random
integers. Let them be:

$s_1 = 1281759$
$s_2 = 63306$
$s_3 = 100742$
$s_4 = 647983$

Next V chooses a binary vector $e = (1, 1, 0, 1)$ and computes:

$$w_1 = (-1)s_1^{-2} \equiv 559476 \bmod 1507801$$
$$w_2 = (-1)s_2^{-2} \equiv 1445404 \bmod 1507801$$
$$w_3 = s_3^{-2} \quad \equiv 663524 \bmod 1507801$$
$$w_2 = (-1)s_2^{-2} \equiv 120740 \bmod 1507801$$

The vector (w_1, w_2, w_3, w_4) is the public identification information of P and is registered with TA. When P wishes to prove herself to V, both parties execute t iterations of the protocol. We are going to show a single iteration only. P starts by choosing at random $r = 736113$ and sends her commitment $u = r^2 \equiv 887797 \bmod 1507801$. V replies with his 4-bit challenge, let it be $(1, 0, 1, 0)$. P responds with $v = rs_1s_3 \equiv 1045302 \bmod 1507801$. Next V verifies whether

$$u \stackrel{?}{\equiv} \pm v^2 w_1 w_3 \bmod N.$$

Clearly $\pm v^2 w_1 w_3 \equiv \pm 620004 \equiv 887797 \pmod{1507801}$. The check holds so V goes to the next iteration.

13.5.3 Guillou-Quisquater Identification Protocol

The Guillou-Quisquater (GQ) identification protocol is a modification of the FS protocol and it is described in [223]. The security of the protocol relies on the assumption that factoring is difficult. An attractive feature of the protocol is that it is identity based so the verifier need not use any certified elements except the publicly accessible identity of the prover and the public key of the trusted authority.

GQ identification protocol

TA Precomputations: TA holds its public modulus N where $N = pq$ and primes p and q are secret. Next TA generates two exponents d and e such that $d \times e \equiv 1 \bmod \varphi(N)$ where $\varphi(N)$ is Euler's totient function. The modulus N and exponent d are public. The factors of N and the exponent e are secret.

Registration: 1. P is assigned a unique identity ID_P. The identity is converted into a unique integer J_P $(1 \leq J_P \leq N - 1)$ that is called the shadowed identity. The conversion is public.

2. TA takes J_P and signs it, using its secret key e. The signature

$$\sigma \equiv J_P^{-e} \pmod{N}$$

is communicated to P. P verifies the signature by checking $\sigma^d \overset{?}{\equiv} J_P^{-1} \bmod N$. The integer σ is kept secret by P and TA.

Message Sequence: P introduces herself to V as an entity with ID_P. V converts her identity to the corresponding numerical shadowed identity J_P. The identification process takes t iterations. A single iteration runs as follows:

1. $P \to V : u \equiv r^d \bmod N$ where $r \in_R \{1, \ldots, N-1\}$.
2. $V \to P : b$ where $b \in_R \{1, \ldots, d\}$.
3. $P \to V : v \equiv r \times \sigma^b \bmod N$.
4. Verification: V checks whether
$$J_P^b \times v^d \overset{?}{\equiv} u \bmod N.$$
   V stops on failure or continues otherwise.

After t successful iterations V accepts.

TA sets up an RSA system with public elements (d, N). TA uses its secret key e to sign J_P. The certificate σ is kept secret by both TA and P as it is further used by P to prove herself to V. The public information accessible to Victor is Peggy's ID_P and her shadowed identity J_P.

A single iteration starts from the random selection of r by Peggy. She next sends her commitment $u = r^d$ to Victor. Victor chooses his challenge b at random and communicates it to Peggy. Peggy responds by sending $v = r \times \sigma^b$. Victor checks whether $J_P^b \times v^d$ is equal to r^d.

Assume that an opponent, Oscar, tries to impersonate Peggy. First, he introduces himself as Peggy with Peggy's ID_P. Next, at random, Oscar selects r and tries to guess Victor's challenge. Let his guess be g. Oscar sends his commitment

$$O \to V : u \equiv r^d \times J_P^g \bmod N.$$

V sends his challenge b. Oscar has to reply

$$O \to V : v \equiv r\sigma^{g-b} \bmod N.$$

Victor checks whether

$$J_P^b \times (r\sigma^{g-b})^d \overset{?}{\equiv} r^d \times J_P^g \bmod N.$$

Victor fails to detect the impostor if Oscar either has guessed g correctly, i.e., $g = b$, or has computed σ. The first case may happen with the probability d^{-1} per iteration. The retrieval of σ is assumed to be computationally intractable. If the identification takes t iterations, the probability of false acceptance is equal to d^{-t}. Note that if P and V follow the protocol the probability of false rejection is zero.

The GQ protocol is designed with efficiency in mind. Keeping the public exponent d short, preferably smaller than 2^{20}, is recommended. The shorter d is the more efficient the computations for both P and V. For $d \approx 2^{20}$, most practical GQ protocols would require one iteration only $(t = 1)$. On the other hand, a too short d will force P and V to do many iterations to attain an agreed probability of false acceptance.

Consider a toy example. Let TA set up its RSA system with $p = 563$, $q = 719$. The modulus is $N = 404797$ and the Euler's totient function $\varphi(N) = 403516$. Let $d = 23$ then $e = 298251$. The modulus N and d are public. Peggy is assigned her identity ID_P and let her shadowed identity be $J_P = 123456$. TA gives P her secret $\sigma \equiv J_P^{-e} \equiv 79833 \bmod 404797$. P verifies it by checking

$$J_P = 123456 \stackrel{?}{\equiv} \sigma^{-d} = 123456 \pmod{404797}.$$

The check holds so P is sure that σ is valid.

If V now asks P to identify herself, she first presents her ID_P to V and later P and V execute t iterations of the protocol. Consider a single iteration only. P selects $r = 133504$ and sends her commitment $u = r^d \equiv 172296 \bmod 404797$. V chooses his challenge $b = 11$ and forwards it to P. As expected, P sends back her response $v = r\sigma^b \equiv 41169 \bmod 404797$. Now V computes

$$J_P^b \times v^d \equiv 172296 \bmod 404797.$$

which equals u. P and V have completed successfully an iteration of the protocol.

Identification protocols may use zero-knowledge proof systems. The Fiat-Shamir protocol is a classic example of the direct application of a zero-knowledge proof system. To reduce the number of interactions between P and V, a common method used in the Feige-Fiat-Shamir and Guillou-Quisquater protocols is to allow the verifier to challenge the prover by sending ℓ-bit challenges (instead of binary). This increases the efficiency of the protocol but causes some problems. The most important is that the zero-knowledge property becomes harder to prove. Recall that the starting point in proving zero knowledge is the design of an efficient transcript simulator that is indistinguishable from the view ensemble generated by the interactions of the real protocol. The simulator runs in an expected polynomial time only if the length of the challenge string is logarithmic. If the challenge string is superlogarithmic the proof system is not known to be zero knowledge. This becomes apparent when an identification protocol consists of a single iteration that involves three passes only ($P \rightarrow V$: commitment (or witness), $V \rightarrow P$: challenge, and $P \rightarrow V$: response). The single challenge used needs to be long enough so the false acceptance rate can be selected arbitrarily low. This clearly precludes the existence of an efficient transcript simulator.

13.6 Identification Schemes

Consider "three-pass" protocols. From now on, we are going to refer to schemes by indicating that they are short versions of identification protocols with arbitrary numbers of passes. Some authors have introduced other measurements to indicate that identification schemes do not "leak" any information about the secrets held by the provers. These measurements include *no useful information transfer* [167] or *no transferable information with security level* [388]. An alternative approach is to prove that breaking an identification scheme is equivalent to finding a polynomial-time algorithm that solves an intractable problem (such as the discrete logarithm).

13.6.1 Schnorr Identification Scheme

Schnorr [452] designed an identification scheme that is intended to be suitable for smart cards where both memory and computing power are in short supply. The security of the scheme relies on the assumption that the selected instance of the discrete logarithm problem is intractable.

Schnorr identification scheme

TA Precomputations: TA sets up the parameters of the protocol, and TA
1. chooses the modulus p such that p is prime,
2. selects a prime q that is a divisor of $(p-1)$,
3. takes an integer $\alpha \in \mathbb{Z}_p^*$ such that it is a generator of a group of order q, i.e., $\alpha^q \equiv 1 \bmod p$,
4. determines the collection of possible challenges $\{0, 1, \ldots, 2^t - 1\}$,
5. applies its secret key to issue certificates while the corresponding public key is used to verify them, and

6. publishes p, q, α, t and its public key.

Registration: The following steps are undertaken by P to get the certificate from TA.

1. P selects at random her private key $s \in_R \mathbb{Z}_q^*$ and computes her public key $K \equiv \alpha^{-s} \bmod p$.

2. P registers her public key K with TA so TA publishes a certificate (signature) S for (ID_P, K).

Message Sequence: P proves to V her identity in three passes.

1. $P \rightarrow V : ID_P, K, S, u$ where S is the certificate generated by TA for (ID_P, K) and $u \equiv \alpha^r \bmod p$ for a random integer $r \in_R \mathbb{Z}_q$.

2. V verifies the certificate S.

3. $V \rightarrow P : b \in_R \{0, \ldots, 2^t - 1\}$.

4. $P \rightarrow V : y \equiv r + sb \bmod q$.

5. Verification:
$$u \stackrel{?}{\equiv} \alpha^y K^b \bmod p.$$
If the check fails V rejects, otherwise V accepts.

TA provides public parameters of the system. The public key of TA is used to verify the prover's certificate S. The protocol in the scheme takes three passes. P picks a random $r \in_R \mathbb{Z}_q$ and computes her commitment $u \equiv \alpha^r \bmod p$ and sends ID_P, K, S, u, S to V. V checks whether (ID_P, K) and the corresponding certificate S match. If so, V chooses his random challenge b and dispatches it to P. P replies by sending $y \equiv r + sb \bmod q$. V finally verifies whether the response $u \stackrel{?}{\equiv} \alpha^y K^b \bmod p$.

Clearly if P follows the protocol, she is always correctly identified by V. On the other hand, an impostor Oscar can cheat if he is able to guess V's challenge. Let his guess be g. Instead of the prescribed $u = \alpha^r$, Oscar sends his commitment

$$u \equiv \alpha^r \times K^g \bmod p.$$

V sends his challenge b and Oscar has to respond with

$$y \equiv r + (b - g)s \bmod q.$$

He will get away with it if $g \equiv b \bmod q$, as he is able to send a valid response $y \equiv r \bmod q$. The probability of Oscar's correct guess of b is 2^{-t}. In other words, the false acceptance rate is 2^{-t}.

Let us illustrate the protocol using small parameters (the protocol is not secure). TA has the following parameters: $p = 285457$, $q = 313$, $\alpha = 146159$. Peggy chooses private key $s = 237$ and computes her public key $K = \alpha^{-s} \equiv 166428 \bmod 285457$. P registers her identity plus her public key with TA. TA publishes its public key and certificate S of Peggy's (ID_P, K).

Assume that V wishes P to identify herself to him. P selects at random r, let it be $r = 133$, computes her commitment $u = r^2 \equiv 36157 \bmod 285457$, and forwards ID_P, K, S, u to V. V verifies whether the pair (ID_P, K) and the certificate match (this step is skipped). If the check holds, V sends his challenge b, say $b = 167$, to P. P finds $y \equiv r + sb \bmod q$, which is $y = 274$ and sends it to V. V calculates

$$\alpha^y K^b = 146159^{274} 166428^{167} \equiv 36157 \bmod 285457,$$

which is equal to Peggy's commitment u. V accepts Peggy.

The Schnorr scheme is indeed very efficient. The prover (a smart card) needs a single exponentiation modulo p to generate her commitment. The response y involves single multiplication and addition modulo q. The scheme is provably secure against passive attacks under the DL assumption.

13.6.2 Okamoto Identification Scheme

A modification of the Schnorr scheme that is as secure as the corresponding discrete logarithm instance was given by Okamoto in [388]. The scheme is provably secure against active attackers. The scheme works as follows.

Okamoto identification scheme

TA Precomputations: TA sets up the parameters of the scheme. In particular, TA

1. chooses a modulus p where p is prime,
2. takes a factor q of $(p - 1)$ (q is prime),
3. picks up two integers α_1 and α_2 of order q in the group $\mathbb{Z}_p^*$,
4. selects an integer $t = O(p)$, say $t \geq 20$,
5. uses its secret key to issue certificates while its public key is used to verify them, and
6. publishes $p, q, \alpha_1, \alpha_2, t$ and its public key.

Registration: The following steps are undertaken by P to get the certificate from TA.

    1. P selects at random her private key $(s_1, s_2) \in_R \mathcal{Z}_q \times \mathcal{Z}_q$ and computes her public key $K \equiv \alpha_1^{-s_1} \alpha_2^{-s_2} \bmod p$.

    2. P registers her public key K with TA so TA publishes a certificate (signature) S for (ID_P, K).

Message Sequence: P proves to V her identity.

    1. $P \rightarrow V : ID_P, K, S, u$ where S is the certificate generated by TA for (ID_P, K) and $u \equiv \alpha_1^{r_1} \alpha_2^{r_2} \bmod p$ for random integers $r_1, r_2 \in_R \mathcal{Z}_q$.

    2. V verifies the certificate S.

    3. $V \rightarrow P : e \in_R \{0, \ldots, 2^t - 1\}$.

    4. $P \rightarrow V : y_1, y_2$, where

$$y_1 \equiv r_1 + es_1 \pmod{q},$$
$$y_2 \equiv r_2 + es_2 \pmod{q}.$$

    5. Verification: Victor checks whether

$$u \stackrel{?}{\equiv} \alpha_1^{y_1} \alpha_2^{y_2} K^e \bmod p.$$

    If the check holds V accepts, and otherwise rejects.

Let us illustrate the scheme on a simple example. The scheme has the following parameters: $p = 6491$, $q = 59$, $\alpha_1 = 1764$, $\alpha_2 = 4269$, $t = 5$. P chooses her two secret elements $s_1 = 21$, $s_2 = 47$. The public key

$$K = \alpha_1^{-s_1} \alpha_2^{-s_2} = 1764^{-21} 4269^{-47} \equiv 5196 \pmod{6491}.$$

P selects at random $r_1 = 13$, $r_2 = 33$, computes her commitment

$$u = \alpha_1^{r_1} \alpha_2^{r_2} = 1764^{13} 4269^{33} \equiv 1131 \pmod{6491},$$

and sends it to V. V replies with his challenge $e = 12$. P solves the congruences:

$$y_1 = r_1 + es_1 \equiv 29 \pmod{59},$$
$$y_2 = r_2 + es_2 \equiv 7 \pmod{59}.$$

On arrival of y_1 and y_2, V computes

$$\alpha_1^{y_1} \alpha_2^{y_2} K^e = 1764^{29} 4269^7 5196^{12} \equiv 1131 \pmod{6491}$$

which is the same as the commitment. V accepts.

13.6.3 Signatures from Identification Schemes

Identification schemes can be converted into signature schemes [181]. To convert an identification scheme, it is enough to replace the verifier by a hash function. The hash function takes two arguments, a message to be signed and a commitment, and produces a digest (challenge) that is later signed. Consider the Schnorr identification scheme [452]. The signature scheme based on it is presented below.

___

Schnorr signature scheme

Initialization: The TA sets up the scheme and
1. chooses the parameters as in the Schnorr identification scheme so the modulus p is prime $(p \geq 2^{512})$, a prime q is a divisor of $(p-1)$ $(q \geq 2^{140})$, and an integer $\alpha \in \mathcal{Z}_p^*$ is a generator of a group of order q,
2. picks up a hash function $h : \mathcal{Z}_p \times \mathcal{Z} \to \{0, 1, \ldots, 2^t - 1\}$,
3. applies its secret key to issue certificates while the corresponding public key is used to verify them, and
4. publishes p, q, α, h and its public key.

The following steps are undertaken by the signer S to get the certificate from TA:
1. S selects at random her private key $s \in_R \mathcal{Z}_q^*$ and computes her public key $K \equiv \alpha^{-s} \bmod p$.
2. S registers her public key K with TA so TA publishes a certificate (signature) for (ID_S, K).

Signing: To sign a message m, S selects a random integer $r \in_R \mathcal{Z}_q$, computes $u \equiv \alpha^r \bmod p$, and calculates the digest $b = h(u, m)$ for the message $m \in \mathcal{Z}$. The signature is the pair $SG_s(m) = (b, y)$, where

$$y \equiv r + sb \bmod q.$$

Verification: The verifier V takes the message $\tilde{m}$, and its signature $(\tilde{b}, \tilde{y})$, and collects the authentic public key K from TA (together with the necessary public elements). V next reconstructs

$$\tilde{u} \equiv \alpha^{\tilde{y}} K^{\tilde{b}} \bmod p$$

and checks whether

$$\tilde{b} \overset{?}{\equiv} h(\tilde{u}, \tilde{m}).$$

If the check holds V accepts the signature, and otherwise rejects.

Pointcheval and Stern proved [410] that if an existential forgery of the Schnorr scheme is possible then DL in subgroups can be solved. This statement is true in the random oracle model.

Similarly, the Okamoto identification scheme can be converted for signing [388].

Okamoto signature scheme

Initialization: TA sets up the scheme. In particular, TA:
1. chooses the parameters as in the Okamoto identification scheme; in particular, the modulus p is prime $(p \geq 2^{512})$, a prime q divides $(p-1)$ $(q \geq 2^{140})$, and α_1 and α_2 are two integers of order q in the group $\mathbb{Z}_p^*$;
2. selects a hash function $h : \mathbb{Z}_p \times \mathbb{Z} \to \{0, 1, \dots, 2^t - 1\}$;
3. uses its secret key to issue certificates while its public key is used to verify them; and
4. publishes $p, q, \alpha_1, \alpha_2, h$ and its public key.

The following steps are undertaken by the signer S to get the certificate from TA.
1. S selects at random her private key $(s_1, s_2) \in_R \mathbb{Z}_q^* \times \mathbb{Z}_q^*$ and computes her public key $K \equiv \alpha_1^{-s_1} \alpha_2^{-s_2} \bmod p$.
2. S registers her public key K with TA so TA publishes a certificate (signature) for (ID_P, K).

Signing: To sign a message $m \in \mathbb{Z}$, S picks up two random integers $r_1, r_2 \in_R \mathbb{Z}_q^*$, computes $u \equiv \alpha_1^{r_1} \alpha_2^{r_2} \bmod p$, finds out

$$e = h(u, m)$$

and solves two congruences

$$y_1 \equiv r_1 + e s_1 \pmod{q},$$
$$y_2 \equiv r_2 + e s_2 \pmod{q}.$$

The signature for message m is (e, y_1, y_2).

Verification: Victor is given a message $\tilde{m}$ and a signature $(\tilde{e}, \tilde{y}_1, \tilde{y}_2)$. V collects public elements from TA, calculates

$$\tilde{u} \equiv \alpha_1^{\tilde{y}_1} \alpha_2^{\tilde{y}_2} K^{\tilde{e}} \pmod{p},$$

and checks whether

$$\tilde{e} \stackrel{?}{\equiv} h(\tilde{u}, \tilde{m}).$$

If the check holds V accepts the signature, and otherwise rejects.

Okamoto proved that the above scheme is secure against any adaptive chosen message attacks if the discrete logarithm problem is intractable and h is a correlation-free one-way hash function. The existence of correlation-free hash functions is a stronger requirement than the existence of collision-free hash functions (for details consult [388]).

13.7 Problems and Exercises

1. Consider the following identification protocol. Peggy gives her name to Victor. Victor tosses an unbiased coin. If the coin comes up heads, Victor accepts Peggy, otherwise he rejects. Compute the false rejection/acceptance rates. Is the protocol practical?

2. Victor has bought two personal identification machines. One machine uses fingerprints for identification and is characterized by the false rejection and acceptance rates P_{fa1} and P_{fr1}, respectively. The second machine uses face images to identify a person. Its false rejection and acceptance rates are P_{fa2} and P_{fr2}, respectively. Victor is not sure how to combine the machines, but he thinks about the two following schemes:

   (a) In the first scheme, a person is accepted only if the person is accepted by both identification machines.

   (b) In the second scheme, a person is accepted if at least one machine has accepted the person.

   Compute the false rejection/acceptance rates for both schemes (make reasonable probabilistic assumptions if necessary).

3. Assume an identification scheme based on PINs in length 4 digit. What is the probability of guessing the PIN if the attacker is allowed to enter three consecutive guesses?

4. Suppose that passwords are 10 characters in length. Characters are chosen randomly from a given set of elements. Consider that the set of possible elements consists of

   (a) all lower case letters (i.e., $a, b, c, \ldots, z$),

   (b) all letters (i.e., both lower and upper case letters),

   (c) all alphanumerical characters (i.e., all letters plus all digits),

   (d) all characters accessible on a typical keyboard (i.e., the set has 96 lower/upper case letters, digits, and special characters).

What is the probability of guessing a password in a single attempt for each of the cases mentioned above? What is the time necessary to exhaustively search the whole password space for the above cases if it is possible to check 1000 passwords per second.

5. Let passwords be 7 characters in length. The password space contains 26^7 possible elements. Assume that an attacker can access a hashed password file and can run a program that tests 1000 passwords per second. What would be the lifetime of a password selected at random from the password space provided the owner changes the password if the probability of the attacker breaking it becomes equal to 10^{-3} (the attacker continuously runs his program starting from the last change of password).

6. Modify the challenge-response protocol for a shared (secret) key in such a way that it allows the use of timestamps by both interacting parties.

7. Assume that two parties A and B have collected their corresponding public keys from their TA. Design the challenge-response protocol that allows mutual authentication of both A and B. Consider two possible cases: when the public keys are used for encryption and when the public keys are used for authentication.

8. Show that the Fiat-Shamir protocol is sound and complete. Write a transcript simulator for the protocol and evaluate its efficiency.

9. A prover P and a verifier V apply the Fiat-Shamir protocol for identification. They have been using it for some time. An attacker Oscar has collected a transcript of their interactions and discovered that Victor does not select his challenges with uniform probability. In fact Victor's selection of the challenge is described by two probabilities $P(b = 0) = \varepsilon$ and $P(b = 1) = 1 - \varepsilon$ where $\varepsilon < 0.5$. Oscar wants to impersonate Peggy and knows that he will be successful if he guesses Victor's challenge. To guess the challenge, Oscar may apply the two following strategies:

   (a) He chooses his guess according to the same probability distribution as Victor.

   (b) He chooses his guess to be always 1.

   What are the probabilities of Oscar's successful impersonation for the two strategies? Which of the strategies is better? What would be the best possible strategy for Oscar?

10. An attacker Oscar has collected a transcript of Peggy and Victor interactions in the Fiat-Shamir identification protocol. Looking through the transcript, Oscar has discovered that there are two entries (u_1, b_1, v_1) and (u_2, b_2, v_2) for which $u_1 = u_2$ and $b_1 \neq b_2$. What is the probability of the event? Can Oscar use the discovery to break the protocol?

11. Consider the Feige-Fiat-Shamir protocol. Prove that it is sound and complete. Design a transcript simulator for the protocol. Discuss its efficiency and show how it depends on the size of the parameter ℓ (ℓ is the length of the challenge).

12. Given the Feige-Fiat-Shamir protocol, an attacker Oscar has noticed that the verifier V chooses his first challenge according to the protocol (randomly and uniformly from the set $\{0, 1\}^{\ell}$). But the other $t - 1$ challenges are "recycled" from the previous ones. A recycled challenge in the ith iteration is created as follows. Let a challenge in the $(i - 1)$th iteration be $b_{i-1} = (a_1, \ldots, a_{\ell})$, then a recycled challenge is $b_i = (a_2, \ldots, a_{\ell}, a_{\ell+1})$ where the bit $a_{\ell+1}$ is randomly chosen with a uniform probability. What is the probability of false acceptance in the protocol with the recycled challenges.

13. Convert both the FFS and GQ identification protocols into corresponding signature schemes. Discuss their security.

14. Modify the Schnorr identification scheme for the case when the arithmetic is performed in $GF(2^{521})$, and $q = 2^{521} - 1$ is a Mersenne prime. Discuss its efficiency.

15. Consider the Schnorr identification scheme. Let the set of challenges be binary, i.e., $b \in_R \{0, 1\}$. Show that the resulting protocol is sound and complete. Design a transcript simulator for it and discuss its efficiency.

16. In the Okamoto scheme, Peggy selected s_1 at random and assigned $s_2 = s_1$. Discuss the repercussions of her choice of parameters on the scheme. Is the scheme still secure if an attacker knows that $s_1 = s_2$?

17. Consider the Okamoto scheme again. Assume that the trusted authority TA displayed the public parameters with two generators $\alpha_1 = \alpha_2$. Is the scheme secure? Justify your answer.

14 Intrusion Detection

14.1 Introduction

Distributed systems emerged as a consequence of rapid progress in both computing and communication technology. A distributed system combines all computing resources into one "super" computer in which the underlying network provides the necessary communication facilities. The main advantage and, ironically, the major problem of distributed systems is its openness. The openness of the system permits sharing of all resources among users independently of their locations. At the same time, a distributed system is much more vulnerable to a potential attacker due to a distributed nature of the system. The communication network is typically too large to even attempt to protect it via some physical means. Widely used cryptographic methods may either detect illegal activity or render the transmitted data nonintelligent to an attacker. Some channels due to their characteristics may be subject to some specific attacks. For example, all broadcasting channels used for mobile and satellite communication are inherently vulnerable to eavesdropping. An attacker may be aware of some weaknesses in the security guards and choose them to compromise a part of or the whole system. In general, the designers of the security guards try to prevent any illegal user accessing the system. Numerous examples have shown that even the best protection mechanisms may fail because there is a flaw in the design, or more often because the mechanism was not designed to withstand some "exotic," yet, practical attacks. So if the security guards fail, should we succumb and do nothing?

The absolutely last line of defence is an intrusion detection system (IDS). The system assumes that an attacker has outsmarted the security guards and gained an (unauthorized) access. It tries to identify attackers by scanning the behavior of active users. This is possible if an intrusion exhibits distinctive characteristics, those typical of a nonintrusive activity. A nonintrusive activity is characterized by user behavior profiles. A crucial component of any IDS is a database in which these profiles are stored. Auditing that primarily provides information about how and by whom different computing resources are being used can also be used to establish user behavior profiles. Profiles should be continually updated to reflect the current behavior of users. The IDS is in fact an identification system and as such can be characterized by probabilities of false acceptance and false rejection. False acceptance means that the IDS allows intruders to continue their activity, while false rejection typically means that the IDS stops the activity of a legitimate user.

Attackers are classified into three broad categories:

1. *clandestine* – attackers who avoid the IDS or auditing system,
2. *masqueraders* – attackers who impersonate legitimate users,
3. *misfeasors* – legitimate users who abuse their privileges.

Note that misfeasors are just authorized users who are trying to circumvent the access control mechanism. Masqueraders are intruders who somehow manage to convince the identification mechanism that they are legitimate users. A typical example of a masquerader is an attacker who has guessed somebody's password. Clandestine attackers are ones who are usually trying to immmobilize the IDS (and consequently the audit system) so they can act with no trace of their activity in the audit trail.

The IDS works on the assumption that it is possible to identify abnormal user behavior. A behavior observed by the IDS can be abnormal for a user although it may not be harmful and may be typical for somebody else. An abnormal behavior indicates that the user may be a masquerader. In contrast, the IDS may detect a user behavior that violates the rules of the game (the security policy). In this case, the IDS does not need to use the behavior profile to detect the intrusion – the decision is made on the basis of the definition of misuse of computer resources. So there are two possible intrusion detection strategies:

– *anomaly detection* when the observed behavior deviates from the expected one for the user,
– *misuse detection* when the observed behavior indicates an intention to abuse the computer resources.

Anomaly intrusion detection requires the IDS to keep information about typical behavior profiles for each legitimate user. For instance, if a user always accesses his computer from his office during working hours from 8 a.m. to 6 p.m, and sometimes remotely via modem from 7 p.m. to 10 p.m, then an abnormal behavior would be an access to the computer from his office at midnight. On the other hand, misuse intrusion detection demands that the IDS store information about attacks on the security of the system known so far. Note that a user will be marked as an intruder as soon as the IDS comes to the conclusion that he tried to compromise the security using one of the known attack scenarios. Note that the IDS cannot detect intrusions if the applied attack scenarios are not recorded in its database. Normally, managers of the computer systems should update their attack scenario databases as soon as a new attack becomes known.

14.2 Anomaly Intrusion Detection

An IDS based on anomaly intrusion detection is in fact an identification system that uses some measurable characteristics of user activities. A user activity can be characterized by its

1. Intensity – this is reflected by the sheer volume of audit records produced for a user per time unit. A better granulation can be achieved if the intensity is measured in the context of a particular type of activity.
2. Mix of different types of activity – this includes not only the collection of different types of activity but also other more specific information as to the order in which the particular activities take place and the context in which a particular sequence of activities occurs.

The intensity measure is very much related to the type of activity and may be described by many specific parameters. In general, it is possible to use two major intensity characteristics: the number of times a given activity occurs per time unit, or the average amount of time consumed by a single activity. Typical intensity measures for a user are the amount of CPU time, the number of active processes, the number of I/O operations, the number of opened files, etc.

User identity can be characterized by types of activity (for instance, sending e-mails, calling an editor, compiling a program, creating a window, etc.), the order of activities (for example, after login, a user normally first reads e-mails, sends e-mails, saves e-mail copies, uses the Web browser and prints out some Web pages), and the context in which the specific order of activities takes place (i.e., differentiation of a user activity profile depending on whether the user accesses the system from his workstation or from a remote terminal).

14.2.1 Statistical IDS

Implementation of an IDS starts by choosing an appropriate collection of user activity measures. The selection depends on many factors, such as the required probabilities of false acceptance and false rejection, the required memory to store user profiles, the efficiency of the IDS, etc. Assume that the measures chosen are $m_1, \ldots, m_n$. Each user therefore is assigned the collection of random variables $M_1, \ldots, M_n$. Each random variable can be stored in the form of its probability distribution (an expensive option) or in a compressed form that includes the name of the probability distribution together with parameters describing it. The *profile* of a given user consists of the sequence of random variables $(M_1, \ldots, M_n)$ evaluated from the audit trail and stored by the IDS usually in a compressed form. The security policy determines which of the chosen measures are more important and which are less significant. To express the current security policy, the manager provides the IDS with a sequence of weights $(w_1, \ldots, w_n)$ that needs to be used together with the corresponding measures to determine the IDS decision about intrusion.

IDS based on statistical measures

Setup: Manager selects a collection of measures $(m_1, \ldots, m_n)$ and a vector of weights $(w_1, \ldots, w_n)$. For each user, IDS computes and stores the user profile described by $(M_1, \ldots, M_n)$ from the audit trail.

Processing: For a given time interval, the IDS takes the corresponding audit trail and computes the actual profile of the user defined by $(\tilde{M}_1, \ldots, \tilde{M}_n)$. The IDS uses distance functions $d_i = d_i(M_i, \tilde{M}_i)$ to determine the extent of abnormal behavior with respect to the measure m_i. The distance functions need to be treated as functions that operate on pairs of probability distributions and return integers that makes sense of the distance.

Decision: If

$$\sum_{i=1}^{n} w_i d_i \leq d_t$$

then the behavior in the time interval is considered to be normal, otherwise the behavior is abnormal (an intrusion is detected). The integer d_t is the threshold value that determines the boundary between normal and abnormal user behavior.

Action: If an intrusion is detected, the user activities are suspended or/and
the manager is immediately notified. Otherwise, the profile of the user is
updated.

While designing a statistical IDS, the following questions need to be considered:

- how to select a collection of measures $(m_1, \ldots, m_n)$,
- how to define distances $d_i = d_i(M_i, \tilde{M}_i)$,
- how to determine the threshold d_t.

The measure selection also called feature choice is crucial to the quality of
the intrusion detection. Typically, the designer identifies first a collection of all
measures accessible in the system. Let the collection be $(m_1, \ldots, m_\ell)$, then the
designer tries different (if ℓ is small, the designer may try all) combinations of
features that are most sensitive (a good user discrimination) and stable (features
do not change over time).

Once a collection of good features has been selected, the designer has to
define the corresponding collection of distances between two probability distributions (for normal and abnormal behavior). This works well if the accepted
measures are statistically independent. In most cases this assumption does not
hold. A typical solution is to combine related features into one anomaly measure
using covariance matrices [310]. The value of the threshold d_t is selected experimentally as it directly influences the two false rejection and false acceptance
probabilities. It is also a matter of security policy.

Statistical intrusion detection assumes that each user can be assigned a
unique profile that can be effectively compared with the current approximation
of the profile. In general, a user is modeled by a stochastic process that is
stationary or whose parameters do not vary dramatically, so the update of the
profile can cope with the changes of behavior (the process is quasistationary).
More precise models include nonstationary stochastic processes or generalized
Markov chains. Building such models is too expensive to be practical.

14.2.2 Predictive Patterns

Predictive pattern anomaly detection is based on the assumption that it is
possible to identify normal and abnormal user behavior from ordered sequences

of events generated by users. So a profile of a user is a collection of "typical" sequences. The probabilistic nature of patterns of events generated by users can be reflected by assigning conditional probabilities to transitions to other events provided a given typical sequence has occurred. For instance, a typical pattern can be an ordered sequence of events

$$\langle e_1, e_2, e_3 \rangle$$

with $P(e_4 \mid \langle e_1, e_2, e_3 \rangle) = 0.1$ and $P(e_4' \mid \langle e_1, e_2, e_3 \rangle) = 0.9$. This reads: if a user generates the sequence $\langle e_1, e_2, e_3 \rangle$ then only two events e_4 and e_4' may follow it with the probabilities 0.1 and 0.9, respectively. A typical sequence $\langle e_1, \ldots, e_n \rangle$ together with associated conditional probabilities $P(e_{n+1}^{(i)} \mid \langle e_1, \ldots, e_n \rangle)$ for some i is called a *rule*. Note that the rule can be used only if a user applies the correct event prefix $\langle e_1, \ldots, e_n \rangle$.

IDS based on predictive patterns

Setup: For each user, the IDS computes and stores the user profile described by a collection of rules $\{R_1, \ldots, R_n\}$ computed from the audit trail.

Processing: For a given time interval, the IDS takes the corresponding audit trail and computes conditional probabilities associated with the rules stored in the user profile. The IDS uses distance functions d_i $(i = 1, \ldots, n)$ to determine the extent of abnormal behavior with respect to the rule R_i. The distance functions need be treated as functions that operate on the pairs of conditional probability distributions and return integers that makes sense of the distance.

Decision: For weights chosen by the manager, w_i, if

$$\sum_{i=1}^{n} w_i d_i \leq d_t$$

then the behavior in the time interval is considered to be normal, otherwise the behavior is abnormal (an intrusion is detected). The integer d_t is the threshold value that determines the boundary between normal and abnormal user behavior.

Action: If an intrusion is detected, the user activities are suspended or/and the manager is immediately notified. Otherwise, the profile of the user is updated.

A major problem with this approach is that the rules can be only used if they are triggered by their event prefix. If none or a few of the event prefixes were generated by a user, it is impossible to make any reasonable decision, and the IDS simply fails.

Advantages of this approach include the ability of the system to be adapted for misuse detection. A nice property of the system is that it works very well for users whose behavior exhibits a strong sequential pattern [504].

14.2.3 Neural Networks

Neural networks sometimes offer a simple and efficient solution in situations when other approaches fail. To use a neural network for intrusion detection, it is enough first to train the neural net on a sequence of events generated by a user and later to use the net as a predictor of the next event.

IDS based on neural networks

Setup: For each user, the IDS maintains a neural net. The neural net is being trained on a sequence of events generated by the user.

Processing: The IDS repeatedly considers sequences of n events generated by the user. Each sequence is fed to the neural net. The network predicts the next event $\tilde{e}$ and compares it with the event e issued by the user.

Decision: If

$$\tilde{e} = e$$

then the behavior of the user is considered to be normal, otherwise the behavior is abnormal (an intrusion is detected).

Action: If an intrusion is detected, the user activities are suspended or/and the manager is immediately notified.

The selection of the parameter n is an important issue. If n is too small, the network will not be able to predict the next event (many false alarms). On the other hand, if n is too large, then there is no relation between the events at the beginning and at the end of sequence. Evidently, the IDS will fail if a user selects the next event nondeterministically. To fix this, the neural net needs to exit a number of typical events.

14.3 Misuse Intrusion Detection

Note that anomaly intrusion detection always compares the current activity with the expected one defined for a user and can be seen as a user identification. Misuse intrusion detection does not care whether users can be properly identified as long as they do not try to abuse the computer resources. From the IDS point of view, there are only two classes of users: friends and foes. To define the class of foes, it is necessary to determine precisely the meaning of intrusion. This is done by providing a list of intrusion scenarios or attacks (also called *intrusion signatures*). An intrusion signature defines the

– order of events (typically commands),
– resources involved (files, processes, CPU, memory, etc.), and
– conditions on resources and events,

which compromise the security of the system. Intrusion signatures can be categorized into the following classes:

1. Simple signatures – the existence of a single event in the audit trail or/and the existence of a trace of an intrusion attempt is enough to detect intrusion.
2. Event-based signatures – the existence of an ordered sequence of events is enough to conclude that the user is an intruder.
3. Structured signatures – the signature can be written as a regular expression.
4. Unstructured signatures – all signatures that do not fall into one of the above classes.

Having a collection of intrusion signatures, the IDS may apply a variety of different methods to detect that a user has attempted to attack the system using some intrusion scenario recorded in the system as the corresponding intrusion signature. Some typical approaches involve the application of

– expert systems, and
– finite state machines.

An expert system implementation of the IDS encodes the collection of intrusion signatures into `if-then` rules. A rule not only reflects a single intrusion signature (`if` part) but also specifies what action needs to be undertaken when an intrusion is detected (`then` part). The IDS takes an audit trail and investigates it to check whether or not some of the rules are active (or an attack is under way).

In the finite state machine approach, it is required that signatures be translated into corresponding state transitions of the underlying machine. The states of the machine are divided into three classes: save (no intrusion detected), suspicious (advanced in one of the signatures), or intrusion (an intrusion detected and the corresponding signature is active).

14.4 Uncertainty in Intrusion Detection

The most important issue related to an effective intrusion detection is the adoption of an appropriate mathematical model that allows us to generate user profiles efficiently and facilitates an effective and accurate decision-making process for intrusion detection. Due to the nondeterministic nature of user behavior, the decision about intrusive or nonintrusive behavior must take into account all evidence for and against the claim. There are several mathematical models to choose from, two most popular are: the probabilistic model and the Dempster-Shafer model [133, 463]. In the probabilistic model, the decision about intrusion is based on the probabilistic assessment of the body of evidence. The Dempster-Shafer theory of evidence can be seen as a generalization of the probability theory.

14.4.1 Probabilistic Model

Given an event space Ω over random events $e_1, \ldots, e_n$ such that $P(e_1 \cup \ldots \cup e_n) = 1$ or $\bigcup_{i=1}^{n} e_i = \Omega$, the Bayes theorem asserts that for any random event $B \in \Omega$ $(P(B) > 0)$

$$P(e_i \mid B) = \frac{P(e_i, B)}{P(B)} = \frac{P(B \mid e_i)P(e_i)}{\sum_{e_j \in \Omega} P(B \mid e_j)P(e_j)}. \tag{14.1}$$

$P(e_i \mid B)$ is called an posteriori probability, and $P(e_j)$ are the a priori probabilities. From an intrusion detection point of view, the space Ω defines a collection of events that occur with different probabilities for normal and intrusive behavior. Define a hypothesis I "there is an intrusion." The complement $\bar{I}$ reads "there is NO intrusion." Clearly, $P(I \cup \bar{I}) = 1$. From (14.1), we can obtain

$$P(I \mid e) = \frac{P(I, e)}{P(e)} = \frac{P(e \mid I)P(I)}{P(e \mid I)P(I) + P(e \mid \bar{I})P(\bar{I})}. \tag{14.2}$$

To characterize the evolution of the validity of hypothesis I we introduce four parameters: a priori and a posteriori odds, and positive and negative likelihoods. The a priori odds for I are the following ratio:

$$O(I) = \frac{P(I)}{P(\bar{I})}.$$

The a posteriori odds are defined as:

$$O(I \mid e) = \frac{P(I \mid e)}{P(\bar{I} \mid e)}.$$

An odds ratio $O(I)$ is a positive rational. For a hypothesis I such that $P(I) = P(\bar{I}) = 0.5$, the a priori odds $O(I) = 1$. If the value $O(I) > 1$, then $P(I) > P(\bar{I})$. If the value $O(I) < 1$, then $P(I) < P(\bar{I})$. A posteriori odds provide a quantitative measurement of the validity of hypothesis I after the observation of a random event e.

The positive likelihood is the ratio

$$S(e \mid I) = \frac{P(e \mid I)}{P(e \mid \bar{I})},$$

and similarly the negative likelihood is the ratio

$$N(e \mid I) = \frac{P(\bar{e} \mid I)}{P(\bar{e} \mid \bar{I})}.$$

The positive likelihood characterizes the event e in terms of its relation to intrusion. If $S(e \mid I) > 1$ then the event e confirms the hypothesis I, otherwise the event is consistent with the antihypothesis $\bar{I}$. If $S(e \mid I) \approx 1$, the event is neutral.

Consider some properties of the parameters.

Theorem 47. *Given an event space Ω and an event $e \in \Omega$. Then*

$$O(I \mid e) = S(e \mid I)O(I), \tag{14.3}$$

where I is the hypothesis that there is an intrusion.

Proof. According to the definitions, we have the following sequence of equations:

$$\begin{aligned}
S(e \mid I)O(I) &= \frac{P(e \mid I)}{P(e \mid \bar{I})}\frac{P(I)}{P(\bar{I})} \\
&= \frac{P(e, I)}{P(e, \bar{I})} = \frac{P(I \mid e)P(e)}{P(\bar{I} \mid e)P(e)} \\
&= \frac{P(I \mid e)}{P(\bar{I} \mid e)} = O(I \mid e),
\end{aligned}$$

which proves the theorem. □

Theorem 48. *Assume that there is a collection of events* $e_1, \ldots, e_n$ *such that* $P(e_1, \ldots, e_n \mid I) = \prod_{i=1}^{n} P(e_i \mid I)$ *and* $P(e_1, \ldots, e_n \mid \bar{I}) = \prod_{i=1}^{n} P(e_i \mid \bar{I})$, *then*

$$O(I \mid e_1, \ldots, e_n) = O(I) \prod_{i=1}^{n} S(e_i \mid I). \tag{14.4}$$

Proof. Consider the following sequence of transformations:

$$
\begin{aligned}
O(I \mid e_1, \ldots, e_n) &= \frac{P(I \mid e_1, \ldots, e_n)}{P(\bar{I} \mid e_1, \ldots, e_n)} = \frac{P(I, e_1, \ldots, e_n)}{P(\bar{I}, e_1, \ldots, e_n)} \\
&= \frac{P(e_1, \ldots, e_n \mid I) P(I)}{P(e_1, \ldots, e_n \mid \bar{I}) P(\bar{I})} = \prod_{i=1}^{n} \frac{P(e_i \mid I)}{P(e_i \mid \bar{I})} O(I) \\
&= O(I) \prod_{i=1}^{n} S(e_i \mid I),
\end{aligned}
$$

which proves (14.4). If one observes that

$$\frac{P(e_i \mid I)}{P(e_i \mid \bar{I})} = \frac{P(I \mid e_i)}{P(\bar{I} \mid e_i)} \frac{P(\bar{I})}{P(I)} = \frac{O(I \mid e_i)}{O(I)},$$

then (14.4) can be rewritten as

$$O(I \mid e_1, \ldots, e_n) = \frac{1}{O(I)^{(n-1)}} \prod_{i=1}^{n} O(I \mid e_i)$$

□

Consider an example. Let the space $\Omega = \{e_0, e_1\} = \{0, 1\}$. Time is tied up defining a sequence of random variables $E_1, E_2, \ldots$ for the corresponding time instances. We assume that users generate events for every time instance i so $P(E_i = e)$ is the probability that the user generated event $e \in \Omega$ at time i. We also assume that $P(I) = P(\bar{I}) = 1/2$ and $P(E_1 = 0 \mid I) = P(E_1 = 1 \mid I) = 1/2$, $P(E_1 = 0 \mid \bar{I}) = P(E_1 = 1 \mid \bar{I}) = 1/2$.

Normal behavior is characterized by the following conditional probabilities:

$$P_{\bar{I}}(E_{i+1} = 0 \mid E_i = 0) = 1/4,$$
$$P_{\bar{I}}(E_{i+1} = 1 \mid E_i = 0) = 3/4,$$
$$P_{\bar{I}}(E_{i+1} = 1 \mid E_i = 1) = 3/4,$$
$$P_{\bar{I}}(E_{i+1} = 0 \mid E_i = 1) = 1/4$$

for $i = 1, 2, \ldots$. Intrusive behavior differs from the normal one and is characterized by the following conditional probabilities:

$$P_I(E_{i+1} = 0 \mid E_i = 0) = 1/4 + \varepsilon,$$
$$P_I(E_{i+1} = 1 \mid E_i = 0) = 3/4 - \varepsilon,$$
$$P_I(E_{i+1} = 1 \mid E_i = 1) = 3/4 - \varepsilon,$$
$$P_I(E_{i+1} = 0 \mid E_i = 1) = 1/4 + \varepsilon,$$

for $i = 1, 2, \ldots$.

The initial odds $O(I) = \frac{P(I)}{P(\bar{I})} = 1$ can be computed from the assumed probability distribution for I. Similarly $O(I \mid E_1 = 0) = O(I \mid E_1 = 1) = 1$. In fact, the probability $P(I)$ can be selected arbitrarily and the IDS uses the initial odds as a benchmark for further evaluation of the validity of the hypothesis I. Compute the following probabilities:

$$P(E_2 = 0 \mid I) = P(E_1 = 0 \mid I)P_I(E_2 = 0 \mid E_1 = 0)$$
$$+ P(E_1 = 1 \mid I)P_I(E_2 = 0 \mid E_1 = 1) = \frac{1}{4},$$

$$P(E_2 = 1 \mid I) = 1 - P(E_2 = 0 \mid I) = \frac{3}{4}$$

$$P(E_2 = 0 \mid \bar{I}) = P(E_1 = 0 \mid \bar{I})P_{\bar{I}}(E_2 = 0 \mid E_1 = 0)$$
$$+ P(E_1 = 1 \mid \bar{I})P_{\bar{I}}(E_2 = 0 \mid E_1 = 1)$$
$$= \frac{1}{2}(\frac{1}{4} + \varepsilon) + \frac{1}{2}(\frac{1}{4} + \varepsilon) = \frac{1}{4} + \varepsilon,$$

$$P(E_2 = 1 \mid \bar{I}) = 1 - P(E_2 = 0 \mid \bar{I}) = \frac{3}{4} - \varepsilon,$$

$$P(E_2 = 0) = P(E_2 = 0 \mid I)P(I) + P(E_2 = 0 \mid \bar{I})P(\bar{I}) = \frac{1 + 2\varepsilon}{4},$$

$$P(E_2 = 1) = 1 - P(E_2 = 0) = \frac{3 - 2\varepsilon}{4},$$

$$P(I \mid E_2 = 0) = \frac{P(E_2 = 0 \mid I)P(I)}{P(E_2 = 0)} = \frac{1}{2 + 4\varepsilon},$$

$$P(\bar{I} \mid E_2 = 0) = 1 - P(I \mid E_2 = 0) = \frac{1 + 4\varepsilon}{2 + 4\varepsilon},$$

$$P(I \mid E_2 = 1) = \frac{P(E_2 = 1 \mid I)P(I)}{P(E_2 = 1)} = \frac{3}{6 - 4\varepsilon},$$

$$P(\bar{I} \mid E_2 = 1) = 1 - P(I \mid E_2 = 0) = \frac{3 - 4\varepsilon}{6 - 4\varepsilon}.$$

The a posteriori odds are

$$O(I \mid E_2 = 0) = \frac{1}{1 + 4\varepsilon} \quad \text{and} \quad O(I \mid E_2 = 1) = \frac{3}{3 - 4\varepsilon}.$$

So if $\varepsilon > 0$, the event $E_2 = 0$ confirms the antihypothesis $\bar{I}$ and the event $E_2 = 1$ is consistent with the hypothesis I. Knowing a sequence of observations $(E_2, E_3, \ldots, E_n)$, we can compute the corresponding odds to see whether or not they confirm or contradict the hypothesis I.

14.4.2 Dempster-Shafer Theory

The theory is a generalization of the probability theory. Dempster [133] laid the foundations and Shafer [463] later generalized it so it can be used for evaluation of uncertainty. The theory is especially applicable for intrusion detection using expert systems [308].

Let $\Omega = \{e_1, \ldots, e_n\}$ be a set of elements. All elements e_i are disjoint for $i = 1, \ldots, n$. Given a function

$$m : 2^\Omega \rightarrow [0,1]$$

such that $m(\emptyset) = 0$ and $\sum_{\omega \subseteq \Omega} m(\omega) = 1$, the function m is called the *basic probability assignment* or *mass distribution*. From an IDS point of view, the collection Ω can be seen as the set of all elementary events (also called the hypotheses). The observations $\omega \in 2^\Omega$ accessible to the IDS are predominantly complex events involving more than one elementary event. The IDS wants to evaluate the validity of some hypotheses (elementary events).

The *belief* function $Bel : 2^\Omega \rightarrow [0,1]$ is defined as

$$Bel(\omega) = \sum_{\alpha \subseteq \omega} m(\alpha) \tag{14.5}$$

for $\omega \subseteq \Omega$. The belief function measures the probability that a given subset $\omega \in 2^\Omega$ occurs as a separate event or as the superset. The belief function $Bel(\omega) = 0$ if and only if $m(\alpha) = 0$ for all $\alpha \subseteq \omega$. In other words, the event ω never happens.

The *plausibility* function $Pl : 2^\Omega \rightarrow [0,1]$ is defined as

$$Pl(\omega) = \sum_{\omega \cap \alpha \neq \emptyset} m(\alpha) \tag{14.6}$$

for $\omega \in 2^\Omega$. The plausibility function $Pl(\omega)$ indicates the probability of all events α that relate to ω ($\omega \cap \alpha \neq \emptyset$). It is easy to observe that $Pl(\omega) \geq Bel(\omega)$ as each $\alpha \subseteq \omega$ implies that $\alpha \cap \omega \neq \emptyset$. The belief function $Bel(\omega)$ defines the lower bound on the confidence in ω while the plausibility function determines the upper bound.

Let $\Omega = \{a, b, c\}$. Then a possible mass distribution can be expressed by the function m such that

$$m(\{a, b, c\}) = \tfrac{4}{16};$$
$$m(\{a, b\}) = \tfrac{4}{16}; \quad m(\{a, c\}) = \tfrac{2}{16}; \, m(\{b, c\}) = \tfrac{1}{16};$$
$$m(\{a\}) = \tfrac{2}{16}; \quad m(\{b\}) = \tfrac{1}{16}; \quad m(\{c\}) = \tfrac{2}{16}; \quad m(\emptyset) = 0.$$

The belief and plausibility function for $\{a, b\}$ are:

$$Bel(\{a, b\}) = m(\{a\}) + m(\{b\}) + m(\{a, b\}) = \frac{7}{16},$$
$$Pl(\{a, b\}) = m(\{a\}) + m(\{b\}) + m(\{a, b\}) + m(\{a, c\})$$
$$+ m(\{b, c\}) + m(\{a, b, c\}) = \frac{14}{16}.$$

Consider two $Bel(\omega)$ and $Pl(\omega)$. If we define the complement of ω as $\bar{\omega} = \Omega \setminus \omega$, then it is easy to show that

$$Pl(\omega) = 1 - Bel(\bar{\omega}).$$

In other words, $Bel(\bar{\omega}) = 1 - Pl(\omega)$ measures the amount of evidence against the hypothesis (event) ω while $Bel(\omega)$ evaluates the evidence in favour of ω. There are the following possible cases:

1. $Pl(\omega) - Bel(\omega) = 1$. This means that $Pl(\omega) = 1$ and $Bel(\omega) = 0$ or, in other words, all events for which ω is a superset never happen and for the other events, ω is a proper subset. So every single observation contains ω as the constant. It is impossible to say anything about ω itself. There is no evidence against and none for ω.
2. $Pl(\omega) = 0$ (this implies that $Bel(\omega) = 0$). Any event that intersects ω never happens. The hypothesis (event) is false.
3. $Bel(\omega) = 1$ (this implies that $Pl(\omega) = 1$). Any event must be a subset of ω. The hypothesis (event) is true.
4. $Pl(\omega) = \varepsilon_1$ and $Bel(\omega) = \varepsilon_2$ ($\varepsilon_1 > \varepsilon_2$ and $\varepsilon_1, \varepsilon_2 \in [0, 1]$). There is evidence in favor of ω ($Bel(\omega) = \varepsilon_2$) and there is evidence against ω ($Bel(\bar{\omega}) = 1 - \varepsilon_1$).

Observe that in the probability theory always $P(\bar{\omega}) = 1 - P(\omega)$. In the Dempster-Shafer theory this can be translated into the requirement that $Pl(\omega) = Bel(\omega)$.

The centerpiece of the theory is the Dempster rule of combination. Let Ω be the set of elementary events and m_1, m_2 be two basic probability assignments.

Then the combined probability assignment is a function $m_1 \oplus m_2 : 2^\Omega \to [0, 1]$ such that

$$m_1 \oplus m_2(\omega) = \frac{\sum_{\alpha \cap \beta = \omega} m_1(\alpha) m_2(\beta)}{\sum_{\alpha \cap \beta \neq \emptyset} m_1(\alpha) m_2(\beta)}$$

for all $\omega \neq \emptyset$. Briefly, the rule allows us to construct a combined probability assignment from two pieces of evidence (two basic probability assignments).

The more "relaxed" setting that allows us to measure, somewhat independently, evidence against and for a hypothesis provides a convenient tool for IDS systems based on expert systems. For more information on the Dempster-Shafer theory and its applicability to reasoning in the presence of uncertainty, the reader is referred to [308].

14.5 Generic Intrusion Detection Model

One of the earliest proposals for using audit trails and system logs for intrusion detection was presented in [137] in the form of an intrusion detection model. Although dated, the model is still valuable since it accurately describes the architecture of many current IDSs (Fig. 14.1).

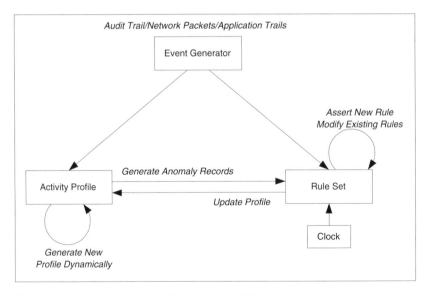

Fig. 14.1. Generic intrusion detection model

The Event Generator in the model is purposely generic, and the events may include audit records, network packets, or other observable activities. The Activity Profile represents the global state of the intrusion detection system, and it contains variables that are used to calculate the behavior of the system based on some predefined statistical measures. The variables are associated with certain pattern specifications, which come into play when filtering the event records. During filtering, any matching records will then provide data to update the values stored in these variables. Furthermore, each variable is associated with one of the statistical measures built into the system, and is therefore responsible for updating the system state based on the information obtained from the matching record.

Using a history of common activities conducted by a typical user, the Activity Profile can develop pattern templates that are then applied to newly created subjects (e.g., users) and objects (e.g., files). When new users of new files are introduced into the system, these templates can be used to instantiate new profiles for them. The Rule Set represents a generic inferencing mechanism, such as a rule-based system. It uses event records, anomaly records, and other data to control the activity of the other components of the IDS and to update their state.

Although the above model of [137] is generic, it does provide the basic framework for the components of an intrusion detection system. Most IDSs follow the basic concept of formulating a statistical metric for identifying intrusions, computing their values, and recognizing the anomalies in the resulting values. IDSs differ typically in three aspects, namely:

– on how the rules making up the Rule Set are determined,
– on whether the Rule Set is fixed a priori or if it can adapt itself depending on the type of intrusion, and
– on the nature of the interaction between the Rule Set and the Activity Profile.

The notion that the Activity Profile module detects anomalies and that the Rule Set performs misuse detection will remain the same in most IDSs. Different techniques may be employed in each of the modules without changing the conceptual view of the model.

Audit trails and system logs represent the main source of input data for IDSs. A wide of range of audit data and log types can be obtained, many of which are dependent on the particular host or network that generated them. Such data can be used in a number of ways [78] in order to:

- review the access patterns to individual objects,
- provide access histories of specific users and specific processes,
- initiate the use of protection mechanisms offered by the system,
- discover repeated attempts by users and outsiders to bypass the protection mechanisms,
- reveal the exercise of privileges when a user takes on a functionality or role with privileges higher than the usual user privileges,
- deter penetrators from repeatedly trying (successfully or otherwise) to bypass the system protection mechanisms, or
- provide assurance to honest users that attempts to bypass the protection mechanisms are being recorded and discovered, and thus are being addressed by system administration.

For the development of trusted systems [145] auditable events are monitored in order to gather auditable data. Events that are typically monitored include (but are not limited to):

- the start and end of user identification and user authentication mechanisms,
- the introduction (deletion) of objects into (from) the user address space,
- actions by system administrators (including operators and security administrators),
- invocation and use of external services (e.g., printer servers and printer devices), and
- all security-related events (depending on the definition of these events in a given environment).

The information collected about events is wide-ranging, but at the very least should include the date and time of the event, the type of event, the identifier of the subject (user/process triggering the event), the success/failure indication, the name/identity of the objects (introduced or deleted), and the description of the actions taken by the system administrator. In the case of specific security-related events, the origin of the request for user identification/authentication must also be noted.

14.6 Host Intrusion Detection Systems

Most host IDSs follow the basic model described in Sect. 14.5. In the following, we briefly review some of the major efforts in host-based intrusion detection. The motivation of this review is to gain an overall understanding of the basic elements that are common in most, if not all, major intrusion detection systems.

14.6.1 IDES

The Intrusion Detection Expert System (IDES) was one of the earliest projects on intrusion detection. Developed in 1985 at SRI International, IDES employs user profiles and an expert system to decide on intrusion events. The general goal of IDES is to provide a system-independent mechanism for the real-time detection of intrusions, hence its focus on providing an expert system that detects anomalous behaviors based on complex statistical methods.

IDES is designed to run continuously, and is based on two beliefs [310]:

1. Intrusions, whether successful or attempted, can be detected by flagging departures from historically established norms of behavior for individual users.
2. Known intrusion scenarios, know-system vulnerabilities, and other violations of a system-intended security policy (that is, an a priori definition of what is to be considered suspicious) are best detected through the use of an expert system rule base.

These two basic assumptions have prevailed in the subsequent prototypes of IDES.

The components of IDES are shown in Fig. 14.2. The Receiver module parses the received audit records and validates them, and the results are deposited in the collection of Audit Data. The two main subsystems of IDES consist of the components related to the anomaly detection and those within the expert system. In the statistical anomaly detector, the audit data is first used by the Active Data Collector that produces Active Data, which consists of information about all user activities, group activities, and remote host activities since the last time the profiles were updated. This data is then used by the Anomaly Detector that compares the data against the existing Profile Data [259]. If an anomaly is found, an anomaly record is created and deposited in the Anomaly

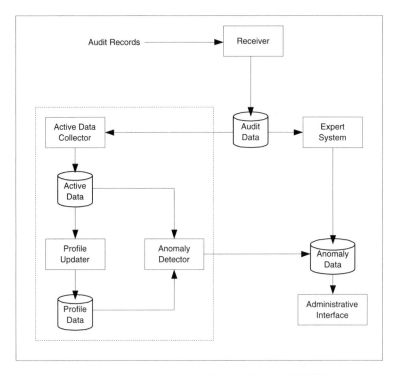

Fig. 14.2. The Intrusion Detection Expert System (IDES)

Data database, which is accessible through the Security Administrator Interface. Daily updates on the profiles are conducted by the Profile Updater. In the meantime, the Expert System works in parallel with the Active Data Collector, receiving the Audit Data as input. The Expert System checks for actions that can be considered intrusions, based on the user's profile. The initial versions of the Expert System suffered from the limitation of working only on known attack methods and vulnerabilities, so subsequent versions of IDES have extended its functions to a networked environment, where several interconnected hosts send the audit information to a central site that performs the intrusion analysis.

IDES was developed by SRI over a number of years. An initial prototype system was developed for Sun/2 and Sun/3 systems to monitor a DEC 2065 that was running SRI's modified version of TOPS-20. The Intrusion Detection Model [137] framework is the basis for the initial IDES prototype system [309]. This early prototype system was modified over many years to incorporate new and more sophisticated detection techniques and interfaces, and it allows for scalability. Furthermore, it was later migrated from an Oracle relational database system using (Pro*C, C, and SQL on IBM/DEC/Sun systems with SunView graphical interface environment) to a C-based Sun Unix environment using an object-oriented X graphical interface library.

14.6.2 Haystack

Haystack is an intrusion detection system developed by the Los Alamos National Laboratories (LANL), with the initial design and system prototyping carried out by Tracor Applied Sciences and Haystack Laboratories. Haystack was not designed to work in a realtime environment, but rather as an offline batch system. Its aim was to aid the US Air Force computer system security officers (SSO) in analyzing data by reducing the voluminous audit data on the Air Force's Unisys 1100/60 mainframes. Initially Haystack existed as two components, one part running on the Unisys mainframe and the other on the Zenith Z-248 PC [480]. The model followed by Haystack was that of [137].

The goals of Haystack were:

- to enable a computer security policy to be enforced by improving the ability to detect and respond to security policy violations,
- to develop a software solution that conforms to POSIX and ANSI standards,
- to enable the SSO to monitor large volumes of raw audit data by summarizing and reporting events deemed suspicious.

The components of Haystack are shown in Fig. 14.3. Here the audit data on the Unisys mainframe is given as the input to a Preprocessor that extracts the relevant details. The result is written to a Canonical Audit Trail (CAT) file and the file is written to a 9-track tape. At a later time the PC will then read the file from the tape, logging any obvious anomalies. A new session history record is created for any users appearing in the file. This history is also used to update a database that contains the user's past behavior. Haystack looks for misuses in the following ways:

Pattern-based analysis. This is used to select important events that occur in the user's session. The audit records are selected based on the following behaviors:

1. Modify Events – these include all successful and unsuccessful events that modify system security.
2. Tagged Events – these are system subjects and objects that have been marked by the security officer as needing more detailed logging and analysis.

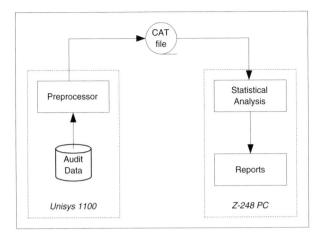

Fig. 14.3. Haystack components

Statistics-based analysis. The statistical analysis is based on two computations (the Cumulative Weighted Multinomial method and the Wilcoxon-Mann-Whitney Rank Test). The first is computed by comparing a user's session with the expected ranges of behavior, resulting in a "suspicion quotient." Any user whose quotient is outside the acceptable range is reported to the security officer. The second is computed by comparing the user's session behavior with previous sessions, with the aim of detecting users who are slowly trying to adapt their profiles over time, effectively modifying a normal behavior pattern to one that is unauthorized.

Although Haystack has provided considerable aid to the security officers in analyzing the audit data, one of its shortcomings is precisely its lack of real time capabilities. This opens a gap in time between the data collection and auditing, which may allow an intruder to break into the system.

14.6.3 MIDAS

MIDAS or Multics Intrusion Detection and Alerting System is an expert system that provides intrusion and misuse detection in real-time. It was designed by the National Computer Security Center (NCSC) for their networked mainframe (called Dockmaster), which is a Honeywell DPS 8/70. The expert system itself has several components, some of which are actually running on a separate Symbolics List machine [462]. Figure 14.4 shows the components of MIDAS.

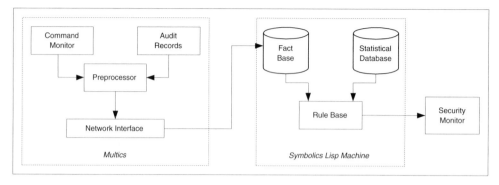

Fig. 14.4. MIDAS components

When the Multics system generates an audit record, the Preprocessor filters the data which are not needed by MIDAS. It then formats the remaining data into an assertion for the FactBase, which is sent to the FactBase through the Network Interface that links the two computer systems. The Statistical Database contains statistics for users and the system, and defines the normal state for Dockmaster. The new assertion that is introduced into the FactBase may result in a binding between the new fact and an existing rule in the RuleBase, and may even cause the firing of several other rules. Thus, the new assertion may change the state of the system and cause a system response to a suspected intruder. Clearly, the performance of MIDAS as a whole is largely dependent on the rules in the RuleBase.

Three different types of rule exist, namely, immediate attack heuristics, user anomaly heuristics, and system state heuristics. The immediate attack rules only superficially examine a small number of data items without applying any statistical analysis. The aim is to find auditable events that are abnormal enough to raise suspicions. The user anomaly rules employ statistical analysis to detect deviations in a user's profile as compared to previous histories. The system state rules are similar to the user anomaly rules, except these are applied to the system itself.

14.7 Network Intrusion Detection Systems

NetworkIDSs are intrusion detection systems that work on the basis of monitoring traffic within a network segment. In contrast to hostIDSs that monitor and detect intrusions within a host, networkIDSs observe raw network traffic and detect intrusions from that traffic information. Unlike hostIDSs that are, in effect, insulated from the low-level network events, networkIDSs can correlate attacks occurring against multiple machines within the monitored network segment. Typically, networkIDSs passively monitor the network, copying packets as they pass by, regardless of the packet's destination.

One major advantage of networkIDSs that carry out passive protocol analysis is that the action of monitoring occurs at the lowest levels of a network's operation, thereby they are both unobtrusive and difficult to evade. In fact, unless an external attacker uses other means to find out the existence of a networkIDS, typically the attacker will be unaware of the networkIDS.

14.7.1 NSM

The Network Security Monitor (NSM) was developed at the University of California, Davis, and performs traffic analysis on a broadcast LAN in order to detect unusual behavior and traffic patterns, and thereby detect possible intrusions (Fig. 14.5). In contrast to host-based intrusion detection systems running on a host and consuming its resources, NSM runs independently of the host being monitored in the LAN. These monitored hosts are in fact unaware of the passive monitoring behavior of NSM. Hence, intruders will also be unaware of the traffic monitoring that is occurring.

NSM is based on the Interconnected Computing Environment Model (ICEM) [360], which consists of six layers arranged in a hierarchical fashion. These layers (bottom to top) are, with one layer providing input for the next layer above it:

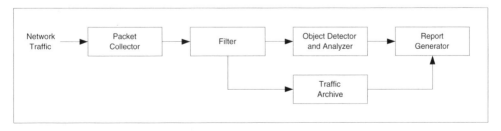

Fig. 14.5. The Network Security Monitor

- *Packet layer* – accepts bitstream input from the broadcast LAN, divides input into complete packets and attaches a timestamp to each packet.
- *Thread layer* – accepts time-augmented packets and correlates them into unidirectional data streams. Each stream represents data transferred from one host to another using a particular protocol (e.g., TCP/IP or UDP/IP) through a given port. The stream or thread is then mapped to a thread vector.
- *Connection layer* – attempts to pair one thread with another to represent a bidirectional stream or host-to-host connection. The pairs are then represented by a connection vector consisting of combinations of thread vectors. After the connection vectors are analyzed, their reduced representation is passed up to the next layer.
- *Host layer* – builds a host vector from the reduced connection vector, representing the network activities of a host.
- *Connected-network layer* – creates a graph from the host vectors representing the various connections between hosts in the network. Subgraphs (or connected network vectors) can be generated and compared against historical connected subgraphs. Here, the user can begin to query the system about the resulting graph (e.g., existence of the path between two hosts through intermediate hosts).
- *System layer* – creates a single system vector from the collection of connected network vectors, representing the entire network.

The host vectors and connected network vectors are used as the first type of input to an expert system within NSM. The components of these vectors that are of interest to the expert system are the host ID, host address, security state (an evaluation value of a given host), number of data paths to a host, and the data path tuples. A tuple has four elements representing a data path to/from a host (other-host address, service ID, initiator tag, and security state).

The second type of input is the expected traffic profile, which is the expected data paths (or connections) between hosts and a corresponding service profile (that is, the expected behavior about things such as telnet, mail, keyboard activity, etc.). The next type of input is a representation of the knowledge of the system regarding the capabilities of the services (for example, a telnet service has more capabilities than ftp). The fourth input is the level of authentication needed for each service. The fifth is the level of security for each of the machines in the host (based, for example, on the ratings by the National Computer Security Center (NCSC)). The last input to the expert system is the signatures of past attacks to hosts.

NSM employs the notion of the security state that represents the "suspicion level" associated with a particular network connection. When deciding on the security state for a connection, four factors are taken into consideration:

1. *Abnormality of a connection* – refers to the probability of the connection occurring (i.e., often or rare) and the behavior (i.e., traffic volume). This is established by comparing against the profile for that connection. Thus, for example, if a connection is rare and traffic is unusually high in one direction, then the abnormality of the connection is high.
2. *Security level used for the connection* – based on the capabilities of the service and the authentication typically required for that service. For example, TFTP (high capability, no authentication) is given a high security level. Telnet (high capability, requires authentication) has a lower security level than TFTP.
3. *Direction of connection sensitivity level* – based on the sensitivity level of the connected hosts and which host initiated the connection. For example, if a low-level host attempts to connect to a high-level host, then the direction of connection sensitivity is high.
4. *Matched signatures of previous attacks.*

NSM has been used with interesting results. During a two-month period at UC Davis, NSM analyzed over 110,000 connections. Within these, NSM correctly detected 300 intrusions, whereas only 1% of the intrusions were detected independently by the system administrators.

14.7.2 DIDS

The Distributed Intrusion Detection System (DIDS) [482, 483] is a project representing an extension of the NSM, with the aim of adding two features missing from NSM. These are the ability to monitor the behavior of a user who is connected directly to the network using a dial-up line (and who therefore may not generate observable network traffic), and the ability to allow intrusion detection over encrypted data traffic. The DIDS project is sponsored by UC Davis, the Lawrence Livermore National Labs (LLNL), Haystack Laboratory, and the US Air Force.

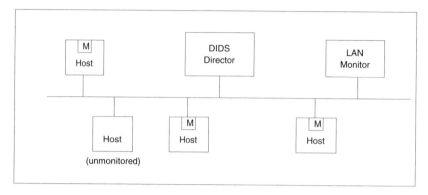

Fig. 14.6. The Distributed Intrusion Detection System (DIDS)

The architecture of DIDS consists of three components (Fig. 14.6), namely Host Monitors, the LAN Monitor, and the DIDS Director. Each host in the monitored domain runs the Host Monitor, scanning their individual audit trails for suspicious events and other events relevant to the network (e.g., rlogin and rsh attempts). The data from these Host Monitors augment the data received from the LAN Monitor, which are then reported to the DIDS Director. The LAN Monitor is used for each broadcast LAN segment. The DIDS Director contains an expert system that analyzes all incoming data related to the monitored domain.

DIDS allows the tracking of users who move around within the domain. It does so by introducing a network-user identification (NID) for all users within the network. This tracking, however, can only be done when users move across monitored hosts. The issue of movements to unmonitored hosts was not addressed by DIDS.

The Host Monitor has two main components, namely, the host event generator and the host agent. The host event generator collects audit records from the host operating system, and scans them for notable or unusual events. These are forwarded to the Director. The host agent is responsible for all communications between the Host Monitor and the Director. The LAN Monitor also has a LAN event generator (currently a subset of NSM) and a LAN agent. The LAN monitor observes all traffic on a given LAN segment, noting network-related events, such as host connections, traffic volumes, and services invoked over the network. The DIDS Director has three components on a single dedicated workstation, namely, an expert system, a communications manager, and a user interface for the security officer. The communications manager handles all communications with the Host Monitors and the LAN Monitor. The Director may in fact request more data from these monitors through the communications manager.

14.7.3 NADIR

The Network Anomaly Detector and Intrusion Reporter (NADIR) [244] is a system for network intrusion detection developed and tailored for the Integrated Computing Network (ICN) at the Los Alamos National Laboratory (LANL). NADIR employs an expert system that analyzes audit data as a supplementary method to the manual audit done by the security officer. From the network audit records, it generates weekly summaries of the activities of the network and of individual users.

NADIR is tailored for the compartmentalized or "multilevel" arrangement of security classifications in the ICN network. Following the Bell La Padula model [21], a computer system may only access computer systems within the same compartment or partition, and those at a lower-classified compartment (the "read-down" rule of the model). The compartments are linked by a collection of dedicated service nodes that carry out many security-related tasks (e.g., access control, file access, file storage, file movements).

Each user account is associated with a value called the level of interest, which indicates the current level of suspicion regarding that account being compromised by an intruder. The weekly summary is generated from data that includes the user's activities. The parameters reported include the host compartment or partition, the host ICN machine number, the destination partition, the destination host classification level, and others. NADIR has a graphical interface, which highlights the suspicious activities and users, bringing them to the security officer's attention.

14.7.4 Cooperating Security Manager (CSM)

Another effort towards developing network intrusion detection is the Cooperating Security Manager (CSM) system developed at the Texas A&M University [526]. One of the primary goals of the CSM project was to move away from the centralized intrusion detection system (as in DIDS). Instead, each host would run the CSM and together the hosts would set up a mesh of the intrusion detection system that shares information in a cooperative manner. Hence, intrusion detection can be achieved in a distributed manner.

The distributed nature of the intrusion detection makes the effort scalable (as compared to the centralized approach). For the distributed intrusion detection to work, however, each of the hosts in the networked environment must be running CSM. When a user at a host in the network connects to another host (both running CSM) the CSMs at both hosts cooperate in monitoring the user's behavior. Hence, if an attacker decides to use one host as a platform for further attacks in a hop-by-hop fashion, the CSMs on the linked hosts work together to detect the intruder.

The basic components of the CSM are shown in Fig. 14.7. The Command Monitor captures the user's input and passes it to the Local IDS that has the task of detection intrusion for that host. Network-related activities are reported to the Security Manager that communicates with other CSMs at other hosts. In effect, the Security Managers coordinate the distributed interaction among the CSMs. When a host communicates to another host, all the user actions at the first host are considered to be occurring in parallel at the second host. Thus, intrusion detection processes occur on both hosts. If a user is connected over several hosts in a chain and one of the CSMs in that chain determines that an intrusion activity is occurring, that CSM will notify all other CSMs along the chain. The Administrative Interface is used by the security officer to query the CSM about the security status of the current host, and to further query

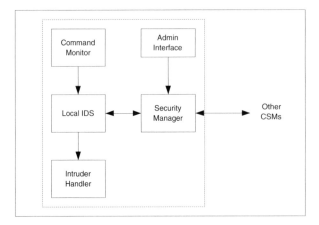

Fig. 14.7. Cooperating Security Manager (CSM)

a (suspect) user's origin and trails. A level of suspicion can be requested for a given user.

Again, for the concept to succeed all the hosts within the network must run the CSM. It is unclear how the concept of the CSM can be implemented in the near future if not all hosts run the CSM and if the origin (or destination) of a connection to or from a CSM-based host does not itself run the CSM. That is, the issue of the interaction at the boundary of a CSM-based network and a non-CSM network remains to be solved.

14.8 Limitations of Current Intrusion Detection Systems

Although a number of research prototypes and commercial IDSs have been developed, in general there are some aspects of IDSs that need to be addressed.

14.8.1 General Limitations

- *Lack of generic development methodology* – The current costs for developing IDSs are substantial, due to the lack of a structured methodology to develop such systems. Although there is a growing body of knowledge about IDSs, not many structuring insights have emerged (at least within the public literature). This may be due to the fact that the field of IDSs is still relatively young, that it is an area that borders on several fields (e.g., artificial intelligence, operating systems, networking), and that there is a lack of agreement on the suitable techniques for intrusion detection.
- *Efficiency* – Some IDSs have attempted to detect every conceivable intrusion, which in many circumstances is impractical. In reality, expensive computations, such as that for anomaly detection, need not be done for every event. Some systems employ an expert system shell that encodes and matches cases or attack signatures. Unfortunately, these shells typically interpret their rule set, and thus present a substantial runtime overhead.
- *Portability* – Many IDSs are developed for a particular target environment, often in an ad hoc and custom-design fashion. This is largely because many of the systems are dependent on OS-specific functions and therefore tailor their detection to that OS. Reuse of an IDS for a different environment is difficult to perform, unless the system was designed in a generic manner (in which case it would probably be inefficient and have limited capabilities).

– *Upgradability* – Retrofitting an existing IDS with newer and improved detection techniques requires a considerable effort in reimplementation. This aspect is related to the lack of a development methodology for IDSs.

– *Maintainability* – Maintaining an IDS typically requires skills in fields other than security. Often modifying or upgrading the rule set requires specialized knowledge about expert systems, the rule language, and some familiarity with how the system manipulates the rules. Such expertise is necessary in order to prevent the added rules from creating undesirable interactions with the rules already present. Similarly, modification of the statistical metrics within the statistical component of the IDS requires equal expertise. This aspect, unfortunately, is difficult to address due to the inherent complexity of AI-based systems.

– *Benchmarking* – Hardly any data on IDS benchmarks exist in the literature, and very little data on the performance of IDSs for a realistic set of vulnerability data and operating environments have been published. Similarly, little coverage data exists about any system. Such coverage data would report the percentage of intrusions detected by an IDS in a real environment. This aspect is difficult to solve due to the inherent difficulty in accurately verifying the types of frequencies of intrusions in large environments. Related to this issue is the difficulty of testing IDSs using a developed set of attack scenarios.

14.8.2 Network-IDS Shortcomings

One major drawback of network-IDSs is their lack of ability in knowing (or determining) the events within a computer system that result from that system receiving a message or packet. That is, although a network-IDS observes (and copies) a packet destined to a particular computer system, there is no direct way for the network-IDS to discover whether the packet was accepted (or rejected), and if accepted, what reaction it caused in the recipient computer system.

When an attacker (internal or external) is aware that an IDS is monitoring his or her activities, the IDS itself can instead become the main target of attack. In the case of a network-IDS, an intelligent attacker will realize that, although he or she may not be able to directly attack the network-IDS to disable it, he or she may still have the ability to cheat or mislead the detection system within the network-IDS. Assuming that an internal attacker has a valid account on the machines in the network (e.g., a malicious valid user or external attacker who has created an undiscovered account), the attacker can send dummy traffic to himself/herself through a valid session. In this manner, the detection system may gradually modify its rule set (if it is dynamic), effectively being cheated by the internal attacker.

There are two main shortcomings of network-IDS [417, 398]:

– *Lack of information* – Typically a network-IDS is a machine separate from those that it monitors. Through passive monitoring, the network-IDS aims to predict the behavior of the networked machines using protocol analysis and its rule set. Although the network-IDS obtains a copy of every packet sent to a machine, it does so in a slightly different timeframe and it is never sure about how that packet was treated by the machine. Hence, a discrepancy can occur between the detection system and the machines it monitors. As an example, consider an IP packet with a bad UDP checksum. Although most machines will reject this packet, some may ignore the bad checksum and accept the packet. The network-IDS must be able to know whether each machine will accept/reject the packet.

– *Denial of service* – Denial-of-service attacks are aimed at reducing the level of availability of a computer system, and if possible to disable the system (i.e., system crash). When discussing the failure of a security system, the issue of the mode (fail-open or fail-closed) of the system after it fails becomes important. In fail-open, the disabled system ceases to provide any protection, while in fail-closed the disabled system leaves the environment still protected. Clearly, a good network-IDS must be fail-closed. As an analogy, consider the firewall. A fail-open firewall that crashes will leave the network available, and thus will leave it open to attacks. From a security perspective, a good firewall must be fail-closed, closing the entire network when it crashes.

There are a variety of possible attacks that can result in the detection system of a network-IDS becoming misled. When an attacker can exploit the use of dummy packets, which the valid destination rejects (but which the network-IDS thinks it accepted), the attacker can effectively insert data into the network-IDS. This problem is due to the network-IDS being less strict than the destination system in its packet processing. To solve this problem, the network-IDS can be tuned to be maximally strict. This approach, however, may lead to the opposite situation where a packet accepted by the destination system is rejected by the network-IDS, leading to an evasion attack.

14.9 The Common Intrusion Detection Framework (CIDF)

The Common Intrusion Detection Framework (CIDF) is a recent standardization effort, which began in early 1997 among all the DARPA-funded intrusion detection projects. The idea of a common framework arose when DARPA decided to make all the intrusion detection systems that it was funding interoperate, and therefore make the benefits arising from these projects more useful and accessible to the wider community.

Although initially confined within these DARPA projects, in April 1998 the work of the CIDF community was put forward to the IETF (LA meeting) with the aim of creating an IETF working group on CIDF. As mentioned in the CIDF specification document, the goal of the CIDF specification is twofold [221]:

1. The specification should allow different IDSs to interoperate and share information as fully as possible.
2. The specification should allow components of IDSs to be easily reused in a contexts different from those they were designed for.

All CIDF components deal in GIDOs (Generalized Intrusion Detection Objects) that are represented via a standard common format. GIDOs are data that is moved around in the intrusion detection system. GIDOs can represent events that occurred in the system, analysis of those events, prescriptions to be carried out, or queries about events.

The CIDF specification covers a number of issues related to the creation of a framework:

- A set of architectural conventions for how different parts of IDSs can be modeled as CIDF components.
- A way to represent GIDOs, where they can
  - describe events that occurred in the system,
  - instruct an IDS to carry out some action,
  - query an IDS as to what has occurred, or
  - describe an IDS component.
- A way to encode GIDOs into streams of bytes suitable for transmission over a network or storage in a file.
- Protocols for CIDF components to find each other over a network and exchange GIDOs.
- Application Programming Interfaces to reuse CIDF components.

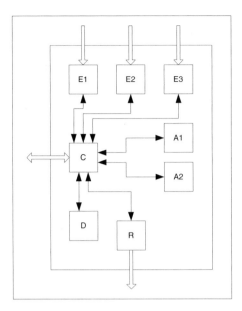

Fig. 14.8. CIDF architecture

The CIDF architecture consists of four main types of components: Event Generators, Analyzers, Databases, and Response units (Fig. 14.8). Correspondingly, the CIDF specification talks in terms of *E-boxes*, *A-boxes*, *D-boxes*, and *R-boxes*. Event countermeasures are also introduced in the form of *C boxes*.

The E-box has the task of supplying information about events to the rest of the system. Events act as the sensory organs within an IDS, and an *event* itself has a wide range of meanings, from high-level complex events to low-level network protocol events. Their role is to obtain events from the larger computational environment outside the IDS and provide them in the CIDF standard GIDO format to the rest of the system. For example, event generators might be simple filters that take C2 audit trails and convert them into the standard format, or another event generator may passively monitor a network and generate events based on the traffic on the network.

Input from the event generators is then analyzed by the A-box, using the analysis method defined in the A-box of the given IDS. These analysis methods can be based on statistical-anomaly detection, graph-based methods, or others. A-boxes obtain GIDOs from other components, analyze them, and return new GIDOs.

The outputs from the A-boxes and E-boxes are stored in the D-box component, which acts as the storage mechanism so that the data may be available at a later time. D-boxes exist to give persistence to CIDF GIDOs, where that is necessary. The interfaces allow other components to pass GIDOs to the database, and to query the database for GIDOs that it is holding. Databases are not expected to change or process the GIDOs in any way. Responses are produced by the R-boxes, which carry out prescriptions, namely, GIDOs that instruct them to act on behalf of other CIDF components. This is where the functionality, such as killing processes, resetting connections, etc., would reside. Response units are not expected to produce output except for acknowledgements [221].

14.10 Partial List of ID Systems

The following is a list of IDS prototypes and commercial systems. The list is not meant to be comprehensive, and the reader is directed to the COAST web pages at Purdue University (*http://www.cs.purdue.edu/coast*) for more information.

Name	Source/Organization	Attributes	References
ADS (Attack Detection System)	University College Dublin, Ireland		[266, 267]
AID (Adaptive Intrusion Detection system)	Brandenburg University of Technology at Cottbus, Germany	Multi-host-based misuse detection	[485] *http://www-rnks.informatik.tu-cottbus.de/~sobirey/aid.e.html*
ALVA (Audit Log Viewer and Analyser tool)	General Electric	Host-based, limited anomaly detection	[349]
APA (Automated Penetration Analysis tool)	University of Maryland at College Park		[225]
ASAX (Advanced Security audit trail Analysis on uniX)	University of Namur, Belgium, and Siemens-Nixdorf Software, S.A.	Multi-host-based, misuse detection	[81, 226, 354, 355, 356, 357] *http://www.info.foundp.ac.be /~amo/publications.html*
Autonomous Agents for Intrusion Detection	COAST Laboratory Purdue University	Multi-host-based, anomaly detection	[116, 117] *http://www.cs.purdue.edu /coast/projects/autonomous-agents.html*
CMDS (Computer Misuse Detection System)	Science Applications International Corporation	Multi-host-based, anomaly and misuse detection. Commercial	[416] *http://www.saic.com /it/cmds/index.html*
Computer Watch	AT&T Bell Laboratories	Host-based, limited misuse detection. Commercial	[160] *http://www.att.com*
CyberCop	Network General Corporation	Network-based, misuse detection. Commercial	*http://www.ngc.com /product_info/cybercop*
Discovery	TRW Information Services	Host-based, anomaly detection	[503]
EMERALD (Event Monitoring Enabling Response to Anomalous Live Disturbances)	SRI International	Network-based, anomaly and misuse detection	[412] *http://www.csl.sri.com /emerald/index.html*
ESSENSE	Digital Equipment Corporation		[512]
GASSATA (Genetic Algorithm for Simplified Security Audit Trail Analysis)	SUPELEC, Cesson Sevigne, France		[332, 333] *http://www.supelec-rennes.fr /rennes/si/equipe/lme /these/these-lm.html*

Name	Source/Organization	Attributes	References
GrIDS (Graph-based Intrusion Detection System)	University of California at Davis	Network-based, misuse detection	[488] http://olympus.cs.ucdavis.edu /arpa/grids
Hyperview	CS Telecom, Groupe CSEE, Paris, France		[130, 131]
IDA (Intrusion Detection Alert)	Motorola, Rolling Meadows, IL		[400]
IDA (Intrusion Detection and Avoidance system)	University of Hamburg, Germany		[182, 484]
IDIOT (Intrusion Detection In Our Time)	Purdue University	Misuse detection	[291] http://www.cs.purdue.edu /coast/coast-tools.html
INSA/Network Security Agent	Touch Technologies, Inc.	Network-based, anomaly and misuse detection. Commercial	http://www.ttisms.com /tti/nsa_www.html
ISOA Information Security Officer's Assistant)	Planning Research Corporation, McLean, VA	Multi-host-based, anomaly and misuse detection	[535, 536]
ITA (Intruder Alert)	AXENT Technologies, Inc.	Multi-host-based, misuse detection. Commercial	http://www.axent.com
Kane Security Monitor (KSM)	Intrusion Detection, Inc.	Commercial	http://www.intrusion.com
NAURS (Network Auditing Usage Reporting System)	SRI International		[372, 373]
NetRanger	WheelGroup, Inc., San Antonio, TX	Network-based, misuse detection. Commercial	http://www.wheelgroup.com
NetStalker	Haystack Laboratories, Inc., Austin, TX	Host-and-network-based, misuse detection. Commercial	http://www.haystack.com
NetSTAT (Network-based State Transition Analysis Tool)	University of California, Santa Barbara	Multi-host-based, misuse detection	http://www.cs.ucsb.edu /~kemm/netstat.html
NID (Network Intrusion Detector)	Computer Security Technology Center, LLNL	Network-based, anomaly and misuse detection	Continuation of NSM [360] http://ciac.llnl.gov/cstc /nid/niddes.html

Name	Source/Organization	Attributes	References
NIDES (Next-Generation Intrusion-Detection Expert System)	SRI International	Multi-host-based, anomaly and misuse detection	Continuation of IDES [259, 309]. See also [6, 7] and *http://www.csl.sri.com /nides/index.html*
NIDX (Network Intrusion Detection eXpert system)	Bell Communications Research, Inc., Piscataway, NJ		[17]
OmniGuard/ Intruder Alert	AXENT Technologies, Inc.	Multi-host-based, misuse and anomaly detection. Commercial	*http://www.axent.com /product/ita/ita.html*
PDAT (Protocol Data Analysis Tool)	Siemens AG, Munich, Germany		[523]
POLYCENTER Security Intrusion Detector	Digital Equipment Corporation	Host-based, misuse detection	*http://www.digital.com /info/security/id.html*
RealSecure	Internet Security Systems, Inc., Atlanta, GA	Network-based, misuse detection. Commercial	*http://www.iss.net /prod/rs.html*
RETISS (REal-TIme expert Security System)	University of Milan, Italy		[76]
SAINT (Security Analysis INtegration Tool)	National Autonomous University of Mexico	Multi-host-based, misuse detection	[542]
SecureDetector	ODS Networks	Network-based	*http://www.ods.com*
SecureNet PRO	MimeStar, Inc.	Commercial	*http://www.mimestar.com*
Stalker	Haystack Laboratories, Inc., Austin, TX	Multi-host-based, misuse detection. Commercial	Evolved from Haystack [480]. *http://www.haystack.com /stalk.html*
Swatch	Stanford University	Multi-host-based, limited misuse detection	[229]
TIM (Time-based Inductive Machine)	University of Illinois at Urbana-Champaign		[504, 505]
UNICORN (Unicos Realtime NADIR)	Los Alamos National Laboratory	Commercial	Evolution from NADIR [244]. See [95] and *http://www. EnGarde.com /∼mcn/unicorn.html*
USTAT (State Transition Analysis Tool for UNIX)	University of California, Santa Barbara	Host-based, misuse detection	[248] *http://www.cs.ucsb.edu /TRs/TRCS93-26.html*

Name	Source/Organization	Attributes	References
WebStalker Pro	Haystack Laboratories, Inc., Austin, TX	Host-based, misuse detection	*http://www.haystack.com /webstalk.html*
Wisdom and Sense	Los Alamos National Laboratory & Oak Ridge National Laboratory	Host-based, anomaly detection	[304]

14.11 Problems and Exercises

1. Discuss possible intrusion detection strategies. Clearly define two broad classes of strategies. What are the advantages and shortcomings of the two strategies?

2. Describe some measurable characteristics that can be used to define an anomaly intrusion detection system.

3. Consider the three anomaly IDS implementations, namely, statistical, predictive-pattern and neural-network IDS. Contrast them, specify their advantages, and point out their limitations.

4. Define intrusion signatures and show how they can be used for intrusion detection.

5. Assume an IDS system is based on the probabilistic model. The event space is binary $\Omega = \{0, 1\}$. The behavior of a legitimate user is described by the collection of conditional probabilities (to simplify the calculations, assume uniform probability distributions). The behavior of an illegal user is characterized by a collection of conditional probabilities that are different by some constant ε from those for the legitimate user. Make the other necessary assumptions. Show the dependency between the length of the event sequence after which the decision about the intrusion is made and the false acceptance/rejection probabilities.

6. Consider the set of events $\Omega = \{e, f, I, \bar{I}\}$ with two basic probability assignments m_1 and m_2 defined as follows:

$$m_1(\omega) = \begin{cases} 0.8 & \text{if } \omega = \{\bar{I}\}, \\ 0.2 & \text{if } \omega = \{I\}, \\ 0 & \text{otherwise,} \end{cases}$$

and

$$m_1(\omega) = \begin{cases} 0.3 & \text{if } \omega = \{e\}, \\ 0.2 & \text{if } \omega = \{f\}, \\ 0.5 & \text{if } \omega = \{e, f\}, \\ 0 & \text{otherwise.} \end{cases}$$

Compute the combined probability assignment $m_1 \oplus m_2$.

7. Choose three IDS implementations published in the literature (printed or electronic). Specify their features, and compare their efficiency versus false acceptance/rejection rates. What are your recommendations as to the applicability of the systems chosen?

15 Electronic Elections and Digital Money

Electronic banking, commerce, and elections are examples of services that are already accessible or will be in the near future on the Internet. Without exaggeration, one can say that most services that require a face-to-face contact will be replaced by their network versions with remote interaction between a client and the parties involved in the service. A distributed system provides the medium for interaction. By its nature, the distributed system allows us to perform the requested services (banking, voting, etc.) by exchange of information only. Needless to say, all stages of service must be converted into protocols, each of which achieves a well-defined goal (such as client-server mutual identification, establishing a secure communication channel, verification of client request, etc.). Network services can be seen as a collection of elementary protocols executed by the parties in order to provide the well-defined service to the client(s).

15.1 Electronic Elections

As soon as computers became widely available, they began to be used during elections to help prepare and run election campaigns, support pooling centers with databases of eligible voters, collect and count votes, and produce the final tally. To observe the election process, the media (press, radio, TV) use computers to gather and store statistical information about voters and their voting tendencies, making guesses as to the election results.

In order to computerize elections from start to finish, there are many legal and technical problems that must be addressed. Most of the published protocols for electronic elections are generic protocols that may not satisfy some legal requirements present in the given country or state. For instance, in countries where voting is compulsory, the election protocol must enable the administrator (government) to identify who did not cast their votes. There are, however, some general properties of election protocols that must always hold. For instance, counting votes during the election has to be error free. It means that all votes cast by those who follow the correct voting procedure must be counted. The votes cast during the election must be anonymous so nobody can associate a given voter with his or her vote. All partisan voters must be prevented from casting their ballots if they deviate from the correct voting procedure. Clearly, noneligible voters must not be allowed to cast their ballots at all and eligible voters must not be allowed to cast their ballots more than once.

In general, the whole election process consists of several stages, such as registration, casting ballots (voting), counting votes, and displaying results. To design a protocol for electronic elections, the following difficulties must be overcome:

- Ballots must be authentic yet untraceable.
- Each voter must be able to check whether or not his or her ballot has been counted without compromising his or her privacy.
- The election protocol must be protected against the illegal activity of both eligible voters and dishonest outsiders.

A typical collection of requirements for a secure electronic election protocol includes [189]:

- *Completeness* – all valid votes must be counted correctly.
- *Soundness* – dishonest voters cannot disrupt the voting process.
- *Privacy* – all ballots must be secret.
- *Unreusability* – no voter can cast their ballot more than once.
- *Eligibility* – only those who are allowed to vote can vote.
- *Verifiability* – nobody can falsify the result of the voting process.
- *Fairness* – nothing must effect the voting.

Chaum [86] was the first to suggest a practical electronic election protocol. Many other protocols have been published. Some are more theoretical, as the underlying assumptions are difficult to meet in practice, and some are designed to be practical for large-scale elections [25, 54, 88, 103, 189, 256, 403]. There are two approaches to implement anonymity (untraceability). The first one uses encryption [25, 256, 445], and the other uses anonymous channels [54, 86, 88, 189].

15.1.1 A Simple Electronic Election Protocol

The protocol is described in Pfleeger [403] and can be used for small elections where all interactions and processing are handled by voters themselves. It is a boardroom voting in which voters pass encrypted messages from one to another while performing encryption and decryption operations till all are confident of the outcome of the election. A characteristic feature of the protocol is that all voters must be known in advance, and if one voter stops following the protocol, the protocol fails. As it is possible that two people may have identical ballots, the protocol must allow people to recognize their own ballots without being able to recognize other people's ballots. For that reason the protocol uses two public-key cryptosystems. Each voter V_i owns two public-key cryptosystems. The first is specified by the pair (E_i, D_i) and the other by (R_i, Q_i), where E_i and R_i are public encryption and D_i and Q_i are private decryption functions.

Now we outline the protocol for three voters only. The reader may easily generalize it for an arbitrary number of voters. Let the three voters be Joan, Keith, and Leo. Their public cryptosystems are described by (E_j, D_j, R_j, Q_j) for Joan, (E_k, D_k, R_k, Q_k) for Keith, and $(E_\ell, D_\ell, R_\ell, Q_\ell)$ for Leo.

Registration stage. Voters agree to follow the protocol and collectively decide who is eligible to vote and what is the order in which the voters will interact. Consequently, each voter knows the ordered list of all eligible voters including their public encryption functions.

Voting stage. A voter V_i prepares a vote v_i and computes $R_j R_k R_\ell(r_i, E_j E_k E_\ell(q_i, v_i))$ where r_i, q_i are two random integers chosen by the voter V_i. Being more specific, each voter takes their vote v_i and the random number q_i and creates the cryptogram $E_j E_k E_\ell(q_i, v_i)$. Next the voter concatenates the cryptogram with the random string r_i and encrypts it using R_j, R_k, and R_ℓ. All voters send their encrypted ballots to the first voter Joan. Joan has received the following cryptograms:

$$R_j R_k R_\ell(r_j, E_j E_k E_\ell(q_j, v_j))$$
$$R_j R_k R_\ell(r_k, E_j E_k E_\ell(q_k, v_k))$$
$$R_j R_k R_\ell(r_\ell, E_j E_k E_\ell(q_\ell, v_\ell))$$

Verification stage. Joan removes one level of encryption from all cryptograms by applying her private decryption algorithm (note that the composition of $Q_j \circ R_j$ is the identity permutation). She obtains the cryptograms:

$$R_k R_\ell(r_j, E_j E_k E_\ell(q_j, v_j))$$
$$R_k R_\ell(r_k, E_j E_k E_\ell(q_k, v_k))$$
$$R_k R_\ell(r_\ell, E_j E_k E_\ell(q_\ell, v_\ell))$$

and forwards them in a random order to Keith. Keith verifies whether his ballot is among the cryptograms and removes one level of encryption using his private decryption Q_k. As a result, he gets the following cryptograms:

$$R_\ell(r_j, E_j E_k E_\ell(q_j, v_j))$$
$$R_\ell(r_k, E_j E_k E_\ell(q_k, v_k))$$
$$R_\ell(r_\ell, E_j E_k E_\ell(q_\ell, v_\ell))$$

Keith dispatches the cryptograms (in a random order) to Leo. Leo checks whether his ballot is among the cryptograms, removes the encryption R_ℓ using his private decryption algorithm Q_ℓ, and extracts the ballots:

$$E_j E_k E_\ell(q_j, v_j)$$
$$E_j E_k E_\ell(q_k, v_k)$$
$$E_j E_k E_\ell(q_\ell, v_\ell)$$

The random integers r_j, r_k, r_ℓ are discarded.

Opening stage. Leo signs all ballots and sends the signature to Joan and Keith and the ballots to Joan. Joan removes the encryption E_j and signs the ballots. The ballots

$$E_k E_\ell(q_j, v_j), E_k E_\ell(q_k, v_k), E_k E_\ell(q_\ell, v_\ell)$$

are communicated to Keith, the signature is given to both Keith and Leo. In turn, Keith peels off his public encryption, gets

$$E_\ell(q_j, v_j), E_\ell(q_k, v_k), E_\ell(q_\ell, v_\ell)$$

and signs the ballots. The ballots are sent to Leo while the signature is forwarded to Joan and Leo. Finally, Leo strips off the last encryption, extracts random number, votes, and publishes the results (together with the random numbers q_j, q_k, q_ℓ for verification).

The protocol uses two cycles of interactions. The first provides anonymity and the other allows us to recover the clear form of the votes. Note that Joan who collects all the encrypted ballots at the beginning of the protocol may trace the origin of each of the ballots. This is impossible for Keith and Leo as they got all ballots in a random order. Leo after removing random numbers r_j, r_k, r_ℓ breaks any link between double encrypted and single encrypted ballots so Joan cannot identify ballots unless she can try all possible random numbers for r_j, r_k, r_ℓ or collude with Leo. The protocol is *complete* as the final result of elections can be trusted if all voters are honest. To prove that the protocol is *sound* we need to define the possible actions of a dishonest voter. The voter can

1. Refuse to vote – this will be detected by the first honest voter.
2. Cast multiple votes – this will also be detected by honest voters as the number of ballots will be greater than the number of voters (this is the *unreusability* property).
3. Substitute ballots – any voter can do this during the first cycle for their own ballots, if an attacker substitutes a ballot of some other voter this will be detected with a high probability unless the attacker has broken the corresponding public-key cryptosystem (this is the *verifiability* property).

Note that the protocol has some drawbacks, including:

- An excessive computation overhead when the number of voters gets bigger (the protocol is not practical for large-scale elections).
- A difficulty with the initialization of the protocol. The agreement about the list of voters must be done collectively as there is no central trusted authority.
- All voters must be present at the same time to execute the protocol.
- The protocol fails if there is a voter who refuses to follow it.

15.1.2 Chaum Protocol

In 1981 Chaum designed a protocol that uses a trusted *mix* to implement an anonymous channel and digital pseudonyms to ensure voter privacy [86].

In most cases, any message sent over a communication network could be traced back to its origin (for instance, in any packet-switching network, it is possible to identify the sender from the headings of the packets). To thwart traceability, Chaum suggested using an *anonymous channel*. The main feature is an active entity called the mix. The mix is a trusted authority that plays the same role as Joan for both Keith and Leo in the previous protocol at the very beginning of the voting stage.

The mix sets up its service by announcing its public encryption algorithm E_x and keeping the decryption algorithm D_x secret. Needless to say, anybody can get the authentic E_x. If a voter V_i wants to send a message m anonymously to another voter, say V_j, V_i follows the following steps.

1. V_i gets the authentic E_x of the mix.
2. V_i creates a cryptogram

$$E_x(r, m, a_j),$$

where $m \in \mathcal{M}$ is the message, r is a random integer used to prevent exhaustive attacks if the message space $\mathcal{M}$ is small, and a_j is the address of voter V_j (the destination).
3. V_i forwards the cryptogram to the mix that decrypts it using its private D_x.
4. The mix sends the message m to the destination a_i.

If V_i cares about the privacy of m, V_i may send m encrypted using the public encryption algorithm of V_j. To prevent attacks based on the knowledge of the sequence of cryptograms coming to the mix, the mix changes the order of outcoming messages. The mix may also prevent reply attacks by keeping the random strings r and checking subsequent cryptograms against it.

A *digital pseudonym* is a public-key used to verify the signature made by an anonymous voter (who holds the matching private key).

Chaum protocol

Assumptions: 1. There is a trusted administrator (authority) TA.
    2. Voters and the administrator communicate via an anonymous channel (there is a trusted mix).
    3. Each voter has a pseudonym.

Initialization stage: 1. TA prepares the information for voting, including the bundle of cryptograms (one cryptogram per voter). Any cryptogram $E_v(r, K, \pi)$ includes the public key K and the pseudonym π.
    2. $TA \rightarrow Mix : \{E_v(r_i, K_i, \pi_i) \mid i = 1, \ldots, n\}$,
    where n is the number of eligible voters.
    3. The mix shuffles the cryptograms and
    $Mix \rightarrow V_i : E_v(r_i, K_i, \pi_i)$
    for $i = 1, \ldots, n$. The mix also conveys general information about how to vote (encrypted using the voter's public key). TA does not know which cryptogram goes to which voter. Clearly, the mix has to have the list of all eligible voters.

Voting and counting stage: 1. Each registered voter V_i prepares their ballot of the form

$$E_v(r_i, \pi_i, E_{K_i}(q_i, v_i))$$

where r_i, q_i are random integers, v_i is the vote, and π_i, K_i is the pseudonym and the public key given by the mix to V_i, respectively.

2. V_i sends its ballot to the mix.

3. The mix collects all ballots and processes them as a single batch and outputs a complete list of valid entries $(\pi_i, E_{K_i}(q_i, v_i))$.

4. The mix communicates the list via a secure channel to TA.

5. TA verifies whether π_i is valid. If so, TA decrypts the second part, re-covers the votes v_i and counts them. All ballots with invalid pseudonyms are rejected.

In 1988 Chaum published a modified version of the protocol [88]. That version uses blind signatures and sender untraceability. For security analysis, we direct the reader to the original papers [86, 88].

15.1.3 Boyd Protocol

The Boyd protocol [53] uses exponentiation modulo a prime p. The security and anonymity depends on the difficulty of computing the discrete logarithm modulo p. The protocol involves registered voters V_i and a trusted administrator TA.

Boyd protocol

Initialization stage: 1. TA selects three complementary keys a, b, c. Two of them, say a and b, are picked at random and are coprime to $p - 1$. The third one c satisfies the following congruence

$$a \times b \times c \equiv 1 \pmod{p - 1}.$$

2. TA makes the key a public and publishes a primitive element $e \in \mathbb{Z}_p^*$.

Registration stage: 1. Each voter V_i creates a message $m_i = (\alpha, r_i, v_i)$ where a string α provides redundancy and should be the same for all voters, r_i is individually chosen by V_i, and v_i is the vote.

2. V_i creates

$$B_i \equiv e^{m_i} \pmod{p},$$

takes the public exponent a, randomly selects a_{i_0}, and calculates a_{i_1} such that

$$a_{i_0} \times a_{i_1} \equiv a \pmod{p - 1}.$$

Further, V_i blinds B_i by computing $B_i^{a_{i_0}}$ and sends $B_i^{a_{i_0}}$ to TA.

3. TA checks the voter identity. If the check holds, TA records that V_i has registered and returns $B_i^{a_{i_0} \times b}$ to V_i.

Voting and counting stage: 1. Voters complete their ballots by using the key a_{i_1} so they compute

$$(B_i^{a_{i_0} \times b})^{a_{i_1}} \equiv B_i^{ab} \pmod p.$$

The ballot B_i^{ab} is sent to TA via an anonymous channel together with the original message m_i.

2. TA retrieves B_i using c as

$$(B_i^{ab})^c \equiv B_i \pmod p.$$

Next TA computes $\tilde{B}_i = e^{m_i} \bmod p$ and verifies whether $B_i \overset{?}{=} \tilde{B}_i$. If the redundancy constant is correct, TA accepts the vote v_i.

3. Finally, TA publishes all messages m_i together with the result of the election. At this stage each voter can check their random number that clearly identifies the message m_i.

The protocol ensures the privacy and authenticity of voters [53]. The main drawback of the protocol is that TA can see the votes and produce a false tally by adding votes of its own choice. The final result of casting is not verifiable.

15.1.4 Fujioka-Okamoto-Ohta Protocol

Fujioka, Okamoto and Ohta described a protocol that is more suitable for large-scale elections [189]. The players in the protocol are voters, an administrator A, and a counter C.

Fujioka-Okamoto-Ohta protocol

Assumptions: 1. The counter communicates with voters via an anonymous channel.

2. Ballots are computed using a bit commitment scheme.

3. Every voter has its own digital signature scheme SG.

4. The administrator uses a blind signature scheme.

The bit commitment scheme uses two functions (f, g). The function f encrypts binary strings into cryptograms (blobs) and the function g decrypts cryptograms (open blobs) and reveals the bits. The blind signature uses two functions (B, U), The function B takes the ballot x and a random integer r and computes the blind message $e = B(x, r)$. The blind message e is then given to the administrator who signs the blind message and returns the blind signature d. The function U allows us to unblind the signature and to retrieve the signature of the administrator as $SG_A(x) = U(d, r)$.

Registration stage: 1. V_i selects its vote v_i, which is typically a binary string, and creates a blob for it, i.e.,
$$x_i = f(v_i, k_i).$$
for a random k_i.

2. V_i blinds x_i, i.e., computes
$$e_i = B(x_i, r_i)$$
using a random integer r_i.

3. V_i signs e_i by calculating $s_i = SG_i(e_i)$ and sends the triple $\langle ID_i, e_i, s_i \rangle$ to A, i.e.,
$$V_i \to A : \langle ID_i, e_i, s_i \rangle,$$
where ID_i is the identity or name of voter V_i.

4. A verifies whether
   (a) V_i is eligible to vote,
   (b) V_i has not already applied for registration, and
   (c) s_i is valid.

   If the three conditions hold, A generates the certificate $d_i = SG_A(e_i)$ and
   $$A \to V_i : d_i.$$
   If any of the three conditions is violated, the registration of V_i is declined.

5. When the deadline for registration has passed, the administrator announces the number of voters and publishes the list $\langle ID_i, e_i, s_i \rangle$ of all registered voters.

Voting stage: 1. V_i retrieves A's signature for x_i by unbilding d_i so $y_i = SG_A(x_i) = U(d_i, r_i)$.

2. V_i checks whether y_i is a signature generated by A. If the check fails, V_i complains by showing the pair (x_i, y_i). Otherwise, V_i sends the pair (x_i, y_i) to the counter C via an anonymous channel.

3. C verifies the signature y_i of the ballot x_i. If the check holds, C puts the triple $\langle \ell, x_i, y_i \rangle$ into a list where ℓ is the consecutive number assigned to the ballot.

4. C publishes the list after all voters have cast their ballots, i.e.,
$$C \to \star : \{\langle \ell, x_i, y_i \rangle \mid i = 1, \ldots, \alpha\},$$
where α is the number of ballots cast.

Opening and counting stage: Each voter V_i checks whether

1. The number of ballots on the list is equal to the number of voters. If the check fails, voters may reveal their secret random numbers r_i and indirectly indicate which ballots are forged.

2. The ballot x_i is on the list. If not, V_i complains by showing the valid pair (x_i, y_i).

If the checks are successful, V_i sends the key k_i with the number ℓ to C via an anonymous channel. C opens the blob x_i using the key k_i and retrieves the vote $v_i = g(x_i, k_i)$. The pair (k_i, v_i) is appended to the entry (x_i, y_i) on the list. Finally, C counts the tally and announces the results.

It is easy to check that if all parties honestly follow the protocol, then the result of the election is correct. The protocol is *complete*. A dishonest voter can disrupt the election process by sending invalid ballots, but this will be detected in the counting stage (*soundness* holds). There is a problem when a voter sends an illegal key at the opening stage as, in this case, it is impossible to distinguish a dishonest voter from a dishonest counter. The *privacy* of voters is ensured by the blind signature as the administrator never sees voters' ballots. As the voters blind their ballots using a random string, the privacy is unconditionally secure. The *unreusability* property holds as each voter can legally obtain one blindly signed ballot by the administrator. The ability to create two different ballots signed by the administrator is equivalent to breaking the blind signature used by the administrator. Note that an outsider cannot vote unless she is able to to break the signature scheme used by voters (*eligibility* is satisfied). *Fairness* holds as counting ballots does not affect the voting (votes are hidden by the bit commitment scheme). The results of voting are *verifiable* as even if both the administrator and counter collude, they cannot change the result of the voting process. The main problem with the protocol is that it requires all registered voters to cast their votes and no voter can abstain from voting. In fact, the failure of a single voter will disrupt the whole election process. Additionally, the vote is fixed after the registration phase.

15.1.5 Other Protocols

Iversen [256] designed an electronic election protocol based on privacy homomorphisms. Players in the protocol are voters, candidates, and the government. The communication between voters and candidates is done over a broadcast channel. Voters may cast their ballots with no need for "synchronization" and there is no need for global computation. The protocol preserves the privacy of votes against collusion by dishonest voters or any proper subset of dishonest candidates, including the government.

Sako and Kilian [445] proposed a voting protocol based on families of homomorphic encryptions, which have a partial compatibility property, generalizing the method of Benaloh and Yung [25]. The protocol has a much lower complexity than protocols using anonymous communication channels. It preserves the privacy of voters as long as the centers are honest. The drawback of the protocol is that if all centers conspire, the privacy of voters is violated. Even worse, if a center accidentally or otherwise produces an incorrect subtally then the verification fails and consequently the entire election will collapse.

Niemi and Renvall described a protocol [374] that prevents the buying of votes. In traditional voting protocols, the buying is prevented as voters cannot prove that they have voted as agreed. In other words, the buyer has no means to verify how the voter has voted. This is mimicked by attaching to the vote v_i an eligibility token e_i. Each ballot must consist of the pair (v_i, e_i). The token e_i is generated collectively by all candidates and the voter. Although the voter V_i is confident as to the authenticity of e_i, V_i does not have any means to prove its validity to anybody. Sako and Kilian in [446] present a receipt-free protocol that also prevents buying votes. Other protocols for electronic elections can be found in [15, 114].

15.2 Digital Cash

Traditional cash has the following properties:

- It is difficult to forge.
- It is untraceable (more precisely, coins are untraceable but paper currency can be traced, at least in principle, because of its unique serial number).
- It is issued centrally by a mint.
- Its lifetime extends beyond a single transaction (coins from 10 to 20 years, banknotes several years).

Cash transactions directly involve two parties: the seller and the buyer. The third party usually is the bank where the buyer withdraws a suitable amout of money to pay for goods offered by the seller, and the seller deposits the money after a transaction. Any single transaction takes three operations: withdrawing money by the buyer, selling/buying process, and depositing money.

In a computer environment, electronic cash (money) must be in the form of a binary string. If a transaction between the buyer and seller can proceed successfully without the direct involvement of the bank, we are dealing with *off-line electronic money*. If a payment protocol requires all three parties (buyer, seller, bank) to interact at the same time, it is called *on-line electronic money*.

The required properties of electronic money include:

Unforgeability – money cannot be forged, i.e., money tokens (coins, bills) cannot be generated illegally.

Unreusability – the same money must not be spent twice,

Untraceability – the bank is not able to identify the buyer from the money deposited by the seller.

Transferability – money can be transferred from person to person.

Divisibility – a money token can be divided into tokens of smaller values.

The next section describes an electronic money protocol that satisfies: unforgeability, unreusability, untraceability, and transferability. The interesting feature is that two characteristics, unreusability and untraceability, are connected, i.e., any double payment of the same coin reveals the identity of the spender. The protocol is an example of off-line payment.

15.2.1 Untraceable Digital Coins

Unforgeability requires that nobody can produce valid digital cash except a bank who knows some secret so it can identify its money. Chaum, Fiat, and Naor [90] showed how to get untraceability when the seller is honest (spends digital money once). If, however, the seller spends the same money more than once, his or her identity will be revealed. Their electronic money takes the form of \$1 coins. Each coin is a pair

$$(x, f(x)^{\frac{1}{3}}) \bmod N,$$

where $f(x)$ is a one-way function, N is an RSA modulus ($N = pq$, p and q are large enough primes), and x is some integer. Note that the factorization of N is known to the bank that has issued the coin. Coins can be forged if the calculation of the cube root is feasible. In other words, unforgeability rests on the assumption that computation of the cube root modulo N is intractable.

Assume that we have three parties. Alice wants to buy an item from Bob. The item costs \$1. Both Alice and Bob use the same bank. The purchase involves three phases. In the first phase, Alice withdraws \$1 from her account u. In the second phase, Alice purchases the item from Bob and pays \$1. Finally, Bob deposits \$1 to the bank.

Issuing a coin (Alice $\leftrightarrow$ Bank)

1. Alice chooses n triples (a_i, b_i, c_i) at random $(i = 1, \ldots, n)$ where n is the security parameter.
2. Alice computes n blind elements

$$B_i = r_i^3 f(x_i, y_i),$$

   where r_i is a random integer used for blinding, and f is a collision-resistant hash function,

$$x_i = g(a_i, c_i)$$

   and

$$y_i = g(a_i \oplus (u\|v + i), b_i),$$

   where $\|$ stands for the concatenation, g is a collision-resistant hash function, and v is a counter associated with the account u. Finally,
   $A \to \text{Bank} : \{B_i \mid i = 1, \ldots, n\}$.
3. Bank picks up a random subset of $n/2$ indices. Let them be $\mathcal{R} = \{i_j \mid j = 1, \ldots, n/2\}$.
   Bank $\to$ Alice : $\mathcal{R}$.
4. Alice $\to$ Bank : $\{r_i, a_i, b_i, c_i \mid i \in \mathcal{R}\}$.
   Bank checks its consistency with B_i. If there is any attempt to cheat, Bank aborts.
5. Otherwise (checks hold)
   Bank $\to$ Alice : $\prod_{i \notin \mathcal{R}} B_i^{\frac{1}{3}}$
   and charges one dollar against her account.
6. Alice extracts the coin C

$$C = \prod_{i \notin \mathcal{R}} r_i^{-1} \cdot B_i^{\frac{1}{3}} \equiv \prod_{i \notin \mathcal{R}} f(x_i, y_i)^{\frac{1}{3}} \pmod{N}.$$

   To simplify our notation, we further assume that the indices that were not in $\mathcal{R}$ belong to the set $\{1, \ldots, n/2\}$ so

$$C = \prod_{i=1,\ldots,n/2} f(x_i, y_i)^{\frac{1}{3}}.$$

In the withdrawal protocol, Bank checks whether or not Alice follows the protocol. After Alice computes her blind elements and commits herself by sending them to Bank, Bank randomly selects half of them and asks her to show all parameters. If Alice cheats she will be caught with a high probability. Note that if Alice does not follow the protocol for a single blind element, the probability of not being (or being) caught is 0.5 and equals the probability that the element will be selected by Bank for checking.

Payment (Alice $\leftrightarrow$ Bob)

1. Alice $\rightarrow$ Bob : C.
2. Bob $\rightarrow$ Alice : e
   where $e = (e_1, \ldots, e_{n/2})$ and each $e_i \in_R \{0, 1\}$. The string e is a challenge.
3. Alice has to reply to the challenge and

   $$\text{Alice} \rightarrow \text{Bob} : \begin{cases} a_i, c_i, y_i & \text{if } e_i = 1 \\ a_i \oplus (u \| v + i), b_i, x_i & \text{otherwise.} \end{cases}$$

4. Bob verifies whether C has the form consistent with the response provided by Alice.

Deposit (Bob $\leftrightarrow$ Bank)

1. Bob deposits the coin C with Bank and forwards his string e together with Alice's response.
2. Bank verifies the correctness and credits \$1 to Bob's account. Bank must keep e and Alice's response for future references (in the case when the coin is spent more than once).

Untraceability is tied up with prevention against multiple spending. A single spending of a coin does not allow Bank to identify the spender. If Alice, however, spends the same coin many times, then there is an overwhelming probability that there is at least one bit e_i for which the buyers have recorded both (a_i, c_i, y_i) (when $e_i = 1$) and $(a_i \oplus (u, v+i), b_i, x_i)$ (when $e_i = 0$). After the coin is deposited with Bank twice, Bank knows both a_i and $a_i \oplus (u, v + i)$ so it can recover the account number u and identify the double spender.

There is a problem, however, when both Alice and Bob conspire and Bob uses the same challenge string e for two different transactions or, equivalently, Bob tries to deposit the same coin twice. Another face of this problem is the case when Alice spends the same coin twice with different sellers who agreed to use the same challenge string e. A simple solution would be to divide the challenge string e into two parts: fixed and random. Each seller would have different fixed parts (imposed by the bank). This would exclude the collusion among buyers and sellers.

15.2.2 Divisible Electronic Cash

This protocol was invented by Okamoto and Ohta [390]. The bank applies a collection of RSA schemes determined by triples (e_j, d_j, N_j) for $j = 0, \ldots, n$ where e_j, d_j are the encryption and decryption keys, respectively, and N_i is an RSA modulus. The RSA system (e_0, d_0, N_0) is used to generate electronic licenses for Bank clients. The other RSA systems are used to generate electronic banknotes (coins) of specific values. For example, the RSA system (e_1, d_1, N_1) is used to generate electronic coins each of value \$100, the RSA system (e_2, d_2, N_2) to issue \$50 bills, and so on. Needless to say, the bank announces public parameters (e_j, N_j) of the RSA schemes. Also, there is public knowledge about which RSA scheme is to be used to produce coins of a given value.

A buyer Alice has an account u_A with the bank and generates her RSA scheme (e_A, d_A, N_A). The pair (e_A, N_A) is public.

An important ingredient of the payment system is a tree structure of coins (bills). Before we show how to design such a tree, we need to introduce some number theory facts. Let $z \in \mathcal{Z}_N$ be an arbitrary integer and the modulus $N = pq$ such that $p \equiv 3 \bmod 8$ and $q \equiv 7 \pmod 8$. Such N is called a Williams integer. Then it is relatively easy to show that among the elements of the set

$$\{z, -z, 2z, -2z\}$$

one element, say z_1, is a quadratic residue (denoted as $z_1 = \langle z \rangle_Q$), one element, say z_2, is a quadratic nonresidue with its Jacobi symbol $\left[\frac{z_2}{N}\right] = 1$ (written as $z_2 = \langle z \rangle_+$), and one element, say z_3, is a quadratic nonresidue with its Jacobi symbol $\left[\frac{z_3}{N}\right] = -1$ (or simply $z_3 = \langle z \rangle_-$).

The coin structure is a binary tree with the top node (a coin) $\Gamma_0 = \langle z \rangle_Q$ (at level 0). At level 1, there are two children Γ_{00} and Γ_{01}. The left child

$\Gamma_{00} = \langle \Gamma_0^{1/2} \rangle_Q$. The right child $\Gamma_{01} = \langle \Omega_0 \times \Gamma_0^{1/2} \rangle_Q$, where Ω_0 is an integer generated by a suitable hash function f_Ω. Now, children become parents and generate their own pairs of children in the same way. The process continues until the necessary depth of the tree is achieved. Note that all nodes in the tree are quadratic residues (belong to $\mathcal{Z}_N^{Q+}$).

Registration (Alice $\leftrightarrow$ Bank)

This stage of the protocol is executed once only when Alice wishes to open her account with the bank. The bank issues a license B.

1. Alice picks up at random (a_i, η_i) for $i = 1, \ldots, n$ where n is the security parameter, and η_i is an RSA modulus (i.e., $\eta_i = p_i \times q_i$ is a Williams integer or $p_i \equiv 3 \bmod 8$ and $q_i \equiv 7 \bmod 8$).

2. Alice $\rightarrow$ Bank : $\{w_i, i = 1, \ldots, n\}$,

   where

   $$w_i \equiv r_i^{e_0} \times g(\alpha_i \| \eta_i) \pmod{N_0},$$

   where r_i is a blinding random integer, g is a collison-resistant hash function and α_i is generated as follows. First, Alice creates a sequence $s_i = u_A \| a_i \| g(u_A \| a_i)^{d_A} \bmod N_A$. Next the sequence s_i is split into two substrings so $s_i = s_{i_0} \| s_{i_1}$. Finally, $\alpha_i = \alpha_{i_0} \| \alpha_{i_1}$ where $\alpha_{i_0} \equiv s_{i_0}^2 \bmod \eta_i$ and $\alpha_{i_1} \equiv s_{i_1}^2 \bmod \eta_i$.

3. Bank chooses at random $n/2$ indices. Let the collection of indices be $\mathcal{R}$ and Bank $\rightarrow$ Alice: $\mathcal{R}$.

4. Alice displays all the parameters used to generate w_i for which $i \in \mathcal{R}$. In other words, Alice shows $a_i, p_i, q_i, g(u_A \| a_i)^{d_A}, r_i$ for all $i \in \mathcal{R}$.

5. Bank verifies the correctness of all w_i for $i \in \mathcal{R}$. If they are not valid, Bank aborts the protocol. Otherwise, the protocol is continued.

6. Bank $\rightarrow$ Alice: $\prod_{i \notin \mathcal{R}} w_i^{d_0} \bmod N_0$.

7. Alice extracts her license by using inverses r_i^{-1} so

   $$B = \prod_{i \notin \mathcal{R}} g(\alpha_i \| \eta_i)^{d_0} \bmod N_0.$$

We simplify our notation by assuming that $B = \prod_{i=1}^{n/2} g(\alpha_i \| \eta_i)^{d_0} \bmod N_0$.

Issuing a coin (Alice $\leftrightarrow$ Bank)

Assume that Alice wishes Bank to issue a bill of value $\$x$. Bank finds the RSA scheme associated with this value, let it be determined by the triple (e_x, d_x, N_x).

1. Alice selects two random integers b and r and
   Alice $\rightarrow$ Bank : $Z \equiv r^{e_x} g(B \| b) \bmod N_x$.
2. Bank $\rightarrow$ Alice: $Z^{d_x} \bmod N_x$
   and charges Alice's account x dollars.
3. Alice extracts the coin
   $$C = r^{-1} Z^{d_x} \equiv g(B \| b)^{d_x} \pmod{N_x}.$$

Payment (Alice $\leftrightarrow$ Bob). Parties use three public collision-resistant hash functions: f_Γ, f_Λ, and f_Ω.

1. Alice computes top nodes (at the level 0) of her coin trees
   $$\Gamma_{i,0} = \langle f_\Gamma(C \| 0 \| \eta_i) \rangle_Q \bmod \eta_i$$
   for $i = 1, \ldots, n/2$. Next she computes two children of $\Gamma_{i,0}$. The left child is
   $$\Gamma_{i,00} \equiv \langle \Gamma_{i,0}^{\frac{1}{2}} \rangle_Q \bmod \eta_i,$$
   and the right child is
   $$\Gamma_{i,01} \equiv \langle \Omega_{i,0} \Gamma_{i,0}^{\frac{1}{2}} \rangle_Q \bmod \eta_i,$$
   where $\Omega_{i,0} = \langle f_\Omega(C \| 0 \| \eta_i) \rangle_+$. The process continues in the same way. The node $\Gamma_{i,00}$ has two children $\Gamma_{i,000}$ and $\Gamma_{i,001}$, and $\Gamma_{i,01}$ has its children $\Gamma_{i,010}$ and $\Gamma_{i,011}$. For the sake of clarity, the rest of the protocol is described for a case when Alice wants to pay $\$75$ using a $\$100$ coin C. Instead of finding the whole coin trees, Alice needs to find two nodes (in independent tree paths) whose sum is equal to $\$75$. Let those nodes be:
   $$\Gamma_{i,00} \equiv \langle \Gamma_{i,0}^{\frac{1}{2}} \rangle_Q \bmod \eta_i \quad \text{worth } \$50,$$
   $$\Gamma_{i,010} \equiv \langle \Gamma_{i,01}^{\frac{1}{2}} \rangle_Q \bmod \eta_i \text{ worth } \$25.$$
   Next she computes their square roots whose Jacobi symbols are equal to -1, thus:
   $$X_{i,00} = \langle \Gamma_{i,00}^{\frac{1}{2}} \rangle_- \equiv \langle \Gamma_{i,0}^{\frac{1}{4}} \rangle_- \bmod \eta_i,$$
   $$X_{i,010} = \langle \Gamma_{i,010}^{\frac{1}{2}} \rangle_- \equiv \langle \Omega_{i,0}^2 \Gamma_{i,0}^{\frac{1}{8}} \rangle_- \bmod \eta_i.$$

2. Alice $\rightarrow$ Bob: $(B, C, \{(\alpha_i, \eta_i, X_{i,00}, X_{i,010}), i = 1, \ldots, n/2\})$.

3. Bob verifies the license B and the coin C. Further Bob checks whether for all $i = 1, \ldots, n/2$, the following conditions hold:

   (a) Jacobi symbols of $X_{i,00}$ and $X_{i,010}$ are equal to -1,

   (b) $X_{i,00}^4 \stackrel{?}{=} d_i \Gamma_{i,0}$, $d_i \in \{\pm 1, \pm 2\}$,

   (c) $X_{i,010}^8 \stackrel{?}{=} d_i' \Omega_{i,0}^2 \Gamma_{i,0}$, $d_i' \in \{\pm 1, \pm 2\}$.

   If any of the checks fails, Bob aborts the protocol. Otherwise, Bob continues.

4. Bob $\rightarrow$ Alice: $\{(E_{i,00}, E_{i,010}), i = 1, \ldots, n/2\}$,

   where $E_{i,00}, E_{i,010} \in_R \{0, 1\}$ for all i.

5. Alice calculates

$$
Y_{i,00} = \begin{cases} \langle \Lambda_{i,00}^{\frac{1}{2}} \rangle_- \bmod \eta_i & \text{if } E_{i,00} = 1, \\ \langle \Lambda_{i,00}^{\frac{1}{2}} \rangle_+ \bmod \eta_i & \text{if } E_{i,00} = 0, \end{cases}
$$

and

$$
Y_{i,010} = \begin{cases} \langle \Lambda_{i,010}^{\frac{1}{2}} \rangle_- \bmod \eta_i & \text{if } E_{i,010} = 1, \\ \langle \Lambda_{i,010}^{\frac{1}{2}} \rangle_+ \bmod \eta_i & \text{if } E_{i,010} = 0, \end{cases}
$$

   where $\Lambda_{i,s} = \langle f_\Lambda(C \parallel s \parallel \eta_i) \rangle_Q \bmod \eta_i$ for $s = 00$ and $s = 010$.

6. Bob checks whether

   (a) Jacobi symbols of $Y_{i,00}$ and $Y_{i,010}$ are equal to -1,

   (b) $Y_{i,00}^2 \equiv d_i f_\Lambda(C \parallel 00 \parallel \eta_i) \bmod \eta_i$, where $d_i \in \{\pm 1, \pm 2\}$,

   (c) $Y_{i,010}^2 \equiv d_i' f_\Lambda(C \parallel 010 \parallel \eta_i) \bmod \eta_i$ where $d_i' \in \{\pm 1, \pm 2\}$.

   If the checks hold Bob accepts the payment of $75.

Deposit (Bob $\leftrightarrow$ Bank)

1. To deposit $75, Bob sends a transcript of his interactions with Alice. The transcript (history) is verified by Bank, and if the checks hold then Bank credits $75 to Bob's account. If the payment is invalid, Bank reveals Alice's secret information s_i.

The major problem of the payment scheme is its low efficiency. The payment involves transmission of a large volume of data. Okomoto [389] suggested a modification that is more efficient. In this protocol, however, Alice can cheat at the registration stage [80].

15.2.3 Brands Electronic Cash Protocol

Brands [57] used the intractibility of the discrete logarithm to design an electronic cash system. The protocol handles coins of the same value, say \$1. All computations are done in the group $\mathcal{Z}_q^*$, q is a large enough prime. Bank sets up the protocol. It picks up at random three generators (g, g_1, g_2) of $\mathcal{Z}_q^*$ and selects a secret $x \in_R \mathcal{Z}_{q-1}$ together with two collision-resistant hash functions H and H_0. Bank publishes (g, g_1, g_2), q, and the descriptions of the hash functions. The integer x is kept secret but its exponent $h = g^x$ is a public key of the bank.

Registration (Alice $\leftrightarrow$ Bank)

1. Alice identifies herself to Bank.
2. She generates her secret integer $u_1 \in_R \mathcal{Z}_{q-1}$ and computes her account number

    $$I = g_1^{u_1}$$

    If $Ig_2 \neq 1$, Alice gives I to Bank while keeping u_1 secret.
3. Bank $\rightarrow$ Alice: $z = (Ig_2)^x$.

Issuing a Coin (Alice $\leftrightarrow$ Bank)

1. Alice identifies herself to Bank.
2. Bank $\rightarrow$ Alice: $(a = g^w, b = (Ig_2)^w)$
    for $w \in_R \mathcal{Z}_{q-1}$.
3. Alice chooses at random (s, x_1, x_2) and computes

    $$A = (Ig_2)^s, \ \ B = g_1^{x_1} g_2^{x_2}, \ \text{and} \ z' = z^s.$$

    Next, Alice selects two integers u, v and computes

    $$a' = a^u g^v \ \text{and} \ b' = b^{su} A^v.$$

    Then she finds out $c' = H(A, B, z', a', b')$.
4. Alice $\rightarrow$ Bank: $c = \frac{c'}{u}$,
    where u is a blinding integer.
5. Bank $\rightarrow$ Alice: $r = cx + w$
    and withdraws \$1 from Alice's account.

6. Alice verifies whether

$$g^r \overset{?}{=} h^c a \text{ and } (Ig_2)^r \overset{?}{=} z^c b.$$

If the checks hold, Alice computes

$$r' \equiv ru + v.$$

The coin is the sequence $C = (A, B, z', a', b', r')$.

Note that everybody can verify the coin by checking whether

$$g^{r'} \overset{?}{=} h^{c'} a', \text{ and}$$
$$A^{r'} \overset{?}{=} z'^{c'} b'.$$

For this reason, the sequence (z', a', b', r') can be considered to be a signature of (A, B). The signature is created by Alice with a collaboration with Bank who contributes by sending $r = cx + w$ (and charges for this $1) where c is a blinded version of $c' = H(A, B, z', a', b')$. Alice publishes r' so Bank knowing the coin is not able to trace Alice provided the discrete logarithm instances are intractable.

Payment (Alice $\leftrightarrow$ Bob)

1. Alice $\rightarrow$ Bob: C
   or Alice pays Bob by sending the coin C.
2. Bob $\rightarrow$ Alice: $d = H_0(A, B, I_{\text{Bob}}, \text{date/time})$.
3. Alice $\rightarrow$ Bob: r_1, r_2
   where $r_1 \equiv dsu_1 + x_1$ and $r_2 \equiv ds + x_2$.
4. Bob verifies whether Alice's response is correct, i.e.,

$$g_1^{r_1} g_2^{r_2} \overset{?}{=} A^d B.$$

Bob saves $(C, r_1, r_2, \text{date/time})$.

Deposit (Bob $\leftrightarrow$ Bank)

1. Bob $\rightarrow$ Bank: $(C, r_1, r_2, \text{date/time})$.
2. Bank recalculates d from the information given by Bob and verifies whether $g_1^{r_1} g_2^{r_2} \overset{?}{=} A^d B$. If the check holds and:
   (a) The coin has never been spent before, Bank stores the transcript $(C, r_1, r_2, \text{date/time})$ in its database for future reference and credits $1 to Bob's account.

(b) Otherwise, the coin has been deposited already. In this case Bank takes the current transcript $(C, r_1, r_2, \text{date, time})$ and the previous $(C, r_1', r_2', \text{date}', \text{time}')$, recomputes d and d', and creates a system of four equations in four unknowns in $\text{GF}(q)$:

$$r_1 \equiv du_1 s + x_1,$$
$$r_2 \equiv ds + x_2,$$
$$r_1' \equiv d' u_1 s + x_1',$$
$$r_2' \equiv d' s + x_2'.$$

After easy transformations, Bank is able to find the secret key of Alice

$$u_1 \equiv \frac{r_1 - r_1'}{r_2 - r_2'},$$

and identify her as $I = g^{u_1}$.

The above protocol can be modified for electronic wallets with observers [57]. An *electronic wallet* is a collection of a user-controlled computer with a tamper-proof unit (such as a smart card) also called an *observer* [91]. It can be argued that the collection is more secure than the computer or observer individually. It is assumed that an organization communicates with the computer and accepts only those messages that have been approved by the observer. Observer cannot directly talk to the organization. The concept of electronic wallets can be used to design cryptographic protocols that are secure against:

1. *Inflow* – if the computer follows the protocol, the organization cannot send any extra information to the observer no matter how the organization and the observer deviate from the protocol.
2. *Outflow* – if the computer follows the protocol, the observer cannot send any extra information to the organization no matter how the organization and the observer deviate from the protocol.

15.2.4 Other E-Cash Protocols

The Brands e-cash drops the *cut and choose* method to formulate coins. This obviously is reflected in increased efficiency. A similar system of e-cash was also designed by Ferguson [176].

The anonymity of the e-cash discussed so far is tied up with preventing multiple spending. It can be argued that in some circumstances anonymity can be a problem, especially when criminals try to exploit it to their advantage. von Solm and Naccache [514] discussed such scenarios, including perfect blackmailing and money laundering. To relax the anonymity of e-cash, Brickell, Gemmell, and Kravitz [62] introduced a trusted party who collaborates during the generation of coins. The party together with Bank can later cooperate to trace the origin of coins. This is e-cash with escrowing. Jakobsson and Yung [258] showed how an ombudsman may be involved in the e-cash protocol to ensure traceability. M'Raihi [358] presented an efficient e-cash system with a blinding office that plays the role of the independent (from Bank) party who on a valid court order can together with Bank suppress the anonymity of coins.

15.2.5 Micropayments

E-cash requires a substantial computational overhead that is an overkill for payments of small charges, say cents per transaction. Examples of such transactions include reading a WWW site, sending a short e-mail, or using white or yellow pages on the Internet. To support micropayment, the cash generation, withdrawal, and deposit must be significantly simplified so the computational overhead is not expensive. Typically, the generation of a one-cent coin should not cost more than several percent of its nominal value. The most expensive operations are digital signatures so micropayment protocols substitute digital signatures with much cheaper hashing whenever possible.

The parties involved in a micropayment protocol are the clients, the vendors, and a bank. Vendors provide services for which clients pay small fees. The bank registers clients and vendors, maintains their accounts, and debits/credits their accounts. Consider a micropayment protocol, called PayWord, introduced by Rivest and Shamir in [426]. Clients, vendors, and Bank use their secret and public keys for digital signatures. H is a collision-resistant hash function. The PayWord protocol involves a client (Alice), a vendor (Bob), and Bank.

Registration (Alice $\leftrightarrow$ Bank)

1. Alice identifies herself to Bank, opens her account and applies for a PayWord certificate.
2. Bank $\rightarrow$ Alice: $CR = (m, SG_B(m))$
   where $m =$ (Bank-ID, Alice-ID, K_A, expiry date), $SG_B(m)$ is a signature generated by Bank for the message m, and K_A is the public key of Alice.

Payment (Alice $\leftrightarrow$ Bob)

1. Alice creates a chain of paywords (each payword is worth 1 cent) $w_1, w_2, \ldots,$ w_n, where

   $$w_i = H(w_{i+1}),$$

   and w_n is a random payword. The element $w_0 = H(w_1)$ is a commitment or root of the chain.
2. Alice $\rightarrow$ Bob: $(w_0, SG_A(\text{Alice-ID}, \text{Bob-ID}, w_0, \text{time}))$
   where $SG_A(\text{Alice-ID}, \text{Bob-ID}, w_0, \text{time})$ is a signature for the root generated by Alice.
3. Bob verifies the signature and stores the root.
4. Alice $\rightarrow$ Bob: (w_i, i),
   where i is initially set to 1 and incremented each time. Alice pays by revealing the next paywords in the chain.
5. Bob verifies consecutive paywords by checking whether $w_{i-1} = H(w_i)$.

Deposit (Bob $\leftrightarrow$ Bank)

1. Bob $\rightarrow$ Bank: $(w_\ell, \ell), (w_0, SG_A(\text{Alice-ID}, \text{Bob-ID}, w_0, \text{time}))$
   where w_ℓ is the last payword obtained from Alice.
2. Bank verifies the correctness of the last payword. If the chain of paywords generate the root, and the signature is correct, then Bank charges Alice's account ℓ cents and deposits this amount in Bob's account.

The security of the protocol depends on the strength of the digital signature and the collision resistance of the hash algorithm. Payments in the PayWord protocol are very efficient. Time-consuming digital signatures are only applied at the beginning of a payment session. Partial payments by paywords do not need digital signatures. Instead they employ much faster hashing algorithms such as MD5 or HAVAL. The second protocol, MicroMint, considered in [426], completely relies on hashing. Some other micropayment protocols can be found in [8, 359].

15.3 Payment Protocols

We are going to review some implementations of e-cash. For more details, we refer the reader to the book by Furche and Wrightson [190] or, alternatively, to the Web sites of the campanies that offer the payment system.

CAFE. CAFE stands for Conditional Access for Europe and it is a project within the European Union's ESPRIT program [47]. CAFE uses smart cards and electronic devices called wallets. The wallet is a portable computer with its own power supply, keyboard, and display. The wallet can house a tamper-proof smart card (observer) but can be used with or without it. Stores have their point-of-sale (POS) terminals. The communication between wallets and terminals is done using infrared light. Smart cards may also be inserted directly into terminals. CAFE is an offline e-cash protocol based on blind signatures to ensure anonymity. To protect against multiple spending of e-cash, an observer (smart card) is included in the wallet. When the observer is not present or is disabled, the identity of the client is incorporated into the e-cash. If the wallet is lost or stolen, the owner can get a refund by revealing some information about their identity, but only after the e-cash has expired.

eCash^{TM}. Digicash commercialized Chaums's anonymous electronic cash and called it eCash. eCash is a protocol that enables a user to withdraw e-cash and to store it on his local computer. The user can spend his e-cash at any shop that accepts eCash money. The shop can later deposit the money to its account. The following banks offer eCash: Mark Twain Bank of St. Louis (US), Deutsche Bank (Germany), St. George (Australia), Den norske Bank (Norway), and Bank Austria.

Mondex. Mondex (*http://www.mondex.com*) implements e-cash using smart cards. E-cash is stored on a smart card. Transfer of cash is possible from one card to another. The devices used in the protocol are a smart card, a balance reader, a wallet, and a phone set with a reader for the card. The wallet supports card-to-card money transfer. The phone set enables money flow between the card and the bank or can be used to make payments. Payments can be done in exact amounts. For security reasons, the card can be locked using a password-like code. The protocol does not use cryptographic techniques.

NetCash. The protocol was developed by the Information Science Institute at the University of Southern California and is documented at *http://nii-server.isi.edu:80/info/netcash*. The protocol uses e-mail as the communication medium. Electronic cash is a simple token (serial number) that is issued by a bank. The holder of a token can spend it by sending it to the shop via e-mail. The shop deposits the token with the bank. The security of NetCash is low and the protocol can be used for micropayments.

There is also a class of protocols that use credit cards as the main payment facility. Some of the existing protocols are briefly discussed.

CyberCash. CyberCash provides a secure credit card transaction service (available at *http://www.cybercash.com*). CyberCash supplies software for customers and merchants. The customer package is called a wallet. The information flow is protected using 1024-bit RSA encryption. After the customer has downloaded the software, his ID must be attached to the wallet and his credit card number must be binded to it. This information is conveyed via a secure channel to CyberCash. On its side, CyberCash verifies the user identity and his card number.

Assume that a customer has decided to buy some goods from a merchant. The merchant sends information about the purchase to the customer. The information is fed to the customer wallet. The customer indicates to his wallet which credit card to use so the wallet sends the card number to the merchant using encryption. The merchant then contacts a CyberCash server, which takes the transaction information and sends the payment order to the merchant's bank. The merchant's bank talks to the customer's bank and provides details of the payment. The result of the talk is sent back to the CyberCash server that then forwards it in encrypted form to the merchant. A single payment takes no more than 20 seconds.

CyberCash also supports the CyberCoin service. This service is aimed at handling small credit card payments below $10. A customer can transfer coins from his credit account to his wallet and make payments. The transfer of Cyber-Coins is done using encryption. The banks involved and the wallet keep records of all transactions.

First Virtual. This is an electronic fund transfer for credit card payments (see *http://www.fv.com*). To use the facility, a user has to open an account with First Virtual. The account consists of a user name, an e-mail address, and credit card details. A user buying goods from a First Virtual shop gives the shop his or her name and e-mail address. The shop ships the goods and sends the bill to First Virtual who charges the buyer's credit card.

SET. Secure Electronic Transaction (SET) is a protocol developed by Master-Card and VISA with the cooperation of many companies, including IBM, Microsoft, and Netscape. The SET protocol supports credit card payments over the Internet. SET is similar to the CyberCash protocol. The communication of messages in the protocol is encrypted. The encryption keys are distributed by trusted certificate authorities.

A typical payment in SET is initialized by a customer who asks the merchant for both her public key and the public key of her bank payment gateway. The merchant provides the certificates of both keys. The customer first verifies the keys, and after successful verification he generates two messages: order information (OI) and purchase instructions (PI). The OI message is encrypted using the merchant's key. The PI message is encrypted using the payment gateway key. The merchant decrypts the OI and forwards the PI together with his certificate. The gateway decrypts the PI, verifies other payment information, and sends the payment authorization to the customer's bank. The bank approves or declines the payment and communicates this to the gateway that relays it to the merchant.

16 Database Protection and Security

Database management systems are an important part of the operations of most computerized organizations. In many instances the data held within a database carry more value than the hardware and software used to manage and maintain the data. Consequently the privacy and security of data stored within database systems represents a major concern for organizations relying heavily on database management systems.

The subject of database security has been investigated by researchers for a number of years. This chapter aims at providing a general overview of such research and other related developments.

16.1 Database Access Control

A database can be seen as a reservoir of information that is necessary for a continued successful operation of the organization. The organization wants to be sure that data items are accessible to authorized persons only (access control) and that the data correctly reflect the reality (consistency and protection against illegal modification). A careful analysis of security threats and risks associated with them is essential to work out an acceptable security policy. The security policy can be further divided into [14]:

– *Access control policy* – defines the collection of access privileges and access rules. There are two broad classes of access control policy: *mandatory* and *discretionary*. A discretionary access control policy specifies users' privileges relating to different system resources. A mandatory access control policy defines user access to system resources using the user security clearance and the security classification of the resource.

- *Inference policy* – determines which data items have to be protected to eliminate a leakage or disclosure of confidential information (this is important in statistical databases).
- *User identification policy* – specifies the requirements for proper user identification.
- *Accountability and audit policy* – indicates a collection of requirements for the audit control.
- *Consistency policy* – defines the meaning of operational integrity, semantic integrity, and physical integrity of databases.

A security mechanism is an implementation of a security policy. It is crucial to verify to what degree the security features have been incorporated into the mechanism. The process of verification of security mechanisms can be performed according to some existing evaluation criteria (see the White Book [382] or Canadian Book [381]).

All resources in a computer system can be divided into (active) subjects and (passive) objects. The way a subject acts on an object is called the access privilege or right. Access privileges can allow a user to manipulate objects (read, write, execute, delete, modify, etc.) or to modify the access permissions (transfer ownership, grant and revoke privileges, etc.). Note that for each pair (subject, object), the access control policy assigns a collection of access rights. The assignment can be explicit (*positive authorization*) or implicit (*negative authorization*). In positive authorization, an entry (subject, object) consists of privileges that are explicitly allowed. In negative authorization, an entry (subject, object) contains a collection of privileges that are explicitly denied.

Now we briefly introduce the basic vacabulary. A *data model* is a general description of the structure of a database, i.e., the data types, relations, and constraints existing in the database. There are two main categories of data models.

- *Physical* (*low-level*) – the data model describes the way data is stored in the computer system.
- *Conceptual* (*high-level*) – the data model reflects the way users see data.

The smallest identifiable entity in a physical database is a *data item*. Typically it is a number or a string of characters that expresses some information (distance between cities, surname of a person, etc.). An entity in the real world is described by providing more specific information about its attributes, such as color, shape, length, etc. An ordered sequence of data items is called a *physical record*. The *physical database* is a collection of stored physical records that also may include pointers that are used to reference other records.

A *relational database model* uses a set-theoretic relation defined over a Cartesian product of domains. Each domain is a set of values. A relation can be seen simply as a table with rows (called tuples) and columns (called attributes).

16.2 Security Filters

The idea of a filter mechanism for database security was probably one of the earliest to appear because of its simplicity. Given a database system to be protected, it is only natural to initially think of a trusted intermediary between the user and the database system in the form of a filter that simply screens-out data according to some policy for labeling data.

Filters can be used to provide security services, such as

− integrity checking,
− concealment of sensitive data,
− access control.

For integrity checking, a checksum is attached to incoming data, and the data, together with the checksum, is stored in the database. If the integrity checking is designed to detect changes due to storage errors, then checksums can be generated by hash functions (such as MD5 or SHA-1, for instance). If data is to be resistant against modification by a malicious attacker, then checksums must be created using MACs (encrypted hash values) or digital signatures. The former option is preferred if the filter uses private-key cryptosystem. The latter option is time- and resource-consuming and can be applied for databases with multiple trusted filters (multiple entry points). Note that integrity checking does not prevent duplication and removal of data.

Concealment of data is normally implemented using encryption. Encryption in databases should be used carefully and is normally restricted to a specific attribute or a sequence of attributes. Note that encrypted attributes cannot be interpreted correctly and therefore query processing is usually impossible for encrypted data.

Filters control access to databases by reformatting user queries. This approach is applied if:

- The modified query can be processed more quickly (say, several queries are merged and processed together for an efficiency gain). The obtained data are later screened out so the users get only the data they are authorized to access.
- The query must be modified, taking into account the user authorization and the previous queries generated by the user. This is especially important in statistical databases where the private data of individuals is protected by law. The filter in this case restricts user queries if there is a possibility that private data may be derived from the current and previous queries.

Stand-alone filters do not make much sense from a management point of view. They have to be integrated with

- The database (creating the so-called *trusted front-ends*). In this case, their security features are part of the overall database security and are governed by the DBMS (database management system).
- The user (incorporated into a user application that creates an interface to the database). The filter may perform a variety of security tasks depending on the security requirements imposed by the user. For instance, the filter encrypts (or decrypts) all data transmitted to (or from) the database for backup purposes (a user traveling with her laptop and using the database for backup).

In discussing the use of filters with checksums to provide data integrity in the database it must be understood that only the detection of illegal modification is possible, and the remedy for this problem is simply to use the backups of the database files. Filters with integrity checking fail to address the following problems:

- Undetected modification for long periods of time. If the illegally modified data is hardly ever used, and thus its checksum is never verified, it can remain in the database for a long period of time and will be present in every backup since the time of the unnoticed modification. This renders the backup useless as a solution to the problem of illegal modification. The solution to this problem is to perform checksum verifications of all modified data before a backup is created.
- High occurrence of illegal tampering. If the backup solution is used to remedy this problem, then a high level of occurrence of illegal tampering means that the backup must be used more often. In real-time systems, this results in an intolerable performance degradation.

Filters with encryption try to reconcile two contradictory requirements: encrypted data should require as little structure as possible but at the same time the structure of the data must be preserved in order to process queries. Apart from this:

– Encryption expands the size of short data items. To avoid unnecessary expansion of data sizes, short data items can be clustered, leading to an evident loss of structure (clustered data are no longer visible for query processing).
– Encryption is unable to detect tampering, such as duplication of (encrypted) data, swapping (encrypted) data, etc. Again, to make tampering detectable, integrity protection must be incorporated.

Access control filters are defenseless against such threats as Trojan Horses, worms, viruses, and groups of conspiring users whose individual behaviors comply with the access control rules while jointly they can break the security.

16.3 Encryption Methods

The use of cryptographic techniques or encryption for database systems represents another important security mechanism. Data is stored in the database system in an encrypted form, hence illegal users cannot read or modify the data. Encryption should be done in a lower-level security mechanism that is applicable independent of the type of policy used in the database system. Although some authors have suggested that, because encryption is very secure, the database system need not be a trusted one [142], encryption should be used together with other security components in an integrated manner. Encryption on its own does not secure the database system since many loopholes may still exist within the operating system and the database system itself. Hence the effective use of encryption depends on the architecture or configuration of the database system that incorporates it. In general, encryption in database systems has other advantages, some of which are:

– Encryption provides the last line of defence against any attack by an opponent.
– Encryption of data in the database presents a "deterrent" to attackers. Access to the encrypted data without knowledge of some suitable cryptographic

information is equivalent to access by an attacker to an encrypted communications line. Without the suitable cryptographic information it may be very difficult or impossible to convert the cryptograms into plaintext.

The disadvantage of encrypted databases is that record searching, particularly in the case of partial-match and range queries, becomes inflexible unless secure auxiliary information that maintains the positions of records or fields in the database is kept.

Encryption can be applied to three levels of data granularity, namely to whole tuples (records), whole attributes (fields) and to individual data elements. The encryption of whole attributes results in the need to decrypt the entire column or attribute in the relation if a single tuple is selected, hence it can be immediately dismissed as being too inflexible and resource-consuming. The next alternative would be to encrypt whole tuples, in which case every record needs to be decrypted during projections of certain attributes. In general, given an unconditionally secure cryptosystem, the best alternative is to encrypt individual data elements. This allows selections and projections in the normal manner. This alternative may result in the expansion of the tuples, and thus the database. With the continual decrease in the cost of storage media this issue will not be a problem. In the following, the various database encryption schemes that have been designed by researchers in the area of database security are presented.

DES-based encryption. In [141] Denning used the DES algorithm [383] for the encryption and authentication of fields within a record. Each field is encrypted using a distinct cryptographic key. The scheme assumes that the unique record identifier in the first field of each record is at most 8 bytes long and is left as plaintext. This ensures that record searching can be performed without loss of flexibility.

The encryption key for each field j of record i with a unique record identifier R_i and field identifier F_j is $K_{ij} = g(R_i, F_j, K)$, where g is a *key generating function* based on a secret database key K. Five ways are proposed to create the key generator g:

- $K_{ij} = E_{K_j}(R_i)$ with $K_j = E_K(F_j)$,
- $K_{ij} = R_i \oplus K_j$ with $K_j = E_K(F_j)$,
- $K_{ij} = E_{K_i}(F_j)$ with $K_i = E_K(R_i)$,

$- K_{ij} = K_i \oplus F_j$ with $K_i = E_K(R_j)$,
$- K_{ij} = E_K(R_i \oplus F_j)$,

where $\oplus$ is the exclusive-OR operator and E_K denotes encryption using key K. By using any of the five key generating functions the unique identifiers are padded until all 8 bytes (64 bits) are filled. Out of the five generators the first and the second provide the highest level of security but are the least efficient. The third and the fourth generators are the most efficient but suffer the problem of multiple key exposures due to key compromises. In addition, all five generators suffer from the possibility of producing weak keys, in which case unused bits in the identifier can be set to 1 or 0 randomly to increase security.

The encryption and decryption of a field M_{ij} uses the DES cryptosystem, and in the case that it is less than 8 bytes long it is simply replicated until all 8 bytes are full. In the case that M_{ij} is longer than 8 bytes, it is encrypted using cipher block chaining with an initialization block I. Since the keys are secret and never repeat, block I need not be distinct for every record, and in this scheme it is proposed that I be set to the all-zero block. This produces the effect of having a single block encrypted in standard block mode being equivalent to that block encrypted in cipher block chaining with it as the first block.

Note that field encryption may cause expansion in the field size. Furthermore, in searching for a particular field j, all the fields must be decrypted first. A possible modification of this scheme is to incorporate a checksum to detect illegal records or field substitution. The checksum for field M_{ij} is computed using a key that is a function of the record identifier R_i, field identifier F_i, and the secret database key K.

Subkeys encryption model. Davida, Wells, and Kam [122] used a subkeys model or method that is based on the Chinese Remainder Theorem. The theorem asserts that given r positive integers $m_1, m_2, \ldots, m_r$ that are relatively coprime and given r integers $a_1, a_2, \ldots, a_r$, then the congruence $x \equiv a_i \bmod m_i$ ($i = 1, \ldots, r$) has a common solution. The idea in the subkeys model is that the equation $C_i \equiv a_j \bmod d_j$ is associated with records and fields. C_i corresponds to the encrypted records, a_j corresponds to the fields within a record, and d_j corresponds to the decrypting keys for field j. Here d_j are large primes and a_j are any integers. Hence d_j become the subkeys in the system and the field values a_j can be recovered by calculating:

$$C_i \equiv \sum_{j=1}^{n} e_j(x_j \| f_{ji}) \bmod D$$

where

$$D = \prod_{j=1}^{n} d_j,$$

f_{ji} is the value for field j of record i (f_{ji} is a data item) and $\|$ stands for concatenation. A random number x_j is generated for field j and is concatenated to f_{ji}. This concatenation must result in a number less than d_j. Encryption is performed by using the key e_j, where

$$e_j \equiv (D/d_j)b_j \bmod d_j,$$

and where

$$b_j \equiv (D/d_j)^{\varphi(d_j)-1} \bmod d_j$$

is the inverse of (D/d_j) modulo d_j and $\varphi(d_j)$ is the Euler totient function of d_j.

In order to decrypt field j in a record C_i using key d_j the following calculation is performed:

$$C_i \equiv (x_j \| f_{ji}) \bmod d_j$$

($j = 1, \ldots, n$). That is, we calculate $C_i \bmod d_j$ to get $(x_j \| f_{ji})$ and we remove the random bits x_j to get the actual data item f_{ji}.

One disadvantage of the system is that the whole record must be re-encrypted after any field is updated. This is done to counter the known plain-text attack by a malicious user. The subkeys method for record encryption was shown to permit some database operations, such as *project* and *join*, in further work by Davida and Yeh [123]. The realization of the subkeys method and further extensions and improvements to increase its security can be found in the results of Omar and Wells [392]. The extensions consist of placing an encryption/decryption (E/D) unit at the user's terminal and a *locator* unit between the database management software and the encrypted database. The subkeys and a user-field capability matrix exist inside the locator. Users are allowed to access the database vertically (fields) and horizontally (records or tuples). Before any interaction with the database management system, a public key scheme is used to ensure the security of key transfers between the locator and the E/D unit. The work by Wells and Eastman in [524] is related to research into the subkeys model, and represents effort on traffic analysis of encrypted databases.

The reader is directed to the last three cited works for further information on the model.

Composed encryption functions. A method put forward by Wagner [516] consists of a two-stage encryption method for databases where no single agency or device can encrypt or decrypt data directly. It allows users to choose their own keys while all data in the database are finally encrypted using a secret key. The system employs a trusted central authority or *Data Distributor* (DD) that holds a complementary key for each user. Before accessing any part of the database a user n must cooperate with another user i ($i < n$) who acts as a *sponsor* to user n. In this scheme the first user (user 1) has a special position in that he or she chooses half of the random key for the database encryption (user 1 is preferably a trusted user, such as the database administrator). User 1 then becomes the sponsor of user 2, and so on. The RSA cryptosystem and DES are suitable as cryptosystems for this model.

The first step in the method is to perform key distribution where user 1 chooses a random secret X and the Data Distributor chooses also a random secret Y. User 1 then chooses his or her encryption key K_1 and finds its inverse (decryption key K_1^{-1}) modulo $\varphi(N)$, where N is a large prime (public). User 1 then calculates

$$Z_1 \equiv K_1^{-1} X \bmod \varphi(N),$$

and sends Z_1 to the Data Distributor who calculates

$$L_1 \equiv Z_1 Y \bmod \varphi(N)$$

secretly. Note that L_1 is in fact

$$L_1 \equiv K_1^{-1} XY \bmod \varphi(N),$$

and all data M is later encrypted as $M^{XY} \bmod N$. The value $L_i \equiv K_i^{-1} XY \bmod \varphi(N)$ is stored in secret and is used later for access to the database by the user i. Also note that user 1 does not have a sponsor, hence he or she should be a trusted user or database administrator.

The key distribution for user n is the following. User n chooses a secret random pair U and V and calculates his or her key $K_n = UV$. He or she then sends V to the Data Distributor. User n then chooses a sponsor user i ($i < n$) and sends U to user i. User i calculates the inverse U^{-1} of U modulo $\varphi(N)$ and calculates

$$Z_n \equiv U^{-1} K_i \bmod \varphi(N)$$

on behalf of user n. In this step, the sponsor has attached his or her own key K_i. The sponsor then sends Z_n to the Data Distributor. The Data Distributor now has both V and Z_n, and proceeds to find the inverse V^{-1} of V modulo $\varphi(N)$. Next, the Data Distributor calculates

$$L_n \equiv V^{-1} Z_n L_i \bmod \varphi(N),$$

and stores L_n in a secure place. This means that in fact L_n reduces to

$$L_n \equiv K_n^{-1} XY \bmod \varphi(N).$$

The storage and retrieval of data M is performed as follows: User n stores data M by encrypting it using his or her key K_n and forms cryptogram $C' \equiv M^{K_n} \bmod N$. This cryptogram is then given to the Data Distributor who further encrypts it using L_n, producing C, where $C \equiv (C')^{L_n} \bmod N$. Thus:

$$C \equiv (C')^{L_n} \equiv (M^{K_n})^{Z_n Y} \equiv M^{XY} \bmod N.$$

User n can retrieve data M by asking the Data Distributor to decrypt C into C''. The Data Distributor first fetches the secret value L_n corresponding to user n and computes the inverse L_n^{-1} of L_n modulo $\varphi(N)$. Then the cryptogram C'' is calculated using:

$$C'' \equiv C^{L_n^{-1}} \bmod N,$$

and the Data Distributor passes C'' to user n. User n then finds M from C'' using K_n^{-1} using

$$M \equiv (C'')^{K_n^{-1}} \equiv (C^{L_n^{-1}})^{K_n^{-1}} \equiv ((M^{XY})^{(K_n^{-1} XY)^{-1}})^{K_n^{-1}} \bmod N.$$

One advantage of this method is the ease in changing the user keys. When user n wants to get a new key, he or she must choose a random secret V and send it to the Data Distributor who calculates its inverse V^{-1} modulo $\varphi(N)$. The Data Distributor then updates the secret L_n corresponding to user n and generates

$$L_n' \equiv V^{-1} L_n \bmod \varphi(N),$$

and user n updates his or her key K_n into

$$K_n' \equiv V K_n \bmod \varphi(N).$$

Another advantage is the restructuring of the list of L_i values when that list is compromised. The Data Distributor simply chooses a secret random W and for each L_i in the list a new one is generated:

$$L_i' \equiv WL_i \bmod \varphi(N).$$

All ciphertext C in the database is then encrypted into $\overline{C}$ by performing $\overline{C} \equiv C^W \bmod N$. Encryption and decryption of data by users then proceeds as before.

Polynomial-based encryption. Cooper, Hyslop, and Patterson [105] suggested a method for database encryption based on polynomials in the field $GF(p)$, where p is prime. The contents of the database are viewed as consisting of fixed-length character strings. These are in turn made up of substrings and users can have access to a select subset of these substrings, as in the usual situation where users may only have access to a subset of the records in the database.

Let the substrings S_i $(i = 1, \ldots, n)$ be concatenated into a single long string S. The long string is then encrypted using the following procedure. For the selected plaintext alphabet, a prime $p \geq c$ is chosen, where c is the number of characters in the alphabet. A bijection is then constructed from the plaintext alphabet to the integers in field $GF(p)$. Hence, under the bijection the representative substring belonging to users will correspond to the set of integers between 0 and $p - 1$. Each sequence of integers S_k is then used to form a polynomial $S_k(x)$ in x of degree at most $d = l - 1$ where l is the length of the representative sequence S_k. A finite field $GF_k = GF(p^l)$ is then generated using an irreducible polynomial $I_k(x)$ such that it contains $S_k(x)$ as its element. Following this, a secret polynomial $R_k(x)$ is calculated for each finite field GF_k, and is multiplied to produce the polynomial $T_k(x)$ as follows:

$$T_k(x) \equiv S_k(x)R_k(x) \bmod I_k(x).$$

Encryption for the representative record S is equivalent to finding a polynomial $A(x)$ using the Chinese Remainder Theorem, where

$$A(x) \equiv T_k(x) \bmod I_k(x)$$

for $k = 1, \ldots, n$. Decryption of a sequence S_k is performed by dividing $A(x)$ by $I_k(x)$, resulting in the remainder $T_k(x)$. This remainder is further multiplied by $R_k^{-1}(x)$, producing the required $S_k(x)$ that can be inverted back to the original plaintext using the initial bijection.

In [42] Blakley and Meadows present an encryption scheme that allows the encrypted data to be used in some statistical computation involving counts, sums, and higher-order moments. Given a Galois Field $GF(\pi)$ where π is a large prime, the ith record of the database is encrypted as the polynomial p_i, where each p_i is constructed so that $p_i(c_j)$ is the jth data element of the ith record $(i = 1, \ldots, d)$. Here the k fields are represented by the elements $c_1, \ldots, c_k$ of the Galois Field $GF(\pi)$.

A user who is authorized to access all the fields in a record can be given one polynomial and all c_j $(j = 1, \ldots, k)$. A user with access to a given number of fields of all the records gets all polynomials but only one c_j. A user who is authorized to know the sum or the average value of the projection of the jth field can calculate

$$\bar{p} = \sum_{i=1}^{d} p_i,$$

and evaluate it at c_j and divide by d. Here the division by d is over the reals and the summation is over $GF(\pi)$. The reader is directed to [42] for further notes on how to encrypt the polynomials and how to do other statistical computations.

Joint encryption and error-control. In [364] Nam and Rao present a database encryption scheme that allows decryption and the control of errors in the database. The scheme is called the Residue-Coded Cryptosystem (RCC) and is based on residue codes that provide an error detection capability based on (n, k) residue codes. Error detection is a very attractive option for distributed databases in which data in the form of records must be sent between sites through a communications medium that is subject to noise and to illegal tampering.

Given a plaintext M that has one field per record, the encrypted ciphertext C consists of n residues, including $(n - k)$ error-control residues. Thus,

$$C = C_1, \ldots, C_k, C_{k+1}, \ldots, C_n,$$

where $C_1, \ldots, C_k$ are the information residues and $C_{k+1}, \ldots, C_n$ are the error-control residues. The encryption stage consists of the selection of n encryption keys $d_1, \ldots, d_n$ (relatively prime integers) for each $C_1, \ldots, C_n$, respectively, where

$$\prod_{i=1}^{k} d_i \geq \max(M) \cdot Z_c$$

and

$$d_{k+j} > d_i$$

for $j = 1, \ldots, n-k$ and $i = 1, \ldots, k$, where Z_c is an integer employed for security and $\max(M)$ is the maximum value of M. Thus, the n pieces of information take the following form:

$$C_i \equiv (Z \parallel M) \bmod d_i$$

for $i = 1, \ldots, n$, where Z is a fixed length random number less that Z_c, and $\parallel$ denotes concatenation.

The decryption stage consists of the calculation of Z concatenated to M as follows:

$$Z \parallel M \equiv (\sum_{i=1}^{k} e_i C_i) \bmod D$$

where

$$D = \prod_{i=1}^{k} d_i.$$

The decryption key e_i is calculated as:

$$e_i = \frac{D}{d_i} b_i,$$

where b_i is the inverse of D/d_i modulo d_i, and

$$\frac{D}{d_i} \times b_i \equiv 1 \bmod d_i.$$

The value M can then be retrieved from the concatenation $Z \parallel M$.

The syndrome computation and error control can be done depending on the setup of the scheme. Thus, for a single residue error correction capability the ciphertext would then require a two-error-control residue. The syndrome vector can be computed in the following manner:

$$S_i \equiv (C - \overline{M}) \bmod d_i$$

for $i = k + 1, n$. Here $\overline{M} = Z \parallel M$ before the M is extracted out of the concatenation. We are assured that no errors have occurred when $S_i = 0$ for all the syndrome vectors. The reader is directed to the work by Nam and Rao [364] for further information on the scheme, and a comparison of the scheme with the Subkeys Model in [122].

16.3.1 Privacy Homomorphisms

A major hassle with encryption for information protection in databases is the necessity for decryption every time information is needed for either processing or retrieval. It can be argued that during processing the decryption can be eliminated if operations can be performed on cryptograms. In other words, instead of clear data, the operation uses ciphertext and generates a cryptogram of the result that can then be decrypted during retrieval.

Given an operation $OP : \mathcal{M}^n \to \mathcal{M}$ that takes n arguments and produces a result from the set $\mathcal{M}$ and a cryptographic algorithm defined by its encryption and decryption functions E_k and D_k, respectively, it is said that a cryptographic transformation-preserves an operation OP on n variables if

$$OP(m_1, \ldots, m_n) = D_k(OP(E_k(m_1), \ldots, E_k(m_n)))$$

for each cryptographic key $k \in \mathcal{K}$. This concept can be extended to algebraic fields when a cryptographic algorithm preserves both field operations $\langle +, \times \rangle$. Different candidates for cryptographic transformation-preserving field operations are discussed in [456]. If processing involves not only addition and multiplication but other operations, such as comparison operations, then the class of cryptographic transformations preserving the operations is rather small and thus its practical usage is limited.

Rivest, Adleman, and Dertouzos [427] defined a broader class of cryptographic transformations that preserve operations and called them *privacy homomorphisms*. The class of privacy homomorphisms is defined as the quadruple

$$(E_K, D_K, OP, OP^*)$$

such that

$$OP(m_1, \ldots, m_n) = D_k(OP^*(E_k(m_1), \ldots, E_k(m_n)))$$

for each cryptographic key k and any sequence of $m_1, \ldots, m_n$ in the message space $\mathcal{M}$. OP and OP^* are operations that are permissible in the message and cryptogram spaces, respectively. Notice that the definition says that we get the correct result after decryption of the operation OP^*.

Recall that the enciphering transformation in the RSA system is $E_e(m) = m^e p \bmod N$, where e is the enciphering key, m is the message, and the modulus $N = pq$ (p, q are primes). Note that:

$$E_e(m_1 \cdot m_2) = (m_1 \cdot m_2)^e = m_1^e \cdot m_2^e = E_e(m_1) \cdot E_e(m_2).$$

Thus, the enciphering transformation of the RSA system has the multiplication property. In other words, it is possible to define the multiplicative homomorphism (E_e, D_d, OP, OP^*) for which E_e, D_d are cryptographic transformations defined in the RSA system and $OP = OP^*$. This privacy homomorphism is as secure as the RSA system.

Other protection methods. An interesting idea was presented by Brandt, Damgard, and Landrock [58] whereby individuals can submit data concerning themselves to a centralized database without the need to trust the register of the database. The data of each individual is protected from the others, and each individual has the power to ensure that data about him or her in the register database is correct and not modified illegally. This scheme applies very attractively in scenarios such as in centralized medical databases with data from various hospitals, and in centralized government taxation databases. Given a number of institutions which have to send data about a particular individual to the centralized database, the scheme aims at keeping the individual *anonymous* and making the registration *verifiable*.

Carroll and Jurgensen [77] present a relational database structure in which access is controlled by cryptographic means, while data in the database are stored in an encrypted format. Information about the clearance of users is placed in individual *user profiles* that can be hierarchical and non-hierarchical. A number of rules concerning *read*, *write*, and *read/write* operations are also suggested. The results of a simulation are also provided, which indirectly point out the practical difficulties of the ⋆-property of the Bell-La Padula security model [19, 20]. Based on the access control mechanism and the database encryption scheme a formal model of systems security is also provided.

16.4 Database Machines and Architectures

Database machines or database computers provide some advantages in security depending on their configuration with respect to the host operating system. Following the work by Hsiao [247] and by Henning and Walker [236], the four database machine architectures that may provide security are:

- *Intelligent disk controller* – Here the database management system resides on the host computer and employs the main memory of the host, but interacts with the intelligent controller. The controller usually has built into it enough processing logic so that raw data can be preprocessed before it is placed in the main memory of the host [247]. The security of the database provided by this architecture depends heavily on the security mechanisms provided by the host operating system. This includes user authentication that is performed by the host operating system. The advantage of this configuration comes from the increase in performance due to the speed of data retrieval by the controller, independent of the data storage mechanisms of the host. In this case it is required that the path between the controller and the host be a trusted one.

– *Host-independent hardware back-end database machine* – All security responsibilities belong to the database machine. All access can be controlled by the machine since it is physically separated from the host (front-end) computer. The database management routines and the online I/O capabilities are built into hardware, thus offering an increase in performance during normal database operations. The back-end machine only receives the queries and returns answers to the host computer [247]. User authentication may be performed independent of the authentication by the host operating system. The back-end machine must rely on the operating system to pass to it data and queries from users, hence a trusted path must exist between the back-end and the host. Such a database machine would be trusted to a level at least equal to the highest level of trust in the host operating system.

– *Software back-end database machine* – A software approach can be taken in the implementation of a back-end database system, in which all database management tasks and online I/O routines are performed by software residing in a standalone general-purpose computer. In this manner the resources of the host operating system are free from any database functions. The security of the database system in this configuration follows the security of the operating system, hence portability to different hosts may prove to be difficult. Additional security measures can be implemented on the back-end computer independent of the security measures of the host.

– *Multiback-end software database machine* – The software-based back-end database machines can be adapted to a multiprocessor multiback-end configuration. The same piece of software can be used in all instances of the back-end without requiring any modifications to the hardware. A software control module is located between the single host and the multiple back-ends. In a multilevel security classification of data each back-end can be used to store data of differing sensitivity. The software control module can then route queries to these back-ends depending on the security clearance of the user. In terms of performance this configuration allows queries to be processed in parallel. However, the very nature of replicated data makes the control of these back-ends difficult. The security of this configuration is no different to that of the single back-end software database machine. However, the fact that one back-end may interact with another in the course of processing a query means that a covert channel may also exist between the back-ends.

16.4.1 Experimental Back-end Database Systems

Two of the early experimental systems using back-end database systems are the *Data Base Computer* (DBC) [13] developed at Ohio State University, and MULTISAFE [510] developed by Virginia Tech and the University of South Carolina.

MULTISAFE. In MULTISAFE [510] the data management system is divided functionally into three major hardware-software modules. These are the *User and Application Module* (UAM), the *Protection and Security Module* (PSM), and the data *Storage and Retrieval Module* (SRM). Logically, each of these modules is separated, but physically they may be implemented on the same underlying hardware. However, performance needs suggest that each module should be implemented on physically different processors. Although the three modules are treated as separate and independent processes, they are precisely connected to achieve a combination of multiprocessing, pipelining, and parallelism.

The UAM is essentially the interface between the user and the system. The UAM can be realized in a number of ways. It can be seen as a large conventional multiprogrammed processor with disjoint user address space or it can be viewed as a collection of intelligent terminals, each with a private memory and processor. Independent of its actual implementation, the UAM has the task of analyzing user queries and formatting results, and providing working storage and computation abilities to the user. The UAM does not provide any security or I/O tasks to the user.

The PSM encapsulates the security mechanism away from the other modules. It makes access decisions based on three dependency classes:

– *Data-independent access* – This access condition depends on user and/or terminal identification information and dynamic system variables.

– *Data-definition-dependent access.* This access depends on attribute names and relations, independent of their actual value.
– *Data-value-dependent access* – This requires the checking of attribute values before any access.

The PSM is dedicated to security-related tasks and is free from any operating system or database system functions. This includes audit-trail maintenance, integrity checking, cryptographic functions, and the control of backup and recovery.

The SRM is dedicated to perform database accesses on behalf of the UAM and PSM. The SRM processor can be realized in terms of conventional computer hardware and/or a conventional DBMS software. Alternatively, a back-end processor or a database machine can be employed. The SRM can perform other additional tasks, such as data manipulation operations and the materialization of database views. Furthermore, it can maintain private files associated with other non-DBMS applications belonging to the user. The reader is directed to [510] for more information on the communication of messages between the modules of MULTISAFE and other security-related issues.

Data Base Computer (DBC). The Ohio State University Data Base Computer (DBC) [13] employs the idea of back-end computers and associative processors. The developers of DBC recognized a number of problems found in common database systems in relation to data security. Some of the problems they set out to solve are:

– the complexity of name-mapping operations in answering queries,
– the performance bottleneck caused by different functional software modules being implemented on the same underlying hardware,
– the data security overhead due to the need to perform multiple name-mapping operations in order to enforce security.

The key design concepts employed in the DBC to overcome these problems include the use of a *partitioned content-addressable memory* (PCAM), the use of *structure and mass memories, area pointers, functional specification, look-aside buffering*, and the *integration of security* into the design. The aim of the PCAM is to reduce the need for name-mapping data structures. The PCAM is implemented by splitting a storage system into many blocks or *partitions*.

Name-mapping data structures for these blocks is based on the *structure memory* concept, in which a *mass memory* holds the information making up the database and contains only *update invariant* name-mapping data structures. The structure memory and the mass memory in the DBC are implemented as PCAMs. Name-mapping data structures are simplified using the concept of *area pointers*. A given area pointer shows which PCAM partition holds a required data item, and no modification needs to be done on an area pointer when data items are moved.

In order to minimize the difficulties met during the modification of name-mapping data structures a fast *look-aside buffer* is employed. Before any change is recorded permanently in the structure memory, it is first recorded in this buffer and is used to satisfy subsequent commands.

To overcome the bottleneck found on many database systems that employ software modules, the DBC has taken the approach of *functional specialization*. Here, components are designed individually to adapt to their specified functions. The DBC has seven major specialized components. These are the *keyword transformation unit* (KXU), the *structure memory* (SM), the *mass memory* (MM), the *structure memory information processor* (SMIP), the *index translation unit* (IXU), the *database command and control processor* (DBCCP), and the *security filter processor* (SFP). The system operation consist of two "loops," namely, the *structure loop* and the *data loop*, which have the DBCCP in common. The incoming request from the *Program Execution Unit* (PES) is passed through the KXU that converts keywords into their internal form, and structural information about the database is retrieved and maintained by the SM. Set operations on the structural information are performed by the SMIP. Both the SM and the SMIP are implemented using PCAMs. The structural information from the SMIP is then decoded by the IXU and the results returned to the DBCCP. The data retrieval and update is then performed in the data loop. The MM contains the database and the SFP performs the necessary security checks.

Although the DBC initially employed the relational model, simulation studies shows that it is also suitable for network and hierarchical data models [234].

16.5 Database Views

The concept and implementation of views in the broad area of database systems has been a topic of research for a number of years [79, 497, 436, 543, 273]. Interest in the use of views for purely security purposes only began in the early 1980s. One of the earliest uses of views was by Griffiths and Wade [220] in IBM's System R as a form of access control. This early work, however, concentrated on a single security classification and attempted mainly to solve the problem of grant propagation in a multiuser database system. The use of views for multilevel security in database systems was independently suggested in 1983 by Claybrook [98] and by the Summer Study on Multilevel Database Management Systems coordinated by the US Air Force Summer Studies Board [104].

In order to understand the possible uses of views as security objects, it is useful to define views and to briefly look at the related terminology. Although views are not strictly defined over the relational data model, the best examples can be given using this data model and the syntax of the Structured Query Language or SQL [121]. The general form of a SQL query is the following:

$$\textbf{select } att_1, att_2, \ldots, att_n$$
$$\textbf{from } rel_1, rel_2, \ldots, rel_m$$
$$\textbf{where } pred$$

Here, att_i are the attributes, rel_i the database relations, and $pred$ is the predicate. The attributes can also be replaced by a (*), meaning that the whole tuple (record) with all its attributes are to be retrieved.

A *view* can be defined to be a preset or predefined named retrieval query that creates a *virtual relation* over *base relations*. The view or virtual relation is not stored in the database, whereas the base relations are the underlying data stored in the database. Once created, a view can be queried as if it were a true relation. Views can be built upon other views, and so on. For example, in [98] Claybrook presents an architecture whereby an internal view is defined over the database, then a conceptual view is in turn defined over the internal view, and finally the multiple user-defined views are defined over the conceptual view.

Using the SQL notation, the following is an example of the creation of a view V, which is then queried by a user:

create view V **as**

> **select** $att_1, att_2, \ldots, att_n$
>> **from** $rel_1, rel_2, \ldots, rel_m$
>> **where** $pred_{view-def}$

> **select** $att_{i1}, att_{i2}, \ldots, att_{ik}$
>> **from** V
>> **where** $pred_{user}$

During query processing, the user query over view V is resolved internally into:

> **select** $att_{i1}, att_{i2}, \ldots, att_{ik}$
>> **from** $rel_1, rel_2, \ldots, rel_m$
>> **where** $pred_{view-def}$ **and** $pred_{user}$

There are a number of concepts and terminology that are often used in discussing views and database security in general. Following the notation found in Wilson [534] and Denning et al. [143] we use the following:

– A *security level* is a pair (H, S) where H is a hierarchical security classification and S is a set of categories or compartments [534].

An example of a classification is *Confidential* < *Secret* < *Top Secret*, and examples of categories include *Crypto*, *NATO*, and others. An alternate notation is given in [143] where a security level is the pair

$\langle SecrecyLevel, SecurityCategory \rangle$

which is also defined to be the *secrecy component* of an *access class*. The *integrity component* of an access class is given as

$\langle IntegrityLevel, IntegrityCategory \rangle$

– The security level (H_1, S_1) *dominates* the security level (H_2, S_2), or

$(H_1, S_1) \geq (H_2, S_2)$

when $H_1 \geq H_2$ and $S_2 \subseteq S_1$.

That is, a given security level L_1 *dominates* the security level L_2 when the set of categories for L_1 is a superset of the set defined for L_2 and categories from L_1 are at least as sensitive as those from L_2. When L_1 *strictly dominates* L_2 ($L_1 > L_2$) we have that ($L_1 \geq L_2$) and ($L_1 \neq L_2$). Hence the symbol $\geq$ denotes partial ordering [534]. Equivalently, *access classes* [143] can be seen as an element of a lattice structure having the $\geq$ partial ordering, where *access class* L_1 *dominates* (or *strictly dominates*) another *access class* L_2.

– A *subject* is an active entity that accesses *objects* in accordance with a security policy.

In the case of views in databases, the subject may be a process executing on behalf of a user, and the objects are various views defined over the base relations and other views [534]. The subject or user has *clearance* or an associated *access class* [143], and the clearance (or access class) of a subject must dominate the *classification* (or access class) of the data before the subject has access to the data.

16.5.1 Advantages and Disadvantages of Views

There are a number of advantages using views for security objects in database systems. The first and foremost is the fact that views express the context of the data over which it is defined, and it is important that both the context and the data itself need to be protected. In its simplest form views present a subset of the database to the user, be it whole tuples or whole field attributes. Any change in the underlying base relation does not require a corresponding modification to the view definition over that base relation. Thus, views are very much static even while the database is dynamically changing. This advantage is derived from the fact that views can be defined independently of the logical structure and design of the database [98].

Views also provide content-dependent security where certain field (or attribute) values can be placed in the view definitions and the records (or tuples) containing those values can be hidden from certain users or groups of users. The opposite effect can be achieved by allowing only tuples containing certain attribute values to be displayed to the user. Content-dependent security further implies that only correct values or values within a given range can be inserted into the database via views. In this way users have less chance of inserting inappropriate values by chance or deliberately.

Another advantage of views is that labeling of attributes and tuples can be done by creating a separate attribute containing the security labels. Thus, the labels can be stored as part of a relation or as a separate relation, and their existence can be hidden away from the user through the use of views. Hence, it is clear that the database system need not have any special mechanism to coordinate labeling of attributes and tuples. An example of an attribute for storing labels is the following [534]:

$$\textbf{create view } V_{level \leq L} \textbf{ as}$$
$$\textbf{select } *$$
$$\textbf{from } R$$
$$\textbf{where } LabelAttribute \leq L$$

In this example R is the relation while $LabelAttribute$ is the attribute of R containing the labels of the tuples in R. If the views are defined using the SQL syntax then conditional expressions can be included in the view definition:

$$\textbf{create view } Salaries_{unclassified} \textbf{ as}$$
$$\textbf{select } Name, DepartmentNumber,$$
$$UnclassifiedSalary =$$
$$\textbf{if } Salary \leq 10000$$
$$\textbf{then } Salary$$
$$\textbf{else } F(Salary)$$
$$\textbf{from } Employees$$

where F can be a function that performs some operation on the $Salary$ attribute. F can also be a *sanitization operation* or function [143] that is defined to be a computation that takes inputs from a source and outputs data that is less sensitive than the source. Besides sanitization functions, other built-in functions can also be used inside the view definition. Examples of these are functions that return the machine time and date, and user identification.

Although views have many advantages, there are some shortcomings. View definitions may contain errors, and the database upon which the views are defined may also contain errors [534]. If content dependence is used in the definition, then errors in the database may cause the downgrade of whole tuples that are accessed by the users. The complexity of view definitions may also result in an overhead in the computing resource usage. Another possible threat comes from users or Trojan horses that attempt to deduce the view definition of data of a higher security classification by doing various insert operations and retrievals through the views. If inserted data cannot be retrieved again by the user due to the view definition, then the user has gained some information through inference about the view definition. In general, the advantages of views outnumber its disadvantages, and views do present some possibilities for high-level protection.

16.5.2 Completeness and Consistency of Views

Although views may contain visible errors in the syntax of their definition, of more concern and interest are the errors arising from the conflict of two or more syntactically correct view definitions. In such cases, one view definition may present some conditions or constraints that must be observed in order for data to be accessed through that view, while another view definition may relax or even contradict the constraints of the first view definition.

Denning et al. [143] distinguishes between a view that retrieves or updates data and a view that classifies data. The first type is referred to as *access views* while the latter is refered to as *classification constraints*. Access views can be used to retrieve data through the user's clearance. The base relation that contains the required data is permitted to have a higher security clearance. Classification constraints are views that specify access classes and the relationship between actual data in the relation and other data derived from it. In this way views as classification constraints can be used to manage content dependencies and context dependencies, to control inference by the users and to perform sanitization of data. A sanitization rule ensures that the access class of the view output (*target*) is dominated by the least upper bound of the access class of the view input (*source*).

Classification constraints must be consistent and complete. A set of classification constraints is *consistent* when no two constraints define conflicting classes and both must be simultaneously satisfied. A set of classification constraints is *complete* when an access class is defined for each valid data element. A more specific definition given by Akl and Denning [4] is the following.

Assume that a multilevel relation R is modeled by the scheme

$$R(A_1, C_1, A_2, C_2, \ldots, A_n, C_n),$$

where C_i is the classification attribute holding the access class labels of data attribute A_i. A classification constraint is then a rule of the form $S = (R, A, E, L)$ that is interpreted as *if E then class(R.A) = L*, where R is the relation, A is one or more data attribute in R, E is an optional expression, and L is the access class.

A set of classification constraints is consistent when any two constraints S_i and S_j are consistent, which in turn requires one of the following four conditions to be true:

1. $L_i = L_j$ – both constraints assign the same access class.
2. $A_i \cap A_j = 0$ – constraints S_i and S_j apply on disjoint attribute sets.
3. $E_i \cap E_j = 0$ – occurs when S_i and S_j cannot be simultaneously satisfied.
4. $E_i \cap E_j \cap D = 0$ – constraints S_i and S_j never simultaneously satisfy all integrity constraints.

Here D is the intersection of all m integrity constraints $I_1, \ldots, I_m$ in the database. A set of classification constraints is complete when for every instance of the database in D, each element is assigned an access class by at least one constraint.

Akl and Denning [4] also present an algorithm based on computational geometry to check for consistency, with a complexity of the order of $O(Nn^2(g+m^2))$, where N is the number of relations, n the number of classification constraints, m the number of integrity constraints, and g is the number of attributes in each relation. An algorithm to check for completeness is also presented in [4], with a complexity of the order $O(Mn)$, with M being the number of attributes in the database.

The algorithms in [4] for secure views are computationally feasible when the constraints are simple and deal only with numeric data. In [534], Wilson proposed the idea of *atomic views* which is a small set of views on which secure views can be built. For a relation R, a view $R_{=L}$ is defined for each security level L that includes exactly the tuples of the relation R classified at level L. Similarly, view $R_{\leq L}$ is defined to include tuples of R that are dominated by L. Then, for each hierarchical classification and for each category C_i, an atomic view $R_{\geq C_i}$ is defined to consist of the set of tuples whose levels dominate C_i. Wilson proposes that atomic views should be defined by the trusted database administrators, while the DBMS should automatically create secure views based on the atomic views. Atomic views guarantees that completeness and consistency are achieved in defining secure views. Atomic views in [534] are more general than secure views in [4] as they are not restricted to numerical values.

16.5.3 Design and Implementations of Views

Although interest in the use of views and research into formal methods of describing views started in the 1980s, only a few projects have been dedicated completely to investigating views for database security. One major project whose results have shaped much of the opinion on secure views is the SeaView project.

SeaView. The SeaView project has its roots in the Summer Study on Multilevel Data Management Security held by the Committee on Multilevel Data Management Security of the US Air Force Studies Board [104]. The project was a three-year joint work by SRI International and Gemini Computers. Its aim is to design a multilevel secure database system fulfilling the A1 class of secure systems as specified by the US Department of Defense Trusted Computer Systems Evaluation Criteria [146].

Within the three-year period of its design, the project by Denning et al. completed a security policy and interpretation [139], a multilevel relational data model [144, 313] that is an extension of the standard relational data model to accommodate labeling, a formal security policy model [140], and a formal top-level specification [315] and its verification [527]. The project also contributed ideas on the assurance of multilevel database systems [312]. The SeaView models extend the relational data model by including in it mandatory security requirements and by supporting data consistency through application-dependent constraints. Data in the base relations and views are hidden from unauthorized users, with different users seeing different instances of a given relation. These multiple instances of the same objects or *polyinstantiations* have different access classes. Thus multiple tuples with the same primary key but different access classes can exist. Similarly, tuples may have multiple values, each having a different access class.

With respect to its architecture, SeaView has ensured that all components of a system that enforces mandatory security are to be isolated in a security kernel. The whole database system with all its support for multilevel relations is to be implemented on a general-purpose operating system kernel enforcing a mandatory security policy in the single-level files and segments [312]. Each multilevel real relation is decomposed into single-level relations defined as single-level kernel objects. These single-level relations are then later combined to provide the multilevel relations for the users. The reader is directed to Lunt et al. [315] for a detailed discussion on the architecture and components of the SeaView implementation.

ASD_Views. Another project on the implementation of views is ASD_Views by the TRW Defense Systems Group [192]. The main aim in ASD_Views is to achieve a suitably sized Trusted Computing Base (TCB) that meets the criteria for the evaluation of class B2 and above. ASD_Views is an attempt to

solve the problem met when views are defined to be objects of both mandatory and discretionary security in multilevel secure DBMSs. In particular, the
major difficulty in a view-based DBMS is that the TCB tends to become very
large because the use of views involves a great deal of the DBMS code. The
requirement of a class-B2 certification as specified in [146] is that only a small
size TCB can be used. Thus, most view-based DBMS will face difficulty in
achieving certification above class B1.

The approach in SeaView [143] is to place the view mechanism over a reference monitor together with a trusted kernel. Each level of data is then physically
stored on its own disk segment and the reference monitor must guarantee that
only data with clearance dominated by the user's clearance is released. The
main problem with this configuration is that the overall performance of the
system rapidly degrades if the mechanism is used for large amounts of data.

ASD_Views takes the simpler solution of restricting the query language that
can be used in the view definition. This limits the complexity of the view definition but ensures that the TCB remains small. The view definition only allows a
subset of rows (tuples) and columns (attributes) from only one underlying base
relation. Joins, aggregate functions, and arithmetic expressions are excluded.
These restrictions allow the processing of the query that defines a secure view
to be done within the TCB perimeters without the need for the creation of
other data structures commonly associated with queries. Thus within the TCB
only a small number of data structures are created for any view definition. Another important point is that ASD_Views do not allow polyinstantiations, so
the complexity of their implementations can be reduced.

The architecture of ASD_Views consists of three general parts. The *SQL
Processor* resides outside the TCB boundary, and it decomposes user queries
into requests to read rows (tuples) from the secure views defined by the TCB.
These reduced queries are then handled by the *Restricted View Processor* followed by the *Read/Write Row Interface*, both of which reside inside the TCB
boundary. The reader is directed to the work by Garvey and Wu [192] for more
details.

16.6 Security in Distributed Databases

Although there is a considerable amount of research material dealing with aspects of distributed database systems and their design, research into the secu-

rity aspects of distributed database systems and distributed systems in general has only begun to take serious form and definition during the last five years. The number of available research results that directly address security in distributed database systems is small, due not to the lack of interest in the topic on the part of researchers, but rather to the complexity of the distributed systems themselves, and the need to do the groundwork on the security of centralized database systems before any consideration can be given to security in distributed databases.

Researchers have addressed the individual security needs of distributed databases as compared to the security of distributed systems in general [408, 330, 316]. The security of some issues and features of distributed databases are now being analyzed, particularly those that have solid research backgrounds from the pure database research point of view.

Such an analysis is exemplified by the work by Downing, Greenberg, and Lunt [161] where the security of serializable transactions has been considered. Two general assumptions that are useful for all distributed transactions have been suggested in this work:

- *⋆-property* – simply requires that a transaction must write only data whose access class equals the transaction class. This is a direct derivation from the Bell-La Padula security model [19, 20].
- *Simple Security Property* – requires that transactions must read only data whose access class is dominated by the transaction class. That is, the "read-down" rule must be observed.

Following these two assumptions the work in [161] proceeds to compare three concurrency control techniques that have been suggested in the pure database research literature, namely, two-phase locking, time-stamp ordering, and optimistic concurrency control. Out of these three concurrency control techniques, only optimistic concurrency control satisfies the two assumptions, and together with some modifications presents the most suitable algorithm for secure transactions, both in centralized and distributed databases.

These research conclusions represent initial steps towards the full understanding of the security requirements in distributed database systems. Such research provides the foundation on which further work and specialized designs can be done in the area of database security.

From the point of view of the use of cryptography for distributed database security, most of the protocols involving cryptography had communications and computer networks in mind (such as the work in [369], [515], and [263]), and they were not geared to solve other more complex security problems in distributed database systems. One notable initiative has been taken by Herlihy and Tyger [237], where the application of cryptographic secret-sharing schemes to data replication in distributed systems has been considered. The parallel between secret sharing and quorum formation for the determination of updates to replicated data is very clear, but successful practical secret-sharing algorithms suitable for distributed databases have yet to be found. Another notable work on cryptographic considerations for distributed systems is by Dolev and Wigderson [159], where the security of multiparty protocols in distributed systems is discussed.

Another approach from the point of view of design methodology has been taken by Bussolati and Martella [73, 72]. The work presents a multiphase methodology for the design of security systems in an integrated and aggregated distributed environment. The approach is a high-level initiative that is suitable for the expression of security policies governing the distributed database system. The use of views in distributed database systems has been considered by Bertino and Haas in [29]. Views over base relations represents a high-level approach to the security of database systems independent of any low-level physical design and constraints of the system. One can easily conclude that if the view approach at individual sites is secure, then views over the distributed database are also secure. However, the proofs and verification of the security of views at a high level does not necessarily eliminate the difficulties and complexities in the underlying design and implementation of the views.

Another approach to secure distributed databases would be to employ an underlying secure distributed operating system, with the database application running on top of the operating system at each site. This approach may prove rewarding since there may be many common mechanisms for controlling distributed processes in both distributed databases and distributed operating systems. An immediate consequence of this approach would be the increase in complexity in the distributed operating system due to the different nature of the data in the two systems. These differences include granularity, the life-span, and the sheer volume of data. Thus, it is probably more useful in the long term to design distributed database systems that infuse security in the whole design, rather than to depend on external components, such as a secure distributed operating system, to achieve a verifiable level of security. The reader is directed to [171, 203, 538] for more interesting work towards the security of distributed databases and distributed systems.

16.7 Security in Object-Oriented Database Systems

Object-oriented systems have recently received increasing attention, and from the point of view of database research many researchers have began to develop object-oriented database systems for various applications. Historically, the idea of *objects* as a programming construct came from the language *Simula*. The fact that it has a programming language background has resulted in the notation and meanings of the terms in object-oriented systems having programming connotations. Thus it is advantageous to maintain a loose definition of object-oriented systems and to use more precise definitions in more specific contexts [375]. In this section the notation for object-oriented database systems will follow that of Banerjee et al. [12]. The reader is directed to this reference and to the work by Kim and Lochovsky [280] for more details on object-oriented systems.

Each entity in an object-oriented system is represented as an *object*. The information about the state of a given object is represented in the *instance variables*, while the behavior of an object is represented by *messages* to which the object responds. The values of the instance variables are objects themselves, and the recursive definition only terminates when *primitive objects* are used. The primitive objects immediately represent their state (they do not have instance variables).

The behavior or actions defined on objects are referred to as *methods*, and a given method performs its actions by sending messages to the objects. Methods themselves can be seen as some code that manipulates or returns the state of a given object, and methods are in fact part of the definition of objects. Usually, a message consists of the name of the method to be invoked, together with a list of objects involved. Thus, sending a message to an object means that the method is to be executed. Objects also communicate with each other using messages. The messages and object name arguments become the interface from the outside world to the objects. *Primitive methods* are used to represent simple actions that can be carried out without the need for messages.

To prevent the consumption of large storage space for objects with their own instance variables and methods, it is natural to group "similar" objects in a *class*. Objects that belong to one class or type are described by the same instance variables and methods, and they all respond to the same set of messages. Each object may have a different state, but the computation type, which is the result of a method activation, is uniform throughout the class. Thus, objects that belong to a class are *instances* of the class, and so a class describes the form (instance variables) of its instances and the applicable operations (methods) of its instances. Note that the class of an object is itself an object, and a class object can create new instances of its own type.

Related to the idea of a class is the notion of a *class hierarchy* and *inheritance* of properties (which are the instance variables and messages) following along the hierarchy. A class and its *subclass* (or *superclass*) are related through an *is-a* relationship. Subclasses of a class inherit all properties defined for the class and, in addition, can have their own local properties. Another possible relationship is the *is-part-of* hierarchy that is used to define *composite objects*, which can consist of objects from different classes [12, 272].

The area of object-oriented systems is a relatively new one, and only very recently has attention been given by researchers to the security needs of object-oriented systems. In discussing the security of object-oriented database systems it is important to realize that security is very difficult or impossible to achieve without an underlying mandatory security kernel. This fact refers more to the implementation aspects of object-oriented database systems than to the conceptual and high-level use of objects in a database system.

The work by Lunt [311] and by Lunt and Millen [314] represents an effort to investigate the problems in defining the meaning of security as applied to object-oriented database systems. Security classifications as described in the work by Lunt [311] are associated with objects and classes. An alternative way to look at the classification of objects is to take the classification itself as being applied to the *fact* that an object or class exists in the database with that given security classification. Similarly, the security classification of the properties (or *facet* in [311]) of an object, which consists of instance variables, messages, methods, and constraints, does not actually apply to the properties themselves, but more to the *association* that exists between the property and the object.

The "read-down-write-up" rule or "$\star$-property" of the Bell-La Padula security model [19, 20] can be transferred quite readily to the object-oriented model of database systems. The following points define more precisely the "read-down-write-up" rule for objects and classes (where L denotes the security classification) [311]:

- All system-defined classes should be classified as *system-low*.
- If object O_1 is a superclass of O_2, then $L(O_1) \geq L(O_2)$.
- If V is a property (facet) of an object O, then $L(V) \geq L(O)$. This is true for all properties of that object.
- If property (facet) V_2 of object O_2 is inherited from object O_1 with the corresponding property (facet) V_1, then $L(V_2) \geq L(V_1)$.
- If two or more of an object's classes have a property (facet) named V, then the object must inherit the property (facet) V having the *lowest* security classification.
- If a subject S sends a message m to an object O to execute method M, then $L(S) \geq L(M) \geq L(O)$ and $L(S) = L(m)$.
- Assume that class O_1 has property (facet) V (which is inherited by its subclasses). If object O_2 belongs to class O_1 and if $L(V)$ in O_1 is dominated by $L(O_2)$, then $L(V)$ in O_2 must be dominated by $L(O_2)$. This is to prevent inference when V in O_1 is visible, yet V in O_2 is invisible, implying that $L(V)$ in O_2 dominates $L(O_2)$.

The above rules show that the notion of security and its associated ideas are applicable to object-oriented database systems. The reader is directed to the following references for further discussion on this area:

- The work by Keefe, Tsai, and Thuraisingham [272] presents the SODA (Secure Object-Oriented Database System) model.
- The work by Fernandez, Gudes, and Song [178] discusses an authorization model for an object-oriented database system.
- The work by Thuraisingham [506] gives a multilevel secure object-oriented data model called SO2.
- The work in [12, 279, 278] and the work in [185, 184, 530] present two implementations of object-oriented database systems, namely the ORION and Iris object-oriented database systems, respectively.

An overview of the research on access control in object-oriented databases can be found in [14].

16.8 Security in Knowledge-Based Systems

The area of artificial intelligence and the application of expert systems has received an explosion of interest in the last decade. Various expert systems have been designed, from research prototypes to commercial versions to be used in real-life situations. Both the business community and the military have found increasing uses of expert systems in daily tasks.

One aspect of expert systems and knowledge-bases in general which has received hardly any attention is that of the security of such systems. Although the differences between the security of knowledge-base systems and database systems are not immediately obvious, further consideration of the different natures of the data in both systems and the use of rules in knowledge-base systems will indicate that they present a somewhat more complex and unresearched problem compared with database systems.

The term *production systems* is best used to represent a model that partitions intelligent processes into rules, data, and a control strategy [28]. Thus, in a multilevel secure production system both data and rules need to be classified, which in turn may require modifications to be done to the existing control strategy.

The work by Berson and Lunt [28] and by Morgenstern [352] represents one of the earlier attempts to consider the application of multilevel security concepts to production systems and knowledge bases. In [28] Berson and Lunt analyze the use of the *noninterference* condition first proposed by Goguen and Meseguer [204] to production systems. The condition requires that besides higher-level data being invisible to lower-clearance users, the effects of the actions, such as the firing of rules, by higher-level users, should also be invisible to lower-clearance users. From this condition emerge four important points that must be taken into consideration when designing secure production systems [28]:

– Rules and data that are classified at a high level must be invisible to lower-clearance users and their lower-level processes.
– The inference engine should function independently of the security classification of the rules and data. Thus, the inference engine should function at a given security level with only the available rules and data of the same (or lower) security level without the need to reference or know of the existence of higher-level rules and data.

– To satisfy knowledge engineering requirements the rules must be created such that they are complete and make sense to any user with a given security clearance. Thus, the user must not be aware of the existence of other rules that have higher security classifications. Immediately related to this point is the need for the lower-level subsets of rules to be closed so that users or processes cannot infer the existence of higher-level rules.
– Any intermediate results of the firing of rules by a user must be classified at the same level as the user's clearance.

The above discussion only represents an introductory note and an example of the direct application of multilevel security policies in database systems to knowledge-based systems. The reader is directed to other studies such as [352] and the efforts by Garvey and Lunt [193, 194] for more work on multilevel security for knowledge-based systems.

16.9 Oracle8 Security

Oracle8 is a commercial database based on the relational model and developed by Oracle, Inc. *Oracle8* is designed for relatively small applications while its version called *Oracle8 Enterprise Edition* targets high-volume online transaction systems or query-intensive data warehouse applications. SQL (structured query language) is used in Oracle for data manipulation. We are going to describe security features implemented in Oracle8. In particular, the following security aspects are studied:

– user authentication,
– resource management (access control),
– Oracle Security Server (OSS).

The reader seeking more details is referred to the Oracle website *http://www.oracle.com* or to [253].

16.9.1 User Authentication

Authentication provides assurance that the alleged identity of a party who wishes to access one or more Oracle database servers is valid. Oracle uses passwords to authenticate users. To enhance the security, the following features are introduced:

– account locking,
– password aging and expiration,
– password history,
– password complexity verification.

Account locking is activated if a user exceeds a designated number of failed login attempts. The number is controlled by the Database Administrator (DBA) via the variable `FAILED_LOGIN_ATTEMPTS`. The user account is frozen for a specific period of time or permanently. The time is determined by the variable `ACCOUNT_LOCK_TIME`. In the latter case with `ACCOUNT_LOCK_TIME UNLIMITED`, the security officer must manually unlock the account. The variables used to control passwords are defined by the DBA in the `CREATE PROFILE` statement. An example of a user `smith` profile is given below.

```
CREATE PROFILE prof LIMIT
   FAILED_LOGIN_ATTEMPTS 4
   ACCOUNT_LOCK_TIME 30;
ALTER USER smith PROFILE prof;
```

It means that the user account is locked for 30 days after 4 failed login attempts.

The variable `PASSWORD_LIFE_TIME` can be used to specify how long the password can be used. When the password lifetime has passed, the user enters the so-called grace period. In the grace period, warning messages urging users to change their passwords are displayed every time users login to their accounts. If a user ignores the warnings, then the password eventually expires and after that the user is unable to use the account. For example,

```
CREATE PROFILE prof LIMIT
   FAILED_LOGIN_ATTEMPTS 4
   ACCOUNT_LOCK_TIME 30
   PASSWORD_LIFE_TIME 90
   PASSWORD_GRACE_TIME 3;
ALTER USER smith PROFILE prof;
```

It means that the user Smith is able to use his password for 90 days. After 90 days, he is given a 3-day grace period for his password change. The password eventually expires (after 93 days).

Oracle restrict the reuse of passwords using two variables: `PASSWORD_REUSE_TIME` and `PASSWORD_REUSE_MAX`. The first varable indicates for how long the current password is not allowed to be reused. The second variable determines the number of times the password must be changed before the current password can be reused.

Oracle also screens passwords for weaknesses and accepts a new password only if it

- is at least 4 characters long,
- is not obvious, i.e., a password must be different to the `userid` and should not match simple words such as welcome, account, database, or user,
- contains at least one alphabetic character, one numeric, and one punctuation mark,
- differs from the old password by at least 3 characters.

Users may login to their Oracle accounts

- Directly via an Oracle database. In this case Oracle performs both the identification and the authentication of users using their passwords. This is a preferred option from the security point of view as Oracle does not rely on any (trusted) intermediary.
- Indirectly via an external service (either an external host or an external network service such as the Oracle Advanced Networking Option (ANO)). The external service is responsible for user password administration and user authentication.
- Via the Oracle Security Service (OSS). This option is available in the Oracle8 Enterprise Edition. The user authentication is done by OSS and is shared among multiple Oracle database servers.

16.9.2 Access Control

Authorization assures that a given party can only operate according to privileges that have been defined for that party by an administrator. To access Oracle resources, users must run database applications and be identified by their valid usernames. A security administrator (SA) is the only person who can create users. To do this, the SA calls the CREATE USER system privilege that specifies the new user default and temporary segment tablespaces, tablespace quotas, and profile. For instance,

```
CREATE USER OPS$smith
IDENTIFIED EXTERNALLY
```

```
DEFAULT TABLESPACE data_ts
TEMPORARY TABLESPACE temp_ts
QUOTA 100M ON test_ts
QUOTA 500K ON data_ts
PROFILE clerk;
```

The user smith is identified externally and the prefix OPS$ indicates the name of the host (operating system) responsible for the identification. If the user creates a schema object and does not specify any tablespace for storing it, the default tablespace is used. A temporary tablespace is used when a user executes a SQL statement that requires storage for segment processing. Oracle stores the requested segments in temporary tablespace. The quotas impose the restrictions on the available space. The last line indicates the profile of the user. Profiles are used to control access to Oracle resources.

A *profile* is a named set of resource limits. Profiles can be

− *created* − the creator must hold the CREATE PROFILE privilege.
− *assigned to a user* − done by using either CREATE USER or ALTER USER privileges.
− *altered* − done by using the ALTER PROFILE privilege.
− *dropped* − executed by the DROP PROFILE privilege.

The following statement creates the profile clerk.

```
CREATE PROFILE clerk LIMIT
CPU_PER_SESSION unlimited
CPU_PER_CALL 6000
LOGICAL_READS_PER_SESSION unlimited
LOGICAL_READS_PER_CALL 100
IDLE_TIME 30
CONNECT_TIME 480;
```

All unspecified resource limits are set by the DEFAULT profile. Note that all limits in the DEFAULT profile are initially set to UNLIMITED.

A *privilege* in Oracle is defined as a right to execute a particular type of SQL statement or a right to access another user object. Oracle uses 80 system privileges each performing a specific database operation. The system privileges are grouped into 23 categories:

− *analyze* − analyze any table, cluster, or index in the database.

– *audit* – AUDIT ANY audits any object in the database and AUDIT SYSTEM turns on/off the privilege audit options.

– *cluster* – CREATE CLUSTER, CREATE ANY CLUSTER, ALTER ANY CLUSTER, DROP ANY CLUSTER.

– *database* – ALTER DATABASE adds files to the operating system via Oracle and DATABASE LINK creates private database links in its own schema.

– *index* – CREATE ANY INDEX, ALTER ANY INDEX, DROP ANY INDEX.

– *library* – CREATE LIBRARY and DROP LIBRARY create/drop callout libraries in its own schema. CREATE ANY LIBRARY and DROP ANY LIBRARY create/drop callout libraries in any schema.

– *privilege* – GRANT ANY PRIVILEGE grants any system privilege.

– *procedure* – CREATE PROCEDURE, CREATE ANY PROCEDURE, ALTER ANY PROCEDURE, DROP ANY PROCEDURE, EXECUTE ANY PROCEDURE.

– *profile* – CREATE PROFILE, ALTER PROFILE, DROP PROFILE, ALTER RESOURCE COST.

– *public database link* – CREATE PUBLIC DATABASE LINK, DROP PUBLIC DATABASE LINK.

– *public synonym* – CREATE PUBLIC SYNONYM, DROP PUBLIC SYNONYM.

– *role* – CREATE ROLE, ALTER ANY ROLE, DROP ANY ROLE, GRANT ANY ROLE.

– *rollback segment* – CREATE ROLLBACK SEGMENT, ALTER ROLLBACK SEGMENT, DROP ROLLBACK SEGMENT.

– *session* – CREATE SESSION, ALTER SESSION, RESTRICTED SESSION.

– *sequence* – CREATE SEQUENCE, CREATE ANY SEQUENCE, ALTER ANY SEQUENCE, DROP ANY SEQUENCE, SELECT ANY SEQUENCE,

– *snapshot* – CREATE SNAPSHOT, CREATE ANY SNAPSHOT, ALTER ANY SNAPSHOT, DROP ANY SNAPSHOT.

– *synonym* – CREATE SYNONYM, DROP SYNONYM.

– *system* – ALTER SYSTEM.

– *table* – CREATE TABLE, CREATE ANY TABLE, ALTER ANY TABLE, BACKUP ANY TABLE, DROP ANY TABLE, LOCK ANY TABLE, COMMENT ANY TABLE, SELECT ANY TABLE, INSERT ANY TABLE, UPDATE ANY TABLE, DELETE ANY TABLE.

– *tablespace* – CREATE TABLESPACE, ALTER TABLESPACE, MANAGE TABLESPACE, DROP TABLESPACE, UNLIMITED TABLESPACE.

– *transaction* – FORCE TRANSACTION, FORCE ANY TRANSACTION.

– *trigger* – CREATE TRIGGER, CREATE ANY TRIGGER, ALTER ANY TRIGGER, DROP ANY TRIGGER.

– *user* – CREATE USER, BECOME ANY USER, ALTER USER, DROP USER.

– *view* – CREATE VIEW, CREATE ANY VIEW, DROP ANY VIEW.

Objects in Oracle are tables, views, sequences, and procedures. The object privileges are

– ALTER,
– DELETE,
– EXECUTE,
– INDEX,
– INSERT,
– REFERENCES,
– SELECT,
– UPDATE.

A *role* is a group of several privileges and roles that are granted and revoked together. Any user with the privilege CREATE ROLE can define his/her own role. The name of a role must be unique and different from user names and other role names. Oracle has nine predefined roles. For instance, the role CONNECT encapsulates the following privileges:

ALTER SESSION, CREATE CLUSTER, CREATE DATABASE LINK,
CREATE SEQUENCE, CREATE SESSION, CREATE SYNONYM, CREATE TABLE,
CREATE VIEW

Note that before a role is executed, it is first authorized. The authorization can be done by Oracle (using passwords), by the host (operating system), or by a network service.

16.9.3 Oracle Security Server

The Oracle Security Server (OSS) supports centralized authorization and distributed authentication in an Oracle environment. To ensure the secure management of database resources:

1. Identities must be named uniquely. A local Oracle server takes care that all local identities differ. This is no longer true in a distributed environment where two local servers may use the same names. To avoid collisions, OSS

creates names according to the X.500 standard (see [112]). The names complying with the standard are called distinguished names (DNs) and are of the following format:

`DN=([Country,][Org,][OrgUnit,][State,] [Locality,] CommonName)`

where `Org` stands for `Organization`.

2. Any subject (active identity) should be able to talk to any server in the Oracle enterprise in a secure manner. The implementation of secure communication requires:

   (a) A secure key establishment protocol. Oracle applies a version of the SKEME protocol described in [288]. Cryptographic operations (encryption and digital signature) are based on RSA,

   (b) A trusted Certification Authority (CA) that provides an authentic cryptographic key typically in the form of certificates (a certificate is a public key signed by CA).

The OSS includes three major components:

– OSS Manager,
– OSS Repository,
– OSS Authentication Adapter.

The OSS Manager is an application of the Oracle Enterprise Manager that administers the OSS Repository. The OSS Manager provides a graphical user interface (GUI) that is used to define and maintain information about identities and the authorizations granted to the identities for usage of database resources within the enterprise. Typically, the OSS Manager runs under Windows NT 4.0 or Windows 95.

The OSS Repository stores all information provided by the OSS Manager and, in fact, acts as the Certification Authority (CA) for the OSS. In particular, the Repository generates and stores the certificates of the public keys of subjects. It also keeps information about certificates that have expired or have been revoked. The Repository is a primary source of Oracle certificates or, in other words, it maintains the public key infrastructure (PKI) for the enterprise.

17 Access Control

A computing environment can be seen as a collection of resources which are shared by user processes under the watchful eye of the operating system. The collection typically includes hardware resources (the CPU, the main memory, disk space, I/O devices, etc.) and software resources (editors, compilers, debugging tools, etc.). Sharing of resources can take on different forms and each form of sharing requires a different degree of operating system attention or control. For example, resources such as printers may be accessed by every process as long as the operating system puts the interested processes in a queue so they can access the printer sequentially in some order. An editor can be accessed concurrently by many processes as long as each process does not modify it. Normally, personal data files can be accessed by their owners only. The main task of the operating system (OS) is to control the access to system resources. The classification of computer entities into resources (passive) and processes (active) is not disjoint as a process can be also a resource to which another process would like to have access. In the access control vocabulary, passive entities or resources are called *objects* and active entities or processes are called *subjects*.

Any type of resource (object) has a well-defined collection of access operations specifying how the object can be manipulated by a subject. A subject can usually be granted a small subset of all possible access operations. This subset defines access privileges (permissions) assigned to the subject. Whenever a subject wishes to access an object to perform some specific operation (read, write, execute, etc.), the OS checks whether the subject has the corresponding access permissions to the object. If the subject holds the appropriate permissions, the OS grants the access, otherwise it denies the access to the object.

The access control can be based on different policies. The choice of a security policy is crucial as it determines the performance, flexibility, and availability of the computer system. The policy is normally defined by the organization and reflects restrictions imposed on access control by the legal and business requirements. Consider the following aspects of an access control policy:

1. *Minimum versus maximum collection of privileges* – The assignment of access permissions can be done using the *minimum privilege principle* where a subject gets assigned the smallest possible collection of access permissions that is enough for the subject to function normally. The other extreme is the *maximum privilege principle* which defines the widest range of permissions for subjects.

2. *Open versus closed access control* – OS has to verify each access request generated by a subject. There are two possibilities. All access requests are allowed unless they are explicitly forbidden. This is an open access control. In a closed access control, all access requests are forbidden unless explicitly authorized.

3. *Granulation of access control* – Each object has to be well defined together with its basic collection of access permissions such as read, write, delete, execute, and create. The permissions may be ordered so if a subject is assigned a privilege of a higher order to an object then the subject implicitly holds all lower-order privileges to the object.

There are three major types of access control:

– *Mandatory access control* (MAC) – Objects (information) are classified on hierarchical levels of security sensitivity (typically, top secret, secret, confidential, unclassified). Subjects (users) are assigned their security clearance. Access of a subject to an object is granted or denied depending on the relation between the clearance of the subject and the security classification of the object.

– *Discretionary access control* (DAC) – Each object has its unique owner. The owner exercises its discretion over the assignment of access permissions.

– *Role-based access control* (RBAC) – Rather than to subjects, permissions are assigned to roles. A subject always acts according to the currently delegated role and therefore acquires the appropriate permissions relevant to the current role. The subject can hold different permissions to objects depending on the role assigned to it.

There is a tendency to use mandatory access control for security policies that are governed by a central authority. Discretionary access control, on the other hand, is set by the owner of an object and can be seen as a decentralized approach to access control.

Role-based access control is gaining attention as a viable alternative to MAC and DAC [179, 448]. Access permissions are associated with roles rather than with subjects. Note that most institutions and organizations are role driven. A person who today is the manager of a branch may be asked to be the chair of a selection committee to appoint new staff or to be the acting chief manager for a day or, perhaps, that person may be suspended as the manager for some time due to a pending investigation. Depending on the circumstances, the person may have new roles or may cease to hold other roles.

17.1 Mandatory Access Control

Mandatory access control, also called *multilevel access control*, originated from research into military security models and deals with the problem of information flow control. The aim of MAC is to ensure that information flows in one direction. Note that most attacks involve interaction between an attacker (a hostile process or Trojan Horse) and a victim process. One would expect that the enforcement of information flows in one direction could decrease the efficiency of attacks or perhaps eliminate some of them.

17.1.1 Lattice Model

Denning [136] developed a formal model of MAC using lattices. In the model, there is a collection of objects $\mathcal{O}$ (typically, files, program variables, data items, records, etc.), a collection of subjects $\mathcal{S}$ (processes), and a collection of security levels $\mathcal{L}$. Security levels are assigned to both subjects and objects.

– *Security clearance* is a level assigned to a subject.
– *Security classification* is a level associated with an object.

Although levels are shared by both subjects and objects their interpretation is different. The decision about whether or not a subject $s \in \mathcal{S}$ can access an object $o \in \mathcal{O}$ is made after looking at the relation between the clearance of the subject and the classification of the object. If the clearance dominates the classification, the access is permitted, otherwise it is denied.

The key issue now is the definition of a relation $\geq$, which can be used to compare two security levels (clearance with classification). It is said that the relation $\geq$ introduces a partial ordering if it is

- transitive, i.e., if $a \geq b$ and $b \geq c$, then $a \geq c$, and
- antisymmetric, i.e., if $a \geq b$ and $b \geq a$, then $a = b$.

A *lattice* is a partially ordered set $\langle \mathcal{L}, \geq \rangle$ in which a pair $a_1, a_2 \in \mathcal{L}$ has

- The *least upper bound* $a_{up} \in \mathcal{L}$, that is

$$a_{up} \geq a_1 \text{ and } a_{up} \geq a_2.$$

If there is an element $c \in \mathcal{L}$ such that $c \geq a_1$ and $c \geq a_2$, then $c \geq a_{up}$.
- The *greatest lower bound* $a_{down} \in \mathcal{L}$, that is

$$a_1 \geq a_{down} \text{ and } a_2 \geq a_{down}.$$

If there is an element $c \in \mathcal{L}$ such that $a_1 \geq c$ and $a_2 \geq c$, then $a_{down} \geq c$.

If the lattice is finite, it contains two distinguished elements: the largest and the smallest in the lattice.

Consider the security levels $\mathcal{L}$ for the case when users are working on different projects and they (their processes) will need to access objects (data) with different sensitivity levels: top secret (TS), secret (S), confidential (C), and unclassified (U). There is a natural ordering among the sensitivity levels, namely, $TS > S > C > U$. It is obvious that for any project there is a specific collection of necessary objects, so for each project there are corresponding clusters of objects called compartments. Let the collection of object sensitivity be $\mathcal{R} = \{TS, S, C, U\}$ and the collection of compartments be $\mathcal{T}$. Then $\mathcal{L} = \mathcal{R} \times \mathcal{T}$ and a security level $\ell \in \mathcal{L}$ is a pair $(\ell_{\mathcal{R}}, \ell_{\mathcal{T}})$ where $\ell_{\mathcal{R}} \in \mathcal{R}$ and $\ell_{\mathcal{T}} \in \mathcal{T}$. A relation $\geq$ can be defined as

$$(\ell \geq \ell') \Leftrightarrow (\ell_{\mathcal{R}} \geq \ell'_{\mathcal{R}}) \text{ and } (\ell_{\mathcal{T}} \supseteq \ell'_{\mathcal{T}})$$

for $\ell, \ell' \in \mathcal{L}$. The relation can be used to control the access. A subject $s \in S$ with its clearance $\ell_s \in \mathcal{L}$ is granted access to an object $o \in \mathcal{O}$ with its classification ℓ_o if and only if

$$\ell_s \geq \ell_o.$$

If this happens, we say that the subject s dominates the object o or simply $s \geq o$. Note that the comparison of subject and object is performed using their labels (security levels).

Consider an example. Given a computer system which is working within a university environment. Let $\mathcal{S} = \{s_1, s_2, s_3\}$ and $\mathcal{O} = \{o_1, o_2, o_3\}$. Security levels are defined as $\mathcal{L} = \mathcal{R} \times \mathcal{T}$ where $\mathcal{R}$ defines information sensitivity levels $\mathcal{R} = \{TS, S, C, U\}$ with the order $TS > S > C > U$, and $\mathcal{T}$ is a collection of the following compartments: $\alpha, \beta, \gamma, \delta$. The compartment α consists of all objects related to student data, β to academic staff, γ to visiting scholars, δ to executives of the university.

Assume the following clearance levels:

$$s_1 \leftrightarrow (TS, \{\alpha, \beta, \gamma, \delta\}),$$
$$s_2 \leftrightarrow (S, \{\alpha, \beta, \gamma\}),$$
$$s_3 \leftrightarrow (C, \{\alpha, \gamma\}).$$

The notation $s_2 \leftrightarrow (S, \{\alpha, \beta, \gamma\})$ reads that s_2 has clearance at level S and can access objects from compartments α, β, and γ. The information classification levels are

$$o_1 \leftrightarrow (U, \{\alpha, \gamma\}),$$
$$o_2 \leftrightarrow (TS, \{\beta, \delta\}),$$
$$o_3 \leftrightarrow (S, \{\alpha, \beta\}).$$

The object o_3 is classified at level S and is stored in two compartments α and β. Denote the clearance level assigned to s as $(s_\mathcal{R}, s_\mathcal{T})$ and the information classification level assigned to o as $(o_\mathcal{R}, o_\mathcal{T})$. The relation $\geq$ can be defined as follows:

$$(s \geq o) \Leftrightarrow (s_\mathcal{R} \geq o_\mathcal{R}) \text{ and } (s_\mathcal{T} \supseteq o_\mathcal{T}).$$

The lattice $\langle \mathcal{L}, \geq \rangle$ has two distinguished elements. The smallest is $(U, \emptyset)$ and the largest is $(TS, \mathcal{T})$. The subject s_1 can access all objects as its label equals the largest element in the lattice. The subject s_2 can access o_1 and o_3. The subject s_3 is permitted to access o_1 only.

17.1.2 Bell-LaPadula Model

Bell and LaPadula [21] introduced a simple model for information flow control which can be considered as a special case of the general lattice model. The collection of subjects is $\mathcal{S}$ and objects, $\mathcal{O}$. The security levels are simply sensitivity levels, or $\mathcal{L} = \mathcal{R} = \{TS, S, C, U\}$ with the order $\geq$. A request generated by a subject is granted if the information flows from lower security levels to higher security levels. The model concentrates on two access permissions: read and write. Note that when:

- a subject reads an object, the information flows from the object to the subject, or

$$s \xleftarrow{r} o;$$

- a subject writes into an object, the information flows from the subject to the object, or

$$s \xrightarrow{w} o.$$

There is no violation of the information flow policy when a subject s_1 with low clearance is allowed to write into an object o_1 with high classification. Clearly, a subject s_2 with high clearance is permitted to read object o_2 with a low security classification. If the two subjects happen to be the same, $s = s_1 = s_2$, then we can write this as

$$o_2 \xrightarrow{r} s \xrightarrow{w} o_1.$$

The rules for information flow control are formulated as follows:

1. *Simple security property* – a subject can read information from an object if the clearance level of the subject dominates the security classification of the object.
2. *⋆-property* – a subject can write into an object if the clearance level of the subject is dominated by the security classification of the object.

In other words, the simple security property indicates the *read-down* property, while the ⋆-property is termed the *write-up* property.

The existence of so-called *covert channels* makes it possible for the information to flow in prohibited directions. Consider an example. Assume that there are two subjects with different security clearances. Two subjects may conspire to create a covert channel that will be used by the process s_L with lower security clearance to read some information from the process s_H with higher security clearance. Both processes can agree before-hand on an object that is rightfully accessible for both of them. Process s_L can write into the objects and s_H can read it. Every time s_H wants to communicate a single bit to s_L, s_H applies or releases a read lock on the object. s_L at the agreed instant in time attempts to write into the object. If the attempt

– succeeds, s_L reads a covert bit 1 (the object is not locked);
– fails, the covert bit is 0 (the object has been locked by s_H).

In general, the elimination of covert channels is expensive. In addition, the progress in hardware means that covert channels have become faster.

17.2 Discretionary Access Control

Discretionary access control assumes that the owner of an object controls access permissions to it. It is at the owner's *discretion* to assign access permissions to objects. Most access control models use a matrix to describe the current protection state.

17.2.1 Access Matrix Model

Lampson [297] introduced the access matrix model for DAC. The model was extended by Graham and Denning [219]. The core of this model is a matrix whose rows are indexed by subjects $\mathcal{S}$ and columns by objects $\mathcal{O}$. A single matrix entry (s, o) contains all access permissions held by the subject s about the object o. Usually, the collection of objects contains all subjects, or $\mathcal{O} \supseteq \mathcal{S}$. The access matrix describes the current protection state defined by the pattern of permissions in the matrix entries. An example of an access matrix is given in Table 17.1. For instance, s_1 is permitted to read the object o_4. The subject s_3 can execute o_4 and read o_5.

Since the contents of the access matrix reflect the current state of protection privileges in a computer system, they must be changed whenever a new privilege has been granted to a specific subject or an existing one has been removed from a specific matrix entry. To modify the protection state, Graham and Denning [219] identified the following collection of protection commands:

Table 17.1. An access matrix

	$o_1 = s_1$	$o_2 = s_2$	$o_3 = s_3$	o_4	o_5
s_1		wait		read	read, write
s_2	signal	execute	send, receive	delete	write
s_3	control	signal, wait	control	execute	read

- Create_object() – create an object (or a subject). Note that $\mathcal{O} \supseteq \mathcal{S}$.
- Delete_object() – delete an object (or a subject).
- Grant_permission(α, s_i, o_j) – grant the permission α to the subject s_i for object o_j.
- Delete_permission(α, s_i, o_j) – delete the permission α to object o_j held by the subject s_i.
- Transfer_permission(α, o_j, s_i) – for the specified object o_j, the command allows one subject to transfer permission α to another subject s_i.
- Read() – display the contents of selected entries of the access matrix.

Create_object() can be called by any subject s_j to create either an object or a subject. The creator s_j becomes the owner of the object o_{new} (subject s_{new}) and has exclusive rights to control the distribution of permissions to that object (subject). In effect, a new column o_{new} is added to the matrix with the owner in the entry (s_j, o_{new}) if the object is passive. If, however, the new object is active, a new column $o_{new} = s_{new}$ and a new row s_{new} are added to the matrix. The entry (s_j, o_{new}) contains the owner permission and the entry (s_{new}, o_{new}), which is the control permission.

Delete_object() is the reverse of Create_object(). The command can be invoked by the owner of the object o_j (subject) only and it means that the object o_j ceases to exist. This implies that the corresponding column (in the case of a passive object) or both the corresponding column and row (in the case of an active object) are removed from the matrix.

Grant_permission(α, s_i, o_j) can be executed by the owner of the object o_j and it grants the permission α to the subject s_i. Granted permissions must be different from the *owner* permission.

Delete_permission(α, s_i, o_j) may be executed in two situations. The owner of the object o_j can delete any permission from any entry of the access matrix column o_j. A subject s_k which controls s_i (the entry (s_k, s_j) contains the control permission) can remove any permission from any entry of the row s_j.

Transfer_permission(α, o_j, s_i) involves two subjects, s_k which intends to transfer the permission α and executes the command, and s_i which is a grantee to whom the permission is to be assigned. The command is executed only if the subject s_k has a *copy flag* associated with the permission α (denoted by α^*). In other words, if a matrix entry (s_k, o_j) contains α^*, the subject s_k may transfer the permission α to s_i.

`Read()` allows a subject to read the current entries of the access matrix.

Needless to say, any choice of permissions and protection commands is to some extent arbitrary. There is a natural tradeoff between the protection and openness of computer resources. If we accept a very limited set of protection commands with a small number of possible permissions, we will presumably get better protection but sharing computer objects will be very restricted. Consider the case with a large number of protection commands and permissions. The first problem with such a protection system would be the design of an efficient algorithm for security verification. Even if it is possible to prove the correctness of our protection system, the complexity of its implementation grows with the number of components (protection commands). On the other hand, if the collection of protection commands allows us to create and destroy objects only, then we get a protection mechanism which provides complete isolation among subjects. The mechanism is extremely inflexible, but it is secure.

Protection commands directly influence the way subjects may share their resources. There are three main levels of sharing:

1. no sharing (complete isolation),
2. sharing data objects,
3. sharing untrusted subjects.

The first and second level can be implemented using the access matrix model presented above. The third level of resource sharing requires new protection commands. Consider the following scenario. Given three subjects s_0, s_1, and s_2. The subject s_0 owns the subject s_2, and the subject s_2 uses an object o according to some permission α. For some reason, the subject s_0 needs to share with s_1 the object accessible to s_2. Although s_1 and s_0 may trust each other, s_1 may not trust s_2. This problem was formulated by Graham and Denning [219] and can be solved by the introduction of a new **indirect** access permission. The permission **indirect** is defined as follows:

– Given three subjects: the subject s_2, its owner s_0, and the acquirer s_1.
– The **indirect** access to s_2 can be granted to the acquirer s_1 by the owner s_0 only.
– The acquirer s_1 can access all objects which are accessible to s_2 in the same way as the subject s_2 (in other words, s_1 holds the same collection of permissions as the subject s_2).
– An **indirect** permission can be revoked by the owner s_0 at any time.

In general, the more flexible the access control the more protection commands have to be defined. Unfortunately, some access control problems cannot be solved using the access matrix model. For example:

1. If a permission α^* is transferred from one subject to another, then the second subject can propagate the permission α with no agreement from the first one.

2. The **read** permission allows a reader to copy the object and to grant friendly subjects **read** access to the copy.

3. If two or more untrustworthy processes conspire, they may exercise their permissions collectively.

17.2.2 Harrison-Ruzzo-Ullman Model

The access control model defined by Harrison, Ruzzo, and Ullman in [233] deals with the set of subjects $\mathcal{S}$, the set of objects $\mathcal{O}$, and the set of generic rights $\mathcal{P}$ which define access permissions held by a subject $s \in \mathcal{S}$ to an object $o \in \mathcal{O}$. M is an access matrix with rows and columns labeled by subjects and objects, respectively. An entry $M(s, o)$ is a subset of $\mathcal{P}$ and defines the access right of $s \in \mathcal{S}$ to $o \in \mathcal{O}$.

There are six *primitive operations* op_i which are used to modify the sets $\mathcal{S}$ and $\mathcal{O}$ together with the entries of the matrix M. They are:

- `enter` r `into` $M(s, o)$ – put an access right r into the entry (s, o) of the matrix M.
- `delete` r `from` $M(s, o)$ – remove an access right r from $M(s, o)$.
- `create subject` s – create a new subject and append a new row and column to the matrix M labeled by subject s with empty entries.
- `create object` o – create a new object and append a new column to the matrix M labeled by subject o.
- `destroy subject` s – destroy the subject s and remove the corresponding row and column from M.
- `destroy object` o – destroy the object o and remove the corresponding column from M.

Obviously, subjects do not have direct access to the primitive operations. Instead, they can be invoked indirectly via the so-called *protection commands*. The generic form of a protection command is:

```
command c(X)
    if r₁ in M(s₁,o₁) and
        r₂ in M(s₂,o₂) and
        ⋮
        rₘ in M(sₘ,oₘ)
    then
        op₁;
        op₂;
        ⋮
        opₙ;
end
```

where X is a collection of formal parameters and $r_i \in \mathcal{P}$ for $i = 1, \ldots, m$.

A configuration of a protection system is a triple $(\mathcal{S}, \mathcal{O}, M)$ where the sets $\mathcal{S}$ and $\mathcal{O}$ are current subjects and objects, respectively, together with the current access matrix M.

The UNIX access control mechanism allows us to manipulate files by providing protection commands equivalent to the following ones.

```
command create_file(s, f)
    create file f;
    enter own into M(s, f);
end
```

The command create_file first creates a file and adds a single column in the matrix M labeled by f and puts the right own into $M(s, f)$. The owner s of an object o can grant the read r access right to a friendly subject s' by invoking:

```
command grant_read(s, o, s')
    if own in M(s, o)
    then
    enter r in M(s', o);
end
```

The owner s of an object o can withdraw the access right r from a subject s' by invoking:

```
command delete_read(s, o, s')
```

```
if  own in  M(s, o) and
     r in  M(s', o)
then
    delete r from  M(s', o);
end
```

Given an initial configuration $Q_0 = (\mathcal{S}, \mathcal{O}, M)$ of the protection system and a collection of protection commands $\mathcal{C} = \{c_1, \ldots, c_u\}$, the protection state will change after application of a protection command $c \in \mathcal{C}$. The evolution of protection states can be captured by the sequence of configurations resulting from execution of the protection commands $(c_1, c_2, \ldots)$, i.e.,

$$Q_0 \vdash_{c_1} Q_1 \vdash_{c_2} Q_2 \ldots$$

We say that a protection system *leaks* access right r from a configuration Q if a command $c \in \mathcal{C}$ leads to a configuration Q' such that the access matrix contains r in some entry (or $r \in M(s, o)$) which previously did not contain it (or $r \notin M(s, o)$).

A protection system is *safe* with respect to r if there is no configuration Q which leaks r. This leads us to the following decision problem [191].

Name: Safety of file protection systems problem.
Instance: Given a protection system with a set of subjects $\mathcal{S}$, a set of objects $\mathcal{O}$, a set of access rights $\mathcal{P}$, and a collection of protection commands $c \in \mathcal{C}$.
Question: Is there any sequence of commands from $\mathcal{C}$ and an access right $r \in \mathcal{P}$ such that the system leaks r?

It turns out [233] this problem is undecidable or, in other words, there is no algorithm which could be used to solve it. Typically, undecidability appears whenever the problem in hand has too many free variables and parameters. If we restrict the form of commands so they consist of no more than a single primitive operation, then the safety problem becomes **NP-complete**. If additional restrictions are imposed, then the resulting problem may be solvable in polynomial time.

17.3 Role-Based Access Control Model

An alternative to the MAC and DAC access control models is the *role-based access control* (RBAC) model. The RBAC model streamlines the access control by first defining *roles* which are given access permissions to objects and later assigning roles to subjects. In most organizations and institutions, the access permissions do not depend on who the persons are but rather where their positions are in the management hierarchy. Normally, the position uniquely identifies a collection of jobs which is associated with it. RBAC allows for a nice packaging of access control permissions necessary for performing specific roles. Roles are treated as subjects whose identity is undefined until specific persons assume them.

The RBAC model allows us to define relations among roles and users. As argued in [449], two roles may be mutually exclusive so they cannot be assumed at the same time by a single user. Roles may exhibit a hierarchical structure in which a higher-level role inherits the permissions of lower-level roles. RBAC directly supports the following security policy principles [449]:

- *Minimum privilege* – a job defines a collection of objects (resources) and access rights which are necessary to perform duties associated with the job.
- *Separation of duties* – if the collaboration of two users is required to complete a job, it is possible to enforce this by defining two mutually exclusive roles for the job.
- *Data abstraction* – low-level access rights (such as read, write, delete, etc.) can be encapsulated into high-level access rights (such as send invoice and receive invoice).

Sandhu, Coyne, Feinstein, and Youman in [449] presented a general RBAC model with role hierarchy and constraints. Given the set of users $\mathcal{U}$, the set of access permissions $\mathcal{P}$, the set of roles $\mathcal{R}$, and the set of sessions $\mathcal{S}$, a user $u \in \mathcal{U}$ is identified with a person. A role $r \in \mathcal{R}$ is a well-defined job function which describes the duty and authority imposed on the person who takes on the role. A session $s \in \mathcal{S}$ is an assignment of different roles to a given user. Users can start up a session during which they assume one or more roles they belong to. A session is always associated with a single user who has started it up. The same user can run many sessions concurrently. The notion of session is equivalent to the notion of subject in the DAC model. A user simply accesses a subset of all roles he or she belongs to. The RBAC model uses the two following relations:

1. *Permission-to-role* – assignment $PA \subseteq \mathcal{P} \times \mathcal{R}$; and
2. *User-to-role* – assignment $UA \subseteq \mathcal{U} \times \mathcal{R}$.

There are two functions:

1. *user*: $\mathcal{S} \to \mathcal{U}$ – each session s is assigned to a single user $user(s)$.
2. *roles*: $\mathcal{S} \to 2^{\mathcal{R}}$ – each session s is assigned to a subset of roles, i.e., $roles(s) \subseteq \{(r|user(s), r) \in UA\}$. In effect, the session s has the permissions $\bigcup_{r \in roles(s)} \{p|(p, r) \in PA\}$.

The basic RBAC model includes the above-defined components $(\mathcal{U}, \mathcal{R}, \mathcal{P}, PA, UA, user(), roles())$.

Consider the set of roles $\mathcal{R}$. If the roles are partially ordered, i.e., there is a relation $RH \subseteq \mathcal{R} \times \mathcal{R}$ with the role hierarchy imposed by $\geq$, then the $role()$ functions can be more conveniently defined knowing that if a user belongs to a role r, then he or she must belong to all roles r' which are dominated by r or $r \geq r'$. Constraints can be imposed on the assignments PA and UA and on the *roles* and *user* functions. For more details refer to [449].

17.4 Implementations of Access Control

Now we are going to consider implementation of access control. The starting point is always a security policy which needs to be enforced by a properly designed access control mechanism. Depending on the environment in which the mechanism is to be incorporated, the designer considers which of the known access control mechanisms could be adopted as the basis for implementation. Let us review some implementations. For alternative discussions on the subject refer to [214, 218, 469].

17.4.1 Security Kernel

This implementation is based on the so-called *reference monitor* concept [297]. The reference monitor is an abstract system that:

1. mediates all access requests,
2. functions correctly, and is tamperproof.

Any access request must go through the reference monitor which grants or denies the access. There must be no way to bypass the monitor. The monitor must work correctly and the correctness must be verifiable. It must also be tamperproof, so modification of its functions by an unauthorized person or process must be possible. Note that the reference monitor concept is policy neutral – it can implement any access control policy (MAC, DAC, RBAC).

It is no surprise to learn that most access control mechanisms based on the reference monitor concept are incorporated as an integral part of the operating system kernel [218]. This part is called the *security kernel*. The Orange Book [145] defines the Trusted Computing Base (TCB) which includes all protection mechanisms (including the security kernel) which enforce the security policy (including the access control policy).

To protect the operating system from untrusted processes, the computer system must have at least two distinct modes of operation:

– *user mode*, and
– *monitor mode.*

All components of the OS are run in the monitor (supervisor) mode. All user processes are executed in the user mode. To enforce two-mode operation, the underlying hardware must have an additional bit called the *bit mode* which indicates the current mode – 0 for the monitor mode and 1 for the user mode. The Intel 80386/486 microprocessors support four modes of operation (protection rings) with two mode bits:

– the kernel is assigned the mode 0;
– the remainder of the operating system – mode 1;
– I/O routines – mode 2;
– user processes – mode 3.

Clearly, the most privileged mode is 0 and the least privileged is mode 3.

Modes of operation alternate from monitor to user and from user to monitor. The switch from monitor to user mode is safe as long as the kernel works correctly. The switch from user to monitor mode must be controlled. To facilitate this, users (or more precisely their processes) are allowed to switch to monitor mode indirectly invoking privileged instructions. Privileged instructions can only be run in monitor mode. When a user invokes a privileged instruction, the hardware does not execute it but generates a trap to the operating system. The operating system starts running from the address given in the trap vector. The address determines the place where the corresponding trap service routine is.

Assume for a while that a user is able to modify the contents of the trap vector. In this case, a user process may replace the address of the trap service routine with an address from the user program space. When the trap occurs, the hardware switches to the monitor mode and transfers control to the user process. In effect, the user process is run in the privileged mode [469].

As a matter of principle, the operating system never allows user processes direct access to I/O routines. It also means that all I/O routines are part of the operating system and are run in monitor mode. Whenever a user process needs to print, it issues a privileged I/O instruction which traps to the operating system, or more precisely to the proper I/O routine.

As the CPU executes a user process, all the CPU references to main memory must be checked to see whether they are within the address space of the program being executed. Any attempt to access the instructions of other processes should result in an error and trap to the operating system. To implement memory protection, a hardware support is again required. The hardware consists of two registers and additional comparison gates. One register stores the base (the memory address where the currently executed program starts). This is the *base register*. The other, also called the *limit register*, indicates the size of the range. Both registers uniquely identify the (legal) address space of the process.

Assume that the CPU is running a process whose code resides in the memory $[a, A]$ where a is the smallest address and A is the largest address of the process. The current content of the base register is a and the limit register contains $A - a$. When the CPU tries to access a memory address x, then the hardware:

- First checks whether $x \geq a$. If so, go to the next step. Otherwise, it traps to the operating system.
- Next compares whether $x \leq A$. If the check holds, the reference is valid. Otherwise, a trap to the operating system is generated by the hardware.

Needless to say, the kernel only can load to the base and limit registers.

The most precious resource in computer systems is the CPU. Once the control over the CPU is passed to a user process, there is no way to take it back until the process either voluntarily releases it or generates an interrupt. This may never happen if, for example, the process has entered an infinite loop. To prevent the CPU from being taken over by a single process, a piece of hardware called a *timer* is necessary. The timer can be accessed by the operating system only. Before a user process gets control over the CPU, the timer is initialized to the amount of time for which the process will be allowed to run. Every clock cycle decreases the contents of the timer until eventually it equals zero. This causes an interrupt and a switch to monitor mode.

17.4.2 Multics

This section is based on the description of Multics given in [395]. The Multics system is an operating system whose access control shows many similarities with the Bell-LaPadula model. In fact, the Bell-LaPadula model evolved from the Multics access control mechanism. Multics is a fully fledged operating system and its description goes beyond the scope of book. We give a brief account of the Multics access control.

All resources are organized in a hierarchy of concentric rings of protection. The innermost ring is $\mathcal{D}_0$. The outermost ring is $\mathcal{D}_N$. A single ring $\mathcal{D}_i$ constitutes a protection domain. $\mathcal{D}_0$ is the most privileged and $\mathcal{D}_N$ is the least privileged domain. Multics treats all resources uniformly as segments (files) arranged into a hierarchical file system. Executable files are subjects (or procedures). Passive objects are data files (data segments). The relation between the protection rings and the hierarchy of files is defined by the security policy. Assume that a process $s \in \mathcal{D}_i$ invokes a process $s' \in \mathcal{D}_j$. The general rule for access control is:

– If $j \geq i$, the access is permitted – a more privileged process s can always call a less privileged one.
– If $j < i$, the access is either denied or controlled, i.e., it is possible via so-called *entry points* or *gates*.

The gate notion is a generalization of system calls. Any attempt by $s \in \mathcal{D}_i$ to invoke $s' \in \mathcal{D}_j$, when $i > j$, will be treated as an error and will generate a trap into s'. The process s' may deliver a service to s only if the process s has suitable permissions.

Multics defines two possible implementations of access control using:

1. access brackets, and
2. call brackets.

Instead of a single ring, a resource is assigned a band of rings (k, ℓ) where $k \leq \ell$. The pair (k, ℓ) constitutes the *access brackets* of the resource.

Assume that a process $s \in \mathcal{D}_i$ wishes to access a data file f with its access brackets (k, ℓ). The access control rules are:

– If $i \leq k$, then the access is granted.

- If $k + 1 \le i \le \ell$, then reading/execution access is granted while writing/append access is denied.
- If $i > \ell$, the access is denied.

If the process $s \in \mathcal{D}_i$ wishes to access a process s' with its access brackets (k, ℓ), then the access control rules are slightly different:

- If $i < k$, then the access is granted and a ring-crossing fault is induced.
- If $k \le i \le \ell$, then the access is granted.
- If $i > \ell$, the access is denied.

Note that in the above access control, if $i > \ell$, all access is denied. To relax this, Multics introduced *call brackets*. A process is assigned three integers (k, ℓ, m) where (k, ℓ) are access brackets and m is a call bracket (or range). Call brackets are defined for subjects (procedure segments) only. The access rules are as above with the following addition:

- If $\ell < i \le m$, then access is granted via specific entry points (gates).
- If $i > m$, the access is denied.

The Multics project was aiming at designing a secure and efficient multiuser operating system. The access control was an integral part of the overall security. The ring structure of protection domains, although conceptually elegant, puts restrictions on access control. Any subject in an inner ring $\mathcal{D}_i$ can access any object from all outer rings $\mathcal{D}_j$ for $i < j$ no matter whether the subject needs the object or not. In other words, the need-to-know principle is not supported in Multics.

17.4.3 UNIX

The UNIX access control evolved from Multics and some Multics features are still present in UNIX. One of them is the tree structure of the file system. There are two basic types of elements in the file system: directories and files. Files can be further classified into data files and executable files. The tree structure is relaxed by the presence of the so-called links which are pointers to files in some other subdirectories. The collection of permissions supported by UNIX are write (w), read (r), and execute (x).

Users are assigned their home directories. It is the user's responsibility to build and maintain his/her own subtree rooted in the user home directory. This responsibility includes assignment of permission to access all files owned by the user. Subjects in UNIX are defined into three broad categories:

1. owner,
2. group the owner is in,
3. universe (all other users).

The listing of a typical subdirectory is given in Fig. 17.1. To describe access permissions to a file or directory, it is enough to give a collection of triplets of the form **rwx** to the owner, the group, and the universe. So each file may have up to 9 permissions. For instance, the **form** file can be read and written by the owner (this is indicated by **rw-**), can be read by the group (see the next triplet **r--**), and is not accessible to the universe (the last triplet **---**). By the way, the first character in the listing specifies the type of file (data file indicated by **-** or directory denoted by **d**). To grant or deny access to a file, the UNIX system checks whether the user who asks for access:

− Is the owner of the file. If she is, then UNIX considers the owner permissions.
− Belongs to the group. If she does, then UNIX compares the requested access with the group permissions.
− Otherwise, UNIX compares the requested access with the universe permissions.

UNIX allows a single user to be a member of different groups. In System V, the command **newgrp** allows users to switch between groups. The owner of a file is always able to set permissions to the file. The command **chmod** can be used for this purpose. Also the ownership of a file can be transferred by the current owner to another user by using the **chown** command.

While creating new files (by copying, editing, or running a process which creates new files), UNIX assigns permissions according to default permissions. They can be controlled by the **umask** command. To modify the default to the

```
$ ls -l
drwxr-xr-x 1 josef    cs-uow    3552 Jun 16 14:06 LIBRARY
-rw-r----- 1 josef    cs-uow    2349 Jun 16 08:43 form
-rwxr-xr-x 1 josef    cs-uow    3292 Jun 18 13:05 shell_script
```

Fig. 17.1. Listing of files in UNIX

requested permission pattern, it is enough to call the command **umask abc** where a,b,c are integers from 0 to 7. So if you execute **umask 037** then

owner	group	universe
rwx	rwx	rwx
000	011	111
rw-	r--	---

By default, any new file created by the owner gets the full range of permissions specified by the application. If the application is an editor, this is typically **rw-**. For executable files, the default is **rwx**. The group can read the new file, i.e., their permissions are **r--**. The universe gets no access or **---**.

Unlike data files, directories play a different role. They are used to partition the file system into subtrees and keep information about them (who can use them and where they are stored on the disks). Consequently, a directory is a list of filenames together with addresses to their *inodes* where the information about their owners, permissions, and location on the disks is kept. Clearly, access permissions for directories are defined differently, and [166]

– **r--** means that the contents of directory can be listed,
– **-wx** means that files in the directory are allowed to be renamed or deleted,
– **--x** means that files in the directory are permitted to be executed.

The UNIX access control uses owners, groups, and the universe to define access permissions. This resembles a three-ring structure. The owner is in the center, the group creates the first ring, and the universe sits in the outer ring. The current list of permissions to an object (file) may be assigned independently by the owner. An obvious restriction in this access control is the weak granularity of the group and the universe. If the owner of a file wishes to allow sharing of it with another user, then the owner must allow the same access to the group the user is in. UNIX also defines the all-powerful *superuser* (root) who is typically the administrator responsible for the maintenance and smooth operation of the system. More details about UNIX and its security can be found in [166].

17.4.4 Capabilities

Consider an access matrix from Sect. 17.2.1 with rows and columns indexed by subjects and objects, respectively. Note that the access matrix normally is sparse as most objects are not accessible to many subjects. It is, therefore, reasonable to split the matrix into smaller and more manageable units. One of the possibilities is to assign to each subject the corresponding row of the access matrix. For a given subject (or protection domain), the *capability list* specifies the collection of accessible objects together with permissions to them. A *capability* is an object representation usually in the form of its name or identifier together with permissions.

It is said that a subject can access an object if the subject possesses an object capability. Capabilities are protected objects themselves and they must be protected against modification by users. There are three basic solutions which have been used to protect capabilities [501]:

- *Tagged architecture* – capabilities are stored in memory with a tag bit switched on indicating that it can be modified by the kernel only.
- *Isolation from users* – capabilities are kept by the operating system so users can refer to them only.
- *Cryptographic techniques* – users are allowed to hold capabilities but any modification will be detected by the operating system.

A capability-based access control has an obvious advantage. It is easy to decide whether to grant or deny the access as subjects must present valid capabilities. Note that it is the subject's responsibility to store and maintain capabilities. The operating system generates and verifies capabilities. For a given object, however, it is difficult to:

- determine which subjects are allowed to access it and what permissions they have to the object,
- revoke permissions to the object.

The above-mentioned difficulties relate to the fact that capabilities are scattered around different subjects.

Let us illustrate how capabilities can be used for access control. The *Amoeba* distributed operating system was designed at the Vrije Universiteit in Amsterdam [361, 500]. The Amoeba access control is capability based. The format of capabilities in Amoeba is shown in Fig. 17.2. The first two fields uniquely identify an object. They, in fact, constitute the object name. The last two are used for access control. The permission field is a binary string (8 bits long), that specifies the collection of operations allowed to be performed by the capability

| Server | Port | Object | Permissions | Check |

Fig. 17.2. Amoeba's capability

holder. The check field (48 bits long) is used for validation of capabilities. The integrity of a capability is enforced cryptographically.

The following operations on capabilities are defined in Amoeba:

– *Creation of an owner capability* – This operation is performed when a new object is created. The owner of the object asks the server (which is a part of the OS) to issue an owner capability. In response, the server creates the capability with all permission bits turned on and with a random string in the check field. The information about the capability is also stored by the server in the file tables for further references. In effect, the owner holds a valid capability and the server registers the new capability.
– *Verification of an owner capability* – The holder of a capability presents it to the server, which retrieves its registration information. Next the server compares the registration information with that provided by the capability.
– *Creation of a derivative capability* – Assume that a user holds a valid owner capability and asks the server to create a restricted capability with the permission bit pattern p. First, the server verifies whether the capability held by the user is valid. If it is, the server takes the random check number x from the owner capability, adds it exclusive-or to p, and the result is input to a one-way function $f()$. The result is the new check string which is returned to the user. In other words, the new check string $x' = f(x \oplus p)$ and the matching permission pattern is p.
– *Verification of a derivative capability* – Given a derivative capability with the permission p and the check value $\tilde{x}$. A holder of a derivative capability asks the server for verification. The server retrieves the information about the owner capability, takes the check value of the owner capability x, adds to it the permissions p from the derivative capability, and calculates the valid check string $x' = f(x \oplus p)$. If the value x' is equal to $\tilde{x}$, the capability is considered valid.

Note that capabilities resemble tokens. The access is granted when a user is able to present to the server a valid capability. The resistance of capabilities against forgery rests on the difficulty of reversing the one-way function and the length of the check field.

The Amoeba access control has the following interesting features:

– *Garbage collection* – when an object is no longer accessible because all capabilities have been lost. This is done by removing all objects which have not been used in the last garbage collection cycle.
– *Revocation of access* – the holder of a capability can always propagate copies of the capability. To revoke the access, the owner can ask the server to invalidate all capabilities by changing the check number stored in the file table.
– *Controlled propagation of capabilities* – a holder of a derivative capability can ask the server to create a capability with more restricted permissions.

There are many operating systems whose access controls apply capabilities. Hydra [539] allows users to define their own (access) operations using the basic ones provided by the system. Those new permissions are called auxiliary rights. The CAP system [371] uses two types of capability: data and software. Data capabilities are standard permissions provided by the system (read, write, execute). Software capabilities, on other hand, allow users to define their own access operations.

17.4.5 Access Control Lists

An alternative to capabilities is the concept of access control lists (ACL). Instead of slicing the access matrix by rows, the matrix is divided by columns. So every object is asssigned its ACL which specifies who (which subject or protection domain) can use the object and how (access permissions). This idea has been adopted in UNIX (Sect. 17.4.3).

Consider how ACLs are implemented in the DCE distributed operating system. DCE, which stands for Distributed Computing Environment, was a project initiated by a group led by IBM, DEC, and Hewlett-Packard. The goal of the project was to develop a version of UNIX for distributed environments [434, 500].

The DCE operating system follows the client/server paradigm. Users are identified by their client processes and services by server processes. All computing resources are clustered together into *cells*. A cell typically covers the resources of a department or division so can it be identified by resources hooked to a single LAN.

Unlike in capability-oriented access control, where the fact of possessing a valid capability is enough to grant the access, ACL-oriented access control requires identification of users (subjects) who issue access requests. The identification used in DCE is based on the Kerberos system. For identification purposes, users are given privilege attribute certificates (PAC), which are simply cryptograms of the message which include the user identity, and group and organization memberships. ACLs are protected entities kept by ACL managers. ACL managers are privileged library routines present in every server.

Objects are divided into two categories: simple objects, such as files, and complex objects called *containers*, such as directories. The collection of permissions is an extension of those present in UNIX and includes

- read (r),
- write (w),
- execute (x),
- change-ACL (c),
- container-insert (i),
- container-delete (d), and
- test (t).

The only permission that is not self-explanatory is test. The test permission allows us to check whether or not the value stored in the protected object is equal to some value without revealing the protected value. For instance, a user who has t permission to the password file, can verify whether the password in hand is equal to the password stored in the file without getting any additional information about the stored password. An example of an ACL is given in Fig. 17.3. The first row indicates the type of the object. The second row identifies the default cell. Next the table specifies the permissions of three users and of the group staff existing in the cell. All other local users can test the object (row 7). Finally, there are two foreign subjects (user and group) whose permissions are given in the last two rows.

Assume that a client (user) wishes to access a file. First the client contacts the suitable server and presents her PAC together with her access request. The server decrypts the PAC, retrieves her identity and memberships, and looks up the appropriate ACL. If her name or groups she belongs to appear on the ACL, the server checks the permissions and grants the access if the request is consistent with the permissions. Otherwise, the request is denied.

sample_data
/.../C=AU/O=UOW/OU=ITACS
user:josef:rwxcidt
user:jennie:rwxidt
user:thomas:rwxidt
group:staff:rxt
other:t
foreign_user:john@/.../cs.qut.edu.au:rwxt
foreign_group:staff@/.../cs.qut.edu.au:rt

Fig. 17.3. An example of an ACL in the DCE system

The owner (creator) of an object typically retains all permissions. The DCE system provides also the ACL editor, which can be called by clients to create new objects and subjects, manipulate the contents of ACLs, etc. Clearly, any call to the ACL editor is scrutinized against the caller's permissions.

Windows NT provides another example of access control based on ACLs. Readers interested in this subject are referred to the book [227].

Let us compare capabilities with ACLs. First consider how the access control is performed.

- *Capabilities* – access is granted if a valid capability is presented. The identity of the capability holder is not verified. The fact that a user holds a valid capability is enough to grant the access. Capabilities, however, have to be protected against modification.
- *ACLs* – access is granted to a user if the name of the user together with suitable permissions appears on the object ACL. Every time users request access, they have to be identified by the operating system.

Capabilities seem to be more suitable for distributed environments. The protection mechanism and naming can be merged making the access control more flexible. Capabilities can be more easily incorporated into programming languages. On the other hand, ACLs offer better protection as users are always identified before allowing the access. It is easier to keep track of who has been using which objects.

18 Network Security

The invention of the telephone by Alexander Bell could be regarded as the starting point of the communication revolution. Very soon after this, the global telephone network made the world the "global village" for the first time in human history. The telephone network also provided the communication infrastructure for computer centers in the late 1970s and 1980s. For example, the first electronic funds transfer systems were built using the telephone network.

The first work on computer network technology was initiated by the famous ARPANET project that started in the late 1960s. The main focus at that time was on the design principles and implementation of communication networks. Unfortunately, the security aspect of communication was not of major concern, mainly because it was not perceived as a "real problem." The discovery of malicious software such as viruses, worms, and Trojan horses has changed the perception. In particular, computer viruses have become the major security problem, especially for personal computers.

18.1 Internet Protocol Security (IPsec)

The "commercialization" of the Internet in the early 1990s and the growing popularity of the World-Wide Web applications put the Internet in a completely new light. The computer network infrastructure was seen by some as a new vehicle for conducting trade and commerce in an open manner, reaching millions of people connected to the Internet. These demands brought to the foreground the issues of security, and, consequently, the designers of computer networks amended the Internet protocols so they provided confidentiality and authenticity of messages.

Since the Internet spans the globe, crossing national boundaries, issues of transborder data flow and national security – from the defense and from the economic point of view – have also come to the foreground. A computer network

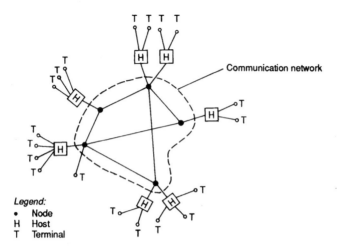

Fig. 18.1. A typical computer network

can be regarded as a single "supercomputer," whose hardware and software resources are distributed over a given geographic area. An especially important
component of this supercomputer is the communication network (Fig. 18.1)
that connects computers. It is susceptible to illegal activity by unfriendly users.
The large physical dimensions of the network make it impossible to protect the
network resources by physical security measures [112, 499, 500]. The application
of access control methods in the computer network has obvious limitations; for
example, it cannot be used to protect information that is being sent through
the communication network. The only class of protection methods that can be
applied is the class of cryptographic methods. It is worth noting that cryptographic protection does not exclude illegal user activity. Its main benefit is the
protection of the computer network against the effects of such activity.

Recent advances in communications have tried to reconcile two seemingly
impossible requirements: unrestricted global access to all communication end-
points and isolation of some parts of the network. The requested isolation is
typically temporary and the configuration of the network may fluctuate from
time to time. This dilemma can be solved by designing two or more computer environments isolated from each other. For example, this solution is often applied
by the military. One computer environment is dedicated to military purposes
while the other is integrated with the public Internet for unclassified infor-

mation. Although quite effective, this solution is also expensive and in most institutions may not be acceptable.

Firewalls can be deployed to control incoming traffic to a protected site (or a local area network). Modern firewalls are fairly sophisticated, combining an extensive range of traffic control mechanisms. The decision about whether the traffic is friendly, unwanted, or simply hostile, is made using a variety of message identification techniques. Typically, firewalls either allow the traffic to pass or the traffic is blocked. Note that the confidentiality aspect is ignored by firewalls.

Therefore, it is possible to distinguish two aspects of networks security:

1. *Protection of network nodes* – data coming into a network node is carefully examined using access control methods, normally placed in firewalls at network boundaries.
2. *Protection of traffic* – data in transit is protected using a variety of cryptographic mechanisms.

When the first networks were constructed and suitable standards for Internet communication developed, the security aspect was overlooked. The Internet Engineering Task Force (IETF) is trying to fix this by development of new standards for secure Internet communications. For more details about IETF see *http://www.ietf.org*. In November 1998, the Network Working Group of IETF published their request for comment RFC2401 [275], in which a security architecture for the Internet Protocol (IP) was detailed. The Internet Protocol security (IPsec) is based on the following two protocols:

1. Authentication Header protocol (AH), and
2. Encapsulating Security Payload protocol (ESP).

The AH protocol provides integrity and authentication services, while the ESP protocol delivers mainly confidentiality. These services are implemented on the network layer (see the ISO OSI reference model [500]). Being more specific, IPsec can be implemented as:

– An integral part of the underlying Internet protocol (this is the case for IP version 6 or IPv6).
– An interface between the IP layer and the network driver. This is also called the *bump-in-the-stack* implementation.

– A separate crypto engine. This is also called the *bump-in-the-wire* implementation.

18.1.1 Security Associations

A *security association* (SA) is a unidirectional secure channel that offers either confidentiality (ESP protocol) or authenticity (AH protocol). If both confidentiality and authenticity are required, two security associations, say SA_{ESP} and SA_{AU}, must be used. The sequence in which these two associations are applied is important. Always the unprotected (clear) message (packet) is first input to SA_{ESP} and later the result is sent to SA_{AU}. In other words, if the clear message is M then $M \rightarrow SA_{ESP} \rightarrow SA_{AU}$. Note that this order of channels saves time and computing resources when the receiving side deals with corrupted packets. They are discarded after failing the authentication checks (which is typically less expensive than decryption). Note also that to establish a two-way channel with confidentiality and authenticity, one would need four security associations. Each security association is identified by the triple: destination IP address, security parameter index, and security protocol used (either AH or ESP).

A security association may be applied in either *tunnel* and *transport* mode. In the tunnel mode, an SA takes an incoming datagram and encapsulates it in a new datagram with a new header. This mode is used for confidentiality services when the incoming datagram is encrypted and the new header is added to enable the destination point to decrypt it. The transport mode typically leaves the basic structure of a datagram intact with some extra fields attached to it.

In other words, the tunnel mode resembles a postal service in which a postcard is put into an envelope at the sender's post office. The destination address on the envelope indicates the post office of the receiver. On arrival at the receiver's post office, the envelope is removed and the postcard is delivered to the destination address. The transport mode can be compared to the registered mail service. A postcard is time-stamped and a number attached to it. The card still looks the same, but some extra information is attached to it.

18.1.2 Authentication Header Protocol

The AH protocol [276] provides authentication of IP datagrams. The Authentication Header is placed directly after the IP header and is structured as shown in Table 18.1. The Next Header field is 8 bits long and specifies the type of

Table 18.1. Authentication Header

Next Header	Payload Length	Reserved
Security Parameters Index (SPI)		
Sequence Number Field		
Authentication Data		

the next payload which follows the AH. The Payload Length (8 bits) field gives the length of the AH in 32-bit words. The 16-bit Reserved field is dedicated for future usage. The SPI field (32 bits) uniquely identifies the security association. The Sequence Number indicates the position of the datagram within the stream of packets sent via the security association. This number is used to prevent the reply attack. The Authentication Data contains the Integrity Check Value (ICV) that is used by the receiver to verify the authenticity of the packet.

The ICV is, in fact, a message authentication code (MAC) generated using:

1. a keyed hashing based on a private-key cryptosystem (such as DES or LOKI),
2. a collision-free hashing algorithm such as MD5 or SHA-1,
3. a signature based on a public-key cryptosystem.

For point-to-point communication, hashing is recommended, while for multicast communication signatures are preferred. In general, the ICV is computed for all immutable parts of the packet. In particular, these parts include: IP header fields, which are immutable, or those whose values can be predicted, the AH header, and the upper-level protocol immutable data.

The AH provides also protection against the reply attack. Any packet transmitted for an active SA has a unique (fresh) sequence number. The sequence number inserted into the AH is always initialized to zero at the initialization stage of a new SA and incremented by one for each consecutive datagram. The first packet is assigned 1 as its sequence number. As the sequence number field contains 32 bits, it is possible to send 2^{32} packets before the sequence number will cycle. To prevent cycles, the SA with its sequence number set to zero (first full cycle is completed) causes the SA to be closed and a new SA is created.

It is interesting to note that an SA with the AH protocol is only typically used in the transport mode. If, however, it is used in combination with the ESP protocol, it can be applied in either the transport or the tunnel mode.

18.1.3 Encapsulating Security Payload Protocol

The ESP protocol is described in [277]. Unlike the AH protocol, the main service delivered by the ESP protocol is confidentiality of transmitted data. An SA based on the ESP protocol can be used in either the transport or the tunnel mode (Table 18.2).

The ESP packet format is given in Table 18.3. The first two fields, SPI and Sequence Number, create the ESP header. The padding section together with Pad Length, Next Header, and Authentication Data constitute the ESP footer. The SPI (32 bits) uniquely identifies the security association of this datagram. For the first datagram sent via the SA, the Sequence Number (32 bits) is initialized to 1 and increased by one for each consecutive packet. If the sequence

Table 18.2. Datagram structure for (a) transport and (b) tunnel modes

IP Header	Datagram Payload

(a)	IP Header	ESP Header	Datagram Payload	ESP Footer

(b)	New IP Header	ESP Header	IP Header	Datagram Payload	ESP Footer

Table 18.3. ESP Packet Format

Security Parameters Index (SPI)		
Sequence Number Field		
Datagram Payload		
Padding		
	Pad Length	Next Header
Authentication Data		

number overflows (is equal to 2^{32}), then this SA is closed and the remaining packets are sent over a new SA. This field is used for reply prevention. The Datagram Body (also called Payload Data) contains the data carried by the original packet. The Padding is necessary to adjust the length of the encrypted data to be a multiple of 32-bit words. The padding cannot be longer than 255 bytes. The Pad Length (8 bits) specifies the number of bytes in the Padding field. The Next Header (8 bits) indicates the type of data in the Datagram Body field. The Authentication Data field contains a MAC (or ICV) calculated for the whole datagram (excluding the Authentication Data).

The ESP protocol is designed for private-key encryption (such as DES) as it is typically faster than its public-key counterparts. The authentication is supported by the same algorithms as in the case of the AH protocol.

18.1.4 Internet Key Exchange

The Internet Key Exchange (IKE) is described in [232]. Two parties called *Initiator* and *Responder* who wish to establish a common SA (secure channel) call the Internet Security Association Key Management Protocol (ISAKMP). The protocol runs in two stages. In the first stage, two peers negotiate a common secure channel called an ISAKMP Security Association (ISAKMP SA). The negotiated attributes include: encryption algorithm, hashing function, authentication method, and the algebraic group for exponentiation (Diffie-Hellman key agreement). Additionally, a pseudorandom bit generator can be negotiated. An ISAKMP SA is a bidirectional channel and provides both confidentiality and authenticity. Note that a normal SA used to transmit data is unidirectional and can provide either authentication or confidentiality. In the second stage, the ISAKMP SA is used to exchange key material for an SA.

The key material SKEYID necessary to establish the ISAKMP SA is derived differently, depending upon the authentication method used. The collection of options is

SKEYID $= PBG(N_i|N_r, g^{x_i x_r})$ for signatures,

SKEYID $= PBG(H(N_i|N_r), CKY_i|CKY_r)$ for public-key encryption,

SKEYID $= PBG(key, N_i|N_r)$ for preshared keys,

where N_i, N_r are payloads of nonce datagrams generated by the initiator and responder, respectively, g^{x_i}, g^{x_r} are public keys of the initiator and responder, respectively, $g^{x_i x_r}$ is the Diffie-Hellman key (common for both parties), and CKY_i and CKY_r are tokens (also called cookies) for the initiator and responder, respectively. The tokens provide a source address identification for two parties. The pair of tokens uniquely identifies the currently valid cryptographic key SKEYID used by the two parties. PBG is an agreed pseudorandom bit generator and H is a hash function. The key SKEYID now is used to generate the three variants

$$\text{SKEYID}_d = PBG(\text{SKEYID}, g^{x_i x_r}|CKY_i|CKY_r|0),$$
$$\text{SKEYID}_a = PBG(\text{SKEYID}, \text{SKEYID}_d|g^{x_i x_r}|CKY_i|CKY_r|1),$$
$$\text{SKEYID}_e = PBG(\text{SKEYID}, \text{SKEYID}_a|g^{x_i x_r}|CKY_i|CKY_r|2),$$

where SKEYID_d is the key used to derive keys for non-ISAKMP SAs (or simply session keys), and $\text{SKEYID}_a, \text{SKEYID}_e$ are the keys used by the ISAKMP SA for authentication and confidentiality, respectively. The exchange of information is authenticated using two strings

$$H_i = PBG(\text{SKEYID}, g^{x_i}|g^{x_r}|CKY_i|CKY_r|SA_i|ID_{ii}),$$
$$H_r = PBG(\text{SKEYID}, g^{x_r}|g^{x_i}|CKY_r|CKY_i|SA_i|ID_{ir}),$$

where SA_i is the entire body of the SA payload minus the ISAKMP header, and ID_{ii}, ID_{ir} are the identification payloads for the initiator and responder, respectively. The IKE has two distinct phases: negotiation and establishment. In the first phase two parties negotiate attributes for the SA and the key material used to establish a common ISAKMP SA.

Negotiation phase of IKE with signatures. Assume that the parties know their true public keys for signature verification. Initiator and Responder are two parties who would like to establish a secure channel. The communication between the parties is as follows:

Initiator	Responder
(1) HDR, SA	$\rightarrow$
(2)	$\leftarrow$ HDR, SA
(3) HDR, KE, N_i	$\rightarrow$
(4)	$\leftarrow$ HDR, KE, N_r
(5) HDR*, ID_{ii}, SIG$_i$ $\rightarrow$	
(6)	$\leftarrow$ HDR*, ID_{ir}, SIG$_r$

HDR is an ISAKMP header and SA is a negotiation payload. The negotiation payload can contain many options if the SA is sent by Initiator. It must have a single option when the SA is sent by Responder. KE is a key exchange payload with the public exponents used in the DH key agreement. N_i and N_r are nonce payloads generated by the parties. HDR* is an ISAKMP header with an encrypted payload which follows the header. ID_{ii} and ID_{ir} are identification payloads for the ISAKMP initiator and responder. SIG$_i$ and SIG$_r$ are the signature payloads for H_i and H_r, respectively. In the first two steps, parties negotiate security attributes. In steps (3) and (4), parties exchange their nonces and public parameters of the DH key agreement. Now the two parties can calculate the main key SKEYID and its variants SKEYID$_d$, SKEYID$_a$, SKEYID$_e$. The two last variants are used in steps (5) and (6) to provide confidentiality and authentication. The exchange can be compressed by allowing the initiator to send messages in steps (1) and (3) in one go and the responder to send messages (2) and (4) in one packet. This is the *aggressive mode* of the IKE protocol.

Negotiation phase of IKE with public-key encryption. This option works under the assumption that the parties know their mutual public keys PK_i and PK_r. The data exchange is given below:

Initiator		Responder
(1) HDR, SA	$\rightarrow$	
(2)		$\leftarrow$ HDR, SA
(3) HDR,KE,		
$\quad \{ID_{ii}\}_{PK_r}, \{N_i\}_{PK_r}$	$\rightarrow$	
(4)		$\leftarrow$ HDR, KE, $\{ID_{ir}\}_{PK_i}, \{N_r\}_{PK_i}$
(5) HDR*, H_i	$\rightarrow$	
(6)		$\leftarrow$ HDR*, H_r

where PK_i and PK_r are the public keys of the initiator and responder, respectively, and $\{m\}_{PK}$ means the cryptogram of message m encrypted using the public key PK.

Negotiation phase of IKE with preshared key. Assume that the parties share the same secret key. The phase takes the form of the following steps:

Initiator	Responder
(1) HDR, SA	$\rightarrow$
(2)	$\leftarrow$ HDR, SA
(3) HDR, KE, N_i	$\rightarrow$
(4)	$\leftarrow$ HDR, KE, N_r
(5) HDR*, ID_{ii} H_i	$\rightarrow$
(6)	$\leftarrow$ HDR*, ID_{ir} H_r

Final phase. This phase is used to obtain the key material for non-ISAKMP security associations (or simply session keys). The information exchange is performed via the ISAKMP SA established in the first phase. In other words, the payloads, except the ISAKMP header, are encrypted. The parties involved in the first phase may act on behalf of their clients. In this case, the identities of the clients may be used together with the identities of the Initiator and Responder. Typically, the internal security policy determines whether or not this is required. To simplify our considerations we assume that the Initiator and Responder do not have clients. The exchange of messages is as follows:

Initiator	Responder
(1) HDR*, H(1), SA, N_i $\rightarrow$	
(2)	$\leftarrow$ HDR*, H(2), SA, N_r
(3) HDR*, H(3)	$\rightarrow$

where H(1)=$PBG(\text{SKEYID}_a, M_{ID}|SA|N_i)$, H(2)=$PBG(\text{SKEYID}_a, M_{ID}|SA|N_r)$, and H(3)=$PBG(\text{SKEYID}_a, 0|M_{ID}|SA|N_i|N_r)$. M_{ID} is the message identity from the ISAKMP header. If the KE payloads are not exchanged, the key material is

$$\text{KEYMAT} = PBG(\text{SKEYID}_d, \text{protocol}|\text{SPI}|N_i|N_r),$$

otherwise

$$\text{KEYMAT} = PBG(\text{SKEYID}_d, g^{x_i x_r}|\text{protocol}|\text{SPI}|N_i|N_r).$$

Note that the key materials KEYMAT are different on both sides as the SPIs used by Initiator and Responder are different. If the key material is too short, the IKE protocol extends it by applying the following iterative procedure:

$$K_1 = PBG(\text{SKEYID}_d, \text{protocol}|\text{SPI}|N_i|N_r), \ldots$$
$$K_{i+1} = PBG(\text{SKEYID}_d, K_i|\text{protocol}|\text{SPI}|N_i|N_r), \ldots$$

18.1.5 Virtual Private Networks

The Internet is a driving force for new network-based applications and services. It spans the globe and connects most organizations and institutions, and many private users. The main weakness of the Internet is the lack of security. The concept of a virtual private network (VPN) repeats a well-known idea for a private network built over insecure leased public communication lines. The Internet provides insecure communication links that can be used to build a secure and private subnetwork using IPsec. IPsec can be used directly (IPv6) or indirectly (jointly with IPv4) to provide authentication and confidentiality.

Consider a collection of basic VPN configurations:

– *host-to-host* secure communication,
– *gateway-to-gateway* secure communication,
– multiple nested secure communication.

The host-to-host configuration is used to create a bidirectional secure channel (with authentication or privacy or both). To implement an authentication channel, two security associations (in each direction) with the AH protocol must be used. To provide authentication and privacy, four security associations have to be applied. This configuration is the basic one which is used for other more complex ones.

Most international companies and organizations have many branches or divisions, each of which is typically supported by one or more LANs with access to the Internet. It is reasonable to assume that a company needs to establish from time to time a secure communication between two or more LANs. Consider the simplest case when two LANs are to be integrated into a single VPN. If the LANs already have access to the Internet, then the traffic to and from the Internet is passing through a nominated host, called a gateway. It is enough to establish a secure channel between two security gateways in order to integrate the two LANs into a VPN.

Assume that we have already two LANs integrated into a VPN. It can be expected that two hosts residing in two different LANs may need to establish a secure channel. In this case, the traffic between the two hosts will be protected locally (within the LANs) and externally (outside the LANs). The local protection is provided by the host-to-host secure channel. The external security is guaranteed jointly by the host-to-host and gateway-to-gateway secure channels.

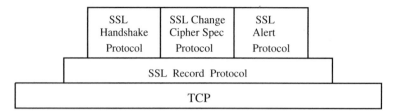

Fig. 18.2. SSL protocol layers

This kind of nested secure channel makes sense if, for example, the authentication channel is requested within the VPN while the transmitted information between LANs is to be kept secret from the outside world.

18.2 Secure Sockets Layer

The Secure Sockets Layer (SSL) protocol was developed by Netscape to provide a secure communication channel between two applications interacting in the client-server mode. The SSL protocol is a suite of protocols arranged in two layers (Fig. 18.2).

– The first one consists of a single protocol which is the *SSL Record Protocol.* It sits on top of a reliable transport protocol such as TCP and provides confidentiality and integrity services for the protocols from the second layer.
– The second layer includes three protocols:
  – *Handshake Protocol* – used for mutual authentication of client and server.
  – *Change Cipher Spec Protocol* – enables parties to choose proper cryptographic options.
  – *Alert Protocol* – exchanges warnings.

18.2.1 States of SSL

The protocol uses sessions and connections.

– A *session* is an association between a client and a server that defines the security environment (such as cryptographic algorithms). A session is established by the Handshake Protocol.
– A *connection* provides a suitable type of service within a single session. Normally, a new connection starts after the Change Cipher Spec Protocol is executed.

Sessions and connections provide a convenient way of splitting the security options negotiated by the parties into two collections: long term (session state) and short-term (connection state). The session state includes the following parameters:

- *Session identifier* – an arbitrary byte sequence chosen by the server to identify an active or resumable session.
- *Peer certificate* – an X509.v3 certificate of the peer. This element of the state can be null.
- *Compression method* – the algorithm used to compress data prior to encryption.
- *Cipher spec* – specifies the bulk data encryption algorithm (such as null, DES, etc.) and a message authentication code (MAC) algorithm (based on MD5 or SHA). It also defines cryptographic attributes such as hash_size.
- *Master secret* – 48-byte secret shared between the client and server.
- *Is resumable* – a flag indicating whether the session can be used to initiate new connections.

The connection state determines the following parameters:

- *Server and client random* – a byte sequence that is chosen by the server and client for each connection.
- *Server write MAC secret* – the secret used in MAC operations on data written by the server.
- *Client write MAC secret* – the secret used in MAC operations on data written by the client.
- *Server write key* – the bulk cipher key for data encrypted by the server and decrypted by the client.
- *Client write key* – the bulk cipher key for data encrypted by the client and decrypted by the server.
- *Initialization vectors* – when a block cipher in CBC mode is used, an initialization vector (IV) is maintained for each key. This field is first initialized by the SSL Handshake Protocol. Thereafter the final ciphertext block from each record is preserved for use with the following record.
- *Sequence numbers* – each party maintains separate sequence numbers for transmitted and received messages for each connection. When a party sends and receives a change_cipher_spec message, the appropriate sequence number is set to zero. Sequence numbers may not exceed $2^{64} - 1$.

18.2.2 SSL Record Protocol

The protocol provides the two basic security services:

- *Authentication* – messages received from higher layers are authenticated and SSL records coming from the underlying TCP protocol are verified. MACs are obtained using a collision-resistant hash function (such as MD5).
- *Confidentiality* – messages are encrypted if they are coming from higher layers or decrypted if coming from the TCP layer. Cryptographic operations are based on a private-key cryptosystem (such as DES) and the cryptographic key is generated by the Handshaking Protocol.

Being more specific, the protocol accepts uninterpreted data of arbitrary size from higher layers, and (Fig. 18.3):

- Splits the data into SSL records of 2^{14} bytes or less. This is called *fragmentation*.

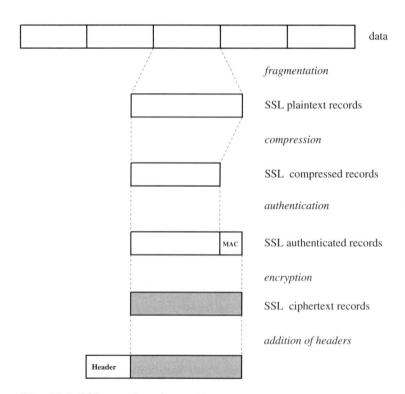

Fig. 18.3. SSL records and operations

– Compresses (this is optional) the received records. Compression must be lossless and may not increase the content length by more than 1024 bytes. Note that one would expect that compression always shortens the length of data. However, for already short records, compression may actually increase the size of the output data.
– Appends MACs to SSL compressed records.
– Encrypts authenticated records (compressed records with MACs).
– Adds headers to SSL records.

The first two steps are pretty obvious and need no further clarification. Consider the next two, as they are essential for this protocol. MACs are generated according to the following formula:

hash(MAC_write_secret‖pad_2‖hash(MAC_write_secret‖

pad_1‖seq_num‖length‖content)),

where ‖ stands for concatenation,

MAC_write_secret is a secret key shared between parties
                 (and generated by the Handshaking Protocol),
pad_1   is a constant character 0x36 repeated 48
                 times for MD5 or 40 times for SHA,
pad_2   is a constant character 0x5c repeated
                 the same number of times,
seq_num   is the sequence number of this message,
hash   is either MD5 or SHA-1,
length   gives the length in bytes of the compressed record, and
content   is the compressed record.

The encryption is performed on compressed and authenticated records using a private-key algorithm (either block or stream cipher). The following cryptographic algorithms are supported:

– *block ciphers* – DES (two variants with 40-bit and 56-bit keys), Triple DES, IDEA, RC2 (with 40-bit keys), and Fortezza,
– *stream ciphers* – RC4 with keys either 40 bits or 128 bits long.

In the last step of the protocol, a header is attached to the record. It consists of four fields (Fig. 18.4), namely:

– *Content Type*, which describes the type of data,

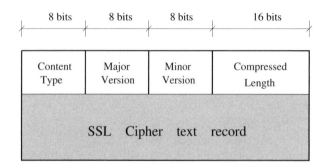

Fig. 18.4. SSL record header

- *Major Version*, which gives the major version number of the SSL. If SSLv3 is used the number is 3,
- *Minor Version*, which allows us to determine versions within the major one,
- *Compressed Length*, which specifies the overall length in bytes of authenticated (and compressed) SSL records. It must not exceed $2^{14} + 2048$ bytes.

18.2.3 Handshake Protocol

The protocol initiates cryptographic parameters of the session state and runs through the following three stages.

Handshake protocol

Initialization: a client and server exchange `client_hello` and `server_hello` messages, respectively, or

    1. Client $\rightarrow$ Server: `client_hello`.

    2. Client $\leftarrow$ Server: `server_hello`.

Attributes established: protocol version, session ID, cipher suite, compression method, and two random values (`ClientHello.random` and `ServerHello.random`).

Mutual authentication and key exchange: server first sends `certificate`, `server_key_exchange`, `certificate_request`, and `server_hello_done` messages. The client replies by sending `certificate`, `client_key_exchange`, and `certificate_verify` messages. In other words,

    3. Client $\leftarrow$ Server: `certificate`, `server_key_exchange`, `certificate_request`, `server_hello_done`.

4. Client $\rightarrow$ Server: certificate, client_key_exchange,
   certificate_verify.

Final: the parties exchange change_cipher_spec and finished messages, or

5. Client $\rightarrow$ Server: change_cipher_spec, finished.

6. Client $\leftarrow$ Server: change_cipher_spec, finished.

Consider the initialization stage in more detail. The first message sent from Client to Server is client_hello together with the following parameters:

Version – the highest SSL version supported by the client.

Random – a random structure generated by the client containing a 32-bit time-stamp and a 28-byte pseudorandom string.

SessionID – a variable-length session identifier. If the identifier is not empty, the value determines an existing session between the same parties whose security parameters the client wishes to reuse. A zero value can be used if the client wants to establish a new session.

CipherSuite – a list of the combinations of cryptographic algorithms supported by the client and ordered according to the client's preference. The session fails if none of the algorithms specified by the client is supported by the server.

CompressionMethod – a list of compression methods supported by the client and ordered according to the client's preference.

If there is no chance to agree on some parameters, the server replies with a handshake_failure message. Otherwise it sends its server_hello message which is accompanied with the same parameters, which are:

Version – the lower of those suggested by the client.

Random – a random structure generated by the server and different (independent) from ClientHello.random.

SessionID – if the identifier is not empty, the server looks in its session cache for a match and reuses it if found.

CipherSuite – a single cipher suite selected by the server from the list suggested by the client.

CompressionMethod – a single compression algorithm selected by the server from the list suggested by the client.

The CipherSuite lists pairs of: a key exchange algorithm and a CipherSpec identifier of the cipher. The following key exchange algorithms can be chosen:

- RSA – a secret key is encrypted using the RSA encryption.
- Fixed Diffie-Hellman – parties exchange messages containing certificates of DH parameters.
- Ephemeral DH – the DH keys are signed by the sender and verified by the receiver.
- Anonymous DH – this algorithm uses no authentication and is insecure against the man-in-the-middle attack.
- Fortezza.

Mutual authentication and key exchange is started by the server who sends its certificate (this is optional). The certificate type must be appropriate for the chosen key exchange algorithm and is typically an X509.v3 certificate. If the server does not have its certificate (or has a certificate only used for signing), then the server_key_exchange message is sent. The message includes the following parameters:

- RSA – the modulus and exponent of the server temporary RSA key.
- Diffie-Hellman – the modulus, generator, and the server public key (this is for anonymous DH). These three elements are signed for ephemeral DH.

A certificate_request message is sent by an nonanonymous server to the client. The message includes two parameters:

- certificate_type – a list of the types of certificates requested (RSA signature only, DSS only, RSA for DH, DSS for DH),
- certificate_authorities – a list of the names of acceptable certificate authorities.

A server_hello_done indicates the end of the message strings generated by the server. After sending it, the server waits for a client response.

The client sends the certificate message only if the server has requested it. If the client has no proper certificate, then it warns the server by transmitting a no_certificate alert. Next the client_key_exchange message is sent. The form of the message depends on the agreed key exchange algorithm and, thus, there are three options:

- RSA – the client generates a 48-byte premaster secret, and encrypts it using the public key (derived from the server certificate or from the temporary RSA key).

– DH – the client sends the public value of the DH key (if it was not already included in the client certificate).

– Fortezza – the client derives a Token Encryption Key (TEK) using Fortezza's key exchange algorithm.

A certificate_verify message asks for explicit verification of a client certificate. This message is sent only if any of the client certificates has signing capability.

The final stage of the protocol starts from a change_cipher_spec message, which sets up the current CipherSpec and is considered to be part of the Change Cipher Spec Protocol. Next the party communicates a finished message, which is cryptographically protected using the just-negotiated algorithms, keys, and secrets.

18.2.4 Change Cipher Spec and Alert Protocols

The Change Cipher Spec Protocol is very simple and consists of a single message, which is encrypted and compressed under the current (not the pending) CipherSpec. The message is a single byte of value 1. Once the message is received, the pending state of CipherSpec is copied into the current state.

The Alert Protocol distributes alerts with the information about their severity (1 byte) and description (1 byte). The severity takes on two forms:

– warning(1),

– fatal(2) – the connection is immediately terminated.

The description of alerts includes:

– close_notify – the recipient is notified that the sender will no longer send any message on this connection.

– unexpected_message – an inappropriate message was received (this alert is always fatal).

– bad_record_mac – this alert occurs whenever an SSL record is received with an incorrect MAC (always fatal).

– decompression_failure – the decompression function received an improper input (always fatal).

– handshake_failure – the sender was unable to negotiate an acceptable set of security parameters (always fatal).

- no_certificate – this alert is normally sent in response to a certificate request if no appropriate certificate is available.
- bad_certificate – a certificate has failed the verification procedure.
- unsupported_certificate – a certificate of a foreign type.
- certificate_revoked – a certificate has been revoked by its signer.
- certificate_expired – a certificate has expired.
- certificate_unknown – some possibly unspecified failure has occurred during validation of the certificate, rendering it unacceptable.
- illegal_parameter – a field (parameter) in the handshake message has been out of range or inconsistent with other fields (always fatal).

18.2.5 Cryptographic Computations

A pre_master_secret exchanged in the Handshake protocol is used to generate the master_secret according to the following formula:

```
master_secret = MD5(pre_master_secret || SHA('A'|| pre_master_secret ||
                ClientHello.random || ServerHello.random)) ||
                MD5(pre_master_secret || SHA('BB'|| pre_master_secret ||
                ClientHello.random || ServerHello.random)) ||
                MD5(pre_master_secret || SHA('CCC'|| pre_master_secret ||
                ClientHello.random || ServerHello.random));
```

Once generated, the master_secret replaces the pre_master_secret.

Further the master_secret is used as a seed to generate key material such as a client write MAC secret, a server write MAC secret, a client write key, a server write key, a client write IV, and a server write IV (IV stands for initial vector). Key material is generated in blocks as follows:

```
key_block = MD5(master_secret || SHA('A'|| master_secret ||
            ServerHello.random || ClientHello.random)) ||
            MD5(master_secret || SHA('BB'|| master_secret ||
            ServerHello.random || ClientHello.random)) ||
            MD5(master_secret || SHA('CCC'|| master_secret ||
            ServerHello.random || ClientHello.random)) || ...
```

18.2.6 Transport-Layer Security

The Transport-Layer Security (TLS) is based on SSL version 3.0 and is documented in the RFC [151]. The differences between TLS and SSL are rather minor but substantial enough to preclude their interoperability. Actually, TLSv1.0 has a mechanism by which a TLS implementation can run SSLv3.0 (but not vice versa). The differences between TLS and SSL are specified in [487].

18.3 Computer Viruses

The discovery of computer viruses was one of the most important factors that put network security issues in the spotlight. It turns out that users of personal computers are all at risk from computer virus infections. Recent developments in computer virus technology, in particular the macro virus that spreads through the exchange of documents prepared using, for example, certain word-processing packages, mean that more computer users than ever before will be affected at some time by a computer virus.

The reader who wishes to further study the topic is referred to [101, 424]. While working on this chapter, the authors were helped by Jeff Horton who made accessible a draft of his PhD thesis [245]. He also read this part and corrected the text. The authors gratefully acknowledge this.

18.3.1 What Is a Computer Virus?

Computer viruses, computer worms, and Trojan horses are all different forms of malicious software or *malware*. Cohen in [99] informally defines a computer virus as

> a program that can "infect" other programs by modifying them to include a possibly evolved copy of itself.

Viruses infect computer programs by changing their structure. The change can take different forms, including:

– *Destroying data* – The Brain virus [240] targeted the IBM PC and was capable of destroying data describing the location of sectors making up files on a diskette and could even overwrite part of a file in the process of infection.

– *Stealing CPU time* – Consider a virus that asks permission before infecting an executable file. The creator of the virus can see it as a useful tool, while users whose work is interrupted by the virus can perceive it as a time-wasting nuisance.

– *Reducing the functionality of the infected program.*

– *Adding new, not necessarily malicious, capabilities to the infected program* – Cohen in [99] discusses a virus that compresses executable files on infection and which decompresses the files on execution.

There is increased research activity related to the problem of detection and removal of computer viruses. Detection of viruses is not easy, as viruses tend to mutate after infection. That is why Cohen used *possibly evolved* in his definition. Designers of computer viruses intentionally create viruses that are able to mutate after infection to make detection of viruses by antivirus software more difficult.

Cohen's definition is too restrictive, as it fails to include a program that is able to attach itself to a host program by some means other than altering the code of the host program, but otherwise would seem well-described by the tag of "computer virus." The *companion* strategy of infection is an excellent example of this. For this reason, the above definition can be extended as follows:

A computer "virus" is a program that can "infect" other programs by modifying either host programs or the environment in which host programs exist. A possibly mutated copy of the virus gets attached to host programs.

The above definition can be further extended by requiring viruses to be capable of further replication. A formal definition of a computer virus is given in [100].

18.3.2 Worms and Trojan Horses

Informally, a *computer worm* can be defined as

a self-replicating and self-contained program that is capable of spreading itself to other machines.

Unlike a virus, a worm does not infect or otherwise depend on a host program. It is self-contained.

The Internet Worm unleashed in November 1988 is probably the most famous example of a worm. The worm exploited a number of known security holes in the UNIX operating system. It consisted of two programs: a grappling hook (or bootstrap) program and the main program [469]. The grappling hook was a short C program. Once established in a foreign machine, the grappling hook compiled and executed. During the execution, it connected to the machine from which it had originated and uploaded a copy of the main program. The task of the main program was to search the Internet for other machines that could be easy victims, i.e., machines that would allow remote execution of the grappling hook without proper authorization.

Recently, the Autostart worm for the Macintosh was reported and is described in [257]. The worm exploited the ability to designate a program on a diskette or hard disk to be executed when the disk was mounted by the operating system. Unlike the Internet Worm, it spread via the transfer of infected disks from one machine to another.

A *Trojan horse* program can be defined as

> a program that claims to perform a particular function sufficiently attractive to the computer user to ensure that the user executes the program. Instead of, or perhaps in addition to, performing this function, the Trojan horse takes some form of undocumented action, often malicious, that was intended by the programmer.

Note that this definition excludes programs that cause destruction as a result of bugs in the program. Trojan horses, unlike viruses and worms, do not replicate themselves. Malicious actions undertaken by a Trojan horse can range from a relatively simple action, such as deleting files, to more subtle activities such as gathering private information about users. It is not difficult to imagine a Trojan horse that collects secret session keys from a user's hard disk and sends this information out over the Internet for collection at a remote site.

18.3.3 Taxonomy of Viruses

The risk of infection greatly depends on the hardware platform in use. Consider the three following platforms:

– *IBM PC* – users of this platform are the worst affected. It is reported in [363] that more than 10,000 DOS-based computer viruses had been created as of November 1996.
– *Macintosh* – users have also been affected by the computer virus problem, but not to the same degree as users of IBM PCs. Estimates vary, but there

are certainly fewer than 100 viruses specifically designed for the Macintosh platform.

– *UNIX* – users are fortunate, as there are no common virus threats against this platform. However, the potential exists for viruses to be written for this platform [99, 101, 162, 331].

Any computer platform where programs are stored on modifiable media is subject to attack by computer viruses. In general, viruses can be divided into two broad classes:

– platform dependent, and
– platform independent.

Platform-dependent viruses normally exploit a specific hardware/software configuration characteristic for the platform. *Macro viruses* are a newcomer in the area and are platform independent. Macro viruses are written in interpreted languages supplied by some common programs (applications) that are available across multiple platforms. A good example of such an application is Microsoft Word. It is available for both IBM PC and Macintosh computers.

Viruses infect only executable files. To activate them, the host program must be executed. A virus can be either:

– *Memory resident* – the virus remains active even after its host program has terminated.
– *Non-memory resident* – the virus becomes active only if its host program is executing.

Writers of computer viruses use two main strategies to make the detection of viruses more difficult. The strategies are:

– *Polymorphism* – a virus changes its form using a variety of techniques, including encryption.
– *Stealth* – a virus tries to conceal its presence in infected objects when executing.

A sequence of bytes considered characteristic of a virus is called a virus *signature*. To detect a virus, it is enough to scan the program for a virus signature. Polymorphism attempts to minimize the number of bytes available for use in a virus signature. There are two parts to the strategy:

– The virus encrypts the main body of the virus code using a variable key when infecting. A range of different simple schemes can be used. Before the encrypted virus can be executed, it must be decrypted.
– In addition to choosing between a variety of different encryption and, hence, decryption schemes, the virus applies equivalent machine instructions, re-ordering instructions (if the new order of instructions leads to equivalent operations), inserting dummy instructions (for instance, no operation instruc-tions), building up a code during runtime (once constructed, the code per-forms the required task), and using intermixing operations [101].

18.3.4 IBM-PC Viruses

This class of viruses is the biggest and can be divided into three groups:

– file-infecting viruses,
– boot-sector-infecting viruses, and
– multipartite viruses (infecting both executable files and boot sectors).

File-infecting viruses. The simplest type of file-infecting virus overwrites part of the host program and does not store the code that was overwritten. The host program before and after infection is illustrated in Fig. 18.5. The virus overwrites the beginning of the file so the virus will get executed every time the host program is invoked. The host program is likely to be so badly damaged that it is unable to function correctly. The viral code may also be placed elsewhere in the file hoping that it gets executed every time the host program is called, leaving most of the host program functions intact.

More sophisticated viruses attach to a host program in such a way that the host program is repairable by the virus. A simple way of infecting an executable

1. Program before infection by overwriting virus.

Program Code

2. Program after infection by overwriting virus.

Viral Code	Program Code

Fig. 18.5. Host program before and after infection by overwriting virus

file so that any changes made are repairable is to append the virus code to the end of the file, save the first few bytes of code for later restoration, and replace them with a jump to the appended viral code. When the host program is executed, the viral code assumes control first, and then can repair the code of its host and call it (Fig. 18.6). It is also possible to prepend the viral code to the host file (Fig. 18.7).

If a virus avoids overwriting, it means that the infected program (the host with the virus) has increased its size. This fact can be noticed by a user or a program monitoring the sizes of executable files. There are, however, ways in which a file can be infected without changing its size, yet the host code can be repaired by the virus at the time of execution.

– A cavity virus finds an area of constant data within the host program that is large enough to accommodate itself, records the value that was originally stored there and replaces the constant data with itself. The Lehigh virus [101] operated in this way.
– A cavity virus might also store itself inside unused spaces within an executable file that exist as a consequence of the format of the file. The CIH virus applies this technique [520].

1. Program before infection by appending virus.

2. Program after infection by appending virus.

Jump to start of viral code

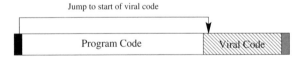

3. On execution, control passes to viral code. Virus repairs program code.

4. Virus executes original program.

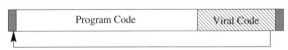

Fig. 18.6. An appending virus

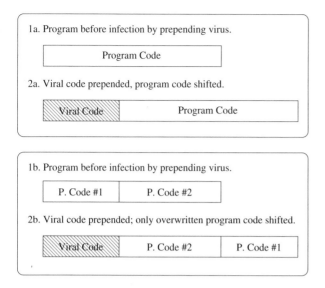

Fig. 18.7. A prepending virus

– A compression virus compresses all or part of the host file contents so it can hide inside the host program without changing the size of the file. The compressed component can be uncompressed at runtime.

Boot-sector-infecting viruses. Every time a computer is switched on, the operating system is loaded from a floppy or hard disk. This process is called *bootstrapping.* The bootstrapping process proceeds in several stages. When the operating system is loaded from a floppy disk, the first sector on the disk, referred to as the *boot sector* or *DOS boot sector*, consists of a small program that is responsible for starting the next stage. If the disk does not contain an operating system, this sector includes a program which informs the user that this is not a bootable disk, prompting for the insertion of another disk.

Hard disks are, because of their large size, often divided into a number of smaller logical parts called partitions. The first physical sector of a hard disk is referred to as the *master boot record* (MBR) or *master boot sector* (MBS) and contains a record of the partitions into which the disk has been divided, together with a small program responsible for locating a bootable partition and booting from that partition. The first logical sector of a bootable partition is then the boot sector that is used to load the operating system (Fig. 18.8).

Floppy Disk Startup:

Hard Disk Startup:

Fig. 18.8. Boot process for floppy and hard disks

Boot sector viruses infect the code found in the master boot record for hard disks or in the DOS boot sector for floppy and hard disks. The infection process normally looks like this. A virus:

- finds the target sector and stores it elsewhere so the virus can continue the boot process,
- loads a copy of itself into the sector.

Examples of this type of virus are:

- *AntiCMOS viruses* – a virus from this family discards the code from the infected sector and attempts to perform the boot functions itself [269].
- *Brain viruses* – a virus infects floppy disks only [240].
- *Monkey viruses* – they infect boot sectors and store the partition tables elsewhere so that infected hard disks are inaccessible if computers are not booted from the virus-infected hard disk [350].
- *Hare Krisna* – they tamper with the location of the partition tables [525].

Companion viruses. Companion viruses do not modify the host programs they infect. Instead, they create their copies as separate executable files. There are two basic types of companion viruses under MS-DOS [49, 246, 318].

- *Regular companion* – a virus of this type creates a file in the same directory as the host program but with a filename extension that usually gets executed before the extension used by the host program. For example, a .COM file with the same name as an .EXE file and in the same directory is executed before the .EXE file if the file extension is not specified.

– *Path companion* – a virus creates a file with any executable extension in a directory that is searched for executable files before the directory containing the host program.
– *Surrogate companion* – a virus renames the host program and replaces it with a copy of itself.

18.3.5 Macintosh Operating System

To discuss viruses affecting some Macintosh platform, we first need to introduce the necessary background about the Macintosh operating system. For more details the reader is referred to [249, 250, 251, 252].

Any Macintosh file has two components:

– data fork,
– resource fork (or resource file).

A characteristic feature of the Macintosh OS is that each file has its:

– type, for example, application (APPL) or ASCII text (TEXT),
– creator, or the application program which owns the file.

Resources within a resource file are described by:

– a resource type (four-letter code),
– an ID number (two-byte integer),
– a name (string of characters).

To identify a particular resource, it is enough to specify a resource type and either an ID number or a resource name. An application resource file stores a variety of information, including:

MENU stores information about the list of options in a particular application menu.
MBAR lists the menus that are present in an application's menu bar.
WIND describes the dimensions and other characteristics of a window created by an application.
CNTL defines a control which is a user interface element such as a button or scrollbar created by an application.
CODE contains the main components of an application executable code.

A loading resource may involve many resource forks. A search path is followed to locate the requested resources. The starting point is always the current resource file and the search ends in the System file that contains resources which are part of the operating system.

Consider the graphical user interface presented by an application. Many of the interface elements such as menus, windows, buttons, etc. are drawn using a *definition procedure* (DP). The executable code of a definition procedure is stored in a resource and loaded by the OS when required to draw a user interface element. The OS provides a default implementation and it can be customized by a user. Examples of definition procedures include:

– *Menu DP* – is stored in an MDEF resource and is responsible for drawing menu items within a menu.
– *Menu bar DP* – is stored in an MBDF resource and is responsible for drawing activities related to the display of menus.
– *Window DP* – is stored in a WDEF resource and is responsible for such tasks as drawing a frame or resizing a window.
– *Control DP* – is stored in a CDEF resource and is responsible, among many tasks, for drawing the control and testing for where the mouse has been clicked by the user within a control.

The INIT is another important type of resource containing executable code. These are resources that contain code that is intended to be executed at system startup. INIT resources can be located within the System file itself or in files of particular types.

The Finder is an application which is a part of the Macintosh operating system. The Finder:

– manages the display of the user desktop,
– keeps track of the location (both on the screen and on the disk directory structure) of files and folders,
– ensures that the appropriate application is used to work with a file created when the file is double-clicked by the user.

Under Macintosh system software prior to System 7 (System 6), "Finder" refers to a version of the software that would permit only one application at a time to execute. That is, users could run the Finder or some other application but not both at once. MultiFinder was a refinement of the Finder that would permit more than one application, including MultiFinder itself, to execute at a time. We will use Finder to refer to a version of the software descended from

MultiFinder – more than one application at a time, including the Finder, may be executed.

Application developers are able to designate an icon for each type of file that is created or owned by the application. These icons will be displayed by the Finder to represent the user documents. Icon information is given by resources from the application resource fork. The Finder extracts this and other information from the application resource fork and stores it in a database for easy access. The location of the application on disk is also stored.

To display the icon for a document, the Finder checks its database for an icon corresponding to the document type provided by the application with the same creator code as the document. When a document is double-clicked, the Finder searches its database for an application whose creator code is the same as the document creator code. If found, the Finder executes that application to process the document.

Macintosh hardware. The first Macintosh models were based on Motorola 68000 microprocessors. We collectively call Macintoshes based on the 680x0 series of microprocessors "68K Macintoshes" and code intended to run on these microprocessors "68K code." The PowerPC series of microprocessors replaced 680x0 microprocessors in new Macintosh models. Models with the PowerPC microprocessor are collectively referred to as "PPC Macintoshes," and the code as "PPC code." Needless to say, the machine code for the 680x0 microprocessors is not compatible with the newer PowerPC microprocessors. Apple has addressed this problem by supplying a 68LC040 emulator as a part of the operating system for PPC Macintoshes.

The executable of an application can be stored within the application file using the following three basic methods:

- Application based on 68K code is split into a number of code segments. These applications can run under emulation on a PPC Macintosh.
- Application based on 68K code is split into code fragments and also contains a small code segment responsible for starting up the code fragment component on versions of the OS that are not able to automatically perform this task. These applications cannot run under emulation on a PPC Macintosh.
- Application based on PPC code is split into code fragments.

Macintosh viruses known so far work by modifying an application based on 68K code segments. This, however, also makes PPC Macintoshes vulnerable, as:

- Most PPC applications contain at least a small component based on 68K code which informs a user that the application cannot be run on a 68K Macintosh.
- Not all viruses attempt to modify the application code directly. Some viruses add executable resources like the MDEF resource to an application. 68K definition procedures added to a PPC application by a virus will still work in a PPC environment.
- There is every reason to expect that such viruses will be written in the future.

Code fragments are typically stored in the data fork of an application file but may also be stored in resources in the resource fork. A resource known as the *code fragment resource* or cfrg resource with identity 0 is used to index the fragments. Applications based on code fragments can also import shared libraries. The code fragments within a shared library could potentially be infected by a virus (although no such viruses for the Macintosh are currently known). A code-fragment-based environment is much more flexible and programmer friendly than the 68K code segment environment.

The structure of an application based on code segments is much simpler (Fig. 18.9). The executable code of a 68K application is divided into a number of segments and each segment is stored in a CODE resource and may contain one

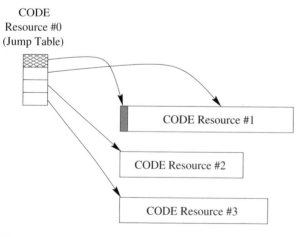

Fig. 18.9. Code-segment-based 68K application

or more routines (note that the second entry of the Jump Table in Fig. 18.9 contains the address of the second routine stored in CODE resource #1). This has the advantage that not all resources are required in memory at a particular time to execute programs.

A mechanism is needed to enable a routine located in one code segment to call another routine. Intersegment calls are handled with the aid of a so-called *jump table*. To invoke a routine in another segment, a jump is executed to the jump table where the addresses of routines are stored. The jump table is stored in the CODE resource with ID 0. The first entry in the table contains the address of the routine which gets executed first. Not all compilers maintain the entire jump table in the CODE 0 resource. Instead, a jump table is constructed in memory on execution.

18.3.6 Macintosh Viruses

Most Macintosh viruses modify the executable code of an application program in some way so that when the program is run, the viral code gets executed. There are two major techniques to achieve this:

− A virus modifies the code segments of the application.
− A virus adds new resources containing a definition procedure that will be invoked implicitly during application execution.

Consider a typical 68K application illustrated in Fig. 18.9. A virus can infect the application by changing the code segments in three ways:

− The virus adds a code segment to the application in the form of an additional CODE resource modifying the first entry of the jump table so it refers to the viral CODE resource. As a result, the viral code gets control when the application starts executing. The original first jump table entry is saved by the virus so that it can return control to the application once it has completed its task. The application original code segments are not modified except from the jump table. The infection process is illustrated in Fig. 18.10. The viruses nVIR [173] and INIT29 [172] are good examples of viruses of this type [174].
− Rather than adding a new code segment to the application, the virus adds its code to the end of an existing CODE resource. The virus need not touch the jump table. Instead, it modifies the first few bytes of a routine in the CODE resource so that when the routine is invoked, the viral code is called. The

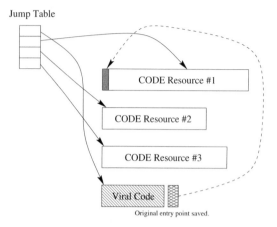

Fig. 18.10. Modifications made by virus that add an additional CODE resource to an application

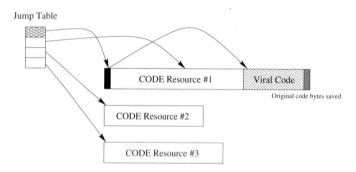

Fig. 18.11. Modifications made by virus that adds its code to an existing CODE resource and modifies a routine to jump to the viral code

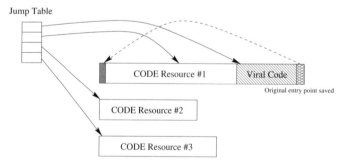

Fig. 18.12. Modifications made by virus that adds its code to an existing CODE resource and modifies a jump table entry

bytes replaced by the virus can be saved and restored after execution of the viral code. Fig. 18.11 presents how the virus works.

- The virus appends its body to an existing CODE resource and modifies the jump table. When the application is executed, the viral code gains control first. The original jump table entry is saved so that control can be returned to the application. This strategy of infection is depicted in Fig. 18.12.

There are several ways in which an application can be infected by the addition of a resource containing the code for a definition procedure. A typical relationship between an application menu and a default definition procedure is given in Fig. 18.13. Consider the following infection strategies for this case:

- The virus adds a viral definition procedure with the same type and identity as a standard DP resource from the System file (Fig. 18.14).
- The virus adds a viral definition procedure with a changed identity (Fig. 18.15).

The WDEF virus [175] deserves special attention. This virus infects using a definition resource. However, the definition resource is not added to an executable file! The WDEF virus adds a WDEF 0 resource containing the viral code to the resource file on each disk in which the Finder stores its desktop database, the Desktop file. This file is opened by the Finder when a disk is mounted. When the user subsequently opens a window within the Finder, the operating system will search for a WDEF 0 resource to perform a drawing operation. As the most recently opened resource files are searched first for resources, the viral WDEF 0 resource stored within the Desktop file will be found and executed in place of the original WDEF 0 resource. All operating systems since System 7 are immune to this attack.

18.3.7 Macro Viruses

A *macro* is a collection of statements in some language that performs a task when interpreted. Many application packages allow users to automate tasks which are common and repetitive, by defining their own macros. Some application packages provide not only a simple scripting language that can be used to control the application usage but also supply an interpreter for a complete programming language. Microsoft Word is probably the best known of these applications. Microsoft Word 6 provided as its macro language a version of

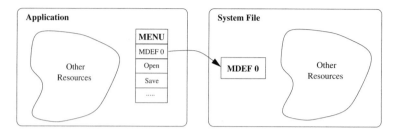

Fig. 18.13. Typical relationship between an application MENU and System MDEF

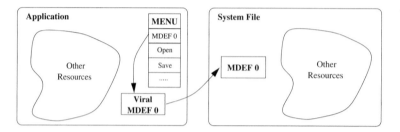

Fig. 18.14. Relationship between an application MENU, viral MDEF, and System MDEF

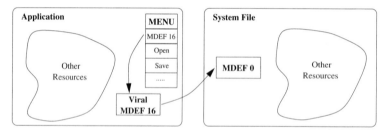

Fig. 18.15. Relationship between an application MENU, viral MDEF, and System MDEF

BASIC that was called WordBasic. Microsoft Word 6 was the first multiplatform implementation for both the Macintosh and the IBM PC.

The concept of a macro virus – a virus written in the macro language – is not new. The possibility of a macro virus was predicted by Highland in 1989 [241]. It was not until 1995 that the first macro virus, Concept, emerged. In March 1999, researchers at the Virus Test Center, University of Hamburg reported almost 600 known macro virus strains (for details see *ftp://agn-www.informatik.uni-hamburg.de/pub/texts/macro*). Most of these macro viruses target versions of Microsoft Word.

Macro viruses are typically embedded within a document file as a ' macro. Because the macros are interpreted by the application package rather than compiled into machine-specific executable code, they can execute within their host application on any computer hardware platform to which the application package has been ported. Macro viruses are potentially more infectious than other viruses especially when the infected documents are distributed via e-mail.

18.3.8 Protection Against Viruses

There are two main strategies to combat viruses:

– preventing viruses from becoming established in a computer system,
– detecting and removing them.

There are many nontechnical solutions to reduce the risk of virus infection and hopefully limit the consequences should it occur, including [242]:

– careful design of the sequence in which the operating system looks for a bootable device,
– reconfiguration of the e-mail system so that a received mail item is opened "safely,"
– removal of all executable programs that have been received from untrusted sources (without executing them),
– systematic backups of the system.

Antivirus techniques can be classified into three major categories,

– scanners,
– integrity checkers,
– behavior blockers or activity monitors.

Scanners. A virus scanner tries to detect the presence of a virus in a file by looking for the signature of the virus. As a virus tends to change its code, scanners need to search a file for parts of the signature which are characteristic for the virus. Once a virus is detected, scanners may attempt to disinfect the infected file by removing the virus. However, in some cases, the original form of the file cannot be restored (when the virus has destroyed a part of the file, for example). A better way is to replace the infected file from a backup. Scanners exhibit some drawbacks, including [101]:

- They can only detect viruses with known signatures.
- Scanners have to be updated every time a new virus is released.
- Polymorphic viruses are difficult to detect using scanners.
- Users must regularly run scanners to check disks for infection.
- There are many false positives when the scanner deals with files written in a foreign language.

The first weakness can be partially eliminated by the introduction of heuristic analysis [222]. Heuristics are sets of rules that can be applied to executable code to determine whether or not it is infected by a virus. Heuristics can be:

- *positive* – code performing operations suggestive of a virus,
- *negative* – code performing operations not likely to occur in virus code.

The difficulties in the detection of polymorphic viruses can be addressed by customizing scanners so they work well for a specific family of polymorphic viruses. A better approach seems to be the application of so-called *generic decryption* [363]. This approach works for viruses which use encryption to change their form. Such a virus must decrypt the main body of its code before execution. Generic decryption attempts to emulate the program under investigation past the point at which the virus code has been decrypted so the virus can be identified from its signature.

To relieve users from the burden of running scanners at regular intervals, a memory-resident scanner component might be provided. This component scans automatically files and disks for viruses when accessed.

Integrity checkers. It is reasonable to assume that a virus must change something when it infects a file. Hashing can be used for integrity checking. Once a file has been created, its hash value is computed. Any modification to it will cause a change of the hash value. Note that integrity checkers detect any changes in a file, not only those created by a virus. So if the hash value has changed, a file may be infected. Obvious limitations of integrity checkers are:

- Viruses introduced before an integrity checker has computed hash values for files will not be detected.
- Integrity checkers fail to detect infection if a file was at the same time modified by the user and infected by a virus.
- Viruses can only be detected after they have spread and inflicted some damage.

The main advantage of integrity checkers seems to be that they are able to detect unknown viral infections including notorious polymorphic viruses. The reader who wishes to pursue this topic is referred to [49, 101, 424].

Behavior blockers and activity monitors. These antivirus programs monitor the computer activity and attempt to detect the presence of a virus. The rationale behind behavior blockers and activity monitors is the hope that it is possible to distinguish somehow between abnormal (viral) and normal behavior. Clearly, this approach has the following drawbacks:

– Most viruses perform entirely legitimate actions rather than exploiting operating system weaknesses.
– Some viruses may try to bypass the antivirus programs. For instance, some Macintosh viruses contain code which redirects traps generated by the virus to ROM code. If successful, the antivirus program will be bypassed, that is, it fails to detect the virus.
– Blocking a suspicious action may result in undesired consequences. For example, files may be left in inconsistent states after a suspicious operation.
– After detecting a suspicious activity, the antivirus program may leave the decision about what needs to be done to the user. This can be irritating especially when it happens frequently.

References

1. C. Adams and S. Tavares. Generating and counting binary bent sequences. *IEEE Transactions on Information Theory*, IT-36(5):1170–1173, 1990.
2. C. Adams and S. Tavares. The structured design of cryptographically good S-boxes. *Journal of Cryptology*, 3:27–41, 1990.
3. L.M. Adleman. On breaking generalized knapsack public key cryptosystems. In *Proceedings of the 15th ACM Symposium on Theory of Computing*, pages 402–412. ACM, Boston, 1983.
4. S.G. Akl and D.E. Denning. Checking classification constraints for consistency and completeness. In *Proceedings of the 1987 IEEE Symposium on Security and Privacy*, pages 196–201. IEEE, 1987.
5. W.B. Alexi, B. Chor, O. Goldreich, and C.P. Schnorr. RSA and Rabin functions: certain parts are as hard as the whole. *SIAM Journal of Computing*, 17:194–208, 1988.
6. D. Anderson, T. Frivold, and A. Valdes. Next-generation intrusion detection expert system (NIDES): A summary. SRI-CSL-95-07, SRI, Menlo Park, CA, 1995.
7. D. Anderson, T.F Lunt, H. Javitz, A. Tamaru, and A. Valdes. Detecting unusual program behavior using the statistical component of the next-generation intrusion detection expert system (NIDES). SRI-CSL-95-06, SRI, Menlo Park, CA, 1995.
8. R. Anderson, H. Manifavas, and C. Sutherland. Netcard – a practical electronic cash system. Technical Report Available at: *http://www.cl.cam.ac.uk/users/rja14*, Computer Laboratory, University of Cambridge, 1996.
9. C. Asmuth and J. Bloom. A modular approach to key safeguarding. *IEEE Transactions on Information Theory*, IT-29(2):208–211, 1983.
10. D. Atkins, M. Graff, A.K. Lenstra, and P.C. Leyland. The magic words are squeamish ossifrage. In J. Pieprzyk and R. Safavi-Naini, editors, *Advances in Cryptology (ASIACRYPT94)*. Lecture Notes in Computer Science No. 917, pages 263–277. Springer, Berlin Heidelberg New York, 1995.
11. S. Bakhtiari, R. Safavi-Naini, and J. Pieprzyk. Practical and secure message authentication. In *Workshop on Selected Areas in Cryptography (SAC'95)*, pages 55–68. Carleton University, Canada, May 18-19, 1995.
12. J. Banerjee, H. Chou, J.F. Garza, W. Kim, D. Woelk, N. Ballou, and H. Kim. Data model issues for object-oriented applications. *ACM Transactions on Office Information Systems*, 5(1):3–26, 1987.
13. J. Banerjee, D.K. Hsiao, and K. Kannan. DBC – a database computer for very large databases. *IEEE Transactions on Computers*, C-28(6):414–429, 1979.

14. A. Baraani-Dastjerdi. *Access control in object-oriented databases*. PhD thesis, Department of Computer Science, University of Wollongong, New South Wales, Australia, 1996.

15. A. Baraani-Dastjerdi, J. Pieprzyk, and R. Safavi-Naini. A secure voting protocol using threshold schemes. In *11th Annual Computer Security Applications Conference*, pages 143–148. IEEE, 1995.

16. F.L. Bauer. *Decrypted Secrets. Methods and Maxims of Cryptology*. Springer, Berlin Heidelberg New York, 2002.

17. D.S. Bauer and M.E. Koblentz. NIDX – An expert system for real-time network intrusion detection. In *Proceedings of the IEEE Computer Networking Symposium*, pages 98–106, 1988.

18. F. Bauspiess. SELANE: An approach to secure networks. In *Proceedings of SECURICOM'90*, pages 159–164. 1990.

19. D.E. Bell and L.J. La Padula. Secure computer systems: Mathematical foundations and model. Technical Report M74-244, Mitre Corporation, Bedford, MA, 1973.

20. D.E. Bell and L.J. La Padula. Secure computer systems (Vols. 1–3). Technical Report ESD-TR-73-278, Air Force Electronic Systems Division, Hanscom AFB, MA, 1973–1974.

21. D.E. Bell and L.J. La Padula. Secure computer systems. Technical Report ESD-TR-73-278, Air Force Electronic Systems Division, Hanscom AFB, MA, 1974.

22. M. Bellare, A. Desai, D. Pointcheval, and P. Rogaway. Relations among notions of security for public-key encryption schemes. In H. Krawczyk, editor, *Advances in Cryptology (CRYPTO'98)*. Lecture Notes in Computer Science No. 1462, pages 26–45. Springer, Berlin Heidelberg New York, 1998.

23. M. Bellare and P. Rogaway. Optimal asymmetric encryption. In A. De Santis, editor, *Advances in Cryptology (EUROCRYPT'94)*. Lecture Notes in Computer Science No. 950, pages 92–111. Springer, Berlin Heidelberg New York, 1995.

24. J. Benaloh and J. Leichter. Generalized secret sharing and monotone functions. In S. Goldwasser, editor, *Advances in Cryptology (CRYPTO'88)*. Lecture Notes in Computer Science No. 403, pages 27–36. Springer, Berlin Heidelberg New York, 1988.

25. J. Benaloh and M. Yung. Distributing the power of a government to enhance the privacy of votes. In *Proceedings of the 5th ACM Symposium on Principles of Distributed Computing*, pages 52–62. ACM, New York, 1986.

26. E. Berlekamp, R. McEliece, and H. van Tiborg. On the inherent intractability of certain coding problems. *IEEE Transactions on Information Theory*, IT-24:384–386, 1978.

27. E. Berlekamp. *Algebraic Coding Theory*. McGraw-Hill, New York, 1968.

28. T.A. Berson and T.F. Lunt. Security considerations for knowledge-based systems. In *Proceedings of the 3rd Annual Expert Systems in Government Conference*. Washington, DC, October, 1987 (preprint).

29. E. Bertino and L.M. Haas. Views and security in distributed database management systems. In J.W. Schmidt, S. Ceri, and M. Missikoff, editors, *Advances in Database Technology (EDBT'88)*. Lecture Notes in Computer Science No. 303, pages 155–169. Springer, Berlin Heidelberg New York, 1988.

30. T. Beth and C. Ding. On permutations immune against differential cryptanalysis. In T. Helleseth, editor, *Advances in Cryptology (EUROCRYPT'93)*. Lecture Notes in Computer Science No. 765, pages 65–76. Springer, Berlin Heidelberg New York, 1994.

31. J. Bierbrauer, K. Gopalakrishnan, and D.R. Stinson. Bounds for resilient functions and orthogonal arrays. In Y. Desmedt, editor, *Advances in Cryptology (CRYPTO'94)*. Lecture Notes in Computer Science No. 839, pages 247–256. Springer, Berlin Heidelberg New York, 1994.

32. E. Biham, R. Anderson, and L. Knudsen. Serpent: a new block cipher proposal. In S. Vaudenay, editor, *5th International Workshop on Fast Software Encryption*. Lecture Notes in Computer Science No. 1372, pages 222–238. Springer, Berlin Heidelberg New York, 1998.

33. E. Biham and A. Shamir. Differential cryptanalysis of DES-like cryptosystems. In A.J. Menezes and S.A. Vanstone, editors, *Advances in Cryptology (CRYPTO'90)*. Lecture Notes in Computer Science No. 537, pages 2–21. Springer, Berlin Heidelberg New York, 1991.

34. E. Biham and A. Shamir. Differential cryptanalysis of FEAL and N-Hash. In D. Davies, editor, *Advances in Cryptology (EUROCRYPT'91)*. Lecture Notes in Computer Science No. 547, pages 1–16. Springer, Berlin Heidelberg New York, 1991.

35. E. Biham and A. Shamir. *A Differential Cryptanalysis of the Data Encryption Standard*. Springer, Berlin Heidelberg New York, 1993.

36. E. Biham and A. Shamir. Differential cryptanalysis of the full 16-round DES. In E.F. Brickell, editor, *Advances in Cryptology (CRYPTO'92)*. Lecture Notes in Computer Science No. 740, pages 487–496. Springer, Berlin Heidelberg New York, 1992.

37. R. Bird, I. Gopal, A. Herzberg, P. Janson, S. Kutten, R. Molva, and M. Yung. Systematic design of two-party authentication protocols. In J. Feigenbaum, editor, *Advances in Cryptology (CRYPTO'91)*. Lecture Notes in Computer Science No. 576, pages 44–61. Springer, Berlin Heidelberg New York, 1992.

38. R. Bird, I. Gopal, A. Herzberg, P. Janson, S. Kutten, R. Molva, and M. Yung. Systematic design of a family of attack-resistant authentication protocols. *IEEE Journal of Selected Areas in Communications*, 11:679–693, 1993.

39. R. Bird, I. Gopal, A. Herzberg, P. Janson, S. Kutten, R. Molva, and M. Yung. The KryptoKnight family of light-weight protocols for authentication and key distribution. *IEEE/ACM Transactions on Networking*, 3:31–41, 1995.

40. D. Blackwell and M.A. Girshick. *Theory of Games and Statistical Decisions*. Wiley, New York, 1966.

41. G.R. Blakley. Safeguarding cryptographic keys. In *Proceedings of the AFIPS 1979 National Computer Conference*, pages 313–317. AFIPS, 1979.

42. G.R. Blakley and C. Meadows. A database encryption scheme which allows the computation of statistics using encrypted data. In *Proceedings of the 1985 IEEE Symposium on Security and Privacy*, pages 116–122. IEEE, 1985.

43. D. Bleichenbacher. Chosen ciphertext attacks against protocols based on the RSA encryption standard PKCS#1. In H. Krawczyk, editor, *Advances in Cryptology (CRYPTO'98)*.

Lecture Notes in Computer Science No. 1462, pages 1–12. Springer, Berlin Heidelberg New York, 1998.

44. L. Blum, M. Blum, and M. Shub. A simple unpredictable pseudo-random number generator. *SIAM Journal of Computing*, 15(2):364–383, May 1986.

45. M. Blum and S. Goldwasser. An efficient probabilistic public-key encryption scheme which hides all partial information. In G.R. Blakley and D.C. Chaum, editors, *Advances in Cryptology (CRYPTO'84)*. Lecture Notes in Computer Science No. 196, pages 289–302. Springer, Berlin Heidelberg New York, 1985.

46. M. Blum and S. Micali. How to generate cryptographically strong sequences of pseudo-random bits. *SIAM Journal of Computing*, 13(4):850–863, November 1984.

47. J-P. Boly, A. Bosselaers, R. Cramer, R. Michelsen, S. Mjolsnes, F. Muller, T. Pedersen, B. Pfitzmann, P. de Rooij, B. Schoenmakers, M. Schunter, L. Vallee, and M. Waidner. The ESPRIT project CAFE – high security digital payment systems. In D. Gollmann, editor, *Proceedings of the 3rd European Symposium on Research in Computer Security, (ESORICS'94)*. Lecture Notes in Computer Science No. 875, pages 217–230. Springer, Berlin Heidelberg New York, 1994.

48. D. Boneh. *Twenty years of attacks on the RSA cryptosystems*. Available at *http://crypto.stanford.edu/dabo/abstracts/RSAattack-survey.html*, 1997.

49. V. Bontchev. Possible virus attacks against integrity programs and how to prevent them. In *Proceedings of the 2nd International Virus Bulletin Conference*, pages 131–141, 1992.

50. J.N.E. Bos and D. Chaum. Provable unforgeable signatures. In E.F. Brickell, editor, *Advances in Cryptology (CRYPTO'92)*. Lecture Notes in Computer Science No. 740, pages 1–14. Springer, Berlin Heidelberg New York, 1992.

51. A. Bosselaers and B. Preneel, editors. *Integrity Primitives for Secure Information Systems*. Lecture Notes in Computer Science No. 1007. Springer, Berlin Heidelberg New York, 1995.

52. J. Bovey and A. Williamson. The probability of generating the symmetric group. *Bulletin of London Mathematical Society*, 10:91–96, 1978.

53. C. Boyd. Digital multisignatures. In H. Beker and F. Piper, editors, *Proceedings IMA Conference on Cryptography and Coding*, pages 241–246. Clarendon, Oxford, 1989.

54. C. Boyd. A cryptographic scheme for computerized general elections. In J.-J. Quisquater and J. Vanderwalle, editors, *Advances in Cryptology (EUROCRYPT'89)*. Lecture Notes in Computer Science No. 434, pages 617–625. Springer, Berlin Heidelberg New York, 1990.

55. C. Boyd. A framework for design of key establishment protocols. In J. Pieprzyk and J. Seberry, editors, *Proceedings of the 1st Australasian Conference on Information Security and Privacy (ACISP'96)*. Lecture Notes in Computer Science No. 1172, pages 146–157. Springer, Berlin Heidelberg New York, 1996.

56. C. Boyd and W. Mao. Design and analysis of key exchange protocols via secure channel identification. In J. Pieprzyk and R. Safavi-Naini, editors, *Advances in Cryptology (ASIACRYPT'94)*. Lecture Notes in Computer Science No. 917, pages 171–181. Springer, Berlin Heidelberg New York, 1995.

57. S. Brands. Untraceable off-line cash in wallets with observers. In D.R. Stinson, editor, *Advances in Cryptology (CRYPTO'93)*. Lecture Notes in Computer Science No. 773, pages 302–318. Springer, Berlin Heidelberg New York, 1994.

58. J. Brandt, I.B. Damgard, and P. Landrock. Anonymous and verifiable registration in databases. In C.G. Gunther, editor, *Advances in Cryptology (EUROCRYPT'88)*. Lecture Notes in Computer Science No. 330, pages 167–176. Springer, Berlin Heidelberg New York, 1988.

59. G. Brassard. Cryptology column – quantum computing: The end of classical cryptography. *SIGACT News*, 25(4):15–21, 1994.

60. G. Brassard and P. Bratley. *Fundamentals of Algorithms*. Prentice-Hall, Englewood Cliffs, NJ, 1996.

61. G. Brassard, D. Chaum, and C. Crépeau. Minimum disclosure proofs of knowledge. *Journal of Computer and System Science*, 37(2):156–189, 1988.

62. E. Brickell, P. Gemmel, and D. Kravitz. Trusted-based tracing extensions to anonymous cash and the making of anonymous change. In *Proceedings of the 6th Annual Symposium on Distributed Algorithms (SODA)*, pages 457–466. ACM, New York, 1995.

63. E.F. Brickell. Solving low density knapsacks. In D. Chaum, editor, *Advances in Cryptology (CRYPTO'83)*, pages 25–37. Plenum, New York, 1984.

64. E.F. Brickell. Breaking iterated knapsacks. In G.R. Blakley and D.C. Chaum, editors, *Advances in Cryptology (CRYPTO'84)*. Lecture Notes in Computer Science No. 196, pages 342–358. Springer, Berlin Heidelberg New York, 1985.

65. E.F. Brickell. Some ideal secret sharing schemes. *Journal of Computer and Systems Science*, 37:156–189, 1988.

66. E.F. Brickell. Some ideal secret sharing schemes. *Journal of Combinatorial Mathematics and Combinatorial Computing*, 6:105–113, 1989.

67. L. Brown. *Analysis of the DES and the design of the LOKI encryption scheme*. PhD Thesis, University of New South Wales, Canberra, Australia, 1991.

68. L. Brown, M. Kwan, J. Pieprzyk, and J. Seberry. Improving resistance to differential cryptanalysis and the redesign of LOKI. In R.L. Rivest, H. Imai, and T. Matsumoto, editors, *Advances in Cryptology (ASIACRYPT'91)*. Lecture Notes in Computer Science No. 739, pages 36–50. Springer, Berlin Heidelberg New York, 1993.

69. L. Brown, J. Pieprzyk, and J. Seberry. LOKI: A cryptographic primitive for authentication and secrecy applications. In J. Seberry and J. Pieprzyk, editors, *Advances in Cryptology (AUSCRYPT'90)*, pages 229–236. Lectures Notes in Computer Science No. 453. Springer, Berlin Heidelberg New York, 1990.

70. M. Burmester and Y. Desmedt. A secure and efficient conference key distribution system. In A. De Santis, editor, *Advances in Cryptology (EUROCRYPT'94)*. Lecture Notes in Computer Science No. 950, pages 275–286. Springer, Berlin Heidelberg New York, 1995.

71. M. Burrows, M. Abadi, and R. Needham. A logic of authentication. *ACM Transactions on Computer Systems*, 8(1):18–36, 1990.

72. U. Bussolati and G. Martella. The design of secure distributed systems. In *Digest of Papers from Spring COMPCON '83: Intellectual Leverage for the Information Society*, pages 492–499. IEEE, 1983.

73. U. Bussolati and G. Martella. Security design in distributed database systems. *Journal of Systems and Software (USA)*, 3(3):219–229, 1983.

74. P. Camion and J. Patarin. The knapsack hash function proposed at CRYPTO'89 can be broken. In D. Davies, editor, *Advances in Cryptology (EUROCRYPT'91)*. Lecture Notes in Computer Science No. 547, pages 39–53. Springer, Berlin Heidelberg New York, 1991.

75. R.M. Capocelli, A. De Santis, L. Gargano, and U. Vaccaro. On the size of shares for secret sharing schemes. *Journal of Cryptology*, 6:157–167, 1993.

76. F. Carettoni, S. Castano, G. Martella, and P. Samaratti. RETISS: A real time security system for threat detection using fuzzy logics. In *Proceedings of the 25th Annual IEEE International Carnahan Conference on Security Technology*, pages 161–167, 1991.

77. J.M. Carroll and H. Jurgensen. Design of a secure relational database. In J.B. Grimson and H.J. Kugler, editors, *Computer Security: The Practical Issues in a Troubled World, Proceedings of the 3rd IFIP International Conference on Computer Security (IFIP/Sec'85)*, pages 1–16, Dublin, Ireland. North-Holland, Amsterdam, 1985.

78. National Computer Security Center. *A Guide to Understanding Audit in Trusted Systems*, 1988.

79. D.D. Chamberlin, J.N. Gray, and I.L. Traiger. Views, authorization, and locking in a relational data base system. In *Proceedings of AFIPS NCC Vol. 44*, pages 425–430, 1975.

80. A. Chan, Y. Frankel, P. MacKenzie, and Y. Tsiounis. Misrepresentation of identities in e-cash schemes and how to prevent it. In K. Kim and T. Matsumoto, editors, *Advances in Cryptology (ASIACRYPT'96)*. Lecture Notes in Computer Science No. 1163, pages 276–285. Springer, Berlin Heidelberg New York, 1996.

81. B. Le Charlier, A. Mounji, and M. Swimmer. Dynamic detection and classification of computer viruses using general behaviour patterns. In *Proceedings of the 5th International Virus Bulletin Conference*, pages 20–22, 1995.

82. C. Charnes and J. Pieprzyk. Linear nonequivalence versus nonlinearity. In J. Seberry and Y. Zheng, editors, *Advances in Cryptology (AUSCRYPT'92)*. Lecture Notes in Computer Science No. 718, pages 156–164. Springer, Berlin Heidelberg New York, 1993.

83. C. Charnes and J. Pieprzyk. Attacking the SL_2 hashing scheme. In J. Pieprzyk and R. Safavi-Naini, editors, *Advances in Cryptology (ASIACRYPT'94)*. Lecture Notes in Computer Science No. 917, pages 322–330. Springer, Berlin Heidelberg New York, 1995.

84. C. Charnes and J. Pieprzyk. Generalised cumulative arrays and their applications to secret sharing schemes. In *Proceedings of the 18th Australasian Computer Science Conference, Australian Computer Science Communications, Vol. 17, No. 1*, pages 61–65, 1995.

85. C. Charnes, J. Pieprzyk, and R. Safavi-Naini. Conditionally secure secret sharing schemes with disenrollment capability. In *Proceedings of the 2nd ACM Conference on Computer and Communication Security*, pages 89–95, Fairfax, VA, 1994.

86. D. Chaum. Untraceable electronic mail, return addresses, and digital pseudonyms. *Communications of the ACM*, 24:84–88, February, 1981.

87. D. Chaum. Blind signatures for untraceable payments. In R.L. Rivest, A. Sherman, and D. Chaum, editors, *Advances in Cryptology (CRYPTO'82)*, pages 199-203. Plenum, New York, 1983.

88. D. Chaum. Elections with unconditionally secret ballots and disruption equivalent to breaking RSA. In C.G. Gunther, editor, *Advances in Cryptology (EUROCRYPT'88)*. Lecture Notes in Computer Science No. 330, pages 177–182. Springer, Berlin Heidelberg New York, 1988.

89. D. Chaum and H. Van Antwerpen. Undeniable signatures. In G. Brassard, editor, *Advances in Cryptology (CRYPTO'89)*. Lecture Notes in Computer Science No. 435, pages 212–217. Springer, Berlin Heidelberg New York, 1990.

90. D. Chaum, A. Fiat, and M. Naor. Untraceable electronic cash. In S. Goldwasser, editor, *Advances in Cryptology (CRYPTO'88)*. Lecture Notes in Computer Science No. 403, pages 319–327. Springer, Berlin Heidelberg New York, 1988.

91. D. Chaum and T.P. Pedersen. Wallet databases with observers. In E.F. Brickell, editor, *Advances in Cryptology (CRYPTO'92)*. Lecture Notes in Computer Science No. 740, pages 89–105. Springer, Berlin Heidelberg New York, 1992.

92. D. Chaum, E. van Heijst, and B. Pfitzmann. Cryptographically strong undeniable signatures, unconditionally secure for the signer. In J. Feigenbaum, editor, *Advances in Cryptology (CRYPTO'91)*. Lecture Notes in Computer Science No. 576, pages 470–484. Springer, Berlin Heidelberg New York, 1992.

93. J.L. Chen and T. Hwang. Identity-based conference key broadcast schemes with user authentication. *Computers & Security*, 13:53–57, 1994.

94. K. Chen. A new identification algorithm. In E. Dowson and J. Golić, editors, *Cryptography: Policy and Algorithms*. Lecture Notes in Computer Science No. 1029, pages 244–249. Springer, Berlin Heidelberg New York, 1995.

95. G.G. Christoph, K.A. Jackson, M.C. Neumann, C.L.B. Siciliano, D.D. Simmonds, C.A. Stallings, and J.L. Thompson. UNICORN: Misuse detection for UNICOS. In *Proceedings of Supercomputing'95*, 1995.

96. R.F. Churchhouse. The ENIGMA – some aspects of its history and solution. *IMA Bulletin*, 27:129–137, 1991.

97. R.F. Churchhouse. The Achilles heel of the ENIGMA cipher machine, and some of its consequences. *IMA Bulletin*, 1993.

98. B.G. Claybrook. Using views in a multilevel secure database management system. In *Proceedings of the 1983 IEEE Symposium on Security and Privacy*, pages 4–17. IEEE Press, 1983.

99. F. Cohen. Computer viruses: theory and experiments. *Computers & Security*, 6:22–35, 1987.

100. F. Cohen. Computational aspects of computer viruses. *Computers & Security*, 8:325–344, 1989.

101. F. Cohen. *A Short Course on Computer Viruses*. Wiley, New York, 1994.

102. H. Cohen. *A Course in Computational Algebraic Number Theory*. Springer, Berlin Heidelberg New York, 1995.

103. J.D. Cohen and M.J. Fischer. A robust and verifiable cryptographically secure election scheme. In *Proceedings of the 26th IEEE Symposium on Foundations of Computer Science*, pages 372–382. IEEE, 1985.

104. Committee on Multilevel Data Management Security. *Multilevel Data Management Security*. Air Force Studies Board, National Research Council, National Academy Press, Washington, DC, 1983.

105. R.H. Cooper, W. Hyslop, and W. Patterson. An application of the Chinese remainder theorem to multiple-key encryption in data base systems. In J.H. Finch and E.G. Dougall, editors, *Proceedings of the 2nd IFIP International Conference on Computer Security (IFIP/Sec'84)*, pages 553–556. North-Holland, Amsterdam, 1984.

106. D. Coppersmith. Another birthday attack. In H.C. Williams, editor, *Advances in Cryptology (CRYPTO'85)*. Lecture Notes in Computer Science No. 218, pages 14–17. Springer, Berlin Heidelberg New York, 1986.

107. D. Coppersmith. Analysis of ISO/CCITT Document X.509 Annex D. Internal Memo, IBM T.J. Watson Center, June 11, 1989.

108. D. Coppersmith. The Data Encryption Standard (DES) and its strength against attacks. *IBM Journal of Research and Development*, 38(3):243–250, 1994.

109. D. Coppersmith and E. Grossman. Generators for certain alternating groups with applications to cryptology. *SIAM Journal on Applied Mathematics*, 29:624–627, 1975.

110. D. Coppersmith, H. Krawczyk, and Y. Mansour. The shrinking generator. In D.R. Stinson, editor, *Advances in Cryptology (CRYPTO'93)*. Lecture Notes in Computer Science No. 773, pages 22–39. Springer, Berlin Heidelberg New York, 1994.

111. D. Coppersmith, A. Odlyzko, and R. Schroeppel. Discrete logarithms in GF(p). *Algorithmica*, 1:1–15, 1986.

112. G. Coulouris, J. Dollimore, and T. Kindberg. *Distributed Systems Concepts and Design*. Addison-Wesley, Boston, 1995.

113. R. Cramer and I. Damgård. New generation of secure and practical RSA-based signatures. In N. Koblitz, editor, *Advances in Cryptology (CRYPTO'96)*. Lecture Notes in Computer Science No. 1109, pages 173–185. Springer, Berlin Heidelberg New York, 1996.

114. R. Cramer, R. Gennaro, and B. Schoenmakers. A secure and optimally efficient multi-authority election scheme. In W. Fumy, editor, *Advances in Cryptology (EURO-CRYPT'97)*. Lecture Notes in Computer Science No. 1233, pages 103–118. Springer, Berlin Heidelberg New York, 1997.

115. R. Cramer and V. Shoup. A practical public key cryptosystem provably secure against adaptive chosen ciphertext attack. In H. Krawczyk, editor, *Advances in Cryptology (CRYPTO'98)*. Lecture Notes in Computer Science No. 1462, pages 13–25. Springer, Berlin Heidelberg New York, 1998.

116. M. Crosbie and E. Spafford. Active defense of a computer system using autonomous agents. In *Proceedings of the 18th National Information Systems Security Conference*, pages 549–558, 1995.

117. M. Crosbie and E. Spafford. Applying genetic programming to intrusion detection. In *Proceedings of the 1995 AAAI Fall Symposium on Genetic Programming*, 1995.

118. J. Daemen, R. Govaerts, and J. Vandewalle. Weak keys for IDEA. In D. Stinson, editor, *Advances in Cryptology (CRYPTO'93)*. Lecture Notes in Computer Science No. 773, pages 224–231. Springer, Berlin Heidelberg New York, 1994.

119. J. Daemen and V. Rijmen. *The Design of Rijndael*. Springer, Berlin Heidelberg New York, 2002.

120. I. Damgård. A design principle for hash functions. In G. Brassard, editor, *Advances in Cryptology (CRYPTO'89)*. Lecture Notes in Computer Science No. 435, pages 416–427. Springer, Berlin Heidelberg New York, 1990.

121. C.J. Date. *An Introduction to Database Systems*, Vol. 1. Addison-Wesley, 1986.

122. G.I. Davida, D.L. Wells, and J.B. Kam. A database encryption system with subkeys. *ACM Transactions on Database System*, 6(2):312–328, 1981.

123. G.I. Davida and Y. Yeh. Cryptographic relational algebra. In *Proceedings of the 1982 IEEE Symposium on Security and Privacy*, pages 111–116. IEEE, 1982.

124. D. Davies. Some regular properties of the 'Data Encryption Standard' algorithm. In R.L. Rivest, A. Sherman, and D. Chaum, editors, *Advances in Cryptology (CRYPTO'82)*, pages 89–96, Plenum, New York, 1983.

125. M. Davio, Y. Desmedt, M. Fosséprez, R. Govaerts, J. Hulsbosch, P. Neutjens, P. Piret, J.-J. Quisquater, J. Vandewalle, and P. Wouters. Analytical characteristics of the DES. In D. Chaum, editor, *Advances in Cryptology (CRYPTO'83)*, pages 171–202. Plenum, New York, 1984.

126. J. Davis and D. Holdridge. Factorization using the quadratic sieve algorithm. In D. Chaum, editor, *Advances in Cryptology (CRYPTO'83)*, pages 103–113. Plenum, New York, 1984.

127. J. Davis, D. Holdridge, and G. Simmons. Status report on factoring (at the Sandia National Laboratories). In T. Beth, N. Cot, and I. Ingemarsson, editors, *Advances in Cryptology (EUROCRYPT'84)*. Lecture Notes in Computer Science No. 209, pages 183–215. Springer, Berlin Heidelberg New York, 1985.

128. M. Dawson and S. Tavares. An expanded set of S-box design criteria based on information theory and its relation to differential-like attacks. In D. Davies, editor, *Advances in Cryptology (EUROCRYPT'91)*. Lecture Notes in Computer Science No. 547, pages 352–367. Springer, Berlin Heidelberg New York, 1991.

129. W. de Jonge and D. Chaum. Attacks on some RSA signatures. In H.C. Williams, editor, *Advances in Cryptology (CRYPTO'85)*. Lecture Notes in Computer Science No. 218, pages 18–27. Springer, Berlin Heidelberg New York, 1986.

130. H. Debar, M. Becker, and D. Siboni. A neural network component for an intrusion detection system. In *Proceedings of the IEEE Symposium on Research in Security and Privacy*, pages 1–11, 1992.

131. H. Debar and B. Dorizzi. An application of a recurrent network to an intrusion detection system. In *Proceedings of the International Joint Conference on Neural Networks*, pages 478–483, 1992.

132. H. Delfs and H. Knebl. *Introduction to Cryptography*. Springer, Berlin Heidelberg New York, 2002.

133. A. Dempster. A generalization of Bayesian inference. *Journal of the Royal Statistical Society*, 30:205–247, 1968.

134. N. Demytko. A new elliptic curve based analogue of RSA. In T. Helleseth, editor, *Advances in Cryptology – EUROCRYPT'93*. Lecture Notes in Computer Science No. 765, pages 40–49. Springer, Berlin Heidelberg New York, 1994.

135. B. den Boer and A. Bosselaers. An attack on the last two rounds of MD4. In J. Feigenbaum, editor, *Advances in Cryptology (CRYPTO'91)*. Lecture Notes in Computer Science No. 576, pages 194–203. Springer, Berlin Heidelberg New York, 1992.

136. D.E. Denning. A lattice model of secure information flow. *Communications of the ACM*, 19(5):236–243, 1976.

137. D.E. Denning. An intrusion-detection model. In *Proceedings of the 1986 IEEE Symposium on Security and Privacy*, pages 118–131. IEEE, 1986.

138. D. Denning and G. Sacco. Timestamps in key distribution protocols. *Communications of the ACM*, 24(8):533–536, 1981.

139. D.E. Denning, T.F. Lunt, P.G. Neumann, R.R. Schell, M. Heckman, and W.R. Shockley. Secure distributed data views: Security policy and interpretation for a class A1 multilevel secure relational database system. Interim Report A002, SRI International, Computer Science Laboratory, November 1986.

140. D.E. Denning, T.F. Lunt, R.R. Schell, M. Heckman, and W.R. Shockley. Secure distributed data views (SeaView): The SeaView formal security policy model. Interim Report A003, SRI International, Computer Science Laboratory, July 1987.

141. D.E. Denning. Field encryption and authentication. In D. Chaum, editor, *Advances in Cryptology: Proceedings of (CRYPTO'83)*, pages 231–247. Plenum, New York, 1983.

142. D.E. Denning. Database security. In *Annual Review of Computer Science, Vol. 3*, pages 1–22. Annual Reviews, Palo Alto, 1988.

143. D.E. Denning, S.G. Akl, M. Heckman, T.F. Lunt, M. Morgenstern, P.G. Neumann, and R.G. Schell. Views for multilevel database security. *IEEE Transactions on Software Engineering*, SE-13(2):129–140, 1987.

144. D.E. Denning, T.F. Lunt, R.R. Schell, M. Heckman, and W. Shockley. A multilevel relational data model. In *Proceedings of the 1987 IEEE Symposium on Security and Privacy*, pages 220–234. IEEE, 1987.

145. Department of Defense. *DoD 5200.28-STD: Department of Defense (DoD) Trusted Computer System Evaluation Criteria (TCSEC)*, 1985.

146. Department of Defense. Trusted Computer System Evaluation Criteria – Orange Book. Pub. DOD 5200.28-STD, US Department of Defense, 1985.

147. Y. Desmedt. Threshold cryptography. *European Transactions on Telecommunication and Related Technologies*, 5(4):449–457, 1994.

148. Y. Desmedt and Y. Frankel. Threshold cryptosystems. In G. Brassard, editor, *Advances in Cryptology (CRYPTO'89)*. Lecture Notes in Computer Science No. 435, pages 307–315. Springer, Berlin Heidelberg New York, 1990.

149. Y. Desmedt and Y. Frankel. Shared generation of authenticators and signatures. In J. Feigenbaum, editor, *Advances in Cryptology (CRYPTO'91)*. Lecture Notes in Computer Science No. 576, pages 457–469. Springer, Berlin Heidelberg New York, 1992.

150. D. Deutsch. Quantum theory, the Church-Turing principle and the universal quantum computer. *Proceedings of the Royal Society*, A400:97–117, 1985.

151. T. Dierks and C. Allen. *RFC 2246: The TLS Protocol Version 1.0*, January 1999. Available at *http://www.ietf.org/rfc/rfc2246.txt*.

152. W. Diffie and M.E. Hellman. New directions in cryptography. *IEEE Transactions on Information Theory*, 22:644–654, 1976.

153. W. Diffie and M.E. Hellman. Exhaustive cryptanalysis of the NBS data encryption standard. *Computer*, 10:74–84, June 1977.

154. W. Diffie, P. Van Oorschot, and M. Wiener. Authentication and authenticated key exchanges. *Designs, Codes, and Cryptography*, 2:107–125, 1992.

155. J.F. Dillon. A survey of bent functions. *The NSA Technical Journal*, pages 191–215, 1972 (unclassified).

156. H. Dobbertin. Cryptanalysis of MD4. In D. Gollmann, editor, *Fast Software Encryption 1996*, Lecture Notes in Computer Science No. 1039, pages 53–69. Springer, Berlin Heidelberg New York, 1996.

157. H. Dobbertin. Cryptanalysis of MD5 compress. Announcement on Internet, May 1996.

158. H. Dobbertin, A. Bosselaers, and B. Preneel. RIPEMD-160: a strengthened version of RIPEMD. In D. Gollmann, editor, *Fast Software Encryption 1996*. Lecture Notes in Computer Science No. 1039, pages 71–79. Springer, Berlin Heidelberg New York, 1996.

159. D. Dolev and A. Wigderson. On the security of multi-party protocols in distributed systems. In D. Chaum, R.L. Rivest, and A.T. Sherman, editors, *Advances in Cryptology (CRYPTO'82)*, pages 167–175. Plenum, New York, 1983.

160. C. Dowell and P. Ramstedt. The Computer Watch data reduction toll. In *Proceedings of the 13th National Computer Security Conference*, pages 99–108, 1990.

161. A.R. Downing, I.B. Greenberg, and T.F. Lunt. Issues in distributed database security. In *Proceedings of the 5th Aerospace Computer Security Applications Conference*, pages 196–203, Tucson, AZ, December, 1989.

162. T. Duff. Experience with viruses on UNIX systems. *Computing Systems*, 2:155–171, 1989.

163. T. ElGamal. A public key cryptosystem and a signature scheme based on discrete logarithms. *IEEE Transactions on Information Theory*, IT-31:469–472, 1985.

164. S. Even and O. Goldreich. DES-like functions can generate the alternating group. *IEEE Transactions on Information Theory*, IT-29(6):863–865, 1983.

165. V. Fak. Repeated use of codes which detect deception. *IEEE Transactions on Information Theory*, IT-25(2):233–234, 1979.

166. R. Farrow. *UNIX System Security*. Addison-Wesley, Boston, 1991.

167. U. Feige, A. Fiat, and A. Shamir. Zero knowledge proofs of identity. *Journal of Cryptology*, 1(2):77–94, 1988.

168. H. Feistel. Cryptography and computer privacy. *Scientific American*, 228:15–23, May 1973.

169. H. Feistel, W. Notz, and J. Smith. Some cryptographic techniques for machine-to-machine data communications. *Proceedings of IEEE*, 63(11):1545–1554, November 1975.

170. P. Feldman. A practical scheme for non-interactive verifiable secret sharing. In *Proceedings of the 28th IEEE Symposium on Foundations of Computer Science*, pages 427–437. IEEE, 1987.

171. J. Fellows and J. Hemenway. The architecture of a distributed trusted computing base. In *Proceedings of the 10th National Computer Security Conference*, pages 68–77, Baltimore, MD, September 1987. NBS/NCSC.

172. D. Ferbrache. INIT29 – infections but your data is safe. Virus Bulletin, December 1989.

173. D. Ferbrache. Virus analysis: nVIR and its clones. Virus Bulletin, October 1989.

174. D. Ferbrache. Mac threats. Virus Bulletin, December 1990.

175. D. Ferbrache. Virus report: WDEF – the hidden virus. Virus Bulletin, January 1990.

176. N. Ferguson. Extensions of single-term coins. In D.R. Stinson, editor, *Advances in Cryptology (CRYPTO'93)*. Lecture Notes in Computer Science No. 773, pages 292–301. Springer, Berlin Heidelberg New York, 1994.

177. N. Ferguson, J. Kelsey, S. Lucks, B. Schneier, M. Stay, D. Wagner, and D. Whiting. Improved cryptanalysis of Rijndael. In *Fast Software Encryption 2000*, 2000.

178. E.B. Fernandez, E. Gudes, and H. Song. A security model for object-oriented databases. In *Proceedings of the 1989 IEEE Symposium on Security and Privacy*, pages 110–115. IEEE, 1989.

179. D. Ferraiolo and R. Kuhn. Role based access controls. In *Proceedings of the 15th National Computer Security Conference*, pages 554–563. NIST, Gaithersburg, MD, 1992.

180. R. Feynman. Simulating physics with computers. *International Journal of Theoretical Physics*, 21(6-7):467–488, 1982.

181. A. Fiat and A. Shamir. How to prove yourself: practical solutions to identification and signature problems. In A.M. Odlyzko, editor, *Advances in Cryptology (CRYPTO'86)*. Lecture Notes in Computer Science No. 263, pages 186–194. Springer, Berlin Heidelberg New York, 1987.

182. S. Fischer-Hübner and K. Brunnstein. Combining verified and adaptive system components towards more secure computer architectures. In *Proceedings of the International Workshop on Computer Architectures to Support Security and Persistence of Information*, Section 14, page 1–7, 1990.

183. R. Fischlin and C.P. Schnorr. Stronger security proofs for RSA and Rabin bits. In W. Fumy, editor, *Advances in Cryptology (EUROCRYPT'97)*. Lecture Notes in Computer Science No. 1233, pages 267–279. Springer, Berlin Heidelberg New York, 1997.

184. D.H. Fishman, J. Annevelink, D. Beech, E.C. Chow, T. Connors, J.W. Davis, W. Hasan, C.G. Hoch, W. Kent, S. Leichner, P. Lyngbaek, B. Mahbod, M.A. Neimat, T. Risch, M.C. Shan, and W.K. Wilkinson. Overview of the Iris DBMS. In W. Kim and F.H. Lochovsky, editors, *Object-Oriented Concepts, Databases and Applications*, pages 219–250. Addison-Wesley, New York, 1989.

185. D.H. Fishman, D. Beech, H.P. Cate, E.C. Chow, T. Connors, J.W. Davis, N. Derrett, C.G. Hoch, W. Kent, P. Lyngbaek, B. Mahbod, M.A. Neimat, T.A. Ryan, and M.C. Shan. Iris: An object-oriented database management system. *ACM Transactions on Office Information Systems*, 5(1):48–69, 1987.

186. National Institute of Standards and Technology. Digital Signature Standard (DSS). *Federal Register*, 56(169), August 30, 1991.

187. R. Forre. Methods and instruments for designing S-boxes. *Journal of Cryptology*, 2(3):115–130, 1990.

188. W.F. Friedman. The index of coincidence and its application in cryptography. Riverbank Laboratories, Publication No. 22, 1920.

189. A. Fujioka, T. Okamoto, and K. Ohta. A practical secret voting scheme for large scale elections. In J. Seberry and Y. Zheng, editors, *Advances in Cryptology (AUSCRYPT'92)*. Lecture Notes in Computer Science No. 718, pages 244–251. Springer, Berlin Heidelberg New York, 1993.

190. A. Furche and G. Wrightson. *Computer Money: A Systematic Overview of Electronic Payment Systems*. DPunkt, Heidelberg, 1996.

191. M. Garey and D.S. Johnson. *Computers and Intractability: A Guide to the Theory of NP-Completeness*. Freeman, New York, 1979.

192. C. Garvey and A. Wu. ASD_Views. In *Proceedings of the 1988 IEEE Symposium on Security and Privacy*, pages 85–95. IEEE, 1988.

193. T.D. Garvey and T.F. Lunt. Multilevel security for knowledge-based systems. In *Proceedings of the Workshop on Object-Oriented Database Security*, University of Karlsruhe, Germany. European Institute for System Security, 1990 (preprint).

194. T.D. Garvey and T.F. Lunt. Multilevel security for knowledge-based systems. In *Proceedings of the 6th Computer Security Applications Conference*, Tucson, AZ, December, 1990 (preprint).

195. M. Gasser, A. Goldstein, C. Kaufman, and B. Lampson. The digital distributed system security architecture. In *Proceedings of 12th National Computer Security Conference*, pages 305–319. Baltimore, MD, 1989.

196. R. Gennaro, S. Jarecki, H. Krawczyk, and T. Rabin. Robust threshold DSS signatures. In U. Maurer, editor, *Advances in Cryptology (EUROCRYPT'96)*. Lecture Notes in Computer Science No. 1070, pages 354–371. Springer, Berlin Heidelberg New York, 1996.

197. J. Gersting. *Mathematical Structures for Computer Science*. Freeman, New York, 1987.

198. H. Ghodosi, J. Pieprzyk, and R. Safavi-Naini. Dynamic threshold cryptosystem: a new scheme in group oriented cryptography. In J. Pribyl, editor, *Proceedings of PRAGOCRYPT'96*, pages 370–379. CTU, Prague, 1996.

199. J. Gibson. Discrete logarithm hash function that is collision free and one way. In *IEE Proceedings-E*, 138(6):407–410, 1991.

200. E.N. Gilbert, F.J. MacWilliams, and N.J.A. Sloane. Codes which detect deception. *Bell System Tech. J.*, 53:405–424, 1974.

201. J. Gill. Computational complexity of probabilistic Turing machines. *Society of Industrial and Applied Mathematicians (SIAM)*, 6:675–695, December 1977.

202. M. Girault. Self-certified public keys. In D. Davies, editor, *Advances in Cryptology (EUROCRYPT'91)*. Lecture Notes in Computer Science No. 547, pages 490–497. Springer, Berlin Heidelberg New York, 1991.

203. J.I. Glasgow, G.H. MacEwen, T. Mercouris, and F. Ouabdesselam. Specifying multi-level security in a distributed system. In *Proceedings of the 7th DOD/NBS Computer Security Conference*, pages 319–340, September 1984.

204. J.A. Goguen and J. Meseguer. Unwinding and inference control. In *Proceedings of the 1984 IEEE Symposium on Security and Privacy*, pages 75–86. IEEE, 1984.

205. O. Goldreich. *Modern Cryptography, Probabilistic Proofs and Pseudorandomness*. Springer, Berlin Heidelberg New York, 1999.

206. O. Goldreich, S. Goldwasser, and S. Micali. How to construct random functions. *Journal of the ACM*, 33(4):792–807, 1986.

207. O. Goldreich, Y. Mansour, and M. Sipser. Interactive proof systems: provers that never fail and random selection. In *Proceedings of the 28th IEEE Symposium on Foundations of Computer Science*, pages 449–460. IEEE, 1987.

208. O. Goldreich, S. Micali, and A. Wigderson. Proofs that yield nothing but their validity or all languages in NP have zero-knowledge proof systems. *Journal of the ACM*, 38(1):691–729, 1991.

209. S. Goldwasser and S. Micali. Probabilistic encryption. *Journal of Computer and System Science*, 28(2):270–299, April 1984.

210. S. Goldwasser, S. Micali, and C. Rackoff. The knowledge complexity of interactive proof-systems. *SIAM Journal of Computing*, 18(1):186–208, February 1989.

211. S. Goldwasser, S. Micali, and R. Rivest. A digital signature scheme secure against adaptive chosen-message attacks. *Society of Industrial and Applied Mathematicians (SIAM)*, 17(2):281–308, April 1988.

212. J. Golić. Intrinsic statistical weakness of keystream generators. In J. Pieprzyk and R. Safavi-Naini, editors, *Advances in Cryptology (ASIACRYPT'94)*. Lecture Notes in Computer Science No. 917, pages 91–103. Springer, Berlin Heidelberg New York, 1995.

213. D. Gollmann. What do we mean by entity authentication. In *IEEE Symposium on Research in Security and Privacy*, pages 46–54, IEEE, 1996.

214. D. Gollmann. *Computer Security*. Wiley, New York, 1999.

215. D. Gollmann, T. Beth, and F. Damm. Authentication services in distributed systems. *Computers & Security*, 12:753–764, 1993.

216. D. Gollmann and W. Chambers. Clock-controlled shift registers: a review. *IEEE Journal of Selected Areas of Communications*, 7(4):525–533, May 1989.

217. L. Gong, R. Needham, and R. Yahalom. Reasoning about belief in cryptographic protocols. In *IEEE Symposium on Security and Privacy*, pages 234–248. IEEE, 1990.

218. A. Goscinski. *Distributed Operating Systems. The Logical Design*. Addison-Wesley, New York, 1991.

219. G. Graham and P. Denning. Protection: principles and practices. In *Proceedings of the AFIPS Spring Joint Computer Conference*, pages 417–429, 1972.

220. P.P. Griffiths and B.W. Wade. An authorization mechanism for a relational database system. *ACM Transactions on Database Systems*, 1(3):242–255, 1976.

221. CIDF Working Group. the common intrusion detection framework. Version 0.6, available at http://seclab.cs.ucdavis.edu/cidf, 1999.

222. D. Gryaznov. Scanners for the year 2000: Heuristics. In *Proceedings of the 5th International Virus Bulletin Conference*, pages 225–234, 1995.

223. L. Guillou and J.-J. Quisquater. Efficient digital public-key signature with shadow. In C. Pomerance, editor, *Advances in Cryptology (CRYPTO'87)*. Lecture Notes in Computer Science No. 293, pages 223–223. Springer, Berlin Heidelberg New York, 1988.

224. C. Günter. An identity-based key-exchange protocol. In J.-J. Quisquater and J. Vandewalle, editors, *Advances in Cryptology (EUROCRYPT'89)*. Lecture Notes in Computer Science No. 434, pages 29–37. Springer, Berlin Heidelberg New York, 1990.

225. S. Gupta and V.D. Gligor. Experience with a penetration analysis method and tool. In *Proceedings of the 15th National Computer Security Conference*, pages 165–183, 1992.

226. N. Habra, B. Charlierand, A. Mounji, and I. Mathieu. ASAX: software architecture and rule-based language for universal audit trial analysis. In Y. Deswarte, G. Eizenberg, and J.-J. Quisquater, editors, *Proceedings of the European Symposium on Research in Computer Security (ESORICS'92)*. Lecture Notes in Computer Science No. 648, pages 435–450. Springer, Berlin Heidelberg New York, 1992.

227. L. Hadfield, D. Hatter, and D. Bixler. *Windows NT Server 4 Security Handbook*. Que Corporation, Indianapolis, IN, 1997.

228. S. Halevi. Efficient commitment schemes with bounded sender and unbounded receiver. In D. Coppersmith, editor, *Advances in Cryptology (CRYPTO'95)*. Lecture Notes in Computer Science No. 963, pages 84–96. Springer, Berlin Heidelberg New York, 1995.

229. S. Hansen and T. Atkins. Automated system monitoring and notification with SWATCH. In *Proceedings of the USENIX Systems Administration (LISA VII) Conference*, pages 145–155, 1993.

230. T. Hardjono and J. Seberry. Authentication via multi-service tickets in the KUPEREE server. In D. Gollmann, editor, *Proceedings of the 3rd European Symposium on Research in Computer Security (ESORICS'94)*. Lecture Notes in Computer Science No. 875, pages 143–160. Springer, Berlin Heidelberg New York, 1994.

231. T. Hardjono and J. Seberry. Replicating the KUPEREE authentication server for increased security and reliability. In J. Pieprzyk and J. Seberry, editors, *Proceedings of the 1st Australasian Conference on Information Security and Privacy ACISP96*, Lecture Notes in Computer Science No. 1172, pages 14–27. Springer, Berlin Heidelberg New York, 1996.

232. D. Harkins and D. Carrel. *RFC 2409: The Internet Key Exchange (IKE)*, November 1998. Available at *http://www.ietf.org*.

233. M. Harrison, W. Ruzzo, and J. Ullman. Protection in operating systems. *Communications of the ACM*, 19(8):461–471, 1976.

234. H.R. Hartson. Database security – system architectures. *Information Systems (GB)*, 6:1–22, 1981.

235. P. Hawkes. Differential-linear weak key classes of IDEA. In K. Nyberg, editor, *Advances in Cryptology (EUROCRYPT'98)*. Lecture Notes in Computer Science No. 1403, pages 112–126. Springer, Berlin Heidelberg New York, 1998.

236. R.R. Henning and S.A. Walker. Computer architecture and database security. In *Proceedings of the 9th National Computer Security Conference*, pages 216–230. National Bureau of Standards/National Computer Security Center. Gaithersburg, MD, September 1986.

237. M.P. Herlihy and J.D. Tyger. How to make replicated data secure. In C. Pomerance, editor, *Advances in Cryptology (CRYPTO '87)*. Lecture Notes in Computer Science No. 293, pages 380–391. Springer, Berlin Heidelberg New York, 1987.

238. A. Herzberg, S. Jarecki, H. Krawczyk, and M. Yung. Proactive secret sharing or: how to cope with perpetual leakage. In D. Coppersmith, editor, *Advances in Cryptology (CRYPTO'95)*. Lecture Notes in Computer Science No. 963, pages 339–352. Springer, Berlin Heidelberg New York, 1995.

239. E. van Heyst and T. Pedersen. How to make efficient fail-stop signatures. In R. Rueppel, editor, *Advances in Cryptology (EUROCRYPT'92)*. Lecture Notes in Computer Science No. 658, pages 366–377. Springer, Berlin Heidelberg New York, 1993.

240. H. Highland. The BRAIN virus: facts and fantasy. *Computers & Security*, 7:367–370, 1988.

241. H. Highland. A macro virus. *Computers & Security*, 8:178–188, 1989.

242. H. Highland. Procedure to reduce the computer virus threat. *Computers & Security*, 16:439–449, 1997.

243. M. Hirvensalo. *Quantum Computing*. Springer, Berlin Heidelberg New York, 2001.

244. J. Hochberg, K. Jackson, C. Stallings, J. McClary, D. DuBois, and J. Ford. NADIR: An automated system for detecting network intrusion and misuse. *Computers & Security*, 12:235–248, 1993.

245. J. Horton. Introduction to viruses. PhD Thesis, School of IT and CS, University of Wollongong, 2000.

246. J. Horton and J. Seberry. Companion viruses and the Macintosh: threats and countermeasures. In *Proceedings of the Fourth Australasian Conference on Information Security and Privacy (ACISP'99)*. Lecture Notes in Computer Science No. 1587, pages 202–212. Springer, Berlin Heidelberg New York, 1999.

247. D.K. Hsiao. Data base computers. In M.C. Yovits, editor, *Advances in Computers*, pages 1–64. Academic Press, New York, 1980.

248. K. Ilgun. USTAT: a real-time intrusion detection system for UNIX. In *IEEE Symposium on Research in Security and Privacy*, pages 16–28. IEEE, 1993.

249. Apple Computer, Inc. *Inside Macintosh: Files*. Addison-Wesley, New York, 1992.

250. Apple Computer, Inc. *Inside Macintosh: Macintosh Toolbox Essentials*. Addison-Wesley, New York, 1992.

251. Apple Computer, Inc. *Inside Macintosh: More Macintosh Toolbox*. Addison-Wesley, New York, 1993.

252. Apple Computer, Inc. *Inside Macintosh: Operating System Utilities*. Addison-Wesley, New York, 1994.

253. Oracle, Inc. *Oracle8 and Oracle8 Enterprise Edition*, 1998. On-line Generic Documentation, Version 8.0.5.0.0.

254. I. Ingemarsson, D. Tang, and C. Wong. A conference key distribution system. *IEEE Transactions on Information Theory*, IT-28:714–720, IEEE, 1982.

255. M. Ito, A. Saito, and T. Nishizeki. Secret sharing scheme realizing general access structure. In *Proceedings of the IEEE Globecom '87*, pages 99–102. IEEE, 1987.

256. K. Iversen. A cryptographic scheme for computerized general elections. In J. Feigenbaum, editor, *Advances in Cryptology (CRYPTO'91)*. Lecture Notes in Computer Science No. 576, pages 405–419. Springer, Berlin Heidelberg New York, 1992.

257. C. Jackson. Worms in the ripe apple. Virus Bulletin, July 1998. see *http://www.virusbtn.com/VirusInformation/autostart9805.html*.

258. M. Jakobsson and M. Yung. Revocable and versatile electronic money. In *Proceedings of the 3rd ACM Conference on Computer and Communication Security*, pages 76–87. ACM, Boston, 1996.

259. H.S. Javitz and A. Valdes. The SRI IDES statistical anomaly detector. In *Proceedings of the 1991 IEEE Symposium on Security and Privacy*, pages 316–326. IEEE, 1991.

260. T. Johansson. Lower bounds on the probability of deception in authentication with arbitration. *IEEE Transactions on Information Theory*, IT-40(5):1573–1585, 1994.

261. T. Johansson and A. Sgarro. Strengthening Simmons bound on impersonation. *IEEE Transactions on Information Theory*, IT-37(4):1182–1185, 1991.

262. T. Johansson, B. Smeets, and G. Kabatianskii. On the relation between a-codes and codes correcting independent errors. In T. Helleseth, editor, *Advances in Cryptology (EUROCRYPT'93)*. Lecture Notes in Computer Science No. 765, pages 1–11. Springer, Berlin Heidelberg New York, 1994.

263. R.W. Jones and M.S.J. Baxter. The role of encipherment services in distributed systems. In F. Pichler, editor, *Advances in Cryptology (EUROCRYPT'85)*, pages 214–220. Linz, Austria, April 1985.

264. D. Kahn. *The Codebreakers*. Macmillan, New York, 1967.

265. J. Kam and G. Davida. Structured design of substitution-permutation networks. *IEEE Transactions on Computers*, C-28:747–753, 1979.

266. I. Kantzavelou and S. Katsikas. An attack detection system for secure computer systems – outline of the solution. In *Proceedings of the 13th International Information Security Conference*, pages 123–135, 1997.

267. I. Kantzavelou and A. Patel. An attack detection system for secure computer systems – design of ADS. In *Proceedings of the 12th International Information Security Conference*, pages 1–16, 1996.

268. E.D. Karnin, J.W. Greene, and M.E. Hellman. On secret sharing systems. *IEEE Transactions on Information Theory*, IT-29:35–41, 1983.

269. D. Karpinski. AntiCMOS – brain damage. Virus Bulletin, August 1994.

270. P. Kasselman and W. Penzhorn. Cryptanalysis of reduced version of HAVAL. *Electronic Letters*, 36:30–31, 2000.

271. A. Kaufmann. *Graphs, Dynamic Programming, and Finite Games*. Mathematics in Science and Engineering. Academic Press, New York, 1967.

272. T.F. Keefe, W.T. Tsai, and M.B. Thuraisingham. SODA: A secure object-oriented database system. *Computers & Security*, 8(6):517–533, 1989.

273. A.M. Keller. Updates to relational databases through views involving joins. In P. Scheuer-
     mann, editor, *Improving Database Usability and Responsiveness*, pages 363–384. Aca-
     demic Press, New York, 1982.
274. R. Kemmerer, C. Meadows, and J. Millen. Three systems for cryptographic protocol
     analysis. *Journal of Cryptology*, 7(2):79–130, 1994.
275. S. Kent and R. Atkinson. *RFC 2401: Security architecture for the Internet Protocol*.
     Network Working Group, IETF, November 1998. Available at *http://www.ietf.org*.
276. S. Kent and R. Atkinson. *RFC 2402: IP Authentication Header*, November 1998. Avail-
     able at *http://www.ietf.org*.
277. S. Kent and R. Atkinson. *RFC 2406: IP Encapsulating Security Payload (ESP)*, Novem-
     ber 1998. Available at *http://www.ietf.org*.
278. W. Kim, N. Ballou, H. Chou, J.F. Garza, and D. Woelk. Features of the ORION object-
     oriented database system. In W. Kim and F.H. Lochovsky, editors, *Object-Oriented Con-
     cepts, Databases and Applications*, pages 251–282. Addison-Wesley, New York, 1989.
279. W. Kim, J.F. Garza, N. Ballou, and D. Woelk. Architecture of the ORION next-
     generation database system. *IEEE Transaction on Knowledge and Data Engineering*,
     2(1):109–124, 1990.
280. W. Kim and F.H. Lochovsky. *Object-Oriented Concepts, Databases and Applications*.
     Addison-Wesley, New York, 1989.
281. L. Knudsen and W. Meier. Improved differential attacks on RC5. In N. Koblitz, editor,
     Advances in Cryptology (CRYPTO'96). Lecture Notes in Computer Science No. 1109,
     pages 216–236. Springer, Berlin Heidelberg New York, 1996.
282. D.E. Knuth. *Seminumerical Algorithms*, Vol. 2 of *The Art of Computer Programming*.
     Addison-Wesley, New York, 1969. Second edition, 1981.
283. N. Koblitz. Elliptic curve cryptosystems. *Mathematics of Computation*, 48(177):203–209,
     1987.
284. N. Koblitz. *Algebraic Aspects of Cryptography*. Springer, Berlin Heidelberg New York,
     1999.
285. T. Kohno, J. Kelsey, and B. Schneier. Preliminary cryptanalysis of reduced-round ser-
     pent. In *Proceedings of the 3rd Advanced Encryption Standard (AES) Candidate Con-
     ference*, 2000. Available at *www.counterpane.com/serpent-aes.html*.
286. K. Koyama, U.M. Maurer, T. Okamoto, and S.A. Vanstone. New public-key schemes
     based on elliptic curves over the ring z_n. In J. Feigenbaum, editor, *Advances in Cryptology
     (CRYPTO'91)*. Lecture Notes in Computer Science No. 576, pages 252–266. Springer,
     Berlin Heidelberg New York, 1992.
287. K. Koyama and K. Ohta. Identity-based conference key distribution systems. In
     C. Pomerance, editor, *Advances in Cryptology (CRYPTO'87)*. Lecture Notes in Com-
     puter Science No. 293, pages 175–184. Springer, Berlin Heidelberg New York, 1988.
288. H. Krawczyk. SKEME: A versatile secure key exchange mechanism for Internet. In *Pro-
     ceedings of the Internet Society Symposium on Network and Distributed System Security*,
     pages 114–127. IEEE, 1996.
289. P. Kumar and R. Scholtz. Bounds on the linear span of bent sequences. *IEEE Transac-
     tions on Information Theory*, IT-29 No. 6:854–862, 1983.

290. P. Kumar, R. Scholtz, and L. Welch. Generalized bent functions and their properties. *Journal of Combinatorial Theory*, Ser. A, 40:90–107, 1985.

291. S. Kumar and E. Spafford. A pattern matching model for misuse intrusion detection. In *Proceedings of the 17th National Computer Security Conference*, pages 11–21, 1994.

292. K. Kurosawa, K. Okada, and S. Tsujii. Low exponent attack against elliptic curve RSA. In J. Pieprzyk and R. Safavi-Naini, editors, *Advances in Cryptology (ASIACRYPT'94)*. Lecture Notes in Computer Science No. 917, pages 376–383. Springer, Berlin Heidelberg New York, 1995.

293. J.C. Lagarias and A.M. Odlyzko. Solving low-density subset sum problems. In *Proceedings of the 24th IEEE Symposium on Foundations of Computer Science*, pages 1–10. IEEE, 1983.

294. X. Lai and J. Massey. A proposal for a new block encryption standard. In I.B. Damgård, editor, *Advances in Cryptology (EUROCRYPT'90)*. Lecture Notes in Computer Science No. 473, pages 389–404. Springer, Berlin Heidelberg New York, 1990.

295. X. Lai, J. Massey, and S. Murphy. Markov ciphers and differential cryptanalysis. In D.W. Davies, editor, *Advances in Cryptology (EUROCRYPT'91)*. Lecture Notes in Computer Science No. 547, pages 17–38. Springer, Berlin Heidelberg New York, 1991.

296. L. Lamport. Constructing digital signatures from a one-way function. Technical Report CSL-98, SRI International, October 1979.

297. B. Lampson. Protection. In *Proceedings of the 5th Princeton Conference on Information and System Sciences*, pages 437–443, 1971.

298. A.K. Lenstra, H.W. Lenstra, Jr., and L. Lovász. Factoring polynomials with rational coefficients. *Mathematische Annalen*, 261:513–534, 1982.

299. A.K. Lenstra, H.W. Lenstra, Jr., M.S. Manasse, and J.M. Pollard. The number field sieve. In *Proceedings 22nd ACM Symposium on Theory of Computing*, pages 564–572. ACM, New York, 1990.

300. A.K. Lenstra and E.R. Verkeul. Selecting cryptographic keys sizes. *Journal of Cryptology*, 14(4):255–293, 2001.

301. H.W. Lenstra, Jr. Factoring integers with elliptic curves. *Annals of Mathematics*, 126:649–673, 1987.

302. L.A. Levin. One-way function and pseudorandom generators. *Combinatorica*, 7(4):357–363, 1987.

303. C.M. Li, T. Hwang, and N.Y. Lee. Threshold-multisignature schemes where suspected forgery implies traceability of adversarial shareholders. In A. De Santis, editor, *Advances in Cryptology (EUROCRYPT'94)*. Lecture Notes in Computer Science No. 950, pages 194–204. Springer, Berlin Heidelberg New York, 1995.

304. G.E Liepins and H.S. Vaccaro. Intrusion detection: Its role and validation. *Computers & Security*, 11:347–355, 1992.

305. G. Lowe. Some new attacks upon security protocols. In *IEEE Computer Security Foundations Workshop*, pages 162–169. IEEE, 1996.

306. J. Loxton, D. Khoo, G. Bird, and J. Seberry. A cubic RSA code equivalent to factorization. *Journal of Cryptology*, 5:139–150, 1992.

307. M. Luby and C. Rackoff. How to construct pseudorandom permutations and pseudorandom functions. *SIAM Journal of Computing*, 17(2):373–386, April 1988.

308. P. Lucas and L. Van Der Gaag. *Principles of Expert Systems*. Addison-Wesley, New York, 1991.

309. T. Lunt and R. Jagannathan. A prototype real-time intrusion detection expert system. In *Proceedings of the 1988 IEEE Symposium on Security and Privacy*. IEEE, 1988.

310. T. Lunt, A. Tamaru, F. Gilham, R. Jagannathan, P. Neumann, and C. Jalali. IDES: a progress report. In *Proceedings of the 6th Annual Computer Security Applications Conference*, pages 273–285. IEEE, 1990.

311. T.F. Lunt. Multilevel security for object-oriented database systems. In D.L. Spooner and C. Landwehr, editors, *Database Security III: Status and Prospects (Results of the IFIP WG 11.3 Workshop on Database Security)*, pages 199–209, 1989. North-Holland, Amsterdam, 1989.

312. T.F. Lunt, D.E. Denning, R.R. Schell, M. Heckman, and W.R. Shockley. Element-level classification with A1 assurance. *Computers & Security*, 7(1):73–82, 1988.

313. T.F. Lunt, D.E. Denning, R.R. Schell, M. Heckman, and W.R. Shockley. The SeaView security model. *IEEE Transactions on Software Engineering*, SE-16(6):593–607, 1990.

314. T.F. Lunt and J.K. Millen. Secure knowledge-based systems. Technical Report SRI-CSL-90-04, SRI International, Menlo Park, CA, August 1989.

315. T.F. Lunt, R.R. Schell, W.R. Shockley, M. Heckman, and D. Warren. A near-term design for the SeaView multilevel database system. In *Proceedings of the 1988 IEEE Symposium on Security and Privacy*, pages 234–244. IEEE, 1988.

316. G.H. MacEwen. Effects of distributed system technology on database security: A survey. In C.E. Landwehr, editor, *Database Security: Status and Prospects (Results of the IFIP WG 11.3 Initial Meeting)*, pages 253–261, Annapolis. North-Holland, Amsterdam, 1987.

317. F. MacWilliams and N. Sloane. *The Theory of Error-Correcting Codes*. North-Holland, Amsterdam, 1977.

318. S. Magruder. High-level language computer viruses – a new threat? *Computers & Security*, 13:263–269, 1994.

319. J. Massey. Contemporary cryptology, an introduction. *Proceedings of the IEEE*, 76:533–549, 1988.

320. M. Matsui. The first experimental cryptanalysis of the data encryption standard. In Y. Desmedt, editor, *Advances in Cryptology (CRYPTO'94)*. Lecture Notes in Computer Science No. 839, pages 1–11. Springer, Berlin Heidelberg New York, 1994.

321. M. Matsui. Linear cryptanalysis method for DES cipher. In T. Helleseth, editor, *Advances in Cryptology (EUROCRYPT'93)*. Lecture Notes in Computer Science No. 765, pages 386–397. Springer, Berlin Heidelberg New York, 1994.

322. M. Matsui. On correlation between the order of S-boxes and the strength of DES. In A. De Santis, editor, *Advances in Cryptology (EUROCRYPT'94)*. Lecture Notes in Computer Science No. 950, pages 366–376. Springer, Berlin Heidelberg New York, 1995.

323. M. Matsui and A. Yamagishi. A new method for known plaintext attack of FEAL cipher. In R. Rueppel, editor, *Advances in Cryptology (EUROCRYPT'92)*. Lecture Notes in Computer Science No. 658, pages 81–91. Springer, Berlin Heidelberg New York, 1993.

324. T. Matsumoto, Y. Takashima, and H. Imai. On seeking smart public-key distribution systems. *Transactions IECE Japan*, 69(2):99–106, 1986.

325. S.M. Matyas and C.H. Meyer. Electronic signature for data encryption standard. *IBM Technical Disclosure Bulletin* 24(5):2332–24, 1981.

326. U. Maurer. A universal statistical test for random bit generators. *Journal of Cryptology*, 5(2):89–105, 1992.

327. U. Maurer. Towards the equivalence of breaking the Diffie-Hellman protocol and computing discrete algorithms. In Y. Desmedt, editor, *Advances in Cryptology (CRYPTO'94)*. Lecture Notes in Computer Science No. 839, pages 271–281. Springer, Berlin Heidelberg New York, 1994.

328. U. Maurer and S. Wolf. Diffie-Hellman oracles. In N. Koblitz, editor, *Advances in Cryptology (CRYPTO'96)*. Lecture Notes in Computer Science No. 1109, pages 268–282. Springer, Berlin Heidelberg New York, 1996.

329. R.J. McEliece. *A Public-Key System Based on Algebraic Coding Theory*, pages 114–116. DSN Progress Report 44. Jet Propulsion Laboratory, California Institute of Technology, 1978.

330. J. McHugh and B.M. Thuraisingham. Multilevel security issues in distributed database management systems. *Computers & Security*, 7(4):387–396, 1988.

331. M. McIlroy. Virology 101. *Computing Systems*, 2:173–181, 1989.

332. L. Me. Security audit trail analysis using genetic algorithms. In *Proceedings of the 12th International Conference on Computer Safety, Reliability and Security*, pages 329–340, 1993.

333. L. Me. Genetic algorithms, a biologically inspired approach for security audit trails analysis. In *Short Presentation, 1996 IEEE Symposium on Security and Privacy*, 1996.

334. C. Meadows. Formal verification of cryptographic protocols: a survey. In J. Pieprzyk and R. Safavi-Naini, editors, *Advances in Cryptology (ASIACRYPT'94)*. Lecture Notes in Computer Science No. 917, pages 135–150. Springer, Berlin Heidelberg New York, 1995.

335. A. Menezes. *Elliptic Curve Public Key Cryptosystems*. Kluwer, Dordrecht, 1993.

336. A. Menezes, T. Okamoto, and S. Vanstone. Reducing elliptic curve logarithms to logarithms in a finite field. *IEEE Transactions on Information Theory*, IT-39:1639–1646, 1993.

337. A. Menezes, P. van Oorschot, and S. Vanstone. *Handbook of Applied Cryptography*. CRC, Boca Raton, FL, 1997.

338. A. Menezes and S. Vanstone. Elliptic curve cryptosystems and their implementation. *Journal of Cryptology*, 6:209–224, 1993.

339. R. Merkle and M. Hellman. Hiding information and signatures in trapdoor knapsacks. *IEEE Transactions on Information Theory*, IT-24:525–530, September 1978.

340. R.C. Merkle. A certified digital signature. In G. Brassard, editor, *Advances in Cryptology (CRYPTO'89)*. Lecture Notes in Computer Science No. 435, pages 218–238. Springer, Berlin Heidelberg New York, 1990.

341. R.C. Merkle. One-way hash functions and DES. In G. Brassard, editor, *Advances in Cryptology – CRYPTO'89*. Lecture Notes in Computer Science No. 435, pages 428–446. Springer, Berlin Heidelberg New York, 1990.

342. R.C. Merkle. A fast software one-way hash function. *Journal of Cryptology*, 3(1):43–58, 1989.

343. S. Micali and C.P. Schnorr. Efficient, perfect polynomial random number generators. *Journal of Cryptology*, 3(3):157–172, 1991.

344. M. Mihaljević. A faster cryptanalysis of the self-shrinking generator. In J. Pieprzyk and J. Seberry, editors, *Proceedings of the First Australasian Conference on Information Security and Privacy (ACISP'96)*. Lecture Notes in Computer Science No. 1172, pages 182–189. Springer, Berlin Heidelberg New York, 1996.

345. G.L. Miller. Riemann's hypothesis and tests for primality. *Journal of Computer and System Science*, 13(3):300–317, 1976.

346. V.S. Miller. Use of elliptic curves in cryptography. In H.C. Williams, editor, *Advances in Cryptology (CRYPTO'85)*. Lecture Notes in Computer Science No. 218, pages 417–426. Springer, Berlin Heidelberg New York, 1986.

347. S. Miyaguchi. The FEAL cipher family. In A.J. Menezes and S.A. Vanstone, editors, *Advances in Cryptology (CRYPTO'90)*. Lecture Notes in Computer Science No. 537, pages 627–638. Springer, Berlin Heidelberg New York, 1991.

348. S. Miyaguchi, K. Ohta, and M. Iwata. 128-bit hash function (N-Hash). In *Proceedings of SECURICOM'90*, pages 123–137, 1990.

349. A. Moitra. Real-time audit log viewer and analyzer. In *Proceedings of the 4th Workshop on Computer Security Incident Handling*. Incident Response and Security Teams – FIRST. 1992 (see http://www.first.org).

350. Computer Virus Information Pages Monkey. Available at *http://www.datafellows.com/*.

351. J.H. Moore. Protocol failures in cryptosystems. In G.J. Simmons, editor, *Contemporary Cryptology: The Science of Information Integrity*, pages 541–558. IEEE, 1992.

352. M. Morgenstern. Security and inference in multilevel database and knowledge-base systems. In *Proceedings of the ACM International Conference on the Management of Data (SIGMOD'87)*, pages 357–373. ACM, New York, 1987.

353. M.A. Morrison and J. Brillhart. A method of factoring and the factorization of f_7. *Mathematics of Computation*, 29:183–205, 1975.

354. A. Mounji and B. Le Charlier. Detecting breaches in computer security: A pragmatic system with a logic programming flavor. In *Proceedings of the 8th Benelux Workshop on Logic Programming*, 1996.

355. A. Mounji and B. Le Charlier. Continuous assessment of a UNIX configuration: Integrating intrusion detection and configuration analysis. In *Proceedings of the ISOC'97 Symposium on Network and Distributed System Security*, 1997.

356. A. Mounji, B. Le Charlier, D. Zampunieris, and N. Habra. Preliminary report on distributed PASAX. Research Report (36 pages). See http://www.info.fundp.ac.be/~amo/publications.html. May 1994.

357. A. Mounji, B. Le Charlier, D. Zampunieris, and N. Habra. Distributed audit trail analysis. In *Proceedings of the ISOC '95 Symposium on Network and Distributed System Security*, 1995.

358. D. M'Raihi. Cost-effective payment schemes with privacy regulation. In K. Kim and T. Matsumoto, editors, *Advances in Cryptology (ASIACRYPT'96)*. Lecture Notes in Computer Science No. 1163, pages 266–275. Springer, Berlin Heidelberg New York, 1996.

359. Y. Mu, V. Varadharajan, and Y.-X. Lin. New micropayment schemes based on PayWords. In V. Varadharajan, J. Pieprzyk, and Y. Mu, editors, *Information Security and Privacy (ACSIP'97)*. Lecture Notes on Computer Science No. 1270, pages 283–293. Springer, Berlin Heidelberg New York, 1997.

360. B. Mukherjee, L.T. Heberlein, and K.N. Levitt. Network intrusion detection. *IEEE Network*, 8:26–41, 1994.

361. S. Mullender, G. Van Rossum, A. Tanenbaum, R. Van Renesse, and H. Van Staveren. Amoeba: a distributed operating system for the 1990s. *IEEE Computer*, 23:44–53, 1990.

362. S. Murphy. The cryptanalysis of FEAL-4 with 20 chosen plaintexts. *Journal of Cryptology*, 2:145–154, 1990.

363. C. Nachenberg. Computer virus-antivirus coevolution. *Communications of the ACM*, 40:46–51, 1997.

364. K. Nam and T.R.N. Rao. Cryptographic models for DBMS communications. In K.H. Kim, K. Chon, and C.V. Ramamoorthy, editors, *Proceedings of Pacific Computer Communications '85*, pages 277–283. North-Holland, Amsterdam, 1985.

365. M. Naor and M. Yung. Universal one-way hash functions and their cryptographic applications. In *Proceedings of the 21th ACM Symposium on Theory of Computing*, pages 33–43 ACM, 1999.

366. W. Narkiewicz. *Number Theory*. World Scientific, Singapore, 1983.

367. National Institute of Standards and Technology (NIST). *FIPS Publication 180: Secure Hash Standard (SHS)*, May 11, 1993.

368. National Institute of Standards and Technology (NIST). *NIST FIPS PUB 185, Escrowed Encryption Standard*, February 1994.

369. R.M. Needham and M.D. Schroeder. Using encryption for authentication in a large network of computers. *Communications of the ACM*, 21(12):993–999, 1978.

370. R.M. Needham and M.D. Schroeder. Using encryption for authentication in large networks of computers. *Communications of the ACM*, 21(12):993–999, December 1978.

371. R.M. Needham and R.D. Walker. The Cambridge CAP computer and its protection system. In *Proceedings of the 6th Symposium on Operating System Principles*, pages 1–10, 1990.

372. P.G. Neumann. Audit trail analysis and usage data collection and processing. Part 1. Computer Science Laboratory, SRI International, 1985.

373. P.G. Neumann and F. Ostapik. Audit trail analysis and usage data collection and processing. Part 2. Computer Science Laboratory, SRI International, 1987.

374. V. Niemi and A. Renvall. How to prevent buying of votes in computer elections. In J. Pieprzyk and R. Safavi-Naini, editors, *Advances in Cryptology (ASIACRYPT'94)*.

Lecture Notes in Computer Science No. 917, pages 164–170. Springer, Berlin Heidelberg New York, 1995.

375. O. Nierstrasz. A survey of object-oriented concepts. In W. Kim and F.H. Lochovsky, editors, *Object-Oriented Concepts, Databases and Applications*, pages 3–21. Addison-Wesley, New York, 1989.

376. K. Nyberg. Perfect nonlinear S-boxes. In D.W. Davies, editor, *Advances in Cryptology (EUROCRYPT'91)*. Lecture Notes in Computer Science No. 547, pages 378–386. Springer, Berlin Heidelberg New York, 1991.

377. K. Nyberg. On the construction of highly nonlinear permutations. In R.A. Rueppel, editor, *Advances in Cryptology (EUROCRYPT'92)*. Lecture Notes in Computer Science No. 658, pages 92–98. Springer, Berlin Heidelberg New York, 1992.

378. L. O'Connor and J. Seberry. *Cryptographic Significance of the Knapsack Problem*. Aegean Park, Laguna Hills, CA, 1988.

379. L.J. O'Connor. An analysis of product ciphers based on the properties of Boolean functions. PhD thesis, University of Waterloo, 1992. Waterloo, Ontario, Canada.

380. A.M. Odlyzko. Discrete logarithms in finite fields and their cryptographic significance. In T. Beth, N. Cot, and I. Ingemarsson, editors, *Advances in Cryptology (EUROCRYPT'84)*. Lecture Notes in Computer Science No. 209, pages 224–314. Springer, Berlin Heidelberg New York, 1984.

381. Canadian System Security Center, Communication Security Establishment, Government of Canada. *The Canadian Trusted Computer Product Evaluation Criteria*. Version 3.0e, January 1993.

382. Commision of the European Union. *Information Technology Security Evaluation Criteria*. Technical Report, Brussels, September 1992.

383. National Bureau of Standards. Announcing the Data Encryption Standard. Technical Report FIPS Publication 46, US Commerce Department, National Bureau of Standards. January 1977.

384. National Soviet Bureau of Standards. Cryptographic algorithm. GOST 28147-89, 1989.

385. Y. Ohnishi. *A study on data security*. Master's thesis, Tohoku University, Japan, 1988.

386. K. Ohta and K. Koyama. Meet-in-the-middle attack on digital signature schemes. In J. Seberry and J. Pieprzyk, editors, *Advances in Cryptology (AUSCRYPT'90)*. Lecture Notes in Computer Science No. 453, pages 110–121. Springer, Berlin Heidelberg New York, 1990.

387. T. Okamoto. A digital multisignature scheme using bijective public-key cryptosystems. *ACM Transactions on Computer Systems*, 6(8):432–441, 1988.

388. T. Okamoto. Provably secure and practical identification schemes and corresponding signature schemes. In E.F. Brickell, editor, *Advances in Cryptology (CRYPTO'92)*. Lecture Notes in Computer Science No. 740, pages 31–53. Springer, Berlin Heidelberg New York, 1992.

389. T. Okamoto. An efficient divisible electronic cash system. In D. Coppersmith, editor, *Advances in Cryptology (CRYPTO'95)*. Lecture Notes in Computer Science No. 963, pages 438–451. Springer, Berlin Heidelberg New York, 1995.

390. T. Okamoto and K. Ohta. Universal electronic cash. In J. Feigenbaum, editor, *Advances in Cryptology (CRYPTO'91)*. Lecture Notes in Computer Science No. 576, pages 324–337. Springer, Berlin Heidelberg New York, 1992.

391. J.D. Olsen, R.A. Scholtz, and L.R. Welch. Bent-function sequences. *IEEE Transactions on Information Theory*, IT-28 No. 6:858–864, 1982.

392. K.A. Omar and D.L. Wells. Modified architecture for the sub-keys model. In *Proceedings of the 1983 IEEE Symposium on Security and Privacy*, pages 79–86. IEEE, 1983.

393. P.C. van Oorschot and M.J. Wiener. A known-plaintext attack on two-key triple encryption. In I.B. Damgård, editor, *Advances in Cryptology (EUROCRYPT'90)*. Lecture Notes in Computer Science No. 473, pages 318–325. Springer, Berlin Heidelberg New York, 1991.

394. R. Oppliger. *Authentication Systems for Secure Networks*. Artech House, Boston, 1996.

395. E.I. Organick. *The Multics System: An Examination of Its Structure*. MIT Press, Cambridge, MA, 1972.

396. D. Otway and O. Rees. Efficient and timely mutual authentication. *ACM Operating Systems Review*, 21(1):8–10, 1987.

397. J. Patarin. How to construct pseudorandom and super pseudorandom permutations from one single pseudorandom function. In R. Rueppel, editor, *Advances in Cryptology (EUROCRYPT'92)*. Lecture Notes in Computer Science No. 658, pages 256–266. Springer, Berlin Heidelberg New York, 1993.

398. V. Paxson. Bro: A system for detecting network intruders in real-time. In *Proceedings of the 7th Annual USENIX Security Symposium*. 1998.

399. T.P. Pedersen. Non-interactive and information-theoretic secure verifiable secret sharing. In J. Feigenbaum, editor, *Advances in Cryptology (CRYPTO'91)*. Lecture Notes in Computer Science No. 576, pages 129–140. Springer, Berlin Heidelberg New York, 1992.

400. K.L. Petersen. IDA – intrusion detection alert. In *Proceedings of the 6th Annual International Computer Software and Application Conference*, pages 306–311. IEEE, 1992.

401. B. Pfitzmann. *Digital Signature Schemes*. Lecture Notes in Computer Science No. 1100. Springer, Berlin Heidelberg New York, 1996.

402. B. Pfitzmann and M. Waidner. Fail-stop signatures and their applications. In *Proceedings of SECURICOM'91*, pages 338–350, 1991.

403. C.P. Pfleeger. *Security in Computing*. Prentice-Hall, Englewood Cliffs, NJ, 1989.

404. J. Pieprzyk. Bent permutations. In G. Mullen and P. Shiue, editors, *Proceedings of 1st International Conference on Finite Fields, Coding Theory, and Advances in Communications and Computing*. Lecture Notes in Pure and Applied Mathematics No. 141. Springer, Berlin Heidelberg New York, 1992.

405. J. Pieprzyk and G. Finkelstein. Towards effective nonlinear cryptosystem design. *IEE Proceedings*, 135(6):325–335, November 1988.

406. J.P. Pieprzyk. How to construct pseudorandom permutations from single pseudorandom functions. In I.B. Damgård, editor, *Advances in Cryptology (EUROCRYPT'90)*. Lecture Notes in Computer Science No. 473, pages 140–150. Springer, Berlin Heidelberg New York, May 1991.

407. J.P. Pieprzyk and X.-M. Zhang. Permutation generators of alternating groups. In *Advances in Cryptology – AUSCRYPT'90*, J. Seberry, J. Pieprzyk, editors, Lecture Notes in Computer Science No. 453, pages 237–244. Springer, Berlin Heidelberg New York, 1990.

408. G.M.J. Pluimakers. Some notes on authorization and transaction management in distributed database systems. *Computers & Security*, 7(3):287–298, 1988.

409. D. Pointcheval. A new identification scheme based on the perceptrons problem. In L. Guillou and J.-J. Quisquater, editors, *Advances in Cryptology (EUROCRYPT'95)*. Lecture Notes in Computer Science No. 9921, pages 319–328. Springer, Berlin Heidelberg New York, 1995.

410. D. Pointcheval and J. Stern. Security proofs for signature schemes. In U. Maurer, editor, *Advances in Cryptology – EUROCRYPT'96*, Lecture Notes in Computer Science No. 1070, pages 387–398. Springer, Berlin Heidelberg New York, 1996.

411. C. Pomerance. The quadratic sieve factoring algorithm. In T. Beth, N. Cot, and I. Ingemarrson, editors, *Advances in Cryptology*. Lecture Notes in Computer Science No. 209, pages 169–182. Springer, Berlin Heidelberg New York, 1984.

412. A. Porras and P.G. Neumann. Emerald: Event monitoring enabling responses to anomalous live disturbances. In *Proceedings of the National Information Systems Security Conference*, 1997.

413. B. Preneel. *Analysis and design of cryptographic hash functions*. PhD thesis, Katholieke Universiteit Leuven, 1993.

414. B. Preneel, W. Van Leekwijck, L. Van Linden, R. Govaerts, and J. Vandewalle. Propagation characteristics of Boolean functions. In I.B. Damgård, editor, *Advances in Cryptology (EUROCRYPT'90)*. Lecture Notes in Computer Science No. 473, pages 161–173. Springer, Berlin Heidelberg New York, 1990.

415. B. Preneel and P. van Oorschot. MDx-MAC and building fast MACs from hash functions. In D. Coppersmith, editor, *Advances in Cryptology – CRYPTO'95*. Lecture Notes in Computer Science No. 963, pages 1–14. Springer, Berlin Heidelberg New York, 1995.

416. P. Proctor. Audit reduction and misuse detection in heterogeneous environments: framework and application. In *Proceedings of the 10th Annual Computer Security Application Conference*, pages 117–125, 1994.

417. T.H. Ptacek and T.N. Newsham. Insertion, evasion and denial of service: Eluding network intrusion detection. Technical Report, Secure Networks Inc., http://www.secnet.com, January 1998.

418. J.-J. Quisquater, M. Quisquater, M. Quisquater, M. Quisquater, L. Guillou, M.A. Guillou, G. Guillou, A. Guillou, G. Guillou, S. Guillou, and T. Berson. How to explain zero-knowledge protocols to your children. In G. Brassard, editor, *Advances in Cryptology – CRYPTO'89*. Lecture Notes in Computer Science No. 435, pages 628–631. Springer, Berlin Heidelberg New York, 1990.

419. J.-J. Quisquater and J.-P. Delescaille. How easy is collision search. New results and applications to DES. In G. Brassard, editor, *Advances in Cryptology (CRYPTO'89)*. Lecture Notes in Computer Science No. 435, pages 408–415. Springer, Berlin Heidelberg New York, 1990.

420. M. Quisquater, B. Preneel, and J. Vandewalle. On the security of the threshold scheme based on the Chinese Remainder Theorem. In D. Naccache and P. Paillier, editors, *Public Key Cryptography (PKC 2002)*. Lecture Notes in Computer Science No. 2274, pages 199–210. Springer, Berlin Heidelberg New York, 2002.

421. M. Rabin. Digitalized signatures as intractable as factorization. Technical Report MIT/LCS/TR-212, MIT Laboratory for Computer Science, January 1979.

422. M. Rabin. Probabilistic algorithms for testing primality. *J. Number Theory*, 12:128–138, 1980.

423. M.O. Rabin. Digitalized signatures. In R.A. DeMillo, D.P. Dobkin, A.K. Jones, and R.J. Lipton, editors, *Foundations of Secure Computation*, pages 155–168. Academic Press, 1978.

424. Y. Radai. Integrity checking for anti-viral purposes: Theory and practice. *http://www.virusbtn.com/OtherPapers/*, 1994.

425. R. Rivest. Remarks on a proposed cryptanalytic attack of the MIT public-key cryptosystem. *Cryptologia*, 2(1):62–65, January 1978.

426. R. Rivest and A. Shamir. PayWord and MicroMint: two simple micropayment schemes. In *Proceedings of RSA'96 Conference*. Available at: *http://theory.lcs.mit.edu/~rivest*, 1996.

427. R.L. Rivest, L. Adleman, and M.L. Dertouzos. On data banks and privacy homomorphisms. In R.A. DeMillo, D.P. Dobkin, A.K. Jones, and R.J. Lipton, editors, *Foundations of Secure Computation*, pages 169–177. Academic Press, New York, 1978.

428. R. Rivest, A. Shamir, and L.M. Adleman. A method for obtaining digital signatures and public key cryptosystems. *Communications of the ACM*, 21:120–126, 1978.

429. R.L. Rivest. The MD4 message digest algorithm. In A.J. Menezes and S.A. Vanstone, editors, *Advances in Cryptology (CRYPTO'90)*. Lecture Notes in Computer Science No. 537, pages 303–311. Springer, Berlin Heidelberg New York, 1991.

430. R.L. Rivest. The MD5 message-digest algorithm. Internet Request for Comments, April 1992. RFC 1321.

431. R.L. Rivest, A. Shamir, and L.M. Adleman. A method for obtaining digital signatures and public-key cryptosystems. *Communications of the ACM*, 21(2):120–126, 1978.

432. J. Rompel. One-way functions are necessary and sufficient for secure signatures. In *Proceedings of the 22nd ACM Symposium on Theory of Computing*, pages 387–394. ACM, 1990.

433. U. Rosenbaum. A lower bound on authentication after having observed a sequence of messages. *Journal of Cryptology*, 6(3):135–156, 1993.

434. W. Rosenberry, D. Kenney, and G. Fisher. *Understanding DCE*. O'Reilly, 1992.

435. O.S. Rothaus. On bent functions. *Journal of Combinatorial Theory*, Series A, 20:300–305, 1976.

436. L.A. Rowe and K.A. Shoens. Data abstractions, views and updates in RIGEL. In P.A. Bernstein, editor, *Proceedings of ACM SIGMOD 1979 International Conference on Management of Data*, pages 71–81, Boston, 1979. ACM SIGMOD.

437. R.A. Rueppel. On the security of Schnorr's pseudo random generator. In *Advances in Cryptology (EUROCRYPT'89)*. Lecture Notes in Computer Science No. 434, pages 423–428. Springer, Berlin Heidelberg New York, 1990.

438. R.A. Rueppel and P.C. Van Oorschot. Modern key agreement techniques. *Computer Communications*, 17:458–465, 1994.

439. B. Sadeghiyan and J. Pieprzyk. A construction for super pseudorandom permutations from a single pseudorandom function. In R. Rueppel, editor, *Advances in Cryptology (EUROCRYPT'92)*. Lecture Notes in Computer Science No. 658, pages 267–284. Springer, Berlin Heidelberg New York, 1993.

440. B. Sadeghiyan and J. Pieprzyk. On necessary and sufficient conditions for the construction of super pseudorandom permutations. In H. Imai, R. Rivest, and T. Matsumoto, editors, *Proceedings of ASIACRYPT'91*. Lecture Notes in Computer Science No. 739, pages 194–209. Springer, Berlin Heidelberg New York, 1993.

441. R. Safavi-Naini and L. Tombak. Optimal authentication codes. In T. Helleseth, editor, *Advances in Cryptology (EUROCRYPT'93)*. Lecture Notes in Computer Science No. 765, pages 12–27. Springer, Berlin Heidelberg New York, 1994.

442. R. Safavi-Naini and L. Tombak. Authentication codes in plaintext and chosen-content attacks. In A. De Santis, editor, *Advances in Cryptology (EUROCRYPT'94)*. Lecture Notes in Computer Science No. 950, pages 254–265. Springer, Berlin Heidelberg New York, 1995.

443. R. Safavi-Naini and L. Tombak. Combinatorial structure of a-codes with r-fold security. In J. Pieprzyk and R. Safavi-Naini, editors, *Advances in Cryptology (ASIACRYPT'94)*. Lecture Notes in Computer Science No. 917, pages 211–223. Springer, Berlin Heidelberg New York, 1995.

444. R. Safavi-Naini, L. Tombak, and J. Pieprzyk. Perfect authenticity and optimal a-codes. In *IEEE International Symposium on Information Theory and Its Applications*, pages 235–238. Sydney, November 20–25, 1994.

445. K. Sako and J. Kilian. Secure voting using partially compatible homomorphisms. In Y. Desmedt, editor, *Advances in Cryptology (CRYPTO'94)*. Lecture Notes in Computer Science No. 839, pages 411–424. Springer, Berlin Heidelberg New York, 1994.

446. K. Sako and J. Kilian. Receipt-free mix-type voting scheme. In L. Guillou and J.-J. Quisquater, editors, *Advances in Cryptology (EUROCRYPT'95)*. Lecture Notes in Computer Science No. 921, pages 393–403. Springer, Berlin Heidelberg New York, 1995.

447. A. Salomaa. *Public-Key Cryptography*. Springer, Berlin Heidelberg New York, 1996.

448. R. Sandhu. Access control: the neglected frontier. In J. Pieprzyk and J. Seberry, editors, *Proceedings of the 1st Australasian Conference on Information Security and Privacy (ACISP96)*. Lecture Notes in Computer Science No. 1172, pages 219–227. Springer, Berlin Heidelberg New York, 1996.

449. R.S. Sandhu, E.J. Coyne, H.L Feinstein, and C.E. Youman. Role-based access control models. *IEEE Computer*, 29(2):38–47, 1996.

450. A. De Santis and M. Yung. On the design of provably-secure cryptographic hash functions. In I.B. Damgård, editor, *Advances in Cryptology (EUROCRYPT'90)*. Lecture

Notes in Computer Science No. 473, pages 377–397. Springer, Berlin Heidelberg New York, 1990.

451. B. Schneier. *Applied Cryptography*. Wiley, New York, 1996.

452. C.P. Schnorr. Efficient signature generation by smart cards. *Journal of Cryptology*, 4:161–174, 1991.

453. R. Schoof. Elliptic curves over finite fields and the computation of square roots mod p. *Mathematics of Computations*, 44:483–494, 1985.

454. A.W. Schrift and A. Shamir. Universal tests for nonuniform distributions. *Journal of Cryptology*, 6(3):119–133, 1993.

455. M.R. Schroeder, editor. *Number Theory in Science and Communication*. Springer, Berlin Heidelberg New York, 1984.

456. J. Seberry and J. Pieprzyk. *Cryptography: An Introduction to Computer Security*. Prentice-Hall, Sydney, 1989.

457. J. Seberry, X.-M. Zhang, and Y. Zheng. Highly nonlinear 0-1 balanced functions satisfying strict avalanche criterion. In *Advances in Cryptology (AUSCRYPT'92)*. Lecture Notes in Computer Science No. 718, pages 145–155. Springer, Berlin Heidelberg New York, 1993.

458. J. Seberry, X.-M. Zhang, and Y. Zheng. Systematic generation of cryptographically robust S-boxes. In *Proceedings of the First ACM Conference on Computer and Communications Security*, pages 172–182. ACM, New York, 1993.

459. J. Seberry, X.-M. Zhang, and Y. Zheng. Improving the strict avalanche characteristics of cryptographic functions. *Information Processing Letters*, 50:37–41, 1994.

460. J. Seberry, X.-M. Zhang, and Y. Zheng. Nonlinearly balanced boolean functions and their propagation characteristics. In D.R. Stinson, editor, *Advances in Cryptology (CRYPTO'93)*. Lecture Notes in Computer Science No. 773, pages 49–60. Springer, Berlin Heidelberg New York, 1994.

461. J. Seberry, X.-M. Zhang, and Y. Zheng. Pitfalls in designing substitution boxes. In Y. Desmedt, editor, *Advances in Cryptology (CRYPTO'94)*. Lecture Notes in Computer Science No. 839, pages 383–396. Springer, Berlin Heidelberg New York, 1994.

462. M. Sebring, E. Shellhouse, M.E. Hanna, and R.A. Whitehurst. Systems in intrusion detection: A case study. In *Proceedings of the 11th National Computer Security Conference*, Gaithersburg, MD, pages 74–81, 1988.

463. G. Shafer. *A Mathematical Theory of Evidence*. Princeton University Press, NJ, 1976.

464. A. Shamir. How to share a secret. *Communications of the ACM*, 22:612–613, November 1979.

465. A. Shamir. A polynomial time algorithm for breaking the basic Merkle-Hellman cryptosystem. *IEEE Transactions on Information Theory*, IT-30(5):699–704, Sept. 1984.

466. C.E. Shannon. A mathematical theory of communication. *Bell Systems Technical Journal*, 27:623–656, 1948.

467. C.E. Shannon. Communication theory of secrecy systems. *Bell Systems Technical Journal*, 28:657–715, 1949.

468. A. Shimizu and S. Miyaguchi. Fast data encipherment algorithm FEAL. In D. Chaum and W.L. Price, editors, *Advances in Cryptology (EUROCRYPT'87)*. Lecture Notes in Computer Science No. 304, pages 267–280. Springer, Berlin Heidelberg New York, 1988.

469. A. Silberschatz and P. Galvin. *Operating System Concepts*. Addison-Wesley, 1998.

470. R.D. Silverman. The multiple polynomial quadratic sieve. *Mathematics of Computation*, 48:329–339, 1987.

471. G.J. Simmons. A game theory model of digital message authentication. *Congressus Numerantium*, 34:413–424, 1982.

472. G.J. Simmons. Message authentication: game on hypergraphs. *Congressus Numerantium*, 45:161–192, 1984.

473. G.J. Simmons. How to (really) share a secret. In S. Goldwasser, editor, *Advances in Cryptology (CRYPTO'88)*. Lecture Notes in Computer Science No. 403, pages 390–449. Springer, Berlin Heidelberg New York, 1988.

474. G.J. Simmons. Geometric shared secret and/or shared control schemes. In A.J. Menezes and S.A. Vanstone, editors, *Advances in Cryptology (CRYPTO'90)*. Lecture Notes in Computer Science No. 537, pages 216–241. Springer, Berlin Heidelberg New York, 1991.

475. G.J. Simmons. A survey of information authentication. In G.J. Simmons, editor, *Contemporary Cryptology. The Science of Information Integrity*, pages 379–420. IEEE, 1992.

476. G.J. Simmons, W. Jackson, and K. Martin. The geometry of shared secret schemes. *Bulletin of the ICA*, 1:71–88, 1991.

477. G.J. Simmons. Authentication theory/coding theory. In G.R. Blakley and D.C. Chaum, editors, *Advances in Cryptology (CRYPTO'84)*. Lecture Notes in Computer Science No. 196, pages 411–431. Springer, Berlin Heidelberg New York, 1985.

478. G.J. Simmons and M.J. Norris. Preliminary comments on the MIT public-key cryptosystem. *Cryptologia*, 1(4):406–414, October 1977.

479. A. Sinkov. *Elementary Cryptanalysis*. Mathematical Association of America, 1968.

480. S.E. Smaha. Haystack: an intrusion detection system. In *Proceedings of the Fourth Aerospace Computer Security Applications Conference*, pages 37–44. IEEE, 1988.

481. B. Smeets. Bounds on the probability of deception in multiple authentication. *IEEE Transactions on Information Theory*, IT-40(5):1586–1591, 1994.

482. S.R. Snapp. A system for distributed intrusion detection scheme. In *Proceedings of IEEE COMPCON'91*, pages 170–176, 1991.

483. S.R. Snapp, J. Brentano, G.V. Dias, T.L. Goan, L.T. Heberlein, C. Ho, K.N. Levitt, B. Mukherjee, S.E. Smaha, T. Grance, D.M. Teal, and D. Mansur. Distributed intrusion detection system – motivation, Architecture and an early prototype. In *Proceedings of 14th National Computer Security Conference*, 1991.

484. M. Sobirey, S. Fischer-Hübner, and K. Rannenberg. Pseudonymous audit for privacy enhanced intrusion detection. In *Proceedings of the 13th International Information Security Conference*, 1997.

485. M. Sobirey, B. Richter, and H. Konig. The intrusion detection system aid. Architecture, and experiences in automated audit analysis. In *Proceedings of the IFIP TC6/TC11 International Conference on Communications and Multimedia Security*, pages 278–290, 1996.

486. A. Sorkin. Lucifer, a cryptographic algorithm. *Cryptologia*, 8(1):22–41, 1984. Erratum: ibid. 7, p. 118, 1978.

487. W. Stallings. *Cryptography and Network Security Principles and Practice*. Prentice-Hall, New York 1999.

488. S. Staniford-Chen, S. Cheung, R.M. Dilger, R. Crawford, J. Frank, J. Hoagland, K. Levitt, C. Wee, R. Yip, and D. Zerkle. GrIDS – a graph based intrusion detection system for large networks. In *Proceedings of the 19th National Information Systems Security Conference*, pages 361–370, 1996.

489. J.G. Steiner, B.C. Neuman, and J.I. Schiller. Kerberos: An authentication service for open network systems. In *Proceedings of the USENIX Winter Conference*, pages 191–202, Dallas, TX, February 1988.

490. J. Stern. A new identification scheme based on syndrome decoding. In D.R. Stinson, editor, *Advances in Cryptology (CRYPTO'93)*. Lecture Notes in Computer Science No. 773, pages 13–21. Springer, Berlin Heidelberg New York, 1994.

491. D.R. Stinson. Some constructions and bounds for authentication codes. In A.M. Odlyzko, editor, *Advances in Cryptology – CRYPTO'86*. Lecture Notes in Computer Science No. 263, pages 418–425. Springer, Berlin Heidelberg New York, 1987.

492. D.R. Stinson. A construction for authentication/secrecy codes from certain combinatorial designs. In C. Pomerance, editor, *Advances in Cryptology (CRYPTO'87)*. Lecture Notes in Computer Science No. 293, pages 355–366. Springer, Berlin Heidelberg New York, 1988.

493. D.R. Stinson. Combinatorial characterizations of authentication codes. In J. Feigenbaum, editor, *Advances in Cryptology (CRYPTO'91)*. Lecture Notes in Computer Science No. 576, pages 62–73. Springer, Berlin Heidelberg New York, 1992.

494. D.R. Stinson. An explication of secret sharing schemes. *Designs, Codes and Cryptography*, 2:357–390, 1992.

495. D.R. Stinson. Combinatorial designs and cryptography. In *Surveys in Combinatorics*. London Mathematical Society Lecture Notes Series, Vol. 187, pages 257–287. Cambridge University Press, Cambridge, 1993.

496. D.R. Stinson. *Cryptography: Theory and Practice*. CRC, Boca Raton, FL, 1995.

497. M. Stonebraker. Implementation of integrity constraints and views by query modification. In *Proceedings of International Conference on Management of Data (SIGMOD'75)*, pages 65–78. ACM, 1975.

498. A.P. Street and W.D. Wallis. *Combinatorics: A First Course*. CBRC, Winnipeg, 1982.

499. A. Tanenbaum. *Computer Networks*. Prentice-Hall, Englewood Cliffs, NJ, 1981.

500. A. Tanenbaum. *Distributed Operating Systems*. Prentice-Hall, Englewood Cliffs, NJ, 1995.

501. A. Tanenbaum and A. Woodhull. *Operating Systems: Design and Implementation*. Prentice-Hall, Englewood Cliffs, NJ, 1997.

502. J. Tardo and K. Alagappan. SPX: global authentication using public key certificates. In *Proceedings of 12th IEEE Symposium on Research in Security and Privacy*, pages 232–244. UEEE 1991.

503. W.T. Tener. Discovery: An expert system in the commercial data security environment. In *Proceedings of the 4th IFIP TC11 International Conference on Security*, pages 261–268, 1989.

504. H. Teng, K. Chen, and S. Lu. Security audit trail analysis using inductively generated predictive rules. In *Proceedings of the 6th Conference on Artificial Intelligence Applications*, pages 24–29. IEEE, 1990.

505. H.S. Teng, K. Chen, and S.C. Lu. Adaptive real-time anomaly detection using inductively generated sequential patterns. In *Proceedings of the IEEE Symposium on Research in Security and Privacy*, pages 278–284. IEEE, 1990.

506. M.B. Thuraisingham. A multilevel secure object-oriented data model. In *Proceedings of the 12th National Computer Security Conference*, pages 579–590. NIST/NCSC, October 1989.

507. J.-P. Tillich and G. Zémor. Hashing with SL_2. In Y. Desmedt, editor, *Advances in Cryptology (CRYPTO'94)*. Lecture Notes in Computer Science No. 839, pages 40–49. Springer, Berlin Heidelberg New York, 1994.

508. L. Tombak. *New results on unconditionally secure authentication systems*. PhD thesis, Department of Computer Science, University of Wollongong, Australia, 1995.

509. M. Tompa and H. Woll. How to share a secret with cheaters. *Journal of Cryptology*, 1(2):133–138, 1988.

510. R.P. Trueblood, H.R. Hartson, and J.J. Martin. MULTISAFE – a modular multiprocessing approach to secure database management. *ACM Transactions on Database Systems*, 8(3):382–409, 1983.

511. G. Tsudik. Message authentication with one-way hash functions. *ACM SIGCOMM, Computer Communication Review*, 22(5):29–38, October 1992.

512. E.M. Valcarce, G.W. Hoglund, L. Jansen, and L. Baillie. Essense: An experiment in knowledge-based security monitoring and control. In *Proceedings of the 3rd USENIX Unix Security Symposium*, pages 155–170, 1992.

513. J. van Tilburg. *Security-Analysis of a Class of Cryptosystems Based on Linear Error-Correcting Codes*. Royal PTT Nederland NV, PTT Research, Leidschendam, 1994.

514. S. von Solms and D. Naccache. On blind signatures and perfect crimes. *Computers and Security*, 11:581–583, 1992.

515. V.L. Voydock and S.T. Kent. Security mechanism in high-level network protocols. *ACM Computing Surveys*, 15(2):135–171, 1983.

516. N.R. Wagner. Shared database access using composed encryption keys. In *Proceedings of the 1982 IEEE Symposium on Security and Privacy*, pages 104–110. IEEE, 1982.

517. M. Walker. Information-theoretic bounds for authentication systems. *Journal of Cryptology*, 3(2):131–143, 1990.

518. W.D. Wallis, A. Penfold Street, and J. Seberry Wallis. *Combinatorics: Room Squares, Sum-Free Sets, Hadamard Matrices*, Lecture Notes in Mathematics No. 292. Springer, Berlin Heidelbeg New York, 1972.

519. M. Wang and A. Goscinski. The development and testing of the identity-based conference key distribution system for the RHODOS distributed system. In Y. Deswarte, G. Eizenberg, and J.-J. Quisquater, editors, *Proceedings of the Second European Symposium on*

Research in Computer Security (ESORICS'92). Lecture Notes in Computer Science No. 648, pages 209–228. Springer, Berlin Heidelberg New York, 1992.

520. R. Wang. Flash in the pan? Virus Bulletin, August 1998. See *http://www.virusbtn.com/VirusInformation/cih.html*.

521. A.F. Webster and S.E. Tavares. On the design of S-boxes. In H.C. Williams, editor, *Advances in Cryptology (CRYOTO'85)*. Lecture Notes in Computer Science No. 218, pages 523–534. Springer, Berlin Heidelberg New York, 1986.

522. M.N. Wegman and J.L. Carter. New hash functions and their use in authentication and set equality. *Journal of Computer and System Sciences*, 22:265–279, 1981.

523. W.R.E. Weiss and A. Baur. Analysis of audit and protocol data using methods from artificial intelligence. In *Proceedings of the 13th National Computer Security Conference*, pages 109–114, 1990.

524. D.L. Wells and C.M. Eastman. A preliminary study of traffic analysis in encrypted databases. In E.L. Gallizzi, J. Elam, and R.H. Sprague, Jr., editors, *Proceedings of the 18th Hawaii International Conference on System Sciences 1985*, pages 373–382. Hawaii International Conference on System Sciences, Honolulu, 1985.

525. I. Whalley. Hare Krishna: ISKCON too far! Virus Bulletin, August 1996.

526. G.B. White, E.A. Fish, and U.W. Pooch. Cooperating security managers: A peer-based intrusion detection system. *IEEE Network*, 10(1):20–23, 1996.

527. R.A. Whitehurst and T.F. Lunt. The SeaView verification. In *Proceedings of the 2nd Workshop on Foundations of Computer Security*, pages 125–132. IEEE, 1989.

528. M.J. Wiener. Efficient DES key search. Presented at Crypto'93 rump session, August 20, 1993.

529. H.S. Wilf. *Algorithms and Complexity*. Prentice-Hall, Englewood Cliffs, NJ, 1986.

530. K. Wilkinson, P. Lyngbaek, and W. Hasan. The Iris architecture and implementation. *IEEE Transaction on Knowledge and Data Engineering*, 2(1):63–75, 1990.

531. H.C. Williams. A modification of the RSA public-key encryption procedure. *IEEE Transactions on Information Theory*, IT-26(6):726–729, November 1980.

532. H.C. Williams. An m^3 public-key encryption scheme. In H.C. Williams, editor, *Advances in Cryptology – CRYPTO'85*. Lecture Notes in Computer Science No. 218, pages 358–368. Springer, Berlin Heidelberg New York, 1986.

533. C.P. Williams and S.H. Clearwater. *Explorations in Quantum Computing*. Springer, Berlin Heidelberg New York, 1998.

534. J. Wilson. Views as the security objects in a multilevel secure relational database management system. In *Proceedings of the 1988 IEEE Symposium on Security and Privacy*, pages 70–84. IEEE, 1988.

535. J.R. Winkler. A UNIX prototype for intrusion and anomaly detection in secure networks. In *Proceedings of the 13th National Computer Security Conference*, pages 115–124, 1990.

536. J.R. Winkler and L.C. Landry. Intrusion and anomaly detection, ISOA update. In *Proceedings of the 15th National Computer Security Conference*, pages 272–281, 1992.

537. R.S. Winternitz. Producing a one-way hash function from DES. In D. Chaum, editor, *Advances in Cryptology (CRYPTO'83)*, pages 203–207. Plenum, New York.

538. J. Wood and D.H. Barnes. A practical distributed secure system. In *System Security – The Technical Challenge: Proceedings of the International Conference*, pages 49–60, London, October 1985. Online, London.

539. W. Wulf, R. Levin, and S. Harbison. *Hydra: An Experimental Computer System.* McGraw-Hill, New York, 1981.

540. A.C. Yao. Theory and application of trapdoor functions. In *Proceedings of the 23rd IEEE Symposium on Foundations of Computer Science*, pages 80–91. IEEE, 1982.

541. R. Yarlagadda and J.E. Hershey. Analysis and synthesis of bent sequences. *IEE Proceedings (Part E)*, 136:112–123, 1989.

542. D.M. Zamboni. Saint: security analysis integration tool. In *Proceedings of the Systems Administration, Networking and Security Conference*, 1996.

543. C. Zaniolo. Design of relational views over network schemas. In P.A. Bernstein, editor, *Proceedings of ACM International Conference on Management of Data (SIGMOD'79)*, pages 179–190. ACM, Boston, 1979.

544. Y. Zheng, T. Hardjono, and J. Pieprzyk. The sibling intractable function family (SIFF): notion, construction and applications. *IEICE Trans. Fundamentals*, E76-A:4–13, January 1993.

545. Y. Zheng, T. Matsumoto, and H. Imai. Impossibility and optimality results on constructing pseudorandom permutations. In *Advances in Cryptology (EUROCRYPT'89)*. Lecture Notes on Computer Science No. 434, pages 412–422. Springer, Berlin Heidelberg New York, 1989.

546. Y. Zheng, T. Matsumoto, and H. Imai. Structural properties of one-way hash functions. In A.J. Menezes and S.A. Vanstone, editors, *Advances in Cryptology (CRYPTO'90)*. Lecture Notes in Computer Science No. 537, pages 285–302. Springer, Berlin Heidelberg New York, 1991.

547. Y. Zheng, J. Pieprzyk, and J. Seberry. HAVAL – A one-way hashing algorithm with variable length of output. In J. Seberry and Y. Zheng, editors, *Advances in Cryptology (AUSCRYPT'92)*. Lecture Notes in Computer Science No. 718, pages 83–104. Springer, Berlin Heidelberg New York, 1993.

Index

Druck: Strauss Offsetdruck, Mörlenbach
Verarbeitung: Schäffer, Grünstadt